Second Edition

AMERICAN STREET GANGS

Tim Delaney, Ph.D.
State University of New York at Oswego

PEARSON

Boston   Columbus   Indianapolis   New York   San Francisco   Upper Saddle River
Amsterdam   Cape Town   Dubai   London   Madrid   Milan   Munich   Paris   Montréal   Toronto
Delhi   Mexico City   São Paulo   Sydney   Hong Kong   Seoul   Singapore   Taipei   Tokyo

Editorial Director: Vernon R. Anthony
Editor in Chief: Vern Anthony
Acquisitions Editor: Gary Bauer
Editorial Assistant: Tanika Henderson
Director of Marketing: David Gesell
Senior Marketing Manager: Alicia Wozniak
Senior Managing Editor: JoEllen Gohr
Production Project Manager: Debbie Ryan
Art Director: Jayne Conte
Cover Designer: Karen Noferi
Full-Service Project Manager: Soumitra Borkakati
Composition: PreMediaGlobal
Printer/Binder: LSC Communications
Text Font: MinionPro 10/12

Credits and acknowledgments borrowed from other sources and reproduced, with permission, in this textbook appear on the appropriate page within text.

Microsoft® and Windows® are registered trademarks of the Microsoft Corporation in the U.S.A. and other countries. Screen shots and icons reprinted with permission from the Microsoft Corporation. This book is not sponsored or endorsed by or affiliated with the Microsoft Corporation.

Many of the designations by manufacturers and sellers to distinguish their products are claimed as trademarks. Where those designations appear in this book, and the publisher was aware of a trademark claim, the designations have been printed in initial caps or all caps.

Library of Congress Cataloging-in-Publication Data
Delaney, Tim.
  American street gangs / Tim Delaney. — 2nd ed.
      p.   cm.
  Includes bibliographical references and index.
  ISBN-13: 978-0-13-305605-1
  ISBN-10: 0-13-305605-8
1. Gangs—United States. 2. Juvenile delinquency—United States. I. Title.
HV6439.U5D45 2013
302.34—dc23

                              2012040880

ISBN 10: 0-13-305605-8
ISBN 13: 978-0-13-305605-1

BRIEF CONTENTS

CONTENTS

PREFACE

NEW TO THIS EDITION

- Addition of 20 "Connecting Street Gangs and Popular Culture" boxes
- Updated statistics
- Numerous new tables
- Revised chapter content
- Increased discussion on a number of specific gangs, such as the Surenos and Nortenos gangs
- Inclusion of the transnational gangs category
- Revised summaries at the conclusion of each chapter

The very mention of the words *street gangs* and *gang members* conjures images of violence and mayhem. The lives of the citizens who live in gang-infested neighborhoods are constantly interrupted by the terror and intimidation that often go hand in hand with street gangs. In an effort to alleviate the growing problem of street gangs in American society, a number of community leaders and social activists are working hard to keep youths out of gangs; law enforcement and judicial officials along with legislative bodies are performing their societal duty in gang suppression efforts; and a slew of treatment programs have been created in an attempt to break gang members' ties with gangs so that they can become productive members of society. In short, there are many people trying to put to a halt the upward trend in the number of street gangs and gang members.

Most Americans do not have regular, or any, contact with street gangs. And yet, that does not stop them from forming an opinion about street gangs. For some of these folks, their attitude about street gangs is that of indifference. For others, gang members are simply thugs who should be incarcerated. Regardless of one's degree of involvement with street gangs, chances are, the media, and especially popular culture, has helped shape his/her vision of street gangs. The relationship between popular culture and street gangs is deemed significant enough to warrant the addition of 20 "Connecting Street Gangs and Popular Culture" boxes in this second edition of *American Street Gangs*. The world of popular culture and street gangs includes films, television, music (primarily gangsta rap and hip-hop), video games and videos, sports, children's books, and the Internet. In each of the 10 chapters, there are two unique examples of the intersection between popular culture and street gangs.

The addition of popular culture and street gangs boxes represents just one example of the many noteworthy changes in this second edition of *American Street Gangs*. Among the other substantial general improvements from the first edition are updated statistics, the addition of numerous tables, revised chapter content, increased discussion on a number of specific gangs, greater discussion of the Surenos and Nortenos gangs, the inclusion of the transnational gangs category, and revised summaries at the conclusion of each chapter. A number of specific changes are made in each chapter. Chapter 1 changes include updated law enforcement definitions of street gangs; updated statistics on juvenile crime and the number of gangs and gang members; more emphasis on outlaw motorcycle gangs and their role with street gangs; and the continued growth of prison gangs and their influence on the streets. In Chapter 2, there are updates in the historical review of street gangs; the addition of a discussion on street gangs in the South (post–Civil War), Baltimore, Richmond, and New Orleans; and the inclusion of a description of many new cities with gang problems in the contemporary era. In Chapter 3, there are many additions to the coverage of social disorganization theory, anomie/strain theory, and social control theory. There are many substantial changes in Chapter 4, including updates in the shifting labor market, including new statistics; the addition of the topic of social stratification along with the discussion of the underclass; updates on poverty, single-parent families, and the feminization of poverty, including new statistics; updates on the role of education; and significant updates in the areas of drug and alcohol use, firearms, the mass media, and "the rush." Many updates, including the race/ethnicity typology, are included in Chapter 5. There have been many major changes made to Chapter 6, including a new opening section called "Gang Proliferation"; a new section called "Rural and Suburban Street Gangs"; updates on local gangs in Syracuse, Rochester, and Buffalo, New York; updates on the coverage of nation gangs; most importantly, a new section titled "Transnational Street Gangs"; and updates on Asian gangs. There are updates on the coverage of female gangs in Chapter 7. The categorical coverage of gang-related crimes discussed in Chapter 8 represents a considerable improvement from the first edition by expanding the coverage of the many crimes committed by street gangs: violent crime (violence, homicide, robbery, assault and battery, rape, extortion, and witness intimidation); property crime (burglary, larceny-theft, motor vehicle theft, and vandalism); drugs (use, sale, distribution, and trafficking); and nontraditional and white-collar crime (alien smuggling, human trafficking, prostitution, and white-collar crime). Crime statistics have also been updated in Chapter 8. In Chapter 9, the three types of intervention strategies, prevention, suppression, and treatment, have all been updated with new examples of programs and evaluative results. The final chapter also has significant changes. Chapter 10 begins with a brief recap of the previous chapters but now includes a section titled "Trends" to reflect what we can expect from street gangs in the future.

In short, while we were very pleased with the first edition of *American Street Gangs*, the second edition will impress everyone who teaches courses on street gangs as well as students and nonstudents who want to learn more about street gangs. Law enforcement folks will be impressed by the coverage of criminal activities committed by street gangs. Sociologists and other social scientists will be equally pleased with the discussion on the numerous socioeconomic variables that affect gang members, including the factors involved in joining a gang, the organizational structure of gangs, and the daily activities of gang members. *American Street Gangs*, second edition, provides a comprehensive review of all the critical elements relevant to gang life. It is designed to provide the necessary background material on gangs so that the reader has a clear idea of the cultural and structural components of gang activity. Gangs have become such a major phenomenon that their existence has long become institutionalized—that is, they are now, and will continue to be, a permanent fixture of American society.

My own interest in street gangs grew in earnest during my years as a field supervisor for a major chain of convenience stores in Los Angeles and the surrounding areas. As a field supervisor with stores in gang areas, I often came face-to-face with gang members on a daily basis. One of my most interesting recollections of these regular conversations with gang members is that while my company believed that it owned the property that the store was located on, rival gangs often felt like they "owned" that turf. Although my company had the law on its side, the store personnel who had to work in these stores often realized who had the real power—street gang members with guns (along with any other criminal with a gun). Maintaining the safety of my employees often involved bulletproof cashier enclosures (which do not make the average customer feel too safe when shopping there!) and various techniques of minimizing potentially deadly confrontations. Because of the nearly daily interactions I had with gang members while working in the convenience store business, I came in contact with a number of law enforcement officers from the Los Angeles Police Department(LAPD) and Sheriff's Office. The LAPD offered concerned business persons a chance to ride along with gang task force officers, an opportunity I could not resist. From my interactions with law enforcement in the late 1980s, I learned about their perspective on street gangs. When I decided to go back to college and work on my master's degree, I made the right decision to attend CSU Dominguez Hills where I had the good fortune to take a graduate course on street gangs from John Quicker. Quicker has the distinction of writing the very first book on female gangs (see Chapter 7). He would bring gang members from nearby Compton into the classroom so that students could learn their side of the story. During my years of living in Los Angeles, I observed many gang-related incidents, poverty-stricken neighborhoods, and general mayhem. (This is not to suggest that I am knocking Los Angeles, as it is my favorite city in the world.) When I moved back to New York State, I began to study gangs sociologically as a researcher, including interviewing gang members in Buffalo. I have continued to interview and closely follow the activities of many street gangs throughout the nation but especially in central and western New York and Los Angeles. Some of the information that I learned from these gang members is found throughout this book.

ACKNOWLEDGMENTS

I would like to thank all the fine folks at Pearson, including Vern Anthony, Gary Bauer, Steve Robb, Tanika Henderson, and all those who helped with final editing and production. I am especially grateful to Paul Hahn, who provided the gang graffiti illustrations used in Chapter 6— thanks Paul! As always, very special thanks to Christina.

ABOUT THE AUTHOR

Tim Delaney is an associate professor of sociology at the State University of New York at Oswego. He holds a B.S. degree in sociology from the State University of New York at Brockport, an M.A. degree in sociology from California State University at Dominguez Hills, and a Ph.D. in sociology from the University of Nevada at Las Vegas. He regularly teaches courses on street gangs and shares his personal stories of gang research in Los Angeles and upstate New York with his students.

Delaney has authored, co-authored, or served as a contributing author/editor on 14 books, to date. Among his publications are *Classical and Contemporary Social Theory: Investigation and Application* (forthcoming 2013); *Connecting Sociology to Our Lives: An Introduction to Sociology* (2012); *The Sociology of Sport: An Introduction* (2009, co-authored); *American Street Gangs* (2006); *Contemporary Social Theory: Investigation and Application* (2005); and *Classical Social Theory: Investigation and Application* (2004). He has also published numerous book reviews, journal articles, encyclopedia articles, and chapters in edited books.

Delaney regularly presents papers at regional, national, and international conferences. His commitment to scholarly activity allows him to travel the world and learn firsthand the great diversity, and similarity, found among people from different cultures. Delaney maintains membership in more than a dozen academic associations, has twice served as president of the New York State Sociological Association, is listed in *Who's Who in America*, and is a charter member of the "Wall of Tolerance."

1

What Is a Street Gang?

Nearly every species gathers in groups. Geese fly in flocks, fish swim in schools, wild dogs and hyenas run in packs, and chimpanzees live in societies made up of groups and affiliated cliques. Humans also form groups, and have done so throughout history for safety, basic survival, and companionship. Group formation helps to satisfy the human need for social interaction with others. Social interaction plays an important role for people because individuals want to feel as though they are a part of a group, community, or general society and want to experience a sense of unity with their fellows. Group membership provides individuals with a sense of identity. Each of us belongs to many social groups, but the most important ones are what sociologists refer to as "primary groups." As articulated by Charles Cooley (1909), primary groups are those characterized by intimate, face-to-face association and cooperation. One's family is generally considered a primary group. When people feel close with fellow members of a primary group they are comfortable using the pronoun *we*. This shared sense of "we-ness" reaffirms solidarity and loyalty. Youths commonly form playgroups and these peer groups may become primary groups. For many gang members, especially hard-core members, the gang becomes a primary group.

Although it might be tempting to think of any gathering of people as a group, that would be a mistake, as there are certain parameters that lead to a distinction between groups, aggregates, and categories. "A social group is defined as two or more people who interact regularly and in a manner that is defined by some common purpose, a set of norms, and a structure of statuses and roles (social positions). There are two general requirements that must be met for a number of people to qualify as a group: (1) they must interact with one another in an organized fashion, and (2) they must identify themselves as group members because of shared views, goals, traits or circumstances" (Delaney 2012, 134). In contrast, *aggregate* is a term used to describe a number of people who happen to be clustered in one place at any given time, for example, at bus stops, train stations, outside a convenience store, and at sporting events. As we shall learn in Chapter 9, court injunctions designed to curtail gang members from gathering together in public places must clearly articulate the difference between random gatherings of people (an aggregate) that might be mistaken for gang members and actual gang members (a specific social group). *Category* refers to a number of people who share a particular attribute, but who may have never

1

met. Examples of categories of people include all left-handers, Democrats, Republicans, baseball fans, and so on.

Core members of a street gang would qualify as a group. Gang members may identify one another based on such qualities as wearing certain clothing, tattoos, hand signals, language, jewelry, and the use of graffiti. In addition, when gang members congregate, they do so for a specific reason(s). The gang acts as a primary group for core members because it helps to fill the void resulting from whatever is missing in the lives of so many troubled youths, young adults, and life-long gang members.

Most street gangsters join gangs when they are juveniles. Generally speaking, these juveniles have participated in acts of delinquency before they join a street gang. As a result, we begin our answer to the question "What is a street gang?" by acknowledging the role of delinquency and gangs.

DELINQUENCY AND GANGS

The concern over delinquency and gangs stems from the reality that most individuals first join a gang in their youth and that a large number of gang members are juveniles. *Delinquency* itself refers to violations of juvenile law by juveniles. Juvenile delinquency refers to a wide variety of violations ranging from minor offenses, such as drinking and truancy, to more serious violations, such a murder and robbery, committed by youths that make them subject to action by the juvenile court. Delinquent offenses range from minor offenses—such as drinking, making prank phone calls, and truancy—to more serious violations, such as murder and robbery. There is no set standard for what ages are considered juvenile, although a majority of states consider persons as juvenile until they reach the age of 18, at which point they legally become adults. Children under the age of 7 are not held accountable for any criminal acts they may commit (Champion 2004). Some juveniles commit acts of delinquency infrequently, but others commit acts of delinquency so often that they are referred to as lifestyle, repeat, or chronic delinquent offenders (Siegel, Welsh, and Senna 2003).

In 2009, there were an estimated 1.9 million juvenile arrests (OJJDP 2011a). The OJJDP (2011a) reports that there were 5,804 arrests for every 100,000 youths ages 10 through 17 in the United States. There were 262 arrests for the "violent crime index" offenses for every 100,000 youth between 10 and 17 years of age. The juvenile arrest rate for all offenses reached its highest level in the last two decades in 1996, and then declined 36 percent by 2009. Seventy percent of all juvenile arrests are committed by males. Of the total estimated juvenile arrests, less than 5 percent fall under the "violent crime index" category, just under 22 percent fall under the "property crime index" category, and rest (73.6%) fall under the umbrella term "nonindex" crime category (see Table 1.1).

TABLE 1.1 2009 Estimated Juvenile Arrests by Index Category		
Index Category	**Number**	**Percentage**
Violent crime index	85,900	4.5
Property crime index	417,700	21.9
Nonindex	1,403,000	73.6

Source: OJJDP (2011a)

TABLE 1.2 2009 Violent Crime Index Juvenile Arrests by Category and Gender

Category of Crime	Male	Female
Murder and nonnegligent manslaughter	1,193	7
Forcible rape	3,098	2
Robbery	31,690	10
Aggravated assault	49,875	25

Source: OJJDP (2011a)

Crimes that make up the violent crime index consist of murder and nonnegligent manslaughter, forcible rape, robbery, and aggravated assault. As the data in Table 1.2 reveal, the vast majority of juvenile violent crimes are committed by males. Property crime index offenses include burglary, larceny-theft, motor vehicle theft, and arson. Larceny-theft is by far the most common of all property crime index offenses and like violent crimes it is far more likely to be committed by males (see Table 1.3). Nonindex crimes are numerous in subcategories and include other assaults, forgery and counterfeiting, fraud, embezzlement, stolen property (buying, receiving, possessing), vandalism, weapons (carrying, possessing, etc.), prostitution and commercialized vice, sex offenses (except forcible rape and prostitution), drug abuse violations, gambling, offenses against family and children, driving under the influence, liquor law violations, drunkenness, disorderly conduct, vagrancy, suspicion, curfew and loitering, and runaways.

The Development of a Juvenile Status

It is important to note that the juvenile status—identifying persons based on age categories—is a historically new distinction. As Siegel et al. (2003) indicate, during the Middle Ages (A.D. 700 to A.D. 1500) in Europe, the concept of "childhood" as we know it today did not exist. The patriarchal nature of society left final authority to the father of a family to discipline children and control his wife. Children who did not obey were subject to severe punishment and in some cases death. Young children were expected to obey the rules of the family and seldom did formal law interfere with the punishment of violators. Champion (2004) explains that in biblical times, Roman law gave nearly exclusive responsibility for disciplining their children and established age 7 as the cutoff from those too young to be held accountable for criminal offenses. Much was the same during the Middle Ages where English common law under the monarchy upheld the power of parents over children. During the Middle Ages, English common law established under the monarchy adhered to the same standard. Children of medieval times faced an abrupt passage

TABLE 1.3 2009 Property Crime Index Juvenile Arrests by Category and Gender

Category of Crime	Male	Female
Burglary	74,789	11
Larceny-theft	317,655	45
Motor vehicle theft	19,883	17
Arson	5,287	13

Source: OJJDP (2011a)

into adulthood. As soon as they were physically able to perform work tasks, they were expected to do so. There was no "childhood" status and certainly no distinction of "life as a teenager." Education and leisure pursuits were luxuries reserved for children of the elites. Children age 7 and older were expected to be productive members of the family and society. Attitudes toward children were most likely shaped by the grim demographic realities (i.e., high infant mortality rate, high death rates, short life expectancies) that may have forced the adults to regard the young with indifference. Children were often ignored and abandoned during medieval times.

In colonial America, the family remained as the source and primary means of social control of children. Children who violated the law were sent back to their families for punishment. Because of the agrarian lifestyle during the colonial era, children were relatively valuable as a cheap form of labor. Colonial children were not pampered. In part because the concept of "original sin" (a religious belief that a child is born "flawed") was prevalent during this primitive time, violent punishment was common, especially caning and other forms of public beatings. Since the colonial period, however, the state has slowly taken the power and responsibility of disciplining children out of the hands of parents and into its own. By the end of the nineteenth century, the government had established a juvenile court to assume responsibility and care for wayward youth. The court was based on an old English doctrine of *parens patriae*, the right of the crown to intervene in natural family relations (Bartollas and Miller 2001). The term *juvenile delinquency* was first coined in 1818 by the Society for the Prevention of Pauperism and was initially used to describe the disapproved activities of neglected immigrant children who roamed the streets of New York City (*Encyclopedia Americana* 1998). Citizens were growing concerned about abandoned children and wanted the government to do something about them.

In the past three centuries the role of the state in the control and discipline of children has increased and the role of the once-central father has dramatically decreased. After the formation of houses of refuge (created by the "child-saving movement") came the creation of reform schools, which were established to supervise unruly juveniles. Thus, America was going through an ideological and cultural change in its attitude toward strategies of social control of children during the nineteenth century. The first juvenile court was established in Cook County, Illinois, in 1899. Progressive reformers hoped to find more "beneficial" ways of dealing with juvenile delinquency, such as forming agencies that helped to keep children off the streets and provide them with a place to go after school and before their parents returned home from work. Community-based private agencies such as Hull House, established in Chicago by Jane Addams in 1889, provided an opportunity of something to do for immigrant children who would otherwise be unsupervised while their parents worked long hours.

It is also important to recognize the role of economics in family life. The economic shift from the agrarian lifestyle to one based on the industrial model had a dramatic effect on family life. With the rise of industrialization, most adults were now primarily working in factories. Child-labor laws prohibited children from working in such places. With this economic shift, children now had something that few children had ever had before—free time. In the past, children had always been too busy working to have free time, but all this changed with industrialization. Improvements in medicine ensured that children lived longer (lower mortality rates) and faced fewer life-threatening diseases, and the overall perception of children began to change. Parents began to pay closer attention to the individual personalities of their offspring, and society as a whole became more sympathetic to the plight of children. Thus, in the eighteenth and nineteenth centuries a separate stage of human development became recognized—childhood. Childhood was now viewed as unique phase of life, and children were seen as needing both protection and education (Thornton and Voight 1992). Compulsory education provided control over young people's lives and helped to change their status identification from that of a small adult to that of a child.

After the passage of compulsory school attendance, truancy laws were established as a means of keeping children in school, but equally important, they were a means of keeping children off the streets where they might commit delinquent behavior (Champion 2004). Sports participation became another tool used by social control agents to occupy the free time of children. For example, in 1929, store owners in Philadelphia banded together to solve a common problem of "teenagers with nothing to do," who were committing acts of violence and vandalism, by instituting a youth football league (Powell 2003, 4). In fact, from the latter half of the nineteenth century people in both Europe and North America have used sports participation in a controlled environment as a means to organize children's lives, especially so that boys and girls would develop into productive adults in the rapidly expanding capitalist economy. Sports and physical activities designed to keep boys busy were organized for boys in schools, playgrounds, and by church groups. The discipline and organization of formal sports were designed to instill ideals of cooperation and team work among boys from working class. Sports for middle and upper classes would instill the same ideals but also emphasize the importance of leadership roles. Girls were being socialized to take over feminized roles of motherhood and homemaking. Until the 1970s, girls had been generally discouraged from participating in sports and were instead taught domestic skills. It should come as no surprise that as women have increasingly made headway in the corporate world, the importance and value of sports have been taught to young girls and that their sports participation levels have never been higher.

As the role, and perception, of children changed in society, the judicial system reflected these changes. "Special courts were subsequently established to adjudicate juvenile matters. The technical language describing inappropriate youthful conduct or misbehaviors was greatly expanded and refined. These new courts were also vested with the authority to appoint probation officers and other persons considered suitable to manage juvenile offenders and enforce new juvenile codes" (Champion 2004, 19). Thus, where historically children over age 7 were held criminally accountable for their actions (subject to the authority of the father and punishment from the family), this was no longer the case. The creation of the concept of juvenile delinquency had also led to the creation of the concept of childhood as a separate stage of life, a buffer if you will, between infancy (0 to 7) and adulthood (generally 18).

The development of a juvenile status (the category of childhood) and the changing role of the family, especially the role of the father, throughout the past few centuries have had a dramatic effect on juveniles. The traditional importance of a strong father figure in the family, especially for the purpose of disciplining children and assuring their conformity to society's expectations, has nearly vanished. The link between this and the disappearance of the father from many contemporary households may be attributed, at least in part, to the taking away of his authority in the family by the state. Furthermore, as Bartollas and Miller (2001) indicate, there is little reason to believe that the 300-plus years legacy of taking authority away from the family is likely to change, at least in Western societies. The lack of a strong male presence in the family is critical to the examination of gang behavior, especially for male gang members. Taking personal responsibility for one's own behavior and correcting the social injustices that often contribute to one's decision to join a gang remain two other vital components to the study of gangs.

The (relatively) historically new designation of a juvenile status as it pertains to law is especially relevant to the study of gangs in that gang leaders recognize that juveniles are treated differently in the court system. As a result, gangs often designate a variety of tasks (e.g., drug running and thievery) for the younger members because they will receive much more lenient punishment than adult street gang offenders if they are caught committing a crime. It is this juvenile status that makes nonadults attractive to street gangs and assures that minors will be welcomed to join.

The Organization of Delinquency

Delinquents may be categorized in various ways, ranging from *loners* to *formal organizations*, but many organize as *peers* (Best and Luckenbill 1994). *Loners* are individuals who commit delinquency on their own and not in association with others. Examples of loner delinquency include most murderers, rapists, check forgers, embezzlers, amateur shoplifters, pedophiles, and art forgers (Best and Luckenbill 1994). "Loners choose deviance because they face situations where respectable courses of action are unattractive, not because they want to rebel against their socialization. For example, a loner may decide to commit a deviant act because the costs of breaking a norm seem less than the costs of respectable conduct" (Best and Luckenbill 1994, 16). Gang activity implies group behavior; consequently, loners are not applicable to the study of street gangs. More applicable to the study of street gangs is Best and Luckenbill's terms *colleagues* and *peers*. *Colleagues* are people who share some common activity or profession. Medical and academic doctors are examples of legal colleagues. Some colleagues engage in illegal activity such as arms and drugs trafficking. Deviant colleagues do not make as much contact with each other as legal colleagues. When deviant colleagues come in contact with one another, they build a body of shared knowledge that leads to the development of a subculture (Best and Luckenbill 1994). Gang members, although possessing a subculture similar to that of deviant colleagues, act as *peers*. *Peers* are people of equal value to one another or status with age as the most common variable that categorizes such a distinction. Elementary-aged children, junior-high, high school, and college students represent different peer group classifications. Although the ages of the members of any particular gang may vary quite a bit, most individuals join at the same age as their fellow peers.

In sum, delinquents can be divided into three categories: loner, colleagues, and peers. And while gang members may commit delinquency and criminal acts on their own, they generally commit most of their illegal activities with their peers, their gang. Best and Luckenbill, and this author, make it clear that all delinquents are not gang members, in fact, most are not. However, the most dangerous criminal youths tend to be street gang members.

DEFINITION OF A GANG

Most people believe that they understand what the words *gang* and *gang member* means. But defining the term *gang* is not as simple as one might think. In fact, there is no single definition, although every definition includes some mention of the word *group*. Nonetheless, establishing clear parameters of what constitutes a street gang is sometimes difficult. For example, is a group of young people hanging out together a gang? What if this group is hanging outside a convenience store talking loud and acting proud? What if this group creates a name for itself, starts identifying members with specific clothing, and uses secret hand signals and handshakes and intimidating nicknames such as "killer" and "assassin"? And what if this group also commits a number of deviant and/or criminal acts? Although these descriptions may fit the parameters of a "gang," they may also describe some sports teams, fraternities, and sororities.

The word *gang* is a variant of *gangue* or *gangr* (Old Norse), which originally meant a band or group that formed together for a journey (*The American Heritage Dictionary* 2000). Over time, the definition of gang has shifted from a group of people who band together for any number of reasons (beyond taking a journey) to a focus on the collective action of a group of people, especially those engaged in delinquent or criminal activities. Since many crimes or acts of delinquency committed by juveniles are done in groups, a core aspect of any definition of a street gang involves the word *group*. Most definitions emphasize the importance of territoriality (protecting "turf"). Contemporary definitions modify turf to include the concept of a "marketplace" for selling drugs. The idea of turf as a necessary component for a definition of a street gang muddled by the reality that most Asian gangs do not claim a specific street turf (Curry and Decker 2003). Other essential aspects for defining a "gang" involves the inclusion of gang members' habits of flashing hand signs, identifying by specific colors or gang emblems, and using a name to identify themselves.

The fact that dictionary editors, gang researchers, and gang members themselves cannot agree on the definition of a "gang" is not nearly as important as the fact that law enforcement agencies across the United States do not have a common definition. Consequently, accurate tracking of gang-related statistics is often difficult. The Office of Juvenile Justice and Delinquency Prevention (OJJDP) is considered one of the leading trackers of street gangs and gang statistics (The FBI [Federal Bureau of Investigation] is the other leading tracker of street gangs). In 2000, the OJJDP identified a number of criteria that must be met in order to classify a group as a youth gang:

- The group must have more than two members. Gangs always have more than two members.
- Group members must fall within a limited age range, generally acknowledged as ages 12 to 24.
- Members must share some sense of identity. This is generally accomplished by naming the gang (often referring to a specific geographic location in the name) and/or using symbols or colors to claim gang affiliation. Hand signals, graffiti, specific clothing styles, bandannas, and hats are among the common symbols of gang loyalty.
- Youth gangs require some permanence. Gangs are different from transient youth groups in that they show stability over time, generally lasting a year or more. Historically, youth gangs have also been associated with a particular geographical area or turf.
- Involvement in criminal activity is a central element of youth gangs. While some disagreement surrounds this criterion, it is important to differentiate gangs from noncriminal youth groups such as school and church clubs, which also meet all of the preceding criteria. (Esbensen 2000, 2–3)

Law enforcement jurisdictions generally incorporate many of the aspects of gangs described above. The California Penal Code (Section 186.22), for example, defines a street gang (in part) as "any ongoing organization, association, or group of three or more persons whether formal or informal . . . having a common name or common identifying sign or symbol, and whose members individually or collectively engage in or have engaged in a pattern of criminal activity." Albuquerque, New Mexico, state penal code (Section 11-9-4) defines a street gang as "any ongoing organization, association in fact, or group of three or more persons, whether formally or informally organized, or any sub-group thereof, having as one of its primary activities the commission of one or more criminal acts or illegal acts, which has an identifiable name or identifying sign or symbol, and whose members individually or collectively engage in or have engaged in a pattern of criminal gang activity for a one-year period." The state of Alabama (Section 13A-6-26) defines a street gang as "any combination, confederation, alliance, network, conspiracy, understanding, or other similar arrangement in law or in fact, of three or more persons that, through its membership or through the agency of any member, engages in a course or pattern of criminal activity." The state of Florida defines a gang (Section 874.03) as "a formal or informal ongoing organization, association, or group that has as one of its primary activities the commission of criminal or delinquent acts, and that consists of three or more persons who have a common name or common identifying signs, colors, or symbols and have two or more members who, individually or collectively, engage in or have engaged in a pattern of criminal street gang activity." In Georgia, it is unlawful "for any person employed by or associated with a criminal street gang to conduct or participate [in such a gang] through a pattern of criminal gang activity" (Code Ann. 16-15-4). In all cases, a criminal street gang member is a person who meets the legal definition of any particular jurisdiction.

It is important to note once again that the definition an agency uses affects the numbers that measure gangs, gang members, gang-related criminal activities, gang crimes, and so forth. It is also important to realize that gangs are not solely criminal organizations. Most of the time gang members simply "hang out" or engage in other nondelinquent behaviors (watching television, going on dates, etc.).

For the purposes of this book, I use a definition that incorporates the ideas of many other researchers along with ideas influenced by personal street gang interactions: A street gang is a group of individuals whose core members interact with one another frequently; they possess an identifying group name; generally wear certain types of similar clothing specific to their gang; can usually be identified by specific colors; are most likely to claim a neighborhood (or turf) or marketplace; and often engage in violent, criminal, or other delinquent behavior.

There are a number of terms related to street gangs that the reader should know. For example, the terms *posse*, *set*, or *crew* may be used to describe a street gang. Street gang members are also known as **gangbangers** or **gangsters**. Participating in gang activity is referred to as **gangbanging** behavior. Criminal **gang activity** refers specifically to gang-based crime. The term *gang-related crime* is applied if either the criminal or the victim is a gang member.

GENERAL DESCRIPTION OF GANGS AND GANG MEMBERS

Once again, conjure up an image of a gang member. Is your assessment accurate? Are gang members mostly inner-city minority males who love to fight, wear certain clothing, have tattoos, wear "bling-bling," and sell drugs? In many cases, the answer is "yes" to all of these stereotypical images of gangs. In other cases, gang members look much different from the stereotypical image most people have of gangs. The fact is there are a wide variety of gangs and gang members. Some of them are unique; others neatly fit the general "profile" of how many people think a gang member looks. This section is a brief review of some of the general descriptions of gangs and gang members.

One of the most basic questions regarding gangs is where do they come from? The simplest answer is based on the fact that ties of friendship link gang members to one another and the fact that many gang members knew each other before joining a gang. Researchers call this type of gang formation *spontaneous*. "A characteristic which may be regarded as typical of all gangs, as distinguished from more formal groups, is its spontaneous and unplanned origin" (Thrasher

1963/1927, 40). As with nongang members, young children grow up together and play and go to school together. When they enter adolescence, some may decide to give themselves a name and become a club, or a gang. There is a much greater likelihood of this occurring if there are already older gang members in the neighborhood. The youths may look up to and admire the existing gang members. Through imitation they quickly learn the subcultural values of gang members. Gang members are peer groups bound by informal ties and generally identified by a group name and distinctive clothing. For example, the Crips, a Los Angeles–based national gang (discussed in greater detail in Chapter 6), are associated with the color blue and wear blue bandannas, or handkerchiefs. The primary rival of the Crips is the Bloods. The Bloods are associated with the color red. Their bandanna (or do-rag) is symbolically equivalent to a national flag; it is to be protected at all times and is never to be lost in battle.

Interaction among gang members varies with the size and complexity of the gang. In larger gangs it is common for interaction to be limited to immediate cliques, or sets (a close-knit group). Hard-core members associate with one another almost exclusively, while peripheral members may associate with people outside the gang, along with other gang members. On important occasions such as a gang-sponsored dance or fight with a rival gang, the entire gang may mobilize collectively. The collective mobilization of the entire gang increases group cohesiveness (Klein 1995). However, day-to-day activities typically involve "traveling cliques" or close friends within the gang who are on patrol of their turf or involved in some criminal activity (e.g., selling drugs, robbery, auto theft). The gang is dependent on shared activities; they are its lifeblood. As with any group, if the members of the gang stop associating with one another, it risks dissolution. Gangs are not created for the sole purpose of engaging in criminal behavior; instead, it becomes one of the activities that the members carry out as peers.

Social interaction among gang members allows for the transmission of subcultural beliefs and attitudes. Younger gang members learn such values not only from older gang members, they are products of the surrounding adult culture as well. Thus, gang members from lower economic social classes tend to take on the values of the greater community, where such traits as toughness, street smarts, and excitement are dominant core values. For this reason, many gang members act, dress, and attempt to look tough. They often possess arrogant and defiant attitudes. Above all, they value their reputation of being tough and aggressive. They must never "punk out." For male gang members, ideals of manhood and masculinity are central aspects of their personality. Gang members are defined culturally and vary according to ethnicity and social class (Schneider 1999).

People in lower socioeconomic classes possess limited resources, and they are expected to defend the items that they do possess. Thus, the importance of toughness comes into play. The limited possession of material objects adds to the importance of protecting home territory, or turf. Members of the outside community may wonder why anyone would risk death to protect a ghetto-like neighborhood, but economically poor gang members view turf as their top possession. Material goods like gold chains, diamond earrings, and large finger rings (bling-bling) are items that lower-class gang members highly desire. Visible tattoos that reflect a gang member's allegiance are symbolic of loyalty to the group. Thus, expensive jewelry and tattoos are often signs of gang membership (*Youth Gangs and Juvenile Violence* 2003).

Clothing is an integral aspect of gang membership. Beyond the obvious distinction of red bandannas for Bloods and blue bandannas for Crips, a wide variety of posse paraphernalia is associated with specific gangs. A great deal of gang apparel is borrowed from the sports world.

Consider the following list as a mere sampling (other examples of gang-related clothing will be discussed in Chapter 6):

- The Fresno Bulldogs (CA) wear Fresno State sports apparel and have adopted the college's red color for its own and bark like dogs.
- Florencia 13 wear the Florida Marlins cap because of the letter "F." When the franchise relabeled itself in 2012 as the Miami Marlins the clothing was still appropriate because the letter "M" shows respect toward the Mexican Mafia, the prison gang that Florencia is aligned with.
- Gangster Disciples, a Chicago-based gang, wear Duke University apparel because they interpret *DUKE* as meaning "disciples utilizing knowledge everyday."
- The Playboy Hat is popular with the Vice Lords, sworn enemies of the Gangster Disciples, because they claim the Playboy icon as one of their gang symbols.
- Bomber jackets are popular with Asian gangs.
- The Vice Lords also wear Chicago Bulls apparel because of the black and red colors.
- The Gangster Disciples wear Detroit Lions caps because of the prominent letter "*D*."
- LA Kings apparel is popular with the Latin Kings street gangs.
- The Philadelphia Phillies cap is popular with the People Nation, an alliance of many street gangs based out of Chicago.
- University of Nevada Las Vegas (UNLV) clothing is popular with the Vice Lords because the letters UNLV are read backward to mean "Vice Lords Nation United."
- The Indiana University logo of the letter "*I*" imposed over the "*U*" appears as a pitchfork and is adopted by Gangster Disciples and the Folks Nation.
- Calvin Klein clothing is popular with the Bloods because CK represents "Crip Killer."
- Crips prefer going to Burger King over McDonald's because BK is interpreted as "Blood Killer."
- The Star of David is very important to the Gangster Disciples and the Folk Nation because it is both a six-pointed star (the Folks identify with the number 6) and because their founder, David Barksdale, considered himself a star and wore a Star of David necklace.
- Like most gangs that wear red, but especially those who have a name beginning with the letter "N," the Northside Mafia (in Denver) wear Nebraska Cornhuskers apparel because of both the color red and the big "N" logo for the university.

Stereotypes of Gangs

The image many people have of a gang member is greatly influenced by the media. A large segment of the population remains relatively removed from the daily problems that gangs represent in certain communities. The information that people have on gangs is usually limited to that provided in newspaper articles and news reports. Often, the journalistic slant relies on many stereotypes regarding gangs and gang behavior. There are a number of stereotypes of street gangs, some based on current realities, others based on popular culture and media presentations of gangs.

1. Gangs are a black or Hispanic problem: Gangs today, like gangs since their early days, reflect societal prejudice and discrimination; that is, any category of people being victimized by society is most likely to dominate the gang world. Gang domination began with the Irish, continued with other white ethnic groups, and switched to blacks and then Hispanics as the white ethnics became assimilated to society. Thus, the gang problem is a societal problem, not a black or Hispanic problem.

2. Only males are gang members: While the vast majority of gang members are male, there are female gang members and independent female gangs as well.
3. All gang members come from poor, "broken" families: There are gang members from all socioeconomic backgrounds, but most are from lower SES, fatherless families.
4. Street gangs are an inner-city problem: While it is true that street gangs are an inner-city problem, the problem is not restricted to the inner city; there are gangs in rural, suburban, and urban areas, and on Native-American reservations.
5. Street gangs are the same today as in the past: Many contemporary gangs are far removed from their historic roots as ethnic groups of juveniles protecting their neighborhood from outsiders. Today, many gangs dominate the drug trade in their communities and the level of violence is higher than ever before.
6. Once in a gang, you are in for life: In many gangs (especially rural, suburban, and local urban), individuals can voluntarily leave. In many such gangs, the individual will be subject to some sort of violation ceremony (e.g., a beating from the gang, or be forced to commit a crime in front of gang members). There are a number of gangs, however, that have a lifetime commitment policy.
7. Gangs are too disorganized to run criminal enterprises: While many gangs are loosely organized, there are street gangs operating in the United States that operate as very efficient criminal enterprises, and in some cases, work with foreign drug cartels.
8. All gangs are the same: There is great diversity in street gangs in regard to settings, type of criminal activity, organizational structure, and so on.
9. Gangs are really groups of misunderstood youths akin to those depicted in *West Side Story*: While young recruits are often misunderstood, have a troubled life at home and at school, and experience a sense of hopelessness, recruits do not enter the gang world thinking gang life is like *West Side Story*. The idea of gangsters dancing and singing while fighting (and with mere switchblades) is certainly far from reality. (See "Connecting Street Gangs and Popular Culture" Box 1.1 for a description of *West Side Story*.)

All of the stereotypes described above will be addressed throughout the book. The significance of stereotypes is that they shape the definitions of gangs and therefore determine policies structured to deal with gangs. Often, crimes committed by juveniles are labeled by the police as gang related. On the other hand, some law enforcement agencies, and as a result media outlets, do not describe specific crimes as gang related even though local citizens and those involved in research in this area know that such incidents are gang related.

There are many stereotypes about street gangs that are true. For example, street gang members are generally perceived to be male minority members. Data collected by the National Gang Center and the OJJDP reveal that law enforcement agencies report that the greatest percentage of street gangs members are Hispanic/Latino and African American/black than other race/ethnicities. In 2008, a little more than half of all street gang members were Hispanic/Latino, about 32 percent were black, 10 percent were white, and about 7 percent were from other races (National Gang Center 2009). White gang membership is highest in rural counties (19 percent) and lowest in larger cities (9 percent) (National Gang Center 2009). The National Gang Center (2009) reports that nearly 94 percent of gang members are males (see Chapter 7 for a discussion on female gang members). Earlier, in this chapter, it was mentioned that a large number of gang members are youths. Data analysis of reporting law enforcement agencies indicate that roughly 40 percent of all gang members are youths (National Gang Center 2009). There is also a stereotype that most gang members come from lower socioeconomic classes, and as we shall see throughout this book, that belief is also true.

Box 1.1   Connecting Street Gangs and Popular Culture

West Side Story: An Atypical Presentation of Street Gangs

Based on the 1957 Broadway stage play, the film *West Side Story* was released in 1961 and received critical acclaim in the movie industry, receiving 11 Academy Award nominations and winning all but 1—Best Adopted Screenplay (Filmsite Movie Review 2012). Among the Oscars won by *West Side Story* were Best Picture, Best Director, Best Supporting Actor and Actress, Best Color Cinematography, Best Color Art Direction/Set Decoration, Best Sound, and Best Scoring of a Musical Picture. That *West Side Story* won so many art-related awards is our primary clue that this film was more about artistic presentation (a melodramatic musical) than street gang reality. In fact, *West Side Story* is really a modern-day version of Shakespeare's *Romeo and Juliet*.

Set in the Upper West Side of New York City in the mid-1950s, *West Side Story* is a tale of two street gangs, the Jets and Sharks. The Jets are a white gang and the Sharks are Puerto Rican. The protagonist of the film, Tony (Richard Beymer) is a member of the Jets. He falls in love with a girl named Maria (Natalie Wood), who is the sister of Bernardo (George Chakiris), the leader of the Sharks. Like Romeo and Juliet, their love is "forbidden." Similar to real street gangs, especially of that era, the Jets and the Sharks are fighting for control of a neighborhood. Their battles involve a relative amount of violence, but are mostly devoid of gunfire. Throughout the history of street gangs (see Chapter 2), it was common for gangbangers to use their fists, knives, and other blunt instruments during battle. Guns were seldom used in gang fights. For the past few decades, however, street gangs regularly rely on firearms to settle their beefs. Like today, the Jets and Sharks are regularly confronted by the police. Officer Krupke (William Bramley) and plainclothes policeman Lt. Schrank (Simon Oakland) don't really care if the gangbangers kill each other, just not on their beat.

Maria, who recently arrived in New York from Puerto Rico, works in a bridal shop. Her brother Bernardo sent for her and arranged a marriage for her with Chino, a member of the Sharks. At a school dance, Tony and Maria see each other across the room. They have an instant attraction for each other. Bernardo and other Sharks keep Tony from Maria, but he finds her apartment building and serenades her while she admires him outside her bedroom. (The two would-be lovers will continue singing to each other throughout the film.) Meanwhile, the Jets and Sharks have a "war council" (a meeting) at Doc's drug store. Modern street gangs may in fact hold such "war councils" especially to discuss a truce to end bloody murderous feuds.

The Jets and Sharks decide to rumble (a gang fight) for the right to claim their disputed turf. The two gangs decide to meet the following night under the rules of a "fair fight"—the best man from each gang fights one-on-one, no weapons. On the night of the fight and upon Maria's insistence, Tony tries to make peace between the two gangs, but Bernardo taunts him. Riff, the leader of the Jets, fights Bernardo and they both pull out knives. When Riff has a chance to stab his rival with his switchblade, Tony holds him back. Riff shakes loose and continues his fight, but he is stabbed and killed by Bernardo. Angered over what has happened, Tony takes Riff's knife and kills Bernardo. While this is going on, Maria is dancing on the rooftop thinking about Tony and awaiting his arrival. The two lovers have already discussed marriage. Chino informs Maria that Tony has killed her brother. Maria cannot believe this and prays that it is not true. Tony tries to tell Maria that it was a mistake; that he tried to stop the rumble. Tony tells her that he loves her. He sings to her. And she sings to him. Somehow, she still loves him. Such is love in *West Side Story*.

The Jets learn that Chino has a gun and that he is looking to kill Tony. The Jets vow to protect him. Tony is hiding out in Maria's room. He asks her to run away with him, and she agrees to meet him later for that purpose. Anita, a friend of Maria, but not a fan of her involvement with Tony, tells her to stick to her "own kind" and forget Tony. "A boy who kills, cannot love, a boy who kills has no heart," Anita sings to Maria. Maria sings her praises for Tony to Anita. Anita tells Maria that Chino has a gun and is going to kill Tony. Anita learns that Tony is waiting at Doc's store. The police detain Maria, and she sends Anita to Doc's to ask Tony to wait a little longer for her. Anita goes to Doc's and tells the members of the Jets that Maria was killed by Chino because of her relationship with Tony. The Jets believe Anita. Doc tells Tony and he believes Maria to be dead too. Broken-hearted and feeling as though there is nothing to live for, Tony looks for Chino. Instead of finding Chino, Tony sees Maria in the street. He cannot believe she is alive, and they run toward each other to embrace. Chino emerges from the shadows and shoots Tony. He falls into Maria's arms and dies. Maria grabs the gun and tells both the rival gangs that they are all to blame for the recent deaths. She breaks down and cries. Maria kisses Tony and the Jets carry him away. All the other gang members somberly leave the scene of the crime. The film ends.

West Side Story is a romantic tale of forbidden love, not because of feuding families as in "Romeo and Juliet," but because of two rival gangs. When street gangs fight, people often die. However, what makes this film unrealistic as a gang movie is the constant singing and dancing of the main characters and the gangs themselves. It is not at all realistic to think of gangs in this manner. From the very beginning of the film, with the Jets snapping their fingers (in time to the music) and dancing in choreographed rhythm as if they belonged to a ballet troop, to their first confrontation with the Sharks, the portrayal of the Jets and Sharks as street gangs is mostly comical. In addition, the characters regularly break out into song as they express their feelings and concerns, behaviors that real gangbangers would never display.

In 1980, *West Side Story* was revived as a Broadway play. Over the years, including a 2008 U.K. tour and a 2009 U.S. tour, fans of *West Side Story* still find enjoyment in this classic play. However, as each year and decade pass, the idea of *West Side Story* presenting a realistic view of street gangs becomes less representative of the truth. Street gang life is not romantic. And gangbangers certainly do not sing and dance as they "rumble."

STATISTICS: COUNTING GANGS AND GANG MEMBERS

There are variations of gangs around the world. Some international gangs are formed by political, ethnic, and increasingly religious influences, and other international gangs are "street guerrillas" who challenge the state for control of cities and regions of a nation (see Chapter 10 for a look at the growing global problem of gangs). Often viewed as predominantly an American problem, street gangs are flourishing around the world. John Hagedorn (2009) attributes the international proliferation of urban street gangs as a result of the negative consequences of globalization. He believes that gangs have become institutionalized in nations other than the United States as a result of the hopeless cycle of poverty, racism, and oppression that persists in much of the world.

It is the United States, however, that still possesses the most street gangs and street gang members. Gangs exist in all 50 American states, in all socioeconomic classes, and in all racial and ethnic groups. For some citizens, the problems presented by gangs are a daily nightmare. For others, their knowledge of gangs is based on secondhand reports. The first line of defense in combating street gangs is law enforcement agencies. The manner in which they deal with and apprehend suspected gang members is based on agency policy. Agency policy is dictated by the definitions used to describe gangs and gang-related crimes. For example, in Syracuse, New York, the police department denied for years that there were gangs in the city (see Chapter 6 for a further discussion of Syracuse gangs). In 2002, Police Chief Dennis DuVal and other city officials acknowledged that there were gangs in Syracuse and consequently created a gang task force to eliminate them (Sieh 2003).

As stated earlier, there is no single, agreed-upon definition of gangs among the various law enforcement agencies across the United States. Consequently, coming up with accurate statistics on the number of gangs and gang members is relatively difficult. Gang researchers and law enforcement agencies often work together and share information on this subject. Since 1995, perhaps the most cited (and reputable) source for statistics on gangs comes from the OJJDP, a division of the U.S. Department of Justice. The OJJDP sends surveys to law enforcement agencies requesting information on gang activity in their jurisdictions. Through a variety of publications, the OJJDP reports its findings. It is worth noting that "in October 2009, the National Youth Gang Center, which had been funded by the OJJDP since 1995, merged with the National Gang Center, which had been funded by the Bureau of Justice Assistance since 2003. This new partnership recognizes that street gang activities transcend ages of the members and that a balanced, comprehensive approach is needed to reduce gang involvement and levels of crime. Consolidation of the centers has leveraged resources and resulted in a single, more efficient entity, responsive to the needs of researchers, practitioners, and the public" (OJJDP 2011b, 1).

Since 1995, when the OJJDP first started to track gang statistics, "three trends are apparent in the prevalence rate of gang activity: a sharp decline throughout the late 1990s, a sudden upturn beginning in 2001 and continuing until 2005, and a relative leveling off thereafter" (Egley and Howell 2011, 1). Among the key findings of the 2009 Youth Gang Survey:

- There were an estimated 28,100 gangs and 731,000 gang members throughout 3,500 jurisdictions nationwide.
- The prevalence rate of gang activity increased to 34.5 percent from 32.4 percent in 2008.
- Larger cities and suburban counties accounted for more than 96 percent of gang homicides.
- Sixty-six percent of the 167 responding cities with populations of more than 100,000 reported a total of 1,017 gang homicides.
- More than 40 percent of law enforcement respondents reported an increase in gang graffiti, while fewer than 3 percent reported no such incidents in 2009.
- More than half of survey respondents viewed drug-related factors, intergang conflict, and returning inmates as significantly influencing local gang violence. (Egley and Howell 2011)

In 2004, the OJJDP reported that there were approximately 731,500 gang members and 21,500 active gangs in the United States in 2002. As shown earlier, the OJJDP reported in 2011 that there were 28,100 street gangs in 2009; a figure that represents a roughly 30 percent increase between 2002 and 2009. However, the OJJDP also reported that there was no corresponding increase in the total number of gang members (in fact, there was a decrease of 500 gang members in the seven-year period). This may appear odd to the casual observer. After all, if the number of street gangs increased by 30 percent shouldn't the number of gang members also have increased by the same percentage to a figure that would total around 1 million gang members? Statistically speaking, we are talking about two different variables, the number of street gangs and the number of street gang members. Thus, there would not have to be such a corresponding increase in the number of gang members.

The FBI also tracks street gangs. Interestingly, through its National Gang Intelligence Center (NGIC) that prepared a report for the 2011 National Gang Threat Assessment (NGTA), the FBI (2011a) reported that there were 1,140,344 street gang members and 30,313 street gangs in 2011. Although the FBI data estimates 2011 street gang numbers and the OJJDP reported 2009 street gang estimates, the FBI figure of over 1 million street gangs seems more feasible. Like the OJJDP, the FBI collects data from law enforcement agencies. The FBI (2011a) utilized a stratified random sample of nearly 3,500 state and local law enforcement agencies; specifically, they received responses from 2,963 of 3,465 law enforcement agencies.

Los Angeles, the home-base of two of the most ferocious Nation gangs (Crips and Bloods), has the dubious distinction as the "street gang capital" of the world. It is estimated that there are well over 165,000 gang members in Southern California. One-half of all homicides are gang-related, and in Southern California homicide causes more deaths than auto accidents. The average life expectancy for a gang member in Southern California is 19. The notorious 18th Street Gang (see Chapter 6) has an estimated 20,000 members in LA County alone (Maxson, Hennigan, and Sloan 2003).

NON-STREET GANGS: OUTLAW MOTORCYCLE GANGS AND PRISON GANGS

There are many types of gangs and sometimes the distinction between street gangs and non-street gangs is murky. In simplest terms, street gangs conduct most of their criminal activity on the streets. They are visible and leave certain trails of cues (e.g., tagging their turf, identifying their intentions and deeds via graffiti) of their presence. Non-street gangs engage in criminal activities in different settings. Prison gangs, for example, are (mostly) restricted to the boundaries of a correctional facility, and organized crime syndicates attempt to operate in secret within the world of finance.

Organized crime (sometimes called syndicate crime) involves criminal activity committed by members of formal organizations that exist to operate profitable illicit enterprises (e.g., insurance fraud, counterfeiting, tax evasion, and money laundering (Delaney 2012). Stephen Schneider (2002) states, "Organized crime can be broadly defined as two or more persons conspiring together on a continuing and secretive basis, with the aim of committing one or more serious crimes to obtain, directly or indirectly, a financial or other material benefit" (1112). Organized crime exists to meet the demand for certain goods and services (e.g., prostitution, drugs, pornography, gambling, or smuggling) of the public; whereas street gangs exist for different reasons altogether. Wherever there is a demand for prohibited goods and services (e.g., prostitution, drugs, pornography, gambling, or smuggled goods), there is an opportunity for organized crime to become a major supplier (Best and Luckenbill 1994). As a result, the provision of illicit goods and services and systematic extortion are fundamental aspects of organized crime.

Although street gangs generally lack political agendas, highly organized street gangs also provide illicit goods and services to people who demand them. Like organized crime syndicates, highly organized street gangs possess a structured hierarchy characterized by persons with different levels of authority based on ranked position within the hierarchy; they continue to operate over time even when certain members leave the organization (e.g., are killed or imprisoned); use force or the threat of force to ensure operational goals; restrict membership to proven associates; obtain their profits primarily through illegitimate means; provide desired illegal goods and services to those who crave them; use corruption and intimidation to influence public officials and politicians; seek a monopoly; and work under a code of secrecy. In short, organized crime syndicates and highly organized street gangs have many of the same characteristics.

That is why it is important to once again point out that the setting of where these criminal activities occur remains important. Street gangs commit their criminal and delinquent acts in public places, primarily streets and parks, whereas organized crime syndicates commit their criminal activity in the white-collar world. Simon and Hagan (1999) argued that "organized white-collar crime" has traditionally referred to the infiltration of organized crime groups such as the Mafia into legitimate business, but it may also refer to behavior on the part of legitimate businesses that resemble organized crime operations or alliances between organized crime and legitimate businesses" (114). In the 2000s, however, law enforcement has increasingly success-fully prosecuted street gangs using federal laws such as the Racketeer Influenced and Corruption Organizations Act (RICO), which is dependent on proving street gangs act as criminal enter-prises. The RICO Act was created to fight organized crime, but it has been used with greater frequency to combat the growth of street gangs (see Chapters 6 and 8). The American Civil Liberties Union (ACLU) believes that the use of RICO arrests against street gang members is illegal, primarily, because there is a distinction between street gangs and organized crime syn-dicates. Organized crime syndicates include such groups as the Russian Mafia, the Irish Mob of Boston, and the Italian Mafia/La Cosa Nostra. But these organizations are not the focus of this book. Two other entities, outlaw motorcycle gangs and prison gangs, however, are within the pa-rameters of this edition but are not the focus of study. A brief review of both outlaw motorcycle gangs and prison gangs is provided in this chapter, and they will be discussed throughout the book when their activities intersect with street gangs.

Outlaw Motorcycle Gangs (OMG)

The world of popular culture thinks of *OMG* as "Oh My God," but the FBI uses the abbreviation *OMG* to refer to **Outlaw Motorcycle Gangs**. According to the FBI (2011a), "OMGs are organiza-tions whose members use their motorcycle clubs as conduits for criminal enterprises" (2).

Members of motorcycle clubs such as the Hells Angels, Outlaws, Vagos, and Sons of Silence do not consider themselves gang members nor do they believe that they should be subjected to the same behavioral restraints as gangs. The Ventura County (California) Fair Board voted in July 2003 to ban gang attire in the hope that gang violence would decrease during the annual fair. A Hells Angels member, wearing a leather vest sporting the group's trademark winged skull (or "death head"), was denied admission to the fair and protested that the ban should not apply to him because the Hells Angels are not a gang. Motorcycle gangs first appeared on the American scene in the 1950s. They had a great influence on American pop culture, and some of the more notorious ones were linked to numerous violent crimes. OMGs emerged following World War II when lower- and working-class males began to form motorcycle clubs without registering their bikes with the respected American Motorcycle Association—an organization that governs the sport of motorcycling riding (Best and Luckenbill 1994). These bikers became known as "outlaws" because of their independence from registered motorcycle associations. It wasn't long after when these outlaw bikers began to commit criminal acts. OMGs are some-times referred to as "One Percenters" because they represent the minority (1%) of bikers who engage in unlawful behavior. They also became frightening popular culture icons as the focus of such movies as *The Wild One* (1953) and the *Hell's Angels* (1930). The frightening aspect of the Hells Angels is attributed to their appearance, their wearing of "colors" (e.g., denim or leather vests or jackets with club insignia), disruptive behavior, stories of illicit drug use and violence, and the loud Harley-Davidson motorcycles they ride.

Despite the "outlaw," nonconformist nature of biker gangs, the more sophisticated ones (e.g., Hells Angels) have a formal operating structure. Wolf's (1991) participant observation study of the Edmonton (Alberta, Canada) Rebels motorcycle club revealed the strong sense of belonging to a brotherhood among the members, but it also revealed its formal structure. The Rebels had a written constitution filled with membership requirements, club officers, and regu-larly scheduled meetings and required that members pay dues. "This formal structure reflects the difficulty of maintaining organizational stability. Bikers find themselves under perpetual threat of attack. The respectable world, especially law enforcement, seeks to constrain, if not eliminate, outlaw clubs. Moreover, members may have to defend their club's territory from attacks by rival clubs. Finally, there is the danger of violent, uncontrolled internal disputes among the club's members" (Best and Luckenbill 1994, 56). In order to deal with these problems, it was important for the biker club to find a clubhouse to serve as a refuge from external enemies (Wolf 1991). As with street gangs, biker gangs often branch out. Such an affiliation and federation generally involves clubs that are separated by some distance from each other. This is important in order to eliminate conflict and the inevitable competition for resources among the affiliates.

The most famous and dominating biker gang is the Hells Angels. The Hells Angels were founded by Ralph "Sonny" Barger (called "Sonny" from the Italian tradition of calling the firstborn son by that name). According to his autobiography, Sonny had difficulty with authority figures and was continually getting suspended for his mischief in school. Taking on the role of a gang leader began at an early age. While he was still at Oakland (California) High School, Sonny organized a small street corner club named the Earth Angels, after the hit song by the Penguins. Barger (2001, 21) explained that the gang "didn't stand for anything, it was just something to belong to. . . . It was all about belonging to a group of people just like you." Sonny's words reflect an important aspect of street gangs, which is the tendency for them to be homogenous in nature, even when they are found in heterogeneous neighborhoods. Sonny's gang spent the majority of their time smoking marijuana and getting into fights at school. Sonny's first experience with a motorcycle club, the Oakland Panthers, was short-lived due to the lack of solidarity (Barger 2001). Some experts on gang behavior believe that individuals seek out gang membership because they are looking for a substitute family that contributes the same kind of support, security, and caring that the "traditional" intact nuclear family is supposed to provide (Siegel et al. 2003). Sonny's search for a substitute family would soon find it in a motorcycle club, the Hells Angels.

On the surface, the Hells Angels possess many of the characteristics of a street gang, including the common name, common identifying symbols, and common activities among members. The Hells Angels are a mix of races and ethnicities, although most of the members are white. Barger (2001) describes the original members of the Hells Angels as "young high school dropouts in our early twenties who didn't have two nickels to rub together . . . all we owned was the clothes on our back and the bike between our legs" (32). Brotherhood and fraternity are the hallmarks of the Angels. It was an unwritten rule that if you messed with one Hells Angel, you messed with them all. Furthermore, if a Hells Angel was locked up in jail, the other members would raise money for bail. The origin of the Hells Angels name is linked to the U.S. Army's 11th Airborne Division. They were "an elite group of paratroopers trained to rain death on the enemy from above, drifting in behind the lines of battle" (Jamison 2000, 2). Barger (2001) states, "The term 'Hell's Angels' had been bouncing around the military as far back as World War I, when a fighter squadron first took on the name. During the twenties in Detroit, a motorcycle club affiliated with the American Motorcyclist Association named themselves Hell's Angels. . . . WWII had a few groups called Hell's Angels, including an American Air Force bomber company stationed in England" (28–29). A veteran of the Airborne was wearing his "modified Air Force-like patch" while bike riding. Barger and the rest of the club liked the design and made matching patches for everyone in the club. The Hells Angels motorcycle club was formed.

Beyond the brotherhood that the Hells Angels provide, recreational opportunities were among the more important reasons that an individual chose to join the motorcycle gang. These characteristics—brotherhood and recreational opportunities—are common with street gangs as well. "They swap girls, drugs and motorcycles with equal abandon. In between drug-induced stupors, the Angels go on motorcycle stealing forays" (Thompson, Hunter S. 1999, 25). Sonny's own criminal record supports Thompson's claims. From 1957 to 1987, Barger's record includes numerous charges of possession of narcotics and marijuana, oftentimes with the intent to sell. In fact, throughout his autobiography, Sonny describes the continuous cycle of partying (drinking and drugs), bar brawls, and women. Barger believes that women are attracted to outlaw bikers because of their tough-guy image. Law enforcement officers and the townspeople who come in contact with outlaw bikers such as the Hells Angels describe the chaos and criminal activity that accompany them. The bikers refute such accusations, protesting that their actions are merely innocent fun. Aggravated assaults, theft, and drug and alcohol-related offenses are the most common criminal violations committed by biker gangs. Sonny Barger's own criminal history, however, supports the accusations, as his record shows numerous aggravated assaults, most involving deadly weapons.

The structure of the Hells Angels is similar to that of a business or corporation. First, there must be a strong leader if the organization is going to survive and flourish. This leader must demonstrate that he/she can deal with any problem that may arise. Disputes in the Hells Angels were handled by Barger, who not only introduced the structure and rules of the biker club but enforced them as well. Sonny insisted on weekly meetings, and if anyone missed a meeting, he paid a monetary fine. Barger also created tactical rules such as a separation of 50 miles between all charters (with one exception—the Oakland and San Francisco charters are less than 10 miles apart). Because of the "pick up and go mentality" of the biker gang, it is hard for members to secure steady employment. Consequently, the majority of the members partake in illegal activities to support themselves. Selling drugs and stolen property (e.g., guns and auto parts) are among the more profitable illegal activities biker gangs participate in. The Hells Angels also provide illegal services such as protection and offer demolition of property services. In one well-documented example, the Rolling Stones hired the Angels to provide security at the California Altamont Speedway concert in 1969. Stones frontman, Mick Jagger, criticized the Angels after a biker stabbed to death a spectator who had pulled a gun during a melee; the killing was ruled self-defense and the charges were dropped (James 2009).

Among the identifying features of the Hells Angels are the numerous tattoos that they sport and the wearing of leather. Angels may use the letters "H" and "A" and "81" to represent the letters' numeric locations in the alphabet, and often wear red and white colors as a contrast to their black leather clothing. A very important characteristic of the Angels is their commitment to their motorcycle—the Harley-Davidson. They generally park their spotlessly clean machines inside their homes at night. Thompson (1999, 85) claimed that the Hells Angels are pathetic without their motorcycles but further stated that there is nothing pathetic about an Angel on his bike. The relationship between an Angel and his bike is obvious even for those who know nothing about motorcycles. The most identifying feature of the Hells Angels is the death's head patch affixed to the back of all members' jackets. The patch is respected in the same manner as a patriot respects the national flag or a gangbanger protects his colors (e.g., bandanna). The Angels make it clear that only members are to be seen wearing the patch. If a nonmember is discovered wearing the patch, severe consequences will occur.

The bar brawling, partying, renegade, free-spirited, deviant, and criminal Hells Angels described above represents their old image. Today, when law enforcement discusses the Hells Angels, they are referring to the criminal organization that controls drug trafficking across the world's most unprotected border. It is rather common knowledge in the study of gangs that the Hells Angels rules the Canadian-American border and will stop at nothing to control the flow of drugs into the United States. A primary staging point for the Hells Angels is Montreal, a city just 45 miles north of the U.S. border. Throughout Montreal, the Angels own businesses and run prostitution and cocaine rings. For the Canadian Hells Angels, Canada is a mecca because of its money-making opportunity as a base to run drugs into the United States (Gangland 2009a). The Canadian Hells Angels make cocaine deals in metric tons and earn hundreds of millions of dollars annually (Gangland 2009a). Today, there are Hells Angels chapters throughout Canada. In the west, they deal mostly in very high-potent marijuana, back east, it's mostly cocaine. The western Hells Angels are responsible for a great deal of the $6 billion annual marijuana trade into the United States (Gangland 2009a). But it is the story of Hells Angels in Montreal that highlights the shift in this OMG mentality. In 1977, the New York City chapter of the Angels first sent members up north to start a prostitution and drug trafficking ring. These gangsters represent the "old guard," the ones who want to make money, but enjoy partying and fighting just as much. The met the challenge of the Outlaws, a rival gang, during their first couple of years in Montreal. The Angels grew in size and in the mid-1990s were challenged by another rival OMG, the Rock Machine. During the couple of years these two gangs warred against one another more than 160 people were killed and 200 more were injured (Gangland 2009a). The Hells Angels won the battle, but needed more recruits. These new recruits would develop into the "new guard," as they were more concerned with making money and using violence to protect their criminal enter-prise and not for fun. The Montreal Angels split based on these two distinctions. While the new guard made huge sums of money, the old guard were sloppy and not as productive. The New York branch sent the word for the new guard to take out the old. Indeed, we had Angels killing Angels—so much for the brotherhood between all chapters. The new guard won the battle, and since that inner dispute the Angels have concentrated their efforts on making money, primarily through drug trafficking. The Canadian Angels uphold many of the old traditions of the original Hells Angels, including riding Harley-Davidsons, wearing the identifying patches and tattoos, and other identifiers. The Hells Angels are the most powerful OMG in North America, and they completely dominate the drug flow into the United States from Canada.

The Vagos motorcycle club is based out of San Bernardino County (California), the largest county in the United States, filled with hundreds of acres of empty desert. There are an estimated 500 members of the Vagos OMG. The term *Vagos* is a Spanish word for *wanderer* and pays hom-age to the Hispanic origins of this OMG. (Today, the majority of the members are white.) The Vagos (also known as the Green Nation) have a logo of the Norse god Loki. The Vagos wear a variety of patches including a green "22" for the letter "V" in the alphabet and a green "13" as a nod to their role as marijuana and methamphetamine distributors and traffickers. The 1953 pop culture movie *The Wild One* is based on a 1947 incident involving a Vagos biker rally party that got out of hand and led to days of rioting. This incident also led to the American Bikers Association claim that only 1 percent of bikers are non-law-abiding and thus the claim among OMG that they are "One Percenters." The Sons of Silence OMG has a home turf of Colorado Springs, Colorado. With a nickname of "Sons of Violence," this biker gang commits a wide range of crimes, activities including drug trafficking and distribution. The gang's logo is inspired by the Budweiser beer logo (an eagle with a capital "A") with their own interpretation of the Latin phrase to mean, "we don't part until we die." The Sons of Silence have a number of patches, including the "13" to represent the letter "M" in methamphetamine.

The FBI (2011a) estimates that there are 2,965 OMGs with a total membership of 44,108. The Angels claim to have clubs in 27 countries, with 125 charters in Europe alone (Hells Angels 2012). When OMGs are combined with street gangs, the FBI estimates a total membership of 1,415,578. When the collective membership of street gangs and OMGs are divided by geographic region, we can clearly see that the largest number of gang members

TABLE 1.4	2011 Estimated Street and OMG Gang Membership by Region	
Region		**Number**
North Central		260,022
Northeast		159,158
South Central		167,353
Southeast		117,205
West		480,715

Source: FBI (2011a)

reside in the west (see Table 1.4). With Los Angeles as the prime location for street gangs, it is not surprising to learn that such a large number of gangs are found in the west. The North Central region, which includes the state of Illinois, has the second largest number of street gang and OMG members. This is also expected as Chicago is the home of the other two nation-based street gangs, the People and Folks (see Chapter 6 for a discussion on the People and the Folks).

PRISON GANGS

A discussion of prison gangs is relevant to the study of street gangs because so many gangbangers end up in prison and continue their gangbanging lifestyle behind bars. Violence and angry confrontations directed against rivals on the street often continue in prison. According to the FBI (2011a), "prison gangs are criminal organizations that originated within the prison system and operate within correctional facilities throughout the United States, although released members may be operating on the street. Prison gangs are also self-perpetuating criminal entities that can continue their criminal operations outside the confines of the penal system" (2).

Prison gangs are known to be in existence in nearly all of the prisons in the United States. They are especially prominent in the Illinois and California prison systems because these two states represent the home base of the four primary nation gangs (People and Folks in Illinois and Crips and Bloods in California). According to Fong (1990), prison gangs first formed in 1950 when a group of prisoners at the Washington Penitentiary in Walla Walla organized and took the name of the **Gypsy Jokers**, so for more than 60 years prison gangs have been present in the United States. The enactment of tougher laws against gang-related crimes, beginning in the late 1980s, has directly led to an increase in the number of gang members in prisons. The judicial system was relatively successful in getting gang members off the streets, but their incarceration has led to increased problems for prison officials. Over the years, prison gangs have become more prevalent (Martinez 1999). They are also responsible for the majority of problems within correctional facilities. The increasing reality is that today's street gangs are becoming tomorrow's prison gangs; and correctional facilities will have to deal with inmates who are more violent and have better connections to illicit activities outside prison walls (Welling 1994).

Prison gangs are similar to organizational crime syndicates. "The emergence of prison gangs has added to the crisis already being experienced by many correctional systems. Prison gangs pursue more than self-protection; they evolved into organized crime syndicates involved in such activities as gambling, extortion, drug-trafficking, prostitution, and contract murder"

(Fong 1991, 66). For example, Larry Hoover, a reputed leader of the Gangster Disciples, was convicted of running a large cocaine enterprise from within a state prison (Tyson 1997). Beyond drug trafficking, organized crime often leads to violence. In Texas, 62 percent of inmate murders recorded between 1979 and 1985 were committed by prison gangs, and overall, prison gangs account for over 50 percent of all problems and violence in America's prisons (Fong 1991).

Some prison gangs are very powerful and command respect among inmates and street gangsters alike. Prison gang leaders keep in contact with outside gangbangers in a number of ways, including through individuals who visit gang leaders in prison and receive commands; correctional officers and other staff members who have been bribed, coerced, or extorted; and direct contact with street gangsters via phone calls from prison gang leaders behind bars. As unthinkable as it would seem, some prisoners actually have cell phones and make regular calls to their outside contacts. As Cory Godwin, president of the gang investigators association for the Florida Department of Corrections stated, "contraband equals power" (Danitz 1998). Judicial intervention in correctional administration has systematically stripped away the legitimate authority of prison officials to discipline and control inmates, experts claim. The existence of this organizational crisis has created an atmosphere conducive to the proliferation of inmate gangs (Fong 1991). Thus, judicial intervention, which has the effect of weakening control over inmates, has created an era in which inmate gangs have begun to dominate the prison setting and that has also led to an escalation of violence in prisons (Fong 1990).

Prison gangs flourished throughout the 1990s and were responsible for increased levels of crime in correction facilities from coast to coast. During this period states such as Illinois had facilities where as much as 60 percent of the prison population belonged to gangs (Danitz 1998). Goodwin identified 240 street gangs operating in the Florida Department of Corrections (Danitz 1998). Street gangs are viewed as an emerging problem in East Coast prisons; they are already a problem in West Coast and Southwest prisons. Texas officials estimated that of the 143,000 inmates in their prisons, 5,000 had been identified as gang members and another 10,000 are under suspicion. Prison gangs are not great in number in Texas, but they are highly organized and possess a paramilitary-type structure (Tyson 1997). In other state prison systems, officials have noticed that the gang problem is very serious. In Illinois, there were prisons (Statesville, in Joliet) with gangs so powerful that they ran a profitable drug trade inside the prison with the help of corrupt guards (Tyson 1997). Chicago super gangs, such as the Vice Lords and Gangster Disciples, exert great control over gallery and cell assignments through intimidation in the Illinois prisons. Gangs dominate inmate organizations and some are allowed to paint their cells with gang colors and insignia and enjoy special privileges such as wearing expensive jewelry and their own clothing. This would be allowed in cases where inmates have otherwise conformed to prison rules. It serves as an incentive for conforming behavior.

It is critical that correctional facilities identify gang members upon arrival at their institutions. In many cases, gang members will be housed separately from other inmates in order to ensure the safety of other inmates, correctional officers, and other staff. Because most gang members have gang tattoos, it is easy to identify many gangsters. During the intake process, it is important for correctional facilities to identify the spoken languages of inmates to assure that a correctional employee who speaks the same language is readily available should circumstances dictate. Correctional facilities are also concerned about the languages spoken by inmates to avoid any type of language-related mishap that could lead to future lawsuits (Skarbek 2012). Trying to recognize gang members during the intake process is merely the first step in helping to identify potential gang problems inside the prison. Correctional facilities also employ a number of separation tactics, such as dividing inmates by their gang affiliation or putting known gang members in an isolation area akin to a lockdown status. Some facilities use behavioral "management units" where inmates are awarded limited privileges with good behavior (Trulson, Marquart and Kawucha 2006). Hardcore, or extreme troublemakers, may be isolated by 23 hours-per-day lockdowns where inmates are given just 1 hour a day of recreation (Morgan 2009). Understandably, this type of separation tactic may cause psychological and emotional problems for inmates. Another hazard of this approach reveals itself after an inmate has been released from incarceration and has trouble reintegrating back into society (Winterdyk and Ruddell 2010). Furthermore, there are those who suggest that the correctional officer is exposed to greater danger by inmates who are housed in 23-hour lockdowns because the inmate can get very edgy. While housed in the correctional facility, gang members have to be monitored by correctional officials. Monitoring is an essential technique for ensuring the inclusive safety of a correctional facility. Every correctional facility has some form of monitoring, or supervising, the activities of its inmates including listening to inmates' forms of communication (e.g., telephone calls, visitation conversations, letters received in the mail, discussions between fellow inmates), searching their cells (looking for forbidden materials, contraband, shanks, and journals that describe gang activities), and collecting and compiling information from the searches. Gang intelligence officers examine confiscated materials and look for hidden messages by decoding cryptic printed materials and piecing together key words used in verbal conversations, including phone messages.

The nature of street gang activities are always subject to change. It is important, therefore, that correctional officers go through constant training. Training of officers begins during their extensive training in the academy. They are taught gun control, how to handle emergencies, and how to identify gang affiliations. Once stationed at a particular prison, or correctional facility, officers annually go through additional training if there is a new threat in the prison (e.g., members from a particular gang at war with other housed gang members). Officers are also trained to be wary of influences from gang members outside the prison as family members of inmates will often move to the surrounding area of the prison so that they can visit more often and possibly to help smuggle goods in and out of the prison during visitation hours. Administration must be careful when hiring correctional officers in order to avoid possible assistance to inmates by facility personnel. Inmates will often threaten the lives of correctional officers' family members, so administrators must be on guard for that too. Sometimes, in reaction to threats, a correctional officer may assist an inmate and other times, officers may take financial bribes from inmates. Thus, administration must be on the watch for **corruption**. If an officer is discovered helping inmates he/she will be fired and face legal consequences.

As a resident of Auburn, New York, home to a maximum security correctional facility, I have long known about the perils that face prison guards. My own grandfather, a prison cook, was stabbed during a riot in the Auburn prison many years ago. I have many friends who are correctional officers. It is common for officers and their families to live outside the city and it is routine that their phone numbers are kept confidential. In the case of my sister, whose husband is a correctional officer, their phone number was under her maiden name. Every time there is a problem in the prison, and there often is, family members worry about their loved ones working inside the walls.

The FBI (2011a) estimates that there were 231,136 prison gang members and an undeterminable number of prison gangs operating in U.S. prisons in 2011 (this figure is based on reports from 32 states). The FBI (2011a) estimated that in 2011 there were a total of 1,415,578 gang members, which included prison gang members, OMGs, and street gangs in the United States (see Table 1.5). The National Criminal Justice Reference Service (NCJRS) (2011), a branch of the U.S. Department of Justice, reports that the line between prison and street gangs is becoming

TABLE 1.5	2011 Total Estimated Gang Membership	
Category	**Members**	**Gangs**
Street	1,140,344	30,313
OMG	44,108	2,965
Prison	231,136	N/A
Total	1,415,578	33,278

Source: FBI (2011a)

increasingly muddied as gang members flow in and out of the correctional system. Consequently, the U.S. Department of Justice has established the "Anti-Violence Crime Imitative," which is designed to develop and coordinate information-sharing strategies among corrections, parole, probation, and law enforcement agencies with regard to offenders who are of particular interest to each of them. "For example, police gang units may supply state prison officials with information about gang affiliations and activities of offenders from their jurisdiction who are sent to prison. In exchange, prison officials may alert local police when gang-involved offenders are about to be released from prison, and describe their gang activities while confined (NCJRS 2011, 1). It should also be noted that a number of juvenile gang members are in prison.

In the following sections, a number of the more powerful prison gangs are briefly discussed. We begin with the three most familiar ones—the Mexican Mafia, the Texas Syndicate, and the Aryan Brotherhood—and continue with a description of Neta, the Black Guerilla Family, the Five Percenters, and La Nuestra Familia.

La Eme (Mexican Mafia)

The largest of all prison gangs is the Mexican Mafia, which has a highly organized and para-military-type of structure. The **Mexican Mafia**, or **La Eme** (*eme* is Spanish for the letter "M"), was started around 1957 at Deuel Vocational Institution, a center for youthful offenders in Tracy, California. The original leaders, believed to be Joe "Peg Leg" Morgan and Rodolfo (Rudy) "Cheyenne" Cadena, formed a gang of about 20 Mexican-Americans, mostly gang members from the Maravilla area in Los Angeles. The initial reason for the formation of La Eme was for protection against African-American inmates. As more Los Angeles Hispanics came into prison, they were recruited into La Eme. As La Eme grew in members, it was soon the hunter and not the hunted. Backed by the threat of violence, La Eme members began robbing other inmates of their possessions and luxuries, such as cigarettes and drugs (Skarbek 2012). The early years of La Eme were portrayed in the movie *American Me* produced and directed by Edward James Olmos, who played the central character as well. Current members of La Eme vehemently deny that the film is factual. They were especially upset about a scene that suggested the rape of one of their leaders, as they are dead set against homosexuality in any form, declaring it violates their creed of *machismo*. (See "Connecting Street Gangs and Popular Culture" Box 1.2 for a description of the film *American Me*.)

By the late 1960s, La Eme began to exert its power over the outside community. La Eme has a dual purpose: ethnic solidarity and the control of drug trafficking. Violence, extortion, vandalism, and pressure rackets are the tools La Eme uses to control drug trafficking. Commands given from inside the prison are carried out by street gangs. Street gangs must pay the Mexican Mafia

Box 1.2   Connecting Street Gangs and Popular Culture

American Me and La Eme

American Me (1992) was inspired by the real life events that led to the formation of La Eme (meaning, the "M"—for Mexican Mafia) at the Deuel Vocational Institution, a center for youthful offenders in Tracy, California. *American Me* was produced and directed by Edward James Olmos, his first film as a director. Olmos also stars in the film, taking on the film's protagonist role of "Montoya Santana," a character based on Rodolfo Cadena, founder of La Eme. The film begins with a warning that the events it describes are brutal and very violent. *American Me* uses a documentary-style format (the occasional voice-over narration is in rhyme) in telling the story of "Santana's" life beginning with a flashback to the youth of his parents during the 1943 "Zoot Suit" riots (see Chapter 2 for a description of the riots). Santana's father was being assaulted by sailors while his mother was being raped. This event would have a profound influence on Montoya's relationship with his father. In a poignant scene midway through the film, Montoya tells his father, "Whatever I did to you or to mama . . . to make you hate me, I'm sorry." His father Pedro replies, "Your mother was a beautiful woman. She made me feel proud. She was 19 years old. Raped . . . by sailors. After it happened, we never talked about it. Then we got married and we tried to forget. When you were born, I tried to love you. But every time I looked at you, I wondered who your real father was. I wondered which sailor's blood you carried inside of you." Always feeling distanced from his father, Montoya and his friends talk about their need for respect and desire to start their own street gang. (They acknowledge the powerful White Fence gang, to be discussed in Chapter 2.)

Growing up on the streets of East Los Angeles, Montoya hangs out with other delinquents, often getting in trouble. Santana and his closest friends, J.D. (Steve Wilcox as a young J.D. and William Forsythe as the adult J.D.) and Mundo (Pepe Serna as a young Mundo and Richard Coca as an adult Mundo) form their own gang. Eventually, their criminal activities lead to incarceration at juvenile hall. The viewer is shown the ritualistic strip searches that all inmates are required to endure when entering "juvie." On his first night, Santana is raped by a fellow juvenile inmate at knife point while he lay in bed. Immediately after, Santana beats the rapist and kills him. For committing murder, Montoya is given a sentence of imprisonment at Folsom as soon as he turned 18. But he had gained the respect of all the other incarcerated Mexican juveniles. Montoya forms a gang of Mexicans, La Eme. When his friend J.D. shows up a year later he is allowed to join the gang even though he is white.

As the film progresses and years have gone by, Santana and his buddies are flourishing in Folsom. They take control of the "black market" to provide goods and services such as drugs, gambling, and prostitution. They use extortion and violence to maintain their power. Santana has successfully transformed his gang into the Mexican Mafia. Santana forms an alliance with the Aryan Brotherhood to expand his power and to have leverage against the black gangs, especially the Black Guerrilla Family. Over a period of time, La Eme members are released to the streets. They continue to follow the orders of Santana as he makes it clear the power of the gang resides in the prison, not on the streets. The Mexican Mafia created the idea of, "if you control the inside, you control the outside." Years later, Santana is released from Folsom. The gang he formed continues to flourish without him. On the streets Santana takes over the drug trade in East Los Angeles from the Italian mafia. In one scene, La Eme members rape the son of the Italian mob boss to send a message that the streets belong to them. (As juxtaposition, Santana is shown having his first sexual encounter, including anal sex, with a young Mexican woman.) As retaliation, the mob boss lets pure heroin reach the streets and more than 30 tecatos (Mexican heroin users) overdose. Controlling the streets of East Los Angeles is not so easy. In one scene the La Eme drug dealers are confronted by the Black Guerrilla Family, who have made a deal with the Italians. La Eme is forced to retaliate. Each retaliation is met with a counter move. Inevitably, Santana is sent back to prison. While incarcerated, younger gang members, trying to make a name for themselves, kill Santana. Back in East Los Angeles, a newly recruited youngster is shown shooting at random rivals as part of his gang initiation. The film ends with the message that in 1991 there were more than 3,000 gang-related murders. There is also a message that states, "Although this film was inspired by a true story, specific characters and certain events are fictional." *American Me* successfully manages to capture the never-ending cycle of drugs, violence, and death that is a natural product of street and prison gang life.

American Me is factual in many ways. References to the Aryan Brotherhood, the Black Guerrilla Family, and White Fence are all based on reality. The Zoot Suit riots did occur in Los Angeles in June, 1943 and involved white sailors attacking Mexican Zoot Suiters in East Los Angeles who took part in the pachuco culture. The character of Montoya Santana was modeled after Cadena, who was a founding member of La Eme, and he was stabbed to death by rival gang members from La Nuestra Familia. The real La Eme reveres Cadena and was infuriated by the film's portrayal of him being raped. The machismo culture of Hispanic gangs refuses to acknowledge any form of gay sex and La Eme insists Cadena was not raped nor would they have raped the son of the Italian mob boss. Court documents show that Olmos was extorted for money and property by La Eme prison gang members (Lopez 1996). Shortly after the release of the *American Me*, two consultants on the movie were murdered because La Eme felt it had been disrespected by the film (Lopez 1996). Other sources, including a *Sixty Minutes* report, indicate that three *American Me* consultants were murdered (Lombardi 1998). One of the consultants, Ana Lizarraga, commonly known as "the Gang Lady" was slain in Boyle Heights, an East Los Angeles community. She was shot by Jose Gilbert Gonzalez, a member of the Hazard Street Gang (in the *American Me* film the young Montoya and his gang had a confrontation with Hazard), which operated in the Ramona Gardens housing project for years. Gonzalez was on parole from Folsom prison at the time. He had been sent to Folsom for assaulting a police officer with a deadly weapon (Ford 1993). *American Me* was released more than 20 years ago, but it remains as an insightful look into the relationship between street and prison gangs, especially La Eme.

a "commission fee" to sell drugs in what La Eme considers its outside territory. The gang frequently resorts to murder as a means of intimidation and gaining respect. Why would outside gang members obey the commands of a prison gang? A simple answer: Most gang members either end up dead or in prison. Going against the Mexican Mafia outside the prison means dealing with the repercussions on the inside. Additionally, members of other gangs who cooperate with La Eme while on the outside will be protected in prison for their loyalty.

The organizational structure of the Mexican Mafia consists of a specific, military-style chain of command. Instructions from generals are carried out by captains, lieutenants, and foot soldiers. Membership is based primarily on race and is open to Hispanics; members are identified by a large "M" tattooed on their chest, back, or arms. Like most gang members, La Eme takes pride in showing off their tattoos. A common tattoo involves a single handprint, usually in black. The five fingers of the hand represent vengeance, terror, death, valor, and silence (Valdez 2009). Other tattoos include the Eme symbol of eternal war, the initials "MM" (for Mexican Mafia) or just "M" along with a more elaborate tattoo of an eagle holding a snake in its mouth with the letter "M" or phrase "Eme Mexican" tattooed along with it (Florida Department of Corrections 2009; Valdez 2009). It is believed that in order to become a member of La Eme one has to kill another prisoner. The members of La Eme are considered members for life, and it is very difficult and dangerous for a member to try to leave the gang. Among the rivals of La Eme are La Nuestra Familia, Arizona's New Mexican Mafia, and Northern Structure. Some of the allies of La Eme are the Aryan Brotherhood and Arizona's Old Mexican Mafia.

Since its formation and through the 1990s, it is estimated that the Mexican Mafia was responsible for more than 700 murders, both inside and outside prison walls. In 1997, this crime syndicate was weakened by a racketeering and conspiracy trial in Los Angeles Federal Court (Ramos 1997). Using the federal RICO Act, prosecutors were able to get convictions of 13 members of La Eme on 26 counts of murder, conspiracy to commit murder, drug dealing, and extortion. They were also found guilty of "shaking down" actor Edward James Olmos. In San Diego, La Eme members commit crimes on both sides of the border, making it more difficult to apprehend them. In November 1997, Mexican Mafia hit men were arrested for the slaying of a Tijuana journalist who was a vocal advocate for stronger sanctions on La Eme members (O'Connor 1997).

Despite the legal setbacks of the late 1990s, La Eme continues to grow in power, influence, and criminal activity. The La Eme prison gangs are responsible for various forms of violence and drug trafficking between the streets and prisons, and then for trafficking inside the prison. There are variations of the Mexican Mafia in most prison systems throughout the Southwest region of the United States. In Texas, the La Eme prison gangs are known as Mexikanemi (which means "soldiers of Aztlan") or the Texas Mexican Mafia (TMM). In 2011, the FBI arrested six San Antonio TMM members on federal drug indictments for conspiracy to distribute heroin. The FBI claimed that the San Antonio TMM members were responsible for the distribution of at least 48 kilograms of heroin (Mafia Today 2011). In 2012, the U.S. Attorney's Office (Western District of Texas) convicted San Antonio TMM members for RICO violations that included aiding and abetting in the murder of Jose Damian Garza, and for substance charges of conspiracy and violent crimes (FBI 2012a). A federal grand jury in San Diego handed up 17 indictments and the U.S. Attorney's Office for the Southern District of California filed eight criminal complaints charging a total of 119 Mexican Mafia defendants with federal racketeering conspiracy, drug trafficking violations, and federal firearm offenses in January 2012. FBI Federal Agent in Charge Keith Slotter commented on the arrests as "one of the largest single takedowns in San Diego FBI history. The FBI and our law enforcement partners stand unified in our efforts to protect this county from the violence, drug trafficking and extortion schemes employed by the Mexican Mafia and its affiliates. San Diego is inherently safer today because of the cooperation between our agencies working together to disrupt and dismantle the criminal activities of these dangerous individuals" (FBI 2012b, 1). San Diego County Sheriff Bill Gore commented on the arrests, "This is a traditional case of dishonor amongst thieves. Gangs were made to pay 'taxes' in order to facilitate their trafficking and violent behavior. We answered with a one-two punch: a strong and experienced multi-agency investigation, armed with the RICO statute. The results speak for themselves" (FBI 2012b, 1).

These two examples of crackdowns against the Mexican Mafia represent a mere sampling of law enforcement efforts to curtail their criminal activities behind prison walls as well as their influence on the streets. That the FBI and multiple law enforcement agencies must work together in an attempt to lessen the power and influence of La Eme speaks volumes about the gang's presence within the correctional system.

Texas Syndicate

The **Texas Syndicate (TS)**, also known as **Syndicato Tejano**, originated in California's notorious Folsom prison in the early 1970s. It was established in direct response to the other California prison gangs—especially the Aryan Brotherhood and the Mexican Mafia—that were attempting to prey on native Texas inmates. The Texas Syndicate's membership, which consists primarily of Mexican-American inmates in the Texas Department of Corrections institutions, has been consistently increasing due to expanded recruitment efforts. Since its formation in California, the TS is strongest in Texas but also has a presence in the Florida Department of Corrections system.

TS has a solid organizational structure. A TS member is called a "carnal," a group of members is called a "carnales," and a TS recruit is called a "cardinal." The institutional leader, called the "Chairman," oversees the vice chairman, captains, lieutenants, sergeants, and soldiers. Just as with La Eme, the TS attempts to avoid intragang conflict by having a ranking member automatically revert to the status of soldier when prison officials reassign him to a different facility. TS members generally have TS tattoos located on the back or the right forearm, but they also have been found on the outside calf area, neck, and chest. As with nearly all organized gang syndicates, the TS has precise rules of conduct, which are outlined in its constitution:

1. Members must be a Texan.
2. Once a member, always a member.
3. The Texas Syndicate comes before anyone, and anything.
4. Right or wrong, the Texas Syndicate is right at all times.
5. All members will wear the Texas Syndicate tattoo.
6. Never let a member down.
7. All members will respect each other.
8. Keep all gang information within the group. (Fong 1990)

As mentioned earlier, the TS was originally designed as a means to protect fellow Texans from other gang members. It is violent and resorts to extreme methods of violence, including murder, to deal with its enemies. As with the Mexican Mafia, the TS attempts to expand its crime base beyond prison walls by participating in drug trafficking. TS members who are released from prison and secure an income are expected to contribute 10 percent of their earnings to the syndicate.

Similar to La Eme, the FBI has been cracking down on the criminal activities of the Texas Syndicate. The United States Attorney's Office describes TS as a "criminal organization that operates inside and outside jail and prison facilities as a criminal enterprise with the purpose of enriching the members and associates of the gang through the distribution of narcotics and robberies" (FBI 2009a, 1). In September, 2009, the Houston Division (Southern District of Texas) of the FBI announced that 10 members and associates of the Texas Syndicate had been sentenced to lengthy prison terms for engaging in a pattern of racketeering activity: three counts of murder; two attempted murders, conspiracy to commit murder; five aggravated robberies and trafficking in cocaine and marijuana, all through the aid of the criminal enterprise (FBI 2009a). In January 2010, the Dallas Division (Northern District of Texas) of the FBI announced that the last of 36 TS defendants were convicted for operating a major drug trafficking conspiracy in the Fort Worth area. The defendants were sentenced for conspiring to possess with intent to distribute and distribution of cocaine, methamphetamine, and marijuana. The distribution ring extended to Mexico where TS associates smuggled the illegal drugs into Texas, including Texas correctional facilities in the northern District (FBI 2010a). In October, 2011, the San Antonio Division (Western Division of Texas) of the FBI announced that 23 Hondo- and Uvalde-based TS members and associates were arrested for RICO violations that included participating in a criminal organization whose members engaged in acts of violence, including murder, extortion, robbery, and drug distribution. "During the conspiracy, the defendants were allegedly responsible for trafficking in the Hondo and Uvalde areas in excess of five kilograms of cocaine, 100 kilograms of marijuana, and three ounces of methamphetamine" (FBI 2011b, 1).

These three examples of crackdowns against the TS represent a mere sampling of law enforcement efforts to curtail the Texas Syndicate's criminal activities behind prison walls as well as their influence on the streets. And, similar to La Eme, that the FBI and multiple law enforcement agencies must work together in an attempt to lessen the power and influence of the TS provides us with a glimpse of TS's power within the correctional system.

La Nuestra Familia (Norte)

La Nuestra Familia (NF) originated in Soledad Prison in California in the mid-1960s. It was established to protect younger, rural Mexican-American inmates from other inmates. NF is the primary rival of La Eme. The cultural and social differences between urban and rural Mexican-Americans are the main reason for the split between these two Hispanic prison gangs. The Los Angeles gangsters disrespected the Northern members by calling them farmers and busters—terms used in a derogatory manner. When one gang member sees a rural gang member, he is to kill him right away. Thus prisons have had to separate gang members from La Eme and La Nuestra. NF represents northern California Chicano inmates. The Nuestra, or Norte, gang members brand themselves with the letter "N" as a symbol of their allegiance and also to separate themselves from La Eme, which uses the letter "M" for tattoos. Additionally, since the letter "N" is the 14th letter of the alphabet, La Nuestra incorporates the number in its graffiti and symbolism. (Delano, or Bakersfield, California, is generally recognized as the dividing line between Northern and Southern prison gangs.) The Nuestra Family prefers large tattoos, usually on their backs. Among the most popular are "NF," "LNF," "ENE," and "F" (Florida Department of Corrections 1999). La Eme members will often wear the color blue; consequently, La Nuestra members wear red. The color red is also symbolic of the United Farm Workers and Cesar Chavez, a champion of civil rights for migrant workers.

Norteno members are much fewer in number than their counterparts the Surenos (in Southern California), but they are much more organized. Battles between the two prison gangs are common in California institutions. In response to their deficit in numbers, especially because of La Eme's allegiance with the Aryan Nation, Norte has an alliance with the Black Guerilla Family (Valdez 2009). The struggle to gain power has led NF to increase its participation in criminal activities. La Nuestra is attempting to control the introduction of contraband into facilities. Membership in NF extends beyond the prison setting. The prison gang problem is of such concern in California that in 2004 state policy dictated the racial segregation of inmates for the first 60 days of imprisonment. California Assistant Attorney General Frances Grunder argued that the policy is strictly a matter of safety, because mixing white and black inmates in their early prison time could lead to riots and other disturbances. Many white inmates join the Aryan Brotherhood because of their minority status within the prison system. Blacks often join black gangs.

NF is similar to the other prison gangs previously discussed in that they too engage in a number of criminal activities that extend beyond the confines of prison walls and reach the streets. For example, according to the Sacramento, California, branch of the FBI (Eastern District of California), "NF members and associates were responsible for distributing large amounts of illegal drugs, including methamphetamine, cocaine, marijuana, and ecstasy in the Eastern and Northern Districts of California with supply lines from Mexico and distribution channels throughout the United States" (FBI 2011f, 1). More than 20 members were operating outside the prison in cooperation with the prison gang. These affiliates of NF face drug trafficking charges.

Neta

The **Neta Association** was established in 1970, in the El Oso Blanco Prison (Rio Piedras, Puerto Rico) by an inmate named Carlos Torres-Irriarte (a.k.a. *La Sombra*—"the Shadow"). Torres-Irriarte vocally advocated against the injustices experienced by fellow inmates at the hands of prison officials and other prison gangs. Among the more significant prison gangs in Puerto Rico was **Grupo (Group) 27**. As Torres-Irriarte became more popular among prison inmates, the gang leader of Group 27 (G27) ordered his execution. On March 30, 1981, the hit was made. Seven months later, members of Neta executed G27 gang leader *El Manoto*. During the 1980s, the Neta Association would continue to grow in strength and numbers.

Members of Neta view themselves as victims of American oppression. They are strongly patriotic and have associated themselves with revolutionary groups in Puerto Rico. It is their hope that Puerto Rico will some day become an independent nation, free from American involvement and citizen status. They have aligned themselves with numerous street gangs in order to bring anarchy to the streets. All Neta members are required to procure 20 prospective recruits for the gang in order to guarantee its growth.

A classic Neta technique of survival in prison is to keep a "low profile" while other Hispanic gangs draw attention to themselves. In this manner, members of Neta are often underestimated by prison officials and work "beneath" the watchful eye of correctional officers. The Neta have quietly entrenched themselves in the drug trade and use the common tactics of extortion, violence, and threat of violence against their enemies. The Neta have become so violent that they perform "hits" for other gangs. They attack and kill without regard to the consequences. Neta members wear the colors of red, white, and blue, although black may be substituted for blue. Common clothing of Neta street gangsters includes wearing beads, bandannas, white tops, and black shorts. Neta is actively recruiting new members in correctional facilities and rapidly climbing up the ranks of the most feared prison gangs. They are primarily found in Northeastern prison systems such as New York, New Jersey, Massachusetts, and Connecticut.

In 2010, the U.S. Attorney's Office in Massachusetts arrested 12 street gang members in the city of Chelsea with ties to Neta on federal and state drug and firearm charges (U.S. Attorney's Office—District of Massachusetts 2010). The Chelsea and Neta gang members have an alliance with the Bloods street gang and were engaged in weapons and drugs violations in the Bellingham Square area in Chelsea. The Neta alliance with the Bloods is explained by the reality that they are "cousins" with the Latin Kings (see Chapter 6). Many of the Neta prison gang members come from the Latin Kings street gang. And like the Latin Kings, Neta has a hierarchical structure of gang membership.

Black Guerrilla Family

The **Black Guerrilla Family (BGF)** is among the dominant African-American prison gangs. It was created by former Black Panther member George L. Jackson in 1966 at San Quentin State Prison. The most politically oriented of the major prison gangs, BGF was formed as a Marxist/Maoist/Leninist revolutionary organization with three sociopolitical goals: to eliminate racism, to maintain dignity in prison, and to overthrow the United States government. The gang was primarily established because Jackson believed that the Black Panther Party was not responding or fulfilling the needs of black prison inmates. At first, the gang was called the "Black Family" and its members were solicited by being told that the crimes they had committed were the direct result of white oppression and a white political-economic system. Jackson then changed the name of the gang to "Black Vanguard" once a sizeable membership had been established. The name stuck until 1971 when Jackson was shot and killed by a prison guard sniper during an escape attempt (Valdez 2009). After his death, the membership continued to grow and the name was changed to what it is today, the Black Guerilla Family. Lifelong allegiance is a requirement of BGF membership. Members are identified by tattoos with the initials BGF, crossed sabers and a shotgun, and, more elaborately, by a dragon overtaking a prison or prison tower. They are allies of La Nuestra Familia, the Black Liberation Army, the Symbionese Liberation Army, the

Weather Underground, and black street gangs (including the Bloods and the Crips). Their enemies include La Eme and the Aryan Brotherhood. Members in the BGF are traditionally drawn from the black inmate population.

The BGF has members nationwide in both state and federal prisons and is strongly represented on both the East and West coasts of the United States. Its membership grew rapidly throughout the 1990s due to its alignment with black street gangs. Recently, a rift has developed between the older members, who see the BGF as a political group, and the newer members, who see the BGF as the "New Man/New Woman" association. The BGF is believed to have created a paramilitary subgroup known as the New Afrikan Revolutionary Nation (Black Guerilla Family 2003).

According to the FBI, over the years, the BGF has increasingly become involved in "a pattern of criminal activity, including: narcotics trafficking, robbery; extortion; bribery; retaliation against witness or informant; money laundering; and commercial robbery" (FBI 2011e, 1). BGF members use violence and threats of violence to coerce incarcerated persons to pay protection fees to BGF. In Maryland, for example, BGF members arrange to have drugs, tobacco, cell phones, food, and other contraband smuggled into prison facilities, sometimes recruiting and paying employees of prison facilities, including corrections officers, to assist BGF and its members in smuggling contraband (FBI 2011e).

The Five Percenters

Another powerful Black prison gang is the **Five Percenters** (slang name for members of the Five Percenters is "Godbody"). The Five Percenters are a loose-knit religious organization that split from the Nation of Islam (NOI) in 1964. Founded by Clarence 13X Smith (also known as "Father Allah") in Harlem, New York, the Five Percenters believe that 5 percent of the population is righteous and teach and know about "truth," 10 percent try to hide the truth, and 85 percent have not yet received knowledge of the truth. Smith was expelled from the NOI for disagreeing with some of the group's teachings. Five Percenters believe that blacks are the original people of Earth, that blacks founded all civilization, and that black men are gods (women are known as "earths" and children as "seeds"). They also believe that whites have deceived the whole world, causing it to honor and worship false gods and idols.

The Five Percenters, also known as the Universal Flag of Islam (Anti-Defamation League 2005), have become a presence in the form of prison gangs throughout the East, especially in New York, New Jersey, Massachusetts, Ohio, North Carolina, and South Carolina. In New Jersey, there are an estimated 400 prison inmates who belong to the Five Percenters; 60 are identified as gang members. To many prison officials, the Five Percenters are simply a violence-prone black-supremacist prison gang. The Five Percenters teach that white people are devils, a teaching that corrections officials find dangerous behind prison walls. Despite prison officials' efforts to suppress the teachings of the Five Percenters, the U.S. Supreme Court (in 1987) held that prison walls "do not form a barrier separating prison inmates from protections of the Constitution" (*Turner v. Safley*, 482 U.S. 78, 84). On September 22, 2000, President Clinton signed the Religious Land Use and Institutional Persons Act (RLUIPA), which enhanced the religious rights of prisoners. Although the RLUIPA protects religion, it leaves it to the courts to define what beliefs actually constitute a religion. New Jersey, for example, has been able to levy restrictions on the Five Percenters on the basis of their designation as a "security threat group" rather than as a religion (*Fraise v. Terhune*, 283 F.3d 506, 3d Cir. 2002). In South Carolina, prison officials also prevailed against Five Percenter inmates in a pre-RLUIPA suit (*Inmates Designated as Five Percenters*, 14 F.3d 464, 4th Cir. 1999) (Levin 2005).

Aryan Brotherhood

Prison gangs break down along racial lines: white, black, and Hispanic. Whites make up a small percentage of the prison population and become automatic targets inside prison walls. If their criminal offense was nonviolent, other prisoners are especially tough on them. White inmates are often beaten, raped, and sold from gang to gang (Selcraig 1999). If they are to survive their prison terms, white inmates need protection. This was especially true in the turbulent 1960s as the nation's racial unrest spilled into the nation's prisons. Gangs formed by white inmates in the California prison system were among the early gangs whose roots were entrenched in state penitentiaries. The **Aryan Brotherhood** (AB) gang originated in 1964 in San Quentin State Prison, Marin County, California. The early members were mostly motorcycle bikers and a few neo-Nazis. The gang's founding fathers were Irish-American bikers who adopted the three-leaf clover with a swastika background and initials "AB" imbedded in the clover, as their official symbol. United together, the Aryan Brotherhood decided to strike against the blacks, who were forming their own militant group called the **Black Guerrilla Family** (BGF). "Initially, the whites called themselves the **Diamond Tooth Gang**, and as they roamed the yard they were unmistakable: pieces of glass embedded in their teeth glinted in the sunlight" (Grann 2004, 158). The Aryan Brotherhood continued to grow throughout the 1970s and by 1975 they expanded into most of California's state prisons, waging a full-fledged race war (Grann 2004).

The Aryan Nation is organized into two groups, one in the federal prison system and the other in the state prison systems. The various AB gangs are unaffiliated splinter groups, although some are loosely affiliated to one another. The Aryan Brotherhood is strongest in California and Texas, but also has a presence in Nevada, Arizona, New Mexico, Missouri, Arkansas, Alabama, Florida, Mississippi, Georgia, Kansas, Ohio, and Colorado. The AB has a paramilitary ranking structure with a commission overseeing each faction of the AB. In Arizona, for example, the AB members are known as "kindred" and organize into "families." A council controls the families' activities. Each splinter AB gang uses the name of its state with the name "Aryan Brotherhood," for example, the Aryan Brotherhood of Texas (ABT). In the Texas prisons alone, there are over 300 identified full-fledged members of the Aryan Brotherhood. Most members are white, of course, and the vast majority express white-supremacist, neo-Nazi characteristics and ideology and identify themselves in such ways as wearing racist tattoos. Among the more common tattoos are the "AB" abbreviation, "666," Nazi symbols such as the "SS" sig runes (the Nazi symbol of victory taken from the Norse meaning of the sun) and swastikas, spider webs near the elbow, Vikings, shamrocks, and other Nazi and/or Celtic iconic markings. It is estimated that the total AB population in prison is about 30,000 members, a small percentage of the prison population.

The primary reason the Aryan Brotherhood exists within prisons is for protection from non-white gangs (especially African-American gangs) and to get high. As with other prison gangs, they attempt to secure contraband. They are especially concerned with attaining drugs and therefore work in cooperation with a few other prison gangs, most commonly Mexican-American gangs such as La Eme. The Aryan Brotherhood are particularly against black gangs and because of their loose alliance with La Eme, are likely to join with Hispanic gangs in prison racial confrontations. They are involved in violence and are known for committing murder against their enemies. Law enforcement officials have uncovered evidence that the Aryan Brotherhood, sometimes called The Brand (Grann 2004), is involved in an increasing level of violence behind prison walls. In California, for example, authorities report that the Aryan Brotherhood, all convicted felons, have "gradually taken control of large parts of the nation's maximum-security prisons, ruling over thousands of inmates and transforming themselves into a powerful criminal organization" (Grann 2004, 158). Upon their release from prison, Aryan Brothers are expected to continue to assist or score drugs for the members remaining in prison. They abide by the creed "blood in, blood out," which means you spill someone's blood to get into the Brotherhood, and your own blood will be spilled if you try and leave the Brotherhood.

Speaking about the hatred that AB members have toward blacks, an AB gang member was sentenced to 450 months in prison in connection with a hate crime involving the arson of a historic African-American church as part of an effort to murder a disabled African-American man (FBI 2011c). The fire was set to the Faith in Christ Church in El Paso, Texas, in 2010 and it was linked to a series of racially motivated arsons that Steven Scott Cantrell perpetrated in his attempt to gain status with the ABT (FBI 2001c). As their admiration of Nazi culture would indicate, the AB also hates Jews. AB gang member Timothy Lee York pleaded guilty to violently assaulting a Jewish inmate in a federal correctional facility in Texas in 2007; he was sentenced in 2012 (FBI 2011d).

Although The AB is the most noted white-supremacist prison gang, there are others in the prison system. In Colorado, for example, the 211 Crew, a 300-member prison gang, participates in various crimes including murder, assault, and racketeering (*Syracuse Post-Standard* 2005). In 2008, a 211 Crew member was convicted on charges of conspiracy, assault, distribution of drugs, and witness tampering (Anti-Defamation League 2008). In 2010, 211 Crew members faced charges of rape and extortion (*Denver Westword News 2011*). The Department of Justice considers 211 Crew a dangerous white-supremacist Colorado prison gang.

European Kindred

The relatively new prison gang **European Kindred (EK)** is the most feared white-supremacist gang in the Pacific Northwest (Holthouse 2010a). Founded by David Patrick Kennedy, the EK had at least 300 confirmed members in the Oregon prison system plus another 100 to 125 members on the streets of Portland, as well as other cities and towns in Oregon in 2010 (Holthouse 2010a). Kennedy was raised to be a criminal as his father was a member of the **Gypsy Jokers**, an outlaws motorcycle gang founded in 1956 and based in Oregon and Washington (Holthouse 2010b). While in elementary school, Kennedy's older brother was killed in a gunfight and Kennedy witnessed his mother's murder. Kennedy began his life of crime as a teenager. Among other things, he was a debt collector for his father's motorcycle gang. In 1998, Kennedy was sentenced to prison at the medium-security Snake River Correctional Institution for a second burglary conviction. That same year, Kennedy formed the EK on April 20 in honor of Adolf Hitler's birthday (Holthouse 2010a). Kennedy formed the EK to "serve and protect our own people in the joint" (Holthouse 2010a, 27). The EK lives by the code of "14 Words"—a white-supremacist phrase: "We must secure the existence of our people and future for White children." In less than two years, the EK spread to all four other medium-security prisons in Oregon. As is the case with other prison gangs, the EK extended its reach outside prison walls as members were released from correctional facilities.

The EK is especially active in Portland. EK gang members commit hate crimes, murders, rapes, home-invasion robberies, commit identify theft, distribute illegal drugs, and operate dog-fighting rings (Holthouse 2010a). Rene Denfeld (2006) of EK wrote in the *Portland Tribune*, "Picture gun-toting ex-convicts with swastikas on their arms, and you have the EK . . . Members see themselves as Viking warriors with freedom to pillage." Although committing home-invasions is modus operandi for the EK, they also like to target drug dealers. They rob drug dealers who have sold their drugs and are carrying large sums of money. The gang realizes that drug dealers cannot run to the police to report the robbery. The EK is infamous for assaulting witnesses, including tying victims to chairs and keeping them captive for days (Denfeld 2006). Law enforcement agencies throughout Oregon recognize the danger EK presents, but they are not alone as the FBI has conducted their own investigations on this prison/street gang. In 2010, the FBI earned convictions against Kennedy and his wife Christina Marie Allen following their pleas of guilty to knowingly providing a firearm to a convicted felon. Kennedy was sentenced to 90 months in Federal Prison and Allen was given 4 years of probation (FBI 2010d). It is worth noting that many white supremacist groups (e.g., like the Nazis and their use of sig runes) and white prison gangs use Viking folklore symbolism as a part of their gang imagery. The Aryan Circle of Texas, a Texas-system white prison gang, named after a gang of Aryan assassins from the book *The Matarese Circle* (by Robert Ludlum, a *New York Times* best seller) believe that Aryans can be traced back to the Vikings. They admire Viking gods, such as Loki and Thor, believing them to be symbols of white supremacy (Gangland 2009c).

Summary

People have always formed groups, generally for protection, acceptance, companionship, and basic survival. Most of us are born into a family and then form play groups with our peers. During childhood, and especially during adolescence, some individuals engage in delinquent behavior. For some, juvenile delinquency is a precursor to deviance and criminality. The study of juvenile delinquency is relevant to the study of street gangs because most gangsters join a gang while they are juveniles. The gradual historic development of a "juvenile status" led to the creation of a judicial system that affords juveniles certain freedoms from responsibility not given to adults. In turn, street gangs recognize this loophole and recruit juveniles to perform a number of gang-related tasks.

There is no single definition of a gang, but a number of characteristics are common in all descriptions. As a result, we can define a street gang as a group of individuals whose core members interact with one another frequently; possess a group name; generally wear certain types of similar clothing specific to their gang; can usually be identified by specific colors; are most likely to claim a neighborhood or turf (marketplace); and often engage in criminal or other delinquent behavior. Although law enforcement agencies vary in their definitions of street gangs, that does not hinder efforts to count the number of street gangs and gang members. In 2011, the OJJDP reported that there were 28,100 street gangs and 731,000 gang members throughout 3,500 jurisdictions nationwide in 2009. The FBI, however, reports much higher numbers—30,313 street gangs and more than 1.1 million gang members in 2011. With more than 315 million Americans, street gang members represent less than a half percent of the total population. Although their numbers are relatively small, their impact on society, especially in particular neighborhoods, is immense.

In addition to street gangs, this chapter provides a review of OMGs and prison gangs. OMGs are quite distinct from street gangs, but there is an overlap between the two as motorcycle gangs, especially the Hells Angels, are linked to drug distribution with street gangs. Prison gangs are relevant to the study of street gangs because so many gangbangers end up in prison and continue their gangbanging lifestyle while incarcerated. In addition, prison gangs, such as La Eme (the Mexican Mafia) were formed in prison and have influence on the streets as well. This influence is reflected in La Eme's motto of, "When you control the inside, you control the outside."

2

A History of Street Gangs

As stated in Chapter 1, people have formed groups since the beginning of human history. This is also true of youths. As was also explained in Chapter 1, the designation of young people as a special group—children—is recent. Children were expected to obey their parents unconditionally and they worked to earn their keep. Many children were treated very poorly and in some cases orphaned or abandoned by their parents. Children learned that there was safety in numbers and that group formation increased their odds of survival. Much has changed in the modern era. Most children have a great deal of free time and few are expected to work 8–10 hours a day—a typical occurrence in the past, especially in agricultural families. Today, children still form groups primarily for play, games, organized sports, and a wide variety of activities. Sometimes they organize as youth gangs.

Street gangs are not, however, a recent phenomenon. Documentation of gangsters and street thugs dates back many centuries. The concept of "street thugs," or the original word *thugz*, dates back to India (A.D. 1200) and refers to a band of criminals that roamed the country, raiding towns along their path (Savelli 2000). They were famous for strangling people. These thugs used their own symbols, hand signs, rituals, and slang. Savelli (2000) also suggested that pirates should be considered gangs because they engaged in similar types of brutal behavior. The idea of pirates as a type of criminal gang is not so far-fetched when one considers that pirates have been active off the coast of Somalia throughout the 2000s. But clearly, their pirating activities are not performed on the streets. Evidence supports the existence of youth street gangs committing criminal acts in Europe throughout the Middle Ages (Hay, Linebaugh, Rule, Thompson, and Winslow 1975). There were numerous gangs in London during the fourteenth and fifteenth centuries, including the Mims, Hectors, Bugles, and Dead Boys, who enjoyed violent acts such as breaking windows, demolishing taverns, and assaulting the watch (a sort of law enforcement) and wore colors similar to contemporary gangs as a means of identifying their affiliation (Pearson 1983). Research has also shown that street gangs engaged in criminal activities in France and Germany during the Middle Ages through the eighteenth century (Covey, Menard, and Franzese 1992).

There are references (Sanders 1970) to gangs in colonial America, but these "gangs" were mostly orphans who banded together, forming a substitute or surrogate family, with the simple idea that there is greater protection in numbers. Research has led to the documentation of at least 500 gangs (vigilante groups) between 1760 and 1900 (Gurr 1989). Taylor (1990, 1–2) stated that "gangs have existed in the United States since the Revolutionary War. The infamous Jean Laffite led his band of buccaneers against the British in Louisiana in support of General Andrew Jackson. Countless gangs rode during the early days of the Wild West." Sante (1991) concurs that there were a number of gangs in the United States on the East Coast following the American Revolution. During the early 1790s, gang members in Philadelphia participated in the activity of flying candle kites, a harmless behavior until the candle kites crashed down into buildings and caused fires.

"By the early 1800s teenage gangs were a fixture, albeit unwanted, of most large cities" (Grennan, Britz, Rush, and Barker 2000, 3). Researchers agree, however, that most of these early adaptations of gangs would not meet the modern interpretation of a street gang. As a result, most gang researchers agree that the first "real" street gang in the United States was the Forty Thieves, founded in New York City around 1826. This Irish-American immigrant gang consisted of youths and adults, a common characteristic of the early Irish gangs in New York City during the early to mid-1800s.

THE EARLY 1800s: THE BIRTH OF STREET GANGS

In 1820, there were approximately 123,000 inhabitants of New York City, most of whom were concentrated in lower Manhattan, below Fourteenth Street. These city residents were native-born Americans and Protestants (sometimes referred to as "Yankees" or "natives"). The once-major ethnic division between citizens of English and Dutch ancestry had subsided by this point (Lardner and Reppetto 2000). New York was a relatively peaceful city, lacking in street gangs, drug dealers, and the threat of street gun violence. There were no police forces as well. Local newspapers were more interested in reporting information like ship departures and arrivals, treaty negotiations, and legislative debates than they were in writing about crime. Citizens appeared to be reasonably satisfied with the level of public safety provided by the local watch (Lardner and Reppetto 2000).

The fate of New York City changed with the opening of the Erie Canal in 1825. "It was Mayor-turned-Governor Clinton's 'Big Ditch,' connecting the Great Lakes to the Hudson River, that turned the city into something more than a provincial port. With the opening of the Erie Canal, in 1825, transportation to, from, and within the new nation evolved into a hub-and-spoke system with just about everything and everybody passing through New York" (Lardner and Reppetto 2000, 7). Dramatic changes in all phases of transportation coincided with the rapid rise of industrialization. Cheap labor was necessary in order to build the Erie Canal and the railroads. Many labor-intensive jobs would be filled by the numerous immigrants entering the United States through New York. The city grew quickly, and its growth was accompanied by a lack of any logical planning. Apartment tracts sprung up on streets lacking sewers and safe drinking water. Drastically overcrowded living conditions and the lack of proper sanitation gave birth to medical (e.g., cholera, yellow fever, typhus, and tuberculosis) and criminal epidemics. Newly arrived immigrants, lacking education and English proficiency, continued to pour into densely populated ethnic ghettos. By 1850, there were so many immigrants in the United States that all the largest cities in the Northeast were comprised of a majority of immigrants. In New York, Boston, and Chicago more than 75 percent of the population was composed of immigrants (McCorkle and Miethe 2002).

Among the immigrants entering New York in the 1820s, the largest number was the Irish. The Irish immigrants, poor and Catholic, were America's first urban ethnic group. Attempting to maintain their ethnic heritage, the Irish opened their own cheap "green-grocery speakeasies" throughout their ghetto neighborhood, known as the Five Points. The first street gangs of the United States arose in the **Five Points** and neighboring Bowery. The Five Points was an area, in the Paradise Square district, where five streets (Cross, Anthony, Little Water, Orange, and Mulberry) once converged (today there are just three streets that converge in this area and Columbus Park now resides where the Mulberry slum, razed in 1831, once resided). The unsanitary conditions of the Five Points ghetto were partly the result of the aforementioned poor developmental planning of city officials. At one time, Collect Pond (or Fresh Water Pond) was located in this area. The pond provided city residents with fresh water and fish, but the advent of industrialization and the corresponding polluting of the pond by industrialists (e.g., Coulthards Brewery and Nicholas Bayard's slaughterhouses) caused great environmental health hazards. As a result, Collect Pond was transformed into a landfill. The landfill was poorly conceived and buried vegetation began to release methane gas in the area. Couple this with a lack of storm sewers and the removal of once–middle-class homes from their foundations. The unpaved streets were routinely filled with mud and human and animal excrement. Mosquitoes bred in the area, causing more problems. The middle-class folks left by the early 1820s, opening the way for immigrants, initially the Irish. Often lacking fresh food and water and unable to afford basic necessities at the established markets, the Irish opened their green groceries. Most of the green groceries concocted their liquor and sold nearly, or fully, rotten vegetables and meats. The green-grocery speakeasies were little more than "fronts" for illegal activity that was conducted in back rooms. The first of these speakeasies was established on Center Street, just south of Anthony Street, by Rosanna Peers. Getting fresh fruits and vegetables to the Five Points was difficult. The Irish speakeasies would carry the discarded fruits and vegetables from the Yankee groceries in display racks outside the store hardly drawing the attention of shoppers. But, Rosanna enticed customers into her back room with cheap home-made liquor (a type of moonshine). Before long, all sorts of persons of ill-repute would patronize her store. Among these thugs, murderers and thieves were the members of New York's first, definitive, acknowledged street gang, the **Forty Thieves**. Rosanna Peer's back room would become the headquarters for the Forty Thieves and their leader, Edward Coleman (Asbury 2002).

Coleman is presumed to have been quite literate as he took the name for his gang in honor of "Ali Baba and the Forty Thieves" from *Arabian Nights*. The Forty Thieves dominated the Five Points for a decade, until 1836, when Coleman was arrested for murdering his wife, for which he was hanged in 1838. The rising gang activity in this urban ghetto led to all Irish being labeled "no good." The **Kerryonians**, composed of natives from County Kerry, Ireland, were also a result of Peers's enterprise. The Kerryonians were territorial, seldom venturing from Center Street. It was their hatred for the English that kept them united as a gang (Asbury 2002).

A number of other gangs were organized and met in different green groceries, including the Chichesters, Roach Guards, Plug Uglies, Shirt Tails, and the Dead Rabbits. The **Roach Guards** took their name from a local grocery owner, Ted Roach. The Roach Guards were formed as a protective gang. They protected the liquor sellers of the Five Points (Yablonsky 1997). The Roach Guards wore a blue stripe on their pants as a form of identification. One evening, while the Roach Guards gathered at their green grocery headquarters, a member of a dissident faction of the gang threw a dead rabbit into the crowd. From the Gaelic tradition, a dead rabbit was a type of warning from a man to be greatly feared (Sifakis 2001). The dissent faction of the Roach Guards took this as a sign to form their own gang, the Dead Rabbits. Naturally, the Roach Guards were not pleased by this split and declared the Dead Rabbits as their sworn enemies. The two gangs would cease their conflict only when they aligned to fight the Yankee Bowery gangs.

The **Dead Rabbits** were organized to honor the Five Points neighborhood's Irish residents. The Dead Rabbits wore a red strip on their pants while their leader carried an impaled dead rabbit on a spike. This was especially intimidating when they went to battle with rival gangs. Their initial leader was Tom Walsh, who was also the foreman of Engine Company #21 fire department. Company #21 often fought battles against Hose Company #14, a fire company manned by the rival Bowery Boys. The **Plug Uglies** are described as very large Irishmen and they were said to have some of the toughest gangsters of the Five Points. The **Shirt Tails** were recognized because they wore their shirts outside of their trousers, similar to the Chinese men of that era. The Shirt Tails also wore large plug hats, stuffed with wool and leather similar to the Plug Uglies.

The Bowery was a slum area to the north of the Five Points. Here, many young men worked as butcher boys (a term that became associated with a rowdy) in the numerous slaughterhouses located throughout the Bowery. There were native-born Yankee gangs and Irish-American gangs. Among the most distinguished Bowery gangs were the Bowery Boys, the True Blue Americans, the American Guards, and the Atlantic Guards. Asbury (2002/1927) described how the Bowery Boys and the Dead Rabbits regularly waged war against one another in the Five Points area and on such sites as the ancient battleground of Bunker Hill, north of Grand Street. The feud between these two gangs lasted until the Draft Riots of 1863 (to be discussed later in this chapter). While the Bowery Boys had an alliance with other Yankee gangs, the Dead Rabbits often aligned themselves with the Plug Uglies, the Shirt Tails, and the Chichesters. Such alliances foreshadowed the alliance mentality that shaped the formation of nation gangs in the late 1960s and early 1970s (see Chapter 6). The battles between these two gangs lasted for days on end, with participants using any sort of object (e.g., bricks, knives, bats, bludgeons) as a weapon. Women supporters of both gangs stood nearby, ready to assist their men with injuries, supplying new weapons, or joining in the fracas themselves. One of the most legendary Irish women gangsters of this era was Hell-Cat Maggie, a fierce battler who fought alongside the Dead Rabbits. Hell-Cat honed her teeth razor-sharp so that she could inflict extreme pain into her victims as she bit them. She also wore artificial fingernails made of brass to further cause harm to her enemies.

So fierce were these early street gangs that law enforcement, such as it was, and the National Guard were no match. As a result, the regular army was often sent in to break up the battles between these rival gangs. A great deal of attention would be directed toward the growing gang problem in the following decades. Newspapers had already begun to change their focus to issues related to crime and the rise of street thug gangs. News reports indicate that there was an average of one murder per night for a 15-year period in the Old Brewery tenement (the former Coulthard's Brewery building) until the Five Points was demolished in 1852 (Dale 1997/2002). The high number of homicides has since been disputed by *New York Times* archives research (Blumenthal 1990). The number of homicides in the entire city would reveal that the high murder rate in the Five Points was exaggerated. But murder, or lack of a value for life, was so commonplace that when a little girl was stabbed to death over a penny she had begged for that her body lay in a corner for five days in a small basement room shared with 25 others (Asbury, 2002/1927; Blumenthal 1990). Five days after her death, the child's mother dug a shallow grave for her.

MID-1800s: THE ESCALATION OF STREET GANGS

The population of New York had risen to 300,000 by 1840. It was a city besieged by street thugs and rampant criminal activities (e.g., pickpockets, street robbers, violent attacks on merchants and tourists). New York was not the only city claiming a gang problem. In Philadelphia, for example, there were approximately 100 street gangs between the 1840s and 1870s. It was New York City, however, that remained the gang capital of the nineteenth century. According to Spergel (1995), there were an estimated 30,000 men who owned allegiance to gang leaders in New York City in 1855. The media took notice. The rise of the "penny press" allowed more citizens access to news events covered by local newspapers. Noteworthy is the fact that the penny press often covered stories about the city's elites and their misdoings. However, the focus of most newspaper reports rested with street crime. The citizens needed someone to blame, a scapegoat, for all the ills of society. Longtime inhabitants of New York and the other Northeastern cities had their target—the Irish.

Old World/New World Rivals

The Irish had been a visible presence in New York since the early 1820s. Irish laborers worked on steam-propelled vessels that left England for America. When they arrived in the United States, many would stay. These very early Irish immigrants were most vulnerable to fraud and abuse by the local citizens (Fitzgerald and Lambkin 2008). However, due to dramatic events in Ireland in the mid-1840s, the presence of the Irish greatly increased in the United States, especially in New York. This dramatic event was the Irish potato famine. The potato famine set off the greatest migration that the world had ever witnessed, with more than 2.5 million Irish leaving their homeland in a single decade. Most of the Irish moved to the United States, and more than 1 million settled in New York. Facing poverty, the Irish took any job available. But the native-born Americans, the Yankees, resented and feared the Irish immigrants. "Framing the threat in apocalyptic terms, the Know-Nothing Party proposed a twenty-one-year naturalization period for immigrants, a ban on Catholics in government, and the deportation of foreign-born criminals and paupers. Of the various foreign elements capable of getting the city riled up in those years, however, nobody topped the British. Worshipped by many upper-crust New Yorkers, they were loathed by the working class, regardless of ethnicity" (Lardner and Reppetto 2000, 26). The Irish and anti-Irish gangs suspended fights against one another to fight the English. English snobbery and the Protestant religion were in direct conflict with the Irish, Catholics, and other ethnic poor groups that were migrating in great numbers to New York.

To better understand this New World conflict, it is beneficial to understand the long history of resentment between the Irish and English in the Old World. For centuries, the English dominated the Irish, militarily, culturally, and economically. The English treated the Irish like barbarians and less than human. During eighteenth- and nineteenth-century occupation, the English army stored their horses in Irish churches. More relevant was the Irish potato famine, referred to in Irish as Gorta Mor, or the Great Hunger, because while there was a failure of the potato crop in Ireland in the 1840s, it was not the cause of the Irish famine. In fact, there was enough food grown in Ireland to feed its own people, but the Irish were forced to pay food as "rent" to England. Most of the more than 1 million Irish who starved to death could have been spared if not for the yearly demand of 15 million pounds worth of wheat, oats, barley, beef, mutton, pork, poultry, eggs, butter, milk, fruit, and vegetables grown by the Irish that was collected by England. The Irish who refused to pay this rent were evicted from their land, and their homes were destroyed. The potato "famine," as perpetrated by England, that occurred in Ireland from 1845 to 1850 is an equal rights violation similar to genocide and slavery. Because of England, 1 million Irish died and more than 2 million were forced to flee.

Needless to say, the Irish brought with them a great deal of cultural "baggage" and resentment toward the English. In America, the English were still trying to tell the Irish how to behave.

The young Irish-Americans fought back via gang participation. Condemned to the ghettos of New York's Five Points district, many of the newly arrived Irish were willing to take any job offered as a means of improving their lives in the New World. Others joined the existing street gangs. Battles between the Irish Dead Rabbits and the native Bowery Boys waged on throughout the 1850s. A famed riot occurred in 1857, leaving more than a dozen combatants dead. Shortly afterward, Charles Dickens visited the Five Points and declared that it was much worse than the slums of London, which he made famous in *Oliver Twist*. In his 1942 book *American Notes for General Circulation*, Dickens describes the Five Points as an area filled with squalid streets and homes rotting due to the debauchery of its inhabitants.

The Rise of Law Enforcement

In addition to the emergence of street gangs in the early and mid-1800s were a number of riots that swept through the Northeast. There were so many civil disobedience riots (e.g., anti-abolitionist) in New York in 1834 that it was dubbed "the year of the riots" (Miller 1977). There were Irish gang riots in Boston in 1837 and scores of riots in Philadelphia in 1842 and 1844 (Gaines and Kappeler 2011; Kappeler and Gaines 2011). The presence of street gangs and the many riots revealed the ineffectiveness of day and night watch systems in cities. No wonder, as the night watch consisted primarily of citizens who were supervised by constables, many of them inept, assigned to various districts. "Major problems with this system were that they operated only at night, enforcement was erratic, and inefficient, and the competence and character of the individuals selected or forced to serve [by judicial courts] were often suspect" (Kappeler and Gaines 2011, 65).

Demands among the citizenry for more law and order and control over the gangs led to the formation of local police forces. Professional law enforcement agencies are relatively new phenomena. Throughout most of human history, law and order was maintained by community elders, tribal leaders, armies loyal to a monarch, or some other variation of "might makes right." Most citizens were powerless against existing social hierarchies, and the concept of innate human rights was something left to philosophers to debate. With industrialization, modernity, a longer life span, and democratic societies came the idea that citizens should have certain basic rights. Primary among these rights was granting citizens certain protections under governmental supervision (e.g., the right to own property free from threat that others may take or destroy it). Professional (governmental) law enforcement rose to serve this function. As described earlier, the "watch" profession was proven to be ineffective, and as a result, a permanent, full-time, professional police force was deemed necessary. New Yorkers looked to London, and its police system, as the solution.

The first professional police force was London's Metropolitan Police Force, established in 1829 by Sir Robert "Bobbie" Peel (Safir 2003). These policemen were referred to as "Bobbies" in honor of Peel. At this same time, New York City still relied on volunteer patrolmen and night watchmen who walked informal beats. These early New York cops—called roundsmen—were armed with nightsticks, rattles, and whistles, but not firearms (Safir 2003). With the quick and stunning rise of street gangs in the 20 years prior, New York City established its first, and the nation's first, police force—The Metropolitan Police (established in 1845) (Johnson 2003). In comparison to London's metropolitan police, the early New York police force was a bit disorganized and not always professional (e.g., citizens often had to make payoffs to the police to get stolen property returned). Part of the confusion in New York is attributed to the existence of two competing police forces, the Municipal and Metropolitan police. The two forces would soon unite into the New York Metropolitan Police—the first recognized police force in the United States. Other American cities followed the lead of New York and created their own organized police forces: New Orleans and Cincinnati in 1852; Boston and Philadelphia in 1854; Chicago in 1855; Baltimore in 1857; and St. Louis in 1861 (Kappeler 1989). By the mid-1860s every major and some smaller American cities had their own police forces (Johnson 1981).

During the 1840s, the police seldom used firearms because of the simple fact that they did not work very reliably—often backfiring or exploding in one's hand during use. Companies such as Colt, Derringer, and Smith & Wesson were already working on guns that would kill more efficiently and that would ultimately become integrated as a common component of the police-man's arsenal. Even so, the reality of a police force was met with a great deal of reluctance by the majority of New Yorkers. Many New Yorkers were worried about the growing crime rate, but the idea of a "standing army" in the city was something that most Americans were against. New Yorkers worried that a professional police force was too similar to an established army patrolling the streets. A standing army, for New Yorkers, was like a symbol of the Old World class distinctions that Americans had fought a revolution against. The concern among Americans about the need for a standing army is firmly entrenched in Amendment II of the U.S. Constitution, ratified in 1791. The "founding fathers" of the United States hoped that it would be unnecessary to have a standing army, but just in case, they wrote that "a well regulated Militia, being necessary to the security of a free State, the right of the people to keep and bear Arms, shall not be infringed." Clearly, the Constitution was granting the right for a future army (a well-regulated militia) to bear arms. New York citizens of the mid-1800s, not exposed to the evils of guns on the streets, were greatly dismayed to see police (or anyone else) armed.

The gangs were not impressed by the early New York police forces and often attacked them with great intensity. For the Irish gangs, the disdain shown toward the police was more personal and reflected their cultural baggage from the Old World. The early New York police dressed in uniforms that attempted to imitate the English bobbies, something that further fueled the Irish–English rivalry. The name *cop* for a police officer dates all the way back to this era as well, as for several years the police appeared on the streets with no other form of identification on their uniform other than a star-shaped copper shield, hence the names *cops* and *coppers*. Through assimilation into the greater culture, the Irish eventually infiltrated the ranks of the police and would come to dominate their numbers.

Politics, Fire Brigades, and Gangs

In 1850, the population of New York City had soared to well over one-half million residents. There were an estimated 30,000 gang members at this time. During the mid- and late 1800s, street gangs directly shaped the outcome of New York's political elections. Political institutions such as Tammany Hall used gangs to control elections. The gangs received favors from elected officials; in return, they would scare people away from the voting polls.

> The political geniuses of Tammany Hall were quick to see the practical value of the gang-sters, and to realize the advisability of providing them with meeting and hiding places, that their favor might be curried and their peculiar talents employed on election day to assure government of, by, and for Tammany. Many ward and district leaders acquired title to the green-grocery speakeasies in which the first of the Five Points gangs had been organized, while others operated saloons and dance houses along the Bowery, or took gambling hous-es and places of prostitution under their protection. The underworld thus became an im-portant factor in politics, and under the manipulation of the worthy statesmen the gangs of the Bowery and Five Points participated in the great series of riots. (Asbury 2002, 68–69)

Having cleverly purchased the green groceries in the Five Points and the saloons and dance halls in the Bowery, several politicians (including ward and district leaders) knew that the gangs would need someplace to gather. Politicians provided meeting places and catered to the vices (alcohol, gambling, and prostitution) of the gangs. In turn, the politician had purchased "muscle" for themselves as they sought reelection (Haskins 1974).

The police force was equally corruptible. Politicians such as Fernando Wood learned how to use both the gangs and the police to their political advantage. Born in Philadelphia in 1812, Wood came to New York with his family and went into the liquor and cigar business as a young man. Through the backing of Tammany Hall, Wood was elected to Congress in 1840. After losing his 1850 bid for New York mayor, Wood learned how to use the new emerging "political games" to his advantage. "His more serious innovations had to do with getting votes and collecting graft. . . . In the 1852 primary, gangs had seized ballot boxes and barred entrance to the polls while the cops did nothing. Control of the police was estimated to be worth 10,000 votes in a mayoral election; at a time when fewer than 100,000 votes were cast . . . Wood was not subtle. While his predecessors had tried to maintain a certain veneer of respectability, he openly ran city government to benefit himself and his Tammany Hall cohorts" (Lardner and Reppetto 2000, 37). Wood was one of the first politicians to pursue the Irish vote. The Irish, large in numbers, represented a huge political block of votes. Newly arrived immigrants were sent to Tammany Hall, naturalized, and given the right to vote—something that the Irish did proudly, as they were not allowed to vote in Ireland because of English domination. The corruption of Wood's administration led to the creation of rival police forces and the governor's (John King) attempt to serve Wood a summons. Street gangs were amused by the whole ordeal.

Another interesting development during the mid-1800s in New York was the creation of fire brigades. Before the Civil War, fire brigades generally consisted of gang members, most of them Irish and loyal to Tammany Hall. Fire companies did not work cooperatively with one another; instead, they were in competition. As a result, a number of rival fire companies were formed. Prominent politicians (even George Washington was once the head of a New York department) aligned themselves with various fire brigades. The bitter rivalry between the fire departments often led to disastrous results. Insurance companies paid compensation to only one fire department that fought a fire. When members from rival companies met at the scene of a fire, they would fight one another over the right to fight the fire. Sometimes entire buildings burned to the ground while the firemen did battle. Another dysfunctional fire-fighting tactic involved the practice of early arrivals at a fire of covering the fire plug with a barrel, disguising it from the rival company until one's own members arrived. If the fire plug was discovered, the battle ensued until the rest of the brigade arrived. The fight for fire plugs frequently resulted in the building burning down before anyone even attempted to put it out.

Gangs in the Southern Cities

Most gang research of the mid-1800s centers on New York City and, to a lesser extent, Philadelphia and Boston. Thrasher, in his much referenced *The Gang* (1927), mentions Chicago and St. Louis as cities with gangs but even he ignored the cities of New Orleans, Baltimore, and Richmond. (It should be noted that Baltimore was considered a Southern city in this era; it would not be considered as such today.) In Baltimore, for example, Irish and German immigrants arrived to this port city in large numbers. "Between 1830 and 1860, their numbers pushed Baltimore's population from 80,000 to 212,000. Nearly 25 percent of the city had become foreign-born" (Ford 2008, 1). Gangs such as the Plug Uglies, Rip Raps, American Rattlers, and the Blood Tubs arose in Baltimore (Ford 2008). Like the immigrants of the Northeast, they were poor, lacked job skills, did not speak English, and were Catholic.

New Orleans and Baltimore experienced riots just as the aforementioned Northeastern cities of New York, Philadelphia, and Boston. In fact, researchers and local historians have concluded that fire brigades and Irish gangs often traveled from city to city to cause trouble. Baltimore gang members arrived in Philadelphia via passenger ship to intimidate and disrupt local elections in the mid-1850s (Melton 2005; Scharf 1874). During this same time period, native gangs in Baltimore and New Orleans fought immigrant Irish and German gangs and the newly formed police forces of these respective cities. And, just like their Northeastern counterparts, the Southern gangs aligned themselves with political parties and/or local politicians expecting favors in return. Knox (2000) describes how gangs could be used to maintain hegemony in voting patterns and that a pattern of quid pro quo was established between gangs and politicians. Gang researchers have described the two-decade transformation of street gangsters from fire fighters and street thugs to patronage-based political muscle in the mid-1800s in Baltimore and New Orleans (Greenberg 1998; Melton 2005). In Baltimore, the anti-Irish, anti-German, and anti-Catholic sentiment of the native whites led to a wide variety of intimidation and violent acts designed to keep favored politicians in power. For example, Irish, German, and Catholic men (only men could vote in this era) were subjected to "coopings." In brief, these immigrants were kidnapped by native gangs and kept in cellars or sheds—"coops" where they would be held, often forced to drink large quantities of alcohol, robbed, and beaten, until election day when they would be transported to the polls to repeatedly cast preordained votes (Ford 2008). In the antebellum (pre–Civil War) New Orleans, street gangs also aligned themselves with political parties and local politicians. And once again, native gangs fought with the Irish and other immigrant gangs (Gleeson 2001) and fought with the local police (Gleeson 2001; McGoldrick and Simpson 2007). Many of the native street gangs that existed in antebellum New Orleans were around after the war and caused much of the resistance, including rioting, during the Reconstruction era. There were over 30 documented gangs in Richmond during the mid-1800s, consisting mostly of white, middle-class boys (Mordecai 1860; Wallace 1938). Boys from the upper classes of Richmond also formed gangs as they had idle time to do so (Wallace 1938). As immigrants began to settle in Richmond their youth would form gangs and fight the native gangsters. Black youths also formed gangs in Richmond following the Civil War.

As in New York, rival fire-fighter companies fought each other for the right to fight fires and collect the insurance money. As Ryan (1998) explains, open warfare between immigrant gangs (and fire brigades) and native gangs and the newly formed police forces on the streets was commonplace in larger urban cities. The Southern city gangs, like street gangs found in other cities, were formed based on ethnic/racial and social class distinctions. Towers (2004), however, indicates that street gang formation of this era can also be attributed to "the emerging domestic ideals of middle-class culture that sought to tame masculine aggression in public and private settings" (p. 128). Towers's idea of street gang formation as a result of a rejection of middle-class ideology and an embracement of male masculinity and toughness is reflected in Walter B. Miller's theory of focal concerns (see Chapter 3).

The chaos caused by street gangs in the Southern cities had a connection to the Civil War as well. The political parties intent on maintaining white power (through such techniques as "coopings") and keeping slavery legal were alarmed by the immigrant gangs and the attention they drew to the mistreatment of the non–power groups. The Southern aristocracy also viewed democracy as a failure, in part, because of the violence caused by immigrant gangs, and they pointed to gang formation as another justification to secede from the Union. The Southern pro-secession movement was intent on maintaining law and order through a system of white-privilege mastery.

THE CIVIL WAR PERIOD-1900

By the mid-1800s, the United States, despite its growing street gang problem, was experiencing a great deal of growth. Manufacturing and industry dominated the North and large-scale, plantation-style agriculture fueled by slave labor dominated the South. The growing abolitionist sentiment in the North concerned many Southerners fearful that slavery was in jeopardy. The election of anti-slavery Republican Abraham Lincoln as president in 1860 resulted in seven Southern states seceding from the Union. As Lincoln took office in March 1861, Confederate forces threatened the federal-held Fort Sumter in Charleston, South Carolina. On April 12, the Confederates fired artillery at the fort, thus starting the Civil War between the North and South. Seemingly, the North had a big advantage; with 23 states belonging to the Union, it had an enormous population advantage and manufacturing advantage (to produce arms and ammunition). But the Confederates (the South) had a strong military tradition and they were fighting for a cause they strongly believed in, and were willing to die for. On January 1, 1863, Lincoln issued the Emancipation Proclamation, freeing slaves. This proclamation changed the face of war, from preventing secession of the Southern states to freeing the slaves. The North was now fighting for the freedom of black slaves. As the war continued, it was clear to Lincoln that the North still needed additional troops. As a result, the nation's first draft was initiated.

The outbreak of the Civil War had a profound effect on the residents of New York City. "There was considerable antiwar sentiment in New York. To the Irish, the abolition of slavery raised the specter of more low-wage workers competing for scarce jobs. (In 1853, Black workers armed with revolvers had been hired as scabs after Irish laborers struck against the Erie Railroad, seeking a salary of $1.25 a day and a limit of ten hours)" (Lardner and Reppetto 2000, 43). Other outspoken opponents of Lincoln going to war were Fernando Wood (who had become mayor again in 1859), New York Governor Horatio Seymour, and Tammany leader William "Boss" Tweed. Speaking in front of a predominantly Irish crowd in 1863 and flaming the feelings of resentment against the impending draft, Seymour stated that "the bloody, treasonable and revolutionary doctrine of public necessity can be proclaimed by a mob as well as by government" (Lardner and Reppetto 2000, 43). The trouble about to occur in New York City was preceded by a riot in Syracuse, New York. On March 17, 1863, dozens of young men and boys encouraged perhaps by the revelry of St. Patrick's Day assaulted blacks on the streets. The riot followed "local elections a week earlier where Copperhead Democrats won most of the city's positions in a show of anti-Republican, anti-Lincoln, anti-war and most likely, a degree of anti-Emancipation sentiments. It was stated that false rumors had been circulated among the local salt workers, prior to voting, that freed slaves were going to be sent north to take jobs as salt boilers" (Connors 2012, A-6). Mining salt was so prevalent in Syracuse it has long been called the "Salt City." Fearful of losing their jobs to blacks, the Irish rioted.

The draft was enacted in July 1863. Male citizens between the ages of 20 and 35 and unmarried men between 35 and 45 years of age were required to register for the draft. Black males were not subjected to the draft because they were deemed non-citizens by the U.S. Supreme Court as a result of the (1857) *Dred Scott v. Sanford* case (60 U.S. 393). The draft was initiated to fill the ranks of the Union Army. Any time a draft is in existence the government risks a negative backlash; this is especially true if citizens are not completely behind the war in question (e.g., the Civil War, the Vietnam War). As unpopular as this draft was, it also included a highly discriminatory "buy-out" clause for those draftees who were willing to pay $300 in order to avoid serving their country. No working-class persons could afford such an amount, but clearly the wealthy could buy their drafted sons' freedom from the military. Immigrants (mostly the Irish) who had the misfortune of arriving in New York at this time were welcomed, made American citizens, and told that they were drafted into war. During the draft registration process, signs of trouble emerged.

The Draft Riots

On the third day of the draft, Monday, July 13, 1863, an unruly crowd began to disturb the draft procedures at Forty-Sixth and Third streets. The state militia, which had been assigned to maintain law and order during draft announcements, had been summoned to Gettysburg to help stem Lee's invasion of the North. This left the local police to defend the draft office. They were unsuccessful. Rioters burned the office to the ground and fought the police. Mobs destroyed telegraph lines and broke into a gun factory. They attempted to overtake the *Tribune* office, primarily because of its support for the war. For days, rioters fought with the police, who were eventually supported by a company of soldiers (returning from the Battle of Gettysburg) with orders to kill every man with a club. The rioters were originally expressing their opposition to the draft, but they soon found other targets, including the wealthy and blacks.

"The riots had started out as a protest against the draft. As they continued blacks were more and more often the main targets. They were attacked everywhere mobs found them. . . . The police and troops showed no mercy, nor did the rioters. An army colonel, himself a local Irishman, fired artillery at a mob and then unwisely went home, where he was caught and tortured to death" (Lardner and Reppetto 2000, 48). In all, 100 buildings were burned to the ground and the city was nearly taken over by the rioters. Authorities speculated that the draft riots were stirred up by Southern agents attempting to cause havoc. They used the gangs to fight the police while they sought out blacks.

Interestingly, Asbury (2002, 63) noted that during the draft riots it was the women who inflicted the most fiendish tortures upon blacks, soldiers, and policemen captured by the mob, "slicing their flesh with butcher knives, ripping out eyes and tongues, and applying the torch after the victims had been sprayed with oil and hanged to trees." The most famous of the female battlers was Hell-Cat Maggie, who ran with the Dead Rabbits during the 1840s. The gangs of New York during the mid-1800s and the draft riots served as the primary subject of the film *Gangs of New York*, 2002 (see "Connecting Street Gangs and Popular Culture" Box 2.1).

Drug use among gang members became predominant in the post–Civil-War period and is directly linked to technological innovations and discoveries, such as morphine (1803), the hypodermic syringe, cocaine, chloral hydrate (1868), and heroin (1898), by the medical profession. At this time, medicine was crude at best and its inability to cure disease led physicians to turn to narcotics for their anesthetic properties. "Proprietary medicines containing morphine, cocaine, and laudanum could be bought at any store or ordered through the mail. In addition, many soldiers from both the North and South had become addicted during the war and returned to their communities heavily addicted to morphine, and spreading addiction even further by recruiting new users" (McCorkle and Miethe 2002, 41). Gang members increasingly turned to cocaine, and as many "as 90 percent of members may have been cocaine addicts" by the late nineteenth century (McCorkle and Miethe 2002, 41).

Post–Civil-War gang activity extended to the South in the form of the Ku Klux Klan. The Klan was started by Civil War veterans.

Box 2.1   Connecting Street Gangs and Popular Culture

Gangs of New York: A Dramatic Presentation

Directed by Martin Scorsese, *Gangs of New York* (2002) provides a mostly socio-historical accurate look at the Irish immigrant gangs of the Five Points district located in New York City in the mid-1800s. As Ted Chamberlain (2003) of the *National Geographic News* quotes historian Tyler Anbinder, "Scorsese knows much more about history than is portrayed in the movie. He wants to make a dramatic statement; he didn't want to make a documentary" (p. 3). And what a dramatic presentation Scorsese provides us. *Gangs of New York* earned 10 Academy Award nominations including Best Picture, Best Director, and Best Actor. The sociological and historic significance of the film is quite outstanding, as viewers are given a sense of what it must have been like to have lived in one of the worse slums in American history. The Irish, as the first identified ethnic group of the United States, immigrated to the United States, most of them via New York, by the millions throughout the nineteenth century. They did literally have to fight for their lives to protect their turf so that they could claim a home in the new land. The Irish also formed the first street gangs in the United States in the slums of the Five Points. The film depicts the unsanitary, filth-ridden housing that the Irish crowded into. And although most of the Irish worked honest jobs, there were indeed brothels in every building (Chamberlain 2003). The gangs shown in this film were chosen by Scorsese after he read Herbert Ashbury's 1927 book *The Gangs of New York*. Among the gangs described in this text and appearing in the film are the Bowery Boys, Dead Rabbits, Plug Uglies, and the Shirt Tails. The film begins in 1846 and then jumps to 1862 leading up to the Draft Riots.

At the start of *Gangs* we see the protagonist Amsterdam Vallon (Leonardo DiCaprio) as a child in 1846. His father, Priest Vallon (Liam Neeson) is preparing to wage war as the leader of the Dead Rabbits. His crew walks out of the Old Brewery and congregates in Paradise Square. The streets are dirty and pigs have pens outside building doorway entrances. The Plug Uglies, Shirt Tails, Chichesters, and Forty Thieves join under the rabbit-on-a-stick flag. These are the fiercest of the Irish gangs and they await Bill "the Butcher" Cutting (Daniel Day-Lewis) and his gang of natives. The two armies of gang members are fighting for the right to control the Five Points. The battle will continue until one of the leaders is killed. The Irish are fighting for their new land turf but many of the native gang members are butchers and skilled with all types of cutting knives, large and small. Most of the gang members are adults and not youths. A brutal battle ensues with all sorts of camera angles reflecting the violence of such a brutal affair. Hell-Cat Maggie (Cara Seymour) fights alongside the Irish gangs. Her teeth are razor-sharp and she wears sharpened and long extending nails on her fingers. There are bodies everywhere and people screaming in agony. Eventually, "the Butcher" confronts the Priest and stabs him multiple times. Young Amsterdam runs to his father's side and watches him as he dies. As the victor, "the Butcher" proclaims that the Dead Rabbits are done and outlawed. He permanently bans anyone from ever mentioning the Dead Rabbits again. Body parts such as ears and noses are gathered by the nativist gangs as spoils (trophies) of victory. As a result of his being an orphan, Amsterdam is sent to reform school.

After 16 years of reform school, Vallon returns to the Five Points. He narrates about the Civil War being in its second year and he describes New York City as dominated by tribes and war chiefs. He marvels at an Irish band brigade being a part of a parade. Politicians warn about Lincoln wanting to enslave white people and shout that New York should secede from the union ring out. The seeds for racial disharmony and future draft war riots are sown. Tammany Hall (Political Society of Democrats) representatives greet Irish immigrants who are still arriving by the thousands on a regular basis. The natives are not pleased with the "Irish invasion of New York" and compare it to the North's invasion of the South. Boss Tweed helps to feed the Irish; in return, he receives votes for the Democratic Party and its politicians. The Butcher still hates the Irish and controls the Five Points. He profits from all criminal activity as no one dares to challenge him. The Butcher and Tweed work out a symbiotic relationship wherein they both profit. They both discuss the ineptness of the police while declaring that the illusion of law and order should be maintained. The cops are corrupt as well and demand their take from the profits of criminals. The rival fire brigades fight each other for the right to put out fires and be paid by the insurance companies. Such is the corrupt nature of New York City.

Amsterdam is reunited with a childhood friend named Johnny Sirocco (Henry Thomas). From Johnny, Amsterdam learns about all the current gangs in the Five Points. He has hatred for the Butcher and his loathing for the Butcher is heightened when he learns that the Priest's death is celebrated annually. Johnny introduces Amsterdam to his gang of thieves who pay gratuity to the Butcher. Over time, Amsterdam gains the trust of the Butcher. One evening, an Irishman attempts to assassinate the Butcher but Amsterdam saves his life (he wants the pleasure of killing Cutting for himself). Meanwhile, the Irish are still arriving in New York but by now the draft has been instituted. The Irish are given their citizenship papers and the males are drafted into the war and given uniforms for the North.

The conclusion of the film is quite exciting and spectacular. Amsterdam resurrects the Dead Rabbits and he unites all the Irish gangs of the Five Points to confront the Butcher and his native gangs. With the draft riots as the backdrop, the impending confrontation between Cutting, Vallon, and their gangs occurs. Amsterdam succeeds in avenging his father by stabbing the Butcher to death. Although artistic liberties are taken in Scorsese's *Gangs of New York*, the viewer is exposed to all the prime happenings of New York City in the mid-1800s—specific gang references and gang fights, dirty politics, immigration and its sociological significance, ethnic/racial fighting, the controversy of the Civil War, and the draft riots.

The Late 1800s

In the world of gangs, the Irish dominated the streets for decades and made "claim" to a number of notorious characters, beginning with the Forty Thieves founded in 1826 and ending with Edward Delaney, alias Monk Eastman. At the end of the nineteenth century, Eastman was the boss of 1,200 men (Borges 2002, 89–90). Tammany politicians hired Eastman (Delaney) to stir up trouble. Eastman had set prices for "jobs" (e.g., $19 to break an arm or leg, $25 to stab someone, and $100 to kill someone). However, by the late 1800s, the Irish, for the most part, had assimilated into American culture. They were now the "natives" and "flag-wavers" of the country. They dominated the police force. Their immigrant status had all but disappeared, and their reign as street gangsters vanished along with their former status.

Replacing the Irish as a "menace" to society were the new immigrants arriving in the United States via New York. By 1910, New York City's population reached a staggering 2 million. These people faced the same obstacles as the Irish—living in ghetto conditions, difficulty speaking the language, lack of job skills, and so on. As with the Irish, these immigrants formed ethnic street gangs, eager to cut out a piece of territory and respect for themselves and their people. As in New York City in the late 1800s, youth gangs flourished in the slums of such cities as Philadelphia, Boston, Chicago, St. Louis, Detroit, New Orleans, and Pittsburgh.

THE EARLY 1900s: THE SPREAD OF STREET GANGS

The early 1900s witnessed the spread of street gangs to many urban cities in the Northeast and Midwest. The use of guns increased the level of violence. Many would-be gangsters were taken off the streets and placed in the military during World War I, in part, because they were drafted into service, or because they volunteered for service. The postwar period initially brought about economic opportunities for adult males, lowering the average gang member's age. During Prohibition and the Depression years, two distinct types of gang activity occurred: Street gangs were committing petty crimes, and organized crime syndicates were making huge amounts of money selling liquor. During Prohibition, law enforcement efforts were concentrated on such characters as Al Capone, the Bonnie and Clyde gang, and the Ma Barker gang. For some reason, the public seemed to glamorize and support these criminals (the "Robin Hood" scenario), and decades later Hollywood immortalized these thugs in film. With the end of Prohibition in 1933, organized criminals lost control of the streets, and street gangs flourished once again until World War II.

New York City

At the turn of the century, the Irish still had a presence in the New York gang world and were led by politician/theatrical impresario "Big" Tim Sullivan, who was successful not only in legitimate business and politics but also as an overlord of crime. "From his headquarters inside the Occidental Hotel . . . Sullivan oversaw gang activities, delivering votes, jobs and graft opportunities—doing more for the downtown poor than other politicians of his day" (Vergano 2002, 8D). His position with Tammany Hall provided Sullivan with opportunities to champion the voices of the common person, even in such matters as the fight against police brutality and their use of excessive force. In 1909, Sullivan "sponsored a state legislative bill banning police use of blackjacks, brass knuckles, and other unorthodox weapons. Although opponents claimed the bill was designed to protect gangsters allied with Tammany Hall, Sullivan insisted that the law was necessary to prevent police from establishing a 'rule of armed terrorism' in his district" (Johnson 2003, 96). As Sullivan demonstrated, the perception of what constitutes acceptable forms of violence is in the eye of the beholder. The power and influence of Tammany Hall was still quite strong in the 1910s. The only time in New York State history that a governor was removed from office occurred in 1913. According to historians, then-governor William Sulzer wasn't removed because of a citizen's revolt (as in the recall of California Governor Gray Davis in 2003); it was because he turned his back on the Democrats of Tammany Hall who got him into office (Case 2003).

Following the lead of the Irish, young males from the emerging immigrant ethnic groups began to form street gangs. In fact, from this point on in U.S. history, a noticeable trend emerges: The most recent immigrants, and those most marginalized from society, tend to dominate the gang world. By 1910, the Irish gangs were all but replaced by Jewish and Italian gangs. The Eastmans, who were mostly Jewish and resided east of the Bowery, formed one gang confederation; the Five Pointers, who were mostly Italian and resided to the west, represented the other major gang confederation of New York. The Eastmans and Five Pointers often waged battle with one another sometimes using handguns. The Five Points Gang was led by Italian immigrant Paolo Antonini Vaccarelli, also known as Paul Kelly, and his second-in-command, Johnny Torrio. Torrio later became a significant member of the Sicilian Mafia (La Cosa Nostra) and recruited street hoodlums from the Five Points Gang. The Five Points Gang gained a reputation as a type of "farm club" for the Mafia. The most notorious recruit was Alphonse Capone, who later gained a notorious reputation and became known by his nickname, "Scarface." In 1919, Capone was summoned by Torrio to move to Chicago, where his assistance was needed in maintaining control of the Chicago mob territories (Savelli 2000).

The post–Civil-War period saw an increased use of guns among criminals and gang members. In 1911, the Sullivan law made the possession of guns without a permit a crime—a move that greatly aided the fight against gang-related crimes. Two years later, Mitchell was elected mayor of New York City, and he became instrumental in prioritizing the NYPD's commitment to containing the street gang problem. The beginning of the twentieth century was a period when reform efforts were instituted in an attempt to control the power of gangs, especially in relation to political elections. "In the early 1900s, reform efforts targeted widespread police corruption, just as election laws eliminated the uselessness of gangs. The cops took after the gangs, driving their most entrepreneurial members underground" (Vergano 2002, 8D). These reform efforts certainly did not eliminate gangs. To eliminate gangs completely (a seemingly impossible goal), numerous socioeconomic issues would have to be addressed, and with the huge numbers of immigrants arriving in the United States, it became obvious that gangs would become a permanent fixture of society. The early 1900s witnessed such events as the Tong Wars, which involved gangs from Chinatown; the emergence of Italian gangs, which would eventually evolve into organized crime syndicates; and Jewish street gangs.

The Gorilla Boys: New York's Dominant Jewish Gang

At the beginning of the twentieth century, there were a number of Jewish street thugs who engaged in a variety of criminal acts. Richard Cohen (2002) chronicled the life of Louis "Lepke" Buchalter, born in Williamsburg, Brooklyn, in 1897 to Russian-born Jews, in his book *Tough Jews* (1998). His mother called him *Lepkeleh*, a Yiddish variation of "Little Louis." His friends would simply call him Lepke. The Buchalters were a large, middle-class family with 14 children, and Louis, the youngest brother, sought attention that his parents could not provide. Whenever he had the chance, Louis would sneak away and roam the immigrant streets looking for adventure and excitement. Lepke's father died when he was 13, and his mother, feeling distraught, moved to Colorado, leaving Louis under the guidance of an older sister. Lepke paid little attention to his sister, skipped school often, and fell into a group of older gangsters (e.g., Joseph "Doc" Stacher, Louis "Shadows" Kravits, Hyman "Curly" Holtz, and Phil "Little Farvel" Kovolick). These men taught him various criminal acts: how to be a pickpocket, roll a drunk, spy on cops, and so on (Cohen 2002). As Albert Fried (1980, 130) described Lepke at this age, "he was, to put it candidly, a delinquent—an audacious and ruthless one, according to the sparse accounts we have—who spent most of his time across the river on the Lower East Side where he committed petty thefts and extortions and other random acts of violence."

Louis Buchalter's criminal career officially began in 1915, "the year of his first arrest and conviction on a felony charge (for stealing luggage in Bridgeport, Connecticut, where he had gone to work for an uncle). From then on he was true to his calling. One arrest followed another, and he shuttled back and forth between the various punitive, retributive, and rehabilitative agencies" (Fried 1980, 131). When he returned to the Lower East Side, Lepke began stealing pushcarts. During one robbery, he met Jacob "Gurrah" Shapiro, a notorious downtown figure. Shapiro's very presence and mannerisms identified him as a street gangster. Shapiro "had come to New York as a boy from Odessa, Russia, home of the brutal, farcical Jewish gangsters immortalized in *Odessa Stories* by Isaac Babel, whose descriptions could apply as well to the Jewish hoods of New York as to those of Russia" (Cohen 2002, 351). In 1918, Lepke was convicted of robbery and sent to the Tombs (a jail that his gangster friends called "City College"), and then sent to Sing Sing prison. Upon his release, Lepke was reunited with Gurrah. They formed a gang of street criminals that came to be known as the Gorilla Boys. These Jewish gangsters had now gone into the extortion business, threatening merchants unless they paid "protection" fees from such "accidents" as failed deliveries and fires. Lepke and Gurrah especially targeted bakeries. "Over the years they extorted money from the biggest bakeries in New York: Gottfried's, Levy's, Fink's, California Pies, Rockwell's, and Dugans. By the mid-thirties Lepke and Gurrah were receiving about a million a year in tribute from the industry" (Cohen 2002, 352).

New York Jews had a strong presence in the garment industry in the early 1900s. When workers began organizing into unions (one of the first unions in New York was the United Hebrew Trade Union) and went on strike to demand higher pay and safer working conditions, the garment bosses hired Jewish street gangsters to bust them up. "One employer hired Monk Eastman to drive the strikers back to work. Monk and his boys attacked the strike leaders on Allen Street. While breaking strikes, gangsters often beat workers with a length of metal pipe wrapped in newspaper. They called this schlamming. In the coming years, as the nation was rocked by strikes, even the most down-on-his-luck hood could get work as a schlammer" (Cohen 2002, 353). Thus, Jewish gang members were being used to bust up strikes by Jewish garment workers and were hired by Jewish garment bosses. By the 1920s, labor unions began to hire gangsters like Lepke and Gurrah to defend the strikers against the strike busters. And just as the schlammers had taken it directly to the strikers, Lepke's crew took it to the bosses by setting fires and throwing bombs. It was only natural for this tide to turn. The gangsters had far more in common with the workers than they did with the bosses and most of the workers were Jews from Eastern Europe, whereas the bosses were German Jews who looked down on the Eastern Europeans. Street gangsters enjoyed labor racketeering. It offered them economic opportunities that were lacking during the 1920s, and it kept them from having to do factory work. As the power behind the unions, these racketeers had access to union dues and kickbacks from workers—cash in exchange for jobs or promotions. Years later, the federal government would intervene and stop this practice.

Lepke and Gurrah, the Gorilla Boys, would lead an interesting and colorful life as successful gangsters. Their crimes, along with those already described, included murder. Lepke was not one of those glamorous gangsters who lead a high-profile, playboy lifestyle; instead, he was in it for the money and power. Gurrah himself lived in Brooklyn, moving to Flatbush. By the early 1930s, Lepke was more of a businessman than gangster, with young gangsters seeking his help and advice on how to survive in the underworld. Although there would be other Jewish gangs, given the overall success that Jews have experienced in the socioeconomic strata of the United States, their presence in contemporary street gangland is extremely limited.

Detroit Street Gangs

Among the many American cities experiencing a rapid population growth fueled by industrial and economic development at the beginning of the twentieth century was Detroit. As Taylor (1990, 2) explained, "the origin of serious youth gang development is rooted in the shift from agrarian to industrial society. Gangs of young toughs were plentiful in early urban America. From the early 1900s to the mid-1930s, industrial cities experienced drastic population increases. . . . Detroit is a microcosm of urban America. . . . As immigrants entered America, Detroit attracted foreign and domestic job seekers to fill the demand for well-paying jobs. Detroit experienced rapid growth during the 1920s, 1930s and, with the industrial needs of World War II, even more. . . ." By the early 1940s, Detroit was a city faced with numerous racial troubles. "No city expected racial trouble more than Detroit, and none did less to prevent it" (Sitkoff 1971, 673). More than 50,000 Southern blacks moved to Detroit in the early 1900s, and they found a city with severe shortages of housing, recreation, and transportation and an overabundance of agitators and extremists of every color and persuasion (Sitkoff 1971). African Americans had not formed significant gangs during this era in Detroit, but the Jews had.

The Jewish population was another group with minority status that experienced discrimination. "During the industrial boom of the early 1900s to the mid-1930s, many immigrants moved into the city in greater numbers, neighborhoods were established along ethnic lines. The earliest gangs in Detroit can be traced to the dynamics of these ethnic neighborhoods where loose groups of youth banded together to "protect" local merchants and neighborhood residents from outsiders. One of the best examples of a protective youth group was the Jewish gang known as the Sugar House Gang, formed to protect Jewish merchants in the 1920s by Harry and Louis Fleisher and Irving Milberg" (Taylor 1990, 3). Greed would eventually lead them to join forces with Norman Purple and his group. This new gang would be known simply as the Purple Gang. "The Purple gang reaped the financial rewards associated with distilling operations and other organized crime activities. Starting in the 1920s, the Purple Gang represented one of Detroit's first true organized gang syndicates" (Bynum and Varano 2003, 215).

The **Purple Gang** was one of the most ruthless organized crime groups in U.S. history. The Purple Gang provided protection to Detroit's narcotic dealers, and were accused of hijacking (stealing liquor loads from older and more established gangs of rumrunners), bootlegging, extortion, kidnapping, and murder (Kavieff 1999). Whenever Purple Gang members were brought to trial, witnesses were afraid to testify against them, and jurors were afraid to convict them. Witnesses and jurors were often bribed or threatened with death. Detroit prosecutors were unable to gain any convictions against Purple Gang members until the early 1930s. With their predisposition to violence and acts of intimidation, the Purple Gang flourished during Prohibition.

The Purple Gang had its genesis with the Bernstein family. In 1902, a young shoemaker, Harry Bernstein, arrived in Detroit with his wife and their six children. Harry opened a small shoe store located on Gratiot Avenue, in the lower east side of Detroit, not far from the Jewish ghetto district (Kavieff 2000). The east side of Detroit was a typical urban, industrial ghetto, marked by uncontrolled diseases, dense living conditions, poverty, and a high crime rate. Observing how difficult a life their parents had in supporting their family, the Bernstein children took to the streets in an effort to help out the family financially. Abe Bernstein, the eldest of the children, became a skilled card dealer and stick man. Gambling, which was illegal at the time, allowed Abe to meet many corrupt politicians, police officials, and other members of the underworld (Kavieff 2000). Abe's brothers, Joe, Raymond, and Isadore (Izzy), took to the streets, claiming turf. Their territory consisted of the Jewish ghetto that stretched from Jefferson Avenue to East Grand Boulevard. The outer boundaries of their territory stretched for about two blocks east and west of Hastings Avenue. Many of the Purple Gang members would come from this area (Kavieff 2000).

The Purple reign in Detroit began in 1918, when on May 1 the state of Michigan's Prohibition Referendum, which had been approved two years earlier, became law. Detroit was the first major American city to go completely dry (no alcohol) as an experiment to test the new "dry law" for the rest of the country. The Prohibition Act (18th Amendment) was a huge failure. People want alcohol, and wherever there is a need and desire for a good or commodity that is not provided by the government or legitimate business enterprises, a black market will rise to satisfy this need. Prohibition, in effect, gave criminal syndicates financial leverage for legitimate business ownerships, spawned rackets to provide people with alcohol, and corrupted every level of government (Albanese 2002). A great deal of liquor entered Detroit illegally via the Detroit River from Canada. The Purple Gang controlled the waterfront and hijacked deliveries in the area. Although they would run their own liquor transports, they preferred to rob others who ran liquor (Kavieff 1999).

The Purple Gang's rise to power during the mid-1920s was the result of a merger with Charles Leiter and Henry Shorr, two well-established Detroit mobsters who also owned a legitimate corn sugar outlet on Oakland Avenue known as the "Oakland Sugar House." (This would be a transitional stage in the development of an even more vicious version of the Purple

Gang yet to come.) As a result of this merger the **Oakland Sugar House Gang** was established. The Oakland Sugar House Gang was a fiercely violent gang designed to protect Jewish liquor merchants from rival gangs. The gang also became involved with running rackets (e.g., against non-union workers and to keep union members under the rule of the corrupt union bosses). Bombings, thefts, beatings, and murder were among the methods the gang used to enforce union policy (Kavieff 1999). After being acquitted in labor trials, the gang became known again as the Purple Gang.

The Oakland Sugar House gang sought out the services of Abe Bernstein to run the rackets that the new liquor laws inspired. Bernstein and his crew were referred to as the Original Purple Gang (Kavieff 2000). The designations of Original Purple Gang members and the new Sugar House Gang members revealed that there was a lack of complete harmony between the gangs' members and that there was still a gang within a gang allied by friendships and birth. Among the Original Purple Gang members was Jack Selbin, one of the first illegal liquor merchants of Detroit. Charles Auerbach, the elder statesman of the Detroit Jewish mob, was known as "The Professor," because of his appearance and refinement and the fact that he was a self-taught educated man who had a collection of rare books. Mike Gelfeld (a.k.a. One-Armed Mike), a noted racketeer, was one of the leaders of the "Little Jewish Navy"—a faction within the Original Purple Gang. Sam Solomon, a bookmaker, was known as the brains behind the Little Jewish Navy. Raymond Bernstein, known as a ladies' man, who ran rackets, was a noted card dealer, hijacker, and gunman, who was not opposed to violence. Joe Bernstein, who was considered the toughest of the four Bernstein brothers, managed to make a great deal of money. Joe eventually left the Purples to become a legitimate businessman in the oil industry (*The Crime Encyclopedia* 1998). Internal turmoil and power struggles between Purple Gang members eventually led to the downfall of the gang. By 1935, the rule of the Purples was over. At least 18 members of the gang had met violent deaths at the hands of one another.

In 1935, Abe Bernstein, along with several other Purple Gang members, saw the handwriting on the wall and had begun to meet with the Italian Mafia to turn over the Detroit rackets peacefully. Bernstein and his cohorts thought that this was the best way to go about things because the Italian Mafia was growing stronger and would eventually take over the rackets anyway. In addition, the Purple Gang was much weaker as a result of the internal killings and long prison sentences of other members. In return for the rackets, the Italians gave Abe Bernstein enough money to take care of himself for the rest of his life (Kavieff 2000). Abe Bernstein removed himself from Detroit's underworld and attempted to get his brother Raymond out of the prison system, a losing battle that he continued until his death in 1968. Joe Bernstein became a legitimate businessman and eventually moved to California with his brother Izzy. Most of the other Purple Gang members met the same fate as Raymond Bernstein—life sentences in prison for such crimes as murder, conspiracy to commit murder, and racketeering. The Purple Gang had its roots in street crime and flourished under the misguided laws of Prohibition. Its success was due to street smarts and strong-arm tactics. Its failure was a result of high-profile methods, lack of organization, greed, and mistrust of fellow gang members.

THE MID-1900s: AN EXPANSION AND SHIFT IN GEOGRAPHIC GANG DOMINANCE

During World War II, the public was obviously distracted from such issues as street gangs. Most of the young, able-bodied males were off fighting wars on two fronts. As Decker and Curry (2002, 756) explained, "during the Depression and World War II, gang activity declined. When gangs reemerged in the 1950s, they included large numbers of African-American, Puerto Rican, and Mexican-American youths. In addition, levels of violence were higher than in previous periods of gang activity. This can be attributed to the presence of guns and automobiles."

The change in immigration laws and internal geographic relocation during the mid-century led to a focus on the emergence of gangs in the West. The legal migration of nearly 2 million Mexicans to the United States in the twentieth century (beginning during the 1920s) had a major impact on the growing numbers of gangs throughout America's Southwest region. Additionally, and following the pattern established by the Irish more than a century earlier, these Mexican immigrants were low-skilled workers—poorly educated, lacking basic English-speaking and writing skills, and from agricultural, rural areas—who were suddenly thrust into densely populated urban ghettos. These people were met with the same indifference and discriminatory actions as were all the other immigrants prior to their arrival. The big difference was their skin color. They were not black, but not quite white either. Consequently, they suffered from a marginalized status that others (white European immigrants) did not. Derogatory terms such as *greasers* and *wetbacks* (because they had to cross the Rio Grande River in Texas and the All-American Canal in California to gain entry to the United States) were applied to these Mexican immigrants, most of whom resided in Southern California, especially Los Angeles.

Internal migration patterns were also important in the expansion of street gangs. Large numbers of African Americans were moving from the rural South to the North and West. With a history that already included slavery, blacks have historically been discriminated against in the United States. Thus, their marginal status in society had already been well established by the mid-1900s. Seeking a better life and hoping for more opportunities than could be found in the South, blacks moved to the industrial cities of the North and the West.

Northern Cities: 1940s–1960s

New York City was still experiencing a gang problem—the continuing influx of immigrants all but guaranteed it. European ethnic groups still fought against one another, but when Puerto Ricans starting arriving in large numbers, they became the common enemy of white street gangs (see Chapter 1 for a description of *West Side Story* a tale pitting a white gang versus a Puerto Rican gang in the late 1950s). An increasing number of African Americans in the Northern and Midwestern cities also led to more turf battles between rival gangs. In Detroit, the Purple Gang was long gone, and the emerging power on the streets was not organized crime syndicates, but street gangs. Bynum and Varano (2003, 215) explained:

> Many African-Americans migrated from the rural South to Detroit during the 1940s and 1950s. Like many European ethnic groups, African-Americans were attracted to the promise of well-paying factory jobs. There were almost immediately tensions between the growing black population and whites. African-Americans were generally restricted to living in a few neighborhoods in the eastern side of the city, and many found it difficult to gain quality employment. Growing tensions and distrust eventually resulted in two riots that would change Detroit forever.

The Detroit riot of 1943 was caused mostly by segregation and racism and did little to change the economic plight of African Americans (Farley, Danziger, and Holzer 2000). The years following World War II was a boom time for Detroit, especially because of the growing automobile industry. Unfortunately, African Americans did not prosper like their white counterparts. The riot of

1967 had a dramatic and lasting effect on Detroit, as many businesses that were instrumental in Detroit's economy withdrew from the city.

The existence of street gangs in Boston throughout the 1940s and 1950s is documented in Walter Miller's (1958, 1959, 1973) studies of delinquent street-corner groups. Miller's evaluative research was based on social workers' intervention programs with gang members. The gang members committed such delinquent acts as fighting, theft, truancy, and vandalism. Their primary concern was protecting turf. The gangs generally consisted of 50 to 70 youths, ranging in age from 12 to 20 (Miller 1957). "This early research documented the territorial nature of Boston gangs, which for the most part continues today. These groups had clearly defined enemies and allies, and the issue of honor or respect was then, as now, a common cause of conflict" (McDevitt, Braga, Nurge, and Buerger 2002, 55).

One more thing that Miller's research revealed was the fact that gang members were becoming younger in age. In this brief review of the history of gangs, the ebb and flow of the age of gang members has become apparent. When gangs first appeared, they were often comprised of children abandoned or orphaned by their parents. During the mid-1800s, many of the Irish gang members were as likely to be adults as children; and during Prohibition and the Depression, the gangsters were almost always adults. The 1940s and 1950s would be a period in gang history dominated by young gangsters. This was especially true in Los Angeles.

Los Angeles Gangs: 1940s–1960s

Gangs are a relatively recent phenomena in Los Angeles. In fact, before the 1940s, gangs, as we understand them today, did not exist in Southern California. Unfortunately for the residents of Southern California, the late arrival of gangs to their streets would not mean that the gang problem would be less severe than that found in eastern cities. In fact, within a few decades, beautiful Los Angeles would hold the dubious distinction of "street gang capital of the world." The proliferation of gangs in Southern California would be the result of the two-pronged migration of millions of Mexicans from rural Mexico and large numbers of African Americans from rural America. The sheer number of Mexicans, especially compared to the relatively small percentage of blacks in Los Angeles during this period, causes us to turn our attention first to Mexican-American gangs during the mid-1940s rather than African-American gangs in the same period. In the later decades of the twentieth century, however, African-American gangs will be the focus.

Mexican-Americans and Cholo Gangs

Southern California experienced an economic boom in the 1920s that had two distinctive results. On the one hand, the aggressive marketing of California real estate created large enclaves of white, middle-class, conservative Midwesterners in Los Angeles and Orange Counties. These transplants brought with them a strong sense of patriotism, nativism, and the presence of the Ku Klux Klan (*PBS: American Experience* 2002). In turn, the economic prosperity enjoyed by some created the need for workers to perform a large number of low-skilled jobs (e.g., agricultural laborers, housekeepers). Mexicans moved north to fill this void and to find their own economic windfall. Predominantly poor and undereducated, Mexican-Americans have often been victims of prejudice and discrimination by mainstream society. Their reception in Los Angeles was less than friendly, and they were often treated as poorly as African Americans. Because of their poverty, they ended up in neighborhoods near downtown and to the east of downtown. Lacking political power, they often saw their homes destroyed for civic expansion projects such as the

Civic Center in the 1920s and Dodger Stadium in Chavez Ravine in 1951. Many of the poverty-stricken barrios of the mid-1900s have not faded into the past, but still exist today throughout the Southwest.

Immigrants from Asia and Mexico had been working as agricultural workers in California since the time of the Gold Rush of 1848. The 1882 Chinese Exclusion Act and the 1902 Gentlemen's Agreement, which expelled Asian agricultural workers, aided the Mexican immigrants and their search for employment. Mexicans arrived in the United States in large numbers between 1900 and 1929 in a search for economic opportunity especially after the Mexican Revolution and the Depression of 1929. During the 20 years from 1930 to 1950, 5 million more workers arrived under the Bracero Program to assist in agricultural work during World War II. However, beginning in 1954, the political tide turned against Mexican immigrants. "Operation Wetback" was a governmental program designed to expel any Mexicans illegally overstaying their visas. Many legal Mexican-American citizens were forced to deal with unannounced "sweeps" in their homes, workplaces, recreational centers, and churches well through the 1960s.

The Mexicans who moved to Southern California brought with them a tradition known as *palomilla*, which refers to a number of young men in a village who group together in a coming-of-age cohort (Vigil 1990). Within the palomilla tradition there is a general "boys-will-be-boys" attitude about their juvenile behavior. In other words, it was expected within the Mexican culture that boys will bond together for "mischief and adventure." In Southern California, these cohorts identified with a specific parish or neighborhood known as *barrios*. Boys grow up thinking that it is necessary to protect their barrio. These groups of boys would become the forerunners of modern Chicano (Mexican-American) gangs, also known as *cholos* (a Mexican-American, or Chicano, gang member).

Vigil (1990) identified a process of *choloization* (or marginalization) within the Mexican-American community, which suggests that various cultural ingredients make Chicano youths more susceptible to becoming gang members. The marginal status that Mexican-Americans have experienced in Southern California can be traced back to the nineteenth-century American conquest of the indigenous Californian people (Mexicans). In addition, many Mexican-Americans were sent back to Mexico during the Depression era. The more than 1 million who were deported to Mexico became known as *repatriadas*. Since most of these Mexican-Americans were born in the United States, they lived as stigmatized strangers and outcasts in Mexico, where they had to learn the Spanish language because it had been prohibited in the schools of Los Angeles (Hayden 2004). All of this further fueled the negative feelings that Mexican-Americans held toward whites.

The **Zoot-Suit riots** marked the starting point in the growth of Chicano gangs throughout Los Angeles. Joan Moore (1991) has stated the cholo gangs that originated in the 1940s were a product of a climate of hysteria. She uses Cohen's (1980) term moral panic to describe the general feelings toward Mexican-Americans in Southern California. *moral panics* occur periodically and are sparked by waves of fear or outrage that generally originate with reports from law enforcement and the media. Quite often moral panics are directed toward targeted minority groups. Moore identified the Zoot-Suit riots and a gang-related incident, now famous as the **"Sleepy Lagoon"** case, as hugely significant events that sparked white-dominated moral panics, which in turn, solidified the formation of Chicano gangs in Southern California.

The "moral panic" concerning the growing level of delinquency among Mexican-American youths started on June 12, 1942, when 19-year-old Frank Torres was ambushed and shot to death outside a track meet at the Los Angeles Memorial Coliseum. The chaos that ensued nearly led to a riot. Newspapers began writing articles suggesting that wartime juvenile delinquency among

Mexican boy gangs was out of control. The Los Angeles Police Department (LAPD), drastically reduced by the wartime draft, tried its best to control the growing concern and problems with crime in the Mexican-American neighborhoods. On July 27, 1942, a crowd fought back against a police attempt to break up a craps game at the corner of Pomeroy and Mark streets in Boyle Heights. On August 1, 1942, a fight broke out between kids from the 38th Street and Downey neighborhoods near a reservoir on the Williams ranch nicknamed the "Sleepy Lagoon," after a popular song of the times. The Sleepy Lagoon was the larger of two reservoirs used to irrigate crops in what is now Bell, California. For many of the young people in the area, the lagoon was a swimming hole by day and a lover's lane by night, and it was frequented mostly by Mexican-American youths, who were routinely denied access to city-owned recreation facilities.

On the night of August 1, several young couples from the 38th Street neighborhood were parked at the reservoir when they were suddenly and violently attacked by members of the Downey Street neighborhood. After the beating, one of the boys successfully rounded up the 38th Street crew to seek revenge against the Downey boys. However, instead of finding the Downey boys, members from the 38th Street crew found a birthday party on the Williams ranch, where Jose Diaz and other immigrant families worked and lived. Diaz was just a few days short of reporting for induction into the army. The 38th Street gang was convinced that the party on the Williams ranch involved Downey boys—it did not—and they attacked the partygoers. Jose Diaz died during the battle, prompting front-page coverage of the "Sleepy Lagoon" murder. A police dragnet resulted in over 600 people being brought in for questioning. Eventually, the police narrowed the murder suspects to 22 gang members from the 38th Street crew. On October 13, 1942, the criminal case *People v. Zammora* went to trial: including 17 of the 22 defendants (five of the boys' families were able to afford separate trials), it was the largest mass trial in California history. On January 12, 1943, 5 of the 17 defendants were found guilty of assault; 9 were found guilty of second-degree murder and sentenced to five years to life; and 3 were found guilty of first-degree murder and sentenced to life. The five suspects who had secured separate trials were acquitted. The harsh penalties and perceived lack of evidence left Mexican-Americans very upset. They questioned the legitimacy of the court decision and made claims of discrimination. (*Note*: On October 2, 1944, the Second District Court of Appeals overturned the Sleepy Lagoon verdicts, dismissed the case, and cleared the records of all the defendants. Authorities declined to retry the case, meaning that whoever killed Diaz got away with murder.)

Animosity between Mexican-Americans and whites was escalated by the Sleepy Lagoon case. The impending war further complicated the city's social dynamics. White men went off to fight in a segregated military, and women and minorities filled the jobs in the defense industry that were previously reserved for white males. (It is important to note that Japanese-Americans were also highly discriminated against in Southern California, as their homes were taken from them and they were sent to live in *internment camps* set up in the rural West.) Newspaper and radio reports warned the public about Mexican zoot-suit gangs. The *zoot suit* was initially an African-American youth fashion closely connected to the jazz culture. Mexican-Americans began wearing them in the 1940s. "The zoot suit was associated with black urban youth when it appeared on the scene around 1940. Malcolm X's autobiography recounted the importance of his first zoot suit and suggested the style had racial connotations as the preferred choice of hip black men and entertainers. Youth of Mexican and Filipino descent were the prototypical wearers of the garb in Southern California, however" (Daniels 1997, 201).

In an era of segregation and discrimination and unwritten rules which demanded that people of color remain unseen and unheard in public places, the zoot suit, with its broad shoulders, narrow waist, ballooned pants, and long coats, seemed to defy conventional expectations of proper behavior. Those who wore zoot suits were often called *pachucos*. Blacks and Mexican-Americans who wore zoot suits generally referred to them as "drapes" and "chukes," probably from the word *pachuco* (Daniels 1997, 202). The zoot-suit ensemble included a felt hat with a long feather in it, called a *tapa* or *tanda*. The baggy pants were referred to as *tramas* and the shirt as a *lisa*. A *carlango*, a long, loose-fitting coat, was worn over the shirt and pants. The shoes, called *calcos*, were always well shined. To complete the style, the zoot-suiter had to have a long chain attached to the belt loop and hanging past the knee and into the side pocket of the pants. Zoot-suiters walked with a confident swagger that seemed to derive from the fabric itself. The amount of material and tailoring required for the suit made them a luxury item that even upset older, conservative Mexican-Americans.

Resentment toward Mexican-Americans who wore zoot suits was not simply because they were presumed to be gang members, it was also grounded on the fact that during the war there was a garment shortage and a limit was placed on how much fabric could be allocated for civilian clothing. Since an excessive amount of fabric was used to make zoot suits, wearing such outfits was considered unpatriotic. Police routinely conducted raids on neighborhoods inhabited by zoot-suiters. On December 31, 1942, reports that a policeman was shot and killed by "a drunken Pachuco" led to weekly clashes between young Mexican-Americans and police and military personnel. (See "Connecting Street Gangs and Popular Culture " Box 2.2 for musical popular culture references to pachucos and the Zoot-Suit riots.)

Box 2.2   *Connecting Street Gangs and Popular Culture*

"Zoot-Suit Riots" and "Hey Pachuco": Using Music to Voice Racial Angst

As Gene Sherman (1943) of the *Los Angeles Times* wrote on June 2, 1943, in Los Angeles, a "zoot suit" is considered a "badge of delinquency" and public indignation was the general attitude of white Californians toward those who wore them. Although Sherman also acknowledged that many non-delinquents also wore zoot suits, the public perception of those who wore them was very negative as it was viewed as a slap to the face against those fighting in, and supporting, World War II and the ban on excessive clothing garments. Confrontations between zoot suiters and servicemen had become commonplace in 1943. Sailors on leave often found a release of their pent-up frustrations by attacking Mexican-Americans who wore zoot suits. Outside of California, the Zoot-Suit riots were generally condemned. First Lady Eleanor Roosevelt, for example, commented, "The question goes deeper than just [zoot] suits. It is a racial situation. It is a problem with roots going a long way back, and we do not always face these problems as we should" (*Los Angeles Almanac* 2011). The *Los Angeles Times* responded with a June 18 headline, "Mrs. Roosevelt Blindly Stirs Race Discord." The editorial page accused her of communist leanings (*Los Angeles Almanac* 2011).

The sentiment among Mexican-Americans was certainly more akin to Mrs. Roosevelt's perspective than it was to the *LA Times*' editorial. In the years since the Zoot-Suit riots, most observers acknowledge the racist overtones. In many ways, popular culture also has acknowledged the racist in-sinuation of the Zoot-Suit riots. As we saw in "Connecting Street Gangs and Popular Culture" Box 1.1, the film *American Me* acknowledged this racist point of view. In 1997, the Cherry Poppin' Daddies, an American band established in Eugene, Oregon, released their most popular selling song, "Zoot Suit Riots." The band, with many different members over the years, produce music that is generally a mix of swing, ska, and rock, characterized by guitars and a strong horn section. During a period of swing revival in the late 1990s, "Zoot Suit Riot" sold over 2 million copies in the United States alone and became a popular radio hit. The opening lyrics set the tone for the album's title track: "Who's that whisperin' in the tree? It's two sailors and they're on leave. Pipes and chains and swingin' hands. Who's your daddy? Yes I am." The chorus of "You're in a zoot suit riot" is repeated three times. It's a catchy tune that describes other events related to Mexican culture (e.g., "jitterbuggin' brown eyed man") and the origins of the riots (e.g., "Now you sailors know where your women come for love"—a reference to the sailors belief that Mexican zoot suiters danced and made love to the servicemen's wives and girlfriends while they fought in war).

Along with the Cherry Poppin' Daddies, a few other swing bands reached the charts in the mid- and late 1990s. Of particular relevance here was the Royal Crown Revue and their song, "Hey Pachuco!" The retro-swinging Royal Crown Revue also relied on guitars and horns for their classic sound. The opening lyrics to "Hey Pachuco!" set the tone for the meaning of the song: "Summer '43 the man's gun-nin' for me. Blue and white mean war tonight. They say damn my pride and all. The other cats livin' down the east side. Tonight there's no place to hide." References to fighting the sailors (e.g., "Well when we hit downtown, we start to throw down") as part of Mexican pride ("They're out to get us, so I stick with that gang of mine") are clearly articulated in "Hey Pachuco!"

Were the Zoot-Suit riots racist in nature? The premiere Mexican newspaper of Los Angeles, *La Opinion*, writing on the Zoot-Suit riots, on June 9, 1943, stated, "This situation, which is prompting racial antagonism between Mexican, Anglo-Saxon and Black communities will undoubtedly have grave international repercussions which will inevitably damage the war effort and thwart the gains made by the Good Neighbor policy. We urge immediate intervention by the Office of War Information so that it moderates the local press which has openly approved of these mutinies and which is treating this situ-ation in a manner that is decidedly inflammatory." This statement indicates that not only were the riots racist, from the Mexican-American point of view, but they were causing an international incident as well. Los Angeles Mayor Fletcher Bowron disagreed with *La Opinion*'s assessment of the riots and informed the State Department in Washington that "we have here, unfortunately, a bad situation as the result of the formation and activities of youthful gangs, the members of which, probably to the extent of 98 percent or more, were born right here in Los Angeles. They are Los Angeles youth, and the problem is purely a local one" (*The New York Times*, 1943).

The Zoot-Suit riots ended when the Navy ordered Los Angeles out of bounds as a place of leave. Maxwell Murray, Major General, U.S. Army, proclaimed that all military personnel of all ranks must understand that no form of mob violence or rioting will be tolerated and that offenses of this nature will result in immediate and drastic disciplinary action (Murray 1943). The Zoot-Suit riots ended but the seeds for Mexican gangs in Los Angeles had been sown.

In light of the Pearl Harbor bombing, Los Angeles considered itself vulnerable to attack. Civilian patrols were established throughout the city, and Los Angeles beaches were fortified with antiaircraft guns. Southern California also was a key military location, and consequently on any given weekend up to 50,000 servicemen could be found in Los Angeles. Many of the single servicemen on leave would attempt to "hook up" with Mexican-American girls. Servicemen who were married or involved in a relationship accused Mexican-American males of taunting their wives and girlfriends. It was also rumored that Mexican-Americans were dancing and dating the girlfriends and wives of servicemen while they were off fighting the war. This atmosphere of "normal" jealousy and an anti-zoot-suiter attitude could only lead to a violent conclusion. What was not so predictable was the extent of the violence. Anglo servicemen on leave in the city engaged in a series of bloody clashes with Mexican-American youths. By spring, the clashes occurred up to two or three times per day. The servicemen did not take the time to distinguish between gang-member zoot-suiters and bystanders who happened to wear zoot suits. As Hickey (2003, 540) explained, "The riot was partly rooted in xenophobia fueled by World War II hysteria. Some thought the Zoot suiters' darker skin resembled the enemy. . . . Servicemen were frustrated and anxious about the war and needed to vent. When the media began focusing on the Zoot suits, tensions soon became explosive."

By May 1943, the rioting boiled over into the Venice Riot. Local high school boys had complained that "Zoots" had taken over the beachfront. A crowd of 500 sailors, soldiers, and civilians appeared at the Aragon Ballroom in Venice on May 1 and attacked Mexican-American young people as they desperately tried to exit the dance. On May 31, approximately 50 sailors clashed violently with Mexican-American boys near downtown. Seaman Second Class Joe Dacy Coleman, U.S.N., was badly wounded. On June 3, sailors on leave from the Naval Reserve Armory revenged the attack on Coleman. They attacked anyone wearing a zoot suit, thus giving the name to the Zoot-Suit riots. On the second night of fighting, Mexican-American young men drove back and forth in front of the armory, hurling obscenities and epithets at the guards. Later in the night, when sailors could not find zoot-suiters, they took the fight into the Mexican-American neighborhoods of East Los Angeles and Boyle Heights. Los Angeles police seemed unwilling to do anything about the fighting. They stood by and even encouraged the servicemen. Police officers had their own problems—they were underpaid and under strength (there were fewer police in 1943 than in 1925 and the wages had not increased during that period). Many were World War I veterans and certainly not likely to arrest servicemen.

Intense fighting between servicemen and Mexican-American gangs (as well as civilians) continued for over a week. The fighting on June 7 was the worst, with servicemen from San Diego traveling to Los Angeles to join in the fracas. Approximately 5,000 civilians and servicemen gathered downtown to fight Mexican-Americans. Young males throughout the barrios organized counterattacks and often lured the sailors into ambushes. When the rioting finally ended, the governor of California ordered the creation of a citizens' committee to determine the cause of the riots. The committee concluded that racism was the key element, but Mayor Fletcher Brown stated that the riots were caused by juvenile delinquents and that racial prejudice was not a factor. One thing most people acknowledge is that both the sailors and the zoot-suiters accused the other of molesting their respective women (Turner and Surace 1956).

"Zoot-Suit" riots were not restricted to Los Angeles in 1943. Daniels (1997) indicated that similar riots took place in such cities as Detroit and New York, where whites not only attacked and beat Mexican-Americans and blacks but stripped them from their zoot suits as well. Before long, the zoot-suit style disappeared. The reservoir known as the Sleepy Lagoon was later filled in as a result of urban sprawl. The primary importance of the Zoot-Suit riots to the gang world was the reaction by Mexican-Americans to the attack by sailors on their neighborhoods. Many of the young Chicano males began to idolize the gang members who fought the sailors and police and treated these Mexican-Americans as heroes. One gang in particular, White Fence, became the symbol of Mexican pride for their battling of the sailors. The name *White Fence* comes from the surrounding barrio; although their original name was *Purisima*, named after the local parish. White Fence still exists today and remains powerful in a number of East Los Angeles neighborhoods. They also have sets located throughout Southern California and Las Vegas. A *set* refers to an affiliated gang of the original gang; a set is a specific subdivision of the overall gang. Another prominent Mexican-American gang that dates back to the mid-1900s is El Hoyo Maravilla, the prime rival of White Fence.

WHITE FENCE Most of the Mexican-American gangs of Los Angeles reside in an area known generically as East Los Angeles, which has the highest concentration of Mexican-Americans in the United States. The **White Fence** gang lived in a city neighborhood called Boyle Heights and was called "White Fence" because of a white picket fence that ran along much of its territory near the Los Angeles River. Boyle Heights was developed before World War I as an exclusive suburb on the heights east of downtown and across the Los Angeles River. Cheaper housing became available during the 1920s, attracting a great diversity of people, among them Armenians, Jews, Russians, and Japanese. The poor Mexicans who migrated to Los Angeles during the 1920s began building shacks in the ravines and hollows of Boyle Heights, and by the 1940s, Mexicans dominated the region. The Japanese population had been forced out of the community and into internment camps during World War II. Most of the Mexican-Americans in East Los Angeles stayed poor, living in shacks without services (e.g., running water, sewers). They were generally reluctant to accept American culture and usually refused to become citizens (Moore 1991, 12). The Mexican-American residents of East Los Angeles during the 1930s and 1940s did not consider their boys to be gang members, but simply "boys from the barrio." Youths hanging out together was a part of Mexican tradition (palomillas), but the original White Fence gang members had a reputation for being very violent.

EL HOYO MARAVILLA To the east of Boyle Heights lies a cluster of neighborhoods known as Maravilla, an unincorporated part of Los Angeles county that Angelenos refer to as East LA. There are several gangs in Maravilla; one of the more prominent calls itself El Hoyo Maravilla (*el hoyo* means "the hole" in Spanish). Mexicans had begun settling in Maravilla prior to the 1920s, but the migration process increased dramatically with the construction of the Belvedere Gardens development. Although postwar Los Angeles experienced an economic boom, it bypassed Maravilla and Boyle Heights, primarily because the Mexican-Americans lacked adequate education and had poor English-language skills. The new industry was mostly in the aerospace field, an industry that demands technological know-how.

The Maravilla neighborhood had a number of gangs, which were named for specific streets, with each territory being quite small. As one of the neighborhoods invaded by servicemen during the Zoot-Suit riots, Maravilla's gang boys fought back and earned the respect of Mexican-Americans in the barrio. The young boys especially admired the gang members who fought back to protect their neighborhood. With the advent of World War II, many of the older gang boys had been drafted, creating an abrupt void of young males to protect local neighborhoods. But in the case of White Fence and El Hoyo Maravilla, the boys (and girls) managed to carry on the traditions and generally surpass the level of violence and staunch determination necessary to defend their neighborhoods. They remain powerful gangs today, with White Fence a highly visible presence in East Los Angeles.

The area of East Los Angeles still suffers from low levels of education and economic success. Its lack of political power has been apparent since the 1940s as the neighborhoods have often been ripped apart in the name of civic improvement—especially the development of freeways in the 1950s. It is worth noting that sensationalized newspaper articles continued to condemn Mexican-American gangs throughout the 1950s.

African-American Street Gangs

African Americans have longed suffered from oppression in the United States. After being granted freedom from slavery, their access to legitimate opportunities in the higher socioeconomic strata of society was severely limited. Seeking a better life than the one offered in the rural South, blacks moved to such places as Southern California. Similar to their Mexican-American counterparts, blacks arrived in Southern California primarily from rural areas (mostly the rural South). They brought with them traditions that involved close family ties and church life. By the late 1920s and early 1930s, African-American street gangs had formed on the east side of Los Angeles near Central and Vernon avenues. They formed clubs in the downtown area of Los Angeles as well. During the late 1930s and 1940s, the black population of Los Angeles moved south from downtown Los Angeles down Central Avenue toward Slauson Avenue. The area between Slauson Avenue and Firestone (Manchester) had been occupied by white residents during the 1920s and 1930s. The African-American population had already been growing in Watts between 92nd Street and Imperial. Thus was created an area known as South Central, the primary residence of the African-American population of Los Angeles.

Among the early black gangs in Los Angeles during the 1920s and 1930s were the Goodlows, Magnificents, and the Boozies. The Boozies were a family of many brothers and friends who ran a prostitution ring and committed robbery. Their turf was the Jefferson Park area. The Magnificents were a group of youths from Central Avenue. These juvenile gangs disappeared by the late 1930s, but during the 1940s, blacks were forming social clubs throughout the African-American community and these clubs eventually evolved into gangs. Among the notable gangs of this era were the Purple Hearts and the 31st and 28th Street gangs. Some of the clubs had been attempts at forming political organizations, but most of them served as a protective mechanism against white gangs. Some of these black crews were involved in petty theft, robbery, and assaults, but murder was quite rare. Weapons of choice were usually limited to bats, chains, and knives, with disputes settled by hand-to-hand combat.

During the 1950s, car clubs modeled after the white car clubs that were popular throughout Southern California were formed by African Americans. Among them were the Low Riders, Coasters, Highwaymen, and Road Devils. Other clubs such as the Slausons, Rebel Rousers, Businessmen, and Watts were tied to area high schools. These clubs were not labeled as gangs by the LAPD. In fact, it was not until the Watts Riots of 1965 that African-American youth groups were considered a serious problem. Before the riots, black people were not on the minds of whites. Johnson and Sears (1971, 698–699) referred to this as "Black invisibility" meaning "a condition describing the perceptual world of the white American. He is physically isolated from blacks, hence they are physically invisible to him, and his few physical contacts with them are structured so that blacks are psychologically invisible to him as well. Thus, Blacks essentially do not exist in the subjective world of the white American." In 1964, blacks had reason to believe that their invisible status would change with the passing of the federal Civil Rights Act. However, California responded with Proposition 14, which was designed to block the fair housing components of the act. This development added to all the other feelings of injustice and despair among inner-city blacks helped to fuel the 1965 Watts Riots.

Watts was a rundown district of Los Angeles, 98 percent black and characterized by numerous social problems (poverty, overcrowding, high unemployment, a high crime rate, etc.). The police force in Watts was nearly all white. The Watts residents viewed the police as an occupying army. On August 11, in the middle of a heat wave, police pulled over a black youth on suspicion of drunk driving. A crowd gathered and yelled angry chants at the police. Eventually, bottles and other items were thrown at the police. When police reinforcements arrived, they were greeted by a hail of stones and bottles. As day turned into night the level of violence escalated. Angry black youths began throwing missiles and Molotov cocktails at white motorists. Stores were looted and buildings torched. Thousands of National Guardsmen were sent in and were met with machine gun fire. News coverage of this six-day riot made Los Angeles look like war-torn Vietnam. When the riots finally ended, 34 were dead, over 1,000 people were injured, and nearly 4,000 had been arrested. **The Watts Riots** sparked other urban uprisings in cities across the United States for the next two years. The importance of the Watts Riots cannot be understated as the 1965 riots did for black gangs what the Zoot-Suit riots did for Chicano gangs. Young black males in the Watts area were viewed more negatively by the outside Los Angeles communities than ever before. Borrowing from the traditions of their Mexican counterparts, black gangs in South Central Los Angeles adopted the gang styles of Chicanos. Although some African-American youths (along with some whites) had already begun to copy the cholo style of Mexican-American youths in the 1950s, after the Watts Riots it became more obvious. Blacks began to borrow such Chicano gang traditions as flashing colors, defending turf, using graffiti, hanging out, and jumping in new members. By the 1960s, black gang members began forming alliances with one another, forming "nation gangs." The most notorious gang of all, the Crips, have their roots in the mid-1960s. (For a full description of the Crips, see Chapter 6.)

CONTEMPORARY GANGS (1970s TO THE PRESENT): AN EPIDEMIC

Throughout the history of street gangs, it has become apparent that youths formed protective-type groups in order to increase their odds of survival. This is true whether we are talking about youth gangs from the Middle Ages or colonial America who united for basic survival reasons or ethnic-based gangs beginning with the Irish-Americans in the 1800s. The largest percentage of gang members came from disadvantaged ethnic and racial groups. They were primarily concerned with protecting their turf and protecting their own. However, around the mid-1960s and early 1970s, this philosophy began to change to the reality that is today's gangs; namely, they are now far more *offensive*. They seek larger territories, they have become mobile and conduct such behaviors as drive-by shootings, and they have seemingly taken claim to the economically profitable illegal drug industry. "The spread of crack cocaine in the late 1980s had produced an epidemic of gang-related violence and corruption" (Johnson 2003, 287). Indeed, the culture of gangs has changed a great deal in the contemporary era.

An examination of contemporary gangs is limited in this chapter for a couple of reasons. First, estimates of the total number of gangs and gang members today were provided in Chapter 1. Second, a large number of contemporary gangs (especially those found in Los Angeles, Chicago, and New York City) and their criminal activities will be discussed in greater detail throughout the book, but especially in Chapters 6 and 8. The following pages help to provide a glimpse into the reality of the changing nature of gangs over the years.

During the 1960s, local neighborhood gangs began to merge, forming "nations." The Crips were the first to make alliances. Rival gangs of Crips formed an alliance under the Blood banner. In Chicago, the **Vice Lords**, having started with just eight original members in 1957, had reached the 8,000 mark by the mid-1960s. An offshoot of the Vice Lords, the **Conservative Vice Lords**, had incorporated into a legitimate business in 1967. Chicago Mayor Daly and rival gangs questioned the legitimacy of the "new" Vice Lords and their attempted peace movement, and by 1969, the Conservative Vice Lords had fallen apart. But in response to the formation of the Vice Lords, a number of other super gangs rose in Chicago (e.g., Latin Kings, Latin Disciples, Black

Gangster Disciples), who in turn formed greater alliances of "Folks" and "People." While all of this was going on, the general public did not seem to take notice. There are many reasons that help to explain this. For example, throughout the 1960s and early 1970s there were many events that distracted Americans away from gangs, including many acts of civil disobedience (e.g., civil rights movements, women's rights movements, and anti-war protests); the hippie and recreational drug use movement; inflation; fuel shortages and rising gas prices; assassinations (i.e., John F. Kennedy, Bobby Kennedy, and Martin Luther King, Jr.); and the media-sensationalized killings of Charles Manson and his "family."

The public's attention to gangs would resurface in the 1980s. The primary reason for the earlier lack of a public outcry, or moral panic, was the fact that gangs were still restricted to certain cities and designated neighborhoods within these "gang cities." "Gang activity increased in the 1980s. At the beginning of that decade, gang problems were recognized in only a few large cities, particularly Chicago, Detroit, and Los Angeles. But, by the end of the decade, gangs appeared in large and medium-sized cities as well as in many rural areas. The levels of violence were much higher than in any previous wave of gang problems, corresponding with even more widespread availability of automobiles and firearms" (Decker and Curry 2002, 756). The seriousness of the gang problem has persisted into the twenty-first century.

Los Angeles

At nearly 3.8 million people, the city of Los Angeles is the second-largest city in the United States (U.S. Census Bureau 2012a). Los Angeles County has over 9.8 million people (U.S. Census Bureau 2012b). Although racially and ethnically quite diverse, it is the large Hispanic and relatively small percentage of blacks that highlight the demographic data of Los Angeles and Los Angeles County (See Table 2.1).

Los Angeles and Los Angeles County are home to the most street gangs in the United States (and most likely the world). This reality began to reveal itself in the 1970s. East Los Angeles remained a poor area during the economic boom years of the 1970s and disenchantment grew among the youth. The African-American Crips super gang was in full bloom, and the rise of the Bloods super gang became an inevitable response to the newly found power of the Crips. Mexican-American gangs continued to develop, led by White Fence, and a number of Asian-American gangs (e.g., the Triads and Tongs) emerged, with roots dating back centuries. While African-American gangs were forming alliances with various neighborhood gangs, the Mexican-American gangs, and Hispanic gangs in general, were not. The number of gangs and gang members continued to increase, however, and White Fence remained a highly visible gang among Los Angeles's Hispanic gangs.

TABLE 2.1 2010 Racial and Ethnic Data—Los Angeles (City) and Los Angeles County (Percentage)		
Racial/Ethnic Category	**Los Angeles (City)**	**Los Angeles County**
Black persons	9.6	8.7
Asian persons	11.3	13.7
Persons of Hispanic or Latino origin	48.5	47.7
White persons not Hispanic	28.7	27.8

Source: U.S. Census Bureau (2012a,b)

For the most part, public concern over gangs in Southern California did not reemerge until the 1980s. Gangs were hard to ignore—1980 estimates had more than 30,000 gang members in Los Angeles County, and by 1982, gang members started dealing heavily in narcotics. Crack cocaine sales were huge during the 1980s, and the gang members controlled a large percentage of the market. Gang-related violent crime and murder became a constant topic of discussion in Southern California. The Southern California region (consisting of the seven counties of Ventura, Los Angeles, Orange, Riverside, San Bernardino, San Diego, and Imperial) is the second-largest metropolitan area in the United States, with roughly 15 million residents. "It has become known nationally as an incubator for gangs" (Maxson, Hennigan, and Sloan 2003, 240). There are nearly 40,000 total Crips, Bloods, and 18th Street gang members with an estimated 400 sets in the city of Los Angeles alone (see Chapter 6 for further statistical analysis). With these three gangs as a starting point, there is little wonder that Southern California is the home to over 2,000 gangs and 165,000 total gang members. Los Angeles serves as the home-base for the Crips and Bloods, who have set up affiliations in nearly every large American city as well as a number of international cities. Many of the largest Los Angeles gangs will be discussed in further detail in Chapter 6.

Chicago

Chicago has the distinction of being the "Third City" of the United States in total population at more than 2.6 million city residents and over 5.1 million residents in Cook County (U.S. Census Bureau 2011a). In Table 2.2 we can see that, like Los Angeles, Chicago is very ethnically and racially diverse. However, it is the large African-American population and the relatively even number of whites, blacks, and Hispanics that contrast Chicago from Los Angeles. Chicago's populations are divided into four main categories of white non-Hispanics (31.7%), African Americans (32.9%), Hispanics (28.9%), and Asian Americans (5.5%) (U.S. Census Bureau 2012c). Traditionally, Chicago has been a highly segregated city, with whites living in the north, northwest, southwest, and far south sides, African Americans on the west and south sides (Coldren and Higgins 2003), Hispanics north and south of black communities, and a small pocket of Asians in the southeast.

Chicago has a huge gang problem, second only to that of Los Angeles, and since the mid-1980s, the number of gangs has increased dramatically. The violence and homicide rates are also staggering. The city serves as a home-base to many super gangs, with the People and Folks the most significant (see Chapter 6 for a full description). The Folks and People both are a collection of other, highly identified gangs. For example, Chicago's largest gang (35,000 members) is

TABLE 2.2	2010 Racial and Ethnic Data—Chicago and New York (Percentage)	
Racial/Ethnic Category	**Chicago**	**New York City**
Black persons	32.9	25.5
Asian persons	5.5	12.7
Persons of Hispanic or Latino origin	28.9	28.6
White persons not Hispanic	31.7	33.3

Source: U.S. Census Bureau (2012c,d)

the **Black Gangster Disciples**, who along with the **Latin Disciples** are under the Folks nation. The People's major Chicago affiliates are the Latin Kings (18,000 members) and the Vice Lords (20,000 members). These numbers are estimates from law enforcement and media sources, but it should be made clear that no one knows for sure how many gang members make up these nation gangs.

The Black Gangster Disciples are descendants of the Woodlawn Disciples and are predominant in Chicago's South Side (Block and Block 1993). The Latin Disciples are a racially and ethnically mixed gang (a rarity among gangs, as they tend to be homogeneous) allied with the Black Gangster Disciples, forming the Folks nation. The Latin Disciples are generally found in the northwest part of the city in and around Humboldt Park and Logan Square. The enemies of the Folks nation are the gangs that comprise the People nation: the Latin Kings and the Vice Lords. The Latin Kings are the oldest and largest of the Hispanic gangs and are found in a variety of diverse neighborhoods, but especially on the southwest side. The Vice Lords are the oldest of the four super gangs, dating back to the 1950s, originating from the North Lawndale area of Chicago (see Chapter 6). The Latin Kings and Vice Lords formed an alliance (the People) primarily in response to the formation of the Folks (Block and Block 1993).

The gangs of Chicago are heavily involved in illegal drug distribution and drug sales. Drugs are viewed by many disadvantaged youths as a means of gaining quick and easy money. This has been true since the 1970s and is excellently chronicled in Padilla's *The Gang as an American Enterprise* (1992). As in most of the cities of the North and Northeast, the departure of industry left the poorly skilled and undereducated youths of Chicago with little hope of economic security. In his research of street gangs, Padilla (1992) referred to the Chicago public school system as being among the worse in the United States. The gang members he interviewed described horrible teachers who had prejudged them as "no good" even before giving them a chance. Consequently, many gang members dropped out of school, never earning a high school diploma. Chicago's public schools had a 40 percent dropout rate (Padilla 1992). When hopelessness is added to marginalization, delinquency cannot be far behind. Throw in a neighborhood in a state of despair and with drastic economic shortcomings, and the ingredients for gang formation and participation become fairly evident. (Further discussion of contemporary Chicago gangs will be found in Chapters 6 and 8.)

New York City

The nation's largest city, New York, is more populated than Los Angeles and Chicago combined. According to the U.S. Census Bureau (2012d), there were nearly 8.2 million people living in New York City's five boroughs in 2010. As shown in Table 2.2, there are more white, non-Hispanics than any other racial/ethnic category of persons living in New York, and New York City had the largest percentage Asians of the "Big Three" U.S. cities (see Table 2.2).

As this chapter has revealed, New York City has played a significant role in the development of street gangs. The European, white, ethnic-based gangs of the 1800s have long been replaced by such contemporary gangs as the Bloods, Latin Kings, Netas, Crips, and Mara Salvatrucha (MS-13). Other new immigrant groups (especially from Central American countries) have also formed street gangs. There were an estimated 15,000 gang members in New York City in 2001. The Bloods claim about 5,000 members, but only about half are "blooded in" (the initiation process—discussed in Chapter 5—that makes them "real" Bloods). The Bloods in New York (also known as the United Blood Nation) now outnumber the Latin Kings, once the largest and most violent gang in the city. But the gang scene in New York is anything but monolithic. Prison officials at Rikers Island reported that in 2001, 1,775 of the 15,000 inmates were members of as many as 47 gangs, the major ones being Bloods (600), Latin Kings (300), Netas (151), Five Percenters (80), and Crips (50) (NYPD and Department of Correction 2001). Nation gang members, such as the Bloods, are far different in New York than in Los Angeles. In Los Angeles, most Bloods who live near each other know each other; this is not true in New York (O'Shaughnessy 2001). Thus, Los Angeles street gangs are generally far more organized than New York gangs.

In 2004, Long Island, New York, witnessed a huge, growing gang problem spearheaded by MS-13 (discussed in further detail in Chapter 6). MS-13, a Salvadorian street gang, has challenged all existing street gangs on Long Island and is also rivaled by its fellow Salvadorian street gang Salvadorans with Pride (O'Shaughnessy 2001). In October 2004, six MS-13 members were charged in Nassau County with the murders of two fellow gang members who they believed were informants for law enforcement. MS-13 policy is to "get rid of all the people that are rats," federal officials said (Kessler and Smith 2004). Nassau police reported that 6 of the 22 homicides in 2003 were gang related and that 5 of the 18 homicides from January to October 2004 were also gang related. Law enforcement officials estimated that 3,000 to 5,000 gang members lived in Nassau alone (Dowdy 2004). Another Long Island jurisdiction, Suffolk County, estimated that it had nearly 2,000 active gang members (Dowdy 2004). Federal officials and local officials both agree that MS-13 is responsible for the large increase in gang activity on Long Island. Mexican gangs have also made their presence known on Long Island. Law enforcement officials in Newburgh accused the Benkard Barrio Kings (BBK) gang of operating a street-corner cocaine market and of at least one homicide. An 18-month investigation of the BBK led to the deportation of 23 Mexican nationals and the arrest of 27 others (*The Post-Standard* 2004c, A-12).

As in Los Angeles and Chicago, there exists a long list of street gangs in New York City, and to acknowledge them all, or even a representative sample, would exceed the parameters of this chapter. In 2010, *New York* magazine published a report titled "The New Gangs of New York." Many of the most notorious current street gangs in NYC are not so "new" and include the Bloods, Crips, Latin Kings, and MS-13. The Bloods are still the largest gang in New York and opt for bracelets made with red and black beads instead of bandanna "flags." Many Blood sets run street operations from Rikers Island and prisons in Upstate New York. In 2010, the Bloods were waging war against rival sets in Harlem (*New York* 2010). In Newburgh, Orange County, and New York, the Bloods and Latin King sets had terrorized folks in this troubled city along the Hudson River for years. On May 13, 2010, about 500 federal, state, and local law enforcement officers rounded up 60 suspected Bloods members and 18 suspected Latin King members in a predawn raid (Rivera 2010). FBI Assistant Director in Charge of the Southern District of New York proclaimed that the FBI's Hudson Valley Safe Streets Task Force had made a commitment several years ago to address the problem of gang violence in Newburgh (FBI 2011j). Although Newburgh, a small city of 29,000 located about 70 miles north of Manhattan, has an unusually large crime problem with numerous gangs, the most notorious gangsters located there are Bloods and Latin Kings (FBI 2010e). Newburgh led New York State in violent crimes per capita in 2008 and 2009, and gang violence has been responsible for all but 2 or 3 of the 16 homicides in the city during a 30-month period (Rivera 2010). The 16 homicides for a city this size equates to a 55.2 rate per 100,000, a figure nearly 10 times the national average. Among the Bloods sets identified were the Newburgh Bloods, Bounty Hunter Bloods, G-Shine, and 9 Trey. The Bloods ran the northeast end of town and the Lain Kings the southeast end. The gangsters were arrested on racketeering, murder, assault, robbery, and narcotics trafficking violations (FBI 2011j).

In 2012, the FBI arrested Ronald Herron the leader of the "Murderous Mad Dogs" set of Bloods, a gang that had terrorized a neighborhood in Brooklyn for over a decade. Herron was charged with various crimes, including three counts of murder, three attempted murders, and racketeering. Herron (a.k.a. Ra, Ra Diggs, Ra Digga, and Raheem) had posted a video on the Internet declaring himself as the gang leader of a "murder team" (FBI 2012c). Nationwide, and especially in Los Angeles, the Crips outnumber the Bloods 3 to 1, but in NYC, it is the opposite. The Crips run drug operations in South Jamaica and Far Rockaway (Queens). In April 2010, four people were shot and 56 minors arrested for a wild melee in Times Square that was believed to be part of a Crips initiation rite. In a sign of the changing times, the gathering was organized via Twitter (*New York* 2010). Along with the Bloods, the Latin Kings are considered the most powerful gang on Rikers Island. (*Note*: The Bloods and Latin Kings are "cousins" in the nation-gang alignment.) In June 2010, a Kings set was arrested for running a major heroin operation in Bedford Park. Eighteen Latin Kings members were arrested for throwing Molotov cocktails at the homes belonging to the mother and girlfriend of a member who wanted out of the gang (*New York* 2010). MS-13 (to be discussed in further detail in Chapter 6) is considered so notorious that the FBI developed a task force just to track this brutal gang. MS-13 is found in Jackson Heights and Elmhurst and throughout Long Island. Perhaps the fastest-growing gang in New York City is the Trinitarios, a gang formed by Dominicans in Sing Sing Prison in the late 1980s. The gang wears green and their weapon of choice is the machete. The **Trinitarios** have two primary rivals: the Latin Kings and **Dominicans Don't Play (DDP)**, a rival Dominican gang (*New York* 2010). The Trinitarios and DDP gangs participate in drug-trafficking, robberies, and violent assaults in the Tri-state area (New York, New Jersey, and Connecticut). **Born to Kill (BTK)** is considered the most dangerous gang in Chinatown and consists of a loose consortium of Vietnamese. BTK primarily runs the illegal knockoff vendors on Canal Street. Other gangs in Chinatown include the **Ghost Shadow** on Mott Street and the **Flying Dragons** on Pell Street, who mostly concentrate on low-level extortion schemes (*New York* 2010). It is important to also acknowledge the **Albanian Boys Inc.**, a gang so powerful and organized that the feds treat them as an organized crime syndicate. The Albanian Boys are considered to be the type of gang the Italian Mafia used to be (*New York* 2010).

Boston

Based on 2010 Census data, Boston is a city with 617,594 residents (U.S. Census Bureau 2012e). Of all the major cities discussed in the modern contemporary era, Boston has the largest percentage of white, not-Hispanic persons (U.S. Census Bureau 2012e) (see Table 2.3). The Massachusetts city has long been characterized by small, ethnically/racially identified neighborhoods such as the North End

TABLE 2.3 2010 Racial and Ethnic Data—Boston and Detroit (Percentage)		
Racial/Ethnic Category	**Boston**	**Detroit**
Black persons	24.4	82.7
Asian persons	8.9	1.1
Persons of Hispanic or Latino origin	17.5	6.8
White persons not Hispanic	47.0	7.8

Source: U.S. Census Bureau (2012e,f)

("Northie"), East End ("Eastie"), or South Boston ("Southie"). Boston is a city with a long history of street gangs dating back to the Irish street gangs of the 1830s. With its large white population containing many distinct ethnic groups including a sizeable Irish presence, it is not surprising to learn that Irish gangs still exist today. One researcher, Martin Jankowski (1991), found that Irish-American gangs in Boston followed the traditional link from childhood friendship groups to adult Irish-American social clubs. (Thrasher would label this formation of groups into gangs as spontaneous—see Chapter 3. This is also similar to the Mexican tradition of palomilla.) These gangs came from families in working-class neighborhoods. Gang participation reflected pride in and loyalty to their ethnic heritage. Jenkins's (1995) research revealed that marginalization was the primary reason for gang formation among Boston's minorities. The gangs he studied were loosely organized, neighborhood-based, and involved in typical gang behaviors: drug sales, delinquency, and violence.

The most noted contemporary Boston Irish gang is the Irish Mob. **The Irish Mob** is involved with drug-trafficking and running protection rackets targeting those who run illegal gambling and drug syndicates. A longtime leader of the Irish Mob, James Joseph "Whitey" Bulger, Jr., became an FBI informant where he would provide information on his rivals to the feds and they would turn their backs on his illegal activities. A scandal emerged within the FBI and its dealings with Bulger. Just prior to the FBI's attempt to arrest him on RICO violations, Bulger escaped and went into hiding. He was finally found in a Santa Monica, California, apartment that he shared with his longtime girlfriend.

Boston is also besieged with many of the same gangs found in New York City, including MS-13 and the Trinitarios. In 2005, there were a series of articles written on the *Boston Herald* and *Militant Islam Monitor* (*MIM*) websites about MS-13 and possible links to al-Qaeda and Adnan Shukrijumah (the Saudi-born fugitive from Miramar, Florida). The *MIM* (1/7/05) indicated that the Salvadorian-based street gang MS-13 held meetings with al-Qaeda members to help smuggle terrorists into the United States. Texas Congressman Solomon P. Ortiz, co-chairman of the House Border Caucus, informed the *Boston Herald* that he is "very concerned" about al-Qaeda's link to Mara Salvatrucha, or MS-13, a gang he described as "extremely vicious" (McPhee 2005b). As reported in the *Herald* in January 2005, a set (Loco Salvadorans) from MS-13 had taken control of a number of neighborhoods in East Boston (Maverick Square), prompting police to create a task force to take down the gang (McPhee 2005b). Although the FBI recognizes the threat MS-13 poses to local neighborhoods, it steadfastly denies that this gang has any connection to al-Qaeda (McPhee 2005b). Boston police report that there were more than 100 hardcore MS-13 members operating in East Boston and that there are hundreds more MS-13 gangsters in towns along the North Shore (McPhee 2005a). **The Trinitarios**, a Dominican gang with roots to Sing Sing Prison and New York City, also operate in Boston and neighboring Rhode Island. In 2010, the Boston Division of the FBI (District of Rhode Island) arrested a Trinitarios gang leader in Rhode Island on firearms and drug charges (FBI 2011f). The arrests were the result of the FBI's "Safe Streets Task Force" comprised of agents and investigators from the FBI, the Bureau of Alcohol, Tobacco, Firearms and Explosives (ATF), and an assortment of law enforcement agencies in Rhode Island.

Outlaw Motorcycle Gangs (OMG) also operate in the greater Boston area. In 2010, the FBI arrested 27 members of the American Outlaw Association (AOA) motorcycle gang. The 12-count indictment charged the AOA with participation in a criminal enterprise that includes such crimes as attempted murder, kidnapping, assault, robbery, extortion, witness intimidation, narcotics distribution, illegal gambling, and weapons violations (FBI 2010b). According to the indictment, members of the AOA were planning to retaliate against the Hells Angels for their attack on two Outlaws members.

Detroit

Based on 2010 Census data, Detroit is a city with 713,777 residents (U.S. Census Bureau 2012f). Of all the major cities discussed in the modern contemporary era, Detroit has the largest percentage of black persons and the smallest percentage of white, not-Hispanic, Hispanics and Asian persons (U.S. Census Bureau 2012f) (see Table 2.3). As the demographic data of Detroit would indicate, most of the street gangs in the city are black gangs. Contemporary street gangs generally form for three reasons: racial/ethnic pride and loyalty, protection of turf, and economic gain. The increasing number of gangs and gang members is almost always directly attributed to marginalized status and the lack of economic opportunities (including the lack of desire to pursue economic gain by legitimate means). Recognizing the social problems confronting many of the urban poor in Detroit, rapper Al Nuke, who heads up Operation Hip Hop, a non-profit organization that tours high schools in the area to encourage students to stay in school and organizes drives to provide clothing and school supplies, said, "I came from those types of broken homes; that's why every year I make it my duty to have school supply drives and food drives for homeless shelters" (White 2010, 1). Nuke was among other rappers, including Trick Trick, Roycee, Lodge Boyz, Seven the General, Big Herk, Stretch Money, DJ Fingers, and DJ Streets of WJLB, who participated in a free concert, "Heal Detroit Rally" in June 2010, to draw attention to the increasing need for peace in the various violence-plagued neighborhoods in Detroit.

Street gangs have existed in Detroit for nearly 100 years, dating back to the Purple Gang. Post–World War II provided an economic boom to the area because of the auto industry; an industry that employed many unskilled laborers. Many of these unskilled laborers came from the lower socioeconomic status groups. However, Detroit has been in an economic slump since the early 1970s when the city, along with several other Michigan cities such as Flint and Saginaw, suffered from tremendous cutbacks in the auto industry (due to increased competition from foreign imports and an oil embargo). During this same time, a number of delinquent groups began to take on gang characteristics and identify themselves with street names. By 1975, the loosely organized street gangs were being replaced by structured, confederated street gangs. Mieczkowski's (1986) research linked the increased gang activity to the heroin epidemic that hit Detroit during the late 1970s and early 1980s. The drug trade continues to be an integral aspect of Detroit's gangs today.

The many abandoned buildings and homes in Detroit give refuge to an indeterminate number of gangs and gang members. The nation gangs are all located in the city along with many regional and local gangs. The Detroit gangs have helped the city earn its nickname of "Murder City." One Detroit street gang, **Best Friends**, is so violent (e.g., contract killings) that it earned a spot on a *History Channel* show first broadcasted on March 2, 2009 (Brignall 2009). The feds believe Best Friends has become the first gang to take control over the I-75 corridor, a pipeline for drugs coming into Detroit from Miami (Brignall 2009). To combat Best Friends and their affiliates, Detroit police have teamed up with federal law enforcement agencies, and, in June 2009 alone, more than 36 men from four Detroit gangs (**Latin Counts**, **Folks**, **Surenos**, and the **Jamaican Posse**) were arrested. (*Note*: *Surenos* is the Spanish word for Southerners, as in Southern California, and is applied to groups of loosely affiliated street gang members who pay tribute to the Mexican Mafia.) The local, state, and federal law agencies have also combined forces to combat the Detroit chapter of a nationwide OMG, the Outlaws Motorcycle Club (OMC). Fourteen members of the OMC were arrested in 2009 for racketeering, drug distribution, and firearms violations (FBI 2009b).

Miami

Miami, like Los Angeles, is known for both its laid-back beach life and notoriously violent neighborhoods where mayhem and drugs are commonplace. As portrayed in the hit American cult film *Scarface* (1983), Miami has been a distribution point for illegal drugs for many decades. Detroit isn't the only city that Miami-fed drugs are distributed to; they also head to many other cities in the Midwest, Northeast, and Southeast. Like most other U.S. cities, however, the illegal drug trade in Miami has increasingly shifted from the control of organized drug cartels to street gangs.

Based on 2010 Census data, Miami is a city with 399,457 residents (U.S. Census Bureau 2012g). There are nearly 2.5 million people, however, in Dade County. Miami, primarily because of its large Cuban American community, is mostly Hispanic/Latino, followed by black persons, white non-Hispanic, and Asians (see Table 2.4). The racial/ethnic breakdown in Dade County is similar to that of Miami specifically, but the percentage of Hispanic/Latino decreases by 5 percent and the white, non-Hispanic population increases by about 4 percent. Street gangs exist in Miami for many of the same reasons they exist in all cities, many suburban, and some rural areas. As John V. Gillies, Special Agent in Charge of the FBI's Miami Office says, "In too many neighborhoods, young people are recruited into gangs and fall into a life of crime, drugs, and violence" (FBI 2011g, 1). Once youth adopt the gang mentality, they show little concern for the lives and welfare of conventional folks. Gillies adds, "Gang members have little regard for innocent bystanders caught in the crossfire and subject entire communities to intimidation and fear" (FBI 2011g, 1).

There are nation gangs (e.g., Bloods, Crips, Folks, and People alliances) in Miami and the surrounding counties, but two of the more notorious street gangs to catch the attention of law enforcement officials are the **Krazy Locos (KL)** and **Making Life Krazy (MLK)**. The KL are a gang composed primarily of juvenile and young adult males with an approximate 2007–2009 membership of 40 (FBI 2011g). In 2010, Manuel DeJesus Medina, a member of the KL was sentenced to life imprisonment following convictions for two homicides, robbery, and firearms charges. Medina's prison sentence followed a lengthy investigation by the FBI and a number of other law enforcements agencies (FBI 2010c). The KL work closely with the MLK gang. The KL gang makes money through the sale of controlled substances (prescription drugs such as oxycodone, Xanax, and methadone) and recreational drugs (marijuana, cocaine, and crack). KL gang members have to pay weekly "taxes" to the gang as a sort of membership, or operating, fee (FBI 2010c). To meet their tax obligation most members engage in criminal activity. The FBI (2010c, 2011g) claims that KL is a criminal gang organization whose members engage in acts of violence,

TABLE 2.4	2010 Racial and Ethnic Data—Miami and Kansas City (Percentage)	
Racial/Ethnic Category	Miami	Kansas City
Black persons	18.9	29.9
Asian persons	1.0	2.5
Persons of Hispanic or Latino origin	70.0	10.0
White persons not Hispanic	11.9	54.9

Source: U.S. Census Bureau (2012g,h)

including attempted murder or murder, sale of firearms, drive-by shootings, obstruction of justice, extortion, and distribution of drugs. Another Miami gang of note is the **Miami Gardens Gang** (a.k.a. "Murder Grove Boys"). Miami Gardens is a street gang involved in the distribution and sale of drugs, violence, murder, intimidation, conspiracy to commit crimes, and identity theft. In 2011, eight members of the Miami Gardens Gang were convicted of narcotics, firearms, and identity theft charges (FBI, 2011h). The **Zoe Pound**, a Haitian gang, is also based out of Miami, participates in drug-trafficking, robberies, and a number of other crimes.

To combat criminal activities and especially the growing influence of street gangs in Miami-Dade County, a number of task forces have been created, including "Robbery Investigation Section" (investigates home invasion robberies, strong armed robberies, armed robberies, and domestic robberies); "Robbery Intervention Detail Section" (provides proactive patrol directed at the suppression of robbery); "Robbery Clearinghouse Section" (collects all relevant information from the tri-county area about the crimes the Robbery Bureau investigates and analyzes information collected); "Street Terror Offender Program (STOP) Section" (a joint law enforcement initiative formed to combat heavily armed criminal gangs, especially those involved in home invasions and drug-trafficking); and the "Cargo Crime Section" (designed to stem the increasing theft of cargo from warehouses and transportation facilities throughout Miami-Dade County) (Miami-Dade County Police 2011).

Kansas City

According to the U.S. Census Bureau (2012h), Kansas City, Missouri, had a 2010 population of 459,787 residents. At nearly 55 percent, Kansas City has a larger white, not-Hispanic population than Boston (or any other major city discussed in this chapter) (see Table 2.4). Nearly 30 percent of its residents are black persons and 10 percent are Hispanic/Latino. Although Kansas City has long been witness to groups of juveniles, the "gang" tag did not surface until the early 1980s when members of nation gangs, including Crips, Bloods, Folks, and People, arrived. (*Note*: Nation gangs migrated to other Midwestern cities, such as Des Moines, Minneapolis, Oklahoma City, Omaha, and Wichita, during this same era.) The nation gangs helped to organize the local Kansas City juveniles into criminal street gangs who slowly began to take over the drug-trafficking (Starbuck, Howell, and Lindquist 2001). By the early 2000s, there were approximately 5,000 documented street gang members in the city (Starbuck et al. 2001). Despite the nation influence, most Kansas City gangs are local and many of them are hybrid (ethnically/racially diverse). Starbuck and associates (2001) described the **Athens Park Boys (APB)** as the most well-established street gang in Kansas City. Although the original APB originated in Los Angeles, this gang had little to do with the Los Angeles Bloods. Interestingly, there were two separate APB sets in Kansas City with no connection to the other. The east side APB consisted mostly of African Americans, while the other APB gang consisted of white teens from affluent families in the suburbs. Both APB gangs engaged in a variety of criminal activities, including violence and drug-trafficking.

Reflecting the reality that street gangs in nearly every major city are increasingly taking over the drug trafficking trade through the use of violence and murder, the FBI (2011i) arrested seven members of the **Click Clack** gang in Kansas City in 2011 for their role in a conspiracy to distribute drugs (crack cocaine) and for illegally possessing firearms. The black gang takes its name from the sound of cocking a gun or "racking the slide" (putting a round into a chamber) of a semi-automatic handgun. During their investigation of Click Clack, the FBI found more than 20 firearms, narcotics, and cash. At present, the FBI and local law enforcement agencies acknowledge a number of gangs in Kansas City and many of them have nation roots: Crips, including the 357 Crips and a number of specific street number Crips like the 23rd Street Crips and the 24th Street Crips; Bloods, including numbered streets like the 25th Street Bloods; Folks; Latin Kings; Traveling Vice Lords, and Vice Lords; and a number of local gangs including the Westside Riders, Somos Pocos Para Locos, Sons of Silence MC, Eastside Vato Locos, and Northsiders (National Gang Intelligence Center 2011).

Guilford County, North Carolina

Based on 2010 U.S. Census Bureau (2012i) data, Guilford County, which includes Greensboro, North Carolina, had 488,406 residents (269,666 in Greensboro), with the largest percentage of residents white (54.3% Guilford County, 45.6% Greensboro), followed by black persons (32.5%, 40.6%), Hispanic/Latinos (7.1%, 7.5%), and Asian persons (3.9%, 4.0%) (See Table 2.5). According to the *Guilford County OJJDP Comprehensive Gang Assessment* 2010, "Criminal gangs exist within both urban and rural North Carolina communities and represent a serious criminal justice problem" (p. 75). Statewide, there were 898 street gangs and 13,699 gang members in December 2009. Gang members in North Carolina are predominantly male (93.2%), African American (70.2%), followed by Hispanic/Latino (18.8%), white (8.8%), and Asian (1.3%).

According to data obtained from the Greensboro Police Department (GPD), there were 38 unique street gangs in Greensboro, with 15 sets claiming Bloods affiliation, 14 sets claiming Crips affiliation, and 3 sets claiming to be Mara Salvatrucha (MS-13) (*Guilford County OJJDP Comprehensive Gang Assessment* 2010). The GPD also reported that the following street gangs operated in Greensboro in 2009: the Latin Kings, Mara Norteno, Surenos (Sur, Sur-13), Tarascos (TCS-13), **Tiny Rascal Gang (TRG)**, and the Vice Lords. The Bloods gangs represent the largest percentage of gang members (56.7), followed by the Crips (12.6), and the Latin Kings (11.7). The GPD also indicated that a total of 462 gang members exist within the city limits. Similar to reported gang members statewide, those reported by GPD were typically male (95%). Using a racial/ethnic breakdown, most gang members are African American (64%), followed by Hispanic/Latino (24%) (a figure higher than the state average), whites (7%), and Asian (5%) (*Guilford County OJJDP Comprehensive Gang Assessment* 2010). The Greensboro gang members are young, with over half (54%) between the ages of 18 and 22 and 64 percent who were under the age of 22. About 1 percent of Greensboro gang members are between the ages of 10 and 14.

Another city located in Guilford County is High Point. According to the High Point Police Department (HPPD), there were 51 unique gang sets in 2010. Some of these gangs claim nation affiliation with the Bloods and Crips, but according to the HPPD, the majority of their sets are local neighborhood gangs. Of the 51 unique sets, the Bloods had the largest percentage of gang members (16.3%) followed by the Crips (14.0%), and the Surenos 13 (6.6%) (*Guilford County OJJDP Comprehensive Gang Assessment* 2010). The HPPD indicates that there were 698 total gang members in 2010 and their demographic characteristics followed the state pattern of being predominantly male (93%) and African American (68.5%). In High Point, 28.2 percent of the gang members were white, a figure higher than the state average. Almost half (47.7%) of the identified gangs members in High Point were between the ages of 18 and 22.

The Guilford County Sheriff's Office (GCSO) reported 43 validated youth gangs and 5 associated youth gangs, for a total of 48 unique and active gangs in the unincorporated areas of Guilford County (*Guilford County OJJDP Comprehensive Gang Assessment* 2010). All but a few of the gang members were male and followed the state pattern for race/ethnicity and age breakdown. The vast majority of the Guildford County gangsters claimed an allegiance to the Bloods and Crips, but a few claimed to be MS-13, Latin Kings, Gangster Disciples, **Norte (Nortenos)**, and **Sur 13 (Surenos)**. (*Note*: *Nortenos* is Spanish for Northerners, specifically Northern California, is used to describe groups of loosely affiliated street gangs that pay homage to the Nuestra Familia.) The Tiny Rascals Gang also operates in the unincorporated areas of Guilford County along with the Arab Mafia and Aryan Brotherhood.

As one might expect, the gangs of Guilford County, like the gangs of North Carolina, and street gangs nationwide, are engaged in a number of criminal activities that include homicide, rape, robbery, aggravated assault, vandalism, and drug offenses. Half of the gang-related incidents in Greensboro involved a weapon, with the most frequently used weapons being handguns.

Indianapolis

Our final look at examples of contemporary street gangs is Indianapolis, Indiana. According to the U.S. Census Bureau (2012j), Indianapolis had a 2010 population of 820,445 residents. At nearly 59 percent, Indianapolis has a larger white, not-Hispanic population than even Kansas City (which was the highest percentage of all cities highlighted in this chapter) (see Table 2.5). About 28 percent of its residents are black persons, 9 percent Hispanic or Latino, and 2 percent Asian. With a population as large as Indianapolis, it is not surprising to learn that there are numerous street gangs in the greater metropolitan area including local gangs (generally more loosely structured with no ties to nation gangs) and sets from nation gangs (e.g., Bloods, Crips, Vice Lords, and Black Gangster Disciples). The greatest gang threat in Indianapolis, however, comes from the **Surenos** (Spanish for Southerners) and the **Nortenos** (Spanish for Northerners). The Surenos are also known as Sur and Sur 13 while the Nortenos are also known as Norte.

The Surenos are a collection of loosely affiliated street gangs that pay homage to the Mexican Mafia (La Eme); their primary stronghold is in Southern California, and that explains their name. As Southerners, these gang members come from urban neighborhoods. The Nortenos' stronghold is in Northern California, and most of these gangsters come from rural areas and are farm workers. Even in the conventional world, these two regions are often viewed as rivals. The recognized dividing line between the Surenos and Nortenos is Delano, California (near Bakersfield). The Surenos have affiliates throughout a great portion of the United States, Mexico, Honduras, El Salvador, and Guatemala. Because of their multinational scope, they often come in conflict with MS-13 (to be discussed in Chapter 6). Sureno gang members generally identify with the symbols XIII, X3, 13, and 3-dots. The number 13 is symbolically important because the 13th letter of the alphabet is M and therefore pays homage to the Mexican Mafia.

TABLE 2.5	2010 Racial and Ethnic Data—Guilford County, North Carolina, and Indianapolis (Percentage)	
Racial/Ethnic Category	**Guilford County, North Carolina**	**Indianapolis**
Black persons	40.6	27.5
Asian persons	4.0	2.1
Persons of Hispanic or Latino origin	7.5	9.4
White persons not Hispanic	45.6	58.6

Source: U.S. Census Bureau (2012i,j)

The gang identifies with the color blue and words that play off the notion of being from the South (California).

The Nortenos have an affiliation with the Nuestra Familia prison gang who have an ongoing feud with La Eme. Norte gang members identify with the symbols XIV, X4, 14, and 4-dots. The reasoning is similar to the Surs; only in this case the number 14 represents the 14th letter of the alphabet, N for Nuestra Familia. The Nortenos may also identify themselves with a five-pointed star because it symbolizes the "North" star or the Huegla bird, the symbol used by the United Farm Workers association. Like their Southern counterparts, Norte can be found in nearly every state as well as several European countries.

The small Hispanic/Latino population of Indianapolis contributes to the low number of Spanish-speaking police officers in the city, a reality that Hispanic/Latino street gangs find attractive. Known as the "Crossroads of America" (a nickname bestowed on Indianapolis because it is the hub of several major interstates that crisscross the state of Indiana), nation gangs view Indianapolis as the perfect crossroad location between the Southwest and Midwest to the East and Southeast to operate criminal activities, especially drug-trafficking. To combat the street gang problem in Indianapolis, the city established the "Safe Streets Task Force" that has as its mission to identify and dismantle criminal street gangs within Indianapolis and Marion County (Indianapolis Metropolitan Police Department 2012). Although this task force is designed to take down all gangs, it places "special emphasis on gangs that commit high impact violent crimes, including, but not limited to, homicide, felonious assault, drug trafficking, extortion, and weapons violations" (IMPD 2012). Law enforcement certainly has its hands full in Indianapolis. For example, in 2010 a 17-year-old longtime gang member opened fire on a crowded street during the Indiana Black Summer Celebration, wounding nine people (Wilson 2010). The July 17 shootings stemmed from a confrontation between two rival gangs. In August 2010, a law enforcement partnership between local U.S. Immigration and Customs Enforcement (ICE) and Office of Homeland Security Investigations (HSI), along with assistance from federal, state, and local police, arrested 14 foreign-born gang members from MS-13, Sur 13, and **Zoe Pound** (Fox59 News 2010). On April 11, 2012, the Indianapolis Division of the FBI levied 26 indictments against members of the Imperial Gangsters street gang for crimes ranging from racketeering activity related to drug distribution and trafficking to homicide (FBI 2012e). One day later, the Indianapolis Division of the FBI announced the sentencing of a street gang drug ring found guilty of operating cocaine trafficking operation (FBI 2012f).

This concludes our look at the history of gangs in the United States. It should be clear that street gangs are so commonplace that they have become institutionalized; that is to say, they have become a permanent fixture of American society. Street gangs exist nearly everywhere in this country, including large cities, small cities, suburbs, and many rural areas. They have increasingly taken over the drug distribution trade and use violence and mayhem to control their marketplaces.

Summary

The existence of gangs, in one form or another, has been documented for over eight centuries. Street gangs, however, have a shorter history, with the first one, the Forty Thieves, originating from New York City's Five Points slums in the mid-1820s. The Forty Thieves were a gang with Irish roots and arose as a result of the prejudice and discrimination the Irish experienced as America's first recognized ethnic minority group. The pattern of street gangs being dominated by ethnically/racially categories of persons lacking in full acceptance into American society has continued to this day.

The epicenter of the growing gang epidemic continued to remain in New York City throughout the 1800s. However, by the mid-1800s and late 1800s, street gangs were found in other parts of the Northeast, especially Boston and Philadelphia, and in such Southern cities as New Orleans, Baltimore, and Richmond. By the early 1900s, many larger cities, such as Detroit and Chicago, played witness to street gangs. In the mid-1900s, street gangs began to flourish in Los Angeles and Southern California. The development of the Crips in Los Angeles and their counterparts, the Bloods, led to the formation

of "nation" gangs who developed a loose confederation of affiliates throughout the nation by the start of the 2000s. Meanwhile, in Chicago, two other nation gangs were being formed—the People and the Folks.

By the end of the twentieth century, gangs had proliferated in nearly all geographical areas of the United States. Gangs can be found in all major cities, in most smaller cities and suburbs, and in some rural areas. Street gangs have become increasingly violent and are taking control of a larger percentage of the drug trafficking business in the United States. Rather than representing a passing moment in time, street gangs are now so institutionalized that they have become a permanent fixture of American society.

3

Theoretical Explanations of Street Gangs

Perhaps the most fundamental question involving street gangs is why they exist in the first place. Many people—social researchers, gang experts, law enforcement personnel, school administrators, citizens, and gang members themselves—have given various explanations. In this chapter, a number of theories on juvenile delinquency are presented and analyzed. Since there are very few theories that specifically address gangs, general delinquency theories are applied to gang formation and gangster behavior.

It is very important to examine theoretical explanations of gang formation primarily because the way a particular agency, governing body, or community views a gang directly impacts the programs and types of law enforcement used in relation to them. Champion (2004) believed that the way in which one explains and accounts for juvenile behavior directly affects the way individuals are processed in the juvenile justice system. "Theories are integrated explanatory schemes that predict relationships between two or more phenomena. They provide rational foundations to account for or explain things and help us to understand why juveniles are processed different ways by the juvenile justice system" (Champion 2004, 83). The theoretical approaches employed reflect contemporary social currents and knowledge available at the time.

Researchers committed to the scientific tradition view theory as much more than speculation, for speculation seems to imply uncertainty; and uncertainty is contrasted with established truths (Delaney 2005). Thus, any theory may already be established as true, or factual. From a scientific perspective, a theory should be empirically verifiable and have the ability to explain or provide and account for behavior and become applicable to a general set of related phenomena. *Empirically verifiable* refers to science's commitment to support theory with systematic observation and data collection, known as research. It is a commitment to scientific research that allows researchers to go beyond "common-sense" explanations of gang behavior. Furthermore, a commitment to sound scientific principles greatly assists in the creation and implementation of programs designed to help mainstream gang members. Research offers a cause-and-effect account of phenomena; it provides the "explanation or account" for why something occurs. When the explanation is general enough, it can be applied to "a general class of phenomena," and not just a few cases (e.g., Newton's theory of gravitation).

Theories are used as an attempt to explain and put order to the world that surrounds us. They provide the road map for our daily activities. We anticipate (theorize) how certain people are going to behave in given situations based on past experience and knowledge (research). For example, it is safe to assume (theorize) that if a student falls asleep in class or an employee falls asleep on the job, there will be negative consequences such as a lower grade in class and possible dismissal from work. Research will indicate that this theory is generally accurate. It may be "speculative," but it is also subject to the laws of probability, especially in cases where the student/employee has been warned against engaging in this deviant behavior. Theories that can be tested and are supported by empirical research are the "best" theories.

"Good" theory is always expressed in general terms, with specific tenets supported by social research. Theories of juvenile delinquency and gangs need to be abstract enough to generalize to other gangs but specific enough to concretely address specific issues critical in the scientific analysis of gang formation and gang behaviors.

BIOLOGICAL AND PSYCHOLOGICAL THEORIES

Before the last half of the nineteenth century, little scientific research had been conducted to explain why delinquency and crime occurred. Most explanations reflected moral beliefs and religious ideals. Biologists developed many of the earliest theories on crime and delinquency. They believed that genetic inheritance or other physical attributes were the causes of crime. Although these theories have been shown to be "useless" (Trojanowicz, Morash, and Schram 2001, 7) in explaining criminal behavior, discussion of theoretical explanations of juvenile delinquency and gangs begins with biological theories.

Biological Theories

Many biological theories attempt to link crime and delinquency to genetics, raising controversial issues such as the concept of a "born criminal" and the suggestion that crime is hereditary. Other biological theories have examined body types as a means of determining an individual's character, suggesting that the person "looks like a criminal." A layperson may think that a person looks shifty and must therefore be a criminal. The idea that a person's character could be determined by a physical examination dates to the ancient Greeks and Romans. In medieval times there was a law which specified that if two people were suspected of having committed a crime, the uglier one should be regarded as the more likely guilty party (Curran and Renzetti 1994). Following this ideology was the field of *physiognomy*, which involves the study of faces and skulls and other physical features in order to reveal an individual's natural disposition. The essential aspect of biological theories of crime and delinquency rests with the premise that such behaviors are caused by some mechanism internal to the individual or an outwardly visible physical trait possessed by the individual. As a rule, biological theories can be divided into two classification schemes: the **classical** and the **positive**.

THE CLASSICAL SCHOOL The classical school of criminology emerged in the eighteenth century, and its name is derived from that entire period, known as the "Classical Period." The classical school was not interested in studying criminals; rather, it focused on lawmaking and legal processing (Williams and McShane 1994). The eighteenth century was an era of great social change; faith and tradition were being challenged; and the rise of industrialization and ideals of democracy dominated in the Western world. The classical school of thought was developed by Cesare Beccaria, an Italian nobleman (1738–1794), in his book *On Crimes and Punishment* (1764). He believed that humans were free to choose courses of action and that they are capable of making rational decisions. People can choose whether to follow the rules or be deviant. Thus, an individual is free to choose whether to become a gang member or not. Another important contributor to this school of thought was Jeremy Bentham (1748–1832), an English philosopher, in his book *An Introduction to the Principles of Morals*. Bentham was known for promoting the idea of **hedonism**—humans seek pleasure and avoid pain in their activities. He also believed in utilitarianism—the greatest good for the greatest number.

According to Williams and McShane (1994, 21) the basic tenets of the classical school are

1. an emphasis on free will choices and the human rational
2. a view of behavior as hedonistic
3. a focus on morality and responsibility
4. a concern with political structure and the way in which government deals with its citizens
5. a concern for the basic rights of all people

These generic ideas and concerns when applied to criminal justice produced the concepts of deterrence, civil rights, and due process of law. Within this framework, individuals are expected to conform to the expectations of society, as Bentham held, for the greater good of society. Champion (2004) argues that society can be possible only when individuals are willing to sacrifice a degree of freedom for the collective good. Once a collective sentiment exists, certain behaviors are labeled as "wrong" or "evil" and therefore subject to punishment. Punishments are to fit the crime, with those found guilty of serious offenses the most harshly punished.

From the classical school perspective, since all behaviors are freely engaged upon, the judicial system merely needs to find a way to make crime so unappealing that individuals dare not violate society's rules. Free will allowed people to choose behavior; the judicial system needed to make sure that offenders would "unwill" to commit future crimes. In this regard, one's socioeconomic status (SES) would become irrelevant as an explanation, or justification, for illegal activity. Because norm violators are viewed as having freely chosen to participate in illegal behavior, presumably because they found it pleasurable or rewarding, punishments would have to be severe enough to offset any thought of committing such deeds. As rational beings, individuals should show good sense in choosing between right and wrong (Trojanowicz et al. 2001). The classical approach to crime and delinquency served a useful function in the transition from the old days of rule by monarchy and religion, where punishment varied based on who committed the crime. The idea of creating a rationally based criminal justice system in an effort to fight delinquency and crime represented a good start in establishing a fairer and just social system of justice. However, the ideas that all people act rationally all the time and that legitimate extenuating circumstances do not exist are just a few of the flaws in this approach.

THE POSITIVE SCHOOL   The classical school consisted mostly of writers and philosophers. The proponents of the positive school were generally scientists, mathematicians, doctors, and astronomers. Where the classicalists believed that humans possess a rational mind and were therefore capable of making rational choices, the Positivists saw behavior as determined by an individual's biological, psychological, and social traits. The Positivists have a deterministic view of the world, concentrate on criminal behavior, and promote protocols that can lead to the prevention or treatment of offenders. The Positivists' rejection of the idea that people were free to make their own decisions in life led them, in effect, to view offenders of the law as being "sick." The belief that such offenders were "sick" implied that researchers needed to find the "cause," or determinants, of such social pathology among individuals. Whether these determinants were biological, psychological, sociological, or cultural, once they were identified, treatment would involve altering one or more of the determinant factors that contributed to unlawful behavior.

Although the true roots of the positive school are hard to ascertain, given the fact that the attribution of criminality and delinquency to biological causes dates to prebiblical times, it is the work of Italian physician and criminologist Cesare Lombroso (1835–1909) that generally receives credit for influencing the beginnings of the positive school (Champion 2004). Lombroso, a trained psychiatrist but known as the "father of modern criminology," is best known for his early views on the "born criminal." The "born criminal" concept, as the name would suggest, works on the assumption that certain people are born to deviate from the norm and inevitably commit crime. Lombroso believed that less-developed (evolutionarily speaking) individuals are the ones most likely to be born criminals because they were incapable of abiding, or unwilling to abide, by the laws and norms of conventional society. Using research common to the time in which he lived and by those who studied criminals from the positivist perspective, Lombroso attempted to categorize anatomically atavistic (most primitive of humans) types. In the first edition of *The Criminal Man*, Lombroso labeled criminals on the basis of physical characteristics (e.g., thickness of the bones in the skull, pigmentation of the skin, hair type). Lombroso believed that criminals were products of heredity; that is, behavioral predispositions toward criminal conduct or antisocial proclivities were passed down through successive generations of blood lines. Lombroso went so far as to state that criminals possess a certain type of physical appearance, and because of this, one could label a criminal or deviant simply based on his/her looks. Only through severe social intervention could such people be restrained from their biologically determined predisposition to commit delinquency.

The logical flaws of biological determinism alone should have been enough to stop this school of thought from becoming as influential as it did. Furthermore, with our knowledge of white-collar crime and the criminals who commit such offenses, the idea of some sort of biological or physical characteristics as indicators of criminals can easily be dismissed. In addition, each culture determines what is deviant or criminal and consequently the positivist perspective violates the scientific notion that theory must be applicable to a general class of phenomena. However, the positive school did, and continues to, contribute to the field of knowledge in crime and delinquency.

Among the more bizarre attempts to link body types to delinquency is the use of somatotype. A *somatotype* refers to the overall shape of the body with particular attention paid to relative development of the various parts of the body in comparison with each other. Practitioners who used this approach believed that delinquency could be explained in terms of body shape and structure of individuals (Shoemaker 2000). William H. Sheldon was one the proponents of this perspective. Sheldon (1949) provided three categories of body types: the **mesomorphs** (strong, athletic, aggressive, and extroverted individuals), **ectomorphs** (thin, frail, and introverted individuals), and **endomorphs** (fat, jovial, and extroverted persons). Sheldon believed that the mesomorphs were the most likely to commit crime. Although it is true that some criminals fall into the mesomorphs category, research, of course, has never been able to substantiate a correlation between these body types and criminality. As hard as it is today to believe that anyone took Sheldon's work seriously, the positive school did enjoy relatively high esteem. Sheldon also attempted to link body shape and intelligence. Beginning in the early 1900s, it was common for frontal and profile nude photos to be taken of generations of elite college students. All freshmen at some colleges—including Ivy League schools—were required to pose in the buff (e.g., former President George H.W. Bush, Hillary Rodham Clinton, Diane Sawyer, and George Pataki). For some time, the photos were available at the Smithsonian Institution, where the public had access to them—they have since been destroyed or made unavailable. Most scientists today consider Sheldon's work as "quackery" (*Billings Gazette* 1995, 1A).

In the late twentieth century, biological explanations of the connection between crime and delinquency have attempted to link specific characteristics (e.g., chromosome analysis and gene identification, brain activity) to behavior. At one time, students who did poorly in school might have been labeled slow, feebleminded, dumb, or uninterested in schoolwork and preferring to cause trouble. In the early 1960s came the "discovery" of "learning disabilities" and the realization that individuals learn differently from one another. There are several forms of learning disabilities, with the most common being dyslexia, aphasia, and hyperkinesis. Thus, descriptions of many of the students once labeled "impulsive" and "unwilling to learn" were inaccurate. "In short, children with learning disabilities are thought to have a breakdown in the usual sensory-thought processes that enable other children to understand societal punishment-reward systems attached to behavior. Thus, the general effectiveness of sanctions on behavior is lessened" (Shoemaker 2000, 35). Many of today's delinquents in schools may in fact suffer from some learning disability. If the disability can be properly identified and dealt with, then many of these delinquents will do better in school and may not end up in a gang.

The only way biological theories will serve any use and purpose in the field of criminality (and the social sciences, for that matter) is if they can clearly link genes and chromosomes to crime and delinquency. Studies involving the **XYY syndrome** have attempted to show that the presence of a Y chromosome signals the secretion of the male hormone testosterone. Testosterone has been linked to aggressiveness. Consequently, it is theorized that the presence of an extra Y chromosome will lead to increased aggressiveness and, by implication, increased levels of criminality. Studies have shown that XYY males are disproportionately found among the institutionalized. "Nevertheless, it must be kept in mind that most studies of XYY males to date have utilized small, selective samples which may have seriously compromised findings. More importantly, even if criminality is associated with this abnormality, XYY syndrome can account for only a tiny proportion of crime. The vast majority of crimes are still committed by chromosomally normal XY males" (Curran and Renzetti 1994, 66).

The biological approach to the study of crime and delinquency has changed quite a bit since its humble roots. No longer are delinquents viewed as evolutionary misfits; instead, personality factors and environmental factors are considered. Nonetheless, biological theories have had little impact on explaining gang behavior. There are two primary reasons for this. First, making a claim that certain persons are destined to be gang members based on physical or biological characteristics would most likely lead to charges of racism in contemporary society. It is true that the vast majority of present-day gang members are either Hispanic or African American. But they do not possess a predisposition, or genetic trait, for this behavior—there is no such thing as a "gang gene." Furthermore, gang members represent a very small percentage of the total population so there are far more Hispanics or African Americans that are not gang members than there are those who are gang members. Second, history (see Chapter 2) has already shown us that in the nineteenth century the vast majority of gang members were white. Did whites lose their gang gene? Of course not. Socioeconomic conditions changed for the ethnic white gangs.

Psychological Theories of Delinquency

Psychological theories, although not as fundamentally sound as sociological theories on gang behavior, represent an improvement over biological explanations. Psychological theories of delinquency start with the premise that there are individual differences in intelligence, personality, and learning.

INTELLIGENCE-BASED THEORIES   At their most basic level, intelligence-based theories on crime and delinquency center around the idea that certain individuals are mentally deficient, possess some hereditary degeneration, are feebleminded, or are just too plain dumb to understand the consequences or meanings of their delinquent behaviors. The development of the concept of insanity, particularly moral insanity, represents the earliest attempt to link psychological or mental aspects of the individual to criminal behavior (Fink 1938). "It was typically suggested that criminals and delinquents were deficient in basic moral sentiments and that, furthermore, this condition was an inherited trait and contributed to the fusion of biological and psychological properties in the explanation of criminality" (Shoemaker 2000, 47). With the introduction of intelligence tests in the early twentieth century, attempts were made to attribute criminality to those who were unable to comprehend their actions. However, these early intelligence tests worked with the assumption that intelligence was somehow an inherited trait, and thus these theories were as much biological as they were psychological.

Hereditary studies attempted to explain criminality as some form of mental deficiency. "At the heart of the early hereditary studies was the belief that intellectual inferiority or low intelligence was a basic cause of crime. With the development of Alfred Binet and Theodore Simon's *Scale of Intelligence* in 1905, numerous studies conducted on prison inmates tested the hypothesized relationship between low intelligence, especially feeblemindedness, and crime" (Thornton and Voight 1992, 143). Goddard reported in his *Feeblemindedness: Its Causes and Consequences* (1914) that 89 percent of one inmate population under study was feebleminded, but only 29 percent in another study (cited in Vold 1958). During this same period, Charles Goring published his study *The English Convict* (1913), in which he found no evidence to support Lombroso's theory of atavism. "However, he found that criminals were abnormally low in intelligence and he took this as an indication of hereditary inferiority" (Curran and Renzetti 1994, 91). This represents quite a jump, for even if convicts are, as a whole, less intelligent than the general population, how does that prove heredity had anything to do with it? The general feeling of the early twentieth century researchers who studied criminality was that criminals were lacking in intelligence and morality.

In 1912, a German psychologist named W. Stern revised Binet's method for calculating general intelligence by introducing the idea of dividing mental age by chronological age, arguing that this gives a better estimate of degree of deficiency. Through division, the resulting score ended up being a fraction, so Stern multiplied the quotient by 100 to get rid of the decimal point and thus gave birth to the concept of the intelligence quotient, or IQ (Curran and Renzetti 1994). There have been numerous adaptations of intelligence tests over the years. Psychological theories of delinquency no longer assume that criminality is a result of mental deficiency and have instead come to the conclusion that socialization and school experiences are important factors in criminality. Psychological theories in the modern era believe that personality and learning techniques are correlated to delinquency.

PERSONALITY TRAIT THEORIES   In order to develop a personality-based theory of delinquency, the concept of personality must be defined. *Personality* refers to the total characteristics of an individual that shape one's pattern of interactions with the environment. These characteristics include patterns of thoughts, feelings, motives, past experiences, and perceptions of reality. This definition, which has not been adopted by all psychologists, still does not solve the problem of how personality develops and how it changes. Among the more famous psychologically based theories of personality is Freud's psychoanalytical theory. Freud did not study delinquency, because he did not feel delinquents and criminals were worthy of his attention (Ewen 1988). Instead, his theory has been applied by others to crime and delinquency. Freud felt that the personality consisted of three parts: the id, ego, and superego. The theory is based on the belief that the *id* component of the personality is concerned with satisfying primal needs, such as sexual gratification and aggressive tendencies. The *superego*, which is the personality trait that symbolizes society's expectations of proper behavior, comes in conflict with the id. Consequently, the *ego* attempts to find the balance between individual needs and society's rules and expectations on how to best attain them. The theory suggests that if a child was not properly taught how to incorporate the superego into the personality, then the child's id would become overly active, ultimately leading to delinquent behavior. Later in life, "the youth may demand immediate gratification, lack compassion and sensitivity for the needs of others, disassociate feelings, act aggressively and impulsively, and demonstrate other psychotic symptoms. Antisocial behavior then may be the result of conflict or trauma occurring early in a child's development, and delinquent activity may become an outlet for violent and antisocial feelings" (Siegel, Welsh, and Senna 2003, 84). Thus, the *underdeveloped superego* syndrome leads to a personality that is more conducive to crime and delinquency. An *overdeveloped superego* may also lead to deviancy—feelings of guilt leave the child with a need for punishment. Among the many criticisms of this theory is the realization that there are those who did not suffer from childhood trauma and yet still end up committing delinquent and/or criminal acts. Additionally, there is no way of empirically testing such a theory as Freud's.

Personality-based theories on deviant behavior have led to the development of such concepts as *neurosis* and *psychosis* being applied to criminality. People who are dominated by their primitive id are known as *psychotics*. Their behavior may be marked by bizarre and inappropriate behaviors. *Schizophrenia* is the most common form of psychosis and is characterized by an illogical thought process (e.g., hearing voices that are not really there). The field of psychology has convinced nearly everyone of the validity of the phenomenon of individuals with multiple personalities. Erik Erickson speculated that delinquents suffer from an *identity crisis*. Multiple personality disorder is believed to be caused by severe childhood trauma, in particular sadistic child abuse. "In order to deal with the abuse, the individual disassociates from it by separating into different selves, each of which has its own way of thinking, feeling, and acting" (Curran and Renzetti 1994, 115).

Many of these disorders are used successfully in courtrooms to excuse improper social behavior. Terms such as *psychopath* and *sociopath* often arise when discussing delinquency, even though attempts by the American Psychiatric Association to standardize the meaning of these concepts have not been successful (Thornton and Voight 1992). The sociopath represents a personality type that has surfaced in biopsychology research. The sociopath possesses an "antisocial personality." "The *sociopath* is thought to be a dangerous, aggressive person who shows little remorse for his or her action, who is not deterred by punishments, and who does not learn from past mistakes. Sociopaths often appear as someone with a pleasant personality and with an above-average level of intelligence. They are, however, marked by an inability to form enduring relationships" (Lyman and Potter 2000, 70). Gang members would not appear to be sociopaths. They do, in fact, generally display little remorse for their actions and are not deterred by punishments; however, they do form loyal, life-long relationships with their fellow gang members.

SOCIAL LEARNING THEORIES   Like sociological theories, psychological social learning theories are based on the idea that delinquency, as with nearly all behaviors, is socially learned. "Traumatic early childhood experiences may be important determinants of subsequent adult personality characteristics, but the primary factors influencing whether one conforms to or deviates from societal rules are those experiences youths have while learning from others such as their parents. Adults in any institutional context (e.g., schools, churches, homes) provide role models for children to follow" (Champion 2004, 94). In simplest terms, children learn to become delinquents based on interaction with significant others. Children model the behavior of the adults that they are in close contact with, especially parents, and also the behaviors they see on television and in the movies. "By implication, social learning suggests that children who grow up in a home where violence is a way of life may learn to believe that such behavior is acceptable and rewarding. Even if parents tell children not to be violent and punish them if they are, the children will still model their behavior on the observed parental violence. Thus, children are more likely to heed what their parents *do* than what they *say*" (Siegel et al. 2003, 87).

Social learning generally takes place through two primary methods: reinforcement of behavior and modeling of behavior. The relationship between **reinforcement** and delinquency is both predictable and, perhaps, surprising to some readers. First, when aggression is rewarded instead of punished, the odds of aggressive delinquency increase (Bandura and Walters 1963). Second, "parents of aggressive youths are more inclined to encourage and condone aggression in the home than the parents of nonaggressive youths. The reinforcement of aggression toward siblings or other children at home can cause the child to be aggressive outside the home, at school, and in the community" (Thornton and Voight 1992, 146). Reinforcement is the result of contact between a great number of people in society, and although parents and the immediate family are the most important agents of socialization, when the child reaches a certain age (around the third grade) the reinforcement of peers becomes very important. If the child associates with a number of other delinquents, the reinforcement of deviant activity becomes stronger and may take hold as a significant modifier of behavior. When a child becomes identified with a particular subculture, the reinforcement becomes stronger.

Along with reinforcement, the child learns behavior through **modeling**. Direct contact between the child and the person who serves as a model is not needed in order for the child's behavior to be influenced. Simply observing how others behave represents a learning opportunity. Thus, a child may learn how to play ball by observing the older kids or by watching professional athletes on television. Thus, one may serve as a model without knowing it, or without wanting to serve as a role model. This happens to athletes a lot—they may not see themselves as role models, but children regard them as such anyway. Delinquents in the neighborhood have a direct influence on younger children. This is especially true in the gang world. Many youngsters grow up as "wannabes"—meaning that they want to be a gang member when they grow older. In fact, the psychological theory involving the impact of modeling on gang participation seems to have a high degree of validity—certainly not as a cause of gang participation, but as a partial explanation as to why youngsters grow up wanting to be gang members. When young children growing up in poverty see gangsters with new clothes, shiny jewelry, and cash, they see a "role model."

SOCIOLOGICAL THEORIES

Sociological theories of crime and delinquency are often applied to the study of gangs. They generally incorporate a diverse, multicausal framework in their explanation of criminality. Sociological theories are grounded by the belief that delinquency is caused by environmental factors. They are supported by empirical data and represent, by far, the most scientific approach in explaining crime and delinquency. Let us begin with the social disorganization theory, which emphasizes that certain neighborhoods are more likely to produce crime and delinquency.

Social Disorganization Theory (the Chicago School)

Social disorganization theory developed from the early ecological research on urban development conducted by sociologists at the University of Chicago during the 1920s and 1930s. Established in 1892, the University of Chicago is home to the first academic department of sociology in the United States. Until the mid-twentieth century it was one of the most dominant forces of socio-logical thought. The city of Chicago was experiencing dramatic change due to rapid industrial growth and a high migration rate at the turn of the twentieth century. The social problems of high-density urban life presented a golden opportunity for researchers to use the city as a sort of living social laboratory. Many of the new residents of Chicago were from rural areas and were not able to cope with the social problems that urban life presented. The researchers at Chicago attempted to provide some sort of explanation for why certain neighborhoods produced high rates of crime and delinquency, including gangs, while others did not.

Robert Park, Ernst Burgess, Louis Wirth, and others from Chicago identified several areas of the city that expanded outward in a pattern of **concentric circles**. The outlining areas (Zones 4 and 5) were populated predominantly by white, middle-, and upper-class homeowners who had lived in their communities for many years and were well integrated into the dominant culture of society. In an area between the center of the city and the outlying districts (Zone 3) were working-class neighborhoods occupied mostly by second- and third-generation immigrants. In the area closest to the center (Zone 2) were found the poor, the recent immigrants, and transients who faced poor housing conditions. This is the area where the ghettos were found. The core of the city (Zone 1) contained the downtown area where businesses and government buildings were located. "The Chicago sociologists observed that not all urban zones were plagued equally by alcoholism, high rates of mental illness, and other similar problems. Indeed, the further one moved away from the city center, the lower the incidence of social problems. According to the Chicago School, this was the result of the social disorganization that characterized city areas" (Curran and Renzetti 1994, 136). Social disorganization most directly affects those people experiencing poor living con-ditions. Feelings of hopelessness foster deviant manifestations. No zone was found to be free from delinquency, but the highest rates were found in Zone 2. However, the farther one moved away from the center of the concentric zone, the fewer social problems were confronted. Because all cities do not grow in the same manner, other models were created to explain delinquency in dif-ferent cities (the other two popular models are the sector and the multinuclei). The importance of the concentric zone model is that it stimulated subsequent research to analyze delinquency rates by incorporating fundamental environmental factors such as neighborhood location.

Social disorganization was believed to be caused by social change that was too rapid for the smooth operation of the social system. In socially disorganized areas, the dominant values and norms are in contrast to the new emerging norms and values. Social cohesion breaks down, social deviance increases, and social disorganization results. Social disorganization can occur when a large number of people become unemployed. Significant social problems in any area can cause social disorganiza-tion. During the early 1900s, social disorganization became the primary explanation for the emer-gence of crime. In neighborhoods where the family and friendship groups were solidly grounded, neighborhoods were stable and cohesive, and where people had a loyalty to the neighborhood, social organization existed. Without these elements, a neighborhood becomes socially disorganized, and normal social control, which prevents delinquency, becomes ineffective (Williams and McShane 1994). Sampson and Groves (1989) outlined four elements that constitute social disorganization:

1. Low economic status
2. A mixture of different ethnic groups

3. Highly mobile residents moving in and out of the area
4. Disrupted families and broken homes

The high degree of mobility, and implied lack of stability, is a major factor in the disorganization of an economically poor neighborhood.

Social disorganization stimulates the creation of subcultures that are in opposition to the dominant cultural values and norms. Delinquent and criminal subcultures tend to flourish in poor areas (Zone 2) that, over time, lead to a subculture of deviance that has values in contrast to conventional ones. Frederic Thrasher is considered the pioneer of gang-formation research. His classic work in *The Gang* comes from a social disorganization perspective. He believed that gangs grew naturally from spontaneous play groups. Thrasher (1927, 32) stated that gangs originate from "the spontaneous effort of boys to create a society for themselves where none adequate to their needs exists. What boys get out of such associations that they do not get otherwise under the conditions that adult society imposes is the thrill and zest of participation in common interests, more especially in corporate action, in hunting, capture, conflict, flight, and escape." Threats from youths outside the neighborhood provided delinquents with the rally call of coming to arms to protect the neighborhood. Protecting the neighborhood would work only with the involvement of other cohorts. Thrasher believed that play groups of youths shared a number of significant characteristics, most of which were centered around the idea of loyalty to the group. This loose affiliation would evolve into a close-knit gang when confronted by outsiders.

Thrasher was firmly entrenched within the Chicago School/social disorganization tradition. He systematically documented gang activity and rigorously attempted to analyze all facets of gang activity—an accomplishment probably never equaled. He identified at least 1,313 gangs with a total membership of nearly 25,000. His studies allowed him to distinguish between what activities are normal for adolescents and what activities are unique to gangsters (Trojanowicz et al. 2001). Thrasher (1927) found that gangs tend to flourish in areas of the city that he called "interstitial"—those areas that lie within the "poverty belt" within a city. For Thrasher, the poverty belt was an area of the city characterized by deteriorating neighborhoods and mobile residents. He believed that gang membership provided many youths a sense of self, an identity, and status and maybe even increased their self-esteem. The gang often becomes a substitute family for its members. Their loyalty to the gang supercedes their loyalty to the greater community or society as a whole.

Research conducted on the **Mongrel Mob** gang of Gisborne, New Zealand, in 2011 reflects the social disorganization perspective. James Ihaka found that Mongrel Mob members either came from families with members already in a gang or from "families that can't provide enough security or support so the gangs become their kind of surrogate family" (*New Zealand Herald* 2011, A6). Some suburbs of Gisborne have numerous social problems; in Kaiti specifically, 40 percent of youths come from single-parent families and 40 percent of adults have no formal qualifications (for employment) (*New Zealand Herald* 2011). Like the pattern established in socially disorganized areas of the United States, major businesses left the Gisborne area, causing high unemployment and the trickle-down effect associated with the lack of employment opportunities. The Maori (indigenous New Zealanders) were especially hit by the social disorganization caused by the negative economic realities, and their youth turned to the Mongrel Mob to fill the void. Kaiti, located on the eastside of Gisborne, is separated from the Central Business District by the Turanganui River. Nearby Kaiti Beach is of great socio-historic interest to New Zealand, as Captain James Cook, the first European to have set foot on New Zealand soil, landed there in 1769.

The social disorganization theory, or Chicago-school approach, is known as an ecological theory. Social ecological theory concerns itself with the organization and structure of society and its impact on localized environments, or communities. "Even at the height of its popularity, the ecological school recognized that American crime patterns might be different from those found elsewhere in the world and that crime zones might exist in city areas other than those surrounding the core" (Schmalleger 2004, 209). Thus, it is important to note that social disorganization theory, which was initially applied to Chicago gangs, is mostly applicable to cities with large urban populations. But even in larger urban cities, social disorganization theory fails to account why some disadvantaged areas produce street gangs while others do not. Katz and Schnebly (2011) came to this conclusion in their study of Arizona gangs. Papachristos and Kirk (2006) found that social disorganization theory helped to explain and predict gang homicide, but not nongang homicide.

Schmalleger (2004) believes that the most significant and lasting contribution from ecological theorists of the Chicago School was its "formalized use of two sources of information: (1) official crime and population statistics and (2) ethnographic data. Population statistics, or demographic data, when combined with crime information, provided empirical material that gave scientific weight to ecological investigations" (209).

Anomie/Strain Theory

Anomie theory, sometimes called *strain theory*, was articulated by Robert Merton, who borrowed Emile Durkheim's term *anomie*. Durkheim was very concerned with what he perceived as the decline of common morality in French society. "Industrialization in particular, according to Durkheim, tends to dissolve restraints on the passions of humans. Where simple societies—primarily through religion—successfully taught people to control their desires and goals, modern industrial societies separate people and weaken their social bonds as a result of increased complexity and the division of labor. Durkheim believed that members of Western society are exposed to the risk of *anomie*" (Delaney 2004a, 101). The term *anomie* comes from the Greek *anomia*, meaning "without law." In his 1893 book *The Division of Labor in Society*, Durkheim used the word *anomie* to refer to a condition of "deregulation" occurring in society. "By this he meant that the general procedural rules of a society (the rules that say how people ought to behave toward each other) have broken down and that people do not know what to expect from each other. This deregulation, or normlessness, easily leads to deviant behavior" (Williams and McShane 1994, 87). Feelings of normlessness lead members to deviant behavior because a common morality of society no longer exists. It was in *Suicide* (1897) where Durkheim used *anomie* to describe a general state of moral deregulation, which had left people inadequate moral controls over their behavior.

> Individuals are confronted with *anomie* when they are not faced with sufficient moral constraint, or do not have a clear concept of what is and what is not acceptable behavior. . . . Durkheim viewed *anomie* as a pathology. By thinking of *anomie* as a pathology, Durkheim was saying that deviant behaviors and the problems of the world could be "cured." Thus, the proper level of regulation, both in terms of issues of morality and civility, would guarantee a cohesive and smoothly operating society. (Delaney 2004a, 101–102)

In short, *anomie* refers to the breakdown of social norms and rules and a condition in which existing norms no longer control the activity of individuals.

Robert Merton was intrigued by Durkheim's notion of anomie and how persons adapt to the *strain* of chaotic social conditions. In 1938, Merton borrowed Durkheim's concept of anomie and used it in an attempt to explain deviant behavior in the United States: "Whereas Durkheim conceived of anomie as a problematic social condition resulting from sudden and rapid social change, Merton saw it as an endemic feature of the everyday operation of certain types of societies" (Curran and Renzetti 1994, 149). Merton conceived of society as consisting of two primary components: the cultural structure and the social structure. The *cultural structure* consists of society's goals—what all members are supposed to strive to attain; whereas the *social structure* refers to the institutional means of attaining these goals. Merton believed that functional societies have an integrated blend of these two aspects. Dysfunctional societies, however, place an undue emphasis on one of the societal components. Merton viewed the United States as a dysfunctional society because it places great emphasis on cultural goals—primarily economic and material success—but is characterized by a social structure that does not provide everyone with an equal opportunity to reach these goals.

Merton's "goals-means" scheme of describing different societies shines a light on how good a job a particular society does in providing its members with opportunities to reach desired ends. Merton contends that every society teaches its citizens to seek culturally approved goals (e.g., economic stability, pursuit of happiness, consumer goods) and provides a number of avenues to achieve these goals. However, Merton counters that these opportunities for success are not equal for all societal members. When people feel that their chances of attaining cultural goals through legitimate means have been blocked, that will pursue illegitimate means. Merton realized that social systems found throughout the world differ a great deal. Some societies do not value capitalism and materialism while others do. Democratic societies present the greatest opportunity for all individuals to achieve some level of success, while repressive ones create strain for their citizens as they pitifully attempt to gain some sense of autonomy. Merton argued, then, that deviance is the result of the social strain anomie created. Deviance is a symptom of a social structure that has not provided an equal opportunity for all members to attain cultural desired goals. Thus, the dissonance between a desired goal and the means to achieve said goal may result in deviance. Conventional folks and gang members alike may experience strain as a result of this dissonance but what differentiates them from each other is the path that they choose to follow in their attempt to reach desired goals. Once again, an individual who has a goal but rejects legitimate means to achieve it and instead pursues illegitimate means (e.g., criminal acts) would be considered a deviant from this theoretical perspective.

One of the most sought-after goals in American society is success. And while success has many meanings for people, it generally involves some level of economic fulfillment. The anomie/strain theory suggests that there are millions of people in the United States who do not have an equal chance of becoming successful for reasons beyond individual incompetence. Instead, anomie/strain theorists would suggest that the social institution is designed to disadvantage certain categories of people (especially those found in the lower social classes and racial/ethnic minority members). Americans struggling to reach culturally approved goals experience strain and anxiety; many of these people will pursue illegitimate, or illegal, means of getting ahead.

According to Merton (1968), when individuals are faced with the strain caused by anomic conditions they have a choice between five **modes of adaptation**. Three of these behavioral adaptations are considered deviant (innovation, retreatism, and rebellion), while the other two (conformity and ritualism) are generally not. (Note that many social scientists consider ritualism as a deviant adaptation.) A description of Merton's modes of adaptation is provided here:

MERTON'S MODES OF ADAPTATION

1. *Conformity*—Involves accepting things as they are. Conformists have accepted the goals of society and the prescribed ways of attaining them. According to Merton, this is the most

common mode of behavior. Furthermore, this reality helps to explain why, no matter how high the crime rate is in some neighborhoods, most citizens are not criminals.

2. *Innovation*—Involves an emphasis on striving for the approved goals of society but legitimate means have been replaced by illegitimate ones. Innovation represents the most common deviant adaptation of behavior. For many members of society, deviant adaptation (e.g., bank robbery) may actually represent a more efficient means of reaching a goal than the approved means to do so (e.g., working hard at a menial job making minimum wage). It is this reasoning that has a direct effect on why a disproportionate number of street criminals are from the lower socioeconomic classes (e.g., a successful businessperson has little need to rob a convenience store for $50).

3. *Ritualism*—Ritualists reject goals but work toward less lofty goals by institutionally approved means. "In this mode the means can become the aspirations of an individual, as when one may attempt to treat a job (means) as a form of security instead of using the job as a means of achieving success. In this example, keeping the job has become a goal by itself, resolving the frustration of unsuccessfully chasing the original goal" (Williams and McShane 1994, 92). Clerks and petty bureaucrats are examples of ritualists. Ritualists simply go through the motions day after day, are never really happy with life, but have found salvation through scaled-down ambition. Deviant behavior occurs when clerks exercise a sense of power by breaking the rules. For example, a clerk may give out private and confidential information to reporters or to people who offer bribes.

4. *Retreatism*—Occurs when people reject both society's goals and the means of attaining them. Rather than innovate, or simply accept society (conformity), these people choose to cut themselves off from the world (e.g., hermits, drug addicts, street people, and bag ladies). This mode of adaptation seems to be more common today than in Merton's era.

5. *Rebellion*—This mode of adaptation interests those persons who are so strained by society that they wish to replace both the goals and the means of attaining them (e.g., anarchists, militant groups).

One other variation of strain theory worth mentioning comes from the work of Cloward and Ohlin in *Delinquency and Opportunity* (1960). These researchers believed that special circumstances (social problems) confront certain members of society and therefore block their opportunities in the pursuit of culturally determined goals. This leads to feelings of frustration and poor self-concepts which in turn may lead to delinquency. Frustrated youths, in particular, may come to view the gang life as their best way to overcome blocked opportunities. They are willing to participate in violence, crime, and drug use.

Culturally frustrated youths are disproportionately found in the lower economic social classes. Within these environments exist greater opportunity and reinforcement to commit acts of delinquency and crime. Thus, there is a difference in opportunity to commit crime based on one's social class. Cloward and Ohlin used the concept of *differential opportunity structure*, meaning that there is an uneven distribution of legitimate and illegitimate means of achieving society's success goal. This "opportunity theory" stressed the importance of the social environment in determining which opportunities individuals choose. Youths from wealthy families have more legitimate opportunities afforded to them, whereas youths from poorer neighborhoods have far fewer legitimate and realistic means of attaining desired goals. The fact that the largest percentage of gangs can be found in lower-class neighborhoods would seem to give validity to anomie/strain theory.

Subculture/Cultural Deviance Theory

By the 1950s and early 1960s, sociologists were studying juvenile delinquency in the context of the new sociological term *subcultures*, which represented an evolutionary step in the study of gang behavior. Subcultural theories offer great insight into gang behavior, as the gang is most definitely a subculture of the greater society. "Subcultural theorists perceive delinquency to be simultaneously a reaction to the larger cultural value system and an adherence to group norms. Subculturalists maintain that delinquency is an expression of standards espoused by one's reference group—in this case, other members of the subculture. For subculturalists, delinquency constitutes behavior consistent with a set of norms" (Thornton and Voight 1992, 171). In brief, a subculture is a group of people found within the greater society. They generally share many of the same ideas and values of the greater society, but go about things differently. If the subculture group participates in deviant behavior, new members will feel the pressure to conform to deviant norms. Subcultural theory concentrates on this group dynamic. As Goldstein (1991, 12) explained, "Subcultural deviance theory holds that delinquent behavior grows from conformity to the prevailing social norms experienced by youths in their particular subculture groups."

Subculture/cultural deviance theories were influenced by the Chicago School tradition (looking for the relationship between community and delinquency), Merton's anomie theory, and even social disorganization theory. When individuals attempt to adopt subcultural values and norms, they may come in conflict with the prevailing cultural values; in essence, the deviant individual has adopted the norms and traditions that emerged within neighborhoods most affected by social disorganization.

During the 1950s, along with the term *subcultures* came the concept of **reference groups**. In many ways, reference groups are similar to subcultures; in fact, it is this "reference point" idea that leads to the formation of subculture. Subcultures are formed when reference group members share a number of common goals and traits. The reference group serves as the point of reference in making comparisons or contrasts, especially in forming judgments about one's self. Reference groups provide points of comparison in evaluating one's own status. The reference group concept is particularly useful in accounting for the choices made among apparent alternatives, particularly where the selections seem to be contrary to the "best interests" of the actor. "The concept of reference group can . . . greatly facilitate research on the manner in which each actor's orientation toward his world is structured" (Shibutani 1955, 562). Within the framework of the reference group, members feel a great sense of loyalty to each other, they aspire to gain or maintain acceptance, and consequently, group norms take on a higher value than society's. When these events occur, a subculture has been formed.

Among the more significant theorists of the subcultural format of explaining crime and delinquency is Albert Cohen. "Delinquent subcultures exist, according to Cohen, within the greater societal culture. But these subcultures contain value systems and modes of achievement and gaining status and recognition apart from the mainstream culture" (Champion 2004, 100). Cohen's *Delinquent Boys: The Culture of the Gang* (1955) is one of the first versions of cultural deviance theory that explains how delinquent subcultures form. Cohen began his analysis with a simple premise, that everyone seeks social status. Unfortunately, not all youths can compete equally for status. "By virtue of their position in the social structure, lower-class children tend to lack both material and symbolic advantages. As long as they compete among themselves, the footing is relatively equal; it is in competition with middle-class children that lower-class children fall short" (Williams and McShane 1994, 108). Cohen did not imply that delinquency is a product of lower SES, rather that lower SES children are at greater risk of being influenced by the subculture of delinquency that contrasts itself from the middle-class ideal. It is this "middle-class measuring rod" against which many youths of lower SES fall short.

Cohen's (1955) subcultural deviance theory works with the following assumptions:

1. A high proportion of lower-class youths (especially males) do poorly in school.
2. Poor school performance relates to delinquency.
3. Poor school performance stems from a conflict between dominant middle-class values of the school system and values of lower-class youths.
4. Most lower-class male delinquency is committed in a gang context, partly as a means of meeting some basic human needs, such as self-esteem and belonging. (Shelden, Tracy, and Brown 2001, 173)

Working with these assumptions, Cohen (1955) identified five central characteristics of lower-class delinquent gangs, which, when combined, comprise the **delinquent subculture**:

1. *Nonutilitarianism*—The acts of delinquency committed by delinquents are not always done for a specific purpose (utilitarianism). Instead, profound satisfaction from committing crimes, such as theft, may come from the act itself—being delinquent.
2. *Maliciousness*—A great deal of delinquency is committed simply for the purpose of being mean and the corresponding rush and thrill of committing deviant acts. Vandalism is a primary example of malicious behavior.
3. *Negativism*—The delinquent subculture is not only at odds with the greater society, it attempts to take its norms and turn them upside down.
4. *Short-term hedonism*—There is little planning in regard to long-term goals; instead, gang members live for the moment and immediate gratification.
5. *Group autonomy*—Delinquents, and especially gang members, do not recognize any authority figure (e.g., parents, teachers, agents of social control) other than those in charge of the gang. (Curran and Renzetti 1994, 153–154)

Cohen concluded that gang members are at complete odds with the middle-class goal structure (e.g., delayed gratification, good manners, self-control, being a productive member of society). When the schools try to impose such goals, they rebel. The strain caused by middle-class expectations placed on lower SES youths causes **status frustration** (Cohen 1955). The fact that some neighborhoods produce more delinquents than others can be explained (at least partially) by Cloward and Ohlin's use of the concept of **degree of integration**. As this term implies, the degree to which delinquents are, or are not, tied to the community will impact their degree of delinquency. Where individuals are at great odds with the prevailing value system, a high degree of delinquency and gang activity will most likely be found. The greater the degree of integration, the lower the rate of delinquency and crime.

Richard Cloward (1959), noting Merton's anomie theory, developed a "differential opportunity theory." Cloward believed that there exist both a legitimate opportunity structure toward desired societal goals and an **illegitimate opportunity structure**. This illegitimate opportunity structure served as the backdrop for a theory Cloward proposed with Lloyd Ohlin in *Delinquency and Opportunity: A Theory of Delinquent Gangs* (1960). Their theory is known as *differential opportunity theory*. Cloward and Ohlin argued that "whereas legitimate opportunities are generally available to individuals born into middle-class culture, participants in lower-class subcultures are often denied access to them. As a consequence, illegitimate opportunities for success are often seen as quite acceptable by participants in so-called illegitimate subcultures" (Schmalleger 2004, 218). The inference is that delinquent (and gang) behavior may result from the availability of illegitimate opportunities and their acknowledgment, within the subculture, as acceptable. Cloward and Ohlin described three types of delinquent subcultures:

1. criminal subcultures—criminal roles are readily available for adoption
2. conflict subcultures—participants seek status through violence
3. retreatist subcultures—groups that participate in drug use and/or withdrawal from the predominant society

The works of Walter B. Miller represent a significant influence on subcultural theory. Miller argued that Cohen's analysis of gangs from the perspective of the middle class resulted in his missing important aspects of gang life. Miller believed that gang members did not see their activities as nonutilitarian, malicious, and negativistic. Instead, Miller believed that gang behavior supports and maintains the basic features of lower-class values and a way of life. Miller (1958) identified six basic features that characterized the lower-class value system. He referred to them as **focal concerns**. Focal concerns are features or aspects of a subculture that require constant monitoring, attention, and care. Miller's (1958) focal concerns are trouble, toughness, smartness, excitement, fate, and autonomy. The cornerstone belief of Miller's focal concerns centers on the idea that lower-class delinquents are overly concerned with immediate gratification rather than delayed gratification encouraged by middle-class values. The pursuit of immediate gratification allows delinquents to ignore the reality that committing crimes will ultimately lead to incarceration in favor of instant fulfillment. Thus, getting in trouble, fighting, committing crime, and possessing street smarts are valued because they bring instant happiness. In contrast, the middle-class ideology encourages youth to pursue academic smarts, sports, cultural arts, and so forth, all the while concentrating on future success. Miller argued that the gang subculture reflected the lower-class value system and that gang participation provided a means to an end.

Subcultural theories had substantial impact on American policy because they offered hope to a new generation of liberal-thinking people in the early 1960s. The Kennedy and Johnson presidential administrations attempted to implement the major concepts of opportunity theory by spending millions of dollars on the Great Society and War on Poverty efforts, especially the Peace Corps.

Control/Social Bond Theory

There are many variations of control theory; its roots date back to the late nineteenth century, but its greatest impact on the field of delinquency developed in the 1950s and 1960s. Lamar Empey (1982) suggests that the nineteenth- and twentieth-century theories designed to explain individual deviance that relied on psychoanalytic explanations were really early prototypes of "control" theory. Travis Hirschi (1969) believes that control theory can be traced back to Durkheim.

> Most often, however, control theories of delinquency are equated with self-concept research and social control mechanisms, such as family and school experiences. In this context, control theories may be historically placed in the 1950s and early 1960s, with the development of Walter Reckless' self-concept or containment explanation of delinquency. In the late 1960s Travis Hirschi extended Reckless' ideas to broader social contexts, thus leading to the social or psychological perspective, which became synonymous with control theory. (Shoemaker 2000, 159)

Social control theories of crime and delinquency examine the standard variables studied by sociologists: family, education, peer groups, SES, and so on.

The common link among social control theories is their rather unusual way of examining delinquent behavior. Whereas most theories of delinquency ask why people commit acts of crime and delinquency, social control theorists ask, "Why doesn't *everyone* commit acts of crime and delinquency?" Control theorists, as explained by Curran and Renzetti (1994), have adopted a Hobbesian view of human nature; that is, everyone is basically a criminal at heart and everyone is equally capable of violating the law and committing acts of violence. Within this perspective, the control theorist would also ask, "Why do people *obey* the rules of society?" Although most of us can think of people whom we know that would shock us to learn that they had committed mass murder, control theorists would point out that anyone is capable of such a deed (e.g., an otherwise mild-mannered mother who fights back against intruders to protect her young children). In fact, it seems as though every time we hear of a murderous rampage the neighbors, friends and family members of the guilty party respond in complete disbelief. Consider, for example, the 2012 case of Robert Bales who was accused of massacring 16 Afghan civilians while serving as a Staff Sergeant in the U.S. Army while stationed at Kandahar, Afghanistan. Friends and teachers described him as a caring, gregarious, and self-confident man before he snapped. One childhood friend said, "That's not our Bobby. Something horrible, horrible had to happen to him" (Brooks 2012, A-12). When otherwise reasonable people suddenly act horribly different, we have to wonder whether or not it's simply in our nature to be violent killers. Some religions use the idea of "original sin" to suggest that all humans are flawed. Although connecting such a concept to a religious belief in an "Adam and Eve" as the source of original sin is all but impossible to prove, secular notions of original sin, such as the one presented by Gilbert K. Chesterton (in *Orthodoxy*), suggest that the doctrine of original sin is the only part of Christian theology that *can* be proved (Brooks 2012). The implication, of course, is that all of us are capable of committing sin because we are all born with this predisposition.

If we are all born with a disposition that allows us to commit sin and harm others, it is worth repeating the question, "Why doesn't everyone commit acts of crime and delinquency?" Control theorists argue that it is a person's ties, links, attachments to conventional social institutions, such as family and school, that inhibit us from acting on criminal motivations. Thus, social control theorists emphasize that individuals must form a bond with society, and in that manner they are less likely to deviate from cultural expectations. The key to forming bonds and attachments to society rests with proper socialization. When people are socialized properly they will conform to societal expectations, and when they are not socialized properly they will deviate from the norm. Delinquency, then, is the result of the weakening, the breakdown, or absence of effective social controls.

Juvenile delinquents are youths who have not developed bonds to the society that spawned them. Juveniles that remain unattached to society's norms are free to engage in a variety of deviant activities, including delinquency. In other words, control theorists say, delinquency occurs because it is not prevented (Nye 1958). In order to prevent delinquency, adequate controls must be placed on youths. According to Thornton and Voight (1992), there are two general categories of controls: personal, or inward, and societal, or external. For example, a youth who refrains from stealing an item from a store because his/her conscience forbids the breaking of laws has expressed personal or inward control. On the other hand, a child who has developed a healthy respect for the authority of the police and refuses to steal, fearing arrest, has displayed external control.

There are a number of variations of control theory, but they all assume one basic point: "Human beings, young or old, must be held in check, or somehow controlled, if criminal or delinquent tendencies are to be repressed" (Shoemaker 2000, 160). In the following pages, a brief review of some of the major variants of social control theory is presented.

As mentioned earlier, the roots of control theory can be traced back to the works of Durkheim. It should first be noted that Durkheim believed that society will always have a certain number of deviants. His idea that even in a "society of saints" there would still be sinners is a perfect example of this belief. In this type of society, there would be no crime as we know it, but even saints may be guilty of committing crimes like failing to say a blessing before a meal or using the Lord's name in vain. "If crime represents harm to society, such behavior for the saints could threaten their social order. Controls, then, are necessary for order to exist and for people to understand the boundaries of accepted behavior" (Williams and McShane 1994, 184). Durkheim's analysis of anomie was related to the existence of controls. According to Durkheim, a normal (nonanomic) society is one in which social relationships are working well and society's norms and expectations (regulations) are clearly defined. "When relationships and norms begin to break down, the controls they create begin to deteriorate. Durkheim noted that a breakdown of those controls leads to crime and suicide. He was particularly concerned with situations in which uncontrolled rising aspirations lead to suicide. Whenever anomie exists in society, controls begin to disappear" (Williams and McShane 1994, 184). Durkheim argued that the extent to which society is integrated (bound to one another morally) and committed to common goals—thus forming a *collective conscience*—the more deviant behavior is controlled. In Durkheim's view, society exerts social control over individuals through custom, tradition, laws, and religious codes. "When members of a society accept and internalize these guidelines for behavior, conformity exists. Durkheim thus explained suicide through the bonding of the individual to the norms of society. Some criminologists have developed theories of juvenile delinquency from this model. The basic premise of social control theories of delinquency is that juveniles who accept societal goals and feel a moral tie to others will engage in less delinquency that those who are not committed to social goals and are not attached to important others" (Thornton and Voight 1992, 179).

Personality-oriented social control theories, such as the one developed by Albert Reiss, Jr. (1951), are based on the idea that social control efforts have gone through dramatic changes since the time of Durkheim. Reiss combined concepts of **personality** and **socialization** with the work of the Chicago School and created a version of social control theory that suggested there are three components of social control that explained delinquency:

1. A lack of proper internal controls developed during childhood
2. A breakdown of those internal controls
3. An absence of, or conflict in, social rules provided by important social groups (the family, close others, the school). (Reiss 1951, 196)

These three elements have appeared in almost every version of social control theory from the time Reiss first presented them. Reiss believed that delinquency was behavior that represents a failure of personal and social controls to produce behavior in conformity with the norms of the social system. Since individuals learn core values during early childhood (via the family and school), delinquency is the result of a failure of primary socialization. Reiss (1951, 197–200) found that delinquents on probation who were most likely to fail to live up to the terms of their probation usually came from the following types of circumstances:

1. They came from a home supported by welfare.
2. The parents were divorced, or one parent was deceased.
3. There was an open breach or gross incompatibility with the natural parents.
4. Unfavorable moral ideas had been institutionalized.

Reiss concluded that the parents and family play a critical role as to whether or not a youth becomes a delinquent. But the family is not the only agent of socialization, and therefore, the peer group also has a great impact on whether a youth becomes delinquent.

Another variation of social control theory comes from Walter Reckless and his **containment theory**. Reckless (1961) described delinquency as a character disorder on the one hand and as a social pursuit on the other. "Reckless's approach represents a socio-psychological synthesis. According to Reckless, not everyone is susceptible to the 'pull' of certain delinquent and criminal activities because some individuals are contained or restrained from these behaviors through various **outer** and **inner containments**" (Thornton and Voight 1992, 180). Delinquency is explained as the interplay between these two forms of control (containment). Reckless believed that inner containments are self-controls that develop during the socialization process. Although he never clearly articulated the term *inner containment*, Reckless (1961) provided a number of its characteristics: self-control, self-concept, ego strength, tolerance of frustration, identification with lawfulness, goal-directed, and realistic objectives. Outer containment was equated to society and the agents of socialization. Reckless believed that in order to avoid delinquency a child must avoid the external pressures from deviant subcultures. A child with a positive self-image and a sense of direction in life will more easily be able to avoid the deviant temptations confronting him/her, whereas a child who does not possess a positive self-concept, or who is drifting aimlessly, becomes more susceptible to a deviant way of behavior.

Gresham Sykes and David Matza (1957) proposed that one becomes free to commit deviant acts when one has found a way to justify one's behavior. Their famous description of the **techniques of neutralization** (a concept that all sociology and criminology students are taught) illustrates how delinquents and norm violators attempt to rationalize their deviant behaviors. "These techniques allow individuals to neutralize and temporarily suspend their commitment to societal values, thus providing the freedom to commit delinquent acts" (Williams and McShane 1994, 186). In their 1957 article, "Techniques of Neutralization: A Theory of Delinquency" and in Matza's book *Delinquency and Drift* (1964), Sykes and Matza argue that delinquency cannot be explained simply as an absence of social controls, instead it must also involve a "will to delinquency." Sykes and Matza believed that lower-class males are especially prone to delinquency because of their feelings of desperation. They supplement their role as passive societal victims through perceived positive acts of delinquency. Not feeling tied to society, these individuals manage to justify their deviant behaviors through neutralizing techniques.

The five techniques of neutralization that individuals use to justify their delinquent behavior described by Sykes and Matza are as follows:

1. *Denial of Responsibility*—The first of any deviant defense is simply denying that involvement in the act of delinquency under question. It can also refer to cases when an individual attempts to escape responsibility by means of insanity (temporarily, or otherwise). Thus, gang members might claim that they did not commit certain delinquent or criminal acts, even though a witness and/or the police saw them do it.
2. *Denial of Injury*—Occurs when individuals can neutralize any guilty feelings they might have for committing deviant acts as long as no one was hurt. Gang members will justify many behaviors when people are not harmed (e.g., theft, selling drugs, painting graffiti on buildings).
3. *Denial of the Victim*—When offenders retaliate for previous acts of a victim, they justify their behavior by denying the "victim status" of their enemy (victim). Gang members use this technique often by saying things like "he/she had it coming" or "we were just getting even."

4. *Condemnation of the Condemners*—Another tactic used by deviants is to attack those who disapprove of their behavior. Delinquents, gang members included, will accuse the police of being corrupt and teachers as playing favorites. "The effect is an attempt to shift attention away from the delinquent's own actions and to neutralize the normative sanctioning system these authority figures represent" (Thornton and Voight 1992, 182).

5. *Appeal to Higher Loyalties*—Many deviants (as well as extremists) use this technique of neutralization. They disobey society's rules and values in favor of some other "higher" authority. Gang members claim a higher sense of loyalty to their gang than to society's laws. Religious extremists claim a loyalty to God, or Allah, or some other deity in order to justify their criminal behavior (e.g., a person who kills a doctor who performs abortions because he/she believes God commanded him/her to do so). Terrorists justify their behavior using the same illogic. Inadequate socialization leads many people to believe that they can pick and choose which laws, if any, to obey.

In his later work, Matza (1964) used the term *bond to the moral order* to mean the tie that exists between individuals and the dominant values of society. Once individuals use the techniques of neutralization to justify their delinquent behavior, they are in a state of limbo or **drift** that makes deviant acts permissible. The key to rehabilitating deviants is to find some component of society that they can attach themselves to through reinforcement and the rewarding of proper behavior.

The most popular version of social control theory is the one presented by Travis Hirschi. In his book *Causes of Delinquency* (1969), Hirschi gave his analysis of empirical data he had collected on delinquency. (Hirschi conducted a survey of 4,000 high school students in California.) He believed that deviant acts are the result of an individual's weakened or broken bond to society. Especially important is the youth's relationship with the family. "Regardless of their social class, the most delinquent youths were least attached to their parents, as reflected by low levels of parent-child intimacy and communication. Beliefs reflected by such things as lack of respect for the police and the law, and lack of involvement with homework were other predictors of delinquency" (Trojanowicz et al. 2001, 72). Like Durkheim, Hirschi believed that behavior reflects varying degrees of morality. "He argued that the power of internalized norms, conscience, and the desire for approval encourage conventional behavior. As did Sykes and Matza, Hirschi saw that a person becomes 'free' to engage in delinquency. Instead of using neutralizing techniques, however, he blamed broken or weakened bonds to society" (Williams and McShane 1994, 188).

Consequently, Hirschi promoted the idea that individuals must form a solid bond with society. Hirschi (1969) specified four elements of the social bond: attachment, commitment, involvement, and belief. They are described below:

1. *Attachment*—A tight connection to significant others (especially parents and peers) and to the school provides the best mechanism on constraining delinquent behavior by youths. Affection to parents and family is a positive sign of attachment. The importance of attachment to significant others rests with the realization that primary socialization takes place while youths interact with parents and family members. When children attend school, they interact a great deal with peers and other agents of socialization (secondary socialization). Developing an attachment to society can be achieved a number of ways, including sport participation. (See "Connecting Street Gangs and Popular Culture" Box 3.1.)

2. *Commitment*—Involves the amount of time that individuals spend with conventional behavior and their dedication to long-term goals (delayed gratification). The reasoning here

Box 3.1   Connecting Street Gangs and Popular Culture

Escaping Street Gangs and Violence through Sport Participation

One of the most pervasive social institutions of societies around the world is sport (Delaney and Madigan 2009). Perhaps only the family and religion have as many adherents. That billions of people love sport is a testament to its role in society as a facilitator of indoctrinating citizens into cultural norms and values. Notions such as cooperation and team work, fair play, hard work leading to rewards, physical fitness, dedication, personal excellence, obedience to rules, commitment and loyalty, and delayed gratification are among the positive attributes promoted by the institution of sport and its supporters. There are informal sports, such as bike riding, skateboarding, cross-country skiing, and running, and there are formal sports, such as football, baseball, basketball, and hockey. Youths of any age can participate in informal sports, whereas formal sport generally begins around the same age that some kids have attained the "at-risk" category (around age 8 and older) of street gangsters (see Chapter 5 for a discussion on "at-risk" youths). Parents, teachers, coaches, school administrators, and community leaders often proclaim formal sport participation as a good way to avoid the negative temptations found in many neighborhoods and communities. In addition, formal sport participation affords youths an opportunity to bond with others who are forming an attachment to local schools and communities specifically and society in general.

For many youths from lower SES backgrounds, sports is viewed as an avenue to possible economic success. We hear stories all the time on how playing sports helped youths escape street gangs and violence through sport participation. Lyrics from Notorious B.I.G. "Things Done Changed" rap song help to illustrate this point; this line in particular—"Either your slingin' crack rock or you got a wicked jump shot." Youths and young people from wealthy families do not have to rely on sports as a path to success; they will find economic stability in the workplace. Consider the contrast between the lyrics of Notorious B.I.G. and the chant shouted by Harvard students at sporting events: "It's alright, it's okay, you'll all work for us some day!" Clearly, a different perspective on the role of sports on economic success. Historically, and generally speaking, street gangs don't bother youths who are athletes and want to lead a conventional life. Unfortunately, this is not necessarily the case any longer. In some instances, nongang youth athletes get caught up in the world of street violence.

When we think of street gangs, our attention often shifts to California. In Oakland, a city known for its violence and street gangs, youths have turned to sports for decades as a way to escape the mean streets. Citing FBI statistics on violent crime, *Business Insider* ranked Oakland as the sixth most dangerous city in the United States (Goldman and Lincoln 2011). In 2011, Oakland had 1,530 violent crimes per 100,000 and 712 robberies per 100,000, a rate six times the national average. In a wonderfully insightful special report for *Sports Illustrated*, George Dohrmann (2008a) describes in great detail how kids in Oakland often turned to sports to escape gangs and violence but noted that recently that is not necessarily the case. Instead, Oakland has witnessed a decline in kids' commitment to sports. In 2008, Fredrick Pugh, the president of the East Bay Warriors Pop Warner football program, said, "It used to be that if you played sports, everyone protected you. Now it is open season on everybody. The neighborhoods are that devastated" (Dohrmann 2008a, 56). Many athletes in Oakland who have tried to stay away from trouble have been killed or severely wounded. Dohrmann (2008a) indicates that more than one coach laments that he attends more funerals than games. Todd Walker, coach of the Berkeley Cougars youth football program, believes that if his athletes are not fully divested from street life by age 11 or 12 it is too late. Walker states, "That is when the hard head sets in. By then they've been to, like, 30 funerals. All that death, all that violence, and no one helps them deal with it" (Dohrmann 2008a, 59).

In Richmond, California, a city about 12 miles to the north of Oakland and with less than a quarter of Oakland's population of 420,000, there were 47 homicides in 2007—the highest homicide rate per capita in California cities of 100,000 residents or more. Based on FBI statistics, Richmond was the 20th most dangerous city in the United States in 2011 (Goldman and Lincoln 2011). Richmond had 1,134 violent crimes per 100,000 in 2011. The gang-related murder of Oregon-bound football star Terrance Kelly in 2004 underscores the cavalier attitude toward life in Richmond and it also "extinguished what should have been an uplifting story of a teen using sports to overcome adversity" (Dohrmann 2008b, 58). In the case of Kelly, Richmond youth have become so disenchanted with life that they look down on anyone striving for a better life. Terrance's father Landrin Kelly said, "A lot of kids gave up after Terrance got killed. They gave up sports and turned to the streets. They stopped feeling they could make it" (Dohrmann 2008b, 59).

In a special report, "Gangs and Sports: Protecting Athletes from Growing Violence," aired on *The Early Show*, December 1, 2011, athletes in Los Angeles face the same problems as their northern counterparts. The message was similar to that of Oakland and Richmond; gangs used to leave athletes alone. But athletes, like other youths, are identified with their neighborhoods and if one gang doesn't recognize the athlete as a member of their gang, the athlete is presumed to belong to a rival gang. In Compton, California, there are 34 active gangs and more than 1,000 gang members. Dannie Farber, an All-City wide receiver for Compton's Narbonne High School football team, was sitting down to dinner at a Louisiana Fried Chicken in Compton with his girlfriend during Memorial Day weekend in 2009. With surveillance cameras running, a young black male approached Farber and his girlfriend and asked, "Where you from, cuz?" meaning, what gang do you belong to (the male intruder was "gang banging on him")? Dannie stood up and asked, "What?" He was immediately shot three times at point-blank range. He collapsed to the floor and died (*The Early Show*, 2011). After an eight-month investigation, police arrested Arlon Watson, a known member of the Crips. Farber had simply been mistaken by Watson for a rival gang member. Farber's dream of playing football for the University of Southern California was gone as quickly as a speeding bullet(s).

In 2012, number two nationally ranked Syracuse University reached the "Elite Eight" of the NCAA basketball tournament. Two of its stars, Antonio "Scoop" Jardine and Dion Waiters were from the mean streets of South Philadelphia. Both Jardine and Waiters credit playing basketball as youths as their ticket out of street gang life. Jardine describes "real" fear as the streets of Philadelphia, where four of his cousins had died during his childhood and none of them was older than 19. Jardine's neighborhood was a place where young people gravitate to a drug life destined to end with a bullet, either stray or intended (Ditota 2012). Jardine proclaimed, "I was afraid growing up, of becoming a statistic" (Ditota 2012, B-1). Jardine spent a great deal of time on the streets, but his mother, and then his grandmother, would keep him busy by encouraging him to play basketball. Scoop recalled that his peers ridiculed working men in the neighborhood. They idolized NBA players, rappers, and drug lords—the people with money, not the working stiffs. His peers thought about the NBA, but never thought about attending college. As a result, they sold drugs and resorted to violence. Scoop credits his grandmother for helping to keep him on the straight path, a path that led to Syracuse University and a college degree. (He was attending graduate school during the 2011–2012 season). Scoop's grandmother (Deb Jardine) also helped to save Waiters. (Waiter's and Jardine's grandmothers are step-sisters.) Waiters was raised by a single mother who had him at age 17; his father was in jail when he was born (Thamel 2012). Known for his bravado and swagger, Waiters proclaims, "Philly brings that out in you. Philly is a different breed. It helped me with that, period" (Thamel 2012, C-10). Waiters spent much of his teen years with Scoop and his grandmother playing basketball for hours upon hours. Spending time at Deb Jardine's home kept Waiters and Jardine away from the drugs, gangs, and the temptations associated with hanging out on the streets (WHEN-CBS 2012). Waiters, just a sophomore at Syracuse, entered the NBA draft immediately following the 2011–2012 basketball season.

With their college careers over, Jardine and Waiters had both benefited from their sports participation. They had formed an attachment to the conventional lifestyle. For other athletes, such as Farber and Kelly, even sports could not save them from the violence of gang life.

is simple: The more time that individuals spend with conventional activities, the less time is available for delinquency. Engaging in conventional activities (e.g., sports, spelling bees, dance and music lessons, planning for college) teaches people that there are rules, that they must be followed, and that there are negative consequences for violating these rules. In short, individuals who possess a commitment to conventional activities are less likely to engage in delinquent activities.

3. *Involvement*—Participation in conventional activities, such as doing homework, working at a job, or doing chores, generally means less time for delinquency. In other words, if a youth has too much free time, he/she is more likely to eventually commit deviant acts.

4. *Belief*—The final element of Hirschi's social bond refers to the simple belief in the law, especially the morality of the law. Successful socialization can take place only if the individual has a willingness and belief in the ideals of law and order. Thus, individuals come to realize that stealing, littering, and similar acts are just wrong and know better than to engage in them. Obviously, from Hirschi's perspective, those who do not believe in law and morality are more likely to commit deviant acts.

Hirschi believed that these bonds are interrelated. From the perspective of control theory, the most critical element of proper parenting is creating a social bond between their children and society. When this bond is strong, delinquency is less likely to occur; conversely, when the bond is weak, delinquency is more likely to occur.

Social Learning/Differential Learning Theory

As the name *social learning theory* implies, individuals *learn* how to become delinquent. "One of the first theorists to associate the origins of crime with a learning process was Gabriel Tarde. In his book *The Law of Imitation*, Tarde argued that crime results from one person's imitating the actions of another. Although he also took into account biological and psychological factors, he believed that crime is essentially a social product" (Kratcoski and Kratcoski 1996, 56). An individual learns behavior through interaction with others. For example, the reason children speak their native tongue is that they were taught that language. In fact, without socialization, people would not act like fellow humans, nor would they develop language. Consequently, social learning theory has a great deal of credibility for the simple reason that all behaviors are learned. Through interaction with others, individuals learn of the norms, beliefs, attitudes, and values treasured by the interactants. According to this perspective, individuals become delinquent not only through direct contact with delinquents but also through exposure to various values, beliefs, and attitudes that are supportive of criminal and delinquent acts (e.g., through the media and music). However, direct association with deviant others, especially over a period of time, is the most likely way to elicit delinquent behavior according to social theorists.

From the social learning theory perspective, youths learn to become delinquent through three related processes: acquisition, instigation, and maintenance. *Acquisition* refers to the initial introduction to a deviant form of behavior. This opportunity allows for reinforcement through modeling. Thus, if a youth is introduced to violence at home or at school, and finds this behavior positively rewarded (or negative sanctions lacking), he/she is more likely to imitate it. *Instigation* occurs when the individual actually participates in some form of delinquent behavior (e.g., beating someone up at school as an initiation requirement to join a gang). *Maintenance* refers to participating in the delinquent behavior consistently over a period of time. This is the only way that criminal or delinquent behavior will persist. "In order for delinquent or criminal behavior to persist, there needs to be consistent reinforcement or *maintenance*. Social learning theory suggests four specific kinds of reinforcement: (1) direct reinforcement, (2) vicarious reinforcement, (3) self-reinforcement, and (4) neutralization of self-punishment" (Shelden et al. 2001, 178).

Edwin Sutherland is considered the most prominent of all the social theorists. He developed a theory of **differential association**, which he first introduced in the third edition of his textbook *Principles of Criminology* (1939). The final version appeared in 1947, after he had made revisions based on criticisms and comments on his first version. Sutherland was highly critical of biological and psychiatric theories of crime. "Sutherland expressly incorporated the notion that all behavior is learned and, unlike other theorists of the time, moved away from referring to the varied cultural perspectives as 'social disorganization' and used the term 'differential social disorganization' or 'differential group organization.' This allowed him more clearly to apply the learning process to a broader range of American society" (Williams and McShane 1994, 75–76). Sutherland recognized that many youths are introduced to, and associate with, a diversity of people, some of whom will encourage and participate in conventional behaviors and others who engage in delinquent and criminal behavior. Individuals exposed to such diverse groups of people may experience internal conflict in trying to decide which set of values, attitudes, and codes of behavior to accept and internalize. Many young people who attempt to embrace society's conventional norms, but who grow up in gang-infested neighborhoods and experience the pressures to join a gang, deal with this internal conflict on a daily basis.

Sutherland put together nine basic and formal theoretical propositions that, when taken together, constitute differential association theory, which is reminiscent of Tarde's imitation theory (Thornton and Voight 1992). The final version of Sutherland's differential association theory is as follows (Thornton and Voight 1992, 165–166):

1. Criminal behavior is learned.
2. Criminal behavior is learned in interaction with other persons in a process of communication.
3. The principal part of the learning of criminal behavior occurs within intimate personal groups.
4. When criminal behavior is learned, the learning includes (a) techniques of committing the crime; (b) the specific direction of motives, drives, rationalizations, and attitudes.
5. The specific direction of motives and drives is learned from definitions of the legal codes as favorable or unfavorable.
6. A person becomes delinquent because of an excess of definitions favorable to violation of law over definitions unfavorable to violation of law.
7. Differential associations may vary in frequency, duration, priority, and intensity.
8. The process of learning criminal behavior by association with criminal and anticriminal patterns involves all the mechanisms that are involved in any other learning.
9. While criminal behavior is an expression of general needs and values, it is not explained by those general needs and values, since noncriminal behavior is an expression of the same needs and values (from Sutherland and Cressey 1978, 80–82). (*Note:* Donald R. Cressey was a former student of Sutherland's and worked on the final modifications of differential association theory.)

The point that Sutherland makes repeatedly is that criminal behavior is learned and not an inherited trait. It is learned through socialization. In short, if the greatest number of associations that youths have are the positive, conventional ones of society, the more likely they are to embrace those values. Conversely, if the primary associations that youths have are with delinquents, the greater the likelihood they will become delinquent.

The primary criticism of this theory is related to the vagueness of the term *association*. Sutherland and Cressey (1978) admitted that their differential association theory was not precise enough to undergo rigorous empirical testing; thus, the theory is difficult to prove or disprove. But differential association theory remains one of the most popular theories of delinquent and criminal behavior. It has worked its way into everyday thinking, as reflected by the familiar instruction of parents to their children. "We don't want you hanging out with that person, or group of people, because they are a bad influence on you."

Labeling Theory

The labeling perspective does not examine how or why people become delinquents and criminals, rather it concentrates on the effect of being labeled a delinquent or criminal. Labeling theorists attempt to uncover the processes that lead to who gets to decide what is deviant and criminal (the labelers) and how it is that certain behaviors come to be labeled criminal while others are legal. For example, why is tobacco legal when it kills over 400,000 Americans a year, and marijuana illegal when no deaths have ever been attributed to it? Somehow the tobacco smoker is not generally considered a deviant but the marijuana smoker is. The answer, of course, lies with economic-political factors. Thus, individuals are subjected to the demands of conventional behavior, and if they fail to embrace these cultural ideals, they risk being negatively labeled and stigmatized.

No one wants to acquire a label that he or she considers an inaccurate assessment of his/her character. Everyone attempts to *negotiate* his/her *role-identity*. Generally, individuals have a stake, and want a say, in the outcome of the role-identity allocation process (Spencer 1987, 131). However, the allocation of labels is often determined by external social control agents, and there are times when these attached, unwanted labels come to consume the identity of individuals. For example, a child who is truly interested in learning at school and repeatedly pesters the teacher might then be labeled by the teacher, and ultimately by the school, as a "troublemaker." In an attempt to restore and maintain cherished identities, individuals often engage in the use of *disclaimers* as a means of fighting unwanted identities and labels (Hewitt and Stokes 1975, 1). Similar to disclaimers are *accounts*. "An account is a linguistic device employed whenever an action is subjected to valuative inquiry. . . . By an account, then, we mean a statement made by a social actor to explain unanticipated or untoward behavior—whether that behavior is his own or that of others, and whether the proximate cause for the statement arises from the actor himself or from someone else" (Scott and Lyman 1968, 46). Accounts, then, like other techniques of neutralization, represent the efforts of labeled individuals to modify their image to the outside world. Scott and Lyman (1968, 47) identified two general types of accounts: *excuses* and *justifications*. Excuses are used when mitigating circumstances are involved with the behavior in question. Justifications are accounts in which an individual admits to some undesired behavior but denies the pejorative quality associated with the act in question.

A label having been attached to a person means that the person must now find a way to neutralize it. Individuals can no longer go about their daily business in the same manner prior to being labeled. As Fontana (1973, 179) explained, "labeling places the actor in circumstances which make it harder for him to continue the normal routines of everyday life and thus provoke him to 'abnormal' actions." Once labeled, the individual's self-identity may not change immediately, but the way that others see that individual may. "The degree to which youngsters are perceived as deviants may affect their treatment at home and at school. Parents may consider them a detrimental influence on younger brothers or sisters. Neighbors may tell their children to avoid the 'troublemaker.' Teachers may place them in classes reserved for students with behavior problems, minimizing their chances of obtaining higher education" (Siegel et al. 2003, 124).

One of the first to reveal the consequences of official labels of delinquency as potentially negative was Frederick Thrasher in his work on juvenile gangs. "A few years later, Frank Tannenbaum (1938) introduced the term 'dramatization of evil,' in which he argued that officially labeling someone as a delinquent can result in the person *becoming* the very thing he is described as *being*" (Shoemaker 2000, 196). Tannenbaum suggested that delinquents were not the result of a lack of adjustment to conventional society, but the fact that they had adjusted to a special group. "Tannenbaum (1938) wrote that a 'tag' becomes attached when a child is caught in delinquent activity. The tag identifies the child as a delinquent, may change the child's self-image, and causes people to react to the tag, not the child. Thus, his argument was that the process of tagging criminals or delinquents actually helps create delinquency and criminality" (Williams and McShane 1994, 133). From the labeling perspective, when an individual continually receives negative feedback from significant others and then begins to accept the negative label, a **self-fulfilling prophecy** has been created. When people take to heart the labels bestowed upon them and then act according to those labels, they have come to see themselves as others have labeled them. In his book *The Gang as an American Enterprise* (1993), Padilla described in great detail how negative school experiences negatively influenced the gang members he studied (the fictitiously named "Diamonds"). These negative experiences and labels contributed to their transformation into delinquency.

Labeling is an important factor in the creation of a deviant identity. When conventional society shuns delinquents, the deviant group will accept them and teach them to reject their rejectors (similar to the neutralization technique of condemning the condemners). The deviant subculture teaches the newly arrived delinquents to show contempt toward those who labeled them. "These actions help solidify both the grip of deviant peers and the impact of the labels" (Siegel et al. 2003, 125). Edwin Lemert (1951) developed the concepts of *primary* and *secondary* deviance to illustrate the transitional status of labeled delinquents. *Primary deviance* refers to individuals who are guilty of committing acts of deviance but whose actions are undetected, or unrecognized by others. With *secondary deviance*, the actor has been identified and labeled as a deviant. The process of moving from primary to secondary deviance is often complex, but the critical determinant is societal reaction and identification.

Howard Becker is a significant contributor to the labeling perspective. In his book *Outsiders: Studies in the Sociology of Deviance* (1963), Becker explained that "social groups create deviance by making rules whose infraction constitutes deviance, and by applying those rules to particular people and labeling them as outsiders" (9). Becker adds that we should "view deviance as the product of a transaction that takes place between some social group and one who is viewed by the group as a rule-breaker" (1963, 10). Individuals are subjected to the rules created by social control agents, and if they fail to meet the demands of others, they risk being negatively labeled. "Once a rule has come into existence, it must be applied to particular people before the abstract class of outsiders is created. . . . This job ordinarily falls to the lot of professional enforcers who, by enforcing already existing rules, create the particular deviants society views as outsiders" (Becker 1963, 162–163). Individuals who accept, or believe in, the labels that are attached to them will begin to see themselves differently. They *are* different in the eyes of mainstream society. As these labeled people think of themselves more as deviant, they may view themselves as more "outside" than other outsiders. They may also view themselves as more outside than do those who labeled them in the first place (Becker 1963).

Becker was concerned with who the labelers are and who and why certain people are singled out as outsiders. Not surprisingly, he found that those who control power control the labeling process. The rule makers can be thought of as "moral entrepreneurs" (Becker 1963). Moral entrepreneurs are people who try to correct the wrongs—as they see them—of a society. Becker believed that power people create rules for one simple reason: personal gain. The 1983 film *The Outsiders* (based on the novel of the same name written by S.E. Hinton) provides us with a look at the effects of societal labeling. The wealthy, more powerful people of the community have labeled certain youths as "good" (the Socs) and have labeled others as delinquent white trash (the Greasers). See "Connecting Street Gangs and Popular Culture" Box 3.2 for a closer look at the film *The Outsiders* from the labeling perspective.

Increasingly in society it is law enforcement that is responsible for labeling criminals and delinquents. This is especially true for gangs. The decision whether or not to label a particular group of juveniles as a gang, or just a group of delinquents, directly impacts the manner in which the police and judicial system will deal with them. Labeling theorists examine the criminal justice system, especially the legislation that describes behaviors that will ultimately be labeled criminal or delinquent. Quinney's (1970) theory of the *social reality of crime* presents a clear look at crime and criminal behavior from a labeling perspective. He based his theory around six interrelated principles:

1. Crime is a definition of human conduct that is created by authorized agents in a politically organized society. This is the starting point of any theory on criminal behavior. Defining a particular behavior as criminal reveals the fact that crime is not inherent in behavior.
2. Criminal definitions describe behaviors that conflict with the interests of the segments of society that have the power to shape public policy. The people in a position to define certain behaviors as criminal have the *power* to translate their interests into *public policy*.
3. Criminal definitions are applied by the segments of society that have the power to shape the enforcement and administration of criminal law. As Quinney (1970, 18) explained, "the probability that criminal definitions will be applied varies according to the extent to which the behaviors of the powerless conflict with the interests of the power segments."
4. Behavior patterns are structured in segmentally organized society in relation to criminal definitions, and within this context persons engage in actions that have relative probabilities of being defined as criminal. "Once behavior patterns are established with some regularity within the respective segments of society, individuals are provided with a framework for developing *personal action patterns*" (Quinney 1970, 21).
5. Conceptions of crime are constructed and diffused in the segments of society by various means of communication. The most critical conceptions are those held by the power segments of society because these are the conceptions that are certain of becoming incorporated into the social reality of crime.
6. The social reality of crime is constructed by the formulation and application of criminal definitions, the developments of behavior patterns related to criminal definitions, and the construction of criminal conceptions. The first five propositions are collected into a composite. "The theory, accordingly, describes and explains phenomena that increase the probability of crime in society, resulting in the social reality of crime" (Quinney 1970, 23).

Box 3.2   *Connecting Street Gangs and Popular Culture*

Labeling Theory and *The Outsiders*

The Outsiders is a 1983 American drama directed by Francis Ford Coppola and an adaptation of the novel with the same name written by S.E. Hinton. The film is loaded with up-and-coming stars, including C. Thomas Howell, Rob Lowe, Emilo Estevez, Matt Dillon, Tom Cruise, Patrick Swayze, Ralph Macchio, Diane Lane, Michele Meyrink, and Sofia Coppola. The film's story takes place in a small southern town in rural Oklahoma during the mid-1960s. The protagonist, Ponyboy Curtis (played by Howell) is the youngest of three orphaned boys who hang out together with

WARNER BROTHERS/Album/Newscom

local delinquents that include Ponyboy's two older brothers, Sodapop (Lowe) and Darrel (Swayze), along with Johnny Cade (Macchio), Dallas Winston (Dillon), Two-Bit Matthews (Estevez), and Steve Randle (Cruise). These boys come from the lower socioeconomic class and are labeled the "Greasers." They commit a number of delinquent acts. The Greasers have a rivalry with a gang of wealthier kids from the south side of town that are labeled as the "Socs" (pronounced "soashes"). Because of their higher SES, the Socs are viewed more favorably by the community and as incapable of doing any harm. Because of their privileged backgrounds, they are likely to succeed as adults even if they are delinquents as juveniles. Conversely, the Greasers' life chances are limited to working-class, low-wage jobs that will keep them at or near the poverty level.

The film begins with Ponyboy writing a school essay that he titles "The Outsiders." After the opening credits the scene shifts for a look at the Greasers, Dallas and a couple of his crew members, as they go through their daily activities of delinquency. At night, they are at a drive-in. A couple of the Socs, Bob and Randy, are drinking liquor from a bottle in their car; they just had an argument with their girlfriends, Cherry and Marcia, who have just walked away. Shortly afterward, Dallas flirts with Cherry. Marcia whispers to Cherry, "that's the boy who was in jail." Dallas has been labeled a delinquent and his role-identity is associated with his past behavior despite his efforts to downplay (negotiate) his own sense of self. When Cherry asks Dallas to be nice, he says, "I'm never nice." He has come to accept the negative label bestowed upon him; he is in the process of fulfilling a negative prophecy. Finally, Cherry yells, "Get lost hood." She is using a negative label to cast Dallas in a very unflattering light. Dallas walks away; Cherry spots Ponyboy and views him as a nice boy. When Ponyboy tells Cherry who he really is, she says, "What is a nice boy like you doing hanging out with that trash?" Cherry did not perceive Ponyboy as a Greaser, but after he tells her that Dallas is his friend she changes her perception of him. He is now simply a Greaser. Dallas returns with sodas for Ponyboy, Johnny, and the two girls. But Cherry wants nothing to do with him and throws the soda in his face. Angrily, Dallas walks away again. Cherry and Marcia invite Johnny and Ponyboy to sit next to them because they are not "dirty" like Dallas. Johnny tries to defend Dallas' reputation to the girls. He tells the girls that Dallas is really nice, once you get to know him. But the girls don't want to take the time to know Dallas; they have already made up their minds about him based on his label of a Greaser and bad boy.

Ponyboy and Cherry go to the concession stand to get popcorn. Cherry asks about the scar on Johnny's face and Ponyboy tells her that he got jumped by a group of Socs. She explains that not all Socs are looking for fights and states, "Not all of us are like that . . . you think that all the Socs have it made. That we are all a bunch of rich kids . . . well, I'll tell you something Ponyboy it might come as a surprise but things are rough all over." Just as Johnny did earlier when he said that Dallas was not really a bad guy, Cherry is using a disclaimer when she says not all the Socs are so bad.

Cherry and Marcia are being walked home by Ponyboy, Johnny, and Two-Bit when their boyfriends Bob Sheldon (Garrett) and Randy Anderson (Dalton) drive up next to them. Bob yells at Cherry for being with "bums." She would rather be with the Greasers than her drunk boyfriend. When a fight almost ensues, Cherry explains how she hates it when people fight. She decides to go home with her boyfriend. She tells Ponyboy, if I see you in school, don't take it personally if I never say hello to you. She has reaffirmed the distinction between her group (the Socs) and his (the Greasers).

Ponyboy and Johnny go to the park; their home lives are so rough that they would rather be outside. Johnny tells Ponyboy that he wished he lived somewhere else, someplace where there were no Greasers or Socs, just people. He is too young to realize that nearly everywhere people are divided, based on labels from others. Nonetheless, they want to move away. A carload of Socs drive by and notice the two Greasers walking in the dark. Ponyboy wonders what the Socs are doing on Greaser turf. But the Greasers are outnumbered four to two by Bob and Randy and two others. Bob and Randy are still upset over Johnny and Ponyboy associating with Cherry and Marcia. The Socs are drunk. Johnny recognizes one of the guys as part of the crew that jumped him and scarred him previously. One Soc says to the other, "you know what Greasers are? White trash, with long greasy hair." Ponyboy replies, "you know what Socs are? White trash with Mustangs and madras." The fight is on. The Socs begin dunking Ponyboy in the park fountain and attempt to drown him, but Johnny pulls out his switchblade and stabs Bob, killing him. Bob's friends all run away. Ponyboy and Johnny go to Dallas and ask him for help. He gives them money and tells them to run away from town and to hide out at an abandoned church. In an attempt to renegotiate their identities, Ponyboy bleaches his hair blonde and Johnny cuts his hair short. Days later, Dallas shows up and takes the two runaways for a car ride to get some food. When they return to the church they are alarmed to discover it is on fire and that children are caught inside. All three risk their lives and run into the burning church to save the lives of children left and trapped in the fire. A church official tells them, "you three are the bravest kids I've seen in a long time." He then asks, "Are you professional heroes or something?" Dallas replies, "We're Greasers." The church official is surprised by this. He seems to be thinking that this is not the behavior of Greasers; but as most of us realize, labels are often deceiving.

Ponyboy's brothers show up at the hospital where the three heroes have been sent. They have a tearful reunion. Darrel says, "I thought we lost you like we did mom and dad." They take Ponyboy home with them. The newspaper has a front-page article on how the three Greasers saved the lives of innocent children. Suddenly, they are cast in a more positive manner. Randy and some Socs see Ponyboy and Two-Bit walking on the street. Randy talks with Ponyboy and tells him that he is surprised about the rescue of the children. Randy states, "I would have let those kids burn to death." Once again, we have an example of someone not living up to the label. After all, if the Socs are so "good" why wouldn't Randy also risk his life for others? Randy is beginning to doubt the whole labeling phenomena. But he does recognize that Greasers will always be kept down in society and the Socs will get all the breaks.

For his good deed, Johnny is bedridden and likely to be paralyzed from the waist down for the rest of his life. And yet, he wants to live now more than ever before. He has had an epiphany; a near-death experience can do that to a person. Meanwhile, the Greasers and Socs are discussing a big rumble for later that night. From his hospital bed, Dallas says, we got to get the Socs for Johnny, "Let's do it for Johnny. We'll do it for Johnny." It is rumble time and as is common with street gangs, all the members of each gang are called upon for the big showdown. Dallas arrives just as the gang war begins. The fight scene is intense and brutal. Both sides incur great beatings. The Socs receive the biggest poundings and run away. Dallas and Ponyboy go back to the hospital and tell Johnny about winning the rumble. But, Johnny is not impressed. He dies immediately afterward. Voicing the sentiment of the adage that "no good deed goes unpunished," a very distraught Dallas says, "So, this is what you get for helping people?" He doesn't want to live anymore; he has lost hope. Dallas leaves the hospital and robs a grocery store at gunpoint (the gun had no bullets in it). He is chased down and shot dead by the police. He fulfilled his negative prophecy. Ponyboy finds a letter from Johnny that said, among other things, that saving the children was worth sacrificing his own life. The film ends, as it started, with Ponyboy writing a school report about his experience as an "outsider." Being negatively labeled can make almost anyone feel like an outsider.

Throughout *The Outsiders* there are plenty of examples of the labeling perspective that illustrate how roles are negotiated, the development of a role-identity, the affects of labels, the use of disclaimers, the making of accounts of behavior, and attempts to neutralize labels. The members of these two distinct gangs generally act in such a manner as to support the labels placed upon them; in other words, they are fulfilling the prophecy bestowed upon them.

In his theory, Quinney attempted to show how a theory of crime can be consistent with some revisionist assumptions about people and society. His theory serves as the foundation of the labeling perspective, a theory with great validity and relevance today—especially in the study of gang behavior.

Marxist/Conflict/Radical Theory

Marxist, conflict, and radical theories are each unique but are linked by a general belief that the capitalistic economic structure is responsible for the formation of gangs. Social conflict theory, according to Siegel et al. (2003, 127), "finds that society is in a constant state of internal conflict, and different groups strive to impose their will on others. Those with money and power succeed in shaping the law to meet their needs and maintain their interests. Those adolescents whose behavior cannot conform to the needs of the power elite are defined as delinquents and criminals." Similarly, Shoemaker (2000, 214) wrote that "the radical theory of criminality argues that criminal behavior is a result of the repressive efforts of the ruling class to control the subject class. The effects of this repression are not only higher instances of crime and delinquency among the subjugated class (the lower class, generally), but also greater tendencies among the middle and upper classes to label the actions of the lower class as criminal in order to facilitate their control." The works of Karl Marx had the greatest impact on the formation of conflict theory. Quinney and Wildeman (1991) used a Marxist perspective to explain delinquency, an expansion on Quinney's earlier work in *Class, State and Crime* (1977), where Quinney linked crime and delinquency to the modern socioeconomic capitalist system.

It is interesting that the general **Marxist paradigm** used to explain crime and delinquency comes from the works of a man who never made law or crime primary topics in his theories. Like the theorists who developed the conflict perspective of social theory, Marxist criminologists must piece together Marx's ideas about conflict in society to formulate a theory on delinquency. Marx paid close attention to forces that gave rise to the capitalistic system; he was especially interested in the role of production and theorized that power was related to one's position in the economic structure. Marx believed that those who controlled the means of production (the bourgeoisie) could exercise their will and power over those who did not control the means of production (the workers, or proletariat). Marx viewed society as basically a two-class system consisting of the workers and of the owners of the means of production. One's relation to production dictated one's relative position in life. Social classes, then, can be understood as conflicting categories of people arising out of the authority structure wherein one category of people, the owners of the means of production, have more power than the workers. Those in a position of authority will want to maintain their advantageous position—this is a matter of common sense. They maintain their power position through the creation of a rationally based political system. Marx believed that the economically powerful are in a position to dominate the political system and therefore are in a position to create laws to maintain their power position over the masses (the economically poor).

In contemporary societies of the West, the masses, of course, are found in the middle class. Nonetheless, the most powerless are still found at the lowest end of the economic strata, and not coincidentally this is where the greatest number of delinquents and gang members are found. Marx, as a humanist, truly hoped that all individuals could reach their full *human potential*, but because of *alienation* (caused by the unequal distribution of power in society) he believed all citizens of a capitalist society would never reach their full human potential. Marx viewed the capitalist society as unnatural and as the primary source of alienation. In this system, the wealthy stood to make great fortunes while the poor were likely to remain poor and powerless. Marx encouraged a workers' revolution that would overthrow the existing capitalist system, hoping to replace it with communism—a political and economic structure in which all people would somehow be treated equally and share equally in society's resources. This naive and utopian ideal, classless system of Marx, in which all people would be treated equally, has never been successfully achieved as he envisioned it, and yet, other utopian idealists have hoped to create such a system.

Contemporary Marxists might be tempted to label street gangs as revolutionary groups attempting to overthrow the existing social structure. Some see gangs as an example of a classless system where all members are created equal. However, even gangs have a structured hierarchy, and, just as in capitalist systems, members are not all treated equally. It should be pointed out that gang leaders do come from the same economic class as members and therefore there is little difference between the leader and the members of the rank and file. Gang leaders, who come from the rank and file, have achieved their position through merit and not some other form of power (e.g., inherited power found in monarchies) and are subject to immediate removal from their leadership position if they prove to be ineffective leaders. Additionally, the gang is a communist society, in the sense that all the activities of the gang are done for the overall benefit of everyone in the gang. Their rebellion against the conventional rules of society can be likened to the proletariat revolution against capitalistic society. Joining a gang generally reduces the alienation that members feel in relation to the greater society through the familial association of the gang and also because gang members benefit directly from what they do. Thus, from a Marxist perspective, it could be argued that the gang is communistic, in the sense that everyone in the gang exists for the good of the gang and its members.

Conflict and radical theories are based on the idea that conflict and contradictions are constant forces in society. Conflict theorists "see consensus as a temporary state of affairs that will either return to conflict or will have to be maintained at great expense. It is the use of power to create and maintain an image of consensus, then, that represents the problems to be studied" (Williams and McShane 1994, 155). For conflict theorists, the most important variable to study is **power**—who has it, and how does he/she maintain it? Those in power will exercise both legitimate and illegitimate means of maintaining their advantageous position—they have a **vested interest** in doing so. On the other hand, the conflict perspective teaches that those without power will want some, and they will find some way of demonstrating what little power they have. This often entails participating in illegal and delinquent activities. Conflict theorists believe that laws are created and enforced because some people have a virtual monopoly on power while others are basically powerless (Quinney 1970).

Because power can be equated with resources, then it seems evident that those who are higher up in the social class structure will be the more powerful members of society. Their influence in the making of social decisions, and their ability to impose values, will also be greater than those of the lower social classes. For conflict theorists, this explains the presence of a dominant middle-class value system in society. Similarly, the important statements of a society, its laws for example, are bound up in middle-class values. This is because, historically, the merchant class helped create the form of society we have today. (Williams and McShane 1994, 158)

The **law** represents one of the most valuable resources that the powerful manipulate to maintain the **status quo**. The poor, on the other hand, have a vested interest in changing the law to better meet their needs and demands. According to social conflict theorists, those in power use the justice system to maintain their high status in society while keeping others subservient. The law protects the interests, including personal property and physical safety, of the rich and powerful and it does so at the expense of the have-nots. Conflict theorists believe that the very fact that a disproportionate number of the poor are arrested for criminal activities and the minority poor claim to be victimized by the police is proof of the imbalance of power found in society. In short, conflict theory views delinquency as a normal consequence of the conditions created by the capitalist system's inherent inequality. From this perspective, the best way to eliminate delinquency is to find quality jobs for the disadvantaged.

Radical theories of delinquency propose that capitalism is the root cause of much criminal behavior, especially of crimes committed by the economically poor. Among the great variety of radical theorists are those who promote such extreme ideas as political anarchy (Tifft 1979). Two of the more prominent radical theorists are William Chambliss and Robert Seidman. Chambliss (1964) focused on the importance of labor, resources, and social control methods as the key ingredients used by capitalists to maintain their position of power. In their 1971 publication, *Law, Order and Power*, Chambliss and Seidman argued that the ruling class maintains its power by exercising control in two ways: through the creation of laws that are focused on controlling the behaviors of the poor and by creating a "myth" that the law serves the interests of everyone.

Donald Shoemaker (2000, 215–216) described the basic assumptions of the radical approach to delinquency as follows:

1. Most behavior is the product of a struggle among the classes within a society, particularly between those who own the tools of production (the bourgeoisie) and those who do not (the proletariat).
2. The economic system of capitalism is primarily responsible for the class divisions within society.
3. The bourgeoisie, either directly or through its agents, such as the State, controls the proletariat, economically, institutionally, or legally.
4. Most official crime and delinquency is committed by the lower and the working classes as a form of accommodation to the restraints placed on them by the bourgeoisie.

For Marxist, conflict, and radical theorists, crime and delinquency are not the result of some individual pathology, or immediate environmental factors, but are instead the result of an economic system that, by its very design, will leave some people behind in a disadvantaged situation in the pursuit of the American dream.

Summary

In this chapter, a number of major theories of crime and delinquency were discussed and applied to gangs in an attempt to understand why they exist. The theories included biological and psychological explanations and the traditional sociological theories: social disorganization (Chicago School), anomie/strain, subculture/social bond, social learning/differential learning, labeling, and Marxist. Psychological theories, although not as fundamentally sound as sociological theories in explaining why street gangs exist, represent an improvement over biological explanations. Psychological theories of delinquency start with the premise that there are individual differences in intelligence, personality, and learning.

Sociological theories of crime and delinquency are the most applicable approaches to explaining gang formation and participation. They generally incorporate a diverse, multicausal framework in their explanation of criminality. Sociological theories are grounded by the belief that gang formation and participation are the result of social factors. Each of the sociological approaches offers great insights into the study of gang behavior. Researchers, professors, and students all have their personal preferences among the various theories, but regardless of one's personal favorite theoretical explanation, the fact remains that there are a lot of diverse reasons why certain adolescents join a gang and others do not.

4

Socioeconomic Explanations of Street Gangs

The theoretical analyses presented in Chapter 3 provided a variety of explanations as to why someone might join a gang. As valuable as social theory is to scientific research, in all the times that I, and other gang researchers, have asked gang members why they joined a gang, none of them have ever cited a theoretical perspective. In other words, gang members themselves will not say something like, "I joined a gang because of the social disorganization theory" or the "anomie/strain theory." Instead, most gang members will cite socioeconomic explanations (e.g., "I need the money" or "I needed protection"). Thus, in many instances, someone chooses to join a gang because of socioeconomic factors. Furthermore, many other juveniles are attracted to street gangs because they find the gangbanger lifestyle so exciting that they experience a rush. An analysis of socioeconomic explanations of why there are gangs can be quite beneficial in our understanding of the prevalence of street gangs.

TRADITIONAL SOCIOECONOMIC FACTORS

Gang researchers and social policymakers have identified and discussed a number of traditional socioeconomic factors that impact on an individual's decision to join a gang. These factors are the shifting labor market, the development of an underclass (a nontraditional explanation, as the term *underclass* is a relatively new concept, but the conditions that led to the development of an underclass have traditional roots), poverty and the feminization of poverty, the breakdown of the nuclear family, lack of a quality education, and the gang's offering of acceptance, protection, and survival.

The Shifting Labor Market

The prime motivator for nearly all actions is security, and, despite those who argue otherwise, security is best accomplished through economic means—money. Although this statement may seem cynical, it is money that allows someone to live in a neighborhood that is relatively free from the daily onslaughts of violence, murder, and mayhem. Money may not be everything, but it is a very important something. Having a good job is the best way of making money. A good job provides workers with the money needed to take care of themselves and their families. Political and social extremist Karl Marx, an economic determinist, believed that all of social life revolved around matters related to economics. For gangs, economics is also a critical element. Because most gang members come from lower socioeconomic status (SES) backgrounds, the search for economic stability takes on prime importance for them.

Clearly, there are other important aspects of life, including love, family, personal security, and happiness, but most of these pursuits come at a cost. As the psychologist Abraham Maslow (1951) explained, there exists a *hierarchy of needs*, which consists of the five basic needs that all humans have and try to fulfill:

1. *Physiological/biological*—The basic survival needs, such as food and shelter, which should be met by the child's parents and family from birth until adulthood.
2. *Safety and security*—Refers to stability, protection, freedom from fear, found in a structured family environment.
3. *Love and belongingness*—Everyone wants to feel as though he/she belongs to a group or family, and especially to have someone special to share in a loving relationship.
4. *Self-esteem*—Feeling good about oneself, self-respect, confidence, and a positive reputation.
5. *Self-actualization*—The stage where one has found peace within oneself, of reaching one's full human potential. One accepts oneself and is relatively independent.

According to Maslow, if the first three needs are met by the family, the adolescent has a good chance of attaining the next two levels. When these needs are not fulfilled by the family, the youth will seek out other groups to provide them. In many cases, youths seek out gangs for these economically driven needs. For gang members, having **respect** is perhaps the most critical need they possess. Any perceived violation of this is often met with extreme prejudice. Being disrespected is one thing that gang members will not tolerate. When a gang member is dissed, he will fight back to maintain his reputation. (*Note*: The importance of respect will be discussed in greater detail in Chapter 5.) Self-actualization can be reached only when the first four needs have been satisfied. Few people reach this level, and for gang members, the likelihood of ever reaching their full human potential is very slim. The constant struggle for economic survival generally means that any chance of self-actualization, according to Maslow's description of the hierarchy of needs, is slim to none.

In our analysis of the effect of economics on street gang participation, the primary concern is with job opportunities. Traditionally, immigrants, minorities, and poorly educated persons could find jobs in factories. Therefore, people with average skills, doing an average job, could earn an average lifestyle (Friedman 2012). Today, however, being average, in terms of job skills, will not assure you any sort of economic stability. The reason for this is the shift in the U.S. labor market from manufacturing to service employment. It is true that the United States still manufactures more goods than any other country in the world—$1.6 trillion worth according to the Federal Bureau of Economic Analysis (*Parade Magazine* 2009)—but an increasing number of manufacturing jobs have been shifted to foreign markets and have been replaced by cheap robotics, cheap software, and cheap automation, eliminating job opportunities for millions of Americans. Capitalists, seeking to maximize their profits, have, for years, moved their industries to foreign countries to get cheap labor, which allows for a higher profit margin. The advent of new technology, however, has fueled the acceleration of the decreasing number of manufacturing jobs in the United States. In the 10 years ending in 2009, U.S. factories have lost so many workers that they have erased all the gains of the previous 70 years; roughly one out of every three manufacturing jobs, or just about 6 million in total (Friedman 2012). According to the U.S. Bureau of Labor Statistics (2012), there were less than 12 million manufacturing jobs in the United States in February 2012.

The shift in the labor market to the service industry can be illustrated in a number of ways. For example, the Institute for Supply Management reports that nearly 83 percent of workers in the private sector are employed in the service industries (*New York Times* 2010). A January 2011 report in *Time* (written by Bill Saporito) indicates that the primary economic growth areas are service related. Business editor Bill Saporito described specific corporations with a need for mechanical engineers, rocket scientists (to work on refrigeration technologies, not rockets), and tax specialists. Saporito (2011) also highlighted the fact that low-end manufacturing jobs are increasingly disappearing. The shifting labor market now provides more opportunities in the service economy, but many of these jobs often require relatively high levels of education. This economic reality has caused many lower-class persons to lose out on opportunities for financial success, especially the poorly educated. (*Note*: We will examine the role of education on street gang participation later in this chapter.)

The shifting labor market did not occur overnight; the signs have been in existence for a long period. Many people took heed of the changing economic reality and prepared themselves for the service, or postindustrial, society. Other people, however, for a variety of reasons, are not as well prepared (Delaney 2012). The economic shift to a service-based economy disadvantages the lower socioeconomic classes, creating greater inequality, higher rates of unemployment, homelessness, and poverty. In all, the economic shift has contributed to the development of an **underclass**.

Social Stratification and the Underclass

All societies are stratified. Sociologists describe **stratification** as the social layers found in society, for an overly simplified example, upper, middle, and lower social classes. We can think of stratification as a ranking system. A critical aspect of social stratification is the built-in corresponding value component that characterizes the higher rank. Think of the cliché, "With rank, comes privilege." Thus, a military general enjoys more privilege and prestige than a private; college seniors enjoy more perks (e.g., earlier course registration) than freshmen; and the starting quarterback of the football team enjoys more prestige than a third-string punter. Because members of a higher rank enjoy more privileges than their lower-ranked counterparts, social stratification may be viewed as institutionalized social inequality. With this in mind, sociologists define **social stratification** as a system for ranking members of a social system into levels with different or unequal evaluations. As a result, social stratification reveals patterns of social inequality found within a society. Sociologically speaking, social stratification may also be viewed as the hierarchal or horizontal division of society based on rank, strata, or social class. This classification system leads to the development of socioeconomic classes. Sociologists use the term **social class** to describe a broad group of people with common economic, cultural, or political status (e.g., the working class or the professional class). Most societies have three major dimensions of stratification: social prestige (what people think about others), political power (the ability to make, or influence, decisions that have a positive effect on a segment of society), and economics (income and wealth). The implications of social stratification are immense. When applied to street gangs, we can see that most gang members come from the lower SES groups, have low levels of social prestige, and very little political power.

The changing nature of America's occupational opportunity structure has dramatically affected many lower SES persons, especially those living in urban areas. The loss of significant numbers of manufacturing jobs has left many inner-city persons without gainful employment opportunities. When people are unemployed, their financial stability is greatly compromised. Anyone who remains unemployed for an extended period of time generally ends up poor. Many of the United States' poor live in the core of America's cities. The term *underclass* (popularized by William Wilson in his 1987 book *The Truly Disadvantaged*) generally refers to the extremely poor, who live in neighborhoods, or census tracts, where the poverty rate exceeds 40 percent. Underclass members are generally poorly educated, unskilled in terms of the economic market, are likely to have been in the poverty category for generations, are dependent on the welfare system, and appear to have little chance to break out of the cycle of poverty (Wilson 1987, 1996). *Underclass* is not meant to refer to a racial or ethnic group, but because the vast majority of the underclass are racial minorities, some oppose the use of the term. The opponents of the term *underclass* believe that it is used to stigmatize persons who already lack in social prestige. But such a criticism is short-sided as the real concern and outrage should be directed toward a social system that contributes to the creation of an underclass in the first place. After all, the persons who fall under the "underclass" umbrella are less concerned about being labeled a part of an underclass as they are about actually rising above the label's parameters. Thus, it is worse to qualify for the underclass restrictions than it is to be labeled an underclass member. Consider, for example, Los Angeles's "Skid Row," which has been renamed (by politicians and other well-meaning folks) "Central City Recovery Zone" (CCRZ). The unfortunate persons who live in Skid Row are not nearly as concerned about changing the name of their living area as they are about rising above its parameters. As another example, a very poor area of Los Angeles that is home to numerous street gangs, South Central, is now known as "South Los Angeles." Changing the name of the area did nothing to improve the lives of the folks living there. It's not the possible stigmatization that concerns poor folks as much as it is the socioeconomic realities of their lives. Another cliché comes to mind when using the term *underclass*, "a rose by any other name is still a rose." People should be more concerned about helping those who are less fortunate than they are about a name for the lower SES persons.

It was during the 1970s that the shift in the labor market began to have a significant negative effect on American blacks. Blacks were heavily represented in manufacturing, and the decline in production in such sectors as automobile, rubber, and steel hurt urban African Americans profoundly. Blacks were also adversely affected by the mechanization of Southern agriculture and the large number of baby boomers and white women who entered the labor market in the 1970s. These socioeconomic factors contributed greatly to adding large number of blacks to the underclass. Thus, Wilson argued, public policies, such as race-based programs and policies, were doomed to fail because they ignored the core economic explanation of poverty, delinquency, and gang membership—the elimination of industry-based jobs. Wilson's use of the term *underclass* was not racist; instead, it was a condemnation of government policies that disadvantaged blacks more than any other group of people. African Americans are overrepresented in the underclass, but generally, they are so because of social and economic forces that they cannot control. Criticism of the term might be a little more appropriate if it were aimed at the person who first coined the term in 1982: Ken Auletta, a writer for *The New Yorker*. Auletta used the word broadly to include individuals with "behavioral and income deficiencies" (Papadimitriou 1998).

Around the same time that Wilson was using the term *underclass* to describe the social conditions that affected many urban blacks, Nicholas Lemann described the prejudice and discrimination that Puerto Ricans faced, especially those living in the South Bronx. Among the larger Hispanic/Latino categories, statistics revealed that Puerto Ricans were far more disadvantaged than Mexican-Americans or Cuban-Americans. Puerto Ricans were more likely to be afflicted by the secondary effects of poverty, such as family breakups and not trying to find employment, which work to ensure that poverty will continue beyond one generation (Lemann 1991). Lemann suggested that the reason Puerto Ricans in New York were so disproportionately poor was the result of two economic factors (unemployment and welfare) and cultural factors (e.g., neighborhood ambience and ethnic history). On the mainland, Puerto Ricans still face a great deal of prejudice, which partially contributes to their being shut out from quality job opportunities, which ensures that they live in poor neighborhoods and instills a defeatist attitude among many Puerto Ricans. In short, persistent poverty is more common among Puerto Ricans than among blacks. Disenchanted Puerto Rican youths are increasingly turning to gangs as a means of gaining economic salvation.

It was the recognition of an "underclass" or if preferred, the growing numbers of urban poor in certain neighborhoods, decades ago that avoided exposing the ill effects on the negative effects of the shifting labor market. Data provided by the U.S. Bureau of Labor Statistics (2009) reveal that in 2008, 116,451,700 (77.2%) of the 150,931,700 jobs were in the service-providing sector of the economy. In contrast, in 1970, approximately 63 percent of all jobs were in the service economy (Godbout 1993). People lacking the necessary job skills are the ones most likely to suffer from the shifting labor market, and many of these folks are found in the inner cities. When industries move (capital flight), they take with them job opportunities and tax revenue necessary to maintain the areas in which they had resided. When economic opportunities disappear, those who can afford to move will also abandon the deprived area ("white" flight—the exodus of middle- and upper-class people, generally white). The consequences of these developments are lower tax revenue and, eventually, impoverished neighborhoods that lack basic civil services, political power, and the representation needed to help the community. The lack of political power is exemplified in a number of ways, including the inability of poorer communities to stop civic projects that rip them apart. The location and building of freeways clearly demonstrate whether or not a community has political power. In *Going Down to the Barrio*, Moore (1991) explained how freeways ripped apart Mexican-American neighborhoods in Los Angeles. Robert Powell, in *We Own This Game* (2003), described how expressways dissected Overtown, a poor section in Miami and a vibrant neighborhood once considered the Harlem of the South.

Inner-city youths recognize the fact that there are few legitimate job opportunities. They are aware of the poverty that surrounds them, and the lure of gangs that calls out to them is often tough to resist. Joining a gang is often viewed as the *only* opportunity to get ahead, especially for those from the underclass. The hopelessness associated with the underclass not only implies that these people will never reach self-actualization; they may also never find economic stability. The gang appears as an attractive alternative.

It is interesting to note that the United States is not the only country to apply the term *underclass* to a group of statistically poor people. In Australia, social researchers have used the term *rural underclass* to describe rural Victoria. Bureau of Statistics data revealed that not a single full-time job had been created in rural Victoria in 13 years (1990–2003), leaving it a land of part-time work despite a decade of solid economic growth in Australia as a whole. The lack of full-time jobs has led to the formation of a rural underclass with countless people in country towns stuck in low-income jobs or unemployed altogether, leaving them caught in a poverty trap—they can't afford to move and they can't afford to stay. The problem is not unique to rural Victoria, as throughout Australia almost two-thirds of all jobs created since 1990 have been part-time (*The Age* 2003). Industrial leaders argue that it is not viable to set up businesses in country towns. It is up to the government to provide legitimate economic opportunities for these citizens to meet their survival needs. Otherwise, Australia may some day have its own significant street gang problem.

In November 2005, rioters torched cars and trashed businesses in the immigrant-concentrated suburbs of Paris, revealing the growing underclass in France (Smith 2005). Drawing parallels between black and white relations in the United States and native French and Muslims from North Africa, France has found itself caught in a three-generation experience of ethnic and religious discrimination. Although not nearly as long-lasting as the urban upheavals of the 1960s in the United States or as devastating as the 1992 Los Angeles riots, the Paris riots may be the first sign of the existence of an underclass in France. Manuel Valls, then a member of French Parliament and mayor of Evry, a troubled suburb south of Paris commented, "We've combined the failure of our integration model with the worst effects of ghettoization, without a social ladder for people to climb" (Smith 2005, A-8). Although the ghettos of France do not compare to the worse found in American cities, large numbers of poor people living in proximity with little hope for upward social mobility are key elements of an underclass. Like many Americans who face prejudice and discrimination, second and third generations of French-born immigrants are coming of age. They have weaker ties to their ancestral homes but feel marginalized in country where they have been taught at school that they are not fully French. Such realizations have led some experts to think "that a structural underclass is emerging" (Smith 2005, A-8).

Poverty

Although most of us have a clear idea of what is meant by the term *poverty*, it is important, especially for governments, to establish clear parameters in order to ascertain the degree and instance of poverty. The World Health Organization (2012a) describes **poverty** in absolute terms of low income and describes a range of key human attributes associated with poverty, including poor general health, due to exposure to greater personal and environmental health risks; people who are less nourished; no household savings; lower learning ability; reduced productivity; and a diminished quality of life. Clearly, living in poverty compromises one's ability to a decent life and any hope of reaching self-actualization. After all, those who are poor must devote all of their resources to meeting the basic needs for survival with very little left over. In extreme cases, people may face destitution—a state of having absolutely none of the necessities of life.

Some people are tempted to blame the capitalistic system for poverty. They claim that the capitalistic system guarantees that there will always be some people at the top and some people at the bottom of the economic hierarchy. Although it is true that there are poor people in countries with capitalism, the reality is capitalism did not create poverty; poverty was inherited from past social systems that created the class distinctions of the "haves" and the "have-nots." Even today, the poorest nations in the world are those without capitalism. In 2008, 9 of the top 10 poorest nations in the world were from Africa, with the Democratic Republic of Congo, with a Gross Domestic Product (GDP) per capita (in U.S. dollars) of $300, as the poorest (see Table 4.1). The Solomon Islands (located in Oceania) was the only non-African nation in the top 10 poorest nations (Maps of the World 2008).

According to the World Bank, in 2010 there are 1.372 billion people in the world who live in constant poverty (defined as living on $1.25 a day or less); 1.345 of these people reside in developing nations (World Bank 2011; World Hunger Education Service 2012). People who live in poverty are personally affected by almost every problem having to do with basic human needs—striving for self-actualization is the furthest thing from the minds of people who suffer in poverty. Worldwide, people living in poverty are generally malnourished; they are refugees, homeless,

TABLE 4.1 Top 10 Poorest Nations in the World	
Country	**GDP per Capita (US$)**
Democratic Republic of Congo	300
Zimbabwe	500
Liberia	500
Guinea-Bissau	600
Somalia	600
Comoros	600
Solomon Islands	600
Niger	700
Ethiopia	700
Central African Republic	700

Source: Delaney (2012); Maps of the World (2008)

or have inadequate shelter; they have no health care; their homes and neighborhoods have little or no sanitation or clean water supplies; they are usually illiterate and have no access to education or educational opportunities; they have no energy supplies; they are often unemployed or underemployed; and because they are generally powerless, they have the least amount of human rights. Additionally, many of the poor people around the world face severe environmental problems, such as deforestation, desertification, soil erosion, and inadequate drinking water. The World Hunger Education Service (2012) states that climate change is increasingly contributing to hunger and poverty: "Increasing drought, flooding, and changing climate patterns requiring a shift in crops and farming practices that may not be easily accomplished are three key issues" (3).

In the United States, which possesses a sizeable middle class as the result of capitalism, many people are economically secure. The socioeconomic system of the United States has attracted people from around the world for 200 years. As we learned in Chapter 2, the first significant number of ethnic Europeans arrived in America from Ireland beginning in the early 1820s. Although highly discriminated against, the Irish eventually assimilated to American culture and began to flourish. Ever since the arrival of the Irish, poor immigrants have continued to migrate to the United States. Although immigrants do not believe that American streets are literally paved in gold, they have a perception of the United States as the land of plenty. And in many cases, people have flourished here. Most "rags to riches" stories generally take a few generations, but for those who are willing to work hard, gain an education, and embrace opportunities when they present themselves find economic security. Unfortunately, there are large numbers of Americans who have not attained economic security for a variety of reasons. Many of these people end up poor, and poverty is often correlated with gang involvement.

Historically, gangs have developed in economically depressed neighborhoods. Poorer neighborhoods are characterized by high rates of unemployment, high population density, and transients. Growing up in poverty leads many youths (and adults) to seek unconventional means of making money. Schools in economically depressed areas generally experience higher crime and drug problems. Students in lower SES schools may lack the readiness and interest to learn when compared with students from more affluent neighborhoods (Siegel, Welsh, and Senna 2003). School districts in poorer neighborhoods may face greater difficulty in hiring and retaining the most qualified faculty. Furthermore, parents may not have the time nor resources to become actively involved in their children's school projects and homework assignments. Combine all these factors and we have the making of an environment that undermines the goals of the educational institution.

The lack of job opportunities not only contributes to the formation of an underclass, it helps to create conditions of poverty. Conditions of poverty, in turn, cause increasing harm to youths who find themselves caught in a continuous downward spiral. Poverty causes human suffering and stunts human potential. It is a major cause of social unrest, crime, and even revolution. A study conducted at the University of Virginia has shown that poverty can lower a child's intelligence quotient (IQ) score a number of points. Impoverished children struggle to reach their full intellectual potential; inadequate nutrition during early life can also stunt a child's potential for learning. The findings of the IQ and nutrition studies reveal the importance of environment over genes for mental development (Kotulak 2003).

Acknowledging poverty as a national concern, President Lyndon B. Johnson declared a "War on Poverty" during his first State of the Union Address in 1964. A number of social programs such as Head Start, food stamps, work study, Medicare, and Medicaid, all of which still exist today, were put in motion as machines to stamp out poverty. In an attempt to measure the progress of the War on Poverty, poverty scales, or thresholds, were established by the federal government—specifically the Office of Economic Opportunity (Delaney 2012). The key variable to determine poverty thresholds was the cost of food. As a result, poverty in the United States is measured primarily by the cost of food for various family sizes (Weinberg 2006). A researcher for the Social Security Administration, the U.S. Department of Agriculture determined that food represented about one-third of after-tax income for the typical family. This yielded a measure of a "multiplier" by three to attain poverty thresholds. Every year the government computes a low-cost food budget and multiplies by three. Families whose incomes are less than this amount are considered poor; while those earning above this figure are considered "not poor." The 2010 Poverty Guidelines are provided in Table 4.2.

According to the U.S. Census Bureau, the official poverty rate in 2010 was 15.1 percent, up from 12.1 percent in 2002. In 2010, the people below the official poverty thresholds numbered

TABLE 4.2 2010 Poverty Guidelines

Number of Persons in Family or Household	Forty-Eight Continuous States and Washington, DC ($)	Alaska ($)	Hawaii ($)
1	10,830	13,530	12,460
2	14,570	18,210	16,760
3	18,310	22,890	21,060
4	22,050	27,570	25,360
5	25,790	32,250	29,660
6	29,530	36,930	33,960
7	33,270	41,610	38,260
8	37,010	37,010	42,450

Source: U.S. Department of Health and Human Services (2011)

46.2 million (*American Educator* 2011; *New York Times* 2011). The number of Americans in deep poverty—those with incomes below half of the poverty line—reached the highest level on record at 20.5 million people or 6.7 percent of the population (*American Educator* 2011). The poverty rate for children was 22.0 percent in 2010, a rate that had not been reached since 1993. Because most gang members "turn" in their youth, this high poverty rate for children is especially alarming. Poverty rates were the highest for African Americans (27.4%) and Hispanics (26.6%). The poverty rates for non-Hispanic whites were 9.9 percent and for Asians 12.1 percent. The perception of poverty often involves an image of the urban poor, but it should be noted that the poor can be found in rural areas and in the suburbs. The Brookings Institution reports that the number of poor grew by 25 percent in the suburbs from 2000 to 2008—a growth rate nearly five times higher than that for the nation's largest cities (Stith 2010). In 2010, the suburban poverty rate hit 11.8 percent, the highest rate since 1967. It is not surprising to find that joblessness is the main reason so many Americans are living in poverty. According to a Census official, about 48 million people aged 18–64 did not work a single week out of the year in 2010 (*New York Times* 2011). When people are out of work, they are generally without health insurance as well. In 2010, there were a record number 49.9 million people without any health insurance (*American Educator* 2011).

As the data in Table 4.2 indicate, the federal poverty level for a family of four was $22,050 (in the 48 continuous states) in 2010. It takes, however, double the income considered "poverty" level of most families to provide their children with adequate and basic necessities, such as food, stable housing, and health care. The families that live in the "gray" area, between poverty and the realistic minimum income necessary to function, face material hardships and financial pressures. Families with income in this gray area make too much money to qualify for public benefits but too little to provide all the necessities of family life. Thus, for every child living in poverty, there is twice that number of children living in low-income families. This figure represents nearly 40 percent of all American children. So, as the statistics reveal, there are millions of poor children in the United States. However, it is also obvious that the greatest percentage of poor people are not gang members; consequently, poverty alone does not lead an individual to gangs.

Single Parent Families and the Feminization of Poverty

The fastest-growing family form in the United States is the single-parent family. Such families may be the result of a woman giving birth out of wedlock, divorce, or the death of a spouse. Most typically, single-parent families are the result of single women having children. The number and proportion of all births that occur out of wedlock has increased tremendously since the 1960s. Between 1980 and 2007, the proportion of births to unmarried women in the United States has more than doubled from 18 percent to 40 percent (National Center for Health Statistics 2009). In 2008, the percentage of births to unmarried women climbed to 41 percent, further illustrating the trend (Pew Research Center 2010). In 2008, the share of births that were nonmarital was highest for black women (72%), followed by Hispanics (53%), whites (29%), and Asians (17%) (Pew Research Center 2010). In poor areas, the number of children being raised by single parents increased, especially for African Americans. As a result, the majority of black children in inner-city urban areas are raised by a single female, who is generally poor. Because single parents must be employed for long hours, they are often less involved in their children's lives. In addition, because many single-parent families reside in neighborhoods with a high concentration of similarly economically poor families, the probability of children becoming delinquent or turning to gangs increases (Ambert 2001). Many gang members come from poor, single-parent, female-headed families. It has long been the contention that young males seek out gangs because they are looking for the male presence that is missing in their lives. Clearly, there is not a cause-and-effect relationship between being raised by a single mother in a poor area and male youths turning to a gang, but it is a risk factor.

Many single-parent poor women who are conscientiously trying to put food on the table for their children will work two or more jobs (most likely, low-paying and part-time jobs). This is highly commendable behavior. Unfortunately, the result of single-parent women spending many hours away from home working is that their children have many unsupervised hours of time at their disposal. Furthermore, because the jobs these women are working at are low paying, they still end up poor. Since women are more likely to be poor than men, sociologists generally use the term *the feminization of poverty* to describe the huge number of women living in poverty, most of whom are single mothers or heads of families. Thio (2003) explains that men can more readily escape poverty by getting a job, whereas women find it harder to escape poverty because of the gender-segregated labor market that often places women in lower-paid, lower-status jobs. The term *feminization of poverty* was popularized by Diana Pearce in her 1978 article "The Feminization of Poverty: Women, Work, and Welfare." In this article, Pearce cited data to support her claim that almost two-thirds of the poor over the age of 16 were women entering the labor force between 1950 and the mid-1970s. She argued that the blame for this feminization of poverty belonged to the government because it did not find a way to support divorced and single women.

Women are far more likely than men to be poor. Women who are single parents and women of color are especially vulnerable to poverty. Consider these 2007 statistics: "28.3 percent of households headed by single women were poor, while 13.6 percent of households headed by single men and 4.9 percent of married-couple households live in poverty" (National Poverty Center 2009). That women are more than twice as likely to be poor than men means that single parenthood has affected women's poverty rates far more dramatically than it has men's. Among the problems facing single-parent women living in poverty are they often have bad credit, or no credit of their own established, their own health care and nutritional needs become secondary to their children's, and they lack sufficient access to education and support services. There are many possible explanations as to why women are more likely to be poor than men. Pearce (1978) argued that one of the consequences of women's fight for independence from men has led to their pauperization and dependence on welfare. A contributor factor to the rise of single-parent families is the dramatic increase in the number of divorces. Thus, the various changes in family structure (especially the large number of children born out of wedlock) have contributed to the feminization of poverty. The poorest of the poor females come from generations of poverty, and when these single women have children, they almost guarantee themselves a life of poverty—especially if they fail to receive a quality education or job training. Many of these poor women do not have families to support them and are left with one primary option, government support. Putting off having children until they have a quality job would solve this problem, but since unplanned pregnancies are fairly common, abortion is often used as a method of birth control. However, the increased feminization of poverty coincides closely with the period when abortion became increasingly legalized. Some have argued that the availability of abortion should help reverse this trend, because job loss due to childbirth would be avoided, as would the burdens of child care which so clearly contribute to the impoverishment of women. This has not been the case as abortions still occur, but the number of women and children living in poverty continues to increase.

The socioeconomic effects on children being raised in a single-parent (especially those headed by a woman in poverty), inner-city environment are often devastating, with abuse and neglect frequently the end result. Consequently, this is another contributing factor to youths who seek out the comfort of a gang.

The Role of Education

The changing nature of America's occupational opportunity structure has dramatically and negatively impacted the chances of many lower SES persons in their attempt to become upwardly mobile. **Social mobility** refers to the degree to which an individual, family, or group changes its status within the stratification system over a period of time. There are two primary categories of social mobility: intragenerational mobility (within a generation) and intergenerational mobility (across generations). *Intragenerational mobility* is defined as changes in SES over a single lifetime—someone born into a lower SES family who rises to a higher SES level. *Intergenerational mobility* occurs when lower SES persons provide the means for their children to rise above their SES level. One of the best ways to become upwardly mobile is through education.

Formal education involves training and developing people's knowledge, skills, intellect, and character, in structured and certified programs. **Formal education** can be viewed as "a process of teaching and learning in which some people (e.g., teachers and professors) cultivate knowledge, skills, intellect, and character, while others (students) take on the role of the learner" (Delaney 2012, 356). The value of a formal education is not only the knowledge one gains but the provisions of credentials (e.g., diplomas, certificates, security clearances) that are needed in a technologically advanced society characteristic of the growing service industry. There is a direct correlation between one's level of education and the amount of money earned (see Table 4.3). As the information in Table 4.3 clearly indicates, as one's level of education increases, the higher one's salary will be (on average). The U.S. Bureau of Labor Statistics does not clarify what is meant by a professional degree or how it differs from a doctoral degree, but, generally, a Ph.D. is considered a research doctorate and a professional degree prepares a person for a specific profession, such as engineering or law. In 2011, a person with a professional degree earned more than someone with a doctoral degree—historically; this has not been the case.

TABLE 4.3 2011 Median Weekly Earning by Level of Education	
Level of Education	**Median Weekly Earnings ($)**
Doctoral degree	1,551
Professional degree	1,665
Master's degree	1,263
Bachelor's degree	1,053
Associate's degree	768
Some college, no degree	719
High school graduate	638
Less than a high school diploma	451

Source: U.S. Bureau of Labor Statistics (2012)

TABLE 4.4 2011 Unemployment Rate by Level of Education	
Level of Education	**Unemployment Rate (%)**
Doctoral degree	2.5
Professional degree	2.4
Master's degree	3.6
Bachelor's degree	4.9
Associate's degree	6.8
Some college, no degree	8.7
High school graduate	9.4
Less than a high school diploma	14.1

Source: U.S. Bureau of Labor Statistics (2012)

There is an inverse correlation between one's level of education and the unemployment rate (see Table 4.4). That is, as the level of one's education increases, the likelihood of unemployment decreases.

As the data provided in Tables 4.3 and 4.4 reveal, education is important for economic purposes. Couple this reality with the shifting labor market discussed earlier in this chapter, we can see why it is so important to encourage all youths to attend college. Youths who not perform well in school, or do not like school, are more likely to be involved in delinquent behavior. Youths who are seriously delinquent report that their school experiences were negative ones. Who is to blame for this? Ideally, schools are institutions where youths learn about society's rules and earn an education.

Unfortunately, some school environments are not very conducive to learning. In some cases, the teachers and/or administrators are incompetent and guilty of labeling certain children as no good (or other negative labels). In many more cases, the students who come to school do not come properly prepared to learn. Parents are responsible for the child's readiness and preparation to perform and behave properly in the classroom. Especially important are language skills. Immigrant children often perform poorly in the schools because of their lack of adequate English language skills. When English is not spoken in the home, immigrant schoolchildren will have an even more difficult time mastering the materials necessary to earn good grades in school. If children have not been properly socialized to accept education as a vital aspect of their future, even the best teachers will not be able to motivate them. If a youth is struggling in the classroom, it is hard to persuade him/her to continue education despite the prospect of a life of continuing poverty. Many gang members have reported that going to school felt like a form of incarceration.

Disenchanted with school, youths may become truants, the first step on the path to delinquency. When youths are out of school during scheduled hours, they find and associate with other deviants. For many, the gang is now just one step away. Parents, teachers, school counselors, school administrators, and community organizations all need to come together with some effective plan for keeping children in school and fostering an environment conducive to learning for all youths.

Dishion, Nelson, and Yasui (2005) found that there are three specific factors in predicting whether school kids turn to gangs: academic grades, reports of antisocial behavior, and relationships with peers. Dishion and associates measured later gang involvement via self, peer, teacher, and counselor reports. The researchers hypothesized that academic grades and relationships with peers would predict the likelihood of being involved in a gang by eighth grade, and that European American (non-Hispanic whites) males and females and African-American males and females would be equally involved in gangs by the eighth grade. (*Note*: They did not study Hispanics.) There were 714 adolescent subjects and their families, from an urban ethnically diverse region in the northwestern United States. Dishion and colleagues found that black males followed by black females were the two groups most likely to become involved in gang behavior. However, the difference between male and female involvement was large—males were much more likely to become involved in gangs. They also found that blacks were far more likely to join a gang than whites. As for academic grades, the researchers found that academic grades were the strongest predictor in gang involvement, in that the lower the GPA, the more likely the youth was to join a gang. Youths who felt socially distanced from their peers in school were also more likely to seek out a gang (because these peers share their outlook on life). Antisocial behavior (e.g., various forms of delinquency and/or criminality) was a factor in predicting gang involvement as well (Dishion et al. 2005). The findings of this study seem to confirm what most gang researchers believe, that blacks, especially males, are more likely to join a gang than whites, and that antisocial behavior and social distance from peers are risk factors.

It is very important that youth attend school to help secure an economically rewarding future. But they also need to attend school, if for no other reason; to stay out of trouble—trouble that can include the allure of street gang life. Once again, we have to add an "unfortunately" to our discussion on the role of education and gangs. Youths are joining gangs at an early age and as we shall see in Chapter 5, youths are considered "at risk" at *age* 8, an age much earlier than those in *grade* 8—the age of the youths Dishion and associates focused their attention on. Schools are breeding grounds for street gangs, as new gangs can be formed by school peers or existing gangs may recruit kids in school. Because of this, schools are no longer perceived to be the safe, neutral zones they were once believed to be (Ramsey, Rust, and Sobel 2003). Some schools have a persistent problem with violence and gang activity. Many students do not feel safe in schools, as turf and territorial issues have surfaced within them. When at-risk youth don't feel safe in school, they tend to accept the idea that they might just as well belong to a street gang because it provides acceptance, protection, and survival.

Acceptance, Protection, and Survival

In simple terms, many youths turn to the gang for **acceptance**. Youths who experience alienation and a sense of powerlessness from their environment find acceptance in a gang. Mexican-Americans develop, in the words of Diego Vigil, a "cholo style." The *cholo style* refers to the way in which Mexican-Americans present themselves by the way they walk, talk, dress, and their overall demeanor. Other aspects of the cholo style are the use of nicknames and graffiti, getting tattoos, listening to certain genres of music, tricked-out cars, and dancing (Vigil 1997). Gangs present an outlet for youths whose culture has been suppressed in the school and discriminated against by society. Gang members form their own subculture, including a style of dress, mannerisms, and communication, sometimes called *slanging*. Today, a number of gang members and nongang members alike use the term *swag* to describe their demeanor and attitude about life. (*Note*: The word *swag* may also be used instead of *bling* as in "the Academy Awards presents presenters, performers, and nominees with swag bags to describe gift bags.") The simple activity of hanging out—something that gang members do more than anything else—provides physical evidence of their existence and establishes turf. As gang expert Irving Spergel summarizes, "gangs often form out of need for acceptance in a culture that tends to shun poor, first-generation

Americans" (Duffy 1996a, A16). Spergel's own research on Chicago gangs and his analysis of the growing presence of the Latin Kings in Syracuse led him to believe that Latino gangs in particular form out of a need for acceptance, but that this is no different from what Irish youth did nearly two centuries ago.

In many high-density urban areas throughout the United States, a youth's motive for joining a gang can be described in one word: **survival**. Existing rival gangs attempt to recruit new members on a regular basis. Consequently, even when a youth tries to remain neutral and stay out of the gang life, he/she may be perceived as a member of a rival gang because he is not a member of "your" gang. In other words, if he's not one of ours, he must be one of theirs (such was the case described in "Connecting Street Gangs and Popular Culture" Box 3.1, when Compton football player Dannie Farber was mistaken for a gang member and killed). To survive on the streets, one generally needs **protection**. Within the gang, youths believe they are safe from attacks by other gang members or conventional youths who are bullying them. Therefore, the threat of being beaten or shot by rival gangs is often an important reason youths join gangs. The gang becomes a substitute family that offers not only acceptance but also protection and the opportunity to survive in a neighborhood filled with dangerous obstacles.

KICKS AND THRILLS

Delinquency is not without its appeal. Youths often feel as though everyone is telling them what to do and how to do it. A desire to violate norms crosses the minds of most people, at least from time to time. The allure of the deviant culture comes from many sources. Some youths are tempted by the drug and alcohol subculture. Firearms in the hands of those once abused or beaten are a source of comfort and provide a sense of power. Media-induced glamorization of delinquency and gang behavior attracts other youths. And at the simplest level of all, some people simply find delinquency and gang behavior exciting, fun, and thrilling.

Drug and Alcohol Use

Drugs and alcohol have a fascinating appeal to most adolescents. Sneaking a drink while underaged is far more exciting than having a drink when you are in your forties. Consuming the forbidden drink gives youths a thrill and a sense of excitement because they feel that they are getting away with something. If the first-time experience of drinking is pleasurable, youths are likely to continue the behavior.

It is not surprising that youths take drugs; after all drugs are often promoted as solutions to all sorts of problems. Have a headache? Take an aspirin. Need a boost to get through the day? Take an energy drink (filled with drugs) or a cup of coffee or soft drink (caffeine). Two of the most popular drugs worldwide are caffeine and aspirin. Caffeine is the most addictive psychoactive drug in the world (Majithia 2012). A study conducted by *New Scientist* magazine indicates that 90 percent of North American adults consume some form of caffeine on a daily basis and its widespread use coupled with its lack of nutritional value has attracted condemnation from many dietary purists (Majithia 2012). Many people take prescription drugs, including youths and especially those youths diagnosed with attention-deficit hyperactivity disorder (ADHD). Prescription drugs are abused more than non-prescription drugs and cause more deaths.

The dangers of tobacco use are so well documented that it is puzzling how cigarettes remain legal. Tobacco consumption causes the deaths of more than 443,000 Americans every year, costing the nation $96 billion in health care costs annually (Centers for Disease Control and

Prevention [CDC] 2009). Secondhand smoke is even more dangerous to those exposed to its deadly effects. This is especially important as nearly half of all nonsmoking Americans are regularly exposed to secondhand smoke (U.S. Department of Health and Human Services 2006). Although cigarette smoking may precede alcohol use for many youths, the Centers for Disease Control and Prevention (2010) states that alcohol is used by more young people in the United States than tobacco or illicit drugs. Among youth, the use of alcohol and other drugs has been linked to unintentional injuries, physical fights, academic and occupational problems, and illegal behavior (CDC 2010). Alcohol and drug use contributes markedly to infant morbidity and mortality (CDC 2010).

Most teenagers will try alcohol and a slightly smaller percentage will try some sort of illegal drug. However, it should be clear that the number of adolescents who go on to become serious delinquents, or gang members, is small. Those youths who find drinking and taking drugs exciting and continue their use are at the greatest risk of becoming delinquents. The problem lies with the fact that the consumption of alcohol and drugs may encourage or facilitate other criminal behaviors such as committing acts of violence and aggression and may result in the user demonstrating impaired judgment, lowered inhibitions, and general reckless behavior (Curran and Renzetti 1994). Heavy drug users with no source of income to support their habits often resort to crime (e.g., theft, robbery). The type of drug used will dictate behavior that, at times, may be violent (e.g., especially under the influence of PCP). Historically, gang members' participation in drugs was limited to using for the purposes of partying. In the past few decades, however, street gangs have begun to take control of drug sales on the street and distribution and trafficking of drugs. The most common drugs sold by gangs are crack cocaine, marijuana, powder cocaine, methamphetamine, and heroin (see Chapter 8).

Marijuana is the most commonly used illicit drug among youth in the United States. Current marijuana use decreased from 27 percent in 1999 to 21 percent in 2009. Current cocaine use increased from 2 percent in 1991 to 4 percent in 2001 and then decreased to 2 percent in 2009 (CDC 2010). Citing 2009 statistics, youths also engage in inhalant use (12%), ecstasy (7%), methamphetamines (4%), heroin (2%), and hallucinogenic drugs (8%) (CDC 2010). Youths also abuse prescription drugs, and rates of nonmedical use of prescription and over-the-counter (OTC) medication remains relatively high. The prescription medications most commonly abused by youth include pain relievers, tranquilizers, stimulants, and depressants. In 2009, 20 percent of U.S. high school students had taken such prescription drugs as Oxycontin, Percocet, Vicodin, Adderall, Ritalin, or Xanax, without a doctor's prescription. Youths also misuse OTC cough and cold medications, containing the cough suppressant dextromethorphan (DXM), to get high (CDC 2010).

Like many adults, getting high and being drunk are ways that delinquents cope with their unhappiness in conventional society. They find drinking and taking drugs enjoyable alternatives to their unpleasant realities. Taking drugs does not cause a youth to become a gang member, but the delinquency that generally accompanies alcohol and other drug use become another risk factor.

Firearms

Firearms are generally classified into three broad categories: handguns (e.g., revolvers, pistols, and derringers), rifles, and shotguns. Rifles and shotguns are both considered "long guns." Handguns are weapons designed to fire a small projectile from one or more barrels when held in one hand with a short stock designed to be gripped by one hand. A semi-automatic firearm fires one bullet each time the trigger is pulled and automatically loads another bullet for the next pull of the trigger. A fully automatic firearm (sometimes called a "machine gun") continuously fires bullets as long as the trigger is pulled. According to the National Rifle Association (NRA) (2011), there are nearly 300 million privately owned firearms in the United States, including nearly 100 million handguns. The number of firearms rises over 4 million annually. The NRA (2011) reports that there are 70–80 million U.S. gun owners, that 40–45 million own handguns, and that 40–45 percent of American households have firearms. Data provided by the FBI (2012d) in its annual Uniform Crime Reports reveal that there were 12,996 homicides in 2010 and 67.5 percent were caused by firearms (68.5% of these homicides involved handguns). Compared to other high-income countries (Western nations such as Australia, Canada, France, Germany, Italy, Japan, and the United Kingdom), the U.S. homicide rate is 6.9 times higher and the U.S. firearm homicide rate is 19.5 times higher (Richardson and Hemenway 2010). (*Note*: Richardson and Hemenway used the World Health Organization's definition of "high income" to determine the nations under study.) For 15- to 24-year-olds, the firearm homicide rate in the United States is 42.7 times higher than that in other high-income nations (Richardson and Hemenway 2010). The U.S. firearm homicide rate is approximately 3.6 (per 100,000), and although this is, by far, the highest among Western nations, it is lower than the non-Western nations of South Africa (74.6), Colombia (51.8), Thailand (33.0), Guatemala (18.5), Paraguay (7.3), Zimbabwe (4.7), and Mexico (3.7) (Nation Master 2012).

People who are comfortable handling guns—and this includes military and law enforcement personnel, hunters, people who shoot at firing ranges, and gangbangers—get a certain rush of power when they possess a firearm. For criminals, especially gangbangers, having a gun not only represents a sense of power, it is exciting and thrilling. Possessing a gun gives gangsters automatic respect because they know people will do almost anything that is asked of them when there is a gun pointed at their head. Gangbangers find this form of intimidation very exhilarating. Gang members have been known to laugh at their victims while watching them shake in terror. Firearms are often used during the commission of a crime and are regularly used in disputes with rivals. Relaxed regulations of gun sales in the United States make it very easy for gang members to find guns. "The easy availability of guns has contributed to a stunning upsurge in killings by teenagers and young adults. Since 1985, the homicide rate has declined among older adults but has soared among young people. . . . Most of these killings take place in large cities' poor neighborhoods, where many teenagers carry guns, a relatively new phenomenon" (Thio 2003, 144). According to the Centers for Disease Control and Prevention (2011a), from 1991 to 2007, homicide rates were consistently higher among persons aged 10–24 years than among all ages combined. On the positive side, the number of juvenile murder victims has decreased from the peak year of 1993, when there were 2,900 juvenile deaths from firearms. The homicide rates among persons aged 10–24 years dropped from 15.6 deaths per 100,000 in 1991 to 9.1 deaths per 100,000 in 2007 (CDC, 2011a). Homicide is still the second leading cause of death among youth aged 10–24 years in the United States (CDC, 2011b). Nearly half of all homicide deaths among youths were from firearms. Most homicide victims are males, and from 2005 to 2007, firearms were the leading mechanism for homicide among males aged 10–24 years. The firearm homicide rate among males aged 10–24 was highest for non-Hispanic blacks with 55.5 deaths per 100,000 and lowest for non-Hispanic whites (see Table 4.5). As the data in Table 4.5 indicate, males aged 10–24 are far more likely to be victims of homicide via firearms than any other cause. In addition to homicide victimization, in 2009 a total of 650,843 young people aged 10–24 years were treated in emergency departments for nonfatal injuries sustained from assaults (CDC, 2011b). Many of these assaults also involved the use of firearms.

TABLE 4.5	Homicide Rates* among Males Aged 10–24, by Race/Ethnicity, United States, 2005–2007		
Race/Ethnicity	Firearms	Cut/Pierce	Other
Non-Hispanic white	2.4	0.5	0.5
Non-Hispanic black	55.5	3.0	1.6
Hispanic	17.3	2.2	1.2
Non-Hispanic American Indian	11.5	3.3	2.0
Non-Hispanic Asian/Pacific Islander	5.7	0.8	0.5

Source: Centers for Disease Control and Prevention (2011c); *per 100,000

There is a great debate in the United States over the availability of firearms and whether harsher restrictions should be placed on the purchase and possession of firearms. The debate over the right to bear arms stems from the Second Amendment of the U.S. Constitution. Amendment II (ratified December 15, 1791) states, "A well regulated Militia, being necessary to the security of a free State, the right of the people to keep and bear Arms, shall not be infringed." This relatively simple, one-sentence amendment has been dissected by lawyers and organizations with their own agendas. Some people take the historical meaning of "a well-regulated militia" as a standing army or a national guard (since the colonists did not have a standing army) that has the right to exist to protect American citizens. Other organizations, such as the National Rifle Association, point to the part of the Constitution that reads: "the right of people to keep and bear arms shall not be infringed" as their reasoning for why all citizens should be able to own firearms. According to the NRA's "Fact Sheet," the right to bear arms is a form of self-defense and, therefore, is an individual right, which cannot be infringed upon. Although the Second Amendment does not use the exact terminology of a "right to self-defense," the Supreme Court ruled in *District of Columbia v. Heller* (2008) that "the inherent right of self-defense has been central to the Second Amendment right" and that "the individual right to possess and carry weapons in case of confrontation" (NRA 2011). Earlier Supreme Court decisions (*U.S. v. Cruikshank*, 1876; *Presser v. Illinois*, 1886; *U.S. v. Miller*, 1939; and *U.S. v. Verdugo-Urquidez*, 1990) have also recognized the individual's right to bear arms. Other organizations and people (e.g., social workers, law enforcement groups, and some politicians) believe that there should be stricter gun laws. And in some states it is relatively difficult to obtain a gun legally; in other states, people can legally carry guns with them in their automobiles or on their persons.

Even those who promote the right of citizens to bear arms cannot deny the harmful effects of firearms in the wrong hands (e.g., gang members and other criminals), but when they weigh these considerations against the fear of not being able to protect themselves against the wrong people, they remain steadfast with the idea of firearms for all individuals. It is not the intention here to take a side on right to bear arms controversy, but rather point out the obvious, that firearms in the hands of gangbangers is a source of power, a means of intimidation, and often the cause of homicide. (*Note*: Chapter 9 includes a further discussion on weapons-related crime and homicide.)

Popular Culture and the Mass Media

Popular culture refers to the items (products) and forms of expression and identity that are frequently encountered or widely accepted (mass produced), commonly liked or approved, and characteristic of a particular society at a given time. Popular culture is viewed as the culture of the people. In contrast, high culture is not mass-produced nor is it meant for mass consumption. The **high culture** generally belongs to the social elite and includes such things as the fine arts, opera, theater, and high intellectualism. Popular culture involves aspects of social life in which the greatest number of people in any given society are actively involved in. Popular culture is determined by the interactions among people in their everyday activities: current clothing and hairstyling, fashions and fads, sports, the use of slang, greeting rituals, and the foods people eat are all examples of popular culture. A major component of popular culture is the **mass media**— including television, radio, film, cyberspace (e.g., social network sites, YouTube), news outlets including televised news and newspapers, books, magazines, and sound recordings. The *mass media* is a collective term used to describe the vehicle by which large numbers of people are informed about important, or popular, happenings in society. As an agent of socialization, the mass media helps to shape public opinion on a variety of subjects, including street gangs. The relationship between popular culture and street gangs is deemed so significant that this text includes numerous "pop culture" boxes that provide readers with a view of street gangs not presented in other publications. The world of popular culture and gangs intersects through a variety of mass media mediums, including films (movies), music (primarily rap and hip-hop), sports, video games, and the Internet. Throughout this text a number of examples have been, or will be, provided to illustrate this point. As a result, a brief overview will be provided here.

People's attitudes and beliefs about crime and criminals are often shaped and influenced by media representations of crime. These opinions carry over to other aspects of the social world. "What people believe about crime and criminals influences Supreme Court decisions, criminal justice policies, the election of public leaders, and routine activities of the public" (Thompson, Young, and Burns 2003, 206). Gang violence has become "one of the most prevalent crime news topics of the past two decades. . . . News stories that focus on gangs have influenced attitudes and opinions by providing vivid public images of gang crime and criminals. Gang news not only presents information, it also articulates ideological messages concerning the meaning and definition of gangs" (Thompson et al. 2003, 206). As described below, we will see how the gang culture is often glamorized in popular culture via films, music, video games, cyberspace, and even in holograms.

A number of **films** have depicted street gang life:. We have already learned about street gang portrayal in *West Side Story*, *American Me*, *The Gangs of New York*, and *The Outsiders* in earlier chapters. A few other films made about gangs include *The Godfather*, *The Chinese Connection*, *Boyz in the Hood*, *Scarface*, and *The Departed*. *The Godfather* is presented as a trilogy with the first film released in 1972. It is an American epic crime film from Mario Puzo's novel of the same name. *The Godfather* glorifies the Italian Mafia through the fictional Corleone family headed by Vito Corleone (played by Marlon Brando). The story spans the years 1945 to 1955 and centers on the ascension of Michael Corleone (Al Pacino) to his rise as Mafia boss while chronicling the Corleone family under the patriarchical rule of Vito. For many years, *The Godfather* was the highest-grossing film of all time. The first movie won three Academy Awards (Best Picture, Best Actor—for Brando, and Best Adapted Screenplay). Although this film trilogy centers on an organized crime syndicate and therefore may appear unrelated to our study of street gangs, its relevance is evident in numerous ways. For example, many gangs incorporate the title of "godfather" in their hierarchal structure, and the organized fashion in which the Corleone family ran its street and drug operation is similar to many gangs that attempt to do the same today. That the Corleone family was always defending its turf and attempting to expand its territory are other similarities to contemporary street gangs. The recent use of the RICO Act to prosecute street gangs as criminal organizations represents another similarity.

Another popular crime film released in 1972 was *The Chinese Connection* starring Bruce Lee as Chen Zhen, the film's protagonist. The film is set in the early twentieth century in Shanghai and pits Japanese martial artist gangs against the Chinese Zhen. Of all the American street gangs, the Asian gangs are the most likely to use martial arts in their battles. The aura of secrecy reigns true for Asian gangs of any era.

A number of films have been made about African-American gangs; among the more popular or influential was the 1991 film *Boyz in the Hood*. Even the film's title's usage of "boyz" instead of "boys" has cultural significance. Long considered an insult to call a black person "boy" but playing off such insults, the black gang culture has popularized misspelling words to take ownership of their meaning. Thus, the film's title is a reference to Los Angeles's South Central neighborhood male street gangs. The film does a wonderful job of depicting life in the lower SES South Central (now known as South Los Angeles) neighborhoods. In 1991 the film was nominated for both the Best Director and Original Screenplay Academy Awards, making John Singleton the youngest person ever nominated for Best Director and the first African American to be nominated for the award. *Boyz* has long served as an inspiration to African-American street gangs because of its accurate and realistic portrayal of street life. *Boyz* begins with an ominous printed on-screen message: "One out of every twenty-one Black American males will be murdered in their lifetime. Most will die at the hands of another Black male." *Boyz* is a film about three buddies coming-of-age in Crenshaw. Among the interesting portrayals of ghetto life was how the film ended. The two brothers, Ricky and Doughboy, raised by a single mom with an absent father were killed in gang violence before graduating from high school. Ricky had a baby boy of his own, who would now be raised without a father. Tre, who was raised next door from the two brothers during his adolescent years by his father, was able to stay out of the gang and made it out of the 'hood by leaving for college in Atlanta with his girlfriend.

Leonardo DiCaprio stars as an Irish gangster once again (he starred in *Gangs of New York*) in the 2006 film *The Departed*, a crime thriller directed by Martin Scorsese. *The Departed* won several awards, including four Oscars at the 79th Academy Awards (Best Picture, Best Director, Best Adapted Screenplay, and Best Film Editing). The film describes organized crime led by the Irish Mob in Boston. Boston represents one of the few contemporary cities with a remaining Irish gang presence, and depiction of criminal activities presents a relatively romantic view of gang activity. The movie contains strong, vicious violence and crude language, but it is necessary to the story and character development. The harsh, in-your-face manner in which it is shown draws the viewer emotionally into the lives of the characters committing the violence and suffering from the pain.

The glorification of criminal street gang life in film almost pales in comparison to that of the world of music. The music most often associated with gangs is known as "**hip-hop**" or "**gangsta rap**." "Rap" music is the forerunner of hip-hop and gangsta rap. Cheryl Keyes (2002, 17) defined rap as "a confluence of African American and Caribbean cultural expressions, such as sermons, blues, game songs and toasts and toasting—all of which are recited in chanted rhyme or poetic fashions." Keyes traced the rap style in music to the "jive-talk" popularized by jazz musicians and Harlem Renaissance writers in the first half of the twentieth century. Radio disc jockeys, such as Daddy-O Daylie (Holmes Bailey), Doc Hep Cat (Lavada Hurst), and Rufus Thomas, would rhyme over the music while it played on the air (Keyes 2002). Cummings and Roy (2002) suggest that the history of rap music dates back to the beat and rhythms that were brought to the Americas by African slaves. Over the centuries, African slaves mixed their beats with American music and formed a new rhythm that would one day turn into what we now know as rap (Cummings and Roy 2002).

The "rap style" was embraced by two diverse groups in the 1960s. Hippies used the term *rap* to mean a form of communication. A common expression would be "Let's rap about it, man." Their idealistic outlook on life incorporated a belief that people should rap (talk) about problems and differences rather than go to war and use violence on one another. Counselors employed the technique of "rap sessions" with their clients as a treatment method. By the late 1960s, African Americans began expressing a new racial consciousness that promoted Afrocentrism in all spheres of social life, including the arts. African-American writing workshops began to spring up throughout the nation. Poetry and rhymes were performed live and were generally accompanied by African music or drum beats. Performers like *The Last Poets of Harlem* gained national prominence. By the early 1970s, soul and funk artists like Barry White and Isaac Hayes began to incorporate raps into their songs (Keyes 2002). In the mid-1970s, another, now common aspect of hip-hop began to emerge: the DJ (disc jockey). The DJ spun records at clubs and private parties. Over time, DJs developed such techniques as "phasing," "back spinning," and "scratching" (Keyes 2002).

The hip-hop rap music style emerged from South Bronx with the purpose to provide an avenue for African Americans to express themselves when faced with discrimination and socio-economic issues. The early raps were created to put down other rappers or done in "battle style." The 2002 film *8 Mile*, featuring Eminem, clearly displays the rap battle style wherein participating rappers were supported by their own gangs in the audience as they battled, through lyrics, against one another. The growth of rap music extended to Washington, D.C., and Philadelphia shortly after it emerged in South Bronx (Basu 1998). Communities dominated by territorial street gangs were immediately influenced by the battle style of rap. Street gang attendance at rap concerts made security a problem for audience members and would-be rap artists. On other occasions, the gangs provided security to assure rap battles on stage. One such early famous rapper, Grandmaster Flash (and his group the Furious Five), used his gang "The Casanova Crew" to provide security for his shows. When describing his crew's role at his shows, Grandmaster Caz (as he was known) said, "they were kicking n*gger's asses" (Henderson 1996).

By the mid-1980s, rap had become popular in urban neighborhoods throughout the country. On the West Coast, however, hip-hop was replaced by a distinctive version of rap known as "gangsta rap" that became increasingly preoccupied with violent tales of the inner city. The gangsta rap style is attributed to rapper Ice Cube when he was with his original band, Niggaz With Attitude (NWA). With their *Niggaz4life* album, NWA became the first gangsta rap act to reach number one on the Billboard pop album chart in June 1991. Gangsters from Compton, California, NWA is generally acknowledged as the pioneer of the gangsta rap style (Baker 2011). This style includes lyrics that glorified violence and often disrespected women (women are often referred to as bitches and ho's). As an industry, it is estimated that rap music earned over $600 million in revenue in the early 1990s (Basu 1998). Throughout the 1990s, several rap artists went platinum, including Dr. Dre, Snoop Dogg, Salt 'N Pepa, and Ice Cube (Quinn 1996). Snoop Dogg's *Doggy Style* sold over 1 million units in its first few months (Baker 2011). By the mid-1990s rap was a billion-dollar industry. In 1997, Sean "Puffy" Combs was voted the Best Artist on the *Rolling Stone* Critic's List. Combs was more than a rapper himself; he was the president of the well-known music company Bad Boy Management. As president of this company, he managed several multi-platinum artists, including the late Notorious B.I.G., Lil' Kim, and Maze. Popular artists from Los Angeles rapped to the nation about defending territories, demanding respect, and drug dealing in South Central. Gangsta rappers would also make lyrical references to keeping one's allegiance to a gang and/or refer to violent images such as drive-by shootings. LA-based rappers also portrayed, through their music, the idea that respect and loyalty to the people and community where one comes from as the utmost importance (Grant 2002).

Many rappers such as the late Easy-E and Tupac Shakur along with current rappers Dr. Dre and Snoop Dogg have used their actual gang and street credentials to give their lyrics legitimacy—"keeping it real" (see "Connecting Street Gangs and Popular Culture" Box 4.1 for a discussion on Tupac Shakur). Rap music had now been transformed into gangsta rap and gangsta rap is all about street credibility.

Box 4.1   Connecting Street Gangs and Popular Culture

Tupac Shakur: The Relationship between Gangsta Rap and Street Credibility

COLUMBIA PICTURES/Album/ Newscom

The story of Tupac Amaru ("2Pac") Shakur sheds light on the relationship between gangsta rap and street cred- ibility. Born on June 16, 1971, Tupac was the son of Afeni Shakur, a former Black Panther and prison inmate who was once charged with conspiracy to blow up sev- eral Manhattan buildings. Tupac became a gangsta rap- per and part-time poet and thug. Before his premature death, Tupac became famous for his hit rap albums and his appearance in three movies. Shakur's track "Brenda's Got a Baby" from his solo debut album, *2Pacalypse Now* reached as high as number three on the Billboard Hot Rap Singles chart. His second album *Strictly 4 My N.I.G.G.A.Z.* crossed over to the pop charts with singles "I Get Around" and "Keep Ya Head Up." The album went platinum. His next two albums *All Eyez on Me* and *Me against the World* also sold millions of copies. Shakur also appeared in popular movies, including *Juice, Poetic Justice*, and *Above the Rim*. While 2Pac became a rap sensation, he was being condemned for his explicit violent lyrics. His lyrics included references to police officers he may have shot in Atlanta, the child he might have shot in 1992, the woman he sexually assaulted in New York, and the rival rappers he assaulted with bats, fists, and guns (Solotaroff 2002, 256). He was living up to his gangsta persona with several arrests for violent offenses in the 1990s. In 1994, he spent several days in jail for assaulting director Allen Hughes.

Tupac's troubles with the law included six arrests, convictions for assault and sexual abuse, and an eight-month prison term. In 1994, he was shot five times but lived. In September 1996, he was shot four times and died (Carlson 2003). On the night of September 7, 1996, Tupac was in Las Vegas to watch the Tyson–Seldon fight. He arrived with Marion "Suge" Knight, the head of Death Row Records. Suge worked with Dr. Dre, the creator of the Death Row gangsta sound, basically inventing a genre, which brought in a South-Central (Los Angeles) kid named Snoop Dogg to get the label off the ground (Solo- taroff 2002). Suge was a Blood from Los Angeles and he hung out with a crew called MOB (Members of Bloods). Tupac had his own road entourage and bodyguards, the Outlaw Immortalz. Flanked by their crews, Suge and Tupac headed toward their fourth row VIP seats inside the MGM hotel. Members of the rival Crips gang were already sitting in Tupac and Suge's seats; a minor confrontation took place but ended quickly. Early in the first round, Tyson knocked out Seldon. As the spectators left the arena, Tupac and his crew met up with members of the Crips outside the hotel and a fight between these rivals started in earnest. The MOB crew beat up a Crip, and when MGM security arrived, they let Tupac and his crew leave and detained the beaten Crip.

Las Vegas is a city with at least 5,000 gang members, most of whom came from Los Angeles. "The cops even have a joke about it: They migrate here for the dry heat to spell the rheumatism that comes from having bullets lodged in your spine or skull. But their sense of territory is dead serious and testy—what with other guys always coming over from LA" (Solotaroff 2002, 260). Feeling good about themselves, Suge and Tupac drove around the Vegas strip and were eventually confronted by assailants in a white Cadillac who opened fire on Suge's BMW 750. Tupac died shortly after. Tupac's death started a chain reaction, beginning with the murder of Notorious B.I.G., or Biggie Smalls, Tupac's East Coast rival, in Los Angeles. Quite a few incidents between East Coast affiliates and West Coast affiliates took place in such diverse cities as Los Angeles, New York City, Salt Lake City, and Omaha. The deaths of rappers Shakur and Notorious B.I.G. represented a turning point and the coming-of-age of a hip-hop generation (Kitwana 2002).

A number of rapper gangsters have followed the lead of Tupac and B.I.G. Some of them live on and some of them suffer the same fate of an early death. Soulja Slim (born James Tapp), considered the Tupac of New Orleans, is another example of a real gangster and not a "studio gangster" (a term used to describe a poser rapper created by a record label). Soulja, who went by the gang name of Magnolia Slim, was a gangster from Magnolia Street in New Orleans's notorious Ward 3 district. At age 25, he was shot down in the face in his mother's front yard. No one was ever found guilty for Slim's death (*Gangland* 2008b).

As demonstrated by the story of Tupac Shakur and rappers like him, gangsta rap is all about street credibility. The claims of contemporary artists such as 50 Cent—who says he has been shot nine times—add to the allure for youths who see delinquency and gang behavior as something to emulate. Interestingly, rap music itself has become more conventional, with suburban white kids listening to it and creating it. Rapper Eminem is one of the few white performers who have credibility in this genre. While former rapper Vanilla Ice was long ago revealed as a poseur, the absence of white women in rap speaks volumes about their lack of credibility on the streets. This review is not meant as a condemnation of rap music—after all, most people who listen to rap do so simply because they enjoy it. In the 1970s, white kids were condemned for listening to Led Zeppelin—the "Devil's music"—and some of those juveniles, such as this author, turned out to be college professors.

Another aspect of the popular culture and the media that has an influence over a mass audience is **video games**. Among the video games that highlight street gangs are *Grand Theft Auto: San Andreas, True Crime: New York City, The Warriors, 50 Cent: Bulletproof, Crime Life: Gang Wars, Saint's Row, 25 to Life*, and *The Getaway*. These games involve missions where the gamer attempts to take over territory, sell drugs, dress characters in certain gang clothing, spray paint graffiti, commit homicide, and perform other acts of violence on rival gang members and innocent citizens. Although there is no conclusive link to playing violent video games and becoming a violent person and specifically a gang member, critics of video games that incorporate street gangs worry that youths may become desensitized to street gang violence or gaming may stimulate desires to perform acts of violence in real life. (*Note*: There is a "Connecting Street Gangs and Popular Culture" box in Chapter 8 that describes street gang video games in greater detail.)

News coverage of street gangs may also influence impressions of viewers. While conventional persons are likely to look at street gang crime negatively, certain depictions of gang members as bad asses might actually conjure romanticized views of street gangs among younger viewers. Gang members themselves often take pride in being shown in the news or being documented in a news special because they feel as though their toughness has been immortalized. In other words, it's like a "badge of honor" among gangsters to be acknowledged by the "outside" world. With this in mind, gang members may encounter reporters or researchers who want to get information from them. Gang members usually have no problem with this because they want the gang to be in the spotlight, to be in the headlines, and to have their moment of fame. Gang members also realize that news reporters and researchers will get only the information that they offer to them. As Jankowski (1991) found decades ago, gangs that are studied realize that the media is interested in running stories on them; therefore, they offer information, but they regulate its flow in terms of depth (degrees of intimacy) and quantity. Thus, a number of street gangs use the media for their own gain—they are playing the media. The media provides advertisement for business because news outlets depict a particular gang as being in control of a specified territory. This is like a type of "yellow pages" because the gang has been named as an existing organization that is trafficking and selling drugs.

On the other hand, many gangsters do not want to appear on film, especially if they are committing a crime as it may lead to their arrest and incarceration. Some gangsters are not pleased with the way they end up being presented by the media—they discover *they* were the ones played by the media. Gang members acknowledge that the negative portrayal of street gangs in the media can work against them in the criminal justice system, as the public already perceives all gang members guilty of criminal acts.

For news organizations, documenting and sensationalizing crime, including street gang stories, helps the bottom line of profitability. News broadcasts need to fill time slots, but they also need to constrain their financial costs in order to be profitable. Airing stories that involve drama and display public vulnerability attracts viewers. News stories that are relatively simple to follow also attract mass audiences. Examples of crime are commonplace in nearly all viewing areas. Furthermore, many law enforcement agencies have their own full-time public relations spokespersons readily available to help describe and explain crime stories. It is not surprising then that crime stories comprise a large share of the news (Callanan 2012). Although news organizations commonly fill their time slots with crime stories, some are reluctant to identify gang-related crimes as such. In other words, they may engage in gang denial (see Chapter 6 for a description of gang denial).

In contemporary society, it is very common for people to spend a great deal of time communicating with one another in the virtual world (cyberspace) rather than in face-to-face interactions. This is accomplished via the **Internet**. Our fascination with the virtual world did not develop overnight, even though for some it may seem that way. For many decades now, people have been increasingly socialized into using (or relying) on computers. We use computers for nearly everything, and most businesses are nearly completely dependent upon them. Trying to conduct a transaction with a company when its computers are down is sometimes impossible. Internet usage is certainly not limited to conducting business, as billions of people worldwide socialize via this mechanism. The electronic socializing aspects of the Internet include such devices as email and social network sites such as Facebook, Twitter, and MySpace. Socializing online is the norm for an increasing number of people. Facebook alone will have more than 1 billion users by the end of 2012. People love to post comments (2.7 billion "likes" and comments), upload photos (250 million daily), generate revenue for the host ($3.7 billion in 2011), and communicate with people who use different languages (Facebook is available in 70 different languages) (*The Post-Standard*, 2012a). In 2010, Twitter, with 96 million users, surpassed MySpace in online traffic for the first time. By the start of 2012, Twitter had nearly half as many users as Facebook, with over 462 million registered users and 125 million active users (Bennett 2012). Like, Facebook, the number of Twitter users is expected to continue to climb and it is likely there will be 500 million folks on the social network site. As this brief look at the Internet indicates, social network sites and all sorts of electronic mediums of communication are fully entrenched in the world of popular culture. It should come as no surprise then that street gangs also use the Internet and its many electronic alternatives as a means of communication. "Connecting Street Gangs and Popular Culture" Box 4.2 provides a quick look at this phenomenon.

Box 4.2   Connecting Street Gangs and Popular Culture

The Internet: Keeping Street Gangs Connected in the Cyber World

There was a time when if one wished to conduct research on any topic, he/she would go to a library or conduct a field study where he/she could observe behavior from a distance or up close and interview subjects. For some time now, people have easily found all sorts of information via the Internet (e.g., "a Google search"). The Internet certainly helps to speed the research process. Of course, one has to be careful to ascertain what bits of information are accurate and which ones are not. One of the most popular sources of online information comes from Wikipedia, a free online encyclopedia, that allows anyone to post information—until it is, or may be, eventually verified. It is best to just skip the entry's text and go to the sources listed below it that are more reputable (e.g., academic sources and government sites for statistical data). Nonetheless, starting with a Google search on almost any topic generally bears fruit. For example, type "street gangs and the Internet" and you will find a vast array of links, starting with StreetGangs.com. This site has a great number of links, including politics, features, race, news, photos, policing, Hispanic gangs, gang injunctions, Crips, Bloods, Asian gangs, forums, and DVDs. And each of these links has a number of links or drop-down menu options offering even more information. The StreetGangs home page has a stern copyright warning against copying or distributing their information. They are not clear, however, who *they* are and therefore we have no idea if the information found on this site is reliable.

If you want information on the Crips or the Bloods, or most any other gang for that matter, why not go right to the source? After all, many street gangs have websites. Type www.crips.com or www.bloods.com and you will find the home pages of these Los Angeles–based nation gangs (see Chapter 6 for a discussion on the Crips, Bloods, and other "nation" gangs). The Crips site provides YouTube videos with links to news stories, interviews with prison gang members, shootings between the Crips and their rivals, and so on. If you go to these sites, you can discover for yourself who is really behind them.

Authorities have known, however, for quite a while now that street gangs do indeed use the Internet to communicate. And many gangbangers are quite Web-savvy, showcasing illegal exploits, making threats, and honoring killed and jailed members on a "digital turf." "Crips, Bloods, MS-13, 18th Street and others have staked claims on various corners of cyberspace. 'Web bangers' are posting potentially incriminating photos of members holding guns, messages taunting other gangs and boasts of illegal exploits on personal Web sites and social networking sites" (Glazer 2006, 1). Individual members are likely to host websites displaying their colors and proclamations. George W. Knox, director of the National Gang Crime Research Center, has trained hundreds of police officials in how to attain intelligence of gang membership, rivalries, territory, and lingo from gang Web pages (Glazer 2006). The tendency for gang members to brag about their exploits on Web pages, especially when compared to other criminals, is an asset for law enforcement authorities. Five or six years ago, MySpace was very popular with gang members. Today, Twitter and Facebook are more popular. In 2006, Chicago police arrested a teenager accused of spraying his gang nickname on a church by tracing his moniker to his MySpace.com account (Glazer 2006). They were able to do this because his online profile included his address, photo, and real name. New Jersey police traced a pair of Bloods gang members who had targeted a "snitch" after they posted messages on MySpace where court records showed that they shared messages back and forth with one another, concluding with LOLs (Queally 2011). The last laugh was on the Bloods members, and not with them, however.

Street gangs use the Internet to recruit new members, to issue challenges to rival gangs, and to post cyber memorials for fallen brethren. Cyber gang-banging is a good way for existing gangs to recruit young kids who are at the at-risk stage by showing them that gang life is like a family that cares about its members and who enjoy having parties. Texas Attorney General Greg Abbott has a PowerPoint presentation titled "Gangs and the Internet" that he uses to train law enforcement officials on the cyber exploits of gang members and how to use their information against them. In its 2011 National Gang Threat Assessment, the FBI addressed the emerging trend of street gangs on the Internet and trained its personnel on tactics to combat street gangs that use the Internet (National Gang Intelligence Center 2011a). According to the National Gang Intelligence Center (2011) street gangs are becoming increasingly savvy and are embracing new and advanced technology to facilitate criminal activity and enhance their criminal operations. Gang members use prepaid cell phones, social networking and microblogging websites, voice over Internet Protocol systems (e.g., making phone calls from one's computer), virtual worlds, and gaming systems that enable them to communicate globally and discreetly. Street gangs are also increasingly employing advanced countermeasures to monitor and target law enforcement while engaging in a host of criminal activity.

As this snapshot analysis of street gangs and the Internet reveals, the level of sophistication used by gangbangers is increasing. And law enforcement officials are doing their best to keep up with them.

In 2012, an emerging form of media—the use of **holograms**—was revealed. A hologram of Tupac Shakur performing on stage at the 2012 Coachella music festival stunned audience members. After all, as discussed in Box 4.1, Tupac has been dead since 1996. The hologram of the late rapper shocked over 100,000 concert attendees as it appeared alongside fellow rap heavyweights Snoop Dogg and Dr. Dre. Snoop and Dre remained silent before the concert about Tupac's hologram appearance. The promoters announced that Tupac would likely "go on tour" with rappers in the future. El Ulbrich, the chief creative officer of Digital Domain, the company that created the illusion, said, "This is just the beginning. Dre has a massive vision for this" (Hom 2012). The use of holograms has longed appeared in popular culture via film and, to lesser extent, television. It may just be a matter of time before holograms become more commonplace, with street gang members and conventional folks alike.

The media has often been criticized for its glamorization of violence in the movies, television, and video games. The great debate regarding the impact of the media's portrayal and glamorization of violence on the behavior of youths has not reached a conclusion. But it seems logical to believe that it does have an impact, greater for some than for others. As Thio (2003, 144) explained, "Media violence may not *cause* violence among the majority of young men, but it is likely to turn the few susceptible, violence-prone youngsters to violence." The media do exercise a great influence on the American public, and it shapes our perception of events. The media have great control over the manner in which they describe events to the public. "Contemporary society can be characterized by a *mass-mediated culture*, that is, a culture in which the mass media play a role in both shaping and creating cultural perceptions. The media do not simply mirror society, they help shape it" (Delaney and Wilcox 2002, 201). One area in particular that the media seem to have an impact on is elevating the public's fear of criminal victimization (Callanan 2012). Among the explanations for this are the realization that the mass media distorts the reality of crime by disproportionately focusing on random violent crimes which helps to raise viewers' assessment of risk (Gerbner and Gross 1976; Reiner 2007) and the realization that most people experience crime via the mass media rather than personal experience (Graber 1980; Surette 2007). Fear of victimization, fear of crime, and perceived risk of victimization of crime have sociological implications for health, behavior, and social status (Adams and Serpe 2000; Shippee 2012).

Nearly everyone enjoys at least one aspect of the media. In contemporary society, most people enjoy social network sites. Some wake up in the morning to check messages on cellular phones or log on to a social network site like Facebook. Others may wake to an alarm clock set to a favorite news or music station and then turn on the television to watch the news or catch up on sports on ESPN. During the day, people may read newspapers, magazines, or a book. Others will play video games. Some listen to music in the car on their way to work or school. Later in the day, many people may go see a movie or attend a ballgame. In short, most people find some form of the mass media exciting and enjoyable, so it should come as no surprise that this is true for youths, some of whom are juvenile delinquents at risk of becoming a gang member, or already a gang member. The effects of the media on juveniles are usually much different than on adults, because juveniles are much more susceptible to the influence of the media. Wannabe gangsters are heavily influenced by gangsta rap and movies that glorify gangs. The content of material that youths are exposed to is important and should be monitored by responsible adults.

The Rush

By this point, a number of socioeconomic explanations have been presented to explain why youths turn to gangs. Chapter 3 provides many theoretical explanations. Perhaps one of the simplest, and most overlooked, reasons why people commit acts of deviance, criminality, and join delinquent groups is that they find it fun and exciting. Deviant behavior has its appeal, to young and old alike. The oldest bank robber in U.S. history, "Red" Rountree, was asked why he robbed banks. As retold in newspapers, Rountree replied, "You want to know why I rob banks? It's fun. I feel good, awful good. I feel good for sometimes days, for sometimes hours" (Carter 2004, A13). Rountree committed his first bank robbery a week before his 87th birthday, on December 9, 1998, in Biloxi, Mississippi. He was arrested within minutes and eventually given three years' probation. Less than a year later, Rountree robbed his second bank, in Pensacola, Florida. He was quickly caught and sentenced to three years. At age 87, he became the oldest inmate in the Florida prison system. Two months after his Florida release, Rountree was arrested for his third bank robbery, in Abilene, Texas. Rountree stated, "I know I'm going to die in here. That's OK. I've led a good life and I have no regrets" (Carter 2004, A13). Red Roundtree did die in prison in 2004; he was 92 years old at the time of his death (*The New York Times* 2004). Clearly, criminal behavior does not have an age limit. However, behavioral indiscretion is more common with the young.

Preteens and teenagers enjoy testing the bounds of acceptable behavior. Sometimes lacking a mature sense of morality, young people, far more often than the elderly, are attracted to deviant forms of behavior. For some, the gang becomes symbolic of taboo behavior that is viewed as exciting, thrilling, and fun. Thus, it is this writer's contention, after speaking with many gangbangers, that a great number of individuals join gangs, at least in part, simply because of the lure of the rush of excitement that the gang provides. This idea should seem fairly logical—after all, nearly everyone seeks excitement and thrills and this is especially true for youths. Jankowski (1991) suggested that gangs provide individuals with entertainment opportunities much as a fraternity does for college students. Many youths join gangs because they represent the primary social institution of their neighborhood capable of delivering such a desirable want and need. Many gangs throw huge parties just as college fraternities do. They may have a clubhouse or meeting place where they all hang out and party. Such a meeting place might come equipped with a bar, pool tables, video games, dart boards, and even slot machines. Bryon Johnson, a Violence Prevention Coordinator with the Marion County Health Department in Indianapolis, Indiana, conducted research on the motivating factors of gang affiliation among diverse gang members and found that 31 percent of respondents (n=198) identified "fun" and 30 percent identified "excitement/ adventure" as motivational factors (Johnson 2012). When fun becomes a key motivating factor for gang participation, nearly all the other theoretical and socioeconomic explanations for gang participation take a back seat. Additionally, it makes the challenge of steering youth away from street gang participation all the more difficult as it now becomes necessary to find means of fun and excitement in the conventional world to deter youths from turning to gangs.

Having fun and excitement contributes to rush feelings. That is to say, gang members get off on the rush of often flirting with death. Although most people understand what is meant by a **rush**, fewer know how to explain its occurrence. A neuropsychological explanation of the rush is that an individual experiences an increase of adrenaline, cortisone, and testosterone, which are released into the bloodstream. This explains how military personnel are able to push on despite fatigue or how athletes are able to play through extreme pain immediately after experiencing an injury. The individual is loaded with adrenaline. Adrenaline is also known as epinephrine, the substance that medics inject into the heart of an individual who has experienced heart failure. It is meant to be a short-term response to a threatening situation. **Epinephrine** is a hormone important to the body's metabolism. It is a *catecholamine* (any of several compounds occurring naturally in the body that serve as hormones or as neurotransmitters in the sympathetic nervous system), and together with *norepinephrine* (a neurotransmitter that mediates chemical communication in the sympathetic nervous system, a branch of the autonomic nervous system) is secreted by the medulla of the adrenal gland. The body's sympathetic nervous system activates arousal by directing the adrenal gland atop the kidneys to release the stress hormones (Myers 1998). The physical body endures a number of changes during this arousal period. The pupils dilate, widening to allow in more light; the heart beats faster; breathing speeds up; and blood sugar rises, providing the body with more energy to act. Digestion will also slow down so that blood flow can be diverted from the stomach and intestines to muscles, all with the purpose of preparing the body to respond quickly to danger, threat, and excitement (Wade and Tavris 2002). The heightened secretions, caused by such reactions as fear and anger, result in an increased heart rate and the hydrolysis of glycogen to glucose. This chemical reaction, often called the fight-or-flight response, prepares the body for strenuous activity.

The fight-or-flight response is critical for survival, as many times people who are victimized freeze and fail to react to signs of danger. The "flight" response is the reaction to run from danger. Individuals not trained for combat are best advised to use this tactic when confronted with a hostile situation. Thus, if one senses trouble or notices visible signs of impending danger (e.g., gang members emerging from a dark alley), a basic survival strategy is to run for safety. Even gang members, police, and military personnel recognize the wisdom of surviving to fight another day when the odds are better. The "fight" response is the more typical response among military, law enforcement, and gang members alike. For many gangbangers, fighting and combat are the very elements that enticed the individual to join the gang in the first place. Gang members will fight rivals even when greatly outnumbered rather than risk being labeled a punk for running. In Chinese gangs there exists the "Red Pole Member," whose sole duty in the gang is to fight and protect the other members (Booth 1999). An abundance of adrenaline rushes has a direct correlation to violence (Klinteberg 1989). In addition, higher levels of testosterone are found in both men and women with aggressive tendencies, something that is necessary to the fight in the fight-or-flight response (Harris, Rushton, Hampson, and Jackson 1996). Aggression, linked to testosterone, can range from simple irritation to full-blown rage.

When some people exhibit rage, they swear. Other people swear when they drop a hammer on their foot, burn their hand on a stove, or when a referee seemingly makes a bad call in a sporting event. Research conducted by Stephens, Atkins, and Kingston (2009) indicates that when people invoke foul language it helps them to withstand a painful experience. The researchers found that swearing increased pain tolerance, increased heart rate, and decreased perceived pain compared with not swearing. Stephens and associates attribute swearing as a trigger that induces the fight-or-flight response and, thus, nullifies the link between fear of pain and pain perception.

Some studies have found that testosterone levels have been linked to levels of anger in adolescence (Archer 1991). High testosterone and cortisol levels, contributors to increased aggression and violence, have been linked to prefrontal cortex dysfunction. The prefrontal cortex is essential in executive cognitive functioning. It controls working memory, planning and organization, and, most importantly, self-regulation and inhibition. A prefrontal dysfunction may cause a breakdown of regulatory control and cause permanent antisocial behavior. Adolescents who do not learn to channel their emotions properly risk involvement in deviant and criminal behavior. Furthermore, it is during adolescence that males experience an increase in testosterone. The hormone testosterone is released at high levels during puberty, and it does not begin to decline until around 23 years of age (Martin 2000). The adolescent years are also the high-risk years for males to join a gang. The gang provides an outlet for the feelings of rage and anger experienced during adolescence. That younger males have higher levels of testosterone than older males leads some critics of the testosterone level link to anger to suggest that there is merely a correlation between the two and not a cause-and-effect principle at hand. Nonetheless, young males, some more than others, *do* possess higher levels of testosterone than older males and they are the ones most likely to be attracted to the thrill that the street gang way of life of violent confrontations presents.

The brain consists of millions of cells. These cells include neurons. Neurons are important because they allow certain regions of the brain to interact with one another through a process known as *neurotransmission*. Messages that are transmitted through the neurons are electrical impulses that are produced when the neurons are stimulated. The neurotransmitters travel across the synapse and relay information. Some of the neurons in the brain produce serotonin. **Serotonin** and the serontoninergic system is known to modulate mood, emotion, sleep, and appetite in humans and therefore is implicated in the control of numerous behavioral and physiological functions (Williams 1998). Serotonin also plays a role in sexual arousal, memory and learning, and the control of pain (Schmid 2009). Decreased serotoninergic neurotransmission has been linked to depression (Williams 1998). Beyond conducting research on the effects of serotonin in humans, scientists report that the effects of this chemical have also been shown to transform easygoing desert locusts into terrifying swarms that ravage the countryside (Schmid 2009). Malcolm Burrows of the University of Cambridge in England states, "Here we have a solitary and lonely creature, the desert locust. But just give them a little serotonin, and they go and join a gang" (Schmid 2009, A-8). Under certain conditions, locusts triple the amount of serotonin in their systems, changing the insects from loners to pack animals (Anstey, Rogers, Ott, Burrows, and Simpson 2009). One of the co-authors of the study on the effects of serotonin on locusts, Swidbert Ott, states, "Serotonin profoundly influences how we humans behave and interact, so to find that the same chemical in the brain is what causes a normally shy anti-social insect to gang up in huge groups is amazing" (Schmid 2009, A-8). The serotonin effect on locusts may also have the same effect on gang members and their sometimes swarming behavior. At the very least, it is something that scientists may want to consider researching.

Norepinephrine, like other neurotransmitters, is released at synaptic nerve endings to transmit the signal from a nerve cell to other cells. Norepinephrine is almost identical in structure to epinephrine, which is released into the bloodstream from the adrenal medulla under sympathetic activation, usually in response to short-term stress. The activation of epinephrine and norepinephrine causes an increased heart rate as well as blood pressure. As a stress hormone, norepinephrine affects parts of the brain where attention and responding actions are controlled. Along with epinephrine, norepinephrine also underlies the fight-or-flight response, directly increasing heart rate, triggering the release of glucose from energy stores, and increasing blood flow to skeletal muscles. Norepinephrine can also suppress neuroinflammation when released diffusely in the brain from the locus ceruleus (Heneka et al. 2010). Other actions caused by the release of norepinephrine include increased glycogenolysis (the conversion of glycogen to glucose) in the liver, increased lipolysis (the conversion of fats to fatty acids) in adipose (fat) tissue, and relaxation of bronchial smooth muscle to open up the air passages to the lungs. These combined reactions mobilize the body's resources to meet a stressful challenge. Thus, the rush that one experiences is actually a release of hormones that the body creates naturally in response to stressful situations (Stamford 1987).

It is important to note the potential harmful effects of catecholamines on individuals. Stamford (1987) states that the chronic release of catecholamines due to psychological stress may cause a wear-and-tear effect on the individual's body, which in turn increases the risk of coronary heart disease, hypertension, and ulcers. That mild exercise helps to produce an acute tranquilizing effect and increases metabolism to use up the excess catecholamines produced by stress is why people are told to work out when they feel stressed and anxious. The more intense the exercise, however, the more catecholamines are released, which creates a state of arousal and the release of even more catecholamines. "This is why taking a walk is a successfully calming solution to a stressful situation, whereas running an intense mile is not" (Stamford 1987, 184).

Chemical reactions in the body affect individuals differently. Furthermore, the rush experience is different from one person to the next. Consequently, all gang members do not share the same rush experience, but this theory (that youths join a gang in part because gang life provides a rush) does help to explain why wealthy kids join a gang—they are looking for thrills and excitement. It would be interesting to conduct research experiments to determine whether chemical reactions among gang members vary compared to those with more conventional lifestyles. It might also be interesting to test for gender differences. For example, are males more likely to experience the rush than females, considering that a larger percentage of conventional males than conventional females engage in dangerous activities? According to Walker-Barnes and Mason (2001) a higher percentage of males report that they joined a gang because they found it fun and exciting. But this does not indicate whether males experience the rush more than females. Gang members certainly feed off of the energy created by catecholamines and generally thrive in violent crisis situations. Conversely, conventional citizens prefer to avoid volatile and violent situations.

There appears to be a decreasing level of civility in society today, although historians and sociologists will state there have always been great levels of incivility throughout history. Perhaps what has really manifested itself lately is an increasing number of outward displays of rage that so many people feel today. Bonnie Berry (1998) warned about the increased levels of rage years ago, and it seems as though incidents and varieties of rage have only continued to increase throughout the 2000s. A prime example of the outward display of rage today is road rage. Road rage takes many forms, from such behaviors as aggressive driving so that another driver cannot pass or turn off and waving the middle finger in hostility to cutting someone off, getting in fist fights, and drive-by shootings. A great number of people exhibit car rage—old and young, male and female—who are otherwise mellow individuals. So why do drivers become so irritated by the slightest perceived form of disrespect? Is it the anonymity of the situation by which the individuals involved feel the incident is so isolated that it does not impact their personalities? Is it related to the fact that when driving a car, especially one made of steel, drivers feel power—power that they might not possess in any other social sphere? Perhaps it's because we live in an instant-gratification society where patience is considered by more and more of us to be equivalent to subservience and weakness. The answers are complex and multiple. But the implication is almost scary. Only gang members seem to take being disrespected so seriously that it warrants a physical retaliation. Perhaps conventional citizens are becoming more like gang members than gang members are becoming like regular citizens.

Rage is an emotional response to stimuli. It is an "expression of a primitive explosive affective state" (Cartwright 2002, 22). The emotion of rage may be the result of a number of factors: the trauma associated with growing up in a bad neighborhood, being a victim of abuse, the lack of a trusted family member to turn to when in trouble, and victimization outside the home. As an emotion, rage is more intense than hatred (Berry 1998). Rage can be personal and it can also be social, as when a number of people focus their rage at a social event, phenomenon, or social category of people (Berry 1998). Some people find rage to be an irrational behavior, whereas others view it as a final, desperate, but calculated undertaking perpetrated by individuals to reach a desired end. Intolerance toward others is generally involved with rage. The person displaying the rage is deeply upset with the actions of someone else or simply the very presence of the other. Gang members are very intolerant of rivals, and they almost always display violent rage toward rivals. The very presence of rival gang members is enough to set off gang members. Violence is the only way they know to deal with confrontation: It is taught, accepted, and carried out on a regular basis. Rage is the very life blood of many gangsters.

Certain people, sometimes called **rage junkies**, seem to feel much better when their system is operating on increased levels of adrenaline. Rage junkies have become addicted to the "drug-like high" that the adrenaline rush provides. It intoxicates the rage junkie. Highly violent people experience this rush of adrenaline; in fact, they feel far more comfortable with this high stress level. The adrenaline high combined with hate is deadly. Hard-core gang members are especially high-strung and will act violently at the slightest provocation. There are many **rage junkies** in American society, as there are in all societies. Most are violence-prone and angry. They are angry over personal and socially defined failures and they need a target at which to direct their anger. Usually these targets are **scapegoats**—readily available, often weaker persons blamed for society's wrongs (e.g., immigrants).

Rage is a form of retribution, but it is not therapeutic. For example, murder victims' families generally do not feel better or even satisfied when the condemned are executed (Verhovek 1997). Rage is a type of "expressive justice" that generally does not satisfy the people who vented the rage and intolerance although they expected that it would (Anderson 1995). Thus, rage seldom provides the relief anticipated by conventional people. Conventional people, those who have developed a strong bond to society, will find positive ways to deal with their rage by taking out their aggressions on a punching bag or participating in some other rigorous activity as a means of blowing off steam. However, gang members appear to receive great satisfaction from rage aimed at rival gang members as well as toward law enforcement.

Jack Katz, in his book *Seductions of Crime* (1988) described how individuals experienced "sneaky thrills" through various property crimes. "A common thread running through vandalism, joyriding, and shoplifting is that all are sneaky crimes that frequently thrill their practitioners" (Katz 1988, 53). Katz explained that the sneaky thrill is created by a series of three events:

1. ***Being seduced to deviance***—The person flirts with the idea of committing a crime. "In most accounts of shoplifting, the shoplifters enter with the idea of stealing but usually do not have a particular object in mind" (Katz 1988, 53). When a situation arises where it appears to be easy to steal, the seduction becomes stronger.
2. ***The ability to create an aura of "normal appearances"***—Amateur thieves often draw attention to themselves because they become so self-centered that they believe everyone is looking at them. "At some point on the way toward all sneaky thrills, the person realizes that she must work to maintain a conventional, calm appearance up to and through the point of exit" (Katz 1988, 59). Remaining cool under pressure is a trait desired by criminals as well as by conventional persons.
3. ***Appreciation of success***—When the criminal has successfully accomplished the crime, a feeling of elation is derived. This is when the thrill is completely experienced. "Usually after the scene of risk is successfully exited, the third stage of the sneaky thrill is realized. This is the euphoria of being thrilled" (Katz 1988, 64).

Katz (1988, 73) concluded that deviant persons appreciate the act of doing evil because "it is literally wonderful." In order words, the thrill of committing acts of delinquency may be enough of a stimulus to entice certain individuals to engage in criminal pursuits.

Committing property crimes is not nearly exciting enough for some people; they seek more extreme forms of thrills. For these people, "thrill killing" is the ultimate expression of criminality. If the reader has a hard time understanding how someone could kill for the "thrill of it," consider that research conducted by McDevitt, Levin, and Bennett (2002) led to the conclusion that some hate crimes are committed simply because the individual reported having nothing better to do. Two-thirds of hate crimes committed were done merely for the thrill and immature desire to display power and to experience the rush at the expense of someone else (McDevitt et al. 2002). If simply being bored and having nothing better to do can lead to hate crimes, then taking the next step of actually killing another living being becomes a little more understandable. There are many types of **thrill killers**. Poachers represent one category of thrill killers. Poaching is the illegal taking or possession of any game, fish, or nongame wildlife. Hunting out of season or out of the district for which one has a valid license, hunting at night with a spotlight, taking more than the legal limit, and a nonresident buying a resident license all fall into the poaching category (*Colorado Department of Natural Resources* 2003). Poaching is a big problem in places like Colorado. Poaching and thrill-killing of game animals leaves more dead and wounded animals than those killed by licensed hunters. Poachers kill for a trophy. According to John Bredehoft, chief of law enforcement for the Colorado Division of Wildlife (DOW), most poachers are not poor people trying to feed their families. They kill for the thrill of killing, for trophies, and for profit—since trophy heads, antlers, and bear gall bladders are worth thousands of dollars (*Colorado Department of Natural Resources* 2003). Colorado authorities have found poachers to range from sophisticated and well-organized crime rings to groups of teenagers who wantonly kill elk, deer, and antelope for the sheer "fun" of it.

Serial killers represent another category of thrill killers. A serial killer is someone who murders many victims with some common trait in a designated time frame. There is a common perception that serial killers are almost always white males in their early twenties to forties who lack a strong family environment. According to the FBI (2005), the majority of serial killers are not reclusive, social misfits who live alone. They are not monsters and may not appear strange. Many serial killers hide in plain sight within their communities. Furthermore, many serial killers have families, own homes, and are gainfully employed. They appear to be normal members of the community. It is because they are so easily able to blend in that they are often overlooked by law enforcement and the public. The FBI (2005) also states that it is a myth that serial killers are predominantly white. Instead, serial killers span all racial groups and their racial diversification mirrors that of the overall U.S. population.

A mass murderer is not the same as a serial killer, as mass murderers kill a large number of people during a state of rage, often in quick succession, but then do not kill again (e.g., Michael McDermott, the 42-year-old employee of Edgewater Technology in Wakefield, Massachusetts, who opened fire on his co-workers, killing seven of them; and Eric Harris and Dylan Klebold of Columbine High School). Serial killers find a far greater thrill in killing by instilling fear into the general public. "Serial killer Andrew Cunanan terrified the nation during the summer of 1997 by staying on the loose after he killed people in Minnesota, Illinois, and New Jersey. More than two months later, Cunanan committed suicide in Miami Beach, but not before he shot to death his final victim, fashion designer Gianni Versace" (Fox and Levin 2002 1037). There are four types of serial killers: the *visionary*, who kills because he feels internally compelled to do so; the *missionary*, who kills to rid his world of perceived evil; the *thrill-motivated* killer, who does so simply because he enjoys it; and the *lust-motivated* killer, who has sexual motivations for killing. Thrill killers represent perhaps the most dangerous of the serial killers, as the motivation to kill comes from the enjoyment it brings to the killer—it makes them feel good. Thrill-motivated serial killers are also the most likely ones to commit gory murders, often after they have tortured their victims in some heinous fashion. Thrill killers enjoy the rush of the hunt as much as the thrill of the kill. They love running from the police, and if they receive media attention, their thrill level increases all the more. They are truly addicted to adrenalin and need more and more of it because their bodies have become conditioned to adrenalin rushes. Murder represents the ultimate rush for thrill killers.

Although a large number of street gangsters will not commit murder, there are many gang members who will. Consequently, gang members may also represent another category of thrill killers. These gangsters are the hard-core members whose very existence and sense of self are dependent on their gang identity. They will engage in whatever behavior is necessary for the maintenance of the gang. Not all gang members are thrill killers, but nearly all of them will indicate that they get a thrill from gang life, a high that is often incomparable to anything else they have ever experienced. Gang members involved in drive-by shootings state that the desire for excitement provided the necessary momentum to carry out their cowardly deed. When taunts from rivals precede the drive-by shooting, gang members are especially aroused and motivated to action (Davis 1995). Hard-core gang members enjoy life in the fast lane, as there is a rush of power and excitement from living on the edge.

Activities that qualify as **living on the edge** vary from one group to another. For adults in the conventional world just finding a way to pay the bills each month on a salary constitutes life on the edge. For children, self-mutilation and self-injury constitute living on the edge. Self-mutilation includes such activities as burning the skin, taking multiple punches to the arm or body, smoking, multiple piercings, and tattoos. Young people are especially susceptible to thinking that these behaviors are somehow cool. They are activities utilized by adolescents as a means of showing their independence from parental and societal rules and expectations. Gangs recognize that these behaviors draw impressionable youths to the gangs and take full advantage of self-injury by requiring gang recruits to go through a physical initiation and brand themselves with gang tattoos. Individuals who can justify self-mutilation have a much easier time justifying injuring others, especially rival gang members.

One need not be a delinquent to understand the lure of excitement from living on the edge, or enjoying life in the fast lane; many conventional people embrace this ideology and consider themselves to be "adrenaline-rush junkies." They seek the rush in such legitimate ways as rock and mountain climbing, skydiving, parachuting, swimming with sharks, surfing huge waves, riding on roller coasters, auto racing, playing chicken with on-coming traffic, hopping trains, watching scary movies, playing video games like *Grand Theft Auto: Vice City*, and so on. When someone climbs Mt. Everest, he/she is commended, even though there is the constant risk of death. Large ocean swells can be very dangerous, but for surfers, the lure of waves caused by ocean storms or surfing the Pipeline in Hawaii or Mavericks in Northern California are the ultimate rush. Many people wish that they could fly. Skydiving and parachuting are forms of human flight. Trapeze performers are able to temporarily fly in the air. The artists who perform their daring feats high above the crowd and without a net are both excited and scared at the same time. Their hearts beat fast as they swing on the trapeze. For a moment in time, when they let go of the trapeze and wait for their partner to reach out and grab them, they are experiencing human flight. They have achieved "air and speed," a rush that is difficult to match. Stunt fliers who perform such feats as cutting the power to their engines while tumbling toward the ground and restarting just in time to swoop safely upward speak of the rush of adrenaline and fun they receive from performing their tricks. Driving a car fast on an open expressway is a rush that many common (non-adrenaline-rush junkies) people enjoy. People who enjoy riding on roller coasters do so because they find it both fun and semiterrifying—it gives them an adrenaline rush.

Endorphins also provide individuals with an adrenaline rush. Endorphins are morphine-like substances in the brain that block pain, heighten pleasure, and have been associated with some addictions. "Narcotics are thought to mimic or enhance the activity of endorphins, which are proteins produced by the brain that control pain and influence other subjective experiences" (Schmalleger 2004, 416). Endorphins are neurotransmitters produced in the brain, which function to transmit electrical signals within the nervous system. In humans, there are at least 20 types of endorphins. Stress and pain are the two most common factors leading to the release of endorphins. When the morphine-like substances are released, our perception of pain dissipates. Endorphins may lead to feelings of euphoria, modulate appetite, release sex hormones, and enhance our immune response. Endorphin release varies among individuals. This means, two people experiencing the same stimuli (e.g., physical exercise, or physical threat) may release different levels of endorphins and therefore act unlike one another. The runner's high that some people experience and others do not is explained, in part, by the varying release of endorphins among runners. Endorphins may be stimulated into action by a variety of seemingly harmless behaviors. For example, friends of mine who belong to a hot chili club state that eating hot chilies provides them with a rush. In other words, people who enjoy eating hot chilis seek to "ride the endorphin rush." Eating chocolate for some people may cause the release of endorphins. That chocolate can release endorphins helps to explain why some people crave it when they are stressed. Sex, acupuncture, and massage therapy may also release an endorphin rush. Research published by Steven Feldman and associates (2004) reveals that tanning is addictive because it appears that the exposure to UV rays triggers the release of endorphins. In their research on tanners who utilize tanning beds, participants reported that they could not go more than a few days without another tanning session or they would feel depressed (Feldman et al. 2004). Tanning may be viewed as addictive (defined as any behavior that makes you feel good but is unhealthful and is a habit that is hard to break without significant effort) because tanners *need* the endorphin rush provided by UV rays. Thus, the reason that people tan extends beyond the perception of improved appearance (the belief that people look better tanned than pale) to the possibility of a physiological effect of UV rays that drives tanning behavior (Feldman et al. 2004). Another example of a mundane trigger of endorphin release may be found in the workplace. Workaholics experience a rush from taking on tasks and challenges with a high stress level. They get off on doing large amounts of work. A great number of law enforcement officers and military personnel report that they receive a rush from performing their jobs because of the realization that they face potential death on a regular basis. In short, many people seek the rush; it should not be surprising that this same idea can be applied to gang behavior as well. In my own interviews with gang members, it is clear to me that many gangsters enjoy the violence of gang activity because they get a rush from it.

Clearly, many people have incorporated legitimate ways of satisfying their need for thrills and the rush. Conventional people fantasize about ways of filling their otherwise boring lifestyles with excitement. An extreme form of "fantasy rush" (as I call it) was detailed in a 2002 *Newswire* report. Controversial Detroit rapper Mr. Scrillion, a.k.a. Adam Thick, offered "extreme kidnapping adventures" to hard-core thrill seekers. The rapper began kidnapping people for his profit and their fun. Extreme kidnapping takes thrill seeking to new heights. The rapper stated, "This service caters to the extreme sports adventurer who is bored with what's currently available; this takes it to a whole new other level. . . . The kidnappings are very realistic, and not for the faint of heart, as every nuance and detail of an actual kidnapping are replicated to provide the most intense experience possible" (*Newswire* 2002, 1). Three different kidnap scenarios are available, and each kidnapping comes with a videotape copy of the adventure so that the client can relive the experience. Extreme kidnapping hardly seems like the type of activity society would like to promote as a means of alleviating boredom.

Clients of extreme kidnapping share something in common with criminals and gang members—they do not go about fulfilling their cravings for the adrenaline rush in ways that mainstream society would prefer. With this idea in mind, it should be understandable why criminals and delinquents have a high disregard for their own safety and the safety of others. In *The Unknown Darkness* (McCrary and Ramsland 2003, xv), former FBI agent Gregg McCrary describes a case where two fugitives, driving from Ohio to Buffalo, had a fully functioning but unstable bomb in their car. "What made it really dangerous was that the shunt of the blasting cap was unprotected. This meant that any extraneous radio transmission or static electricity could have detonated the bomb. They could easily have blown themselves up and some of the bomb techs who dismantled the device were surprised that they hadn't." The fugitives found the ordeal very exciting and reported getting a rush from it all. And that is the way many gangbangers feel about their lives in the gang. They feel as though no one cares about them, so why should they care about themselves. They turn cold and are capable of watching people bleed and die without feeling any remorse. Their disregard for life coupled with the rush that they receive from gangbanging is far more rewarding to them than the alternative, conventional, poverty lifestyle. Furthermore, the fact that people from all socioeconomic classes, races, and ethnicities enjoy experiencing a rush helps to explain why youths from good neighborhoods turn to crime and delinquency. In an attempt to experience a rush, both legitimate and delinquent opportunities are available.

Summary

There are a number of socioeconomic reasons that entice gang members to join a gang. The shifting labor market has left many unskilled workers without work, which in turn has led to the development of an underclass in many urban inner-city neighborhoods. Economics remains a guiding force that lures youths into a gang. Growing up in poverty will stimulate many to take the path that leads directly to a gang lifestyle. The lack of a male role model remains a contributing factor that influences a young male to join a gang. Staying in school and eventually earning a college degree has become increasingly important for most people if they hope to be economically successful in American society. Many youths drop out of school. This free time often leads to a life of delinquency and in some cases joining a gang. Staying in school in some neighborhoods is also problematic, as gangs often attempt to recruit youths frustrated with their life circumstances. Gang life is also attractive to many youths because it provides acceptance, protection, and survival.

Beyond the traditional socioeconomic explanations of gang formation is the reality that many gang members simply enjoy gang life and would lead no other. Owning a firearm provides gang members with a sense of power, something that they lack in the capitalistic system. Feeling a sense of hopelessness, some youths, including gang members, engage in alcohol and other drug use. In many instances, gang members sell drugs to earn money. The mass media, in all of its mediums, often romanticizes gang life, and consequently, making gang participation appealing. Gang members generally experience a rush from gangbanging activity. In short, gang lifestyle is fun, exciting, and dangerous—it provides gangsters an endorphin rush. The adrenaline rush experienced by gang members would be difficult to duplicate by legitimate means. Thus, the "rush factor" becomes a potentially major contributing explanation of why an individual chooses to join a gang.

5

Gang Structure and Process

Based on the information provided so far in this book, it should be clear that there is no such thing as a "typical" gang. However, when focusing solely on street gangs, it is possible to describe the basic structure and the processes that are common to most of them. This chapter analyzes the organizational structure of gangs, gang typologies, and the processes involved in turning to a gang. Beyond all, gang members demand respect—it is the "code of the street."

GANG STRUCTURE

Typically, gangs develop spontaneously, or, as Thrasher (1927) explained, they emerge from playgroups. Children in playgroups hang out with one another for a large portion of their free time and maintain their friendships as they grow up together. These friendship cliques can be viewed as basic building blocks of street gangs. Cliques and friendship cohorts organizing into street gangs are more likely in urban environments. Cohort gang groupings are called *klikas* (the term *clique* is more common) in cholo gangs and *sets* in African-American gangs (Reiner 1992). The degree to which they organize into gangs is dependent on many factors.

The Organizational Structure

Organizational structures of street gangs have varied widely over time, and vary extensively from city to city and even within cities (Regoli and Hewitt 2003). The Vice Lords, based out of Chicago, are an example of a highly organized gang, having created an administrative body called the "board" designed to deal with matters affecting the entire Vice Lord Nation. Keiser (1969) found that the Vice Lords held regular meetings with representatives from all the subgroups present. The gangsters were given printed membership cards with the Vice Lords insignia (a top hat, cane, and white gloves). But the highly organized structure of the Vice Lords is more the exception than the rule, as most gangs are not nearly so established. At the opposite extreme of the Vice Lords' structural arrangement are gangs that Yablonsky (1959) described as "near groups." The term *near groups* is applied to street gangs when their organizational structure is so rudimentary that they fall far short of the criminal demands of a more organized or stable group. Other researchers, such as Short (1974), argue that gangs fall somewhere in the middle. In my research I found that most of Upstate New York's (Syracuse, Rochester, and Buffalo) gangs are loosely confederated, with the exception of local Crips gangs in Buffalo, which possessed many structured qualities.

The Commonwealth of Virginia Department of State Police (2008) compares the organizational structure of sets of Bloods gangs to paramilitary and Mafia-style organizations. For example, the Southside Brim Bloods of Petersburg (Virginia) have this hierarchy:

1. Triple OG (original gangster)
2. OG
3. Baby OG
4. OYG (Older Young Gangsters)
5. Youngster Gangster
6. OBG (Older Baby Gangster)
7. Baby Gangster

The Virginia State Police also provide the structure of the Nine Trey Gangsters, Blood sets found in numerous Virginia cities, and indicate that this hierarchy is common with a number of Blood sets outside of Virginia as well:

1. Godfather
2. BIG 020
3. Low 020
4. 5 Star General
5. 4 Star General
6. 3 Star General
7. 2 Star General
8. 1 Star General

Blood gang sets may use additional organizational structures, including ranks of ministers, captains, and lieutenants. At the top is the Original Gangster (OG) or Godfather. The set leader is typically a proven member of the gang, an OG (Commonwealth of Virginia Department of State Police 2008). Blood sets share set names with larger West Coast and East Coast Bloods and may not all be directly connected to the greater nation but they usually have knowledge of Bloods' history and rules.

As discussed throughout this text, the sizes of street gangs vary a great deal. We will learn much more about the different size of gangs in Chapter 6. However, regardless of the size of any particular gang, or a set from a larger gang, most gangs have a core number of members (that may range from about 10 to 12 in smaller gangs and as many as 30 to 40 in larger ones) who form the nucleus of the gang. The core members oversee the activities of the total unit. The core clique generally consists of the most violent members, and it is from this group that a leader emerges. Like any organized, or quasi-organized, group, gangs have leaders. This is not surprising as all groups and organizations have a difficult time carrying out their duties without some form of leadership. Gang members, however, seldom resemble corporate executives. Instead, they are more like captains of a sports team, a role that can change from one circumstance to another or from one time period to another. The more established the gang, the more established the leadership role of the gang leader. In less established street gangs, the leadership role is far more informal in character.

The **gang leader** is usually a longtime member who has climbed the ranks and is generally looked up to by the other members. The stereotype of the gang leader as someone who is tough, possesses a long criminal history, and holds a strong influence over members is an accurate portrayal of most gang leaders. The gang leader is expected to remain calm under pressure and lead by example. In most cases, the leader gains his/her position based on reputation, as opposed to any "voting-in" procedures by the members. (*Note*: This "might makes right" mentality exists in the animal kingdom, for example, an alpha male in dog and gorilla packs.) As might be expected, the leadership role is a fleeting one. As Klein (1995) explains, "the typical leader does not maintain influence over a long period of time. Leadership tends to be very situational. . . . This is because gang leadership, as with most groups, is a function of the group rather than individuals" (63).

Nonetheless, gangs have clear leaders, and when a gang leader loses the leadership position, another gang member will step in to take over. As with many organizations, there are different types of leaders. Some leaders are charismatic, ruling by the dynamics of personality. A gang led by a **charismatic leader** has certain differences from a gang led by a militaristic leader.

The charismatic leader possesses a personality and charm that is appealing to group members. Charismatic leaders pay close attention to details by scanning and reading their environment, and are good at picking up the moods and concerns of others. The charismatic gang leader is revered by his/her fellow gang members. Like all charismatic leaders, they use a wide variety of methods to manage their image and to assure their position of power. Charismatic gang leaders will, on occasion, manipulate other gang members into aggressive or violent actions just to meet their own selfish needs. Charismatic leaders rule the gang for as long as their members buy into their charms and accept the identity of the gang under their leadership.

In gangs that are more highly structured, the leader is more militaristic, or Mafia-styled. The **militaristic leader** gives orders to the next in command, who in turn transmits them throughout the ranks by a chain-of-command system (Regoli and Hewitt 2003). The militaristic leader rarely provides praise and frequently employs criticism as a means of maintaining power. In the corporate setting such a leadership style undercuts morale and job satisfaction. With street gangs, like the military, such a style is designed to maintain a clear sense of who is in charge and who makes final decisions on group matters.

Historically, turf protection appears to be the most common reason that gangs organize in particular neighborhoods. This has been evident since the formation of Irish gangs in New York City in the early and mid-1800s. The more traditional the street gang and the longer the gang has been in existence, the more important is the notion of protecting turf, or the neighborhood.

Over the past couple of decades, the idea of protecting a specific neighborhood, park, housing project, or school because such an area was the stationary home of street gangs has been somewhat replaced as automobiles make gangs more mobile, families of gang members relocate, and the incarceration of gangsters. The growth of prison gangs has also impacted the structure of street gangs, as over the past several years the two have become more closely intertwined. Prison gangs such as the Aryan Brotherhood (AB), the Mexican Mafia, Nuestra Familia, the Black Guerilla Family, and the Texas Syndicate recruit and train street gang members into their more established and structured organizations (Welling 1994). The influence of organized prison gangs added to the increased mobility of gangs, and their growing control of the illicit drug market has made it clear that street gangs have evolved from their early, simple goal of protecting turf. According to Welling (1994, 148), "it is difficult to find a community or correctional system whose local gangs have not been influenced by outside groups. As a result, local street gangs are evolving into multi-jurisdictional drug organizations throughout the nation."

As stated earlier, some gangs have a militaristic style of leadership. These gangs tend to be similar in organizational structure to the military in other ways besides leadership. A closer examination of the military reveals some of the similarities to gangs.

ORGANIZATIONAL PARALLELS BETWEEN STREET GANGS AND THE MILITARY   Among the similarities between street gangs and the military are the reasons members join, ceremonies of induction and violation ceremonies for disobeying rules, specific clothing and style of dress, a ranking structure, the use of symbols and acronyms, and protection of turf.

The U.S. Army was established on July 14, 1775. Gangs have existed in the United States in one form or another since the colonial era. In some cases, people have been drafted into the armed services, just as some youths find themselves "drafted" (or recruited) into the local gang (youths as young as age 8 are considered at risk in certain large urban neighborhoods). In most cases, however, people have volunteered their service to the military, just as most youths voluntarily join the gang. Sociologists have identified a number of specific reasons why youths join a street gang: identity, discipline, recognition, love, belonging, and money (Nawojczyk 1997). Young people join the army for these same reasons.

Induction into the military and the street gang involves **initiation ceremonies**. Gang members are typically "jumped"—beaten severely to find out how tough they are and to determine if they can take a beating—as a form of initiation. Other ceremonies of initiation may involve acts that range from robbery to shooting someone. Once youths have satisfactorily met the demands of initiation, they become a member of the gang. The military puts its recruits through nine weeks of basic training (boot camp). (*Note:* A Syracuse gang that calls itself "Boot Camp" will be discussed in Chapter 6.) When recruits have successfully met the physical requirements, they graduate into the military. Graduation is accompanied by a ceremony held to recognize the accomplishments of the recruits. Gang members likewise hold celebrations. When gang members violate a group rule, they risk a violation ceremony (a form of punishment) that may involve a physical beating or some form of compensation. Military personnel who violate rules are subject to the loss of privileges and risk possible military imprisonment.

Clothing and **style of dress** are important elements and a means of identification for both the military and the gang. There are different uniforms for each branch of the military and specific uniforms that are to be worn for certain occasions and ceremonies, along with guidelines as to how they are to be worn, and camouflaged-colored uniforms to be worn in specific environments in order to blend into the background. Among the restrictive rules governing military dress (as dictated by the *Officer's Guide*) are these: "There is authorized material as to weave, color, weight, design, and manner. The uniforms will be worn when on duty as to represent the United States military" (*Officer's Guide*, 115). In wearing the cotton uniform or BDU (Battle Dress Uniform) there are certain ways to wear the uniform. "Socks must be knee length, sufficient to provide for a turnover of 2½ to 3 inches at top, to reach a point about 1 inch below the bottom of the knee cap. The shirt worn must be cotton, with 8.2 ounces brown in color, Army shade No. 1; and appropriate dress wear is expected at social functions" (*Officer's Guide*, 130). Clearly, military personnel dress in a manner that distinguishes them from the civilian population. Gang members also dress in a manner that distinguishes them from the general population. Military clothing is worn just loose enough to break up the silhouette of the body; it is not so loose that it nearly falls off the service person or presents an unprofessional look. Gang members, however, wear their clothing loose to help conceal weapons. Although gang members are often stereotyped as wearing baseball caps backward, big necklaces with crosses and stars, and gold jewelry, this look can be deceiving, for many wannabes also dress in this manner. Gang colors and clothing are a trademark of street gangs. In Schneider's (1999) research on gangs, he found that "most gang members employed some insignia or wore some item of clothing that, like colors on a ship, declared the wearer's allegiance" (145). The African-American super gangs the Bloods and Crips are known for their colors of red and blue, respectively. The flashing of colors is most notable in the wearing of bandannas. The bandanna is often treated with the same level of respect the military pays to the American flag. In time of battle, the flag, or bandanna, is never to be left behind for enemy capture. Tattoo branding is another notable method of displaying one's loyalty to a specific gang, or branch of the military. Nearly all gang members, male and female, have had extensive ink done as a way of displaying their gang affiliation.

The military shares another characteristic typically found in street gangs, **rank** and **structure**. The military's very foundation is built on a strict hierarchical structure with a clear-cut ranking system. Orders are to be followed without question and individuality is completely lost. At the bottom of the ranking system is the private, and at the other extreme is the general. Promotion through the ranks is possible after years of service and distinguished performance. As in any organizational structure, the higher the rank, the greater the responsibility. Gangs are also built around a hierarchical structure, although this ranking system varies greatly. As mentioned, the Vice Lords are known to be a highly organized gang with a clear-cut stratification system. Examples of the many different typologies of gangs will be presented later in this chapter.

Symbols and **acronyms** are common to both street gangs and the military. The primary function of symbols and acronyms is in communication between personnel. Effective communication is essential in the military. One example of an attempt to avoid confusion includes associating words with letters of the alphabet during radio and phone transmission (e.g., *Alpha* equals A, *Bravo* is used for B). Symbols and acronyms allow the military to code messages so that enemy personnel cannot steal important information. Gangs rely heavily on symbolism, especially when communicating through the use of graffiti. "Graffiti serves three main purposes for gangs: It defines turf; it provides the opportunity to issue a challenge or a warning; and it reports the neighborhood news" (Schneider 1999, 151). A great deal of information can be learned about gangs through their use of graffiti (see Chapter 6 for further analysis). Street gang members use **hand signals** to flash gang signs as a means of representing their gang membership and to challenge rivals to identify themselves. (See "Connecting Street Gangs and Popular Culture" Box 5.1 for a description of the use of gang signs in an episode of the television show Seinfeld.) Military operations often involve personnel using hand signals when they wish to be stealthy but still need to carry out instructions to fellow members.

In Chapter 6 we will learn about the distinction between rural, small city, regional, national, and transnational gangs. Nation gangs, such as the Crips and Bloods, have affiliations or sets of interrelated gangs throughout the United States. The military has bases throughout the country. Transnational gangs have sets throughout multiple nations, so too does the U.S. military have bases around the world. Furthermore, the military is divided into divisions: Army, Navy, Air Force, Marines, and Coast Guard. The Folks and People, two Chicago-based street gangs, have divisions. For example, the Vice Lords and Latin Kings are a part of the People nation.

Protecting **turf** remains important for many gangs, but as mentioned earlier that concept has changed for some street gangs. However, as gangs continue to take control of the drug market, protecting their expanded turf remains important. As for the military, its primary function and reason for existence is the protection of turf—American territories—to protect U.S. citizens from their enemies and external threats to basic democratic freedoms.

All these characteristics reveal that street gangs and the military share many similarities. In addition, by their very design, both the military and street gangs are violent entities, value camaraderie and group goals and values, seek goals, insist on respect for internal authority, demand respect and honor, and appear to be permanent fixtures of society. But despite the many similarities between street gangs and the military, there is at least one glaring difference: The military is a legitimate social institution, whereas street gangs are illegitimate in purpose and design.

> ## Box 5.1 *Connecting Street Gangs and Popular Culture*
>
> ### *Seinfeld* and the Van Buren Boys: Kramer Inadvertently Flashes a Gang Sign
>
> Among the more popular microsociological perspectives is symbolic interactionism. Symbolic interactionism is based on the idea that social reality is constructed in each human interaction through the use of symbols. Symbols include such things as words and gestures. Our very ability to communicate with one another is predicated on shared understandings of the meaning of symbols. Motorists, for example, must have a shared meaning on the significance of *yield* and *stop* signs, symbols designed to convey specific messages to all participants involved. It is critical that motorists understand that green lights mean *go* and red lights mean *stop*. If people misunderstand the meanings of these symbols, trouble and potential chaos may occur. There are many occasions where any one of us may mistake the symbolic communication of others. For example, an attractive person from across the room suddenly waves at you, so you happily wave back only to learn that the wave was intended for the person behind you. You walk by someone sitting on a bench who loudly yells an obscenity that you believe is directed at you. Turning around, you find that the person is yelling into his phone at the person on the other end. In these two examples, participants have demonstrated the ability to modify their behaviors to meet the needs of the present and immediate environment. In other cases, however, people are not so quick or willing to process the meanings of perceived symbolic communication. For example, in 2008, a Portland, Oregon, high school banned its students from shaving vertical lines into their eyebrows because school authorities considered it gang related. In reality eyebrow shaving was a tribute to hip-hop star Soulja Boy, a trend he had made popular (*The Citizen* 2008). I recall a story I read in the *Los Angeles Times* many years ago wherein a motorcycle at a red light with two riders who were communicating with one another through the use of hand signs. Standing nearby were a group of gang members who misinterpreted the flashing signs for gang signs from their rivals, so they opened fire, killing the two on the bike. As it turned out, the two riders were deaf students from a nearby college and they were merely using actual sign language to communicate. The point of these stories is to highlight the symbolic interactionist perspective reminder that while social reality is constructed in each human interaction, effective communication occurs only when all parties involved clearly understand the messages being conveyed.
>
> Language is a very critical element in human interaction. Language allows individuals to discuss and understand ideas and events that transcend the immediate environment and place and time. For example, if a Latin King gang member wanders into an unknown neighborhood and notices pitchfork graffiti, he knows that he is in Gangster Disciple territory. Even if he does not notice any of his rivals in the immediate vicinity, the Gangster Disciple pitchfork is a clear symbol that danger is imminent. Street gangs rely heavily on symbolic communication, and symbols such as pitchfork graffiti are a clear message to anyone who can read graffiti. Graffiti serves many symbolic purposes, including declaration of territory, warnings to rivals, and remembrances for fallen brethren. Gang members identify with one another in a variety of ways, including the use of colors (to be discussed in Chapter 6) and the use of secret hand signs.
>
> One of the more interesting examples of popular culture to provide us with a look at street gangs comes from one of the most popular television shows of all time, *Seinfeld*. Once described as a show about "nothing," this author has argued in *Seinology: The Sociology of Seinfeld* that *Seinfeld* was really a show about "everything." Sociology is an academic discipline about everything found in the social world and *Seinfeld* seemingly covered nearly as many topics, including street gangs. In the "Van Buren Boys" episode a number of basic elements of gang life, such as the importance of group loyalty, the use of secret hand signals, and initiation rites, come to life.
>
> In the "Van Buren Boys" episode, Kramer retells an experience to Jerry and Elaine in Jerry's apartment about his recent visit to Lorenzo's Pizzeria. Kramer was at Lorenzo's adding spices to a slice of pizza when he notices someone giving him the "stink eye." Kramer responds by giving the guy the "crooked eye." Kramer notices that this guy is not alone and it dawns on him that he is suddenly about to be

confronted by the Van Buren Boys (VB Boys), a white street gang. Jerry asks Kramer, "There's a street gang named after President Martin Van Buren?" Kramer replies, "Oh yeah, and they are just as mean as he was." Kramer tells Jerry and Elaine that he made a move for the front door but the VB Boys blocked it. He tries to find sanctuary in the bathroom but the door is locked. The VB Boys back Kramer up against the wall and all of a sudden they just stop. Elaine asks why. Kramer explains that he was still holding the garlic shaker that he was using to sprinkle garlic on his pizza. He had eight fingers showing (a thumb and pointer finger on one hand are covered by the shaker). As it turns out, Kramer had inadvertently flashed their gang sign—eight fingers. The VB Boys were named after Martin Van Buren, who was the eighth president (and first native-born president) of the United States, because they so admired him. When the gang sees Kramer flash the "8" sign they believe him to be an OG (original gangster, or original member of the gang) because he appears to be flashing their secret gang sign. Modifying their perception of Kramer, the VB Boys immediately back off and let him go about his business. The ability to modify one's interpretation of symbols is a basic tenet of symbolic interactionism. It is also common behavior for gangs to show respect to fellow gang members, OGs especially. Kramer was lucky that he happened to flash a sign that this particular gang respected and that he did not flash a sign from a rival gang.

The "Van Buren Boys" episode proceeds to include George Costanza. George is working for his late wife's foundation and is charged with finding a worthy high school scholarship recipient. Initially George chooses an "average Joe," Steven Koren (the name of one of show's writers and producers), instead of a high achiever, but then changes his mind after he feels as though he was disrespected by the youth. Steven is so distraught he joins the VB Boys. When George is confronted on the street by the gang he tries to act like an OG and attempts to flash, what he believes to be, gang signs. The gangsters tell George that he is not flashing the correct signs. Feeling uneasy being confronted by a gang that includes a youth, he just disrespected by taking away his scholarship, George says, "It was (the sign) when I was bangin'." The gang challenges George. The leader says, "If you are really one of us, take the wallet of the next guy that walks by." This is a type of initiation process to demonstrate group loyalty. Nervously, George agrees. The next people to walk by are Jerry's parents, Morty and Helen. As the gang hides in the alley, George quietly tries to tell the Seinfelds to play along with him and let him take Morty's wallet. Not understanding what George is up to, the Seinfelds walk away. In an act of desperation, George tries to take Helen's handbag from her, but she slaps George and tells him that he is being very rude. Jerry's parents walk away. George is empty-handed. Sensing impending danger from the VB Boys, George runs away; a good tactic for anyone not skilled in fighting a street gang.

COMPARING STREET GANGS TO A VIOLENT TRIBE In their 1997 book *Waorani: The Contexts of Violence and War*, Clayton and Carole Robarchek compare street gangs to the Waorani tribe, found near the Amazon River in Ecuador. Anthropologists have described the Waorani as the most murderous people on Earth. "Virtually no one lived to old age. Entire families were routinely wiped out with 9-foot spears. And the notion of killing a child was no more abhorrent than the notion of killing a snake. A staggering six out of 10 Waorani deaths came at the hands of another Waorani" (Fiore 1997, A1). As the Robarcheks (1997) explained, the Waorani did everything necessary, including engaging in brutal warfare, to keep themselves isolated from other tribes in the Amazonian Ecuador. They regularly engaged in lethal vendettas among themselves well into the second half of the twentieth century. In the past century, more than 60 percent of Waorani deaths have been the result of homicide; consequently, anthropologists consider the Waorani as the most violent society known to exist (Yost 1981). A few clans of Waorani still remain hidden in the vast expanse of the rainforest that spans the disputed frontier between Ecuador and Peru and are still at war with each other and with outsiders (Robarchek and Robarchek 1997).

The Robarcheks (1997, 3) used their research on the Waorani to defend their central theoretical premise that human behavior "is not the determined result of ecological or biological or socioeconomic forces acting on them, but, rather, is motivated by what they want to achieve in their world as they perceive and understand it. Within their experienced reality, people make choices based on the information available to them—information about themselves, about the world around them, and about possible goals and objectives in that world." The Robarcheks contend that gang members, like the Waorani, choose to behave violently not because of a biological predisposition or because of socioeconomic reasons. As for the Waorani, their western Amazon habitat has been a violent place for many centuries and predates the Inca's attempt to colonize the eastern foothills and the early incursions by the Spanish colonialists. The Waorani had managed to hold back any attempts of outside intrusion into their society through means of a violent defense of their territory. Gang members, especially those found in violent, urban areas, are also willing to use extreme forms of violence to fight back a perceived enemy trying to intrude into their territory. Further illustrating the comparison between the Waorani and street gangs, the Robarcheks argue that the willingness to engage in warfare is premised on loyalty to the group, territoriality, bravado, blood vengeance, the use of violence, and the instrumental need for self-validation.

The Robarcheks also described how the Waorani, were transformed, virtually overnight, from a murderous tribe to a relatively peaceful people after being convinced by missionaries that less violent behaviors possessed worthwhile benefits. The murder rate fell by more than 90 percent. The Robarcheks believe that the behavior of gang members can also be altered. Critics of their theory have difficulty getting past the comparison of urban gangs to a jungle tribe, finding it racially insensitive. The Robarcheks insist that the two "jungles" are similar in what they lack—a community acting as a moral force that is more powerful than personal impulse. In urban areas, the community is viewed as merely an amorphous and amoral aggregation with no psychological saliency, nor a consistent model with which to identify or build upon (Robarchek and Robarchek 1997). When young people lack psychologically meaningful communities, they create their own and establish a reference group and a sense of identity. Group cohesion is predicated on loyalty and embracing the subcultural norms shared by group members. Some of these norms promote conventional cultural values such as loyalty, courage, and materialism, while other norms promote subcultural values such as intimidation, vengeance, and murder (Robarchek and Robarchek 1997).

COMPARING STREET GANGS TO GREEK LIFE Many subcultural groups identify themselves by wearing matching colors, throwing hand signs, participating in ritualistic behaviors, and using jargon relatively unique to them. Street gangs certainly engage in these behavioral patterns and so do fraternities and sororities. Through socialization and association, individuals decide to join gangs and fraternal organizations to gain a sense of identity. Members of both street gangs and the Greek fraternities identify themselves with specific colors, symbols, use of hand signs, and may often engage in deviant or criminal activities. As described in Chapter 2, gangs have existed, in shape or form, throughout American history and actually predate the formation of the United States. The American academic Greek system has long roots too, dating back to pre-independence. The first fraternity dates back to 1750 at the College of William and Mary in Williamsburg, Virginia. Known as the "Flat Hat Club," the members met periodically in a meeting room of the Raleigh Tavern. Thomas Jefferson, author of the U.S. Declaration of Independence, was a student member of this club (Elon University 2012). (*Note:* Ten of the founding members of the Flat Hat Club went on to form the Freemasons.) The first Greek-letter society was formed in 1776 at William and Mary when John Heath was refused admission into a campus organization known as PDA (a secret organization known publicly as "Please Don't

Ask"). With four friends, Heath organized a society of his own using Greek letters to name it: Phi Beta Kappa (PBK). Before long, the Greek system spread to colleges and universities in rural, suburban, and city environments across the nation. Street gangs also spread across the nation over a period of time.

PBK introduced an essential characteristic of the Greek community, and one embraced by street gangs: secrecy. PBK introduced the idea of initiation process, hand shakes known and used only by members of the fraternity, and a code of laws by which all members were to abide. Street gangs embrace these same traditions. With street gangs, initiations generally involve some sort of physical beating administered by group members in an effort to ascertain the degree of commitment and loyalty of the recruit to the gang. Fraternities have long held initiation ceremonies that traditionally involved some sort of physical beating known as hazing. Today, colleges and universities forbid the use of hazing in the Greek system. Street gangs still value the physical beating process but also opt for the recruit to commit a crime. Members of street gangs wear certain clothing items and colors as a means of identification; members of fraternal organizations wear their colors and Greek letters on jackets, shirts, hats, pins, and so on to demonstrate their membership and unity with a specific organization. Both street gangs and Greek-lettered organizations possess a hierarchical structure, with older members generally ranking above younger ones. Although members may come and go from street gangs and fraternities and sororities, most participants are considered members for life.

The reasons why someone joins a gang have been discussed in Chapters 3 and 4, but in many cases, individuals join for the companionship, camaraderie, and sense of family the organization brings. Students join the Greek system for many of the same reasons except for one glaring difference. With the Greeks, membership represents a great line item for the résumé and may lead to employment opportunities through association. Belonging to a gang does little for one's résumé, especially when seeking employment in the conventional world. PBK was formed for intellectual purposes and possessed the cardinal principles of literature, morality, and friendship (Elon University 2012). Street gangs are not concerned with the pursuit of increased knowledge and are usually composed of high school dropouts. Another difference between the two organizations involves deviancy. While it is true that frats and sororities make the news from time to time for hazing incidents and out-of-control parties, most of their time is spent in productive endeavors, including academic achievement and volunteering in the community. For example, chapters of Lambda Sigma Latino fraternity raise money for AIDS awareness. Street gang activities are primarily destructive and criminal.

Gang Typologies

The structure of gangs can be differentiated in many ways other than their organizational component. Distinctions can be made based on such variables as age (e.g., a baby posse or veteranos), race and ethnicity (Hispanic, African American, Asian, white, Native American, or, in rare cases, mixed), gender composition (all males, all females, or mixed), setting (e.g., streets, prison, or motorcycle), type of activity (e.g., drug sales, protection, violence, turf defense), and degree of criminality (e.g., minor or serious). These distinctions, along with others, provide a number of typologies with which to classify gangs.

AGE-GRADED GANGS   The hierarchical structure of street gangs is often determined by the simple variable of age. Hagedorn's studies of street gangs in Milwaukee revealed that they emerged from ordinary street-corner peer groups (in the same sense that Thrasher described).

Some of the gangs evolved from local dance groups. Conflicts with other groups and the police accelerated the transition from a cohort group to a gang. Hagedorn concluded that Milwaukee street gangs could be classified as **age-graded**. Furthermore, the age of the youth would determine the level of commitment to the gang. Hagedorn (1988) found that there were four main age groupings:

1. The Ancients—20 years and older
2. The Seniors—ages 16–19
3. The Juniors—ages 12–15
4. The Pee Wees—ages 8–11

I conducted research on Buffalo street gangs in the early 2000s and one of the first individuals I interviewed was a former member of the Fruit Belt Posse (FBP). Having emerged primarily as an offspring of the **Mad Dogs**, the **Fruit Belt Posse** (named after an area of Buffalo where the streets are named after fruit trees) has an infamous history in Buffalo (see Chapter 6). As explained to me, the FBP is an example of an age-graded gang, with most members joining the gang in their early youth along with their fellow peers. Joining a gang as peers is common, especially in close-knit communities as kids tend to look out for one another and question the presence of outsiders. This bond of loyalty generally serves as a precursor for forming a gang. The FBP typology is given here:

1. Senior Posse—ages 16–20
2. Junior Posse—ages 11–15
3. Baby Posse—10 and younger

Buffalo street gangs will be discussed in greater detail in Chapter 6.

DEGREE OF CRIMINALITY   Gangs exist for different reasons. In some cases, the primary function is defense, as in defending turf. Other gangs exist to make money, so they sell drugs. And still others find extreme pleasure being on offense; that is, they are criminal and predatory in design. Huff (1989), who studied gangs in Cleveland and Columbus, found that most of them emerged from break-dancing or rappin' groups (informal groups of peers). Other gangs evolved from regular street-corner groups as a result of conflict with rival groups. Some of these Ohio gangs were influenced by gangsters from Chicago and Los Angeles, who brought with them leadership skills learned from larger urban environments. Huff's (1989) typology of Cleveland and Columbus gangs reflects the level of commitment that gang members had to criminal activities:

1. *Hedonistic*—These types of gangs are mainly into drug use and commit little crime, especially violent crime.
2. *Instrumental*—Gangs that commit property crime, use drugs and alcohol, but seldom sell drugs.
3. *Predatory*—Gangs that are heavily involved in serious crime (e.g., robbery, murder), seriously abuse addictive drugs (e.g., crack), and may sell drugs, but not in an organized fashion.

DEGREE OF ATTACHMENT TO AND INVOLVEMENT WITH THE GANG   Vigil (1988a) and Vigil and Long (1990) distinguished four basic types of gang members based on their degree of attachment to and involvement with the gang:

1. *Regulars (hard cores)*—These are members strongly attached to the gang, have few interests outside of the gang, and started in the gang at an early age. These gang members usually had tough childhoods and tend to be very violent as gang members. They usually

lacked a consistent male adult authority figure in their lives. They are often called "hard core" members because their very identity is directly tied to their gang affiliation. They are very influential within the gang structure and have the highest level of attachment and commitment to the gang.

2. ***Peripheral (or associates)***—These gang members have a strong attachment, but participate less often in gang activities than the regulars, or hard cores. They have some interests outside of the gang and hope to eventually get out. Their commitment and attachment level is strong but not lasting.

3. ***Temporary***—These gang members are marginally committed, and joined the gang later in life (e.g., 14 or 15 years old) than the regulars or associates. Their attachment and commitment to the gang is not nearly as intense as the others. They remain in the gang for a short time.

4. ***Situational***—These members are very marginally attached, have limited involvement, try to avoid violent situations, and do so only when called upon by the gang leaders.

In other degree-of-attachment typologies, classifications could include the following:

1. ***OGs***—The original gangsters of a gang. They are members for life.
2. ***Hard cores***—The diehards of the gang, usually comprising only about 10 percent of the gang.
3. ***Regular members***—Like the associates described by Vigil and Long. They usually range from 14 to 17 years of age and have the primary job of robbing and stealing. If they stay in the gang long enough, they will become hard core.
4. ***Wannabes***—Usually 11 to 13 years old, these youths have yet to be initiated into the gang, but they are waiting to be invited.
5. ***Could bes***—Usually kids 10 and younger who are raised in an environment conducive to gang behavior.

Reiner (1992) studied street gangs in Los Angeles and established his own typology, also based on an individual's level of commitment to the gang:

1. ***At risk***—These are youths that are not in a gang presently, but run a high risk of joining a gang in the near future. They can be described as *pregang* youths. They have shown some interest in the gang, either by fantasizing or by experimenting wearing gang attire and talking the talk of gang members.
2. ***Wannabe***—As the term implies, these are youths who know and admire gang members and want to be just like them. They are viewed as future "recruits" of the gang. They are usually of preteen age and are already dressing and acting like gang members. Mentally they are ready to join; they are just waiting for an invitation.
3. ***Associate***—Generally these members are at the lowest level of the gang and are sometimes referred to as "fringe" or "little homies."
4. ***Hard core***—Regular members who spend most of their time in gang-related activities. They have some friends and interests outside of the gang. They are small in number, usually representing no more than 10–15 percent of the total membership of the gang.
5. ***Veteranos/OGs***—Usually men (or women) in their twenties, maybe their thirties, who still actively participate in gang activities. The term *veteranos* is usually used in correspondence to Hispanic gangs; whereas the term *OG* is applied to elder statesmen of African-American street gangs. They may be old, in gang terms, but generally command a great deal of respect. Moore (1991, 27) stated that the term *veteranos* is far more specific and refers to the original clique in any barrio and to men in any gang who have been in prison.

TYPE OF ACTIVITY   Some researchers (Shelden, Tracy, and Brown 2001; Taylor 1990) categorize gangs by the type of criminal activities involved. Four major types of gangs can be identified in this way. (*Note*: Taylor used the first three of these categories and defined gangs in terms of their motivation.)

1. *Scavenger gangs*—Gangs that are loosely organized and prey on the weak. "Members of these gangs often have no common bond beyond their impulsive behavior and their need to belong. . . . They have no particular goals, no purpose, no substantial camaraderies" (Taylor 1990, 4). They sometimes participate in violence for fun and impulsive reasons. They are low academic achievers, found the challenge of school too difficult to handle, and dropped out for a life on the streets where survival of the fittest still implies physical superiority.

2. *Territorial gangs*—These gangs are associated with a specific area or turf. Protecting turf often leads to conflict with rival gangs. Their specific goal is to protect their turf from perceived outside threats. The turf sometimes serves as a business market for illicit activities such as drug sales, which further highlights the importance of protecting it from external threats. Taylor (1990, 6) stated that "when scavenger gangs become serious about organizing for a specific purpose, they enter the territorial stage."

3. *Organized/corporate gangs*—These are the most cohesive of gangs and are heavily involved in regular and well-organized criminal activities. They often represent a corporate type of division of labor and are specifically motivated by generating a profit. "These well-organized groups have a very strong leader or manager. The main focus of their organization is participation in illegal money-making ventures" (Taylor 1990, 7). Gang members are expected to follow strict orders, and promotion is based on merit—as is generally found in the corporate world.

4. *Drug gangs*—These gangs are focused on making a profit, and selling drugs is the business they employ. Padilla's (1992) *The Gang as an American Enterprise* provides an excellent description of a drug gang and the methods employed to maintain its market. The strict division of labor is designed to benefit the group, but the leaders and members found at the top are the ones who generally enjoy the greatest profits—again, similar to most corporations and businesses.

RACIAL AND ETHNIC DISTINCTIONS OF GANGS   One of the most common ways to identify and categorize gangs is by race and ethnicity. Generally speaking, gangs are homogeneous, even in heterogeneous communities; in other words, gangs almost always consist of members from one race (e.g., African American) or specific ethnic group (e.g., Irish, Mexican, or Chinese).

Hispanic/Latino/Chicano Gangs   There is a debate among scholars—and more importantly, among Hispanic or Latino people themselves—as to which term is more acceptable: *Hispanic* or *Latino*. In some regions of the country, especially Southern California, the term *Chicano* is often preferred. Chicanos identify with their indigenous ancestors (Mayans or Aztecs). Those who prefer the term *Hispanic* generally do so because they trace their roots to Spanish and indigenous ancestors who resided in Mexico and the Southwest (before it became a part of the United States), while people who prefer the term *Latino* generally identify with ancestors from Puerto Rico, Ecuador, the Dominican Republic, and other areas of Central America. Based on 2010 U.S. Census data, the U.S. population consists of 16.3 percent of people who describe themselves as Hispanic/Latino, as such; they represent the largest minority category of Americans (U.S. Census Bureau 2012k). In the gang world, the largest numbers of gangsters are Hispanic/Latino/Chicano (slightly more than 50 percent) (see Table 5.1). Regardless of the

TABLE 5.1	Race/Ethnicity of Gang Members in 2008
Race/Ethnicity of Gang Members	**Percentage**
Hispanic/Latino	50
Black	32
White	10
Other	8

Source: National Gang Center (2011)

terminology used, Hispanic gangs are very territorial; the gang is linked to a specific barrio, or neighborhood, and loyalty to one's barrio is often the basis of much intergang violence. Chicano gangs do not identify with colors in the way that black gangs do, but most of them favor colors such as black, white, brown, and tan (Dickie pants are a favorite). Many Hispanic gangsters wear a second shirt over a white t-shirt with just the top button buttoned. Our discussion of Hispanic/Latino/Chicano gangs is limited here because many of their gangs have nation affiliation and will be discussed in further detail in Chapter 6.

African-American/Black Gangs　African Americans have a unique history in the United States because many of the ancestors of black folks can be traced back to slavery. Therefore, blacks have long been discriminated against in the United States. For more than 200 years, Africans suffered as slaves and even after slavery ended they were subjected to prejudice and discrimination during the Jim Crow era. During the 1950s and 1960s, blacks stood up for their rights and challenged the dominant power structure of the United States. Because so many Africans were once slaves, blacks have historically been the largest racial/ethnic category of persons in the United States. Even as the one-time largest minority category of Americans, blacks suffered from inequality. Now that they are no longer the largest minority category of persons, there are those who wonder if blacks will ever reach full equality in the United States. Consider, for example, the fact that politicians once sought the "black vote" but now seek the "Hispanic vote," meaning the needs of blacks has taken a back seat to whites and Hispanics. Today, blacks represent about 12.6 percent of the U.S. population, but they still represent about 32 percent of the gang world (see Table 5.1). According to Perkins (1987), African-American gangs formed in reaction to institutional racism. He also suggested that blacks join gangs for the typical reasons of developing a sense of belonging, identity, power, security, and discipline. Blacks face discrimination not only from a mostly white-dominated socio-political U.S. system but also from Hispanic/Latinos. This is especially true in the gang world, as some of the most heated gang rivalries involve Hispanic gangs fighting black gangs. For example, a Hispanic street gang in Hawaiian Gardens, Los Angeles County, has "waged a campaign of racist violence and intimidation that was designed to drive out the city's African-American residents" (The Southern Poverty Law Center 2009, 3). Nearly 150 Varrio Hawaiian Gardens (VHG) gang members were indicted for racist violence perpetrated against black folks—gang members and nongang members alike—as part of the VHG's desire to rid the city of Hawaiian Gardens of all African Americans. (*Note*: Hawaiian Gardens is 77 percent Hispanic or Latino and 4 percent black according to 2010 Census data.) The VHG members were charged with 476 "overt acts" of racketeering, such as murder, attempted murder, weapons trafficking, and kidnapping (The Southern Poverty Law Center 2009). The Mexican Mafia has directed Hispanic gangs to carry out ethnic cleansing attacks on African-American gangs in South Los Angeles in order to establish purely Latino neighborhoods since 2006 (The Southern Poverty Law Center 2009). The most noted, and widespread, contemporary black gangs are the Los Angeles–based Bloods and Crips. Because of the importance of the formation of the Crips and Bloods and their sheer large number of affiliated sets of gangs across the country, our discussion of American-African street gangs is limited here but will be more fully discussed in Chapter 6.

White Gangs   White ethnic youths once dominated the gang world. As described in Chapter 2, the Irish formed the first real street gangs in the United States; nearly all of the white ethnic immigrant groups that followed the Irish formed gangs as a mechanism for coping with their marginal status in society. Presently, white gangs represent only about 10 percent of the United States' total gang population (see Table 5.1). In Los Angeles, whites represent only about 2 percent of all gang members. In fact, as the area type decreases from larger cities to rural counties, the percentage of white gang members increases (18.9% in rural areas) (see Table 5.2). The data in Table 5.2 also reveal that the only area type in which blacks have a higher percentage of gang members than Hispanics is rural counties. Most of the contemporary white gang members do not belong to street gangs; instead, they belong to such groups as the **Ku Klux Klan (KKK)**, skinheads, and the AB. The KKK was formed immediately after the Civil War and the resulting freeing of the slaves. The KKK attempted to halt the Reconstruction that followed the Civil War. The Klan was against the idea of equal rights being given to blacks, although they have also persecuted and targeted Jews, immigrants, Roman Catholics, communists, homosexuals, and organized labor in addition to blacks. Like street gangs, the KKK has a number of affiliate chapters, or "dens." Today, the KKK has small chapters across the country. They are a model of extreme bigotry and violence. They maintain a commitment to white supremacy and work toward transforming American culture to one based on the Bible, although with their own warped sense of ridding "undesirables" from their idealized perfect society. The number of Klan chapters has been decreasing throughout the 2000s. In 2010 there were 152 chapters; there were 221 the year before (The Southern Poverty Law Center 2012). This should not be interpreted as a sign of ending hatred among white extremists, rather, it represents a shift in philosophy. For example, the second-largest Klan group in America—the Marion, Ohio-based Brotherhood of Klans, with 38 chapters in almost as many states—folded when its leader, Jeremy Parker joined the AB. Most of his followers joined in the AB (The Southern Poverty Law Center 2012).

Another white group with a reputation of being an organization based primarily on hatred is the **skinheads**. Among other things, skinheads vary from street gangs in that they don't necessarily have a neighborhood, or turf, that they call home and find necessary to defend. On

TABLE 5.2   Race/Ethnicity of Gang Members by Area Type in 2008

Race/Ethnicity of Gang Members	Larger Cities (Percentage)	Suburban Counties (Percentage)	Smaller Cities (Percentage)	Rural Counties (Percentage)
Hispanic/Latino	48.1	43.8	49.7	30.2
Black	35.6	32.3	29.6	41.3
White	9.3	14.5	15.3	18.9
Other	6.9	9.3	5.1	9.6

Source: National Gang Center (2011)

the other hand, skinheads are often cited as an example of a white gang. Skinheads are generally identified with shaved head, swastikas tattooed on their bodies, and certain clothing worn to promote their beliefs (e.g., white-power T-shirts). There is an accepted acknowledgment in the academic world that all skinheads are not racists. *Racist skinheads* refers to those who promote "white power" or are neo-Nazis. They dislike Jews, blacks, certain other minorities, and certain religious groups. They dislike these people because they consider them to be inferior in comparison to themselves. Racist skinheads draw directly upon the works of Adolf Hitler, leader of the German Nazis. The skinheads first emerged in Great Britain, especially in London, in the mid- to late 1960s. The post–World War II era was one of turmoil and social change in Great Britain (England, Scotland, and Wales). During the 1970s, the skinheads became more violent and rebellious. By the late 1970s and early 1980s, skinheads had begun to form gangs in the United States as well as in European countries outside of Great Britain. The rise of skinhead organizations in the United States can be credited to many individuals who accepted the British skinhead ideology. Among the skinhead gangs that have caught the attention of authorities is **Volksfront (VF)** based out of Portland Oregon. With a population of three-fourths white, the skinhead movement is big in Oregon. Founded by Randall Krager in 1994, VF chapters throughout the Northwest have participated in a number of hate crimes that generally involve blacks and Jews as targets. VF members are identified by a VF logo that involves a red circle with the letters V and F and an image of a life rune (looks like an upside down peace sign) in between the two letters. Members who wear red shoelaces have spilt the blood of a rival and those who wear white shoelaces do so to indicate white power. Otherwise, they wear traditional skinhead attire such as bomber jackets, combat jeans, and steel-toe Doc Martens.

According to Moore (1993), these individuals suffered from mental and emotional disabilities and had trouble fitting into American society. Obviously, they were not mainstream persons.

The **neo-Nazi** element was most successfully introduced into the American skinhead scene by Thom Metzger of the White Aryan Resistance (WAR). Metzger had read Ian Stuart's *Blood and Honour* and joined the KKK under David Duke. Metzger learned of the skinheads during a visit to Great Britain. Members of the National Front explained to him the value of using skinheads for the white-power movement. Metzger returned to the United States and began recruiting skinheads as his "frontline warriors" (Anderson and Jenkins 2001; Marshall 1994).

Newsday reporter Jim Mulvaney (1993; reprinted in the *Las Vegas Review Journal*) has argued that Greg Withrow is the founder of the skinhead movement in the United States, dating back to 1978. Withrow has stated that he was raised to be a racist: "Some fathers raise their sons to be doctors, some fathers raise their sons to be lawyers. I was raised to be the next Fuhrer" (Mulvaney 1993). While Withrow was growing up in Sacramento, his father made him study the life of Hitler and read hate literature. At age 14, he joined the Klan. Withrow acknowledged to Mulvaney that he knew he held the youth movement in the palm of his hand but he now feels sorry about it. Withrow describes the philosophy of the loose confederation among skinheads as the "100 Hitlers policy." If all the groups act independently, the police can take only one set down at a time while the rest survive to keep the movement alive. Withrow quit the skinheads in 1987 after his father died. Ironically, he fell in love with a woman whose family fled Hitler's Germany. Withrow was then attacked by the skinheads, including his former best friend, beaten, had his throat cut in two places, his jaw broken, his hands nailed into a board, like a crucifix, and told that he would die as a Jew. He survived the beating and later became a lecturer for the Anti-Defamation League.

Today, skinheads can be found all over the country and are generally affiliated with other white-supremacist groups such as the WAR, the National Alliance, the New Order, the White

Student Union, the KKK, the League of the South, the National Socialist Movement (NSM), and the neo-Nazi Creativity Movement. In 2006, neo-Nazis volunteered for Jim Gilchrist's congressional campaign and distributed propaganda at Gilchrist rallies with the full knowledge of the Minuteman Project co-founder and his campaign managers (The Southern Poverty Law Center 2006). The neo-Nazi group, the **Creativity Movement (CM)**, has survived name changes, the death of its founder, and the imprisonment of his successor (Keller 2010). The CM is especially strong in Montana, the home of many splinter paramilitary groups (e.g., the Militia of Montana). The CM believes it is waging a holy war against non-whites and other undesirables. **The League of the South** started as verbal defenders of the South and its old culture but have now grown to viewing themselves as the new soldiers of the Confederacy (Smith and Lenz 2011). This white hate group was formed by academics in 1994 who were obsessively driven to glorify Southern history and culture, endorsing the idea of succession from the United States. Over the years, however, this once bookish group has been transformed to a distinctly racist group promoting the cultural dominance of the Anglo-Celtic people and their institutions (Smith and Lenz 2011). The **National Socialist Movement** is another neo-Nazi white gang that advocates for a "white nation." Its members give stiff-armed Nazi salutes and wave swastika-adorned flags at rallies (The Southern Poverty Law Center 2011). Among other things, the NSM wants all Mexicans and Mexican-Americans living in the United States to return to Mexico.

Although the number of traditional white gangs has decreased since their dominance in the 1800s, there is little chance of white neo-Nazi, quasi-gangs disappearing anytime soon. Just like traditional street gangs, leaders come and go, and sets disappear. But new sets and new movements continue to emerge. The advent of social networking sites such as YouTube has only helped in spreading the word of hate by neo-Nazi groups. As Bretin Mock (2007) points out, groups like the NSM have been using YouTube (and other video-sharing sites) to disseminate propaganda videos and postings since it was founded in February 2005. Anyone who goes online can attest to the fact that there are a lot of "haters" in cyberspace, just as there are in the conventional world.

As revealed in Table 5.1, Hispanic/Latino, blacks, and whites comprise 92 percent of all American street gangs. That leaves 8 percent for other racial/ethnic street gangs. Asian-American street gangs comprise a little more than half of this category, followed by Native-American and a number of smaller categories of racial/ethnic street gangs.

Asian-American Gangs   As with every other category of Americans, Asian Americans are quite diverse. As a recognized racial category, there are numerous ethnic Asians (e.g., Chinese, Japanese, Korean, Vietnamese, and Filipino). As a collective category of Americans, Asians make up 4.8 percent of the total U.S. population; they also represent about 4 percent of all American street gangs. Historically, Asian-American gangs have ties to their ancestral homes; contemporary Asian gangs, however, have established their own identities. Asian gangs will be given further coverage in Chapter 6, for now, it is relevant to note that a typology of Asian ethnic gangs would include such subcategories as Chinese, Japanese, Koran, Vietnamese, Cambodian, and Hmong. The Hmong are a particularly interesting ethnic group, as they have faced prejudice and discrimination in both Asia and the United States. Although the number of Hmong living in the United States is relatively small, there are over 7,000 Hmong gang members and they are known for a high level of violence. It was a Hmong street gang that confronted Clint Eastwood's character of Walt Kowalski in the film *Gran Torino* (2008). See "Connecting Street Gangs and Popular Culture" Box 5.2 for a description of this film and Hmong street gang members. Asian gangs tend to be more secretive in their street dealings and consequently often make it difficult for law enforcement agents to curtail their criminal activities. Asian gang members are also highly entrepreneurial in their dealings (Reiner 1992).

Box 5.2   *Connecting Street Gangs and Popular Culture*

Gran Torino and Hmong Street Gangs

There are approximately 200,000 Hmong people residing in the United States, and although they are often
mistaken for Chinese or Vietnamese they have their own
distinct culture. The 4,000-year culture of the Hmong
values the concepts of honor, commitment, loyalty, and
freedom (Hamilton-Merritt 1993). Most of the Hmong
in the United States live in Minnesota, Wisconsin, and
California. The Hmong originate from the Asian countries of Laos, Vietnam, Thailand, and China. There are

several million Hmong remaining in Asia. Their language is a blend of Asian languages, including Thai,
Burmese, and Mandarin. It is not clear whether they ever had their own language, and if they did, the
Hmong, due to persecution by China, Laos, Thailand, and Vietnam, did not speak it publicly. As detailed
by Jane Hamilton-Merritt in her book *Tragic Mountains: The Hmong, the Americans, and the Secret Wars
for Laos, 1942–1992*, genocide has long been practiced against the Hmong people by the tyrannical
governments of their homelands.

It is important to understand the role of the United States with the Hmong people before we turn
our attention to Hmong gang members. The CIA's "secret war" in Southeast Asia, prior to the Vietnam
War, involved attempts to circumvent the government of Laos by employing Hmong tribes and clans
victimized by the Laotian government. Many Hmong would also assist the United States in its war against
North Vietnam and its allies. When the United States pulled out of Vietnam after the fall of Saigon in
1975, the Hmong people were left to fend for themselves. (*Note*: U.S. military involvement in the Vietnam War and the draft ended in 1973.) Once again, North Vietnam and its puppet government in Laos
targeted the Hmong for genocidal extinction. Many Hmong fled deep into the jungles and found their
way to Thailand via the Mekong River. Beginning in the late 1980s and especially in the early 1990s, the
Hmong arrived in the United States as refugees. Like so many immigrants before them, the Hmong arrived as people who could not speak English, economically poor, and lacking the necessary job skills of
the American employment sector.

The Twin Cities of Minnesota is the home of the largest concentration of Hmong people in the
United States. In an effort to help the Hmong with their transition to their new country and its rather
unique culture, the Hmong American Partnership (HAP) was founded in 1990 in St. Paul (Hmong American Partnership 2009). The HAP provides service in four main ways: education and training, elderly services, employment services, and youth and family services. The Hmong, like most immigrants, have needed
assistance in their transition to American society as many have found it difficult to find socioeconomic
success. Cultural differences have been especially alienating for some Hmong. In 2004, the much publicized
deer hunter killings in Wisconsin highlighted particular cultural differences. In Wisconsin, deer hunting is
a rite of autumn—a sport practiced by thousands of people who scour the woods for nine days each November with hopes of bagging a trophy buck. Many deer hunters hunt from a "blind" in tree stands. One day in
November 2004, several deer hunters made their way through the woods in northern Wisconsin and were
startled to find a stranger in their tree stand. Asked to leave, the trespasser opened fire on the hunters until
his 20-round clip was empty, leaving five dead. The police eventually caught and identified the shooter as
Chai Vang, a member of the Twin Cities' Hmong community. Locals in the Birchwood, Wisconsin, area had
complained before that Hmong often confront hunters and take their stands because the refugees from Laos
do not understand the concept of private property, an aspect of American culture that baffles the Hmong
(*The Post-Standard* 2004d). The Hmong believe that the woods are open land and whatever they find in the
woods they can take, including tree stands and deer from private property. Vang was sentenced to serve six
life prison terms, one after the other, guaranteeing he would never be freed from prison.

The deer hunter story is just one example of Hmong violence as a result of cultural misunderstandings. Most Hmong do not resort to murder, or even crime, due to cultural differences. Nonetheless, a significant number of Hmong youth have turned to street gang life as a means of getting ahead. Hmong gangs first formed in Minnesota in the mid-1980s, shortly after the immigrants arrived. The first Hmong gang in Minnesota, the **Cobra** gang, began as a group of teenage friends who played soccer. Most of them lived in housing projects and banded together to protect themselves and other Hmong youth from the racism occurring in their schools and neighborhoods (Straka 2003). (As Thrasher would say, this group of cohorts spontaneously transformed to a street gang.) The Hmong gangs have evolved from protecting turf to a wide range of crimes, including homicides, gang rapes, prostitution, home invasions, burglaries, auto thefts, and the sale and distribution of illicit drugs (Straka 2003). It is the crime of rape, however, that is most significantly indoctrinated into the gangs' operational structure. In central California, it is the **Hmong Nation Society** that has the strongest gang presence. They have a bitter and violent ongoing feud with a gang known as **Menace of Destruction** (Criminal Justice Degrees Schools 2012).

The 2008 film *Gran Torino* was directed and starred by Clint Eastwood. Eastwood plays the character of Walt Kowalski, a recently widowed Korean War veteran and retired American Ford factory worker who is alienated from his family and angry at the world. He is particularly angry at the cultural changes occurring in his once-white, working-class neighborhood of Highland Park, outside Detroit, to that of one that is now dominated by poor Hmong immigrants. Walt's Hmong neighbors dislike Walt and for good reason as he has no respect for them. A Hmong gang entices Walt's young Hmong neighbor, Thao Vang Lor, to try to steal Walt's prized, mint-condition 1972 Ford Gran Torino as part of his gang initiation. The gang is led by Thao's cousin "Spider" and they have protected him from Hispanic gangs. Reluctant, but feeling the pressure to appease his cousin, Thao agrees to steal Walt's car. However, Walt catches Thao in the act. Thao runs away. The gang is upset that Thao failed in his initiation. When they offer him one more chance to prove himself and join the gang, Thao declines. Feeling disrespected, the gang attacks Thao outside his home. His sister Sue tries to fight the gang off; older family members try to come to Thao's rescue but to no avail. When the fight spills over to Walt's yard, he comes outside with an M1 Garand rifle and chases them off, thus earning the praise of the Lor family and the conventional Hmong community. Hmong folks begin to drop off ethnic food for Walt in appreciation. On another day, Sue is walking down a street with a poseur white gangster. The two are confronted by three blacks who scare off Sue's boyfriend. They are about to hurt Sue when Walt shows up and saves her by pulling a gun on the trio.

Walt drives Sue home and she explains her Hmong heritage. Sue explains that the Hmong do not have their own country but rather reside throughout Southeast Asia. She tells Walt that the Hmong moving to the United States is a "Vietnam thing" because when the Americans left Vietnam the communists started their plan of genocide against them. Walt questions why they would move to cold-weather states when they are from jungles. Sue answers that they are "hill" people, not jungle people. Sue informs Walt that things are not easy for Hmong in the United States and while many of the girls go off to college, most of the boys end up in jail. Walt respects Sue because she does not back down from anyone. The following day, Sue invites Walt over for a family barbeque and some beer. She teaches him many Hmong cultural ways and customs. As Walt slowly learns of the Hmong culture he also begins to accept them. Thao's mom wants him to work off his shame (for attempting to steal the Gran Torino) and insists that he perform odd jobs at Walt's home. Walt takes Thao under his wing and has him perform a number of odd jobs to help clean up the neighborhood. Walt also teaches him how to use a number of tools, a skill that will help him find a job. As he becomes impressed by Thao's work habits, Walt will eventually find him a construction job.

While Walt is being idolized by the conventional Hmong folks, he is still demonized by the gang he once confronted. The gang attacks Thao one day as he walks home from his construction job. They take his tool belt and rough him up. Walt finds out what happened to Thao and decides to pay a visit to the gang at their house. He waits until all but one is alone at the house and beats him up. Walt threatens the gangbanger with death if the gang bothers Thao again. Walt goes home. At night, the gang retaliates with a drive-by shooting of Thao's house injuring Thao. Sue was not home. Walt immediately worries about her. The gang kidnaps Sue and rapes and beats her. Walt is incensed. Having already sensed his own impending death due to deteriorating health and having taken care of his final preparations (e.g., getting his finances in order, getting a shave and haircut, and going to Church confession for the first time in years), Walt decides to go out in a blaze of glory. These final plans involve protecting Thao. Thao wants revenge and asks Walt for help. "Don't let me down" Thao pleads. Walt counters that he needs time to make a plan and promises that he will take care of things. For his own safety, Walt locks Thao in his basement. Walt goes after the Hmong gang on his own. He stands out in front of the gang house daring the gangbangers to shoot him. Walt wants them to kill him so that they will be sent to prison for committing murder. This will shut the gang down and protect Thao and Sue. As the film concludes, all the gang members open fire on Walt. He has sacrificed his own life for the betterment of the Hmong community. Although the events portrayed in *Gran Torino* are fictional, the story is based on all too many daily realities.

Native-American Gangs   There is no other racial/ethnic category as diverse as Native Americans, as there are more than 560 federally recognized Indian tribes (*Daily Herald* 2011; Infoplease.com 2012). However, one major characteristic is shared by all native people: the harsh treatment they were subjected to by Europeans and, later, Americans. It can be argued that native people, who were victims of attempted genocide, were treated worse than African Americans who were victimized by slavery. After facing near extinction, Native Americans are making a comeback, albeit a modest one. Based on data from the 2010 U.S. Census, Native Americans and Native Alaskans (another 2.3 million were American Indian and Alaska Native in combination with one or more other races) comprise only 0.9 percent of the total U.S. population of the more than 308 million people (U.S. Census Bureau 2012k). Life for many of these approximately 3 million native people is often harsh as they endure many social problems. Consider that native peoples have the highest rate of poverty and shortest life expectancy of any category of Americans. The extreme poverty native people experience contributes to other social problems, including high rates of alcoholism, poor health, and high rates of depression and suicide. Based on research conducted by the Robert Wood Johnson Foundation, a non-profit group in Princeton, New Jersey, that studies health issues, 8 of the 10 least-healthy counties in the United States are home to Native Americans in the Dakotas, Alaska, and Montana according to U.S. Census data (Wayne 2012). Sioux County, North Dakota, was the least healthy for the second consecutive year in 2012 (Wayne 2012). Sioux County is the headquarters of the Standing Rock Sioux Nation and among their health problems is the highest rate of premature deaths in the United States. The Pine Ridge Reservation, a Connecticut-sized zone of prairie, has such a high level of poverty and suffocating hopelessness that syndicated columnist Nicholas D. Kristof refers to Native Americans who live there as the "other 1 percent" (A-12). According to Census data, Shannon County, South Dakota, had the lowest per capita income in the United States in 2010; not far behind were several other Sioux reservations in South Dakota (Rosebud, Cheyenne River, and Crow Creek) (Kristof 2012a). As we have already learned, most gang members come from lower socioeconomic status (SES) families. Thus, poor economic status is a contributing factor in one's decision to turn to a gang. It should not be surprising, then, to learn that many native youths turn to gangs in hopes of improving their SES.

The crime rate on reservations has soared in the past couple of decades. Homicides, assaults, robberies, kidnappings, and weapons and drug-trafficking are among the crimes being reported in record numbers. This increased crime rate is attributed to the growing gang presence on reservations. There were 334 federal and state-recognized American Indian reservations in 2010. Gangs have existed on Native-American reservations for at least four decades. "The earliest references to self-identified gangs come from about 1970 in an agency town located near the eastern boundary of the reservation. In that year, one interviewee claims to have formed a gang, the Cruisers, with about a dozen other schoolmates between the ages of thirteen and fifteen. The primary activity consisted of drinking together at the town's drive-in theater on weekends. They shoplifted items 'a bunch of times' to pay for liquor, which they got someone older to buy for them" (Henderson, Kunitz, and Levy 2004, 129). In the 1990s, there were 75 gangs identified on the Navajo Nation reservation (the largest reservation) in Window Rock, Arizona. The Navajo gangs had adopted many of the behaviors as urban street gangs. They find status through the use of violence and they have been known to possess a range of weapons, from .22-caliber handguns to AK-47s. Drug-trafficking provides the capital to help sustain their existence.

On the Pine Ridge Reservation of South Dakota, home to about 20,000 Lakota Sioux, authorities have acknowledged 3,500 known gang members. The village of Pine Ridge is home to 12 gangs alone. Potato Creek, a small town with just 40 residents, has 15 gang members. The gangs have brought a life of terror to this reservation. They exist primarily to deal in drugs, especially cocaine, marijuana, and methamphetamines. Some of the gangs, such as the **Nomads**, have a command structure with a ruling council and a set of laws. The gangs on this reservation are responsible for 70 percent of the crimes—assaults, sexual assaults, intimidation, harassment, burglaries, vandalism, graffiti, and murder. There are 10 to 12 homicides each year on the Pine Ridge Reservation, which includes Wounded Knee in its territory. Gangs are so prevalent at the local schools that most youth simply drop out; in fact, the graduation rate is a dismal 1 percent (Elsner 2003).

Although gangs have existed on reservations for some time now, federal officials have become increasingly concerned with their activities in the past decade. The Native gangs are not only copying the larger nation gangs' mannerisms (e.g., wearing colors, flashing signs, use of nation gang symbols, and adoption of a hierarchical structure) and bravado, they are beginning to take advantage of their strategic geographic location. This strategic geographic location, of course, is the shared international borders of some Indian reservations that make them conducive to trafficking drugs into the United States via Canada and Mexico. In some jurisdictions, Native-American gang members are in partnership with non-Indian gangs and participate in such gang-related criminal activity as drug distribution, money laundering, assault, and intimidation (National Gang Intelligence Center 2011a). A great deal of marijuana produced in Mexico is transported into the United States through the Tohono O'odham Reservation in Arizona largely because there is a 75-mile stretch of lightly patrolled border. Nearly 20 percent of the high-potency marijuana produced in Canada each year enters the United States through the St. Regis Mohawk Reservation in New York. In Chapter 6, we will see how the Boot Camp gang of Syracuse ran its very profitable drug distribution center by working with gangsters in the St. Regis reservation.

Other Racial/Ethnic Street Gangs The Federal Bureau of Investigation tracks a number of other racial/ethnic street gangs, including East African (Somali and Sudanese) and Caribbean (Dominican, Haitian, and Jamaican) gangs. **Somali gangs** exist in many U.S. cities but are most prevalent in the Minneapolis-St. Paul, Minnesota; San Diego, California; and Seattle, Washington, areas, primarily as a result of their border proximity to Mexico and Canada (National Gang Intelligence Center 2011a). Although some Somali gangs have joined, or aligned themselves, with nation gangs, for the most part, they remain independent and adopt names based on clan or tribe. Somali gangs are involved in drug and weapons trafficking, human trafficking, credit card fraud, prostitution, and violent crimes, including homicide. **Sudanese gangs** in the United States have been expanding since 2003 and are located in such states as Minnesota, North Dakota, South Dakota, Nebraska, and Tennessee. They participate in many of the same criminal activities as Somali gangs but they possess weapons and tactical knowledge because of their involvement in conflicts in their native country (NGIC 2011a). Caribbean gangs are located mostly in the eastern states but they are expanding. Dominican gangs include the Trinitarios. As discussed in Chapter 2 the **Trinitarios** and **Dominicans Don't Play**, the two largest Dominican gangs, respectively, are predominant in New York City and surrounding areas. They are known for their violent machete attacks and drug-trafficking. An increase in the Dominican population in several eastern U.S. jurisdictions helps to explain the expansion of Dominican gangs. **Haitian gangs**, such as the Florida-based Zoe Pound, can be found in many East Coast states. The **Zoe Pound** gang, founded in Miami, is a Haitian gang that engages in drug-trafficking, robbery, and related violent crimes. In February 2010, 22 suspected Zoe Pound gangsters were charged with possession of and conspiracy to traffic powder and crack cocaine from Illinois to Florida (United States Drug Enforcement Administration 2010). Two other Haitian gangs of note are the **Haitian Boys Posse** and the **Custer Street Gang**; they are involved with drug and weapons trafficking, robberies and shootings, and homicides along the East Coast (NGIC 2011a). Compared to Jamaican gangs in Jamaica, American Jamaican street gangs lack a sophisticated structure (e.g., no clear hierarchical structure). Jamaican gangs, such as the **Shower Posse** and the **Spangler Posse**, participate in drugs and weapons trafficking and maintain ties to their island nation.

A Typology of Ex-Gang Members   It is generally understood that once a youth decides to become a gang member, four outcomes are possible: death, imprisonment, life-long membership in the gang, and life outside of the gang. Ex-gang members then may include individuals who left the gang but are still incarcerated; those who have found success outside the gang; and those who have struggled (sociologically speaking) due to the fact that they wasted their early lives in a gang and failed to secure the necessary job skills and/or temperament to succeed in the conventional world.

As this review of gangs and their organizational components has revealed, there are great differences among gangs and their structure and purpose for existence. On the other hand, gangs do share a number of common characteristics. First, they are generally upset by their marginalized status in society and view joining a gang as a viable alternative. Second, their marginalized status helps to develop highly competitive behaviors motivated by self-reliance and a survival-of-the-fittest attitude. Third, they have a general distrust of society's criminal justice system, especially the police and the courts. Fourth, because of their self-inflicted social isolation from the rest of society, they have learned to become self-reliant. This self-reliance often directs them toward delinquent and criminal activities. Fifth, their aura of defiance guarantees that their marginal status will continue.

TURNING: THE SOCIALIZATION OF A GANG MEMBER

Interacting with people one feels comfortable with is a behavioral characteristic shared by nearly all humans. Forming, or joining, a group one feels comfortable in is another vital aspect of human behavior. "Social interaction plays an important role in an individual's life. The individual wants to feel that he or she fits into a group or a society. Individuals want to experience a sense of unity with their fellows. Hence, by joining together in groups, the individual becomes a part of a whole" (Delaney 2001, 126). **Socialization** is a process of social development and learning that occurs as individuals interact with one another and learn about society's expectations for acceptable behavior. The socialization process is especially with young people as it is the mechanism that society utilizes to teach its youths how to conform to cultural expectations.

Socialization

Human infants enter the world unable to fend for themselves and are completely dependent on caregivers for survival. These caregivers (e.g., parents, other family members, legal guardians, friends, babysitters) teach the child necessary, basic rules of life designed to assist the infant's survival. Every infant also enters the world with biological urges that must be controlled. The child must learn to conform to societal expectations and abandon, among other things, desires for instant gratification. The child must be taught not to throw temper tantrums just because he/she wants something, like a bottle, or to get out of the crib. The child must also learn that with rights and privileges come duties and obligations and that certain behaviors are likely to elicit rewards and others punishments. When good deeds are rewarded, they are likely to be repeated, and when bad behaviors are punished, they are less likely to be repeated; or so it is hoped. The behaviors of humans, however, are subject to many variables, including social class, gender, race/ethnicity, and past experiences. To properly understand human behavior, one must comprehend the critical aspect of socialization.

Socialization is a learning process by which individuals learn the expectations of society and are taught the proper guidelines of expected behavior. It is a process by which people learn, through interaction with others, what they must know in order to survive and function as a productive member of society. Successful socialization has occurred when the individual internalizes the norms, values, and beliefs of a society. Proper socialization ensures that the norms and values of a society are instilled within a child. Each of us becomes a part of society because of the socialization process. The socialization allows for the transmission of culture to future generations. If people were not socialized to accept the rules and norms of society, there would likely be chaos. It should be noted, however, that over time, any number of norms, values, and societal expectations may change in light of new cultural ideals. Thus, the basic lessons caregivers provide for infants remain relatively the same, but parents may modify the manner in which they socialize their children from the manner they were socialized by their parents. It is often proposed, or reasoned, that improper socialization results in youths adopting behaviors that may contribute to delinquency, criminality, and, in some cases, joining a gang. Juvenile delinquency and criminal behavior, therefore, is the result of poor socialization and/or the individual's unwillingness to accept the rules of society.

The child is exposed to cultural expectations by the **agents of socialization**: parents and family, the schools, peers, the media, religion, employers, and the government. The initial influence on children is the parents (or other guardians) and the immediate family. *Early socialization* is referred to as **primary socialization**. As the primary agents of socialization, parents have a tough job. They must, at minimum, provide food, clothing, and shelter for their children. Parents are also to provide a loving and nurturing environment that will assist their children's mental and physical development as individuals. Early childhood socialization is especially critical for instilling the proper guidelines for acceptable behavior. This fact is underscored by the reality that most youths, even those found in high-crime areas, do not become criminals and gang members. But, primary socialization is not always successful, as many families fail to properly socialize their children and/or they fail to provide the nurturing and loving environment that youths need. When parenting is insufficient, a child's maturational process is compromised.

The family is also a **primary group**. Charles Cooley (1909) viewed primary groups as intimate, face-to-face groups that play a key role in linking the individual to the larger society. The primary group is relatively small and informal, involves close personal relationships, and has an important role in shaping the self. Primary groups become the most important sources of the individual's ideals, which derive from the moral and ethical unity of the group itself (Delaney 2004a). Primary groups include individuals with whom we form our closest relationships, which eventually evolve into a sense of "we" or belonging. Members of a primary group share a sense of "we-ness," involving the sort of sympathy and mutual identification for which "we" is a natural expression. For example, when friends say, "we hung out and watched movies and ate junk food all night," this "we" expression allows individuals to experience a sense of feeling toward the group.

Children generally start school at age 4 or 5. This begins the **secondary socialization** process. The child is now exposed to the influences of both the institutional demands of the school and the interpersonal pressures associated with having peers and attempting to blend into bonding groups. At home, the child was used to being treated as unique, or special, whereas at school, the child is treated in the same manner as all other children. While at school, children may interact with a number of other children and adults with potentially different outlooks on proper behavior, norms, values, and cultural beliefs. These different outlooks may confuse the child, but they may also enhance an appreciation for diversity of thought and courses of action. It is very important, however, for children to learn to get along with their teachers. This represents another important component to proper continued socialization.

Delinquents and gang members almost always report having difficulty with school, either because of the way teachers treated them or because of the manner in which their peers treated them. In Padilla's (1992) gang research on the Diamonds, he reported that a wide range of school-related experiences contributed to the children's negative outlook of the conventional life and a positive view of the gang. Their affirmative judgment of the gang and decision to join were developed over time but resulted because of negative experiences with schoolmates and teachers. In many cases, the Diamonds were told they were no good and delinquent by their teachers. Negative labels by teachers, coupled with the poor English skills of the Diamonds, led to unsatisfactory academic performances in school. These negative feelings would have dire consequences on their future lives. The negative labels assigned to the members of the Diamonds led them to feel stigmatized, which in turn fueled a poor self-image. By the time these youths reached high school, many of them had already joined the gang and participated in gang activity. However, for most of them, turning to the gang occurred when they entered high school.

Dropping out of school and joining a gang will hurt the life chances of youths who hope to gain some measure of socioeconomic success. The changing labor market and the positive correlation between median weekly salary and the unemployment level and one's level of education were discussed in Chapter 4. But it is important to emphasize once again that dropping out of school, especially to join a gang, will hurt the individual in the long run (and often in the short term as well). High school dropouts will earn significantly less income than college graduates. And the number of students dropping out of high school is scary. "Collectively, America's more than 20,000 high schools graduate just 71% of their students. This means 1.2 million young people a year—about 7000 every school day—are dropping out without the necessary skills to get and keep a good job" (Tyre 2009, 10). Dropout rates vary from school district to school district, but students from inner-city public schools face the greatest likelihood of failure. It is important to also note that often the children who do poorly in school are not receiving proper parental help with their schoolwork at home. It is critical that parents work with their children on home-work projects or, at the least, check over homework and quiz their children on assigned school materials. In this manner, children are far more likely to perform adequately in school and thus increase their level of self-esteem and status in non-delinquent ways. Clearly, many children are not being helped properly with their schoolwork by their parents and consequently do poorly in school. Poor school performance is a predictor of juvenile behavior.

As children age, their associations with peers become increasingly important. Children begin to value the company and opinions of their friends more than those of their parents or families. A **peer group** consists of associates of roughly the same age and usually from the same social status and background. Peers enjoy a certain amount of autonomy and egalitarianism, as each friend possesses relatively equal status within the group. Participation in a peer group af-fords members an opportunity to explore the limits of adult rules and expectations. In this man-ner, the child is being socialized into accepting the idea that norms, values, and beliefs are not fixed entities. This sense of freedom becomes exciting for youngsters and helps to explain why they value praise and acknowledgment from their peers. Understandably, for some youths, the peer group becomes a primary agent of socialization. This occurs when the influence of the peer group has led an individual to become more independent of adult authorities, when the individ-ual has embraced the concept of group loyalty, and when friendship and group norms are valued over societal expectations. When peer groups distance themselves from societal and parental ex-pectations, they have freed themselves for delinquent behavior. As explained in Chapter 3, gangs tend to evolve from peer groups—what Thrasher called the "spontaneous" gang. When youth peer groups embrace deviant and antisocial behavior, they begin to cut themselves off from con-ventional associations and institutions. Chronic juvenile delinquents surround themselves with peers who share their antisocial attitudes and behavioral mannerisms. In some cases, such youth may be tempted to join, or start, a gang.

Reasons to Join a Gang

The composition and the purpose of gangs have changed radically over the years. The early street gangs usually consisted of young members who eventually outgrew the gang affiliation by the time they reached their late teens or early twenties. Today, many gang members are in their late twenties and thirties, and they stay in the gang for more years now as well. In the 1950s, it was rare for a boy over the age of 15 to join a gang (Moore 1991). But just one decade later, nearly a third of male gang members joined after age 16. Over the past decades, the idea of protecting one's neighborhood from "outsiders" has been replaced with the idea of protecting marketplaces to sell drugs. As one can imagine, there are many reasons why someone would join a gang. Bear in mind that theoretical explanations of why youths join a gang were provided in Chapter 3. While socioeconomic reasons, including the idea of searching for kicks and thrills, were discussed in Chapter 4, there is an overlap here because of their relevancy to the discussion of why someone would join a gang. Although most individuals join a gang voluntarily, Curry and Decker (2003) point out a distinction between whether one is pulled or pushed into a gang. Youths are "pulled" to join a gang when they view such a lifestyle as attractive, for either the friendship of peers, op-portunities to make money, or the sense of power within the community that gang life symbol-izes. Youths are said to be "pushed" into a gang when they fear for their lives or when they see themselves as powerless to resist the temptations of gang life. Gang members who are pulled to the gang join voluntarily and are more likely to evolve into hard-core members. Gang members who are pushed into a gang generally try to remain neutral but find themselves being victimized by all the rival gangs. These members are less likely to evolve into hard-core members.

The top 12 reasons why someone joins a gang are provided here:

1. *Respect*—There is nothing more important to a gang member than respect. This is understandable as all want to be respected. For gang members, however, they often come from environments where they possess little but their own sense of pride. The gang provides many individuals with a sense of pride and respect. Once in the gang, the individual feels entitled to be respected, or feared, by others. Any form of disrespect is interpreted as a personal affront.
2. *Turf protection*—Historically, street gangs were formed by youths from close-knit communities that adopted an "us" versus "them" mentality. This is especially true of recent immigrant youths who feel disenchanted by new cultural situations and by existing youths, especially those from working-class families, who are not accepting of new residents.
3. *Sense of pride*—The idea of protecting turf and belonging to a group of cohorts instills a sense of pride in gang members. For many members, the gang is their own source of pride, and as a result, the allegiance to the gang is reinforced through collective action.
4. *Peer group influence*—If one's close friends start to join a gang, the pressure, or influence, to join a gang increases. Comments like "Why don't you hang with us anymore" and "Be cool, join the gang" from close friends who have recently joined a gang bear substantial weight.
5. *Protection from bullies*—Bullies have existed since the dawn of humanity as stronger individuals often exert their power over others. If a child is bullied in school, or in the neighborhood, he/she may lack the ability to defend himself/herself from a stronger adversary. As a result, the bullied individual may turn to the gang for help/revenge.
6. *Protection from rival gang members*—When a youth attempts to remain neutral, that is, tries to stay out of the gang life completely, he/she may be mistaken as a member of another gang because he/she is not a member of the local gang. To avoid beatings from a gang outside the home turf, the individual may turn to the local gang for protection/revenge.
7. *Power*—Closely related to the idea of protection from others, many youths join a gang for a sense of power. As a member of a gang, the gangster assumes a level of power over conventional people who lack a figurative army to back them up in times of trouble and turmoil.
8. *Family turmoil*—Problems at home (e.g., physical or emotional abuse) is a leading cause for females to join a gang (see Chapter 7) and for many males.
9. *Economics*—Because most gang members come from lower SES backgrounds, economic fulfillment is an enticement for many poorer residents as they come to see gang members as the ones with money, cars, and material goods (e.g., bling, electronics, and cars).
10. *Protecting the market turf*—The idea of protecting a home neighborhood from outsiders has been replaced by the need to protect the market area where economic fulfillment is being pursued. The most common type of marketplace is the drug turf.
11. *Kick and thrills*—It is certainly worth repeating here that many gang members are first attracted to a gang because of the opportunities to live on the edge. My own research has confirmed that when gang members are asked, "why did you join the gang," they reply, "because it is fun!"
12. *The gang as family*—Years ago, gang researchers claimed that a youth joined a gang because it was a substitute family. Today, however, there are countless cases of gangs consisting of multiple family members, males and females alike. In this regard, the gang and family are one and the same. In other cases, it remains true that for some members, the gang is the substitute family.

That so many youths find turning to a gang more commendable than turning to society, or that joining a gang is the best means of finding socioeconomic success, is a sure sign that there are flaws in the social system.

Recruitment

As the preceding factors have outlined, there are many reasons why a youth may want to join a gang. Eventually, wannabe gang members will be recruited by the local gang(s). The method of recruitment will vary depending on the type of gang. Street gangs, for example, may take the *fraternal* approach by convincing the recruit that gang membership is about companionship and brotherhood (or sisterhood) and that it is the cool thing to do. Street gangs may also attempt to recruit wannabe members by selling them on the concept of an *obligation* to the local community. The recruit should want to join a gang for patriotism, community honor, and local respect. In other cases, street gangs may use a *coercive* approach to recruitment through intimidation. Coercion and intimidation tactics may include both physical and psychological tactics (Jankowski 1991).

Prison gangs have their own techniques for recruiting wannabes. The Texas Syndicate uses a comprehensive and lengthy recruiting process that includes meeting the "homeboy connection" requirement. A thorough background check is conducted on the recruit to make sure he is "clean" (i.e., not a police informant). Upon successful completion of the background check, the entire membership must cast a unanimous vote before admittance is granted. If membership is denied for any reason, the recruit risks being coerced into paying the gang for protection or being used as a prostitute by the gang (Fong 1990). Recruitment into the Mexican Mafia is not nearly as strenuous. If the recruit meets the homeboy connection, passes a poorly conducted background check, and receives a simple majority vote of the entire group, he is granted membership. This loosely structured recruiting procedure is the major factor in the dramatic growth in Mexican Mafia membership found throughout state prisons such as those in Texas and California (Fong 1990).

Initiation

Gangs not only do not share consistent recruitment patterns, they have also developed different rites of passage, or initiation ceremonies, that recruits must pass in order to gain membership. Gang initiation rites, fighting, and drinking are behaviors that are encouraged because they allow young males an opportunity to prove their manhood (machismo) (Vigil and Long 1990). Initiation ceremonies have become increasingly ritualized since the 1950s and 1960s. Moore (1991) reported that few gang members were initiated in the original cholo gangs. The gang asked a youth to join and that was it. Gang initiations have become far more ritualized in the contemporary gang era. "Nearly every documented gang in the United States has an initiation process, and there is variation in how initiation rituals occur. Most are rather crude with few formal aspects to them and involve some form of violence, typically by current members of the gang directed against the initiate" (Curry and Decker 2003, 71). Most gang members, males and females, are "jumped" into the gang to test the recruit's ability to stand up in a fight. Specific initiation requirements vary from gang to gang. Some gangs (e.g., the Crips) will require new members to commit a crime in front of a gang witness. This process is called "loc'ing in." Most gangs have rituals in which they "beat-in" a member—a literal beating—to test the bravado and toughness of the recruit.

Padilla (1992) provides one of the more comprehensive reviews of the physical beat-in in a process that he called the "violation ceremony." Padilla stated that the violation ceremony can take place on three separate occasions:

1. *The "V-in"*—the initiation beating that a recruit receives when first joining the gang
2. *The "V-punishment"*—used when a gang member violates the rules and is punished for such infractions
3. *The "V-out"*—used when the member wants to leave the gang

The **V-in** ceremony involves the recruit taking an extreme beating with fists and feet. This is done in order to test the toughness of the recruit and to make sure that he will not run or panic during times of a gang crisis. Usually a time limit is set in which the inductee will be beat on by a number of gang members. The gang members are allowed to kick and punch. In some gangs, there are rules against blows to the head of the recruit, for the reason that the beating will be easier to hide. The inductee is to willingly take the beating and is not allowed to fight back. If the inductee survives, he/she is accepted into the gang. Recruits who already have a reputation for being tough and getting in fights usually receive a more lenient initiation. In my own research of street gangs, there are cases where the gang initiation involves the recruit walking a gauntlet of two lines of gang members wherein each member punches the recruit. The recruit cannot fight back, and must not drop to the ground. He cannot run the gauntlet either; he must allow all members a chance to hit him as he walks the path. The violation ceremony is more than a physical beating, however. This is a bonding opportunity. Once the recruit is in, he gets to participate in future initiations. And clearly, the primary purpose of a violation ceremony into a gang is to prove one's toughness and willingness to take a beating for the gang. The **V-punishment** will be implemented when gang leaders determine that certain violations of gang regulations warrant a severe punishment in a ceremonial fashion. Violations that may lead to a physical punishment include stealing from the gang, violating a gang-ordered truce on a rival gang, disrespecting gang leaders, and disobeying orders. The **V-out** ceremony involves physical beating as well. It is especially brutal under two conditions: when the exiting member possesses a great amount of information about the gang—to remind him of loyalty priorities—and when the exiting member was a troublemaker who caused problems of some sort for the gang during his tenure.

There are times when gang initiation beat-ins are so brutal that the inductee may die as a result. In September 2004, six teenagers, aged 13–15, were charged with homicide in the beating death of an eighth grader who agreed to the fight as part of his gang initiation. The blows taken by Tarus DeShawn Williams, 15, were so severe that blows to his chest crushed the left chamber of his heart (*The Post-Standard* 2004b).

Leaving the Gang

Despite the "considerable mythology" (perpetrated primarily by the media) that surrounds the topic of "leaving a gang," it *is* possible to do so (Curry and Decker 2003). The mythology that Curry and Decker refer to includes reports that in order to leave the gang one must commit a particularly heinous crime (e.g., kill a parent or police officer). Having conducted interviews with former gang members, Curry and Decker (2003) found that some gangsters simply quit their gang much like people end any association with others. Local gangs in particular are likely to merely let members leave once their interest has waned. Gangs with a long history, however, may not be as easy to leave. The Bloods, for example, have a "blood-in, blood-out" mentality, meaning one has to spill blood (his/her own or a target) while being initiated into the gang and one will have to do the same to leave. The Latin Kings, however, live by the motto: "Once a King, always a King." If a King or Queen tries to run away or hide from the gang they are likely to be killed. **Flipping** is one way to get out of the gang, but it is a dangerous option. Flipping involves a gang member cooperating with law enforcement about issues pertaining to the gang. Generally, when a gang member of an established gang, such as the Latin Kings, flips, a high-ranking member of the gang will put a "hit" on that individual, meaning whenever a Latin King comes into contact with a member who has flipped, he/she must kill that person. There are any number of reasons why a gang member may wish to leave, and range from concerns over violence (they may have inflicted, witnessed, or been victimized by it) to other obligations of life (e.g., becoming a parent, getting older, having a job). As described earlier, if a gang allows a member to leave, they may require that person to endure a physical beating or commit a crime. The primary reason for the beating is to remind the gang member of the link to the gang and/or because wanting to leave is perceived as a sign of disrespect the exiting member is directing toward the gang. High-ranking gang members who leave the gang run the risk of forever being a target of rival gang members, especially those hoping to make a name for themselves.

In the contemporary era, however, many members are choosing not to leave the gang. Instead, they are remaining in the gang throughout their adult life. This is generally a very costly decision, as the more years that a gangbanger remains in the gang, the greater the likelihood of being a homicide victim or of being caught for committing a criminal offense. Criminal conviction, of course, leads to incarceration. The tremendous increase in the numbers of gang members in prison has led to a continuation of street gang affiliation behind prison walls. Active street gang members who manage to escape arrest and/or criminal prosecution run an increased risk of eventually facing their own mortality on the streets. Death on the streets will result in a memorial tribute—the more famous the gang member, the more elaborate the tribute. Tupac Shakur's death illustrates this dreary reality. A memorial was set up for Tupac outside Club 662 shortly after his death. "Aerosoled (spray-painted) in red and blue on the side wall was the title of a Tupac song, 'Shed So Many Tears,' with R.I.P. written backward. The paint was still wet, and there was an overpowering smell of cheap beer on the ground below it: This was a traditional ghetto memorial, pouring out tribute to a dead brother. There was amazingly little glamour here, just a sad, ugly feeling, very creepy, very hollow. No art, no life, just ashes" (Solotaroff 2002, 267). Tupac may have a mythical status, but he no longer has life. A physical beating, or the V-out, may actually represent the easy way out of a gang.

CODE OF THE STREET: RESPECT

Without question, the subcultural value that carries the highest value for gang members is **respect**. Any sign of disrespect shown toward a gang, or gang member, will result in retaliation with extreme prejudice (a militaristic response). The gang subculture becomes a *lifeway* for youths (Vigil 1988b), and this lifeway, or way of life, is learned on the streets. Young children (those who are too young to the join the gang) in tough urban environments learn early on that violence is generally the method of choice used to settle disputes. They may learn this by observing domestic violence in the home, fights at school, and violent events (e.g., robberies, gun battles, police pursuits of suspects) in the neighborhood. Padilla (1992, 62) recounted the story of Tito, a Diamonds gang member, who described how he witnessed many gang fights while growing up. He paid attention to their justifications for the violence too. By the time Tito reached seventh grade he had been socialized into accepting that the way gang members handle their business is by *throwing down* (fighting). Gang members believe that it is their responsibility to protect their turf from other gangs and criminals. The local gang would justify its behavior by proclaiming their ownership of a territory—"this is my hood."

Gang members like Tito learn two important lessons from examples like this. First, you protect your neighborhood, with violence if necessary. This is done because the perception is that these rivals have disrespected you simply because they came into your neighborhood (the neighborhood boundaries include all shopping stores and movie theaters that are found within the protected territory). Second, if one finds oneself on enemy territory, one better be ready to fight.

Entering a rival gang's territory is just one way of disrespecting a gang member. Looking at a gang member the wrong way or stepping on his shoes is among the hundreds of violations deemed disrespectful and offenses deserving of some sort of physical beating. The importance attached to respect is not limited to the street environment; it also extends to the prison setting. Journalist Leon Bing spent four years in the late 1980s interviewing members of the Bloods and Crips in prison. Those conversations formed the basis of her 1991 book *Do or Die*. Portions of this book reappeared in Donohue's *Gangs* (2001). In an interview with gang inmate Monster Kody, Bing inquired about the importance of respect in prison. Kody responded by stating:

> Respect is not negotiable. You get and you give, but you don't get respect unless you give it. In prison you learn one of the virtues of life, and that's reciprocity. You learn to give and you learn to take. It's nothin' one-way about it, it's nothin' about lookin' out for number one. That's individualism, and that mentality disappears in prison, because prison's not about *you*. It's about survival of your unit, your people . . . Flaggin.' Saggin.' Braggin.' Lettin' people know you're part of something that is powerful. (Bing 2001a, 218–219)

So the street sensitivity to anything remotely considered disrespectful has extended to inside prison walls. The obvious disadvantage of having enemies in prison is the fact that the hunted have no place to hide, and, therefore, it is simply a matter of time before the perceived violator is victimized.

The Gang Mentality

Gangs value respect, but they also value other core beliefs that constitute their subcultural identity. Gang members, like conventional people, value a sense of honor and pride (in oneself and in one's neighborhood), reputation, recognition, courage, heart, and loyalty. With street gangs, there is a difference between respect and honor. Jankowski (1991) articulated the difference between respect and honor. *Respect* is something that must be earned and then protected (common with African-American gangs). *Honor* is something that is automatically bestowed upon a person (common with Chicano/Hispanic/Latino gangs, which believe honor has been earned as soon as the youth enters the gang).

Consistent style of dress among members of a gang is another behavior that unifies the group. The unification of a gang helps to establish a "we" feeling. The "we" feeling is overtly displayed by wearing the same colors or style of clothes. The category of "they"—the rival gangs—becomes easily identifiable because "they" will be sporting different colors or styles. Racial and ethnic groups have a history of identifying themselves based on their distinctive "we-ness." The creation of the "we" category provides a sense of community. For street gangs, "we-ness" plays an integral role in the daily lives of gang members. Rival gang members become the "they" group. The designation of one group as a "they" group implies that confrontations between the two are inevitable. Since conflict is inevitable for gang members, they must be willing to fight. Physical strength and prowess in the field of battle are behaviors worthy of automatic respect among gang members.

In brief, the gang mentality is a mindset that has been developed as a result of life circumstances that lead individuals to value the concept of respect above all else. Recall that respect was listed first (earlier in the chapter) as a reason why individuals join a gang. Any interpretation of disrespect is countered by extreme prejudice and may lead to acts of violence perpetrated against the perceived offender. In turn, the importance of respect is directly connected to the idea that any form of disrespect must be met by revenge and intimidation against perpetrators. Gang members, in an attempt to maintain their identities as street toughs, must always demonstrate their toughness and demand for respect.

The Code of the Street

In many lower SES neighborhoods, people have little or nothing at all. Maintaining a good reputation becomes paramount for such folks. This is especially true for gang members, or street-wise people. People wise to the ways of the street have developed a certain mentality that allows them to sustain and thrive where others are intimidated and scared. What develops is a "code of the street" for survival. Street-wise folks and gangbangers understand this code. So too does Elijah Anderson. Anderson shares his years of observations of Philadelphia ghetto street life in his book *Code of the Street: Decency, Violence, and the Moral Life of the Inner City* (1999), which grew out of the ethnographic work he conducted for his previous book *Streetwise: Race, Class, and Change in an Urban Community* (1990). According to Anderson, one of the most salient features of urban life is the relative prevalence of violence. Anderson used Germantown Avenue as a natural continuum of the conduct found in Philadelphia. One end of the avenue is characterized largely by a code of civility, with conventional citizens of society, whereas the other end is regulated by the code of the street. On the "street" end of Germantown Avenue, people are more weary of others and careful to present a sense of self that demonstrates to others they are wise to the way of life on the streets. It's not that people get jumped all the time on the streets, but rather, people being on guard against those sharing space with them. Intimidation and violence are constant reminders to street folks that they face a different daily reality than conventional residents.

Muggings, burglaries, carjackings, and drug-related shootings happen regularly in inner-city neighborhoods, and residents must be on guard against becoming an innocent victim of street crime. The code of streets which also involves the gang mentality of using violence as a way to handle business is also a contributing factor for people to be on guard. Youths who are raised in such a violent environment learn early in life the value of being "streetwise." They must learn to handle themselves in a street-oriented environment.

> This is because the street culture has evolved a "code of the street," which amounts to a set of informal rules governing interpersonal public behavior, particularly violence. The rules prescribe both proper comportment and the proper way to respond if challenged. They regulate the use of violence and so supply a rationale allowing those who are inclined to aggression to precipitate violent encounters in an approved way. The rules have been established and are enforced mainly by the street-oriented; but on the streets the distinction between street and decent is often irrelevant. Everybody knows that if the rules are violated, there are penalties. Knowledge of the code is thus largely defensive, and it is literally necessary for operating in public. (Anderson 1999, 33)

Families who are located in "street" neighborhoods and try to teach their children the conventional rules of society reluctantly find it necessary to also teach them how to negotiate the inner-city environment.

A great deal of violence on the streets is the direct result of someone being disrespected by a rival. The importance of respect has already been discussed in this chapter, but Anderson also described its importance to the code of the street. He insists that at the heart of the code is the issue of respect—loosely defined as being treated properly or being granted one's "props" (or proper due) or the deference one believes is deserved. The code is sometimes complicated as it allows for a framework to negotiate respect. With the right amount of respect granted to one, enough respect may be granted to the other so that both parties can go about their activities without causing the need for immediate violence. When both parties feel as though they have been disrespected, however, there is confrontation.

From a middle-class, or conventional, perspective, the many forms (e.g., maintaining eye contact for too long) of dissin' appear to be very petty and certainly not worth fighting over. Anderson argued that the code of the street can be traced to the profound sense of alienation from mainstream society that many inner-city black people, especially the young, experience. "The code of the street is actually a cultural adaptation to a profound lack of faith in the police and the judicial system—and in others who would champion one's personal security. . . . The code of the street thus emerges where the influence of the police ends and where personal responsibility for one's safety is felt to begin. Exacerbated by the proliferation of drugs and easy access to guns, this volatile situation results in the ability of the street-oriented minority (or those who effectively 'go for bad') to dominate the public spaces" (Anderson 1999, 34). The alienation that inner-city residents experience is attributed to their financial struggles.

The search for some sort of financial security ties back to one's need for respect. Anderson argues that in the inner-city environment, respect can be viewed as a form of social capital; thus it has value beyond the simple fact that each of us wants respect; it becomes akin to monetary value. When people are economically poor, they must secure a sense of value through social capital. Having a great deal of respect in such a neighborhood is like being wealthy. By the time inner-city street youths become teenagers, most of them have internalized the code of the street, or at least learned to comport themselves in accordance with its rules.

> The code revolves around the presentation of self. Its basic requirement is the display of a certain predisposition to violence. A person's public bearing must send the unmistakable, if sometimes subtle, message that one is capable of violence, and possibly mayhem, when the situation requires it, that one can take care of oneself. The nature of this communication is determined largely by the demands of the circumstances but can involve facial expressions, gait, and direct talk—all geared mainly to deterring aggression. . . . Even so, there are no guarantees against challenges, because there are always people around looking for a fight in order to increase their share of respect—or "juice," as it is sometimes called on the street. (Anderson 1999, 72–73)

The code of the streets revolves around one's presentation of self and one's predisposition to use violence when disrespected. All street-wise people know how to present themselves to others that they are capable of violence and possibly mayhem if the situation requires it. Facial expressions are used for communication and assessing a situation wherein aggression will be deemed necessary. Even when one leaves another alone, he/she must be on guard because you never know when people around you are looking for a fight just to increase their share of respect, or "juice," as it is sometimes called on the street (Anderson 1999).

The code of the street concept is very relevant to the study of street gangs. After all, most gangsters come from lower SES neighborhoods where folks have long viewed the conventional life as a dream, not a reality. They learn to develop different norms, values, and cultural expectations from those of the middle class. These new values, highlighted by the code of the streets, underlie the gang structure and process.

Summary

As Thrasher explained, many street gangs emerge from childhood playgroups. Peers have the same experiences as one another and tend to take on the characteristics of a group in a given environment. The social environment produces a wide variety of street gangs and therefore such a corresponding diversity of organizational structures. Some gangs are so highly structured that they resemble the military. At least one pair of researchers believe that gangs are so violent that they could be compared to a violent, murderous Amazonian tribe. The organizational structure of some gangs may resemble the "Greek-letter" organizations (fraternities and sororities) as well. Conversely, some street gangs are very loosely structured with nary a hierarchal structure or expectation of a lifetime commitment. Despite the differences between street gangs, a number of different typologies have been established to categorize street gangs, including age, degree of criminality, degree of attachment to and involvement in the gang, type of activity, and racial and ethnic distinctions.

As with most behaviors, gang behavior is learned. And it is learned through the socialization process. Socialization is the process by which individuals learn the expectations of society. Some people are socialized to accept the prevailing norms and values of the greater society, while others learn to embrace the norms and values of the immediate community, or subcultural group. Whether street gangs form spontaneously or for any other reason (e.g., revenge, protection, recreation), joining a gang always involves the recruit being socialized into accepting the street gang mentality. Although the processes of recruitment and turning to the gang vary from gang to gang, initiations are often brutal and highly violent. If a gang member disobeys an order in a highly organized gang, he/she may expect a violent punishment. In loosely organized street gangs, it is generally not too difficult to leave the gang. In more organized gangs, leaving may not be an option, and if it is, it will involve some sort of punishment or deed. Gang members learn to abide by the "code of the streets," a code that implies being street smart, showing respect, and demanding respect. Perhaps the most universally cherished desire and need of gang members is to be respected. Any form of disrespect will be addressed by confrontation and may result in deadly violence.

6

Street Gangs: Rural, Suburban, Local, National, and Transnational

Gangs come in all shapes and sizes. An increasing number of law enforcement agencies are reporting gangs in rural areas and the suburbs. Urban local street gangs tend to reside in most American cities and have become increasingly organized in an attempt to control drug marketplaces in specific local neighborhoods. In cities such as Syracuse, Rochester, and Buffalo, local street gangs are responsible for a great deal of violent crime, including homicide. Large gangs, or nation gangs, have spread beyond their respective immediate neighborhoods and regions and their influence extends across cities, states, and, in some cases, even countries. Examples of nation gangs include the Bloods, Crips, People, and Folks. Although each of these nation gangs may have sets in countries outside the United States, the category of transnational gangs is used here to describe the 18th Street Gang and the notorious MS-13 because they operate in most U.S. states and numerous countries outside of the United States. Some consider MS-13 as the most dangerous of all street gangs. Asian gangs have unique qualities. Traditional Asian gangs can be traced back to such nations as China and Japan, whereas contemporary Asian-American gangs have taken on their own identities.

GANG PROLIFERATION

There was a time when some law jurisdictions, especially smaller ones, would understate their communities' gang problem. In smaller jurisdictions, gangs are social and fiscal burdens on the local community and law enforcement. Resources are tight in all municipalities, but this is especially true in smaller cities. Money cannot simply be taken from some other sector of the allocated budget to deal with the rising gang-related costs because the operating budget is so small in the first place. Consequently, some communities had engaged in **gang denial** (this was the case, for example, in Syracuse, New York, a decade ago—to be discussed later in this chapter). When a community suffers from gang denial, ineffective prevention of gang growth and development is often a consequence. Local leaders and politicians are sometimes reluctant to acknowledge the presence of gangs in their jurisdictions because they worry about causing undue concern and fear among citizens. Unfortunately, by the time some communities and institutions acknowledge that they have a gang problem, the situation may have already accelerated. Gang denial generally begins in the families of the gang members. The mother of a gang member is especially likely to deny that her child belongs to a gang. Often, the mother is the central figure of the gang member's family; she will deny that there is a problem and will attempt to protect the youth from accusations of criminal, delinquent, or gang behavior. Denial of gang activity in small cities and towns is also the result of a general belief among townspeople that such activities cannot occur in their hometown. Such people understand how gangs are a problem in cities like Los Angeles, New York, Chicago, and Detroit but question their existence in smaller cities, suburbs, and small towns. Public denial of the existence of gangs and a lack of proactive community efforts to control them are major contributing factors to the alarming increase in the number of gangs. When the local media outlets (especially newspapers) and politicians fail to acknowledge the existence of gangs, resources will not be put aside to deal with the problem.

Gangs flourish in areas where they are allowed to conduct their illegal activities because of the lack of police intervention or surveillance. The lack of police involvement may be the result of unawareness of a gang problem in certain neighborhoods because the local citizenry failed to report an emerging problem. Adopting a zero-tolerance policy is the most effective way for small communities to combat gangs (in larger cities, it is nearly impossible to enforce a zero-tolerance policy in all neighborhoods because there simply are not enough resources available and gangs will move from one neighborhood to the next). To be effective, a zero-tolerance program needs the assistance of local citizens' watch groups and individuals who are willing to get involved (by performing such basic tasks as placing anonymous phone calls to the police to report crimes and removing graffiti). The schools need to get involved as well. Many youth gangs form in school; consequently, teachers and administrators should be able to identify those youngsters "at risk" or already active in gangs. Training programs can be designed to help school officials with this task of identification. The schools and local law enforcement agencies can work together on policies related to curbing delinquency and gang activity. The community infected by gang-related crime needs to take a stand against gangs by establishing an even higher community profile than the gang. Community involvement coupled with police intervention (on a local, state, and national level) will help to slow the growth of gangs and may deter gang activity altogether.

In larger cities, gang denial is not an issue, as citizens and law enforcement officials are all too aware of the reality of gangs as quasi-institutional fixtures of the landscape. The gangs of larger cities have a choice. They can remain relatively small with the primary purpose of protecting turf, or they can merge with the larger gang and claim nation affiliation. Los Angeles and Chicago are the home-base of the largest nation coalitions, with the Bloods and Crips having formed in Los Angeles and the People and Folks in Chicago. These gangs have acquired super gang categorical status and are known generically as nation gangs. According to the National Alliance of Gang Investigators Association (NAGIA) (2002), certain criteria must be met in order to qualify as a nation gang. They are as follows:

- Membership exceeds 1,000 members.
- The gang can be documented in multiple states. (*Note*: Although there are not a minimum number of states established to be labeled a "nation" gang, I would argue that they should reside in more than half of the states.)
- The gang maintains extensive drug networks.
- The gang exercises aggressive recruiting strategies.
- The gang has advocated an ambition for power and massive membership.

There are both advantages and disadvantages in a local gang's decision to join a nation coalition. A decision to remain small and independent may lead to constant battles with a great number of rival gangs. Remaining independent may adversely affect a gang's desire to expand a criminal enterprise, such as selling drugs. Smaller gangs risk dissolution and may eventually disappear completely. Additionally, joining a nation coalition often means that a local gang loses its unique identity. On the other hand, a decision to join a nation coalition has its perks. With a national backing, the former small gang is now a force to be contended with in its local neighborhood because it will always have allies to go to war with. It still has rivals—in fact all the rivals of the nation coalition are now the enemies of this former small gang—but its attempt to keep independent status made it a target anyway. It is easier to expand a criminal drug operation through the assistance of the coalition. Furthermore, the lost former identity of the gang will simply be replaced by a more "respected" super gang identity (*Note*: Many of the former small gangs still maintain a degree of localized identity and the local gang can abandon the national alliance and/or join a rival alliance).

Gang denial is mostly a thing of the past because of gang proliferation. Throughout the past few decades there has been significant gang migration from urban communities to suburban and rural locations. The once local- and regional-based Crips and Bloods are found nationwide in large and small population areas. Gang proliferation is so significant that it represents a serious threat to public safety in many communities throughout the United States (FBI 2009c). The primary threat comes in the form of gang members migrating from urban to suburban areas where they engage in a disproportionate amount of criminal activity, especially with regard to trafficking, distribution, and sale of illegal drugs. Among the key findings of the 2009 "National Gang Threat Summary" conducted by the FBI (2009c) are the following:

- The existence of approximately 1 million gang members belonging to well over 27,000 gangs that are criminally active within all 50 states and the District of Columbia as of September 2008.
- Most gangs engage in violence in conjunction with a variety of crimes, including retail-level drug distribution.
- Fifty-eight percent of state and local law enforcement agencies reported that criminal gangs were active in their jurisdictions in 2008 compared with just 45 percent of reporting agencies in 2004.
- Gangs are migrating from urban to suburban and rural areas so that they can expand their drug distribution enterprises.
- Criminal street gangs commit as much as 80 percent of the crime in many communities.
- Street gangs are increasingly taking over the retail-level of drug distribution of most illicit drugs.
- Street gangs are trafficking in drugs internationally (e.g., through Canada and Mexico).
- Street gangs are increasingly using the Internet to recruit new members and to communicate with one another.
- Street gangs are working with outlaw motorcycle gangs to increase their criminal organizations, especially with regard to drug-trafficking.

As we shall learn in this chapter, street gangs have a growing presence in rural and suburban jurisdictions. Regional gangs such as the 18th Street Gang and Florencia 13 in Los Angeles are becoming increasingly powerful. The nation gangs of Crips, Bloods, People, and Folks are still expanding. And, the influence of MS-13 in multiple countries leads to its classification as a transnational gang.

RURAL AND SUBURBAN STREET GANGS

The proliferation of street gangs in rural and suburban areas is explained, at least in part, by the migration of urban gang members to less-populated areas. This gang migration pattern presents a growing concern among law enforcement agencies who were once, seemingly, isolated from the influence of street gangs. As mentioned earlier, the number of law enforcement agencies reporting gang activity to the Federal Bureau of Investigation (FBI) increased from 45 percent in 2004 to 58 percent in 2008. The OJJDP (2008) also gathers gang information from law enforcement agencies and in its 2006 Fact Sheet provides percentage breakdowns of agencies reporting gang problems by rural counties (n = 492), smaller cities (populations between 2,500 and 49,999, n = 695), suburban counties (n = 7400), and larger cities (cities with populations of 50,000 or more, n = 624) (see Table 6.1). As Table 6.1 indicates, slightly more than half of all responding suburban county jurisdictions reported gang activity in 2006 and nearly 15 percent of reporting rural county agencies reported a gang problem.

The most significant increases were in the East and the Southeast regions, most likely the result of the migration of gang members from urban areas such as New York City, Chicago, and Los Angeles to smaller jurisdictions. "In Chicago, gang movement to suburban areas can be attributed to several factors: the breakdown of traditional hierarchical gang structures resulting from law enforcement targeting of gang leaders, the razing of some large Chicago public housing projects, an abundance of wholesale illicit drug suppliers, and the expectation of high profits from new suburban drug operations" (FBI 2009c, 6). Gang migration from urban areas has contributed to the recruitment of new and younger youths from suburban and rural areas. Data compiled by the Bureau of Justice Statistics' National Crime Victimization Survey in 2005 reveal that 21 percent of high school students report gang activity in their schools, an increase from 18 percent in 2001; and 16 percent of rural high school students report gang activity in their schools, an increase from 13 percent in 2001 (FBI 2009c). The increase in gang activity in rural and suburban jurisdictions is attributed to street gangs utilizing middle schools and high schools as venues for recruitment and drug distribution.

Weisheit and Wells (2004, 5) found that in "most rural areas reporting gang activity, the majority of gang members were local youth. Yet, in many jurisdictions, the impact of migrating gang members was substantially greater than their limited numbers alone would suggest; they became an important conduit for the movement of ideas and symbols into these areas." Many of the gang members who move to rural areas and form gangs are, ironically, from families who moved there to escape the urban street gang life. Others have moved to rural and suburban areas specifically to make money by illegal means. While some rural and suburban agencies are prepared to deal with gangs (e.g., departments with at least some officers with gang training), other agencies are ill-prepared due to under-staffing and under-funding. Most agencies that report having a gang problem indicate that they have adopted a zero-tolerance policy of suppression. Nearly all agencies also stressed the importance of prevention and community involvement as means of combating the growth of gangs. (*Note*: Various prevention, suppression, and treatment efforts will be discussed in Chapter 9.)

While law enforcement agencies in rural and suburban areas are (or are becoming) prepared to deal with the increased presence of gang members in their jurisdictions, residents are not. In

TABLE 6.1 Percentage of Law Enforcement Agencies Reporting Gang Problems in 2006	
Law Enforcement Jurisdictions	**Gang Problems Reported in 2006 (Percentage)**
Rural counties	14.9
Smaller cities	32.6
Suburban counties	51.0
Larger cities	86.4

Source: OJJDP (2008)

small, rural towns across the United States, sounds of serenity and/or farm field machinery are being replaced by gang gunfire. For example, in Caldwell, Idaho, a town of 30,000 halfway between Boise and the Oregon line, police responded to more than 100 reports (from July to October 2004) of shots fired. "Two young men have been killed and several more wounded by drive-by shootings. Police believe that most of the violence is gang-related" (*The Citizen* 2004). Residents of places with small-town conservatism and the farming work ethic are alarmed by the "big-city" violence that has infested their quiet slice of America. Authorities in Caldwell claim that most of the gang members come from Hispanic farm working families who have, in increasing numbers, settled in Caldwell year-round instead of working the rotating seasonal schedule. (The recent economic upturn in Caldwell is cited as a reason for this.) A number of poor white youths in Caldwell have also formed gangs in an attempt to combat the growing Hispanic gangs. With a description of Hispanic gang members from a farming background, one would automatically deduce that Norte, or Norteno gangs, are located in Caldwell, as well as other rural and suburban areas of Oregon and Idaho. Such a deduction is accurate. However, once Norte made its mark in Caldwell, Sureno gangs were sure to follow.

The FBI has been aware of the gang problem in rural and suburban Idaho and Oregon for quite a while. In November 2011, six members of the **Northside** street gang, a Norteno affiliate, that operates in Treasure Valley, Idaho (the greater Boise area and bordering Oregon), and four known associates were indicted by a federal grand jury. A fifth associate was indicted a month earlier. They were charged with numerous counts, including drug-trafficking, unlawful possession of firearms, possessing sawed-off shotguns, transferring sawed-off shotguns, and possessing stolen firearms (FBI 2011k). Earlier in the month the feds indicted members of the **Lokked Out Khmer** Norte gang on a variety of drug-trafficking and firearms violation charges (FBI 2011k). In 2012, Shawn Lynn Gordon of Caldwell, an associate of the Northside gang, was sentenced to 121 months in federal prison for distribution of methamphetamine (FBI 2012g).

In 2011, the FBI put the hammer down on 30 members of the **Brown Magic Clica**, a Sureno street gang active in western Idaho and eastern Oregon (Kouri 2011). They were indicted in federal and state courts. The presence of Sureno street gangs in rural Idaho and Oregon is a part of the "Sureno Movement." The rural and suburban Idaho and Oregon Sureno gangs identify with the letter "M" and the number "13" as a tribute to the Mexican Mafia, even though it is unlikely any of these gang members know anyone in the Mexican Mafia. Thirteen of Brown Magic Clica were indicted by the FBI on charges that include participation in a racketeering enterprise, murder in aid of racketeering, attempted murder in aid of racketeering, assault with a deadly weapon in aid of racketeering, distribution of controlled substances, and unlawful possession of firearms. Eleven other members were charged with various racketeering-related crimes (Kouri 2011). As part of its zero-tolerance policy against gangs, Idaho law prohibits individuals from knowingly soliciting, inviting, encouraging, or otherwise causing a person to actively participate in a criminal gang or to engage in crimes committed as a street gang member. Although the Idaho law was challenged as unconstitutional, the state Supreme Court upheld its legality in 2012 (Rodine 2012).

Our review of street gangs in rural and suburban Idaho and Oregon represents a mere sampling of the jurisdictions of this size facing gang problems. Attention now shifts to local street gangs found in urban areas.

URBAN LOCAL STREET GANGS

As we have already learned, all municipalities, no matter how small, are potentially susceptible to gang formation and therefore gang-related problems. Larger cities such as Los Angeles, Chicago, Detroit, and New York generally receive the most attention from gang researchers and the media. Many people across the United States might be quite surprised by the level of gang violence that is rampant in the upstate New York cities of Syracuse, Rochester, and Buffalo (technically, these cities are in central and western New York). The growing incidence of violent crime and homicide attributed to street gangs in Syracuse, Rochester, and Buffalo proportionately rivals that of the more "traditional" gang cities. Because of gang mayhem, these thruway cities (they are linked by Interstate 90) have some of the highest homicide rates in the country. The homicide rates of these three thruway cities are routinely three to five times the national average, and the overall crime rates are much higher than national averages. The primary cause of gang homicide and violence in these cities is drug-trafficking.

The study of gang research along the "thruway corridor" represents an important contribution to the overall understanding of gang activity in general, and urban local street gangs in particular. Since the majority of street gangs develop spontaneously, and this is the case with these three cities, most of these gangs are made up of local youths. There are nation gang affiliates in these cities as well, but the largest percentage of the gang-related crime is committed by local-based gangs.

Syracuse Gangs

Syracuse is New York's fourth-largest city (population of 145,170 in 2010) and is known for its university's sports (which include Division I national championships at Syracuse University in football, basketball, and lacrosse) and long, snowy winters (average annual snowfall is 114 inches). As with any city of significant size, Syracuse has its rough, urban sections, where violence is common and drug deals sometimes end with murder. Based on 2010 U.S. Census Bureau (2012l) data, 52.8 percent of city residents are white, non-Hispanic; 29.5 percent are black; 8.3 percent are Hispanic or Latino; 5.5 percent are Asian; 1.1 percent are American Indian; and 5.1 percent reporting two or more races. A glaring statistic of 31.1 percent of city residents living below the poverty level factors into the gang presence in Syracuse. The median household income for Syracuse is $30,891 compared to $55,603 for the state of New York (U.S. Census Bureau 2012l). There are 25 identified street gangs operating in Syracuse, with an estimated total gang membership around 1,500. The number of homicides in Syracuse fluctuates from year to year, usually going down following a major gang bust for RICO (Racketeer Influenced and Corrupt Organizations) violations, and going back up prior to the next gang busted by RICO indictments. For example, in 2002, the homicide rate in Syracuse was 15.8, nearly three times the national average (the national average generally falls in the 5.2–5.4 range). In 2003, the first Syracuse gang to be brought down by RICO, the Boot Camp gang, triggered lowered homicide rates of 11.7 in 2003 and 11.0 in 2004. In 2008, the homicide rate in Syracuse was 14.4, and in 2010 it was 10.3. Syracuse's violent crime rate in 2009 was higher than the national violent crime rate by 127.9 percent (154.4% higher than the state rate) and the property crime rate was 39.7 percent higher than the national rate (119.1% higher than the state rate) (CityRating.com 2012a). The vast majority of Syracuse's homicides are committed by street gangs; and a disproportionate amount of violent and property crime is committed by street gangs.

Street gangs have existed in Syracuse since (at least) the early 1960s. Similar to many other jurisdictions, Syracuse street gangs have historically been mostly loosely organized. The crack epidemic of the 1980s changed this as Syracuse gangs slowly became more organized in an effort to capitalize on the money that could be earned selling crack and other recreational drugs. Through the assistance of larger gangs originating outside of the city (i.e., Bloods, Crips, and Latin Kings), many local urban Syracuse street gangs began to organize as drug enterprise gangs. The presence of the **Almighty Latin Kings** and **Queens Nation** can be traced in Syracuse at least as far back as the mid-1980s. The Latin Kings insist that they are not about violence and that they care more about community service and serving as a family for those who need them. They see themselves as a "nation of people." Members of the Kings must abide by a large number of formal rules, or codes of conduct. Among their rules are the following: Pee wees (young gangsters) must stay in school, obey curfews, and achieve good grades; married Kings must remain faithful to their wives; homosexuality is prohibited; and members must support each other when outsiders give them trouble. If a King disobeys a rule, he faces a violation ceremony. Membership size is information shared only among Latin Kings. Secret handshakes and phrases help the Kings to identify one another.

The Spanish Action League estimated that King membership in Syracuse in 1996 was about 100 local men and boys (Duffy 1996b). Local officials view the Latin Kings as a gang and not a community provider. Syracuse police reports linked the Kings to at least three shootings during the summer of 1996 in the city's south and near west sides. According to the police, the Latin Kings were involved in a feud with a local gang called the **Gracetown Boys**, who reside on Grace Street and claim Grace Park as their turf. Some Gracetown Boys claimed that members of the Kings tried to kill them in a drive-by shooting. They identified the shooters as Latin Kings because of the beads they wear around their necks. New Kings receive black and yellow beads that they treat with reverence. The colors have special meaning; for example, black is a reminder that Hispanics share a common ancestry, as most Latinos descend from African, Spanish, and Taino Indians—this is especially true for natives of Puerto Rico. "In Syracuse, many Latino immigrants and Puerto Ricans new to the mainland settle on the near west side . . . the neighborhood was ranked the 12th poorest predominantly white neighborhood in the country by *U.S. News & World Report* in 1994" (Duffy 1996a, A16). The West Side District is still home to the majority of Syracuse's Hispanic/Latino community, and while the median household income remains below the city's average, there has been a revitalization of the neighborhood, including an influx of arts and local businesses (City of Syracuse 2012). Despite the information provided by the Gracetown Boys, the police could not identify the Latin Kings as responsible for the shootings or any of the city's murders that year. As of this writing, the Latin Kings remain as a gang in Syracuse.

By the end of the 1990s, local street gangs took control of the tough streets of Syracuse's South Side—a area location for most of the city's street gangs. The South Side gangs are predominantly black, while the Hispanic gangs reside on the near west side. (In recent years, Hispanic street gangs, such as the **Highland gang**, can be found on the north side of the city.) In 1997, increased gang activity in Syracuse caught the attention of many civic leaders. The two most powerful gangs to emerge in Syracuse during this era were the **110 Gang** and **Boot Camp**. The 110 Gang claimed the area around Bellevue Avenue, including most of the southwest side; Boot Camp, the primary rival of 110, claimed the neighborhood around the corner of Midland Avenue and Colvin Street (this intersection is considered one of the most dangerous in Syracuse). These two vicious gangs fight over turf, girls, appearances, and glares that are perceived as a sign of disrespect. The numerous confrontations between the two gangs have led to murder, retaliation murder, and a vicious cycle of continuous revenge shootings.

Both of these gangs, 110 and Boot Camp, are strictly local gangs with no nation affiliation. These gangs care as much about controlling turf as they do about making a profit selling drugs. In 1996, David Kennedy, a researcher at Harvard University, declared that the 110 and Boot Camp gangs were not highly organized drug business enterprises and that they posed no real threat to the stability of the neighborhood. "Kennedy was among a team of experts who visited Syracuse last summer, at the request of the grassroots Youth Violence Task Force of Syracuse and Onondaga County, to help local officials develop a collaborative approach to reducing juvenile gun violence" (*The Post-Standard* 1997b, A8). Kennedy's research in Boston led to the creation of the Operation Cease-Fire Program, which was aimed at curtailing juvenile-related gun violence. Kennedy's conclusion about Syracuse's Boot Camp gang was inaccurate. By 2003,

Boot Camp had become so notorious and well organized that law enforcement officials used the RICO Act to issue numerous arrest warrants against this drug cartel.

Formed originally as the **Fernwood Boot Camp** in 1994 by Tyree "Cav" or "Caviar" Allen in honor of the Hip Hop band **Boot Camp Clik** (see "Connecting Street Gangs and Popular Culture" Box 6.1), a loose congregation of hard-core underground rappers, Allen supplied crack to his foot soldiers on consignment. The foot soldiers were to sell drugs, return the money to Allen, and then receive a cut of the profits. One year after its formation, the Fernwood Boot Camp gang was challenged by a group of younger kids from the same neighborhood after they were denied admission to the gang. Referred to as "Little Boot Camp," and led by Karo Brown, these youths were far more violent than Allen's crew. They were known to march around their neighborhood chanting, "We're Boot Camp" as a means of intimidation (Shepperd 2012). Brown's crew always carried guns and their willingness to use firearms concerned Allen. Following a shoot-out, the two crews merged and formed the **Boot Camp** gang. The Fernwood members, having earned their strips, were honored with the term *Original Gangsters* (OG). Other members on the hierarchy included "soldiers" and "flunkies," who were on the bottom of the totem pole.

On June 23, 1996, Lee Scott, a member of the **East Side** gang, was shot to death on Midland Avenue and Colvin Street (Boot Camp turf). No one was ever charged with the death and the proud members of Boot Camp began to refer to their turf as "Murder Capital." From that point on, Boot Camp gangbangers would cross their middle and ring fingers and spread their index and pinky fingers as a means of representing their gang affiliation. They hold their hand with three fingers pointed down, to form an "M," which represents both Midland (street) and Murder. Boot Camp may also flash the letter "C" for Colvin Street and "Capital" by curling their thumb and grouping the rest of their fingers on the same hand. The Crips make a sign similar to this. Another normal pose for Boot Camp members involves one fist outstretched with a curled finger sticking out, as if they were firing a gun ("Bust your gun" is the expression they use; it means fire your gun). On June 29, 1996, Allen and fellow gang member Orson Starling were killed in a car crash. Allen was out celebrating the birth of his son. Current Boot Camp gang members pay homage to Allen by stating "Word to Cav" as they place their hands over their hearts (O'Brien 2004b). With Allen's death, the Boot Camp gang, led by Karo Brown, became increasingly violent and orchestrated war against rival gangs that attempted to profit from selling drugs on the South Side.

The events leading up to the RICO-enabled arrests of Boot Camp in August 2003 reveal an acknowledgment of the growing gang problem in Syracuse and the commitment level of law enforcement officials to do something about it. As *The Post-Standard* staff writer Maureen Sieh (2003) reported, the Syracuse police department had a policy against even admitting to the existence of street gangs in their city; they described the teens who called themselves Boot Camp and Elk Block (discussed later) as "wannabes." By 2003, however, "Police Chief Dennis DuVal and other officials admitted there are gangs in Syracuse and created a gang task force to root them out" (Sieh 2003, A-1). It was revealed during the 2004 RICO trials of Boot Camp members that Syracuse police were ordered not to use the G-word in their reports. Detective Steven Stonecypher testified in the racketeering trial of accused Boot Camp gang leader Karo Brown that police investigators could not use the word *gang* in their descriptions of criminal activity in their crime reports until the policy changed in 2002 when the city hit an all-time high for homicides (O'Brien 2004a). Syracuse is a prime example of what can go wrong when city officials engage in gang denial.

In 2002, Syracuse Police Chief DuVal declared war on gang members, warning "They know we are coming" (Weibezahl 2003a, A1). Authorities were especially targeting members of Boot Camp and **Elk Block** (McKinley Ave., Elk St. and S. Salina St.), gangs suspected of running highly organized operations selling guns and drugs on city streets (Sieh 2003). The **1500 gang**, which claimed South Avenue and West Colvin Street, was also alleged to be selling and distributing drugs on Syracuse streets. The Syracuse police department's full-time gang task force filed 10,849 charges (from the time of its inception, April 29, 2002, to April 15, 2003) against a total of 5,566 different people—some of them known gang members. The police department reported that it confiscated 187 guns, a major step in combating street gangs. The courts have assisted in the prosecution of violent offenders through the technique of "fast-tracking"—a process designed to streamline a defendant's trip through the criminal justice system and keep him off the streets at the same time (O'Hara 2003).

Despite these numbers, some residents and store owners of the gang-ridden neighborhoods report that they have not noticed a difference. This belief is borne out by the fact that most of the arrests were for minor infractions (e.g., loitering, open containers, noise ordinance violations), with fewer than 3 percent for felony violations (e.g., grand larceny, weapons, attempted murder). Residents also wonder what took authorities so long to acknowledge the growing crisis on the city's South Side. As Sieh (2003, A-1) explained, "these arrests raise questions: How does a group of youths hanging out on the corner become a criminal enterprise in just a few years? When should authorities recognize these groups as gangs? Does a delay in that recognition cause the problems to get worse?" Residents in neighborhoods such as East Division Street on the North Side wonder if the growing level of delinquency among juveniles there indicates the formation of new street gangs. North Side district councilor Steve DeRegis believes that the city should pay close attention to children who drop out of school and hang out on street corners, because these status offenses lead to an increased probability of a youth joining a gang and selling drugs. DeRegis argued that "anytime you're in denial about something, you're not addressing the issue" (Sieh 2003, A-8). Malcolm Klein, a foremost authority on gang research and professor at the University of Southern California, notes that Syracuse was not alone in denying gangs. In fact, Klein (1995) reported that 40 percent of all cities go through a denial stage. Residents of gang neighborhoods notice the problem first and then report it to the police, but the police, politicians, and school officials are often slow to admit to the problem.

On August 8, 2003, two members of Boot Camp were indicted by a federal grand jury on charges of violating the RICO Act by using their membership in Boot Camp to engage in drug possession and murder. Demetrius Elmore, a member of the Elk Block gang, was gunned down in a drive-by shooting by Leonard Holbdy (the driver of the car) and Christian Williams (the shooter), members of Boot Camp, because Elmore was riding his bicycle to see his grandmother who lived in Boot Camp turf. On June 28, 2004, Williams pleaded guilty to shooting Elmore. One month earlier, Holbdy's brother Christopher was among 26 Boot Campers indicted on RICO charges of using systematic violence to control their turf and their drug trade (O'Brien 2003c, A-5). In September 2003, a reward was offered for help in capturing seven members of Boot Camp who were not apprehended when the indictments were served. Among the missing was Karo Brown, the leader of Boot Camp (within months all 26 Boot Camp members were apprehended). Police determined that Brown was the leader by intercepting the letters members of Boot Camp were sending to each other inside and outside prison. According to authorities, Boot Camp called themselves "Gambinos" named after the notorious New York City Mafia crime family. They labeled some of their letters to each other as "War Report." "Police intercepted the letters as part of a federal investigation that led to the incitement of 26 suspected Boot Camp gang members in June. Those gang members are charged with running a criminal enterprise for eight years by using systematic violence to control the gang's drug trade on the city's South Side" (O'Brien 2003, A-1).

By August 2004, 24 Boot Camp members arrested under RICO had pleaded guilty and one had the charges dismissed before going to trial. On August 3, 2004, a federal court jury found Karo Brown guilty of federal racketeering charges (RICO) and that he was responsible for at least two murders or attempted murders. Defense attorneys argued that a federal law designed to bring down mobsters should not apply to street gangsters. They also argued that Boot Camp was not a criminal enterprise as defined by the RICO Act. However, RICO had been used successfully to convict street gang members as criminal enterprises in Los Angeles, Chicago, New York City, Atlanta, Columbus, and Salt Lake City. RICO convictions against Boot Camp have stood as of early 2005.

Boot Camp had grown from a gang that was not considered to be a serious threat and that was lacking in the organizational skills necessary to carry out a criminal drug enterprise (in 1997) to a highly structured organization worthy of federal investigation. Boot Camp was just a local gang, with no nation-coalition affiliation, and yet it developed into a gang capable of controlling a highly profitable drug market. It used acts of intimidation, violence, and murder to enforce its presence and control a neighborhood. Authorities have linked more than 43 crimes to Boot Camp in 1995–2003. "The gang's crimes include two murders, several attempted murders, drug-trafficking and witness tampering. . . . Boot Camp made a profit of between $350,000 and $1 million" (O'Brien 2003, A-1). "The Boot Camp case may be the first in the country in which the RICO violation was based on geography rather than hierarchy against a street gang" (O'Brien 2003a, B5). Other street gangs have been prosecuted under RICO, but apparently not for using systematic violence to protect turf. The lesson provided by Boot Camp should not be lost on local agencies and officials who attempt to deny the presence, and impact, of local gangs in their jurisdiction: Ignoring the growing presence of gangs in the community can lead to damaging repercussions.

The indictments and convictions of the Boot Camp gang members had initial positive results in Syracuse. Early 2004 crime reports indicate that criminal activity has dropped in Syracuse (14%) in the first six months compared with the same period in 2003. There were 17 total homicides in Syracuse in 2004, the same number as in 2003. Police calls and criminal charges were cut in half since the 2002 RICO arrests of Boot Camp members. Despite this evidence, grassroots organizations such as "Families Against Injustice (FAI)" criticized the use of federal racketeering laws that lead to incarceration of disadvantaged youths. The FAI believes that social policies should be created that prevent the social conditions that lead to crime. Gang activity still persists in Syracuse as new gangs attempt to fill the void left by the dismantling of Boot Camp. In March 2004, gang members from the 110 Gang and Lexington Avenue fought a gang member from the Brick Town Gang at the Syracuse Renaissance Academy at Carnegie School. Five members of the Bloods street gang were arrested by a federal-state gang task force in late 2004 in Syracuse. The gang members were arrested on charges of selling crack cocaine in the city over the previous two years.

As described in Chapter 1, incarceration does not end gang affiliation. Correctional facilities are filled with street gang members. Incarcerated gang members merely strengthen their bond to the gang while serving time. Once released to the streets again, an ex-con gang member is likely to go right back to gangbanging. In 2002, information gathered by the Onondaga County Sheriff's Office (Syracuse is in Onondaga County) and published by the *The Post-Standard* (O'Brien and Sieh 2003a) revealed the gangs with the most inmates claiming affiliation in the Onondaga County Justice Center Jail:

1. Bloods—141
2. Boot Camp—98
3. 110 Gang—79
4. Brighton Brigade—75
5. Bricks (or Bricktown)—42

6. Crips—28
7. Lexington Boys (Lex or Lex Diamonds)—22

Nearly 70 percent of the inmates were black, 9 percent were white, 2 percent were Hispanic, and the other 19 percent were other race/ethnicity not listed. Not surprisingly, most of the inmates claiming gang affiliation were young. Fifty-eight percent of the inmates were between the ages of 20 and 25 and another 11 percent were under age 20.

After successfully taking down Boot Camp, at least for the time being, law enforcement authorities turned their attention to Elk Block. Elk Block is another local street gang. Syracuse's Gang Violence Task Force was well aware of the dangers presented by Elk Block but deemed Boot Camp as the most violent Syracuse street gang. The Task Force worked cooperatively with state and federal officials to bring Elk Block down. Federal authorities first targeted Elk Block after the gang imported 70 guns from Georgia for an anticipated battle with Boot Camp (*The Post-Standard* 2009a). With Boot Camp sent away for RICO violations, Elk Block had temporarily won control of the drug market on the South Side. In July 2005, 16 of the most long-term violent members of the Elk Block gang were indicted on RICO charges. Eleven pleaded guilty and the other five were found guilty at trial (Syracuse Police Department 2012). The next gang to take over the South Side drug trade was the **Brighton Brigade** (Cannon St., W. Lafayette Ave., W. Brighton Ave.). Another sweeping RICO indictment resulted in the arrest of 14 members of this local gang. All 14 members pleaded guilty. During the raids officials found loaded hand guns, crack cocaine, digital scales, drug packaging paraphernalia, cookware to process powder cocaine into crack, a bullet proof vest, cash, and a substantial quantity of gang-related items, such as posters, drawings, and clothing (Ramirez and Lee 2006).

The next local street gang to emerge as the power gang of Syracuse was the **110 Gang**. This gang had built itself a reputation as being the toughest since Boot Camp. Researching the origin of the meaning of "110" gang was quite daunting and at times contradictory. One explanation centers on the gang's hangout at 110 Onondaga Ave. while Quashawn Blunt (a.k.a. Qua), the OG for the 110 Gang, presided over the gang. The gang members would say, "Let's go to the 110." And as a result, the police would call them the "110 Gang." Another explanation is connected to the New York State Penal Law wherein Section 110.00 refers to an "attempt to commit a crime." A 110 Gang member informed me that "110" comes from the number of members in the gang, "We are 110 strong." Another reason for the confusion of the gang name's origin is connected to the fact that the gang goes by different names, including "B-Block" and "Face Mobb." *Face Mobb* is a name used to pay homage to 110 Gang member Darone Scott (a.k.a. "Face"), who was shot and killed by a member of the Boot Camp gang, on July 4, 2001. 110 Gang members celebrate every July 4 as "Face Day" to honor Scott (United States District Court for the Northern District of New York 2009). The 110 Gang members also refer to themselves as "B-Block," a reference to Bellevue Avenue, which runs through the heart of 110 Gang territory. The gang uses "110" and "B-Block" (among other things) graffiti to mark its territory. They represent gang affiliation by wearing white bandannas and white t-shirts (Your News Now 2009). The primary gang hand signal is displayed by putting two fingers in the air—which represent "11"—and touching the index and middle fingers to the thumb, thereby forming a circle—which represents "0" (USDC 2009). Like most gangs, 110 uses MySpace websites to glorify and perpetuate itself by posting gang-related photos and writings. Like most of the local gangs in Syracuse, 110 Gang members have a familial affiliation with a current gang member. The 110 Gang had been dealing in drugs for so long that by 1998 it had a firm hierarchical structure. The gang would get drugs from New York City and distribute them among three dealers, who then supplied OG gang members as mid-level dealers, who established lower-level street dealers who would sell eight balls of cocaine and crack to individual customers who were called "licks." The more successful an individual was in selling drugs, the higher in the ranks he would climb. The operation was so big that it eventually caught the eyes of law enforcement and led to federal arrests. In 2009, 12 members of the 110 Gang were indicted on RICO violations for engaging as a criminal enterprise responsible for the distribution of controlled substances in 110 Gang territory and elsewhere and for preserving, protecting, and expanding its territory through use of intimidation, violence, threats of violence, assault, attempted murders, and murders (USDC 2009).

The next Syracuse gang to face RICO violations was the **Bricktown Gang**. The Bricktown gang is located along Salina St. to the west and Interstate 81 to the east, from Burt St. to the north and W. Colvin St. on the South. The four previous gangs busted by RICO all involved violence between rival gang members. Bricktown took the lives of two innocent people. One of these victims was the much-publicized 20-month-old Rashaad Walker Jr. who was killed in November when Bricktown member Saquan Evans fired a gun into the back of a minivan in retaliation for a gang-shooting two days earlier. (*Note*: On May 15, 2012, Evans was given a 25-years-to-life sentence for the murder of Walker Jr.) The second innocent victim was Anthony Ford who was gunned down on his front porch, a victim of mistaken identity (Bricktown members thought he was a rival gang member). Rashaad Walker's father is a member of the 110 Gang and Bricktown believed that 110 was responsible for the killing of their friend and former Henninger High School athlete Kihary Blue. Blue was a gifted athlete and was not a gang member. Blue and his friend Jarrel Williams were shot in a car traveling on Interstate 81 at the Interstate 690 interchange (Baker 2010). (*Note*: Rashaad Walker Sr. was arrested for committing a drive-by shooting and a number of related weapons charges in 2012.) As it turned out, the shooting was not caused by the 110 Gang but the V-NOT gang (to be discussed shortly). The Bricktown gang sold drugs throughout their territory. The gang frequently scrawled gang-related graffiti on buildings in their territory, including "252"—referring to the willingness of members to do 25 years to (thus, 25 years 2 life, or 252) life in prison to support Bricktown (O'Brien 2011). Before long, many of these gangsters lived up to their "252" motto. In 2011, 14 members of the Bricktown gang were arrested for RICO violations, chief among them, for operating as a criminal enterprise involved with drug-trafficking and the use of violence, including murder, shootings, illegal gun possession, and intimidation to defend their territory. By November 2012, all 14 members of Bricktown who were arrested under the RICO Act were sentenced to federal prison for charges that ranged from engaging in a pattern of racketeering, which included murder, drug-trafficking, and robbery (*The Post-Standard* 2012c,d).

In 2012, the sixth local Syracuse street gang in 10 years was brought down by RICO violations, the **V-NOT** gang. V-NOT is a reference to their South Side territory with the "V" for Valley Drive, which goes through the heart of V-NOT turf (which ends at West Seneca Turnpike in the south and reaches West Newell Street as the northern border) and NOT for N-word On Top. The V-NOT gang headquarters is located at 321 Shirley Drive, off of Valley Drive. Authorities estimate that there are at least 90 members of the V-NOT gang. It was V-NOT member Kahari Smith who shot Blue in a car on the I-81. On October 23, 2010, a Bricktown gang member stabbed a V-NOT gang member at North Geddes Street bar. Later that night, a V-NOT member retaliated by firing 21 shots from an AK-47 assault rifle into the home of the Bricktown member. Back and forth went the war between these local gangs. V-NOT was also involved in selling drugs. Like the 110 Gang, V-NOT referred to cocaine junkies as "licks." And, like the other five gangs described here, V-NOT gang members faced the wrath of federal RICO indictments. In 2012, 11 members of V-NOT were indicted on charges of murder, robbery, drug-trafficking, and witness tampering (O'Brien 2012a). By November 2012, two members of V-Not pleaded guilty to engaging in racketeering activity, including murder; drug-trafficking, and robbery (*The Post-Standard* 2012e,f).

As we have learned, Syracuse has problems with local street gangs. Despite the use of RICO to arrest and prosecute one gang after another, street gangs have not disappeared from Syracuse. And they are not likely to anytime soon as the prevailing socioeconomic reasons for their existence have not been addressed. Like the rest of the country, gangs will exist in Syracuse until drastic changes are made in the social system and cultural values of people who view gangs as the best means of becoming successful. By no means have authorities given up on the youth of Syracuse. After spending the past decade putting nearly 100 street gang members behind bars, Federal prosecutors are now working on prevention methods—steering potential gang members away from gang life (O'Brien 2012b). In September 2012, the U.S. Justice Department awarded the Syracuse community a $300,000 grant, one of only nine grants awarded nationally to fund an effort to reduce gang violence. The grant money will be used to start a program called Syracuse Truce, aimed at preventing the proliferation of street gangs (O'Brein 2012b).

Our attention changes now to Rochester, New York, street gangs.

Rochester Gangs

Rochester, with a declining population of 210,565 (2010 Census data), is the third-largest city in the state of New York. This city enjoys a white-collar image and attempts to portray itself as more glamorous than its western (Buffalo) and eastern (Syracuse) neighboring cities. Unfortunately for Rochester, especially its citizens, this city often has the highest homicide rate in the state. Based on 2010 U.S. Census Bureau (2012m) data, 41.7 percent of city residents are black; 37.6 percent white, non-Hispanic; 16.7 percent Hispanic or Latino; 3.1 percent Asian; and .5 percent Native American. Like Syracuse, Rochester has a poverty rate higher than 30 percent (30.4) and a slightly lower median household income than Syracuse at $30,138. Once again, socioeconomic factors contribute to the significant gang problem of this upstate city. In 2009, Rochester's violent crime rate was 158.3 percent higher than the national average (180.9% higher than the state rate), and its property crime rate was 131.4 percent higher than the national average (79.1% higher than the state rate) (CityRating.com 2012b). The homicide rate in Rochester is consistently about four to five times the national average. In 2003, Rochester had 58 homicides. This figure equates to a whopping homicide rate of 26.7 per 100,000 people (a rate more than five times the national rate), by far the highest for any city in New York State with a population over 50,000. In other years, Rochester's homicide rate was 24.9 percent (2005); 23.2 percent (2006); 24.2 percent (2007); 20.5 percent (2008); 13.6 percent (2009); and 20.1 percent (2010) (City-Data.com 2012a). To put the homicide rate in perspective, New York City generally has a homicide rate just above the national average, 6.56 in 2010 (TRF Policy Map 2012). According to the FBI's Uniform Crime Report, the national homicide rate for young black men aged 14–24 is 125 per 100,000 (FBI 2006). In Rochester, the rate is about 520 per 100,000, compared to the rate of 16 per 100,000 for white males of the same age category.

The high homicide rate in Rochester is directly attributed to street gangs. An impoverished area of the city known as "The Crescent" (home to 27% of the city's residents) is the location of 80 percent of Rochester's homicides. There is no specific neighborhood called "The Crescent"; rather, the high-crime neighborhoods together form a crescent (think of the ecological/Chicago School theory described in Chapter 3) when the locations of murders and violent crimes are plotted on a map of Rochester. Thus, the high-crime areas of inner-city Rochester are commonly collectively referred to as "The Crescent." Facing a $50-million budget gap, Rochester City School Superintendent Dr. Manuel Rivera announced that the city would have to cut funding to the schools unless there was an increase in state aid. In light of the gloomy economic picture facing

Rochester's school district and referring to the concentrated poverty in the city's "crescent" neighborhoods—site of the majority of Rochester's 57 homicides in 2003—Rochester Mayor Bill Johnson stated that the problem was like "a noose around our necks" (Oliveiri 2004, 8).

Officials have been aware of the street gang problem in Rochester for years. Information provided by the FBI's *Law Enforcement Bulletin* reveals that "a 5-year study (1990 through 1994) conducted in Rochester, New York, attributed 86 percent of youth violence in that city to individuals involved with the gang subculture. The same study contended that gangs controlled the majority of drug trafficking within Rochester" (Federal Bureau of Investigation 2001). Most of the gangs found in Rochester are local gangs but some, such as the Latin Kings, who operate in the Clinton section (especially around Avenue D) of Rochester, have nation affiliation. The dominant gang in Rochester is **Dipset** (a local gang). The name *Dipset* comes from the "Dipset Anthem," a rap song by The Diplomats (Flanigan 2003b). (See "Connecting Street Gangs and Popular Culture" Box 6.1 for further description.) The Dipset gang has been linked to 8–10 homicides from mid-2002 through 2003. Dipset is also the largest gang in Rochester, with an estimated total membership of 80, most of whom are between the ages of 15 and 21. As with most of the Rochester gangs, Dipset consists of youths who have grown up together (spontaneous gangs) and as they got older began to engage in criminal acts such as drug dealing, robbery, and homicide.

In late December 2003, police arrested 12 members of this northeast Rochester gang. Police Chief Robert Duffy's goal was to make "the Monroe County Jail the largest gang clubhouse in western New York" (Flanigan 2003b, 8A). The suspects were placed on a "fast track" in the criminal justice system (similar to the approach used in Syracuse), with indictments coming just days after an arrest. Six assistant district attorneys along with several police investigators were assigned to make sure that the charges against the Dipset members stuck. Chief Duffy also stated that Rochester gangs appear to be a loose confederation of youths who conspire to commit such crimes as drug sales, robbery, and various acts of violence and lack the formal hierarchy of nation gangs, such as the Crips and Bloods. Another sign of their loose alliance was demonstrated by how quickly members of Dipset were willing to provide information to police in exchange for a reduction in sentences. Nation coalition gang members would never sell out their comrades. Regardless, the members of Dipset were extremely violent. Police believe that they had committed at least 20 "executions"—planned murders.

Box 6.1   *Connecting Street Gangs and Popular Culture*

Hip-Hop and Its Influence on the Local Street Gangs of Boot Camp and Dipset

The Syracuse street gang Boot Camp was formed in 1994 as Fernwood Boot Camp under the leadership of Tyree "Cav" or "Caviar" Allen. A year later, a group of younger gangsters aged 10–12 (Shepperd 2012) from the same neighborhood, calling themselves the "Little Boot Camp," tried to take over Fernwood. A number of fierce gun battles ensued between these youths. By mid-1995, the two factions merged under new leadership (Karo Brown) and a new shortened name, Boot Camp. The origin of the name *Boot Camp* (both as the Fernwood Boot Camp Gang and as the Boot Camp Gang) can be traced to the hip-hop super group "Boot Camp Clik." Cav Allen greatly admired the Boot Camp Clik and their hardcore rap style.

Boot Camp Clik originated in Brooklyn, New York, in 1993. The members of Boot Camp Clik include renowned artists from Brooklyn: Buckshot (from the group Black Moon), a famous underground rapper and leader of Boot Camp Clik; Smif-N-Wessum, also known as Cocoa Brovaz (from Tek and

Steele); Heltah Skeltah (a hip-hop duo with members Rock and Sean Price); and OGC (Originoo Gunn Cappaz consisting of rappers Starang Wondah, Louieville Sluggah, and Top Dog) (U.S. Military 2012). Boot Camp Clik were an immediate success in the underground world of rap. They added personal and social aspects in their lyrics and are considered the first rap group to infuse reggae elements in their music. Buckshot together with the group Black Moon is also credited with establishing the backpacker scenes within underground hip-hop (U.S. Military 2012). Black Moon made it big in the underground world with its 1992 debut single release "Who Got Da Props?" The song also made the Billboard Hot 100 (at #86). After their first release of "Dah Shinin," Boot Camp Clik leader Buckshot and business partner Dru Hu founded Duck Down Records and signed both Heltah Skeltah and OGC to the label. In mid-1995, the entire Clik membership, in all of its variations, signed with Duck Down. Boot Camp Clik enjoyed minor commercial success but great underground respect. Their lyrics glorified life on the streets, acknowledged a reality that gangsters end up in jail, and liberal use of the "n-word."

Boot Camp Clik's rise to glory in the early 1990s inspired many hip-hop artists, thrilled fans, and influenced the name of a soon-to-be notorious urban local street gang in Syracuse, New York, a gang that would be involved in murder, conspiracy, racketeering, and a host of other criminal activities that would eventually lead to prosecution under the RICO Act.

In Rochester, New York, an urban local street gang of infamous reputation, Dipset, was also named in honor of a hip-hop group. The name *Dipset* comes from the "Dipset Anthem," a rap song by The Diplomats (Flanigan 2003b). The lyrics for this song are filled with references to gangsters, drugs, drive-bys, and homicide. The word *Dipset* may be a code word for "run," as in "flee the scene"; or, it can be used as a term for a person who is a sexual play toy. In hip-hop, the word *Dipset* is the popular name for the Harlem-based hip-hop group The Diplomats, founded by Cam'ron and Jim Jones in 1997. Over the course of the following six years, artists joined the Jones brothers' band. In 2003, The Diplomats released the album "Diplomatic Immunity," which featured a remix of "Hey Ma" (a platinum single with Cam'ron's third solo album in 2002) as well as lead single, "Dipset Anthem." Dipset Anthem would reach #64 on the Billboard Hot R&B/Hip-Hop Songs chart. The Dipset Anthem would also influence a group of gangsters in Rochester who would embrace both the message and the name offered via this anthem. The lyrics are quite graphic and not meant for a publication such as this. Suffice it to say, the lyrics make use of the "n-word" and glorify drive-by shootings.

Hip-hop, like its Western counter, Gangsta rap, is all about representing oneself as being tough, not backing down, demonstrating a willingness to shoot a rival and be shot at, is a genre that appeals to urban street gangs. There are, potentially, a large number of street gangs across the United States that were influenced by hip-hop acts such as Boot Camp Clik and The Diplomats (Dipset).

Dipset competes with such rival gangs as **Thurston Zoo** (operating on Thurston Road) and **Plymouth Rock** (which operates on Plymouth Avenue) for control of the lucrative drug market. Plymouth Rock is also known as Plymouth Roc, as in "Roc"-hester. Dipset is so large that its claimed turf includes Hudson, Clifford, and Joseph Avenues, along with Avenue A and North Street (Flanigan 2003a). These gangs are local and have no affiliation with national gangs. They exist as a confederation of youths who conspire to commit such crimes as drug sales, robbery, and physical assault. They are neighborhood kids who grew up together. Residents of the crescent area of Rochester are well aware of the presence of Dipset and their rivals as their graffiti can be found throughout the area.

For the past decade Rochester's street gangs have been responsible for a great deal of violence. Law enforcement officials hope that if they can dismantle the gangs, the high homicide rate in their city will be dramatically reduced. Suppression efforts to control gangs include the 1997 **Youth Violence Initiative**, a coordinated multiagency organization designed to reduce the violence committed by youth between the ages of 13 and 21. The initiative, which became fully operational in July 1998, involves the cooperation between a number of law enforcement and juvenile justice agencies. The Youth Violence Initiative employs a two-pronged approach:

1. Concentrating enforcement efforts on the small percentage of youth who are responsible for the vast majority of violent crimes
2. Identifying those youth who may be at risk of becoming violent offenders and providing them with the appropriate intervention and prevention services (*Source*: Rochester's 1999 *State of the City Report*)

Approximately 14 city and county personnel staff were hired to work on this initiative full-time. One of these agencies, called **Cease Fire**, is a multiagency effort that brings together representatives from local law enforcement, human service agencies, government, and the community to deliver a zero-tolerance message to juvenile offenders and adult gang members who have been identified as most active in youth violence. Offenders are warned of the serious consequences of their continued gang activity and are offered a variety of alternatives that include education, job training, or job placement assistance. This agency meets with local gangs or gang-affiliated individuals on the streets and at the Monroe County Jail. Another component of the Youth Violence Initiative led to the creation of **School Resource Officers**, who are essentially police officers assigned to every middle and high school in the City of Rochester. Although controversial, their presence has greatly reduced incidents of crime, particularly violent crime. The **Truancy Intervention Program** is another of the 14 programs established by the initiative. As in most cities, the idea of enforcing truancy laws is guided by the realization that youths cannot commit crimes during school hours on the streets if they are in schools where they belong (*Source*: Rochester's 1999 *State of the City Report*).

Some community members fear that suppression efforts alone fail to address the root of the high crime rate in Rochester. Sister Grace Miller, executive director of the House of Mercy, a homeless shelter and community outreach center on Hudson Avenue, believes the reason there are so many gang members is poverty and hopelessness. Her belief that intervention strategies are also necessary to combat the growing presence of gangs is shared by many community leaders throughout the nation and is echoed by gang researchers as well. In Rochester, the city developed a program consisting of 11 distinct campaigns to enhance the quality of life for all of its citizens. Collectively, this program is a part of **Rochester's Urban Renaissance** program. Campaign number 3, "Rochester as a City of Compassion and Caring," addresses the issue of street gangs and their impact on the quality of life experienced by Rochesterians. In an effort to improve the physical and mental well-being of its citizens, as well as a sense of pride in the community, the city has developed a number of key strategies. First, reducing the need for human services by increasing the health, safety, and welfare of its citizens; reducing the number of citizens who experience the problems of homelessness, teen pregnancy, alcohol/drug abuse, and poverty; establishing neighborhood resource centers; and reducing public tolerance of drug use, violent behavior, drunkenness, and gangs (*City of Rochester Comprehensive Plan* 2002).

Despite the city of Rochester's firm commitment to winning the war against gangs (e.g., Rochester Mayor Bob Duffy and Police Chief David Moore's 2007 "zero-tolerance policy") and increasing the quality of life for its citizens, Rochester was deemed by the FBI as the 30th most dangerous city to live in in 2007 (Coventry 2007). Rochester has had some success in bringing down street gangs. For example, a multiagency violent crime task force took down the **G-Boys** gang under the leadership of then Office of Public Integrity Director Richard C. Vega. Vega was also instrumental in the initiation of Project Exile. Project Exile is a gun initiative that targets violent offenders who use firearms in the course of their criminal activity (City of Rochester 2009). Beyond local attempts to control street gangs, Rochester has assistance from the Bureau of Alcohol, Tobacco, Firearms and Explosives (ATF). The ATF's New York Field Division, comprised of special agents, investigators, auditors, technicians, and support staff, is committed to reducing violent gangs and their criminal activities in Rochester along with Syracuse, Buffalo, Albany, New York City, and Long Island (Bureau of Alcohol, Tobacco, Firearms and Explosives 2009). As another example of Rochester's attempt to curb gang activity, the Rochester police department and various community leaders held a three-day summit titled "Gangs 101" in August 2011 wherein violence caused by gangs and ideas on how to curtail further gang escalation were discussed (Voorhees 2011).

Buffalo Gangs

Buffalo is another New York State "big" city to experience a continuous drop in population. Like Syracuse and Rochester, and many other cities in the rust belt, the decline of manufacturing jobs has really hurt the Buffalo economy. In 2000, Buffalo had 292,648 residents; in 2010 it had 261,310 (U.S. Census Bureau 2012n). Even with this decline in population, Buffalo remains the second-largest city in the state of New York. Based on 2010 U.S. Census Bureau (2012n) data, 45.8 percent of Buffalo city residents are white, non-Hispanic; 38.6 percent are black; 10.5 percent are Hispanic or Latino; 3.2 percent are Asian; and 0.8 percent are Native American. Nearly 30 percent (29.6) of Buffalo residents live below the poverty line and just like their "Thruway" neighbors, low socioeconomic status (SES) is a significant contributor to criminal urban street gang activity. In 2009, Buffalo's violent crime rate was higher than the national average by 239.8 percent (279.3% higher than the state rate) and 78.8 percent higher than the national property crime rate (180.4% higher than the state rate) (CityRating.com 2012c). Following national patterns, Buffalo gangs are racially segregated. There are at least 35 street gangs in Buffalo with an estimated total membership of more than 2,000. Most of these gangs are neighborhood gangs and are named after the neighborhood streets.

The greatest numbers of gangs are found on Buffalo's impoverished East Side. The most notorious African-American gangs include the **Fruit Belt Posse (FBP)**, **Bailey Street Posse**, **Fillmore Street Boys**, **New Burgh Crew**, **Townsend Boyz**, **Good Year Crew**, **Downtowners**, **Uptowners**, **Loepere Street Crew**, **Michigan Street Posse**, and the **Genesee Street Posse**. Many of the local projects have their own gangs: **Langfield**, **Perry**, and **McCarley Gardens**. The Vice Lords, Gangster Disciples, Crips, and Bloods have affiliation gangs in Buffalo as well. The number of Crips and Bloods continues to increase in Buffalo. Cheektowaga (a Buffalo suburb) police believe that there are about 100 Blood members in the Buffalo area (*Cheektowaga Times* 2003). The Crips in the Buffalo area have the following gangs among their affiliates: **Shot Gun Gangster Crips**, **Rolling Gangster Crips**, **KB Deuce Crips**, **Loso Crips**, **Central Park Crips**, and the **8-Ball Crew Crips**. Many of these gangs have female auxiliary gangs (e.g., **8-Ball Girls**). Among the independent female gangs in Buffalo are the **Mama Thugs** and the **Baby Thugs** (Ernst 2002). The **Hillbillies**, a new all-female gang on Dodge Street, emerged when many men in the Dodge Street Posse were jailed and the gang recruited young women to take over the drug business (Thomas 2004). Hispanic gangs in Buffalo are smaller in number and less notable than black gangs. They are generally found on the West Side of Buffalo, with the **10th Street Gang** and the **14th Street Gangs** as the most notable. These gang members are mostly Puerto Rican.

Street gangs have existed in Buffalo for more than 100 years. For the unacquainted, Buffalo was once a booming city and was one of the top 10 most populated cities in the nation in 1900. This demographic reality helps to explain the longer gang history in Buffalo compared to Syracuse and Rochester. The early Buffalo gangs were similar to other gangs of this era in that they were primarily involved in petty crime and delinquent activities. As in larger urban cities, the rise of contemporary Buffalo gangs had its roots in the general 1960s "civil disobedience" movements. In the 1960s, a gang known as the **Mad Dogs** claimed most of the East Side. The Mad Dogs used drugs (marijuana, heroin, and cocaine) and wore jackets with *Mad Dogs* printed on the back. They were involved in petty crime, such as theft, and fought over turf. Most battles were settled by hand-to-hand combat with the traditional weapons of bats, rocks, bricks, and switchblades. After nearly 10 years in existence, the Mad Dogs' reign over the streets of Buffalo ended. Most of them got factory jobs, as there were plenty of factory jobs in Buffalo in those days (e.g., at Bethlehem Steel).

In the early 1980s, the FBP emerged, mostly as an offshoot of the Mad Dogs. The FBP is a gang from a neighborhood that centers on the intersection of High Street and the Kensington Highway (the 33), with side streets named after fruits (grape, peach, orange, and lemon). For the most part, members of the neighborhood accepted them because they were primarily a co-hort of adolescents who attended the same local public school (Future's Academy School #37 on Carlton). As the years went by, the FBP became increasingly violent. School #37 was experiencing a great deal of disruptive behavior, resulting in several gang members being transferred or expelled. In the 1980s and early 1990s, the FBP was age-graded by three distinct levels:

1. Senior Posse: ages 16 and over
2. Junior Posse: ages 11–15
3. Baby Posse: younger than 11

To become a member of the FBP, recruits had to be initiated by means of a physical beating. Anyone who ran away during the initiation ceremony was a "marked" man. These disgraced recruits would be subject to gang beatings because they were considered a "punk bitch" or "cur" (a person who is scared to fight).

The FBP were known to sell drugs for profit. They fought with rival gangs on the streets and at neutral sites such as the East Ferry New Skating Land. FBP members would walk in packs through the crowd of youths chanting "Fruit Belt, Fruit Belt, Fruit Belt" as a means of drawing attention to themselves and calling out rival gangs and nongang members alike. They were known to dance in a circle as a crew to intimidate others, and they danced with girlfriends from rival gangs to start fights. With the escalation of weaponry, gun battles replaced fist fights as a means of settling disputes. The FBP died out in the early 1990s due to the deaths of many members and the incarceration of most of the remaining members. There is evidence that the FBP has reemerged in the 2000s and is still active today.

The **M&B Crew** rose to power in the early 1990s under the leadership of Donald "Sly" Green and Darryl "Reese" Johnson; the *M&B* refers to gang members from Marshall Street and Barthel Street. The level of violence committed by this infamous Buffalo gang is legendary—the homicide rate hit an all-time high during the early to mid-1990s, with a modern record high of 92 in 1994. A large number of these murders were committed by the M&B Crew as they attempted to control the distribution of crack cocaine in Buffalo. Green and Johnson routinely ordered the executions of rival gang members. A massive law enforcement effort by federal and local police resulted in the arrests of Green, Johnson, and numerous other gang members. Green and Johnson are currently serving multiple life sentences on multiple charges, including murder and drug-trafficking. After Green and Johnson were sent to prison, the M&B Crew was led by Calvin Cornelious, who immediately took control of drug distribution. Cornelious followed the same pattern of murder and drug-trafficking as Green and Johnson. In 1999, he was arrested on 60 counts of federal racketeering and murder. He was already in federal custody for unrelated drug-trafficking and rape charges (*Buffalo News* 1999).

In 1997–2000, Buffalo averaged 40 homicides a year, a relatively low number for the city compared to the era that preceded it. However, at the turn of the century, the Bloods and Crips had found their way to Buffalo. The Blood and Crip recruiters in Buffalo came mostly from New York City (the Bronx) rather than directly from Los Angeles. The signs of renewed street gang activity became quite apparent. There were 66 homicides in 2001, and there were 19 murders alone in the month of May when gangs were fighting over the control of drug-trafficking. As of January 2002, there were only 26 arrests for the 66 slayings (Michel 2002). Buffalo's homicide rate for 2000 was 22.55 per 100,000, a figure that is four times the national average of 5.6 per 100,000 (FBI statistics). The high homicide rate in Buffalo is a common trait that it shares with fellow upstate cities Syracuse and Rochester. Gang shootings terrorize community members who are forced to live in gang territories. In 2001, there were 820 shootings in Buffalo, with most of the victims in their late teens and twenties. A majority of the shootings occurred on the city's East Side, but a handful occurred on the West Side (Thomas and Pignataro 2003). Most of Buffalo's gang homicides occur on the East Side and the victims are generally African Americans. Buffalo Police Department Lt. Jake Ulewski, when describing a rash of shootings in Buffalo in late July 2003, stated, "It's like a wild west show" (Weibezahl 2003b, A1).

While local street gangs like the Downtowners (from the Clinton–Jefferson area) and Uptowners (from the Bailey and Minnesota area) continue to have an influence on the street gang scene, involved in such criminal acts as murder and drug-trafficking, it is the presence of the Crips and the Bloods that commands the greatest concern. Most of Buffalo's gangs are local and neighborhood-based; some are affiliated with such national gangs as the Bloods and Crips. The Bloods and Crips recruit Buffalo's youth to help in the highly lucrative drug trade found in Buffalo. Elsie B. Fisher, the principal at Buffalo's Alternative School, reported in the early 2000s that there were many signs of Bloods and Crips recruiting schoolchildren into their gangs. Some students at the Alternative High School on Oak Street and the Junior High on Fulton Street have tried to wear gang colors to school. As in Los Angeles, the Buffalo Blood gangs wear red plaid handkerchiefs, known as **soldier rags** (do-rags), wrapped around their heads; the Crips wear blue plaid handkerchiefs. The flashing of gang signs and the use of gang graffiti and symbolism are other shared traits between these local Bloods and Crips and their Los Angeles–based brothers and sisters. Officials at the Alternative High School stepped in immediately and banned the wearing of gang colors to school.

In my own interviews with members of the 8-Ball Crips and the Central Park Crips, it became quite apparent that these Crips have many similarities with those of Los Angeles. The 8-Ball Crips are all expected to know their gang history, including such things as the Los Angeles origins and leaders, past and present. These Crips abide by the nation rules and have an alliance with the Folks, whom they consider "cousins," as opposed to fellow Crips who are treated like brothers. The right-left distinction is also abided by, with the Crips slanting to the right out of respect to the Folks. The six-point star is also respected, as are Gangster Disciples' pitchforks. Thus, the 8-Ball Crew will chant "6 poppin', 5 droppin,' " revealing allegiance to the six-star nation and death to five-star-nation gangsters—a six-star member shoots (pops) a five-star gangster (he is going to drop). One of the gang members ("Sam") told me that they generally wear black, especially black bandannas (which is symbolic of a "war flag") when they go into battle. Gang members are never to leave their flag behind—it is the ultimate embarrassment and sign of weakness in battle. Returning to the home-base without your flag is met with extreme prejudice among gang members and a violation ceremony will follow. On the other hand, bringing back a rival's flag is usually proof that you killed an enemy and the member is received with great honor. The flag is extremely important to gang members. As one gang member told me, "It is your heart, you keep it, and you show it off."

Crips refer to Bloods as Slobs as a sign of disrespect. The Crips have a saying, "See a Slob, Kill a Slob." K-Swiss is favorite attire worn by these Crips because the KS is interpreted as "Kill Slobs." Joining the 8-Ball Crips involves an initiation process. One of the most common forms of initiation involves brands and burns on the upper right arm. Many preteens begin their indoctrination into the gang by getting gang burns on their arms. A six-pointed star is burnt into the arm and then a pitchfork is burnt into the leg later. (*Note*: Buffalo Blood gangs initiate recruits with burn marks in the arm as well.) The 8-Ball Crew has a hierarchal organizational structure:

1. Godfather (and sometimes a simultaneously reigning queen)
2. Superiors
3. OG
4. Generals
5. Commanders
6. Foot soldiers
7. Riders

The godfather is the reigning power. As revealed in the typology, women may gain high levels of respect; the queen, the highest-ranking female gangster, commands a great deal of esteem. She is just below the godfather but above most males. This is rather unusual for most gangs, as a woman generally has little authority over males. Superiors are next in the line of command and have status and authority over the OG because of some past or present demonstrated prowess. OG are the oldest active members of the gang. The generals are active on the streets overseeing operations. Generals may sometimes leave the original gang in order to start their own set. This is permissible because they still answer to the godfather. The commanders are the go-betweens between the generals and foot soldiers. The foot soldiers do all the dirty work (petty theft, robberies, serving as "watches," etc.), and the riders are really wannabes and are only semiactive in the gang.

The primary reason for the very high homicide rate in Buffalo is tied directly to gang activity in drug-trafficking. The Buffalo area has become increasingly used as a drug corridor for illegal drugs entering the United States via Canada. Huge amounts of cocaine, heroin, marijuana, and methamphetamines are smuggled into the Buffalo distribution point by gangs and organized crime syndicates in New York City. On November 26, 2003, New York Senator Charles E. Schumer issued a press release stating that the "Buffalo area is smack in the middle of an illegal drug pipeline." Schumer added that Buffalo's proximity to New York City and Canada creates a perfect storm for the convergence of drugs and gangs in western New York. Despite the efforts of local law enforcement officials, Schumer agreed with Buffalo Mayor Tony Masiello and Police Commissioner Rocco Diina that the federal government needed to get involved to combat the threat of gangs and drugs plaguing the area. Schumer referred in his press release to Buffalo and western New York as a distribution point for drugs and stated that the increased federal funding would be used to fight drug-trafficking. If Buffalo becomes designated by the U.S. Office of National Drug Control Policy as a "high-intensity drug-trafficking area (HIDTA)" as Schumer wants, then western New York cities will be eligible to receive millions in federal money to help local law enforcement clamp down on the illegal drug-trafficking that is so prevalent (Schumer 2003). Senator Schumer was indeed successful in securing the HIDTA status for Buffalo and as a result law enforcement efforts have been assisted by federal authorities and federal money (U.S. Department of Homeland Security 2012a). In 2012, for example, the Buffalo Border Enforcement Security Task Force (BEST) made an arrest of a Canadian police officer with the cooperation of U.S. Immigration and Customs Enforcement's (ICE) Homeland Security Investigation (HSI) who pleaded guilty to charges that he used his position to smuggle drugs and other contraband into Canada (U.S. Department of Homeland Security 2012b).

As described in Chapter 1, motorcycle gangs are often involved with drug-trafficking, generally by supplying street gangs with mass quantities of drugs. This is especially true at the U.S.-Canadian border. In the Buffalo area, it's the Canadian Hells Angels who are often involved in trafficking drugs that cross the U.S. border. In 2011, a dozen members of the Afro Dogs motorcycle club were arrested on drug-trafficking charges (*The Citizen* 2011a). The **Afro Dogs** is one of the biggest and oldest African-American motorcycle clubs in Buffalo and all of western New York. Like their Hell's Angels counterparts, the Afro Dogs ride Harley Davidson bikes. Some Dogs are police officers and firefighters. A business owner, Ricky Allen, Sr., a past officer of the club and elected chair of a Buffalo city commission on police reorganization (the Joint Commission to Examine Police Reorganization), was among those arrested. The dirty dozen Dogs were named in a 35-count indictment involving cocaine drug distribution. Officers seized 19 guns, including a high-powered sniper rifle and AK-47 assault rifle, more than $200,000 in cash, and three Harley-Davidson motorcycles during the roundup of the suspects (*The Citizen* 2011a).

In addition to the deadly violence and drug-trafficking of the African-American, Hispanic/Latino, and biker gangs, there are also Chinese gangs who have committed a number of "traditional" Asian gang-related crimes. These Asian gangsters are generally from New York City and come to the Buffalo area to target Chinese restaurants and businesses. They are also known for their brutal home-invasion robberies. Special agents from the Asian Organized Crime Task Force in New York City state that these types of crimes are a common means for Asian gangs to make money (Herbeck 2000).

Gang violence and homicide represent a constant threat to many citizens of the Buffalo area. Law enforcement personnel have done the best they can to fight the growing presence of street gangs in Buffalo. As previously stated, Senator Schumer secured federal funding to help assist the suppression efforts of local officials in Buffalo; in addition to the federal funding the city received money from a COPS (Community Oriented Policing Services) grant, which helped to provide about 25 officers for community policing (Thomas and Pignataro 2003). The Buffalo police have established an intelligence unit to share information among police in the region regarding gang-related activity. Buffalo, like crime-plagued Niagara Falls, has enlisted the help of state troopers and county officers in its attempt to cope with the high rate of violence, due to the reality that many gangs transcend police-district boundaries. Members of the **Buffalo Gang Suppression Unit** coordinate efforts with the **Major Case Squad** and **Flex Unit** and **Narcotics Bureau Detectives**. Suburban police, such as those in Cheektowaga, have joined in the information and intelligence effort to combat gangs. Cheektowaga has witnessed a reemergence of gang members, shootings, and thefts in the western end of the town. **Project Exile** was created, in part, to provide training to local police officers in federal criminal gun charges that sometimes carry more severe prison sentences than state laws. Also assisting Buffalo police with gang information is the **Violent Crime and Career Criminal Task Force**, which includes federal law enforcement agents and police from area municipalities.

Despite the fact that the number of homicides dropped to 43 in 2002, it would appear that the Buffalo gang problem is escalating. In 2003, Buffalo had 63 criminal homicides (21.9 per 100,000, or four times the national average), and in 2004, there were 51 criminal homicides, with investigators solving just 39 percent of them. The weapons being used range from .22- and .25-caliber handguns to shotguns and AK-47s. Many of the shootings are drive-bys. The Bloods and Crips have received much of the blame for the increased level of gang violence in Buffalo in 2004 and 2005. The Bloods claim territory on the East and West sides, including Central Park and the Bailey-Delevan neighborhoods (Thomas 2004). Bloods recruit young, local Buffalo kids while inside juvenile detention centers and the Erie County Holding Center, in the malls, and in local schools. Among the emerging gangs in Buffalo are the **Young Blood Thugs**, described by some officers as Blood gang members in training.

The motives for gang violence are multiple and include attempts by one gang to establish itself in a neighborhood, individual gang members trying to make a name for themselves, a perceived lack of respect, turf, or women. However, one factor sticks out above all else for gang homicides: control of the drug trade and turf. Selling drugs as a means of earning money reflects the socioeconomic realities of a depressed Buffalo region. The lure of quick money from drug-trafficking, the lack of enough properly funded community programs for urban youths, and the overall poor economic condition in Buffalo, specifically, and upstate New York, in general, indicate that more and more youths are likely to turn to gangs.

As the 2000s proceed, the number of homicides in Buffalo remains high: In 2005 there were 56 homicides (19.8 per 100,000); in 2006 there were 74 homicides (26.4 per 100,000, or five times the national average); in 2007 there were 54 homicides (19.7); in 2008 a drop to 37 homicides (13.7); in 2009, 60 homicides (22.3); and in 2010, 55 homicides (20.7 per 100,000) (City-Data. com 2012b). The continued rampant gang problem in Buffalo is the result of increased gang activity among Hispanic/Latino gangs on the West Side of the city. Chief among these threats are the introduction of the **Almighty Latin Kings and Queens Nation** and the continued presence of the infamous 10th Street Gang. The introduction of the Latin Kings to Buffalo became apparent around 2006 as this highly organized street gang attempted to take control of the city's West Side's drug-dealing turf. In 2008, six Latin Kings gang members were indicted on drug-trafficking charges by the **Buffalo Safe Streets** task force and the U.S. attorney's office (Herbeck 2008). Other Latin King gang members were still facing charges at the time. The ringleader of the Buffalo Latin Kings was Joseph J. "King G" Santiago, who was 43 at the time of his arrest, of Newton Street (Buffalo), who was sent to Buffalo to take control of the Buffalo chapter of the Almighty Latin Kings and Queens Nation (Herbeck 2008). The **10th Street Gang**, a local street gang, has responded to the Latin Kings intrusion on their turf and stepped up their game of drug-trafficking, violence, and intimidation. And such activities did not go unnoticed. There have been ongoing federal investigations and arrests of the 10th Street Gang since 2009. In September 2009, a federal grand jury charged six 10th Street Gang members and associates with violent crimes in aid of racketeering and other charges (FBI 2012h). The FBI had already indicted 38 other 10th Street Gang members and associates with a variety of federal criminal offenses. On March 26, 2012, U.S. Attorney William J. Hochul, Jr., announced that 10th Street Gang member Saul Santana, 24, of Buffalo, pleaded guilty to RICO violations (FBI 2012i). As of March 29, 2012, 14 of the 40 10th Street Gang members had been convicted for RICO violations in connection with the ongoing federal, state, and local investigation (FBI 2012h). By the end of May, more than a dozen members of the 10th Street Gang were locked up by federal authorities (Herbeck 2012).

Also in March 2012, U.S. Attorney Hochul announced that six members of **LRGP Gang**, which operates in the area of Lathrop, Rother, Gibson, and Playter Streets (LRGP for short) in the city of Buffalo, were arrested for RICO violations. The LRGP Gang is alleged to be an organization engaged in violent criminal activity, including the distribution of cocaine and crack cocaine and the use of firearms (FBI 2012j). FBI agents have noticed how street gangs in Buffalo are becoming increasingly organized and sophisticated and continue to use violence to control neighborhoods in order to elicit moneymaking schemes (Mobilia 2012). The LRGP Gang has established itself as a gang of note in Buffalo because its members are responsible for many shootings, some resulting in homicides (Mobilia 2012). One of the glaring observations of the LRGP arrests is the range of ages of the accused: 28–52. That 50- and 40-year-olds are still involved in criminal street gang activity is a sure indicator of why the numbers of gang members continuously increase and that the socioeconomic climate in the United States has not changed in such a manner to afford people from lower SES backgrounds opportunities to achieve economic success in the conventional work place. In May 2012, federal prosecutors filed racketeering charges against 17 members of the no-toriously violent **7th Street Gang (a.k.a. the Cheko's Crew)**, as police agencies continued their crackdown against gang-related crime on the West Side (Herbeck 2012). The charges included two murders, six attempted murders, and a robbery. Buffalo's Safe Streets Task Force and other agencies made the arrests. The violence is directly connected to the ongoing battle among gangs for control of the drug market on the West Side. Buffalo police report that the number of shoot-ings (through May 25) in the city was up 70 percent from the same period in 2011.

As this review of Syracuse, Rochester, and Buffalo gangs indicates, there are a number of jurisdictions that have homegrown gang problems. There are local street gangs in most large urban areas. Although local street gangs certainly represent a significant problem in many juris-dictions, they seem to pale in comparison to nation and transnational gangs. Our attention now shifts to nation gangs.

NATION STREET GANGS

There are plenty of urban local street gangs in cities across the United States. Many of them, es-pecially those in larger urban areas, are likely to join a "nation" gang. Nation status is given to any street gang that has affiliations across the United States. The largest of these nation coalitions are the Crips, Bloods, People, and Folks. Discussion of nation gangs begins with the Los Angeles–based Crips.

The Crips

The Crips are believed to be the largest of all the gangs found in the United States. In 2002, the U.S. Department of Justice (2002) estimated that there were over 800 Crips sets with 30,000 to 35,000 members and associate members, including more than 13,000 members in Los Angeles alone. A decade later, the number of Crips has increased, with estimates ranging from 35,000 to 40,000. Their home-base and origin are on the mean streets of South Central Los Angeles. (South Central Los Angeles is now called Southern Los Angeles.) The history of the Crips can be traced to the late 1960s and early 1970s. Some people believe that the formation of the Crips was the direct result of the FBI's crackdown on the **Black Panther Party (BPP)** in the late 1960s, when activism and political organization in the black community were viewed as threats to na-tional security by the FBI and the Los Angeles Police Department (Chambliss 1993). The Black Panther Party was a progressive political organization that sought social change. The Panthers were founded by Huey P. Newton, who viewed the party as a means of meeting the needs of oppressed African Americans under the party slogan of "survival pending revolution." Its first program was the Free Breakfast for Children started at a Catholic church in the Fillmore district of San Francisco. The program was so successful it spread to every city in which the Panthers had chapters. The federal government quickly modeled its own version of this program for the public schools. The Panthers ran a number of other programs within communities as well, and its example influenced future gang attempts to provide social services to the local people. In accordance with partywide rules, chapter members were required to attend political education courses regularly, learn how to use firearms (training was conducted in the Mojave Desert), and learn to perform emergency medical techniques (Black Panther Party 1999).

The Southern California chapter of the BPP was formed in 1968, in Los Angeles, by street gangster Alprentice "Bunchy" Carter (Black Panther Party 1999). Carter (1942–1969), known as the "Mayor of the Ghetto," was the former head of the 5,000-strong Slauson Gang and its hard core, the Slauson Renegades. While spending four years in Soledad prison for armed robbery, Carter became a Muslim and a follower of Malcolm X. Carter met BPP Minister of Defense Huey Newton in 1967 and became a Panther on the spot. He was given the title of Deputy Minister of Defense when he took over the Southern California chapter in 1968. By April 1968, the Southern California chapter was gaining 50–100 new members each week, although not all stayed. As the chapter grew, so did the attacks (from law enforcement) against it. FBI Director J. Edgar Hoover believed the BPP to be the greatest threat to the internal security of the United States. Carter began attending UCLA. On January 17, 1969, he was gunned down at Campbell Hall on the UCLA campus—some say by the FBI, others say by rival members of the BPP. Huey Newton proclaimed the FBI to be behind Carter's execution, either directly or indirectly (by hiring/blaming members of the cultural nationalist U.S. organization led by Ron "Maulana" Karenga). By the end of the decade, 28 Los Angeles Black Panthers had been reported killed by the police. Youths (such as Raymond Washington and Stanley "Tookie" Williams) who were too young to join the Panthers and who were upset by their grim socioeconomic realities began to form their own groups (gangs).

It is worth noting that at present a hate group calling itself the New Black Panther Party exists. This group gained the attention of the mainstream media in March 2012 when they placed a public bounty on the head of George Zimmerman, the white Hispanic who shot unarmed Trayvon Martin (Pitts 2012). The Huey P. Newton Foundation flatly denies that this hate group has any affiliation to the real BPP, saying that "the Black Panthers were never a group of angry young militants full of fury toward the 'white establishment.' The Party operated on the love for black people, not hatred of white people" (Black Panther Organization 2012).

The crackdown on the socio-politically active Panthers upset many blacks, who are generally upset with the political system because they feel they never receive justice. This view gains some credence when looking at the pattern followed by civic projects. Civic leaders considering projects like freeway expansion put a great deal of time and effort into assuring the wealthy and "connected" people that they will not be harmed by the construction. As a result, it is the politically weak who are. The construction of the Century Freeway in Los Angeles, for example, caused the destruction of numerous homes in South Central Los Angeles and led to the building of housing projects. A number of small gangs formed in these projects, among them the **Avenues**. The Avenues, who date back to the early 1960s, became the first dominant African-American gang in Los Angeles. They claimed the areas around Central Avenue.

A 15-year-old high school student named Raymond Lee Washington, who was born in Texas on August 15, 1953, moved to Los Angeles with his family when he was three years old, wanted to join the Avenues but was denied because of his young age. Undaunted, Washington got together with a few of his friends and formed a gang called the **Baby Avenues**, in line with the older Avenues gang. Washington and his crew attempted to preserve the Black Panther aura by forming a quasi-political street gang to represent a new generation of African Americans. Because blacks had long experienced the negative effects of oppression and lack of political influence in American society, the Black Panthers had been a sign of hope to many young blacks, especially in Los Angeles. At the same time that Washington was organizing a powerful gang of young teenagers, Stanley "Tookie" Williams was earning great status as a vicious street gang fighter. Williams had moved to Los Angeles from Louisiana when he was nine years old and learned quickly that the only way to survive and, more importantly, dominate, was to fight.

Williams never backed down to anyone, and no one was tougher. Williams was fascinated with the idea of the Black Panthers and Malcolm X and it was his goal to secure black survival and equality via civil rights organizations (Williams 2004). Inevitably, Williams and Washington met one another. Their great mutual respect led to an immediate alliance and commitment to the idea of "an urban cleansing of the gang element" (Williams 2004, 87). Washington and Williams believed that if they could get all the street gangs to merge into one, they could do great things for black people. Their hope was to form a collective organization more powerful than any other and to become a more political and intimidating force than the Panthers. Things did not go as planned. The local South Central gangs were intimidated and did not want to risk fighting this emerging power. Quickly numerous neighborhood gangs merged with the Baby Avenues rather than risk fighting them.

Around 1970, the Baby Avenues changed their name to the **Avenue Cribs**. The word *crib* was used to describe their youthfulness. Soon after, *crib* got changed to *crip*, for reasons no one knows for certain. Some suggest that Williams's handwriting was so poor his "b's" looked like "p's" and after a while everyone started to think *crib* was *crips*. Others suggest that Washington, who was a poor speller, wanted to change the name of his gang to "crypts" but spelled "crips" instead (Crip History 2003). A television show *Tale of the Crypts* was popular at that time. A more plausible explanation is the statement by one of the original members of the Baby Avenues that the word *crip* stood for "Continuous Revolution in Progress" (Davis 1992, 299). Another play on words has the origin of the name *Crip* coming from a combination of the word *crib* and the acronym R.I.P. (Kontos and Brotherton 2008). The early Cribs wore black leather jackets, walked with canes, and wore earrings in the left earlobe. On one occasion in 1971, several Crib members assaulted a Japanese woman and were described as young "cripples" who carried canes. With a February 10, 1972, article in the *Los Angeles Sentinel* leading the way, the local media picked up on this description and called this young gang of hoodlums the Crips (National Drug Intelligence Center 2002). This story provides yet another explanation as to how the Cribs came to be called the Crips. The term can be used as a verb, *crippin*, which means to steal, but also describes a way of life. Regardless, by the early 1970s, the Avenue Cribs became known as the **Crips**. It was Washington's intent to link his Crip gang to other African-American gangs in an attempt to unify the movement. He worked hard in the early 1970s to organize a number of **crip sets**—gangs that maintained individuality but linked to the greater nation coalition. Washington and Williams initiated black teens throughout the inner city into their Crip gang, starting up the East Side Crips, West Side Crips, Avalon Garden Crips, and the Inglewood Crips. Crips gangs emerged around the Fremont, Locke, and Washington high schools. Much like a colonial or imperialistic empire, the Crips continued to expand their territory throughout the greater Los Angeles area. Local gangs were looked upon as fiefdoms to be conquered.

As the Crips expanded, they came upon other gangs that were less willing to give up their claims to specific neighborhoods. The **Piru Street Boys** was one of the gangs the Crips came across that were uncooperative. During the summer of 1972, the Crips from Compton fought with the Compton Piru Street Boys, who, outnumbered, were beaten badly by the Crips. Looking for revenge, the Pirus turned to the Lueders Park Hustlers for backup, and they agreed. A member of the **L.A. Brim** gang had been murdered by a Crip earlier that year, so the Pirus asked them as well to join in a meeting to discuss a revenge battle. The **Denver Lanes**, **Bishops**, **Slausons**, **Huns**, **Gladiators**, and **Pueblos** also joined the Pirus. All of these gangs were greatly outnumbered by the Crips, so they decided to form a permanent alliance. The Crips were known for wearing blue bandannas, so the Piru alliance decided to wear red bandannas. Eventually they came up with the name **Bloods** for their new gang. Other gangs would join the Blood and Crip alliances until the predominantly African-American neighborhoods of Los Angeles were dominated by one gang or the other. Over the years, political issues became totally irrelevant and making money and gaining respect on the streets became the primary goals of the Bloods and Crips.

The amount of attention in the press that the early Crips received enticed younger boys, who became eager to join a group that provided black teenagers with raw power. For marginalized male youths, joining the Crips was a sign of manliness. Each inductee had to go through the initiation ritual of beating-in by members of the gang. The beating includes fist punches and body kicks, and the recruit is not allowed to fight back—he must simply take the beating willingly. Many modern Crips gangs initiate members by having them commit a crime in front of gang witnesses, a process called "loc'ing in." Chapters 3 and 4 explained some of the many reasons that individuals choose to join a gang. For the Crips, gang activities represent an opportunity to earn an income. Most Crips are involved in such criminal activities as murder, armed robbery, and selling illegal contraband in the underground economy—especially drugs and weapons. By 1978, there were 45 Crips sets operating in Los Angeles; some of these sets produced and distributed PCP (phencyclidine) within the city. They also distributed marijuana and amphetamines (U.S. Department of Justice 2002). The Crips have been involved in the sale and distribution of crack cocaine since it first came on the drug scene in the early 1980s. In the 1990s and continuing into the 2000s, the Crips' involvement in drug-related activity has continued to grow, and they have attempted to set up markets throughout the United States.

The Crips are notoriously violent and do not hesitate to use extreme methods to protect their turf against rival gangs and the police. Crips gang members are generally members for life, whether they are incarcerated in prison or have become rich and famous in the legitimate society. Stanley Williams is an example of the former and Calvin Brodus (a.k.a. Snoop Dogg) the latter. Williams was sentenced to death row in San Quentin State Prison in 1981 having been found guilty of the murder of four people during robberies at a convenience store and a motel in Los Angeles in 1971. He died from lethal injection in 2005. See "Connecting Street Gangs and Popular Culture" Box 6.2 to learn more about Williams's life behind bars, including his authorship of children's books.

Box 6.2   Connecting Street Gangs and Popular Culture
Stanley Tookie Williams: A Nobel Prize Nominee for Writing Children's Books

Stanley Tookie Williams, co-founder of the Crips, was sent to San Quentin State Prison in 1981 after being convicted for gunning down 7-Eleven convenience store clerk Albert Owens in Whittier and killing Yen-I Yang, Tsai-Shai Chen Yang, and the couple's daughter Yu-Chin Yang Lin at the Los Angeles motel they owned (CBS News 2009). Witnesses at the trial said that Williams boasted about the killings, stating, "You should have heard the way he sounded when I shot him" (CBS News 2009). For years, California prison authorities believed that Williams ran the Crip inmate population. In July 2003, authorities at Corcoran State Prison locked down 1,300 African-American general-population inmates in their cells as they investigated whether incarcerated members of the Crips were conspiring to attack prison staffers in retaliation for the anticipated execution of Williams (Warren and Morian 2003, B1). Prison officials had uncovered notes from prisoners, indicating that Crips were going to attack and kill high-ranking prison staff members. Prison officials admitted that any time a Crip attacked a staff member they looked for a link to Williams. And yet, despite his significant role in forming the Crips, a gang that would become a nation gang and directly lead to the formation of the Bloods, many people not directly connected to the world of street gangs held candlelight vigils on the night Williams was to be executed hoping for a stay of execution. Nonetheless, Williams was executed on December 13, 2005, via lethal injection into his muscular arm (apparently struggling to find a vein) (*CBS News* 2009).

Why would people such as singer Joan Baez, actor Mike Farrell, Jamie Foxx, Bianca Jagger, Snoop Dogg, Rev. Jesse Jackson, and other celebrities protest his execution? The answer lies with what Williams did while incarcerated and it has nothing to do with running the Crips from his prison cell. Williams tried to convince people that the person he became in prison was not the same person who was sent there. During the many hours, days, and years Williams spent incarcerated, he had a great deal of time to self-reflect. During this self-reflection he began to see the error of his ways. One of the few luxuries afforded Williams while in solitary confinement was the opportunity to read and educate himself. Given his expulsion from school in his teenage years, Tookie had a limited vocabulary. He remedied this by studying words out of the dictionary. Armed with a vast vocabulary, instead of firearms, Williams became an author of children's books. And although today it seems like nearly every celebrity fancies himself/herself an author, especially of children's books, Williams's stories were quite unique. His books were anti-gang. (*Note*: Williams also wrote an autobiography about his gang and prison lives.)

In 1992, Barbra Cottman-Becnel, a black journalist and author, wrote Williams a letter seeking his audience. She wanted to write a book about the history of California's black street gangs (Williams and Cottman Becnel 2001). Since Raymond Washington, the co-founder of the Crips, was dead, she knew Tookie was the only person with the full history of the Crips. Williams was not interested in her book but agreed to meet with her. After much convincing of prison authorities, Becnel met with Williams. Williams wanted to write children's books. Becnel was skeptical at first, but agreed to help him only if he was serious about it (Rist 1996). Williams wished to stop the madness that he helped to create. He never thought the Crips would spread across California, let alone the entire United States. He regretted the legacy that he had created—black on black genocide—and wanted to extend an olive branch to youths through his writings and children's books. He reasoned that it was the next generation that had to be swayed away from gangs and that's why he targeted children that were pre-"at-risk" age.

Among his writings were "My Letter to Incarcerated Youth, No. 1" an open letter posted on "Tookie's Corner," a website (Williams 1997a). In this letter, Tookie warns youth in juvenile halls and youth detention centers to straighten out their lives so that they do not end up like him. In his letter "The Apology," Williams (1997b) apologizes for creating the Crips. Williams states, "I apologize to you all—the children of America and South Africa—who must cope every day with dangerous street gangs. I no longer participate in the so-called gangster lifestyle, and I deeply regret that I ever did" (Williams 1997b). Williams videotaped himself as well so that his message could be sent to youth everywhere.

In September 1996, the Rosen Publishing group (PowerKids Press) published Williams's eight children's books as a series. These books are all anti-gang in nature. The books have been distributed to libraries, schools, and homes throughout the world. The series includes books with titles such as *Gangs and the Abuse of Power*, *Gangs and Self-Esteem*, *Gangs and Violence*, and *Gangs and Your Friends*. The books gained instant attention throughout the world. They have been used in both schools and juvenile facilities all over the United States. So acclaimed had Williams's books and writings become that in 2001 he was nominated for a Nobel Peace Prize by Mario Fehr, a member of the Swiss Parliament. Fehr made the nomination to the Nobel Peace Prize Committee in Oslo, Norway, on the basis that Williams's books and Internet project ("Tookie's Corner") have had a positive influence on children and encouraged them to resist gangs. It was the first time that a man on death row had ever been nominated for the Prize. The man once, and perhaps still, revered by Crips everywhere had a new acclaim. His nomination for a Nobel Peace Prize added to his mythical status among Crips (Warren and Morian 2003). The Nobel Peace Prize, an award associated with words like prestige, dedication, and brilliance, was now being associated with a gangster and convicted murderer, and such acclaim did not sit well with many people in the conventional world (Severson 2001). Trying to set the record right, Barbara Becnel stated, "He [Williams] is not being rewarded for the bad things he had done. He is being acknowledged for the good things he is trying to do" (Severson 2001). In the following year, Williams was nominated by a Brown University professor for the Nobel Prize for Literature. In all, Williams was nominated five times for the Nobel Peace Prize and once for the Nobel Prize for Literature (Robinson 2005). He did not win any of these nominated awards. However, in 2005, Williams did win an "Outstanding Character of America Award" and a "President's Call to Service Award" from President George W. Bush for his efforts to inspire volunteerism in the United States (*Jet* 2005).

Despite Williams's attempts to stop gang violence, gangism has only increased. The super gang he helped to create has become a social institution that has spread across the United States. Imagine if Williams had stayed in school and had become a children's books author and promoter of volunteerism instead of forming the Crips. Imagine is all we can do as history has been written and Williams's real claim to fame, or infamy, will remain as a co-founder of a brutal gang and not an acclaimed author.

Tookie Williams died in prison in 2005 and Raymond Washington was shot and killed in gang violence in the 1970s.

Calvin Broadus, better known as rap artist Snoop Dogg, helped to transform a criminal lifestyle and a childhood spent in a hostile environment into a style of music known as gangster rap (see Chapter 4 for a discussion on this musical genre). Snoop Dogg claims to have given up his days of *crippin*, but he openly pays homage to the nation coalition of the Crips by immortalizing his criminal past in his rhymes. In one of his songs, "187," Snoop makes numerous references to firearms and praises the killing of police. In his musical videos, Snoop often employs members of his Crip crew, who openly flash gang signs and wear the blue gang color. It is believed that the color blue was chosen because it was the primary color for Washington High School in South Los Angeles (today their school colors are blue and red) (Jah and Shah'Keyah 1995). Crips generally wear blue bandannas. The blue bandanna is symbolically the Crips' "flag." The flag is always to be respected and never left behind during the heat of battle. The Crips may wear black, especially when they are at war.

In one of his songs, Snoop introduces another gang feature, wearing to the right or wearing to the left. Although there is not a universal acceptance among gang members about the right–left distinction, Snoop's lyrics indicate that the Crips identify to the left. His lyrics make mention to displaying his flag (blue bandanna) on the left side of his pants pocket because it is the Crip side. In contrast, the Bloods wear to the right. Rapper "The Game," who identifies himself as a Blood from Compton responded to Snoop's song with lyrics of his own, which includes wearing a flag on the right side because it is the Blood side (Black Perspective and Introspection 2005).

The Crips are known for a specific style of dance known as the "crip walk." Following her Olympic Women's Singles Championship victory over Maria Sharapova, Serena Williams, a native of a Crip neighborhood in South Central Los Angeles (Compton), celebrated by performing the "crip walk" (*The Daily Mail* 2012; *The Post-Standard* 2012g). While most conventional people had no idea her celebratory victory dance was "a gang thing" those "in the know" who try to combat gang violence were highly critical of Williams. Beyond a specific dance style, Crip gangsters refer to each other as "Cuzz" and say things like, "Wuz up cuzz?" (Jah and Shah'Keyah 1995). Crips identify themselves by gang-related tattoos and by wearing other gang-related clothing, for example, clothes representing various sports teams such as the Dodgers because their team color is blue or the Chicago Cubs because of the letter "C" for Crips and British Knights because their initials—BK—represent "Blood Killers." Even Burger King (BK) is preferred over other fast-food restaurants. Since the Bloods are the sworn enemies of the Crips, any time a Crip can wear something that disrespects the Bloods, he will do so. Because of their allegiance to the Folk Nation, Crips may represent by using a six-pointed star and the number 6 (represents "F," for Folks, the sixth letter in the alphabet). Crips may use the number 3 (for "C") in graffiti as well. It is important to note that although the Crips and Folks (and Bloods and People) have nation alliances, such alliances are always subject to vary from gang to gang in specific areas. The U.S. Department of Justice (2002) indicates that nation alliances were established in the 1980s as a means of gang members being better able to protect one another while in prison. The alliance is strongest within the prison system and less effective on the streets.

Gang graffiti is one of the most prevalent ways a gang identifies itself. Among other functions, graffiti is used to mark turf, make certain pronouncements, commemorate the dead, and issue challenges. Gangs generally use their specific colors when spray-painting graffiti. However, because most gang members are poor they will use any color they can get their hands on. **Scratchiti** is another form of graffiti. Scratchiti involves using a sharp object like a knife to scratch painted surfaces, wood, and glass windows. Scratchiti is very common on buses, subway trains, and bathroom stalls. The Crips refer to Bloods as "Slobs" (in graffiti the letter "b" is crossed out) and will use such graffiti slogans as Crip 187 Slobs. The *187* refers to part of the California penal code for homicide; thus, Crips murder Bloods. (See Figure 6.1 for examples of Crip gang graffiti.)

The Crips also use the following chant as a means of disrespecting the Bloods:

Ashes to Ashes
Dust to Dust
In Crips We Trust
In Bloods We Bust
Kill a "Slob" Win a Prize
Kill a Crip and Your Family Dies

Today, the Crips are among the most violent street gangs in the world. They are most likely the largest of all the street gangs. They have extended their reach to nearly every large city in the United States (they are also found outside the United States). They make money through the distribution and sale of drugs, gun trafficking, and a number of other violent and property offenses. The Crips are highly feared because they readily cause harm to anyone who interferes with their goals. It should be pointed out that not all the Crip factions are unified; they are known to fight each other nearly as often as they fight Blood gangs. But despite their growth and spread over the decades, the franchising of Crip gangs (and Blood gangs as well) is nothing like the process of franchising retail stores—they are not *that* organized.

The Crips often employ the letters "BK", which represents "Blood Killer." The letter "B" is crossed out to disrespect the Bloods. The number 3 is for the letter "C".

187SLOBS

The Crips paint "187 Slobs" as a way to disrespect their rival, the Bloods (by calling them slobs and by crossing out the letter "B"); the 187 comes from the California penal code for murder. Thus, Crips murder Bloods.

This hand sign is shaped like the letter "C", for Crips.

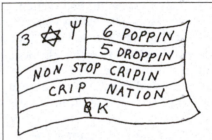

In this Crip graffiti, a six-pointed star and an upright pitchfork is used to show their allegiance to the Folks Nation (who abide by the number 6), the number 3 is for Crips. The slogan "6 poppin, 5 droppin" is a common chant among members of the Crip/Folk Nation, which means a member of the Crips/Folks is shooting at a member of the Blood/People Nation. *Non-stop crippin* refers to the lifestyle of the Crip Nation. "BK" refers to Blood Killer.

Cripin with an arrow represents a Crip gang's turf boundary marker; the letter "P" is crossed out to show disrespect toward the Piru gang (the original Blood gang).

ECCBH

ECCBH is graffiti by the East Coast Crips of Brooklyn Heights.

FIGURE 6.1 The Crips (*Source:* Paul Hahn)

The Bloods

The Bloods are the second gang to gain nation status. They are also the second of the two Los Angeles–based nation gangs. It is generally accepted that the Crips outnumber the Bloods by a 3 to 1 ratio; however, this is not the case on the East Coast. In total, there are an estimated 15,000 to 20,000 Blood members (Commonwealth of Virginia Department of State Police 2008). There are approximately 4,500 Bloods in Los Angeles. The ability of the Bloods to hold their own against the mighty Crips with such a disadvantage in numbers is testimony to the strength and potential brutality of the Bloods. This underdog status contributes to the Bloods elevated status in the gang world. As mentioned, the Bloods originated in and around the Piru Street area in Compton, California. Because the original Blood gang was the Piru Street Boys, the Bloods are often referred to as **Piru gangs**. They are primarily an African-American gang; however, unlike the Crips, the Bloods are more likely to accept other racial and ethnic folks, including Hispanic, white, and Asian.

The Blood nation formed as a protective alliance against the forces of the Crip nation. The rivalry between these two super gangs has been responsible for a great deal of violent crime in Los Angeles, dating back to the early 1970s, and as the years went on, the degree of violence escalated. The sharp increase in assault and homicide attributed to gangs is directly related to the increased use of firepower by gang members and the tactic of drive-by shootings. The Crips claim that the Bloods were the first to use guns in gang fights. This would seem logical, considering they were generally outnumbered by Crips. Like the Crips, the Bloods protect their neighborhoods at all costs. And like most street gangs beginning in the 1980s, the Bloods are heavily involved in the drug trade. The Bloods share a common philosophy of all for one, one for all and have a true devotion to their set and nation. To keep presence in any neighborhood that has a Crip set, the Bloods have expanded to all corners of the country.

During the 1980s, the Bloods had many affiliates in the Midwest, especially in Chicago. It is because of the Chicago Bloods that the Blood nation has an alliance with the People Nation. That the People were already enemies of the Folks, who had already aligned with the Crips, made the Bloods and People logical partners. The gangs originally aligned with the Black P-Stone Nation fell under the People Nation umbrella, and the Black Gangster Disciple (BGD) Nation aligned under the Folks Nation umbrella (Commonwealth of Virginia Department of State Police 2008). Blood sets that recognize the cousin status of the People incorporate the use of symbols tied to the People Nation. These symbols include the number five, a five-pointed star, and a five-pointed crown.

By the early 1990s, the Bloods' presence had reached the East Coast. But it was not until two inmates at Riker's Island correctional facility in New York joined together that the West Coast–based gang gained popularity. At this time, the Latin Kings and Netas gangs dominated the prison system in the East Coast. These Hispanic gangs harassed and intimidated black inmates. In 1983, Omar Portee, known on the street as O.G. Mack, along with Leonard "Deadeye" McKenzie, who were inmates at Riker's, formed the United Blood Nation (UBN) as a way to protect themselves from Hispanic gangs. Portee and McKenzie were also influenced by the Black Panther Party and adopted a gang philosophy that capitalized on the perception of blacks as oppressed people (Commonwealth of Virginia Department of State Police 2008). Although the UBN was formed as a protective unit, like their West Coast brethren, they did not receive a blessing from the West. To this day, the West Coast Bloods do not recognize the UBN as "real" Bloods (Commonwealth of Virginia Department of State Police 2008). Despite their unofficial status, the UBN prospered in the prison systems. This power was transplanted to the streets by Portee upon his release from Riker's. Before long, Portee's Bloods became the largest street gang in New York City, and by 2000, the Bloods were known as the most violent gang on the East Coast (Savelli 2000). The initiation process of the UBN, known as a "Buck 50," was highly frowned upon by the West Coast Bloods. The Buck 50 involved recruits cutting nongang members, or neutrals, in the face to the extent that they would need 150 stitches. West Coast initiations involve rival gang members being attacked, not conventional citizens.

In the mid- to late-1990s, the UBN had become a dominant gang on the East Coast, outnumbering the Crips (Commonwealth of Virginia Department of State Police 2008). In August 1997, in a three-day sweep, New York City police arrested 167 alleged members of gangs, most of whom were Bloods. Police attributed 135 slashings to the gang initiation rituals (Tyre 1997). Two Blood members would approach a stranger on the street or subway, pull out a box cutter, and slash the victim's face. The NYPD launched the sweep in an attempt to stop the slashings and the gang's expansion. The NYPD named this operation "Red Bandanna." Executed by the Citywide Anti-Gang Enforcement unit, Red Bandanna was a multiagency drug-and-gang initiative set up to dismantle street and other violent drug gangs in targeted areas of the city. "The operation was focused in precincts in Upper Manhattan, Southern Queens, Northern Brooklyn, and on Riker's Island. Criminals arrested during this operation were accused of selling drugs, committing armed robberies, weapons' possession, and murder. With 'Red Bandanna's' strategic arrests, we dismantled seven sets of Bloods and one set of Crips and achieved the purpose of the sweep, which was to stop the gangbangers from expanding their activity" (Safir 2003, 181). On April 14, 2003, a federal judge in Manhattan sentenced Portee to 50 years in prison. When Naomi Reice Buchwald of the United States District Court sentenced the Blood gang leader, she noted the amount of violence and lawlessness that he was responsible for and the lack of anything on the positive side of the ledger (Weiser 2003).

Howard Safir (former NYPD commissioner) recounted the epidemic of gang-related crimes attributed to the Bloods in New York City citing their unprecedented violence, especially during initiations that involved random slashings and stabbings, mostly on subways, with box cutters and knives.

> The gang lived by their code of "Blood in. Blood out." To be initiated you had to spill someone's blood; and to get out of the gang your own blood was spilled. Because of the NYPD's enforcement of low-level crimes, many of the gang members had stopped carrying guns, and so slashings and stabbings with box cutters fulfilled most initiation rites and solved some of the disputes that in the past would have involved shootings. (Safir 2003, 180)

In the years since Portee's incarceration, the UBN has fallen apart. McKenzie, the co-founder of the UBN, had disappeared from the gang scene. Other prominent UBN leaders have been either killed or imprisoned, creating chaos at the top. Today, a number of Blood sets in the East Coast have established official recognition from the West. These "real" Blood gangs are found throughout the East Coast and have made a presence in such southern states as Virginia and South Carolina. For example, Columbia, South Carolina, is home to the **Gangster Killer Bloods (GKB)**. The GKB emerged in 1999 and have as a prime rival the Folk Nation member gangs. The GKB chapter in Columbia was formed as a chapter of the East Coast Bloods from New York City. The gang formation of GKB follows the pattern of many other gangs with their roots in the projects, especially Gonzalez Gardens, where so many people live in poverty and dream of a better way of life.

Among the codes of the Bloods is a lifetime allegiance to the gang. Blood gangs have a strict set of rules that members must abide by or otherwise face punishment ordered by the gang leaders. Gang members must follow all orders given to them by their leaders or risk a violation ceremony. Violation punishments may range from menial tasks and physical assault to (in some extreme cases) death. The philosophy of punishment varies from one set to another, with Blood gangs in New England having a reputation for being more structured and rigid than sets in California. The West Coast Bloods do not have a formal written constitution or code of conduct. Members have to learn the rules and regulations either from older members or by interaction over time with the gang. A code of brotherly love exists among members. The implication being that everyone in the gang should be treated as family. It also means that no "brother" should ever be left behind. The name for the gang Bloods is said to come from the idea of "Blood Brother," a term used by blacks since the time of slavery (Kontos and Brotherton 2008).

Recruitment into the Bloods is usually done aggressively and involves an initiation, which generally takes the form of "jumping in." In this ritual, the new member is required to take a beating and is not allowed to fight back. The most common form of initiation involves the recruit "walking the line," which means walking between two lines of gang members with hands behind while the members beat and kick him/her. The goal is to get to the end of the line without falling to the ground; otherwise, the recruit must start all over. To gain acceptance into the gang, the individual must "Blood-in," meaning he/she must spill someone's blood or have his/her own blood spilled. Among the various ways to go about this is to fight, slash, or assault a law enforcement officer or regular citizen. Committing robberies and rape can be another way to Blood-in. Women recruits may be obligated to participate in group sex. As with all other gangs, the initiation process is conducted so that the new member can demonstrate loyalty to the gang. New recruits are also expected to memorize the nation history, organization, and symbolism.

Much of the Bloods' criminal activity consists of drug distribution and sales. The Bloods distribute such drugs as marijuana, LSD, PCP, heroin, and cocaine and make a great deal of money from the sale of crack cocaine, powder cocaine, and heroin. Profits from drug sales allow the gang to prosper and grow. As the Crip nation expanded its turf to increase both its membership and its share of the drug market, the Bloods grew with them. In the early 1980s narcotics trafficking was considered a minor activity of the Bloods and Crips in Los Angeles. But by 1983, both of these gangs had established criminal networks throughout California. Today, they have drug markets throughout the country. The Bloods also have connections with drug lords and traffickers in South America and other drug-producing countries. They regularly participate in such illegal activities as robberies, car thefts, extortions, rapes, and murders. These crimes are committed for a variety of reasons: initiation, general acceptance, to raise money for dues, or for personal benefit.

The Bloods also enjoy a reputation as a vicious prison gang. Incarcerated Bloods are responsible for a great deal of violence inside prisons and jails, primarily stabbings and slashings. In prison, they fight with rival gang members and nongang inmates and work to eliminate any threats or competition to business inside the prison setting. Going to prison elevates the status of gang members on the street. When inmates are released, they usually gain OG ("original gangster" or "old gangster") status.

Bloods can be identified in a number of ways, especially by the color red, graffiti, and gang signs. There are different theories why the Bloods chose red as their color. Some suggest it simply represents a contrast to the Crips' usage of blue. Another theory is that when the Bloods were first established most of their members went to Centennial High School in which their school color was red (San Antonio Police Department 2012). And clearly, a logical theory centers on the reality that the color of blood is red. Nonetheless, the color red is the main identifier; they wear or carry a red bandanna and treat it as if it is their flag. During a battle, a Blood can never leave the fight without his flag; Bloods are willing to risk death to retrieve it. On the other hand, returning from battle with an enemy's flag/rag will result in great honor, as it usually means that a rival has been killed. Some Bloods may use other colors, such as the Lime Street Pirus, who of course wear lime colors. The color a set chooses to wear, other than red, is the result of alliance with some other gang that may identify with such colors as brown, pink, beige, or orange (Washington Regional Threat and Analysis Center 2008). It is worth noting that increasingly over the past few years, gangs that are identified by a specific color, like the Bloods and the color red, are beginning to shun overt displays as they are easy targets for law enforcement. Although most gang members maintain a level of individuality by adopting a nickname or street name (e.g., Killer Dog, 12-Gauge, and Cop Killer), the Bloods have gang-related tattoos to identify themselves. Other forms of identification include gang-related bling-bling and certain types of clothing. Calvin Klein clothing is popular with Bloods because *CK* is understood to mean "Crip Killer." As usual with all gangs, they have adopted certain sport team logos. Some Bloods wear a Pittsburg Pirates ball cap because of the logo "P" on the cap. The "P" stands for Pirus (it is also used by the Bloods' ally, the People Nation). Kansas City Chiefs hats are very popular with Bloods because they are red and the letters CHIEFS spell out "Crips Hated in Every F***ing State." East Coast Bloods are particularly fond of the FUBU clothing line. To them, *FUBU* means "Forever Us Bloods United." When the Bloods paint graffiti, they prefer the color red and will never use the letter "C" because of their hatred for the Crips (thus, they will not wear a Cincinnati Reds ball cap for the letter "C" even though the team color is red). Typical gang graffiti is generally a single color and simplistic in design. Complex and colorful graffiti is generally done by taggers, who are not gang members. Bloods will often draw three round circles to form an upside-down triangle, which represents a dog's paw, and they will paint the word *Crabs* as a sign of disrespect toward the Crips. The Bloods may sport tattoos with three burn marks shaped like an upside down triangle, or a three-pointed star. Although the specific signs that Bloods flash and the symbolism in their graffiti change constantly, their practice is a constant. (See Figure 6.2 for examples of Blood graffiti.) Gang hand signs, common to most street gangs, are used by members to greet one another,

↑ȻKPPw/s

This Blood graffiti identifies the Campanella Park Piru, Westside gang. As a blood gang, they must disrespect the letter "C"; thus, they have crossed out the first letter of their own gang origin and added a "K" to signify Crip Killer.

RxxsȻK

Graffiti of the Rolling 20s Bloods with the letter "R" for Rolling and Roman numerals for the number 20 and CK added (Crip Killer and letter "C" crossed out to disrespect the Crips).

ȻK

The CK graffiti is common among Bloods because it signifies Crip Killer, with the letter "C" crossed out.

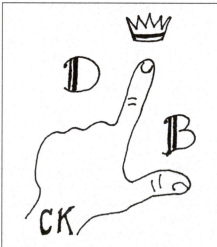

Graffiti of the Denver Lane Bloods features a five-point crown on top to show allegiance to the People Nation and CK for Crip Killer.

PSB PIRUS
RULE
BOMPTON

PSB represents Piru Street Bloods. The Pirus were the original Blood gang and hail from Compton, California. The Bloods do not acknowledge the letter "C" so they spell Compton as Bompton.

FIGURE 6.2 The Bloods (*Source:* Paul Hahn)

give silent warnings, intimidate nongang members and rivals, and as a means of representing themselves as Bloods. Bloods will make hand signs that with the letters "C" and "K" for Crip Killer. They may modify American Sign Language as well as develop their own signs to represent words and messages. This is similar to military personnel in battle situations.

The Bloods remain a real threat on the streets of numerous American cities to rival gangs, civilians, and law enforcement personnel. The police especially worry about the Bloods because they are known to routinely target law enforcement and criminal justice personnel for retaliation or as part of an initiation process (Commonwealth of Virginia Department of State Police 2008). The Bloods continue to grow in number and expand the size of their territory, an expansion fueled by the sale of drugs. Generally, Blood members consider the gang their family and their loyalty to it is very strong. By all accounts, the Bloods look to be a formidable force for years to come. Their competition with the Crips, Folk alliances, and other gangs guarantees that blood will continue to spill.

The People

The next two super-sized gangs to be discussed are the **People Nation** and the **Folks Nation**. The Chicago-based People and Folks are far more diverse than the predominantly African-American, Los Angeles–based Bloods and Crips in at least two major ways. First, there is a greater ethnic and racial mix among the gangs aligned to the People and Folks. Second, whereas the Bloods and Crips consist of individual sets of gangs by the same name (Blood or Crip), the People and Folks nations consist of a number of distinct gangs with their own unique names. Thus, these two umbrella groups are not gangs in and of themselves, but represent a collection of individual gang factions. Using a sports analogy, the People and Folks are like conferences (Big East and Big Ten or the National League and American League). For example, the Folks include such gangs as the **Black Gangster Disciples (BGD)**, **Maniac Latin Disciples**, **Simon City Royals (SCR)**, **C-Notes**, and the **Spanish Gangsters**. The People include such gangs as the **Latin Kings**, **Vice Lords**, the **Almighty Conservative Vice Lords**, **Insane Vice Lords**, **Black P-Stone Nation**, and the **Almighty Gaylords**. It is not uncommon for some gangs (primarily the smaller ones) to change nation allegiance, nor is it uncommon for a gang to rejoin a nation after declaring itself independent. Thus, any listing of gangs belonging to nations is subject to change. The People and Folks are found predominantly in the upper Midwest, especially in Milwaukee and Chicago, and throughout the East.

The SCR, a mostly white street gang that was well known for its burglary rings in Chicago, is generally credited for the formation of nation alliances in Chicago in the 1970s. As SCR members began to get arrested, prosecuted, and incarcerated, they quickly realized how outnumbered they were in the Illinois prison setting. The SCR agreed to provide drugs to fellow inmates who belonged to the BGD in exchange for protection from the Latin Disciples. The alliance between the SCR and the BGD led to the formation of the Folks. The Latin Disciples aligned themselves with other gangs and formed the People. On the streets, the SCR also provided guns to allied gangs in order to secure the Folk alliance. Presently, there are over 30 different gangs that claim allegiance to one of these two nations.

As for why the Almighty Gaylords, another gang affiliated with the People Nation, did not choose to join the SCR and the Folks, the Gaylords had their own history of fights against most of the individual gangs that made up the Folks alliance. On the other hand, their biggest rivalry was against the Latin Kings, the primary member of the People. Latin King members had killed Almighty Gaylord members in the 1970s, 1980s, and 1990s. The Gaylords are a white, Chicago-based street gang, and the alliance to the People Nation was a tough thing for many Gaylord members to accept (in fact, many wonder why the white gangs do not form a national coalition of their own). They were always on guard against their alliance partners, the Latin Kings, because of the way the Kings had pushed fellow alliance member the Insane Deuces too far. The choice to join the People really came down to the fact that the Gaylords had more enemies within the Folks, including the SCR, who had also killed a member of the Gaylords. But their decision to join the People Nation has not really benefited them, because the Almighty Gaylords automatically gained all Folks gangs as enemies. It should be noted that the Folk Nation is larger than the People Nation, and the Gaylords, as a white gang, is already small. Its territories around Palmer Street have now been overtaken by Folks.

The People and Folks distinguish themselves in a number of ways. The People use a five-pointed star or a three-pointed star as a gang insignia and the Folks use a six-pointed star. Thus, the People use in their drawings a five-pointed crown or five-pointed star. The points of the star represent the five pillars of the gang: love, respect, sacrifice, honor, and obedience. The Folks represent their affiliation with the number 6 and/or the six-pointed Star of David. The People and Folks abide by the "left" and "right" rule of dressing, writing, wearing tattoos, and so on in order to show alliance to the gang. But, the left and right distinction becomes cloudy once again. Earlier it was stated that the Bloods wear to the right (as rapper "The Game" indicated in his lyrics) and the Crips wear to the left (as indicated by Snoop Dogg's lyrics). The Bloods are cousins to the People and therefore they should both wear to the same side. However, the People wear to the left (San Antonio Police Department 2012). What this means is that the People gangs wear their identifiers to the left side of the body, including, but not limited to, hats, bling-bling, a rolled-up right pant leg, or hand inside a right pocket. The National Alliance of Gang Investigators Association (NAGIA), a cooperative non-profit organization composed of criminal justice and professional organizations that represent gang investigators' associations with a membership of approximately 20,000 gang investigators across North America, provides, perhaps, the best explanation of the left and right distinction. The NAGIA (2009) states that the West Coast Bloods and Crips abide by original distinctions of Bloods to the right and Crips to the left; however, the Bloods and Crips in the Midwest (i.e., Chicago) and the East (i.e., New York) align with their People and Folks counterparts.

Members of the People Nation can be identified in a number of ways beyond the five-pointed star and the "left–right" rule. The predominant colors of the People are red, black, and white. However, the primary colors of the Latin Kings are black and gold, and they wear black and yellow clothes. Many members of the People wear Chicago Bulls clothing because of their black and red colors. The Latin Kings wear beads with their gang colors as a necklace and also wear Los Angeles Kings apparel. Tattoos for Latin Kings are often symbolic: A teardrop in red means the gangster has killed someone, and a teardrop without color means the gangster has lost someone. The Vice Lords wear Bulls clothing but also always wear a playboy bunny emblem or tattoo. Sports teams such as the Pittsburgh Pirates and the Philadelphia Phillies, because of the prominent letter "P," are favorites among People gangsters. The Vice Lords like to wear the University of Nevada–Las Vegas (UNLV) clothing because of the red-and-black color scheme and because the UNLV letters can be rearranged to read "Vice Lords Nation United." The Vice Lords wear Louis Vuitton hats because they choose to read the initials backward. Primary symbols of the Vice Lords include a pyramid with a crescent moon, the letters "VL," a bunny with a top hat, cane, and gloves, and a crescent moon. The top hat is symbolic of the shelter that the gang provides members; the cane is symbolic of weapon at one's ready and thus, the strength of gang; and the Playboy bunny is symbolic of such traits as awareness and quickness. The crescent moon with the pyramid is symbolic of black power. The Latin Kings can be identified by such symbols as a three-pointed crown (as well as a five-pointed crown), five dots, cross necklace, a king's head with a crown, lions, and the letters "LK." When tagging, they always cross out the "C's" (for Crip) and X-out the "O's" (for Hoover) (as we shall learn shortly, Larry Hoover was the founder of the Folks Nation, the sworn enemies of the People Nation). They refer to Folks and Crips as "Craps"—it is meant as a sign of disrespect to the word *crip*. Since the Folks often use a pitchfork as a major identifier symbol, the People will paint upside down pitchforks as a sign of disrespect toward Folks. (See Figure 6.3 for examples of People graffiti.) The People also identify

The five-pointed star is a staple of People Nation gangs, the pitchfork is upside down to disrespect the Folk Nation gangs, and the "5 poppin, 6 droppin" is a motto to signify a People Nation gang member shooting a Folk Nation gang member.

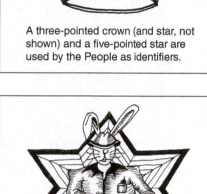

A three-pointed crown (and star, not shown) and a five-pointed star are used by the People as identifiers.

"L" and "K" represent Latin Kings. A three-point crown with the number 5 symbolizes membership to the Latin Kings and the People Nation. The pitchfork is upside down to disrespect the Folks.

Common gang identifiers of the Vice Lords, a gang under the People Nation umbrella, are a bunny rabbit, or Playboy bunny, with a cane and top hat. The top hat equates to shelter, the cane is a sign of strength (used as a weapon), and the bunny represents awareness and quickness. The right ear is pointed down to disrespect the Folks and the left ear upward to represent the People Nation. A five-point star is in the background.

Any combination of these People symbols (five-pointed crown, pyramid, dice, cross, and five-pointed star) along with canes and crescent moon (not shown) may be incorporated into their gang graffiti.

FIGURE 6.3 The People (*Source*: Paul Hahn)

with a crescent moon and a pyramid with 21 bricks to represent the 21 original gangs. They use upside down "6s" to disrespect the Folks and Crips. They also draw a lion (as a symbol of toughness) wearing a five-pointed star.

Among the more significant gangs that make up the People is the **Almighty Latin Kings Nation**, or Latin Kings for short. (There is also an Almighty Latin Queens Nation.) The Latin Kings are one of the oldest and largest Hispanic (predominantly Mexican and Puerto Rican) gangs in existence. They were founded by Hispanic inmates in Chicago during the 1940s to protect themselves against other prison gangs (Safir 2003). The co-founders of the Latin Kings are Raul Gonzalez, who was known by many as "Baby King," and Gustavo Gino Colon, known as "the Gino." On the streets, the Latin Kings were designed to protect the Hispanic communities from being invaded or taken over by rival ethnic gangs and to protect their culture within the neighborhood. Most Latin King members come from lower SES families so they found it important to protect their heritage by any means necessary, including forming a gang alliance that would extend across most of the eastern half of the nation. The majority of Latin King members are Puerto Rican, but many other members come from diverse Central American nations, including Cuba, the Dominican Republic, and Ecuador.

The Latin Kings are a little different than most street gangs. What makes the Kings different is "their mixture of intense discipline and revolutionary politics with a homemade religion called Kingism, adding idealism and a boot-camp rigor to the usual gang camaraderie—a potent mixture for troubled ghetto kids whose lives lacked structure and hope" (Richardson 1997, 32). The Latin Kings developed slowly in Southeast Chicago and the Humboldt Park area throughout the 1950s. There were numerous gangs in Chicago in the 1950s, including many white ethnic gangs. During this time, the Humboldt Park community was a very strong and thriving Jewish community with nearly 75 Jewish temples. By the 1960s, Latinos and blacks were moving into Humboldt Park and South Chicago, effectively dissolving the Jewish community and the local white ethnic gangs. The Latin Kings rose to power as their turf protection skills increased. They also learned to form alliances with other gangs, like the Vice Lords, who shared with them common enemies, and thus began a nation coalition (the People). In 2002, there were an estimated 18,000 Latin King members in Chicago alone (Main and Sadovi 2002). Today, nationwide, there are an estimated 25,000 Latin Kings.

In an attempt to expand their territory, the Latin Kings began to expand to other Eastern cities during the 1980s. They can be found in New York, Connecticut, New Jersey, Iowa, Indiana, Ohio, Florida, and Massachusetts as well as in Illinois and Wisconsin. In fact, wherever there is a sizable Hispanic community, it is likely that the Latin Kings have recruited there. The Latin Kings' presence in New York can be traced back to the mid-1980s. "The New York branch of the Kings was established in 1986 by Luis Felipe, or 'King Blood,' who is currently serving a life term in solitary confinement for ordering hits on several Latin King members in the early 1990s" (Safir 2003, 181).

The Latin Kings are highly organized and well structured and live by a charter constitution. Most sets have a hierarchical structure with military-style titles (high-ranking soldiers are called lieutenants and lower-level ones are known as sergeants). Foot soldiers are used to sell drugs and are required to pay a "street tax" of more than half their drug profits to higher-level gang members (Main and Sadovi 2002). The Latin Kings in Buffalo, for example, hold regular meetings—every Wednesday and Sunday—and require members to pay dues. The dues are $5 a week for members who don't sell drugs and $10 to $20 for those who do (Herbeck 2008). The primary leaders are known as the High Holy Incas, secondary leaders are known as Supreme Caciqua, and leaders third in command are called the Royal Crown. Female members are known as **Latin Queens**. The gang members function in a cooperative manner and work under the ideal of one body, mind, and soul. New recruits are initiated. Current members who violate the gang's rules are subject to "physicals" (a violation ceremony, or punishment). Most Latin King gangs, and especially the Almighty Latin King Nation (ALKN), have the mentality of "Once a King, always a King." The Latin Kings participate in all the regular gang criminal activities: drug and weapons sales and trafficking, assault, robbery, intimidation, property damage, murder, and so on. The Latin Kings are generally considered to be the most violent of the Hispanic gangs. They are notorious for fighting in packs and implement a "911" tactic—the Kings call to battle (Richardson 1997). This inevitably results in constant disputes with rivals, which leads to a high level of violence.

Criminal activity and religious mysticism are intertwined in this street gang. As mentioned, the Kings employ a religious philosophy (Kingism) and have their own prayers and a "good book" that members are expected to follow. Members who don't follow the rules are subject to a violation, which usually means a beating that can last up to five minutes (Herbeck 2008). One of the rules states: "You are not to put God, religion, family or friends before the Latin King nation" (Herbeck 2008). Gays, gamblers, and users of hard-core drugs are not welcomed in the gang, according to the rules, but selling hard drugs is acceptable. The ALKN commonly use a fist over the heart to represent "I will die for you, for you are the flesh of my flesh, blood of my blood, son of my mother who is the universal nature and follower of Yahve, who is the Almighty King of Kings." This passage is found in the book of Genesis in the Bible. The primary symbol of the Latin Kings is the five-pointed crown. As Latin King members explain, slogans and prayers used by the Latin Kings reflect both a secular and a religious flair. Latin Kings pay homage to each other and to God by stating, "Almighty Father, King of Kings, hear us as we come before you, one body, mind, and soul, true wisdom, knowledge and understanding. Give us strong brown wisdom, for we realized you are the best, and the wisest of all seeing eyes." The Latin Kings consider January 6 to be "Kings Holy Day," and the first week of March as "Kings Week." These occasions are celebrated by gang members hanging out and consuming drugs and alcohol. The private notebooks that King members use are referred to as "Bibles" of Kingist teachings.

The Latin Kings are particularly ruthless and are involved in a wide range of criminal acts, including the distribution and sale of drugs, weapons trafficking, murder, assault, armed robbery, kidnapping, extortion, racketeering, public corruption, intimidation, and alien smuggling (NAGIA 2009). Like all the nation gangs, the criminal activities of the Latin Kings in various cities are too numerous to document here. But as an example, the highest-ranking leader nationwide of the Latin Kings, Augustin "Big Tino" Zambrano was sentenced to 60 years in federal prison in January 2012 after being convicted at trial of racketeering conspiracy (RICO) and related charges involving narcotics trafficking and violence that plagued numerous neighborhoods on Chicago's north, south, and west sides (FBI 2012k). The FBI claims that Zambrano ordered and personally participated in the executions of rivals.

Another important gang aligned to the People Nation is the **Almighty Vice Lord Nation**, or Vice Lords for short. The Vice Lords were first known as the Conservative Lads, then the Imperial Vice Lords, and later the Conservative Vice Lords (Dawley 1992). Some of the original Vice Lords had belonged to one of the earliest black gangs in Lawndale, the Clovers. The Clovers dominated the area from around 1951 to 1956. The Vice Lords are an African-American gang with an estimated Chicago membership of 20,000 in 2002 (Main and Sadovi 2002). There are an estimated 30,000 total Vice Lords today. In addition to Illinois, the Vice Lords have a strong presence in such states as Michigan, Ohio, Indiana, Wisconsin, Tennessee, Mississippi, and Minnesota. The Vice Lords are said to have begun in 1958 in the St. Charles Juvenile Correctional Facility by a group of youths from around 16th Street on the west side of Chicago. These early gangsters agreed to pool their gang affiliations so as to become one of Chicago's toughest gangs. The Vice Lords originally called themselves a "club" rather than a gang. As Keiser (1969) explains, the boys formed what was called a "Harding Cottage" within the Illinois Training School in St. Charles. Within this training school were the toughest boys of St. Charles. From the original 66 members of the Vice Lords, the membership quickly grew to over 300 in 5 different sets located in the North Lawndale area of Chicago. During the 1960s they grew to over 8,000 members and 26 different sets. Today, the Vice Lords can be found all over the Midwest and in some Eastern cities. They continue to maintain a stronghold in many Chicago neighborhoods.

The Vice Lords possess a rank structure within individual factions that include general, minister, lieutenant, and foot soldiers. This structure is similar in all sets of the Vice Lords; however, each set's leadership is unique and has no power over members of other factions. A Vice Lord leader's power is not exercised through force, but, rather, through influence. Members of the Lords follow a leader out of respect. The strength of an individual's power is subject to constant fluctuation. Power is based on the number of one's followers, and the following is constantly changing.

There are a number of Vice Lord factions. Among them are the Traveling Vice Lords (TVL), Conservative Vice Lords, Imperial Insane Vice Lords, Renegade Vice Lords, Gangster Stone Vice Lords, Ebony Vice Lords, and Four Corner Hustlers. The **Conservative Vice Lords** were especially prominent in the 1960s as a gang attempting to organize legitimate job opportunities for members of deprived urban communities (the non-profit organization mentioned previously). They worked to eliminate crime and violence in the community, but they were not successful. Local officials did what they could to undermine the authority of the Conservative Vice Lords. Like the Latin Kings, the Vice Lords developed in Chicago communities experiencing rapid social and racial change. The **Traveling Vice Lords (TVL)** have their roots in Chicago's Klondike area (one of the most dangerous areas of the city). The concept of "traveling" is incorporated with the Vice Lords umbrella because of their ultimate goal to extend the gang globally.

Typical of most large gangs, the Vice Lords are engaged in a myriad of criminal activities centered on making money. In 2010, the FBI arrested nearly 100 members of the TVL on drug charges stemming from an operation that involved around-the-clock retail street sales of crack cocaine and heroin that averaged between $3,000 and $6,000 per day, seven days a week (FBI 2010f). The TVL operate on the west side of Chicago according to federal and state charges. Chicago, state, and federal agents worked cooperatively to bring down this drug ring. In 2011, 17 members of the mid-state (Memphis) Tennessee Vice Lords were indicted on drug, conspiracy, and firearms charges (FBI 2011l). According to the indictment, the object of the conspiracy included, among other things, the acquisition of large quantities of controlled substances, including, but not limited to, cocaine and marijuana, for distribution in Middle Tennessee (FBI 2011l). These two examples of Vice Lords' criminal activities represent a mere sampling of their total impact on neighborhoods throughout the mid-region of the United States.

The Folks

As the previous discussion on the People revealed, the Folks are the other dominant nation Chicago-based gang. The Folks are larger in number and equally as brutal as the People. The Folks have aligned themselves with the Crips to counterbalance the alliance between the People and Bloods. The original Folk gang (Gangster Disciples) was started by **Larry Hoover**, and that is why the Folk Nation is sometimes referred to as the **Hoover Nation** gang. Larry Hoover, currently serving a life term in prison, is still considered the chairman of the Folks. Folk gang members display a six-pointed star, which is symbolic of the core beliefs of the Folks: life, loyalty, love, wisdom, knowledge, and understanding.

The most prominent of the Folk gangs is the **Black Gangster Disciples (BGD)**. These gangsters use an upright pitchfork as their primary symbol in graffiti. To disrespect the People (especially the Vice Lords), the Folks draw, in graffiti, a cane handle upside down. The BGD are an African-American gang with a 2002 estimated Chicago membership of 30,000 (Main and Sadovi 2002). Total membership of the BGD is estimated at 45,000. The Disciples have their roots in the Chicago streets (the Englewood neighborhood) dating back to the 1960s. The BGD abide by a strict code of laws. Central tenets of the code include respecting all members of the nation; refusing to tolerate any BGD member socializing with a member of a rival gang; a willingness to sacrifice one's life for the nation; abiding by the commands of the leaders; promising not to fight nation affiliate members; and acknowledging all fellow BGD members with a clenched fist salute (Knox 2004).

In the mid-1960s Jeff Fort united the leaders of some 50 area street gangs into a single alliance called the **Black P-Stone Nation**. The gang was controlled by a 21-man commission, self-titled the "Main 21." The ideal of this gang was to create a socially active organization designed to empower poorer members of the community (similar to the Conservative Vice Lords, who ran a teen center and job-training classes for youths on the West Side). This organization received $1.4 million in federal antipoverty funds, which were actually used to fund the illegal activities of the gang. The misappropriation of funds was discovered and a federal grand jury convicted Fort of the mismanagement of funds and he was sent to federal prison.

Many other gang organizations surfaced and attempted to secure money as the Black P-Stone gang had managed. Two very influential gangs, the BGD, led by David Barksdale, and the Gangster Disciples, led by the aforementioned Larry Hoover, followed Fort's example and unified their gangs to form the BGD Nation. The BGD wear the six-pointed Star of David (the Jewish star) as a tribute to their leader, David "King David" Barksdale, who was seriously wounded in an ambush in 1969 and died of kidney failure in 1974. A gentile, Barksdale wore the medallion because it was his namesake and because he considered himself a star. Throughout the 1970s the BGD Nation controlled the drug trade and became bitter rivals of the Black P-Stone Nation. Their wars were brutal and left many dead or imprisoned. The Gangster Disciples continued their war with the P-Stone Nation inside prison walls. Their war was another major contributor to the formation of the People and Folks Nations in the 1970s. The P-Stone Nation ended up with the People and the BGD with the Folks.

Recruitment and initiation into the Folks nation are similar to that of the other nations. Recruitment is highly encouraged and actively pursued because of the simple premise of there being strength in numbers. The most common initiation is "The Line," which involves the prospective member walking a line between fellow gangsters from whom he takes an extreme beating. The gang has a constitution and a hierarchical structure, with all underlings expected to strictly abide by rules and codes of conduct. Violations result in a physical beating. The BGD are "cafeteria-style" criminals—their crimes include murder, drive-by shootings, robbery, auto theft, home invasions, weapons sales and distribution, and, of course, the sale and distribution of drugs. The BGD, like other gangs, utilize false-front businesses to run their drug distribution syndicate. Music stores, car washes, ice-cream shops, barbershops, and apartment buildings are the traditional locations of either "market places" or money laundering. When Larry Hoover was convicted in 1997, prosecutors estimated that the Disciples were netting an estimated $100 million a year. In fact, (all) gangs have become such a major economic force in Chicago; it is estimated that their annual profit from the sale of drugs is a half-billion dollars. Federal officials in Chicago estimate that the figure is closer to 1 billion dollars—more than 1 percent of Chicago's gross domestic product (Main and Sadovi 2002).

The Folk Nation has many identifiers beginning with the six-pointed star that pays homage to David Barksdale. In recent years, the six-pointed star is viewed more as two triangles, with one pointed up to heaven and the other pointed toward hell. Each point is still symbolic of the six pillars of the Folk Nation (love, life, loyalty, wisdom, knowledge, and understanding). The upright pitchfork is the second most common identifier, especially with the Gangster Disciples. Bull horns, a sign of strength, are another popular identifier. The Folks are dedicated to "right" identification, as in wearing articles of clothing to the right (caps, bandannas, belt buckles, etc.), wearing jewelry to the right, rolling up the right pant leg, putting one hand in the right pocket, and so on. The primary colors of the Gangster Disciples are blue and black. BGD members may wear any of the following types of clothing: apparel with the letter "D" (e.g., the Detroit Tigers cap) for Disciple; the letter "G" for Gangster (especially the "G" on Georgetown apparel); Duke sweatshirts (the letters are read as "Disciples Utilizing Knowledge Everyday"); Denver Broncos clothing (switch the letters to BK—for Black Disciples); and clothing with the University of Indiana logo (because the IU emblem looks like a pitchfork). The Folk Nation really likes the Georgetown Hoya emblem, not just because the letter "G" is prominent, but also because the collar worn by the dog has six studs and is tilted to the right. Other factions of the Folk Nation abide by "the right" rule and the six-pointed star. The **Satan Disciples** have black and canary yellow for their colors, a devil with a pitchfork for a symbol, and wear clothing with the letter "D." **Orchestra Albany** has gold and brown for its colors and the letter "O" over the letter "A" as its symbol and wear Oakland A's and California Angels apparel. **Latin Lovers** have red and yellow as colors and the double letter "L" inside a heart as their symbol and wear Kansas City Chiefs apparel and Chicago Bulls clothing (minus the "BU" in *Bulls*). The **Black P. Stone** gang also wears Chicago Bulls clothing but interprets the lettering to mean "Boy U Look Like a Stone." (See Figure 6.4 for examples of Folks graffiti.)

Located on the North Side of Chicago in the Humboldt Park area is the notorious **Maniac Latin Disciples (MLD)**. MLD has roots to the early 1960s as a social club that, among other things, played city league baseball and participated in petty crime. MLD consists mostly of Puerto Rican gang members whose families immigrated to Chicago in the early 1960s following Puerto Rico's acceptance of an offer to become a member of the United States Commonwealth in 1952. Following the pattern discussed so often throughout this text, these early Puerto Ricans were victims of prejudice and discrimination, and some youth became disenchanted with the mainland's customs and values. The youth were confronted by such white Chicago gangs as the **Simon City Royal**, **Gaylords**, and the **Harrison Jets**. These early gangs and their rumbles resembled gang portrayal of *West Side Story* wherein most of the confrontations consisted of fist fights and gang members running after, and from, each other (*Gangland* 2008a). As freeway construction ripped apart city neighborhoods in the 1960s and opened the expansion of the growth of suburbs, white families fled Humboldt Park by the end of the 1960s. (*Note*: In 2010, whites consisted of just 4.4% of the Humboldt Park population; Hispanics over 53% and blacks nearly 41%.) By the end of the 1960s, the former social club of 12 members decided to name themselves "Disciples." There are different explanations for this; one account claims that the original 12 members saw themselves as symbolically linked to the 12 disciples of Jesus described in the Bible; while the prevailing sentiment is that the name *Disciples* emerged as a result of the pact made between them and the BGD. This pact helped to start the Folk Nation. In 1969, a new leader, Albert Hernandez, emerged and he wanted to add a Hispanic flavor to the gang name and renamed the group the Latin Disciples. Hernandez set up a structural hierarchy, with a council overseeing the 100 members the gang claimed in 1970. The gang instituted a "beat-in" initiation and allowed members to leave via a "beat-out" ceremony. Gang members who disobeyed gang rules were subject to a violation ceremony. Following the death of Hernandez, at the hands of a Latin King, the gang's archrival, a new leader, Peter "The Burner" Correa took charge. In 1973,

Shown here are among the most common gang graffiti items of the Folks: a six-pointed star (a six-pointed crown may also be used), the number 6 (6 for the letter "F"), raised pitchforks (also known as the Devil's pitchfork among the Gangster Disciple coalition).

This six-pointed star is utilized by the Black Gangster Disciples. Gangs often use numbers in place of letters. The numbers 12, 12, 21, 11, 23, and 12 at the tip of each point on the star represent the first letters of the core beliefs of the Black Gangster Disciples: life, loyalty, wisdom, knowledge, understanding, and love. The numbers 2, 7, and 4 written across the middle of the star represent Black Gangster Disciple.

This gang graffiti illustration has the raised pitchforks, the heart with devil horns, and the letters "BGD" for Black Gangster Disciples inside the heart.

The Latin Disciples often incorporate raised pitchforks and a heart with devil horns. The heart with devil horns equates to love and allegiance to the gang.

A raised pitchfork to show respect to the Folk Nation and an upside down 5 to disrespect the People Nation.

King Huva is a tribute to Larry Hoover, the founder of the original Folk gang.

FIGURE 6.4 The Folks (*Source*: Paul Hahn)

Correa changed the name of the gang to the Maniac Latin Disciples, although the gang is still commonly called the Latin Disciples. By 1996, MLD consisted of 1,700 members. The gang was selling drugs like a "McDonald's drive-thru" in Humboldt Park as auto customers literally lined up as they spoke with MLD dealers selling drugs (*Gangland* 2008a). In addition to MLD fighting its rivals, the Latin Kings and the Spanish Cobras, to this day for control of the lucrative drug marketplace that is Humboldt Park, the Maniac Latin Disciples is split into two factions based on allegiance to two major families that fight for control of the gang. Despite all the in-fighting and out-fighting, MLD remains powerful in Chicago.

As with the People, the Folks have extended their territory far beyond the limits of Chicago. Some faction of either the People or Folks can be found in nearly all Midwest and Eastern cities. Their involvement in drug sales and distribution provides them with over a billion dollars with which to enforce their territories. Their willingness to kill anyone who gets in their way, including nongang members, is a hallmark of the Folk Nation. The residents of the Ebbets Field Apartments in Brooklyn (the site of Ebbets Field, home of the Brooklyn Dodgers) were unwilling witnesses to the brutal tactics of Folk gang **Six Tre Outlaw Gangsta Disciples** for years. The Six Tre gang arrived one day at the apartments and simply said they were in charge. Anyone who crossed them was killed. On one day in 2008, a suspected Blood working out at a playground across the street from the apartments was "shot square in the chest," the FBI reports. When members of this gang started to be arrested, the gang reminded residents that "snitching is a capital offense" and anyone who dares testify against the gang will lose his/her life (*Huffington Post* 2012a).

Such are the tactics of nation gangs. It seems hard to believe that any other coalition of gangs could be more brutal than the nation gangs. But let me introduce you to transnational gangs.

TRANSNATIONAL STREET GANGS

There is no single definition of what characteristics constitute a transnational street gang, but various definitions cite one or more of the following characteristics: Such gangs are criminally active and operational in multiple countries; criminal activities committed by gang members in one country are planned, directed, and controlled by gang leaders in another country; such gangs are mobile and seek further expansion; and, the criminal activities of such gangs transcend borders (Franco 2008). In short, a **transnational street gang** is a gang that acts as a criminal enterprise in multiple countries and whose members reside, and/or operate, in multiple nations wherein primary criminal activities take place in public areas (the streets). Presently, there are two recognized transnational street gangs: M-18, or the 18th Street Gang, and MS-13. The letter "M" for both of these gangs refers to the term *mara*, which is a Spanish word for gang. A *marero* means a gang member. With the meaning of *mara* in mind, both M-18 and MS-13 are Hispanic/Latino gangs. Maras make little effort to hide their affiliations and can be easily identified because of their head-to-toe tattoos (*The Economist* 2012).

The 18th Street Gang (M-18) and Florencia 13 (F-13)

In the street gang capital of the world, Los Angeles, it might seem hard for any one gang to stick out, especially in light of the fact that Los Angeles serves as the home-base for the country's two largest nation coalitions, the Crips and the Bloods. The **18th Street Gang** (M-18) is such a gang. They are often described as the most violent and aggressive street gang in the country (Walker 2012). The 18th Street Gang originated in Los Angeles on 18th Street and Union Avenue in the Rampart District. There are an estimated 20,000 members in Los Angeles alone and an estimated total of 30,000 to

45,000 across the United States, with influence and residence in many foreign nations. Their stronghold, and oldest barrio, is located east of the Staples Center (home of the Los Angeles Lakers, Kings, and Clippers) between the Harbor Freeway (east) and Hoover Avenue (west). Two of the more significant barrios of the 18th Street Gang are in South Los Angeles, with one between Vernon (north) and Slauson (South) along Vermont Avenue and the other between Florence (north) and 91st Street (south). The biggest rivals of the 18th Street Gang are Florencia 13, a Hispanic gang that is large in terms of both membership and turf size, and MS-13, a transnational gang to be discussed later in this chapter. (See Figure 6.5 for a sample of the 18th Street and Florencia 13 graffiti.)

Although both the 18th Street Gang and Florencia 13 are under the loosely aligned Surenos coalition (because of their connection to La Eme), the two Los Angeles–based gangs are rivals on the streets (Goldschein and McKenna 2012). **Florencia 13** has control of the streets in the Florence/Firestone area of South Central Los Angeles, an area that runs along Florence avenue, putting it in direct contact with the 18th Street Gang, and extends from Western Avenue (west) to Compton Avenue (east). This is the largest single Hispanic barrio in all of Los Angeles city and county. Mexicans first arrived in South Central Los Angeles in great numbers around the 1930s. By the 1950s cliques of Mexican gangs formed to protect themselves from the then-majority black population. The name *Florencia 13* is derived from its home turf, Florence Street (Florencia in Spanish), and the "13" as homage to the Mexican Mafia. Florenica 13 (F-13), it should be noted, was the first street gang to align with La Eme. As the number of Mexicans and other Hispanics continued to explode in South Central, a bitter turf war escalated between black and Hispanic gangs. By the 1990s, F-13 had become involved in the lucrative drug trade in the area. The number of Florenica 13 cliques expanded and include the Termintes, Jokers, Los Animales, Malditos, Assassins, and Diablos. Today, Florencia 13 dominates its nearly 3 square mile territory and its prime rivals are the 18th Street Gang and the Crips. They have a particular hatred for the blacks in general and the Crips in particular. They refer to Crip members as "Ducks" in a derogatory way and use such slang as "Hey Ese, I popped a duck last night" as a means to inform a fellow F-13 member that a Crip was shot. Their involvement in drug-trafficking, violence, murder, and extortion of local businesses for protection money has not gone unnoticed by authorities. In 2007 more than 100 leaders and enforcers of F-13 were arrested on a variety of RICO violations. In 2009, 10 La Eme–connected Florencia 13 members were convicted in a federal RICO case that included allegations of attempted murder, firearm violations, and drug charges (Girardot 2009). A large component of the case rested on the gang's targeting blacks. In 2010, six Florencia 13 gang members were sentenced to life in prison for a prolonged spate of violence in the Florence-Firestone district brought on by orders from a La Eme prison gang member in solitary confinement 700 miles away in Pelican Bay State Prison (Quinones 2010).

The formation of the 18th Street Gang can be traced back to the 1960s and has its origins in racial prejudice. During this time, the Clanton Street Gang, a second-generation Hispanic street gang, limited membership to those who were American citizens from a pure Hispanic background. Thus, youths who were undocumented immigrants or of mixed ancestry were not allowed to join the Clanton Gang. The Clanton Street gang had been around since the 1940s and had members that were Zoot-Suit Pachucos (Walker 2012). As more and more immigrant Mexicans arrived in Los Angeles throughout the 1960s, their youth wanted to join Clanton. Many of these youths became juvenile delinquents and committed crimes that led to their arrest and incarceration in local juvenile detention facilities. While incarcerated, their membership to the Clanton gang was still denied. As an inevitable result, these rejected youths decided to bond together and form their own gang to rival the Clantons. A youth nicknamed "Glover" did most of the recruiting and purposely targeted mixed-race youths to join the gang. Glover and most of these youths came from

18th Street (just four blocks away from Clanton gang turf), located in the Rampart district of Los Angeles, a notoriously tough area, but they originally called themselves the "Clanton Street Throw-aways." These delinquents became the original members of the 18th Street Gang.

The 18th Street Gang was the first Hispanic gang to break the racial membership barrier. Because of the lax membership criteria, the 18th Street Gang grew very rapidly. It was largely composed of immigrants and multiracial youths. Most of the members are Hispanic, but some cliques include blacks, Asians, whites, and Native Americans. Youths who have developed a reputation for violence are especially recruited and welcomed. Because it is known to recruit elementary and middle-school youths, the 18th Street Gang is sometimes referred to as the Children's Army. The gang attempts to recruit members early on in life by intimidation, including the threat of death (including the deaths of their loved ones) if the recruit attempts to leave the gang. The 18th Street Gang members can be identified by their tattoos. They have ink done all over their bodies, such as on their foreheads and above their eyebrows. The most common tattoo is the number 18 or XVIII, and they sometimes have 666 tattooed on their bodies as well. Popular folklore, along with some religions, considers the number 666 to represent the devil. For example, *Revelation* 13:16–18 states, "And he causeth all, both small and great, rich and poor, free and bond, to receive a mark in their right hand, or in their foreheads: And that no man might buy or sell, save he that had the mark, or the name of the beast, or the number of his name. Here is wisdom. Let him that hath understanding count the number of the beast: for it is the number of a man; and his number is six hundred threescore and six." The early Christians attempted to link Julius Caesar to the devil beast. Caesar, the first Roman persecutor of the Christians, penned the phrase "VENI VIDI VICI." This phrase, when reduced to Roman numerals, converts to VIVIVI, or 666. From this, Caesar came to be viewed as the devil. In gang reality, when the numbers 666 are added together they equal 18, thus, the connection of 666 to the 18th Street Gang. As for identification based on clothing, the 18th Street Gang members generally wear brown or black pants with a white T-shirt. The use of graffiti is also common. (See Figure 6.5 for examples of 18th Street and Florencia 13 gang graffiti.)

The 18th Street Gang is involved in a wide variety of criminal activities: auto theft, carjacking, drive-by shootings, murder, murder for hire, extortion, arms trafficking, and drug sales and distribution. Various intelligence and law enforcement agencies have indicated that the gang has established ties with the Mexican and Columbian drug cartels, which have a big impact on the Southwest border states. The respect that the gang commands on the streets extends inside prison walls, as the 18th Street Gang has ties with both the Mexican Mafia and black prison gangs. The 18th Street Gang not only controls a great number of streets in the drug trade, it also makes a great deal of money through extortion. These gangsters approach local vendors and threaten them unless they pay a "protection tax." If people refuse to pay the tax, they risk bodily harm and death. The FBI considers their protection racket as evidence of the 18th Street Gang and MS-13 as America's new organized crime syndicates that use numerical superiority and sheer muscle brutality to extort "rent" or "taxes" from local business, including legal and illegal vendors (Delgadillo 2008). M-18 has also learned to make money in the white-collar world as well by committing such crimes as forging identification cards and immigration papers, cloning cellular phones, and stealing credit cards, bus passes, and food stamps. National and international drug-trafficking appears to be M-18's biggest money maker. They enforce their drug trade with their own arsenal of weapons, including automatic weapons (e.g., Tech 9s, Mac 10s, Mac 11s, and AK-47s). Law enforcement expect 18th Street Gang members to always carry weapons, and their history of using them adds to the reputation of M-18 as an extremely violent and ruthless gang. In 2007, for example, an M-18 clique, the Columbia Lil Cycos (CLCS), whom federal

SCXV3ST
M18
18
666

Variations of the 18th Street Gang graffiti: On top, the "SC" represents South Central Los Angeles, a specific clique of the 18th Street Gang. "XV3" represents 18 for 18th Street Gang. As a transnational gang with Central American roots, the letter "M", for Mara, may be combined with the number 18 for a shorten version of 18th Street Gang (second row). The numbers 18 and 666 are common gang identifiers in the 18th Street Gang graffiti (rows 3 and 4).

FLORENCIA13
F13
SCF13JOKERS

The Florencia 13 gang name is derived from Florence Street, the heart of gang's territory and the number 13 a nod to the Mexican Mafia (M is the 13th letter of the alphabet). Florencia 13 often identifies simply with F-13 (row 2). The gang graffiti illustration on line three identifies the South Central (SC), Florenica 13 gang, the Jokers. The Jokers are one of the oldest and most respected cliques of F-13 in South Central Los Angeles.

FIGURE 6.5 18th Street Gang and Florencia 13 (*Source*: Paul Hahn)

authorities two years later arrested for racketeering charges, attempted to murder a street vendor near MacArthur Park, California, but instead shot a 3-week-old infant (FBI 2009e). This same clique murdered an innocent man in 2001. The CLCS gang was running street operations at the direction of La Eme (FBI 2009e).

The 18th Street Gang has evolved since its early days as a turf-oriented street gang. Today, M-18 is found in numerous U.S. states and many Central American nations, including Mexico, Guatemala, Honduras, Columbia, and El Salvador. Because of its expansion internationally, M-18 is in competition with MS-13, perhaps the only gang more brutal than the 18th Street Gang. To combat the 18th Street Gang and MS-13, the FBI has put together an international group of law enforcement representatives from El Salvador, Honduras, Guatemala, Canada, and

Mexico (FBI 2009d). This group is known as the Central American Intelligence Program (CAIP). Officials from each participating nation are well aware of the serious problem these two gangs represent. MS-13 alone has 15,000 members in El Salvador, including many in the prison population. CAIP also reports that MS-13 and the 18th Street Gang are constantly developing and changing their methods of operation. CAIP is designed to keep up with the growing threat of these two transnational gangs (FBI 2009d).

Mara Salvatrucha (La Mara Salvatrucha, MS-13)

Mara Salvatrucha, commonly known as MS-13, is also under the Surenos umbrella because of its allegiance to La Eme (NAGIA 2009). Nonetheless, this transnational gang is a rival of M-18 (18th Street Gang) because of its history with this gang. The roots of MS-13 can be traced back to El Salvador and its civil war. Many refugees from this war-torn country fled to the United States in the 1980s. It is estimated that nearly 1 million Salvadorans and Guatemalans attempted migration to the United States through Mexico during the 1980s (Gzesh 2006). Under the Reagan Administration these immigrants, who sought political asylum, were regarded as "economic migrants" and were thus denied legal migration. The immigrants from El Salvador and neighboring Guatemala were detained and deported (Gzesh 2006). It could be argued that MS-13 became a transnational gang as a result of the deportation, as these one-time guerillas and Los Angeles gang members brought their gang mentality back to their home countries with them. The failed socio-political moves of the Reagan administration throughout Central America led to the growing Mara gangs in nations beyond El Salvador and Guatemala and extended to Nicaragua via the U.S.–Contra debacle. The CIA was selling illegal weapons to Iran and using the money to fund the Contras in Nicaragua (Ried 2004). The United States played a large role in what happened to Nicaragua's economy, especially with the American embargo that resulted in poverty, unemployment, and starvation—all essential elements in the creation of violent street gangs.

The concern over these particular immigrants was deemed reasonable by the Reagan administration because some of these refugees were former members of such military organizations as the Farabundo Marti National Liberation Front and were trained as guerrillas, known as Salvatruchas. These rebels had attempted to overthrow El Salvador's government during the civil war. Former California State Senator Tom Hayden attributes the rise of Salvadorian gangs to U.S. military intervention in the El Salvador civil war and President Reagan's misguided use of the military:

> The sudden emergence of these *pandillas* (gangs) was due entirely to U.S. military intervention in El Salvador in the eighties. The same neoconservatives who promoted the wars on gangs and drugs at home were champions of the military policies, which, ironically, would import those wars to the streets of Los Angeles and other cities. When Ronald Reagan was elected in 1980, the civil war in El Salvador was stalemated, with Jimmy Carter's ambassador reporting that Salvadoran leaders wished a political and economic settlement instead of further war. . . . The incoming Reagan administration ignored Jimmy Carter's negotiations-oriented [approach] . . . announcing a doubling of military aid to El Salvador in March 1981. (Hayden 2004, 200–201)

By most estimates, 75,000 Salvadorans died in the civil war, mostly at the hands of soldiers trained or supplied by the U.S. military. The Salvadorian refugee youths in Los Angeles started calling themselves the *la mara loca*, which roughly translates to "the crazy neighborhood." "Soon they were known as *mara Salvatrucha stoners*, and finally *mara Salvatrucha*, the 'Salvadoran neighborhood,' or simply MS. In a larger sense, they were *las frutas de la Guerra*, the fruits of the war, a description that would become a rap anthem of Homies Unidos a few years later" (Hayden 2004, 203). Mara Salvatrucha was indeed a stoner clique when they initially formed around 1980. A year or two later they changed their name from MS Stoners to MS-13. The "Stoners" was dropped and the "13" was added in honor of the Mexican Mafia. The MS-13 gang first formed in the Pico Union section of Los Angeles in the early 1980s (Kelleher and Gonzales 2004). MS-13 and the 18th Street Gang of Los Angeles had a loose confederation until 1992. Salvadorians were welcomed by 18th Street and they formed a very powerful multicultural super gang. No one is exactly sure what led to the split between these two power gangs, but MS-13 has been independent for nearly two decades now.

Rejected by Hispanic gangs (i.e., 18th Street), the vast majority of Mara Salvatrucha gang members are therefore of either first- or second-generation Salvadorian descent. The rest of the members come from other Central American countries such as Costa Rica, Honduras, Ecuador, and Guatemala. MS quickly received recognition for its level of violence and organization. MS-13 is known for making its rivals and targets suffer a slow death; as an example, they often use machetes in gang attacks rather than guns so that the injured die slowly and painfully (Franco 2008). The gang also uses machetes to cut off people's hands or fingers just to teach them a lesson. Although MS-13 has not been linked to any terrorist attacks in the United States, they use similar tactics: a propensity for indiscriminate violence, intimidation, and coercion that transcends borders and targets nation-states (Franco 2008). In addition to its active criminal participation in Central America, MS-13 also operates in Mexico and Canada.

The Mara Salvatrucha gang is commonly referred to as MS-13, "MS" standing for *Mara Salvatrucha*, with "Mara" as a Spanish word for a gang and "Salvatrucha" a term used to honor Salvadorian peasants trained as guerilla soldiers. In a less literal sense, Mara Salvatrucha has come to mean "Forever Salvador" or, more loosely, "Long live El Salvador." As mentioned, MS-13 is well organized and efficiently run. Each local branch is divided into cliques, or **cliclas**. There is not much of a hierarchy within local cliclas except for local leaders and treasurers who answer to the leaders of MS-13. During group meetings, members of MS-13 stand in a circle, signifying that all members are equal. The members will then display the two-handed "M" hand sign and say aloud "La Mara," which is slang for the gang. Group members are allowed to voice their opinions and discussion leads to group decisions. At the end of all meetings, MS-13 members again flash the two-handed "M" and yell "La Mara." Large-scale meetings—those involving multiple cliclas from all regions—are called "universal meetings." These meetings are held yearly on the 13th day of a predetermined month. When the members gather for a universal meeting, they stand in a circle in order to maintain each clicla group's integrity (Rozanski 2003). The number 13 is significant for MS-13 because the letter "M" is the 13th letter of the alphabet. Thus, when using graffiti, or getting tattoos, the letter "M" and the number 13 are popular expressions of gang affiliation. The letter "S" stands for both Salvador and **Sureno**, a Spanish word for "Southerner." The colors of MS-13 are the same as those used in most Central American national flags: blue, gray, white, and black. Blue- and white-beaded necklaces are also common. Sports jerseys with the number 13 are among the favorite items of clothing worn by members of MS-13. (See Figure 6.6 for examples of MS-13 gang graffiti.)

Females are allowed to join MS-13 and they must go through an initiation similar to the males, which involves a violation ceremony where several members of the gang beat the recruit to test his/her ability to take a beating. If a recruit fails the initiation rite of passage, he/she is then murdered for lack of courage and spirit. Females serve as gun and drug runners because the police generally pay more attention to male MS-13 members. Males and females alike must attend local meetings and are expected to pay membership dues. Members of MS-13 consist of both adults and youths as young as age 12. The older members are expected to teach the younger

The most commonly used identifier for the Mara Salvatrucha gang is MS, which represents Mara Salvatrucha along with the number 13 (the letter "M" is the 13th letter of the alphabet). Because of their affiliation with the umbrella Sureno nation, MS-13 may identify as SUR 13. Mara 13 represents the transnational make-up of MS-13.

FIGURE 6.6   Mara Salvatrucha (MS, MS-13) (*Source*: Paul Hahn)

ones to use weapons—especially explosives and explosive devices—car theft, and gang rules and protocols. Much of the advanced military-style training is deemed necessary in order to conduct criminal activities. Because MS-13 maintains ties to El Salvador, it has easy access to sophisticated military weapons and often traffics weapons throughout the United States, but only to people of similar Central American descent and never to whites or blacks. Stealing cars is another important moneymaker for MS-13. Vehicles are regularly stolen by organized groups of MS-13 and then sold to specific junk yards and "chop shops" or sometimes shipped to South America.

There are nearly 12,000 MS-13 members in the United States alone. MS-13, which can be found in 42 U.S. states and the District of Columbia, with the highest threat in the Southwest and Northeast, is considered the most dangerous street gang in the nation (Goldschein and McKenna 2012; NAGIA 2009). The MS-13 gang can be found in Los Angeles, Washington, D.C., and New York City and in such faraway places as Kodiak, Alaska. In 1998, Los Angeles Superior Court Judge Patricia Collins issued an injunction against the Hollywood clique of MS-13. Members were prohibited from gathering in public, blocking sidewalks, and other activities. The injunction also placed a curfew on members under age 18. County Supervisor Zev Yaroslavsky claimed that the gang uses "murder, rape, robbery and extortion" to terrorize residents in the Hollywood area. Local officials believe that the level of violence associated with this drug-trafficking gang is second only to that of the 18th Street Gang. MS-13 is known to have ties with La Eme, the notorious Mexican prison gang (Associated Press 1998). La Eme appreciates and respects MS-13's level of violence and commitment to protecting drug markets; on the other hand, La Eme considers MS-13 to be a "loose cannon" because of its unwillingness to follow organizational rules and ongoing feuds with other Surenos gangs such as the 18th Street Gang.

In the New York City area, the Port Washington police department reported that the MS-13 gang had earned a reputation for violence and drug-trafficking by the late 1990s. It estimated that there were several hundred members of MS-13 in Nassau and Suffolk Counties alone (*Port Washington News* 1998). In 2004, federal prosecutors announced the indictment of 30 gang members from across Long Island, claiming that they were responsible for five murders and multiple stabbings, shootings, and a firebombing. Investigators said that the 30 defendants were members of three different gangs: the Bloods, based in Nassau; the Murder Unit, which operates in Greenport; and Long Island's largest gang, MS-13, based in Nassau. Members of MS-13 in Nassau are affiliated with the growing national MS-13 gang. Law enforcement officials are convinced that gangs and gang violence are "out of control" on Long Island. According to Assistant United States Attorney Andrew C. Hruska, MS-13 has more than 300 members in Nassau and Suffolk counties (Healy 2004) and are found in such suburban villages as Bethpage, Baldwin, and Valley Stream.

MS-13 is a huge problem in Charlotte, North Carolina. It is considered the most violent of the city's gangs, being suspected of seven of the nine gang-related homicides in 2003 (Campo-Flores 2003). In Charlotte, as in other American cities, MS-13 is a recent gang phenomenon that has developed as a result of a wave of immigration which dramatically increased the number of North Carolina's Latinos (Campo-Flores 2003).

The criminal activities of MS-13 in the Virginia suburbs of Washington, D.C., caught the attention of U.S. Attorney General John Ashcroft in 2004. Ashcroft expressed concern that gangs were threatening several communities a short drive from the nation's capital (Johnson 2004), and in fact MS-13 has been identified as responsible for a number of violent crimes in the capital district. For example, in May 2004, a suspected MS-13 gangster was charged in a machete attack on a 16-year-old boy in Alexandria, Virginia.

Despite law enforcement's attempts to curtail MS-13, the gang continues to grow. Some law enforcement efforts since 2004 are given as follows:

- Twenty-four MS-13 members arrested on federal firearms charges and conspiracy to distribute methamphetamine in Omaha, Nebraska (Johnson 2009).
- Fourteen MS-13 members arrested in Nashville on charges ranging from murder to obstruction of justice, 2008–2009 (Johnson 2009).
- Forty-two MS-13 members arrested in Maryland for a variety of racketeering conspiracy charges between 2005 and 2009 (Johnson 2009).
- In November 2011, a MS-13 member was sentenced to 292 months in prison for sex trafficking of teenage runaway girls in the Washington, D.C., area (United States Attorney's Office 2011). MS-13 is known for trafficking runaway teenage girls, and earlier in 2011, the U.S. Attorney's Office prosecuted four other cases involving MS-13 and sex trafficking (United States Attorney's Office 2011). That sex trafficking is occurring at the hands of a transnational gang in the shadows of the nation's capital is particularly disturbing.

MS-13, as a transnational gang, operates in many nations other than the United States. In fact, it is much larger outside the United States. Estimates of the total number of MS-13 and M-18 gangs in Central America and Mexico are hard to determine but range from 70,000 to 100,000 (Franco 2008). A vast majority of these Mara gangsters belong to MS-13. The MS-13 gang operates in El Salvador, Honduras, Guatemala, Costa Rica, Ecuador, Belize, Nicaragua, Panama, Mexico, Canada, and the United States (Goldschein and McKenna 2012; NAGIA 2009). Although MS-13 is included in the FBI's 2011 Gang Assessment, the gang has its own separation section. The FBI also has a special task force—MS-13 Task Force—dedicated to stopping the gang and alerting the public of the threat it poses (Goldschein and McKenna 2012). The FBI is especially concerned about MS-13 because of the gang's potential to wage terrorist attacks in the United States (Franco 2008). In prisons across Central America, MS-13 gang members are housed in separate blocks; in El Salvador they have their own prison. In neighboring Honduras, Mara gangs appeared at the same time and for the same reasons they appeared in El Salvador. The prevalent gang problem in Honduras led to the implantation of strict anti-gang polices under the presidency of Ricardo Maduro, who held office from 2002 to 2006 (Rivera 2010a). The collective legislation known as "Mano Dura"—or "iron fist"—and "Ley Antimaras"—meaning "anti-gang law"—put forth zero-tolerance policies. But these polices were not effective and actually created the formation of a stronger identity among members to the already powerful Mara gangs (Rivera 2010a). Furthermore, the crackdown actually caused MS-13 and M-18 to become more organized in order to survive and flourish.

El Salvador and Honduras are very violent nations in which murders are commonplace. In fact, on April 14, 2012, for the first time in three years, El Salvador did not have a homicide. This news was even reported in Jay Leno's monologue on *The Tonight Show*, the following Monday. Although it would be newsworthy if the United States went a day without a homicide, consider the differences in population. At present, the United States has over 310 million people and approximately 5.6 homicides per 100,000; while El Salvador has a little more than 6 million people but a homicide rate of 66 per 100,000—one of the highest in the world (Renteria 2012). The homicide-free day may be attributed to the truce brokered between MS-13 and M-18 earlier in the month (Aleman 2012; Renteria 2012). The truce was brokered by the two Los Angeles–based transnational gangs in an attempt to reduce the number of homicides in El Salvador and Honduras (the nation with the highest homicide rate in the world) (Aleman 2012). Most of the 12 to 15 homicides per day in El Salvador are attributed to these two Mara gangs. One has to wonder, why would the Maras broker a truce? As speculated in *The Economist* (2012), the gangs may simply be letting businesses recover so that they can be extorted again once they start making profits. Over 60 shops had closed in the year prior to the truce because they could not afford to pay the protection "rent" charged by the gangs.

Law enforcement officials and gang researchers alike doubt that the truce would last any significant amount of time. There is good reason to question any gang truce as logic alone would dictate that any lasting gang truce is unrealistic. Authorities in El Salvador need only to look at nearby Belize, a nation where the maras brokered a truce in August 2011. After a significant decrease in the number of monthly murders for a five-month period, the murder rate in April 2012 soared beyond the pre-truce rate (*The Economist* 2012). The killing of two gang leaders in April sparked a wave of reprisals. And yet, in light of failed law enforcement attempts to curtail the activities of the Maras, a gang truce may be the only hope for peace in El Salvador.

ASIAN STREET GANGS

Asian gangs are something of a mystery to researchers, civilians, and law enforcement personnel. Of all the street gangs, Asian gangs tend to be far more secretive. They are generally clean-cut, act with respect toward law enforcement, and victimize members from their own culture. They seldom represent gang affiliation with visible colors, clothing, and tattoos. Before 1975, Asian gangs were mostly limited to delinquent youths living in the Chinatowns of larger cities. "Prior to the departure of American forces from Vietnam in 1975, the stereotypical American concept of Asian gangs derived largely from the image of San Francisco tongs or triads of an earlier era. Since that time, the image of Asian gangs has changed to include new immigrant groups, such as Vietnamese, Vietnamese-Chinese, Laotian, Cambodian, and Hmong gangs, which can now be found in communities across the nation where recent Southeast Asian immigrants have settled" (Kodluboy 1996, 1). Recent Asian immigrants are frustrated by their lack of instant success in the United States. Some disenchanted youths turn to gangs as a means of escape from their economic deprivation. Asian gangs are also difficult to categorize in the scheme presented in this chapter. Asian gangs are not likely to exist in rural areas or small towns, but will exist in larger cities. There are no nation Asian gangs either. Furthermore, although traditional Asian-American gangs like the triads, tongs, or yakuza can be traced back to Asian nations of ancestral origin, there is no indication that they operate like transnational gangs.

Traditional Asian Gangs

Review of the traditional Asian gangs begins with the Chinese **triads** and **tong** gangs. Triads are secret societies that originally formed during the 1600s in China. Modern-day triads are generally viewed by law enforcement as criminal organizations. As explained by Kenney and Finckenauer (1995), triads were patriotic and nationalistic organizations that formed in the early seventeenth century primarily as resistance groups to the Ching Dynasty, although some exist mainly as criminal groups in Hong Kong and Taiwan. The origin of the word *triad* can be traced to the word *triangle*, with each of the three sides holding symbolic meaning of heaven, earth, and mankind. Among the more prominent triads are the **Green Pang** and the **Hung Pang** (Chin 1986). Other major triad gangs include the **Sun Yee On**, the **Sung Lian**, **Tian Dao Man**, **Four Seas**, and the **United Bamboo** (Posner 1988). The triads have over 80,000 members, with Sun Yee On as the largest (over 25,000). The name *triad* came about as a result of the society's triangular symbol, which consisted of three dots, two on the base and one on the top (thus forming a triangle).

Originally, the triads were known as the "Men of Hung." The word *Hung* was so sacred and secret that it was rarely used aloud or in public. The Men of Hung were separated into three divisions: the Tien-ti Hui, the San Tien Hui, and San-ho Hui. Collectively, these three distinctions represented the "Three Harmonies Society" (Booth 1999). This secret society, or *hui*, was made up of ruthless outlaws—merciless robbers, pillagers, kidnappers, and murderers. The *hui* attacked government offices, barracks and prisons (in order to release fellow triads), imperial supply convoys, and cargo junks. Many Chinese civilians supported the "cause" of the triads, believing it to be an honorable one. Their mix of Confucian, Taoist, Buddhist, and pagan thinking, and goal of eternal happiness attracted many young people to the triads. Their goal was to right the imperial wrongs and address imperial injustice by any means necessary. By the mid-nineteenth century, the triads had become institutionalized into the subculture of Chinese society.

Perhaps the most honored of all the ancient Chinese triads is the Shaolin. The Shaolin Temple trained warriors and housed sacred scrolls, writings, and books. Shaolin monks trained at the temple learned philosophy and meditation techniques to help them achieve enlightenment. Naturally, the emperor viewed the Shaolin as a challenge to him and ordered his soldiers to kill the monks and destroy the temple and all the documents and records (Booth 1999). Five young monks survived the slaughter and carried on the tradition of Shaolin. Today, many of the Shaolin traditions are upheld in martial arts training, thus preserving the ancient culture through triad ceremonial positions and beliefs.

By 2000, in both China and the United States, the triads had begun to act and function more as urban gangsters than as political idealists seeking social justice. Considering that over 60 million Chinese live outside China, the possibility for increased numbers of triad organizations is very real. Furthermore, Chinese communities are often very secluded and closed off to Westerners. The secretive nature of triad gangs reflects the greater Chinese communities' (e.g., American Chinatowns) efforts to distance themselves from the outside world. Chinese officials consider membership in the triads a criminal offense, but because of the secretive nature of the gangs, it is extremely difficult for law enforcement to penetrate them.

Triads are found in most American cities that have a sizable Asian community. Members of triad gangs in the United States are usually between the ages of 13 and 35 and are almost exclusively male. About two-thirds of America's triad gang members are immigrants; the rest are native-born (Chin 1996). Like most gangs, the triads operate in a hierarchical manner, with the "Dai-Lo" as the "big brother" and the "Sai-Lo" as the "little brother." The various sets of triads all use a numbering system beginning with the number 4, which represents the four oceans that were believed to have surrounded China in ancient times and so signifies the universe as a whole.

The initiation of new members involves the recruit taking a number of oaths of privacy and respect. Current criminal activity involving triads includes arms smuggling, credit card fraud, counterfeiting, software piracy, smuggling of aliens, prostitution, gambling, loan-sharking, home invasion robbery, high-tech theft, and trafficking in endangered animals and plants. Extortion is the most common crime committed by the triads and other Asian gangs. Triads extort money from businesses and wealthy members of the Asian community in the form of a "protection" racket. Home invasions and burglary remain as trademarks of the triads and most Asian gangs (Huston 1995). Smuggling of illegal immigrants has become so lucrative and commonplace that the triads and their rival gangs often abduct these aliens and hold them for ransom (Chin 1996).

Tongs is a reference to Chinese social clubs, a place where peer groups gather, that law enforcement have also long suspected of being guilty of serving as fronts for violent gangs (much like the Irish gangs of the early 1800s had the "green groceries" serve as fronts). "The word *tong* refers to a hall or gathering place. The groups called Tongs function as benevolent associations, business associations, ethnic societies, and centers of local politics in Chinese communities in the United States. They engage in a number of activities, including political activities and some protest activities" (Kenney and Finckenauer 1995, 257). The FBI believes that the tongs are used as fronts for vicious Chinese-organized crime groups. Crimes associated with tongs are illegal gambling, extortion, drug-trafficking, robbery, and prostitution for pornography (Keene 1989). The first American-based tong was the Leong Merchant's Association founded in 1849 in San Francisco. **On Leong** is the original tong in New York City, having formed in Manhattan's Chinatown during the 1890s. On Leong ran a lucrative empire of gambling houses, brothels, and opium dens. **Hip Sing**, the primary rival tong of On Leong, also dates back to the 1890s in New York City. Hip Sing was first led by the notorious Mock Duck, who is mentioned in Herbert Asbury's *Gangs of New York* (1927). A particularly violent confrontation between On Leong and Hip Sing in 1909 left more than 50 dead (Century 2004).

The **yakuza**, criminal groups that operate in Japan, Hawaii, and other parts of the United States, are associated with traditional Japanese gangs. Like the Russian "mafia" (or maffya), the *yakuza* is a collective term used to describe criminal organizations that operate to meet the needs of a certain segment of society. Japanese National Police refer to them as the *boryokudan*, or the "violent ones." It is estimated that there are more than 200,000 yakuza members worldwide, making them perhaps the largest of all the gangs. The yakuza trace their roots back to the fourteenth century, when outcasts of the prevailing feudalist society banded together for mutual protection. The name comes from a popular Japanese card game called *sammai karuta*. A yakuza leader is known as an *oyaban* and the general members as *kobun*. The **Yamaguchi** represent the largest faction of yakuza in Japan with nearly 10,000 members. They are all men, as the yakuza do not believe women should be involved; instead, they should be wives and mothers.

Yakuza gangs in the United States are heavily involved in weapons trafficking, with the guns being sold in Japan. Unlike in the United States, the Japanese have very strict gun laws; consequently, there is a flourishing black market for guns. Handguns are especially in high demand. The yakuza are especially active in Southern California, the San Francisco area, and in Nevada. Prostitution is a lucrative business for them. They provide underage girls at sex clubs for wealthy businessmen. In addition to their numerous illegal businesses, the yakuza have financial interests in a number of legitimate American businesses.

The yakuza are an efficiently run organization that uses violence whenever necessary as a means of normal operating business procedures. In the United States, the yakuza have become similar to their triad counterparts. They are a secretive gang and generally commit crimes within their own communities. The yakuza have an interesting way of dealing with members who have offended the gang leader or violated protocol. Violators are not killed; instead, they go through a ritualistic ceremony called a *yubizume* in which the offender cuts off his little finger and presents it to the person he is apologizing to. If the offering is accepted (as it generally is), then the violator is kicked out of the yakuza permanently.

Contemporary Asian Gangs

Most of the contemporary youths who join Asian gangs do so because they feel overwhelmed, lost, depressed, and angry as they try to adjust to living in the United States. They are experiencing the same angst, alienation, and anomie as their Irish, Italian, Jewish, and Hispanic counterparts felt before them. They are new immigrants to a land where their lack of sufficient and relevant job skills, low levels of education, and language deficiency hamper their goals of success. This is especially true among many Vietnamese, Cambodian, Laotian, and Hmong immigrants. (*Note*: Hmong gangs were described in "Connecting Street Gangs and Popular Culture" Box 5.2.) They often feel as though they are victims of racial/ethnic prejudice and discrimination on the part of the greater society, similar to what many in the black and Latino communities feel. Blocked opportunities to success and learned helplessness lead to feelings of frustration. Expecting instant (economic) gratification and lacking the patience to acquire the necessary skills, many deviant youths turn to gangs. There is growing evidence that Asian youth are turning to street gangs in increasing numbers. It is also common for many Asian gang members to have ties to the larger and more formal Asian organized crime groups (e.g., the triads and yakuza).

The makeup and purpose of Asian gangs vary by ethnicity, but nearly all engage in drug-trafficking, prostitution, and extortion. Their specialty, however, is "home invasion." Home invasions occur when the gang breaks into the home of a wealthy family, or family-owned business (especially restaurants), ties up the family members, and terrorizes them until the family produces valuables or money. Common tactics include beatings, torture, and the raping of female family members. Asian families are targets because they are less likely to report such crimes to the police because they fear reprisal by the gang. Recent immigrant families from Asia do not trust the U.S. police, believing that they may work with the gangs. Furthermore, it is common for Asian immigrants to keep their valuables at home rather than keeping them in a bank.

Contemporary Chinese-American gangs have their genesis in the late 1960s and early 1970s. "Youth gangs started to emerge in Chinatown in the sixties and seventies, and they have a distinctive culture—a bizarre mixture of traits borrowed from the Hong Kong triads (secret criminal societies) and the clichés of American and Chinese gangster movies" (Dannen 2002, 298–299). The passage of the Immigration and Naturalization Act of 1965 opened the door for numerous new Asian immigrants to enter the United States. Most of these people were poor and some of the youths joined gangs. They often served as "muscle" for the existing triads and other Chinese crime organizations. Playing the role of foot soldier was viewed by the immigrant gang members as a step toward admittance to the more established organized crime syndicates. Chinese gangs can be found in Los Angeles, Boston, Chicago, Toronto, Buffalo, New York, Vancouver, and especially in San Francisco. The Chinese gangs in Chicago have evolved out of two old and historic community organizations, the Hip Sing and the Tong. The Hip Sing is active in the Uptown community along the lakefront of Chicago. The **Tong** gang members are a South Side group prominent in the more traditional Chinatown at 22nd Street and Wentworth Avenue (Lindberg 2003).

Gregory Yee Mark (2004) stated that the first nationally known American Chinese gang was the **Hwa Chings**, which means "young Chinese," who originated in San Francisco's Chinatown in 1964. "Eventually, branches of this group and other similar types of gangs spread throughout America's Chinatowns. Since the 1970s, due to escalating violence and expanded criminal activities,

Chinese gangs have been increasingly viewed as a major social problem in the Chinese-American community and as a menace to society-at-large. In government reports and popular media, these gangs are blamed for the increasing violence in Chinatowns, shiploads of undocumented Chinese immigrants, and the massive smuggling of illegal drugs to the United States" (Mark 2004, 142). The Hwa Chings consisted of mostly teenaged immigrant youths, the majority from Hong Kong. By 1967, the Hwa Ching were committing violent crimes in and around Chinatown. Two years later, they made national news because of a 1969 issue of *Esquire* magazine, which referred to the gang as "The New Yellow Peril." Other dominant Chinese gangs emerged in the late 1960s, and most of them identified with a tong. "By the end of 1968, the **Tom Tom** gang, the youth gang affiliated with the San Francisco **Suey Sing Tong**, emerged as the strongest gang" (Mark 2004, 146). The Hwa Ching were never seriously challenged until 1989 when the **Wo Hop To** triad from Hong Kong began moving into the San Francisco Bay area. In recent years these two gangs consolidated (English 1995). Various factions of Chinese gangs have aligned themselves with either the Bloods or the Crips as a means of protecting their turf and guaranteeing revenue from criminal activities. Chinatown gangs were formed primarily for protection and street survival from outside rival gangs. "Even today, thirty years later, young immigrants still join Chinese gangs, Samoan gangs, Cambodian gangs, and Filipino gangs for mutual protection" (Mark 2004, 151).

Among the more visible contemporary Chinese gangs found in New York City's Chinatown and nearby Flushing is the **American Eagles** (or **Asian Empire**). The American Eagles (AE) claim the streets of Chinatown and Flushing (especially around Mulberry Street in Chinatown and Main Street in Flushing) and travel in packs, armed with knives. Members wear satin jackets and sport tattoos with dragons on their biceps (McPhee 2003). Local law enforcement consider AE the newest Asian gang since the **Flying Dragons** and **Ghost Shadows** were busted up and sent to jail. According to Century (2004, 88), the Ghost Shadows favor "tight straight-leg black jeans, satin jackets and little kung-fu slippers. And the dead giveaway: Hair tips dyed blond." The AE have 50 confirmed members, who are mostly immigrants from China's Fujian province or ABCs (American-born Chinese). At the end of 2003, the AE were primarily involved with assaults and petty crime.

New York City's Chinatown has recently become home to a growing hip-hop Chinese gang presence. Chinese-American rapper Christopher Louie, a.k.a. L.S., is among the leading hip-hop gangsters. Bragging about being shot and run-ins with the law are just a couple of the similarities between Chinese rappers and black rappers. The lyrics of L.S. parallel the black rappers' well. Infusing Cantonese slang into their hip-hop, Chinese rappers use the word *chink* the way other rappers drop the word *nigga* (Century 2004). As documented in *Blender* magazine, Century (2004) provides examples of the lyrics used by L.S.:

> *Every time they harass me*
> *I want to explode*
> *We should ride the trains for free*
> *We built the railroads.*

Promoted as the Chinese answer to rapper 50 Cent, L.S. has a bullet-scarred torso and gangsta taunts (e.g., "kung fu—we know *gun*-fu"). L.S. uses the term *yellow slums* to reflect the life of urban poor Asian youth, especially the Chinese.

American Vietnamese gangs are the result of the traditional factors that lead recent immigrants into gangs. According to U.S. Census data, more than 900,000 Vietnamese migrated to the United States between 1975 and 1997. During the same period, another 400,000 Vietnamese-Americans were born here. These Vietnamese immigrants were mostly undereducated, under-skilled, and usually unable to speak English. There was no history of organized crime in Vietnam, but the U.S.-sponsored South Vietnamese government and military were riddled with corruption, so recent immigrants had had experience with bribery, corruption, extortion, and violence. "The thousands of Vietnamese who came to the United States in the late 1970s and 1980s did not come from a country with a tradition of organized crime to a great extent; their involvement in organized crime in the United States developed out of their experiences as immigrants here. It was, however, very much shaped by who they were and where they had come from" (Kenney and Finckenauer 1995, 266).

Vietnamese gangs appear to be the most secretive of all the Asian gangs and therefore have a certain intrigue. They are often considered the most violent of all Asian gangs. They have a stronghold in Southern California, especially in Orange County, where the city of Westminster is known as "Little Saigon" because of the huge Vietnamese population—there are more Vietnamese there than anywhere outside Vietnam. The city has over 2,500 Vietnamese-owned restaurants, malls, hair salons, and professional offices in the commercial Westminster community. These businesses are automatic targets for Vietnamese gangs. Among the common criminal activities committed by Vietnamese gangs are extortion, armed robbery, home invasion, prostitution, auto theft, arson, and gambling. The longevity of Vietnamese gangs is often brief. They are known to form a "hasty gang"—a loose, quickly formed, mobile, nomadic gang that forms and disbands following a brief crime spree such as home invasions or burglaries of occupied dwellings (Kodluboy 1996).

Filipino gangs are found mostly in Los Angeles, San Diego, and San Francisco but can also be found in Las Vegas. The largest gangs include the **Santanas, Taboos,** and **Temple Street Gang**. Filipino gangs began in the 1940s in the California prison system, but contemporary Filipino gangs have their roots in the immigration of Filipinos to the United States during the 1970s (Shelden, Tracy, and Brown 2001). William Sanders in his research on Filipino gangs in San Diego traced the Filipino population in San Diego to the military establishment and the nursing profession. "A large contingent of Filipinos who served in the U.S. military, especially during the Vietnam War, was allowed to immigrate to the United States during the 1970s. Likewise, a large number of Filipino nurses immigrated to the United States during the 1970s when a nursing shortage generated a more liberal immigration policy for nurses" (Sanders 1994, 153). These relatively high-paying jobs placed the Filipino immigrants in the middle class, where they were generally accepted by their white neighbors. The Filipinos were politically and socially conservative like much of San Diego suburbia. Not surprisingly, "throughout most of the 1980s the Filipinos were not only low in crime statistics, but no Filipino gangs were recognized by the police. However, by 1988, about 14 percent of all gang-related incidents recorded by the police department's gang detail involved Filipino youths, and by 1991, 18 percent of the drive-by shootings were by Filipino gangs" (Sanders 1994, 153). These Filipino gangs were involved in drug sales, robberies, car theft, and drive-by shootings.

As previously mentioned, Asian gangs are very secretive and will deny that they are gang members if apprehended by police. However, they do use scarring or mutilation to create gang markings (Chin 1996), often burning themselves in strategic places. For example, Filipinos burn their hands, the Vietnamese and Cambodians burn the forearms, the Chinese burn their upper arms, and female gang members have burns on their ankles or feet (Chin 1996). These burns and burn patterns have significant relevance and importance within the gang. A single burn generally means that the individual is willing to engage in criminal activity. Some Cambodian and Hmong gang members in several American cities have adopted the style, dress, slang, nicknames, hand signs, and names of black and Hispanic gangs of the West Coast and Midwest. Recently, a number of Asian gangs have begun to get tattoos. For example, a member of the **Ninja Clan Assassins**, a Vietnamese gang, will be inked with "NCA." Generally, the tattoos are not visible. Although Asian gang members generally maintain a clean-cut image, they are increasingly adopting the style of the Bloods and Crips.

Last, but by no means least, is the **Tiny Rascal Gang (TRG)**. According to the FBI (2009c), TRG is one of the largest and most violent Asian street gang associations in the United States. Based primarily out of Long Beach, California, and Lowell, Massachusetts, TRG is composed of at least 60 sets across the United States, with a total estimated membership between 5,000 and 10,000. Most members of TRG are Cambodian, although there are other Asian nationalities and rarely white and black members. There is a female auxiliary to TRG called the **Lady Rascal Gangsters**. TRG members commonly identify with "TRG" and "Rascal" tattoos and wear grey, although some wear blue in honor of the Crips (a previous ally). The primary rival of TRG is the **Asian Boyz**. TRG participates in street-level distribution of a variety of drugs; assault and homicide; extortion; home invasion; robbery; and theft.

At present, Asian street gangs have been identified in more than 50 metropolitan areas. They are most prevalent in Boston, Chicago, Honolulu, Las Vegas, Los Angeles, New Orleans, New York, Newark, Philadelphia, Portland, San Francisco, Seattle, and Washington, D.C. (FBI 2012l). The FBI has a number of different working groups and initiatives to combat Asian-organized crime and street gangs. And although Asian gangs represent a minority in the street gang world and little attention has been given to them comparatively speaking, they remain a potential threat. The Asian-American population is small but rapidly growing. According to the U.S. Census Bureau there were 5.6 million Asian Americans in 2010, a figure that represents about 5.6 percent of the total U.S. population (U.S. Census Bureau, 2011a). It is estimated that the Asian-American population will increase to 8 percent of the total population by 2050. If much of this increase is the result of poor immigrants moving to the United States, one could deduce that the number of Asian-American gangs will also increase. Only time will tell if this true.

Summary

This chapter began with an examination of the proliferation of street gangs across the United States, some of which have influence in multiple nations. Our look at street gangs began with rural and suburban street gangs. We generally think of street gangs as limited to urban areas of big cities, but this is not reality as an increasing number of rural and suburban law enforcement agencies are reporting problems with gangs. Next, we discussed the impact of urban local street gangs with a focus on gangs in Syracuse, Rochester, and Buffalo, three cities in New York State. The level of violence committed by local street gangs has caused havoc in these three cities, as street gangs have increasingly taken over the drug trade and resorted to murder to defend their marketplace turfs. Large gangs that are found throughout most of the United States are referred to as "nation" gangs and include two Los Angeles–based nation gangs, the Crips and Bloods, and two Chicago-based nation gangs, the People and Folks. The Bloods and People have a loose confederation and so do the Crips and Folks. *The People* and *Folks* are actually umbrella terms used to describe an alliance between many individual gangs. The People, for example, have Latin Kings and Vice Lords among their nation flag and the Folks have the BGD, Latin Disciples, and Simon City Royals under their flag. Nations gangs are the ones we usually hear about in the news as they represent a bulk of all street gangs. Nation gangs are known for specific colors, graffiti, use of hand signals, and so on. Transnational gangs present the most problems for law enforcement because their influence extends beyond U.S. jurisdiction to many Central American nations. The 18th Street Gang, a.k.a. M-18, and MS-13 Gang are the two transnational gangs. The letter "M" in each of these two gangs refers to the term *Mara*, which is a Spanish word for gang. The Mara gangs, although bitter rivals, are a part of the Surenos very loose confederation. Asian gangs are difficult to categorize because their presence is felt only in specific regional areas that have a relatively large Asian populations. Their historic links to Asian countries makes them quasi-transnational accept for the realization that most Asian-American street gangs have no ties to their ancestral homes.

7

Female Gangs and Gang Members

Women have been involved in criminal activity for nearly as long as men, only never to the same extent. Historically, however, little attention has been given to female gangsters, unless their crimes were related to violations of codes of morality (e.g., prostitution, witchcraft). During the 1800s, women like Belle Starr (Myra Belle Shirley) carried guns, robbed stagecoaches, and cavorted with men who were just as devious. Belle came from a wealthy family in Carthage, Missouri, where she attended Carthage Female Academy and excelled in reading, spelling, arithmetic, and the classics. Born in 1848, Belle lived during the Civil War. Her family moved to Sycene, Texas, shortly before Carthage was burned to the ground by Confederate guerillas in 1864 (Women in History 2012). Her brother, John Shirley, died fighting for the confederacy and Belle assisted the confederacy by giving them information on Union troop positioning. A childhood friend of Belle, who fought alongside her brother in the Confederate Army, was Cole Younger, who later became part of the James-Younger gang (riding with the infamous Jessie James). Starr was a fearless, guilt-free murderer and bragged about it. At age 18 (1866), Belle ran off with outlaw Cole Younger, cousin to Jesse James, and committed numerous crimes with him. While on the run from one crime spree to the next, Belle dressed like a man and spent much of her time in saloons, drinking and gambling at dice, cards, and roulette. At times she would ride her horse through the streets shooting off her pistols. Such behavior gave rise to her image as a pistol-wielding outlaw (Women in History 2012). Belle married Samuel Starr in 1880. In 1882, the couple were arrested on charges of stealing horses, a very serious crime in that era. She was sent to prison and later released after time served. On February 3, 1889, she was killed by a shotgun blast to the back near Eufaula, Oklahoma.

Pearl Hart is another example of a female gangster from the 1800s. Like Belle Starr, Pearl Taylor was raised in a wealthy middle-class family; what led to her downfall was her marriage to Frederick Hart, a known gambler and drunk (Weiser 2010). Born in Lindsay, Ontario, Canada, Pearl and her husband moved to Chicago in 1893 where Frederick worked as a sideshow barker and Pearl performed a number of odd jobs. She was especially intrigued by the "Wild West" shows and especially enamored of Annie Oakley, whom she witnessed performing many times. Inspired by seeing strong women perform feats of bravery, Pearl left her husband and traveled to Trinidad, Colorado, where she became a popular saloon singer. While in Colorado, Pearl realized that she was pregnant with Frederick's child and returned to her family in Canada. After giving birth to a son, she left him with her mother and traveled west again, this time landing in Phoenix, Arizona (Weiser 2010). For a short time, she reunited with her husband, gave birth to another child, moved back to Canada, and then out west again. Pregnancy, as we shall discover later in this chapter, affects female gang members, traditionally, as a way out of a gang. But like Pearl, many of today's female gangsters do not let becoming a mother interfere with their criminal activities. As for Pearl, she hooked up with a guy named Joe Boot. Needing money for medical bills that her mother had accumulated back in Canada, Pearl and Boot decided to rob trains, stagecoaches, and targeted men. Pearl would lure unsuspecting men to an area where Joe would rob them of their money and other valuables. This too is something that female gangsters do today, as male gang members use their women to set up unsuspecting guys to rob them. Hart and Boot robbed trains and stagecoaches but were, of course, eventually captured. On one occasion in 1899, Hart escaped from jail and gained fame as the "Bandit Queen." After a long life of crime, in and out of jail, Hart seemingly disappeared. Some reports have her dying in Kansas City in 1925 where she operated a cigar store; other reports indicate that she lived in San Francisco until she died in 1952. Most often, however, she is said to have married a rancher in Dripping Springs, Arizona, where she lived out her final days and died as Pearl Bywater in 1956 (Weiser 2010).

Another influential historical female gangster is Kate Barker; better known as "Ma" Barker. Kate "Ma" Barker, born in 1871, gained notoriety for being a bank robber and kidnapper. The Barker gang often engaged in daring robberies that captivated the American public during the Depression. Banks had instituted high interest rates and often foreclosed on mortgages when people were at their economic lowest. Thus, bank robbers such as Ma Barker gained "Robin Hood" status. Often considered the brains of the gang, Ma Barker masterminded the transition of the gang from bank robbers to kidnappers and extortionists as she orchestrated the abduction of millionaires William A. Hamm Jr. and Edward George Bremer. The gang demanded and received a ransom of $300,000 for the safe return of the two millionaires (Wallechinsky and Wallace 2010). Ma Barker died during a famous four-hour shoot-out with the FBI at a hideout cottage in Florida on January 16, 1935.

During the twentieth century, Bonnie Parker and Virginia Hill gained fame for their criminal activities and immoral activities (Belknap 2001). Bonnie Parker, born in 1910, formed a romantic and criminal relationship with gangster Clyde Barrow. Bonnie once smuggled a gun to imprisoned Clyde, allowing him to escape. The criminal escapades of Bonnie and Clyde, coupled with Parker's ability to write poetry, made them both folk heroes during the Depression. Virginia Hill, born in 1918, dated Joe Epstein, an accountant for the Mafia in Chicago. She moved on to other key Mafia men, including Frank Nitti and Benjamin "Bugsy" Siegel. Hill became a "Mafia queen." In the 1950s, after years of working for the Mafia, she was called before the Kefauver Committee in Washington, D.C., to testify regarding organized crime in interstate commerce. At age 48, she was found dead of a drug overdose—some suspect it was the Mafia's way of keeping her quiet because she knew too much.

Early female gangsters like Belle Starr, Pearl Hart, Ma Barker, and Bonnie Parker displayed many of the tendencies that female gangsters show today. They had to be as tough, perhaps tougher, than their male counterparts to gain any sort of respect as criminals. They acted like male gangsters in order to achieve their personal acclaim and acceptance. As women in most occupations can understand, a woman has to work that much harder than a man to be taken seriously and to get ahead.

Despite these examples of high-profile and notorious women, little attention overall has been paid to female criminals. This is also true of female street gang members. Thoughts about gangs provoke stereotypical images of males committing extreme forms of violence, such as drive-by shootings, and who are involved in the use and sale of drugs, graffiti, rap music, and instilling fear within the communities where they are found. Since these activities are generally viewed as masculine traits, it was therefore presumed that females did not take part in these behaviors (Moore and Hagedorn 2001). However, as this chapter reveals, the number of females participating in gangs has been increasing steadily for years. Furthermore, female involvement in gangs accelerates the decay of the family structure.

FEMALE GANG PARTICIPATION

A number of extensive studies have been made of street gangs, but they generally addressed females as satellites, or auxiliaries, of male gangs, due in part to the belief that female involvement in gangs has historically been considered less important than male involvement (Taylor 1993). But female participation in gangs dates to the inception of gangs (Covey, Menard, and Franzese 1992). In Thrasher's (1927) famous study of gangs, he refers to females as auxiliaries. Of the more than 1,000 gangs he identified, he classified only six as female. In fact, his definition of gangs excludes females as potential participants—"the spontaneous efforts of *boys* to create a society. . . ." Female gang members were usually described in reference to their sexual role. Female gangsters were assumed to be just "sex toys," "objects," or "tomboys" to the male gang members, an assumption that has carried over to contemporary stereotypes of female gangsters. Whether these stereotypes of female gang members as tomboys and sex toys are accurate is difficult to confirm because often these stereotypes do not come from reliable sources (Moore and Hagedorn 2001). A great deal of information on female gang members does not come from gang researchers, but instead from journalists and social workers, who may have their own agenda and motives when reporting on female gang members. In addition, it is important to realize that the way females are treated by male gang members varies a great deal from gang to gang.

After Thrasher's studies of gangs, there was little interest in female gang members until Miller's study in the 1970s. Miller found fully independent female gangs but stated that they represent less than 10 percent of all gangs. Valdez (2007) explains that the primary reason for the lack of coverage on female gangs is law enforcement first encountered gangs composed of females only fairly recently, in the 1970s and 1980s. Forming all-female membership gangs was a way for girls and women to be independent and make their own rules. Valdez (2007) found that female gang members do commit serious crimes such as drive-by shootings, stabbings, and murder, but they do so far less frequently than their male counterparts. In her 1991 publication about Hispanic gang members in Los Angeles, Joan Moore found that one-third of them were female. She too acknowledged that the literature on girl gangs is very limited because much of it assumes that girl gangs are "auxiliaries" to the tightly bound boy gangs and found, on the contrary, that in the late 1930s and the early 1940s girl gangs (e.g., the **Black Legion**, **the Cherries**, **the Elks**, **the Black Cats**, and the **Vamps**) in Maravilla were not only free from association with the boy cliques, they were also not bound to the neighborhoods in the Maravilla barrios. Preceding Moore's findings on female gang participation were two significant studies done in the 1980s, a brief review of which is presented next.

John Quicker's *Home Girls*

The first in-depth look at female gangsters was conducted by John Quicker. In 1983 he published a very short book titled *Home Girls* based on research he had begun in the early 1970s. The title of Quicker's book comes from the gang terms common with Hispanics. "Chicana gang members use the affectionate terms 'homegirl' and 'homeboy' (sometimes shortened in speech to simply 'homes') to refer to other gang members. These terms take on the same affect as 'brother' and 'sister,' reflecting the family-like structure of the group" (Quicker 1983, 6). In *Home Girls*, Quicker examined the role of female gangsters in East Los Angeles. He interviewed girls from 12 different gangs in the notoriously violent barrios of East Los Angeles and concluded that the Chicana gangs were predominantly auxiliaries to the boy gangs. As Quicker (1983) explained, the homegirls never achieved complete independence from the boys although the amount of independence varied from gang to gang. The relationship of females to males in the gang are determined and negotiated by each gang. While Quicker found many gangs with males only, he did not find any female-only gangs. The overwhelming majority of the gangs did have female auxiliaries. The girl gangs studied by Quicker also indicated that their gang name was derived from the boys' name. Quicker was also one of the first gang researchers to note that Mexican older male gangsters are referred to as *chicos* and older females as *chicas*, while younger boys were referred to as *locos* and the younger girls as *locas*.

Quicker noted that the boys appreciated the help and assistance provided by the chicas (the girls often conceal weapons used by the boys) but felt, for the most part, that girls do not belong in gangs and that gangs are for males. As for the girls, they generally believed that the boys liked them hanging around even though they knew that the boys were against female gang members. "Boyfriend/girlfriend relationships further confound these ambivalences. The boys, almost categorically, do not want their girlfriends to join the gang, while making exceptions for other girls. However, if the girlfriend joins, the boy makes little effort to convince her to leave" (Quicker 1983, 12).

The girls whom Quicker interviewed reported that they generally dated only the boys from their own cliques and that they were allowed to date boys in other gangs as long as the gangs were not fighting each other. Quicker learned that dating practices were strongly influenced by the level of cohesiveness found within the gang. That is, the closer knit the gang, the more likely exogamous dating patterns were restricted, whereas loosely organized gangs were more open to exogamous dating patterns.

Quicker found that the girls joined the gang primarily because of their socially marginal status, negative experiences in school, the search for fun and excitement, respect, and the simple fact that they wanted to be close to the boys from their barrio. As Quicker (1983, 80) concludes, "To be in a gang is to be a part of something. It means having a place to go, friends to talk with, and parties to attend. It means recognition and respected status." As for membership, Quicker stated that the gang was not open to all who desired to join it. There were three requirements:

1. The girl must not be interested in joining solely for protection (i.e., to have the gang fight her battles for her).
2. There must be some indication that the girl will not fold under pressure but will support the banner of the gang even under adverse conditions (i.e., she must be willing to acknowledge her affiliation).
3. She must be able to "throw" down (to fight). Girls who are physically weak or unable to defend themselves are not an asset to the gang and often will not be allowed to join (Quicker 1983, 14–15).

Once these requirements were met, she was ready for initiation—being "jumped in." The recruit must take a beating from a group of gang members, although in some cases, a girl might be allowed a "fair fight" by going up against a skilled member of the gang. Leaving the gang is more complicated than entering. Quicker found that there were two basic types of departure, the active and passive. In the active mode, either the girl herself or the gang members initiate procedures that will unequivocally remove her from the gang. Generally, this would involve a violation ceremony; that is, she needed to "throw" down with a number of girls—a battle assumed would be lost by girl trying to leave the gang leaving her beaten and suffering some kind of injury. The passive mode of leaving the gang involved the girl gradually removing herself from the gang by not hanging out with the girls until she eventually slips away. Another passive way to leave the gang was waiting for its eventual dissolution. In the 1970s, it was far more common for local gangs to fall apart, especially female auxiliary gangs.

Quicker made it clear, however, that girls who wanted to leave an active gang were risking permanent injury or scarring. The gang's initials are often carved on her back. One girl that Quicker spoke with told him that she was raped by eight boys from the gang that she was leaving. In most cases, the girls never really leave the gang. Those who get pregnant have the easiest escape because they are allowed to leave the gang without a beating or being raped.

Anne Campbell's *The Girls in the Gang*

In 1984, Anne Campbell published a more substantial book on female gangs titled *The Girls in the Gang*. Campbell began her two-year study of girl gang members in New York City in 1979. She found that at that time there were around 400 gangs with a total membership between 8,000 and 40,000 in the city, with most of the female gangs being auxiliaries to the male gangs. Campbell concluded, as Miller had 10 years earlier, that approximately 10 percent of gang members were female. The female gang members in her study ranged in age from 14 to 30. Some of the females were married and had children. According to Campbell (1984) female gang members are blamed by the males as the inciters of gang feuds.

> They are described as "passive, property and promiscuous." They are accused of being more vicious than any male; they are praised for being among the few with enough power to curb male gang crime. For some they represent the coming of age of urban women's liberation, for others the denial of the best qualities of womanhood. The contradictions of their position have provoked speculation among the police, the media, and public about their reasons for joining, their roles and way of life. Despite the volumes written on male gang members, however, little is actually known about the girls, the standard reason being that girls constitute such a small number of gang crimes. (5)

Campbell found that, like boys, gang girls sought out excitement and trouble because it breaks the monotony of a desperate life that offers little hope for the future. The girls in Campbell studies, like the historical figures of Belle Starr, Pearl Hart, Ma Barker, and Bonnie Parker who preceded them, admired toughness and verbal "smarts." The girls realized they were not going to make it far in life, but reasoned that they should make the most of the life that they had. The female gangsters disliked any form of authority, including in the schools, by their parents, but especially the police. Like their male counterparts, the female gangsters welcomed a confrontation with the police because it livens things up. (This is similar to the idea of getting a rush or thrill from gang life described in Chapter 4.) Campbell found that female gang members had come to accept the lower-class value system and acknowledged their label as "bad girls." Their undisguised interest in sexual relationships left them branded as "sex objects" and/or tomboys (to be discussed in further detail later in this chapter). Campbell (1984) explains, "Sex objects and tomboys have much in common. Both have romantic and sexual relationships with boys in the gang. . . . Both will use their femininity in the service of the gang by acting as spies with other nearby gangs, by luring unsuspecting male victims into situations where they are robbed or assaulted by the boys, and by carrying concealed weapons for the boys since as females they cannot be searched by male officers" (9). As for Campbell's last point, it should be made clear that there were very few female police officers as recently as the 1980s and today there are far more, enough to assure that females can be frisked and searched by law enforcement.

Campbell's conclusion about gangs was that they exist not because they represent a counterculture, but because they represent a microcosm of American society—a distorted mirror image in which power, possessions, rank, and role are major concerns, but within a subcultural life of poverty and crime. According to Campbell, "Gangs do not represent a revolutionary vanguard rejecting the norms and values of a capitalist society that has exploited them. When gang members talk of politics, they talk of the American Dream, of pride in their country. . . . Girl members as women want to be American, to be free, to be beautiful, to be loved. These girls subscribe to the new woman's dream, the new agenda: No more suffering or poverty" (1984, 267). This is a highly romanticized and politicized viewpoint of gangs—as contributors to the numbers of American patriots!

Anne Campbell's study, as Miller's before, agreed with most studies of female gang participation that set the rate at, or around, 10 percent. This number may be an underestimate, however, because many police agencies are reluctant to identify females as gangsters due to their relatively low levels of criminality (Curry 1998). Nonetheless, the 10 percent figure is quite consistent. "Agencies responding to the 1996 National Youth Gang Survey reported that females accounted for eleven percent of gang members" (Interagency Task Force 2003, 1). As Moore and Hagedorn (2001) reported, two other nationwide surveys of law enforcement agencies, conducted in 1996 and 1998, estimated, respectively, that 11 percent and 8 percent of all gang members were female. Schmalleger (2004) states that nationally, 8 percent of gang members are female. Data provided by the Office of Juvenile Justice and Delinquency Prevention (OJJDP) (2000) indicated (based on law enforcement responses to a 1998 survey) that 8 percent of gang members were female. As for a geographic breakdown of female gang members,

> Female gang members were least prevalent in large cities (7 percent) and most prevalent in small cities (12 percent) and rural counties (11 percent). . . . Female gang members were more prevalent in the Northeast (13 percent) than in other regions. Their representation was lowest in the Midwest (5 percent), far lower than in the Northeast . . . . Survey responses indicated that less than 2 percent (1.76 percent) of all gangs in the United States in 1998 were female dominated. . . . Of the 171 jurisdictions reporting female-dominated gangs, 143 reported that these gangs represented only 14 percent or less of total gangs in their jurisdictions. (OJJDP 2000, 17–18)

There is no consensus on the exact number of females currently participating in gangs. Some researchers believe that female gang membership is increasing; others believe it remains around 10 percent. According to a 1999 *Chicago Tribune* article, 16,000 to 20,000 of the 100,000 gang members in Chicago were female (O'Brien 1999), which would be significantly greater than 10 percent. According to information compiled by the Detective Support Division of the Los Angeles Police Department in February 2000, there were 8,076 female gang members in California, with 6,007 living in Los Angeles county (Bing 2001b). This figure falls far short of 10 percent of the total number of estimated gang members overall in California. It is also consistent with researchers' accusations that police authorities tend to underestimate female participation rates. Hunt, MacKenzie, and Joe-Laidler (2004, 49) insist that "estimates of female membership today range from 10 to 30 percent of all gang members." Regoli and Hewitt (2003, 318) reported that "recent studies suggest that girls may comprise anywhere from 4 to 38 percent of all gang members."

In more recent years, research from law enforcement agencies still consistently report that female gang members make up about 10 percent of the total gang population, non–law enforcement research indicates a higher figure, and the larger the population area (large cities compared to small cities and rural areas), the lower the percentage of female gangsters (*Encyclopedia.com* 2009). *The National Youth Gang Survey, 1999–2001*, indicates that 10 percent of gang members are female; the larger the population size, the lower the proportion of female gang members (17% in jurisdictions under 25,000); and the *2007 National Young Gang Survey* indicates that in large cities females account for just 5 percent of all gangs compared to 11 percent in rural areas (*Encyclopedia.com* 2009). If we go with the 10 percent figure, that would mean there are anywhere between 73,100 and 114,000 female gang members in total (recall from Chapter 1 that the OJJDP reports the total number of gang members as 731,500 in 2009 and the FBI counts 1,140,344 in 2011).

The FBI (2009c) reports that female gang involvement is increasing as females assume greater responsibility in gang activities and grow more independent from their male counterparts. Still, the FBI (2009c) reports that the prevalence of predominantly female gangs continues to be a rare phenomenon. The FBI does, however, predict that female gangs, in one form or another, will exist in every American city by 2020 (Grossi 2011).

FEMALE GANGSTERS

We may not know exactly how many female gangsters there are, but we do know they exist. But why do they exist, what do they look like, and what type of activities are they involved in? Females join gangs for many of the same reasons as males: economic considerations, protection, lack of a stable family background, respect, and for fun and excitement. Female gangsters engage in the same types of criminal and noncriminal activities as boys. They can be very violent as well. According to Huizinga (1997), female gang members account for more violent crimes than do nongang boys. "The stereotype of the girl as primarily a sex object, with limited participation in the delinquent activity of the gang, apparently requires reexamination" (Esbensen, Deschenes, and Winfree 2004, 76).

Reasons for Joining the Gang

According to the National Alliance of Gang Investigators Associations (NAGIA), young women are taking active roles in gangs and female gangsters are being incarcerated in increasing numbers. There are many reasons why the number of girls joining gangs is increasing, but the most common one is that girls join a gang for protection—not from other girls, but from the physical and/or sexual abuse of their fathers or other family members. When youths are abused at home, they become subject to possible low self-esteem. Low levels of self-esteem coupled with feelings of alienation and hopelessness can drive young people to search for familial bonds elsewhere, such as a gang (Messerschmidt 1997). Many female gang members bond over the bad experiences, such as abuse, that they experienced in their homes (Nurge 2003). The gangs often accept girls of all shapes and sizes, abused or not, so the feeling of belonging is created by joining the gang (Leibovich 2001). As Moore and Hagedorn (2001) argue, "A gang serves as a refuge for young women who have been victimized at home. High proportions of female gang members have experienced sexual abuse at home" (3). Having conducted research on 74 self-reported female gang members in Champaign, Illinois, also known as the "North End," a poverty-stricken black community, Fleisher and Krienert (2004) found that many girls join a gang because the lifestyle is attractive and serves a refuge for those who are being victimized at home. Fleisher and Krienert (2004) found that the vast majority (76%) of the young girls reported physical abuse and victimization inside the home and 26 of the girls ran away to escape beatings. "The gang becomes a coping mechanism forming around shared abuse and other early life trauma" (Fleisher and Krienert 2004, 611. Two-thirds of the North End female gangsters came from single-parent homes and spent little or no time with their fathers. The median length of time lived with their fathers was 3.5 years and 16 years with their mothers. Fleisher and Krienert (2004) argue that the link between one-parent households and violent behavior has been supported through numerous previous examinations. In addition, Fleisher and Krienert report that of the 74 girls studied, 41 said their mothers were arrested once or more than once and 45 said that their father was incarcerated for most of their lives. The researchers conclude that parental criminality and drug use were found to significantly enhance youth gang membership, drug use, and delinquency.

Archer and Grascia (2006), citing a 1998 study done by the National Council on Crime and Delinquency that reported 92 percent of females surveyed in the California juvenile justice system had admitted to having been victims of some form of abuse, whether physical, emotional, or sexual, argue that the lack of support and the abuse experienced in the home drive many girls to find a way to escape the pain. Some girls turn to drugs or other illegal activities to escape the pain. These risky behaviors become contributing factors that lead abused girls to join a gang. Escapism can lead to running away. And where do runaways turn? In some cases, the answer is gangs.

Generally, abused girls run away from home; sometimes, they run to the neighborhood gang, which offers them the protection they seek. Other female gangsters come from families that are dysfunctional in other ways (e.g., absentee parents); still others join simply to rebel against their parents. The desire to rebel is common among most teenagers, nongang members included. All adolescents want freedom from the rules of their parents. A small percentage of these rebellious youths turn to gangs. Females are more likely to turn to a gang if their boyfriends are already in the gang. "About half of all female gang members report that their boyfriend is also a member of the same gang" (Knox 2001, 16). Female gang members generally report that they feel independent when they belong to a gang. Wearing the colors of the gang can bring them a sense of pride and a (false) sense of security (Landre, Miller, and Porter 1997).

The economic reality facing many youths of lower socioeconomic status (SES) remains a critical motivator for turning to a gang. Male gang members can make huge sums of money selling drugs; the girl gangsters hope to accomplish the same thing. The underground black market in drugs offers ambitious and aggressive gang members plenty of opportunities to make money, and until such drugs are legalized, this will obviously remain true. For many youths, the underground economy is viewed as the *only* economy. If there were legitimate job opportunities for impoverished youths, that would help deter many of them from turning to gangs. But the huge growth of gangs and gang members can be directly tied to the closing of numerous factories and the sending of American business and production overseas, a failure of U.S. political leaders. Unskilled laborers have been unable to find employment in the new service economy. Moreover, many inner-city youths lack the job skills necessary to survive in the changing economic system because of the poor quality of education provided in many inner-city school districts, where schools are generally and drastically underbudgeted and teachers are forced to work under conditions that are far from ideal—*and far from* equal to those of most suburban schools. The continued deterioration of the inner city has formed an underclass that breeds hopelessness. When we add the potentially negative affects of growing up in a single-parent family (as described earlier by Fleisher and Krienert) to education, it is not surprising to learn that many youths skip school regularly and become attracted to gangs (Milidor 1996). In a study of 15 self-reported female gang members residing in a secure residential facility in Texas, only 3 girls completed ninth grade (Milidor 1996). Most of these girls had had a long history of fighting, drug use, and weapons possession charges, all on school ground. After illegally dropping out of school, the girls turned to gangs. Milidor (1996) also found that most female gang members who were in school were at least two school years behind their peers and consistently fell through the cracks of the education system.

The NAGIA (2002) summed up that females most likely to join a gang are between the ages of 12 and 18, have low self-esteem, come from dysfunctional families, and have a history of victimization. Girl gang members are very likely to have been victims of physical and sexual abuse. The gang provides friends, money, drugs, power, excitement, and, perhaps most important of all, a sense of family. In other cases, gangs have become so institutionalized in some communities that some girls have been raised in a gang culture in which their families have been members for generations. The NAGIA also reports that females with friends, boyfriends, or siblings in a gang are most likely to be in a gang themselves.

Recruitment

The girls who join gangs are looking for a strong support system. Gangs provide support through friendship and mutual understanding. Girls who feel lost at home and at school, thus lacking any trusted adult to turn to, look up to the older girl gang members and bond with their peers. A young girl does not just suddenly join a gang; she has looked up to some of the girls while she was still being abused or victimized at home. Thus, exposure to gang life is the first step of recruitment (Miller 2001). Young girls, usually those under 13, see the older girls hanging out with the gang and may become envious of the perceived attractive alternative gang life provides. The second step toward entering a gang is a dysfunctional family life that leads to the girls' avoiding their homes and cherishing time hanging out with the gang. A third step, according to Miller (2001), is related to the influence of gang members over the girl, that is, if she has an older sibling or relative or close friend in the gang who is now encouraging the girl to join. Historically, lower SES girls from abused homes are likely to view gangs in a positive light.

Girls who are "lost" and feel anomie are likely to view a gang as an alternative. Feeling lost is especially difficult for adolescent girls, who experience major biological and emotional changes. Gang girls learn that the only people they can trust are each other. If a gang is not available, a number of girls may decide to form their own gang. Thus, many gangs are formed out of normal friendship groups; they develop spontaneously. Thus, girls are not generally "recruited" in the normal sense of the term, nor are they pressured or coerced. Members come from existing friendship groups in the neighborhood and/or through family ties (Harris 1988). Joe and Chesney-Lind's (1995) study of Hawaiian gangs supported this common understanding that many, if not most, gangs form gradually among youths from the same neighborhood (Chesney-Lind and Shelden 2004). In her study of Hispanic female gangs in California, Mary Harris (1988) found that girls were not pressured or coerced into joining a gang but did so because of friendships and family ties. Miller (2001), however, points out that girls may be targeted or coerced into joining a gang. Their friends in the gang may make gang life seem more attractive than it is and convince them to join; they may make the life miserable of a girl refusing to join; or, they might simply get "jumped."

Initiation

After a female has decided to join a gang, typically, she is initiated. The prime age at which girls undergo initiation appears to be around the ages of 13 and 14 (Eghigian and Kirby 2006). Gang initiation processes vary and a few gangs may not use an initiation process at all. Generally, initiation is completed in one of three ways: being "jumped in" (beaten), "born in" (being naturally accepted because of familial ties), or "trained in" (raped or forced to have sex with several male gang members at once) (Portillos 1997). The first form of initiation, the beating, can include two variations. The first involves the recruit taking a physical beating from the gang members. This is especially important for violent female gangs who routinely engage in fights. The recruit needs to prove that she is tough and is as willing to receive a beating as she is to administer one. The second variation involves the recruit committing some sort of violent or criminal act against a rival gang member or person of authority (law enforcement personnel). Females may be required to participate in robberies or muggings or commit a drive-by shooting. As Taylor (2001) explained, a potential gang recruit may have to show her toughness and willingness to commit criminal acts by participating in such activities as face slashings or, if they are in prison, the killing of an inmate or warden. In a study conducted on female gangs in Columbus, Ohio, Miller (2001) found that 22 percent of the female recruits car-jacked a motorist, beat up a rival gang member, snatched a purse, or got gang tattoos. Milidor (1996) found that gang leaders decided what the initiation would consist of and how long it would last. It was common for her subjects to "walk the line," "pull a train," or get tattoos, and participate in a crime (e.g., robbery or commit a drive-by shooting). Walking the line meant that the girl walked through a double line of gang members who severely punched and kicked her until she comes to the end of the line. There is no "winning;" but, rather, surviving to show one's strength.

Females who are born in to the gang may escape the physical beating and the humiliation and degradation experienced from the "train in." Females who are born in may get away with just being tattooed with gang symbols. Another variation of the born-in initiation is being "blessed in" by gang members praying over the girl (Regoli and Hewitt 2003). For example, the Latin Queens may "bless in" a recruit, who needs only to promise dedication to the Nation's rules and adhere to the five points of the Nation crown, which stand for respect, honesty, unity, knowledge, and love (Taylor 2001). Many gang members are now second-, or even third-generation members; they are the ones who are able to take advantage of the born-in variation of initiation. Clearly, the born in, especially the "bless in," is a much kinder form of initiation.

A third general category of initiation into female gangs is the "train in" or "pulling a train." The *train in* or *pulling a train* means that the girl will have sex with multiple male gang members. This form of initiation almost always leads to a loss of respect for the girl. Any young woman who is "trained in" has a difficult time shedding the negative stigma that is attached to her. It is also highly likely that she will always be viewed as a sexual object, will never have the respect of most of her fellow female gang members, and rarely will gain the respect of the male gang members. "Girls who are sexed into a gang are at much greater risk for continued sexual mistreatment and exploitation and are generally viewed by male and female gang members as weak, promiscuous, and subject to contempt and disrespect" (Regoli and Hewitt 2003, 320). The train-in initiation involves a girl having intercourse with multiple male gang members. The train in is also known as a "roll-in." Under this scenario, a female initiate rolls a pair of dice and whatever number appears determines how many males will have sex with her. The hierarchy of males in the gang determines who is the "engine, the caboose, or somewhere in between" in this type of initiation (Sikes 2001, 103). The film *Havoc* has a scene involving a roll-in. For a further discussion of the roll-in initiation and a description of the roll-in ceremony in *Havoc*, see "Connecting Street Gangs and Popular Culture" Box 7.1.

The female gang members seldom accept those who choose to be "trained in" over jumped in because they displayed submissiveness in sacrificing their bodies instead of fighting (Portillos 1997). Palmer and Tilley (1995) found that female gang members referred to girls who pulled a train as "hood rats." Hood rats were the girls that the boys set up for exploitation (as a means to entrap rival gang members or conventional folks). Hood rats did more drinking and drugs and participated in sex with multiple partners more freely and frequently than the other girls. As a result hood rats were not respected by the males or females. The family they had chosen to replace the biological one that abused them was now doing the same thing.

Box 7.1   *Connecting Street Gangs and Popular Culture*

Female Gang Initiation and the Roll-In Ceremony

There are three primary ways that a female is initiated into a gang and one of them involves a roll-in. *Roll-in* is a slang term for rolling dice. When a roll-in is coupled with female gang initiations, we get the train in option. The other two methods of initiation being jumped in, wherein recruits are either beaten by fellow gang members or required to commit a criminal act; being blessed in or born in to the gang as a legacy (an older female relative is/was in the gang). The train-in option is certainly the most humiliating method of initiation, as it typically involves a recruit rolling a pair of dice to determine the number of males she will have to have sex with. The roll-in process itself is alienating for the female initiate but the second-class status she will have for the rest of her gang life as a result of choosing this option (over the jump in) will be daunting. She will never have the full respect of male or female gang members. The one minute beating "Sad Girl" and "Mousie" endured as their gang initiation in the film *Mi Vida Loca* is certainly a better option than what happens to Emily and Allison in the film *Havoc*.

In the 2005 film *Havoc*, the protagonist characters Allison (Anne Hathaway) and Emily (Bijou Phillips), two wealthy white girls from the up-scale Los Angeles community of Pacific Palisades, are intrigued by the gangster lifestyle and eventually find themselves in the position of being initiated into an East Los Angeles gang via a roll-in. How did girls from a privileged background find themselves in such a position? *Havoc* provides an insight into the often untold story of gang life, that is, not all troubled youths come from lower SES backgrounds. Allison has a virtually non-existent relationship with her parents. Her mom is a recovering alcoholic whom Allison has seen passed out on the floor and would have to call for help. Allison and her dad have an uneasy relationship and like a lot of teenagers and parents they find it difficult to communicate effectively with each other. So, she turns to her peer group for comfort. Her friends are influenced by the hip-hop music they listen to and the culture it glamorizes and act like gangsters. In reality, they are poseur wannabes. They are experiencing *false consciousness* by believing gangsta life is better than the privileged lifestyle their parents have provided (e.g., private schools, vacations, material goods).

One of the white boys, Eric (Matt O'Leary), is a teenage filmmaker, attempting to document gang life. Crew members discuss how they are bored teenagers and claim to hate the rich white culture. One day, at a beach parking lot, Allison, her boyfriend Toby (Mike Vogel), and their crew tangle with a real gang and a brawl ensues. As the police arrive everyone splits. Later that night, the crew hang out and snort cocaine and get drunk. The following night, Allison, Toby, and her friends decide to drive to East Los Angeles for some drugs and encounter a drug dealer named Hector (Freddy Rodriguez) and his crew, the 16th Street Gang. Toby and Hector get into an argument over the drug deal and Hector pulls a gun on Toby. Allison persuades Hector to leave her boyfriend alone. The next night, Allison and her girlfriends go back to Hector's barrio. They are looking for kicks and thrills that their upper-class lifestyle does not provide. They want to live on the edge. They need an adrenaline "rush" to get by in life. Hector invites the girls to a party. The girls think they are cool. The boys just want to hook up with them. Hector invites Allison to a party at a nearby hotel where the crew has rooms they use. Allison declines and the girls go home. The next day Allison runs into Hector again and he shows her around his barrio. The tour is interrupted by a police sweep and Allison is arrested along with Hector's crew. The scene shifts to the jail where we learn that Allison's parents have posted her bail but they are yelling at her for her transgressions. The next day at school, Toby is upset with Allison and they get into an argument. The kids at school think Allison is a bad-ass. She downplays her brief incarceration but she is now fully intrigued by the gang lifestyle.

The night following Allison's arrest, she and her friend Emily meet up with Hector and his gang at the Alvarado motel to party. After getting high, the girls ask Hector if they can join the gang. They are told they will have to do what every other girl did to join the 16th Street Gang. They will have to roll a single die and have sex with the corresponding number of guys. It is common for girls to have to roll a pair of dice instead of just one as the 16th Street gang mandated. Allison is lucky; she rolls a one and pairs off with Hector, the guy she wanted to hook up with anyway. Emily has thrown a "three" and she eagerly hooks up with the first guy. The two girls are in separate beds in the same bedroom. Allison has second thoughts and pleads Hector to stop before they have sex. He does, but he is angry about it. Allison tries to convince Emily to leave the bedroom with her but she says she wants to go through with the initiation. Allison is kicked out of the bedroom. Hector is the second guy to be with Emily. He invites the third guy to join in and he copulates with her anally. Emily screams out in pain and fear. This is much more than she bargained for; reality has sunk in; being a bad girl is not so glamorous after all. Allison runs back into the bedroom, grabs Emily, and they are allowed to leave. In many gang initiation situations like this, they would not have gotten off so lightly. On the drive home Emily is freaking out and looks dazed and lost. At school she is distant. She goes home early because she is feeling sick.

Allison does something really dumb the following night and returns to the same hotel room to speak with Hector. Hector swears at her and asks, "What do you want?" Allison wants to talk. Gangsters in this type of situation want nothing to do with "talking." Allison tries to lay a guilt trip on Hector and tells him, in essence, to "get real." Hector says there is nothing real about Allison and tells her she does not belong in his world. The scene changes to Emily at the police station with her parents where she has accused members of the 16th Street Gang of gang raping her at a party. She is too embarrassed to admit she volunteered to roll the dice as an initiation. Emily looks at mug shots and points out Hector as a suspect. The police ask Allison to corroborate the gang rape. Allison is upset and says, "I can't believe that you think my friend was raped and I hung out and watched." This is Allison's way of saying, Emily was not raped. She adds, "This is insane, I don't know anything about a *rape*." Allison visits Emily at her home. She is trying to rewrite history. Emily tells Allison that the gang must have put something in her drink(s) and that they took advantage of her. She wants Allison to testify that it was a gang rape and not consensual. Allison is not comfortable with this; she knows they both willingly went along with the gang initiation and agreed to have sex with the number of guys the die rolled up. Allison tries to tell her parents that it wasn't rape, that the girls went there and agreed to a roll-in. But they do not believe her.

The police arrest Hector. The 16th Street Gang goes looking for revenge in Pacific Palisades but they get lost in Bellaire instead. Toby is very upset that Allison hooked up with gangsters in a seedy hotel. He has vowed revenge against the gang. Allison tries to intercede, saying over and over that Emily was not raped but Toby does not care. Things are really getting out of hand now so Allison goes back to Emily's house. She tells Emily's parents about the roll-in and how they asked to join the gang and agreed to roll the dice and voluntarily went into the other room with the cholos. Understandably, Emily's parents are in shock. Emily is mortified that her parents have found out the truth. She contemplates suicide. Meanwhile, Toby's crew busts into the hotel room where the incident occurred. They are heavily armed and ready to kill. They start shooting. But the gang is not there. Instead, it's a couple of women and a baby. Unwilling to kill innocent people, they leave. On their drive home, the two crews cross paths. The two crews exchange glances and as the screen fades to black we hear the sounds of tires squealing, people shouting, and gunfire.

Havoc is not a typical story of a female roll-in initiation. Most gangstas want out of the 'hood and these white girls wanted in the 'hood. For many, the choice is not theirs to make. Life circumstances often dictate courses in life. But *Havoc* does provide us with a graphic look at what a female roll-in initiation is all about.

Gang Membership

Once in the gang, female gangsters are usually quite distinguishable from conventional girls. Although it is necessary to point out, once again, that gangs vary a great deal, it is common for gang girls to wear the colors of the gang, to have multiple tattoos (nothing like that of conventional girls), and to dress in dark colors, especially black, blue, and brown. Some Hispanic gang members wear the same uniform as their male counterparts, which is Pendleton shirts and khakis or Levis. They may also wear a white tank top ("wife beater"). Female gang members rarely dress femininely (skirts and dresses) but instead dress like males. Hispanic female gang members are likely to wear bandannas or make them some part of their daily outfit. Their hair is usually worn long, especially if they are in an auxiliary gang, and is sometimes dyed red or blonde. Female gang members wear thick makeup to make their skin appear lighter. Eye makeup is usually thick and dark. Tattoos generally include their boyfriend's name. Hispanic female gang members may have tattoos of crucifixes and rosaries on their chest or back to signify they would die for their gang (Landre, Miller, and Porter 1997).

Leaving the Gang

Females have a tendency to leave the gang at an earlier age than males, with the most common and acceptable reason being pregnancy. In cases other than pregnancy, leaving the gang can be difficult and, as described earlier in the discussion of Quicker's study, subject to a violation ceremony. The girl who decides to leave the gang must have a support system, ideally, family members, who will help her in her transition back to conventional life. Once the decision is made to leave the gang, the former member will have to remove herself from the neighborhood as she is likely to be jumped by her former gang members and rival gang members or, she may be tempted to rejoin the gang. If the girl has too much information on the gang, especially with regard to criminal activities, her exit may be a permanent one, meaning, of course, she will be killed.

Gang life, more likely than not, will have taken a big toll on the female gangster. Her life was rough at home and then in the gang. What will the future hold? Will she be able to raise her baby (if she becomes a mother)? Will she ever be able to break completely free of the gang? Will she be able to find a conventional job if she does? What about her gang tattoos, will they hinder her pursuit of a conventional lifestyle? Or will all the conventional life challenges be so daunting that she turns back to the gang? For each female, the story is slightly different, but in most cases, belonging to a gang presents more challenges than solutions. As Katherine Kirby, executive vice president for the Chicago Crime Commission, and Mars Eghigian, a contributing researcher and writer, state, "Although it may appear to a girl member that the gang provides her with protection, the reality is that when the exit is handled well, it is always safer to be out of the gang."

TYPES OF FEMALE GANGS

Female gangs can be placed in general categories according to their level of affiliation with male gangs and by class and race. There are three general types of female gang involvement: (1) as female auxiliaries of male gangs, (2) regular membership in a male gang as a coed, and (3) as independent female gangs. Supporting this categorization scheme, Regoli and Hewitt (2003, 318) add, "While the majority of gang boys are in all-male gangs, most girls who join gangs join mixed gangs (which tend to be dominated by boys), female gangs affiliated with male gangs, or independent female gangs."

Female Gangs as Auxiliaries

When John Quicker (1983, 1999) first conducted his research on female gangs in the 1970s, he did not find a single independent gang. Independent female gangs are still few in number, but there are more now than ever before. It is a little more difficult to determine whether there are more auxiliary or coed female gangs, but it would appear that auxiliaries constitute a little more than half of the total. Eghigian and Kirby (2006), for example, found that the vast majority of female gang members were categorized as being auxiliary members of male gangs. The researchers noted that although a few may rise to be marginally independent of some male authority, they are usually subservient to male gang objectives. Further, auxiliary gangs are usually of lower status and treated with little respect by their male peers, some of whom consider the females to be weak (Eghigian and Kirby 2006).

Let's do a quick recap as to why a girl has decided to join a gang. Raised in an environment of broken or abusive homes that offered little hope and incentive to achieve, most gang girls experience low levels of self-esteem. Negative family relationships lead many to seek personal relationships elsewhere. Gang girls find these needed friendships with their fellow gang members. Their sense of loyalty to each other is very strong. Often lacking a loving relationship with their fathers and consequently seeking to replace that missing love with empty sexual relationships, it is very common for gang women to have children at a young age; many times they have children by multiple fathers. When girls join a gang, the gang is usually already affiliated with a male gang, meaning it is an auxiliary gang. Even newly formed female gangs are almost always preceded by a male gang, and they usually take a feminized version of the male's gang name. Auxiliary gang members are usually of the same ages as the males. Although there is not necessarily a formal female leader of the auxiliary gang, some members have more clout than others (Chesney-Lind and Shelden 2004).

Auxiliary gang members perform integral gang duties, such as serving as lookouts and drugs and weapons couriers, luring rivals for ambushes, and providing alibis (Eghigian and Kirby 2006). Although auxiliary gangs are seen as subordinates to their male peers, they are afforded a certain number of freedoms, including opportunities to define their own roles within the auxiliary gang. Nurge explains that female auxiliary gangs are neither completely at the mercy of the male gang members nor are they completely free of their influence. Female auxiliary gangs, then, are quasi-independent, in that they have their own name but since this name is tied to the male gang's name, they do not have complete autonomy. For example, the Vice Ladies are the auxiliary female gang to the Vice Lords.

The **Vice Ladies** are essentially the female version of the Vice Lords (Keiser 1969). The Vice Ladies carry out whatever assignment the Vice Lords give them (Dawley 1992). The Vice Ladies are considered highly valuable for they serve many functions, especially when it comes to carrying and concealing weapons. (As noted earlier, however there are plenty of women law enforcement officers today who are available to frisk female gang members.) Dawley (1992) describes how the Vice Ladies enjoyed the gangbanger lifestyle as much as the males and carry all sorts of weapons, including razors, chains, and anything else they can hide in their bras. If Vice Lady gang members were in a fight, the Vice Lords would not intervene, unless a male joined in to help the competing gang. (See "Connecting Street Gangs and Popular Culture" Box 7.2 for a look at auxiliary female gangs in films.)

Box 7.2   *Connecting Street Gangs and Popular Culture*

Auxiliary Female Street Gangs in Films

Auxiliary female gangs are directly connected to a male street gang, and the male gang always forms first. Often, the auxiliary gang will take a feminized version of the male gang's name. For example, the Almighty Latin Kings have a female auxiliary called the Almighty Latin Queens and the Vice Lords have a female auxiliary called the Vice Ladies. Auxiliary gang members may serve numerous functions for the males both during times of criminal gang activity and while the gang members are simply hanging out together. Some auxiliary gangs are more autonomous than others and generally they are not at the complete mercy of the male gang nor do they have complete freedom. Thus, they are quasi-independent.

ZUMA Press/Newscom

There are a number of films that depict auxiliary female street gangs, including *Grease* and *Mi Vida Loca*. *Grease*, released in 1978 and staring John Travolta and Olivia Newton-John, is a film, based on Jim Jacobs's 1971 musical of the same name, about two lovers in a 1950s California high school. The film begins with a local teenager, Danny Zuko (Travolta) and vacationing Sandy Olsson (Newton-John) from Sydney, Australia, hanging out together at the beach. The two have fallen in love with each other, both assuming that when the summer ends, their romance will end as well. Sandy has no idea that Danny is "greaser" (a street tough) and the leader of the T-Birds because he has let his guard down to romance her. The T-Birds are a local street gang. They all wear white t-shirts and black leather jackets. With the start of the new school year, Danny embellishes his summer love to the boys in his crew. A group of girls, known as the "Pink Ladies," serve as an auxiliary to the T-Birds. Betty Rizzo (Stockard Channing) is the leader of the Pink Ladies. The Pink Ladies wear pink jackets with their gang name stitched on them. Sandy befriends Frenchy (Didi Conn), one of the Pink Ladies. Sandy begins to hang out with them. Frenchy asks Rizzo if Sandy can join their group, but Rizzo says, "She looks too pure to be pink." In other words, Sandy is too goody-goody to be a member of Pink Ladies. Although Sandy will end up as a member of the Pink Ladies, there was no apparent initiation. Danny is surprised to see Sandy at his school. He learns that Sandy's parents decided not to move back to Sydney and have enrolled her at Rydell High School.

Grease is similar to *West Side Story*, in that this film is more of a musical that involves gangs than it is a film about the gritty street life of urban gang warfare. Nonetheless, the basic idea of an auxiliary female gang is portrayed. The Pink Ladies are no Latin Queens. They spend most of their time engaged in juvenile delinquent behavior, including smoking and drinking at a sleepover at Frenchy's home. The T-Birds show up at Frenchy's house and entice some of the girls to go out partying. This is one of the roles of auxiliary female gangs, to entertain the boys. Rizzo, as the leader, is willing to serve as a sex object. She wants kicks and thrills. She wants excitement. And the T-Birds provide it. Rizzo, her sights set on Kenickie (Jeff Conaway), the second in command with the T-Birds. Kenickie downplays his relationship with Rizzo and tells Danny that girls are "only good for one thing." This comment reflects the adage that male gang members look at girls as sex objects.

On their way to the local hangout, the Frosty Palace, a burger and ice cream joint, the T-Birds notice their gang rivals, the Scorpions, driving wildly in their pride and joy automobile nearly running people down in the streets. Danny comments to Kenickie that something has to be done about the Scorpions. Kenickie and Rizzo get into a fight and break up. Rizzo wants to teach Kenickie a lesson. As is often the case with female gang members, Rizzo adds fuel to the gang rivalry when she rides off with Leo, the leader of the Scorpions. Kenickie retaliates by dating Leo's girlfriend, Cha-Cha. The Scorpions crash a Rydell High School dance and the two gangs nearly rumble. The auxiliary girls are ready to do their part as well. As time moves on, Rizzo believes she is pregnant. Kenickie wonders who the father is and tells Rizzo that he takes responsibility for his "mistakes." Hurt by this, Rizzo says, "It's someone else's mistake." Kenickie is hurt by this. But the news certainly adds to his hatred of Leo and the Scorpions. As a result, Kenickie challenges Leo and they agree to race each other's car for "pinks" at "Thunder Roll." Racing for pinks is slang for pink slips, or car ownership rights. Thunder Roll is the paved, usually dry Los Angeles River (a location spot for many other films). The T-Birds and the Scorpions both have their respective female auxiliary gangs there to cheer on their favorite. They are also ready to rumble if necessary. In the "no rules" race to the second bridge and back, Leo uses dirty tactics to take the lead but Danny outsmarts him and wins the race. The Pink Ladies celebrate with the T-Birds. The gang confrontation is over, for now. The film ends with Sandy shedding her goody-goody image by donning an all-leather outfit. She is willing to be a "bad girl" to get Danny. Interestingly, Danny was willing to go clean to get her back. Rizzo, who, as it turns out, is not pregnant, reunites with Kenickie. In fact, many of the Pink Ladies and T-Birds have paired off. At their graduation party, the gang agrees to always be there for each other.

The 1993 film *Mi Vida Loca*, which includes the first film appearances of Salma Hayek and Jason Lee, tells a story of a female auxiliary Mexican-American gang from Echo Park. Echo Park is east of Hollywood, near downtown Los Angeles. It is a place where in the 1920s, Hollywood stars had love nests in the hills. Echo Park, once a white suburb of Los Angeles, is now a Hispanic neighborhood. Like most gangsters, the gang is proud of its neighborhood, and they feel the need to protect it from outsiders. They use the expression "Life in the Echo." *Mi Vida Loca* is told primarily from the perspective of two homegirls "Mousie" (Seidy Lopez) and Sad Girl (Angel Aviles). They belong to an auxiliary of the Echo Park Gang (EPG). Their initiation was a one-minute "jump-in" wherein both of the girls were beaten by the rest of gang. Once the jump-in was over, they were members of the auxiliary.

As is often the case, Mousie and Sad Girl have had sex throughout their teens and are both single-parent mothers as teenagers. Their homeboys talk about needing to work to help pay for their babies, but ultimately it is up to the girls to raise their babies and try to find ways to secure the essentials. Of the two, Sad Girl gets pregnant first, and to complicate matters, it is by Mousie's boyfriend, Ernesto (Jacob Vargas). Ernesto is the leader of the EPG. He sells drugs to make money. One day, he purchases a mini truck that is all tricked out. He got the truck from an older homeboy who is in prison. Ernesto has put a great deal of money into the truck, including a custom paint job. With all the financial needs of Sad Girl and Mousie, he hides this fact from the girls. Meanwhile, El Duran (Jesse Borrego), the leader of River Valley, the rival gang of Echo Park dating back to the days of the Zoot-Suit riots, has told Ernesto that he has a claim on the truck. El Duran claims that while he was in prison with the EPG homeboy the truck was promised to him instead. This seems odd but Ernesto makes it clear, that someone will have to kill him to take the truck. Such foreshadowing will serve as an important element in this film. Before Ernesto is killed, in a drug deal gone bad, he has hooked up with Mousie and she too will become pregnant with his baby.

One day, the Echo Park girls go to prison to pick up one of their Original Gangsters (OGs), Giggles, who is being released after four years in the joint. Baby Doll, one of the Echo Park girls, is driving a car that belongs to her boyfriend, a member of the River Valley gang. One of the EPG girls, Whisper, asks Baby Doll, "you're going out with a Vato from a neighborhood we don't get along with? That's f*cked up bitch." Baby Doll justifies her behavior by saying that no Vato from Echo Park has a car as nice and says that girls got to do what girls got to do. Sad Girl points out that it would be nice to have a car to get groceries and take the baby places. Once again, we have a scenario where an auxiliary girl dates a guy from a rival gang and justifies the behavior. The gang is so excited to have Giggles out on the streets. They think her knowledge and experience will help them with life on the streets. Giggles does offer quite a bit of advice. When Giggles finds out that Sad Girl and Mousie almost killed each other, she says,

"Girls, you don't ever throw down with your homegirl over a guy. Guys come and go. They ain't worth it." Mousie tells Giggles that Ernesto was killed by a white girl during a drug deal. Giggles is surprised to hear this as the word in prison had the River Valley gang responsible for Ernesto's death. Ernesto's brother Shadow is running the gang now. Shadow and the EPG still believe River Valley murdered Ernesto. They will not take the word of Whisper because she is a girl. Shadow has inherited the truck. The Echo Park girls had no idea about the truck and yet Giggles has heard about this in prison. She tells the girls to talk to Shadow to sell the truck and use the money to raise the kids. Mousie agrees that they should have the money because they are relying on welfare. Giggles tells the gang that she learned quite a bit while in prison. She points out that homegirls need new skills because their boyfriends or husbands are either injured, in prison, or dead by the time they are 21. We need to take care of our futures, Giggles says. And she says matter-of-factly that computers are the future and she hopes to find a job in the computer field. The Echo Park girls are disappointed that Giggles wants to go straight, and Whisper comments in a film voiceover that the EPG girls no longer respect their OG because prison has made her a goody two-shoes. Later, Giggles discusses with another female OG how things have changed in the gang, that back in their day auxiliary girls never dated boys from different gangs, sold drugs, dyed their hair blonde (like Whisper), and so on.

Sad Girl and Mousie take a sneak peek at the truck that is hidden in Shadow's garage. They discuss all the things they could do with the truck, like taking the kids to Disneyland or getting groceries. They seek Shadow to ask him about the truck. At the local coffee shop, the girls ask Shadow about the truck but he tells them that it is too dangerous to drive the truck because River Valley is after it. Giggles walks by and the EPG girls flash their gang signs. Giggles just waves back and the gang girls are upset that she did not "throw back" signs to represent. Whisper is making money selling drugs but it all goes back to the boys. Such is the nature of being an auxiliary gang member. She does comment that she should just start her own "operation" because she is better at it than Shadow. But one night Giggles and two homeboys are busted for selling drugs. The cops photograph Whisper but Giggles (who had been nearby) points out that it is against the law to photograph minors. Whisper respects Giggles for helping her. Giggles has dinner with a male OG from EPG named Big Sleepy. Big Sleepy did the paint job on the truck. Giggles points out that the truck should be sold and the money given to the locas for their babies. Big Sleepy replies that the decision has already been made by the locos and the locas have no say in what happens. Giggles is upset that such a big decision involving the auxiliary gang is made without their input. Such is the way of the world of an auxiliary gang. At the end of the film Baby Doll convinces some of her locas to go to a River Valley gang party. Predictably, this cannot end well. The EPG will be upset with their locas. And Shadow is already gunning for El Duran. The EPG show up at the party and kill El Duran. A couple days later, some locas from River Valley drive up to Shadow who is standing on the sidewalk in front of a bodega and shoot at him. They miss. Instead, they kill a little girl riding a tricycle nearby. The little girl is Big Sleepy's daughter. Even when the OG thought he was safe by outing out of the gang, his daughter is killed in a gang-related drive-by.

Mi Vida Loca provides an accurate look at street gangs in the early 1990s. Giggles commented on the significant changes in gang life during her four years in prison. Undoubtedly, if she had been in prison for 24 years instead, she might be shocked by the changes in the behavior of female gangsters today.

Coed Membership

In some cases, females and males are integrated into the same gang. There are many gangs across the United States that are coed. Although the true number of coed gangs is difficult to determine, the figure could be as high as 40 percent. Arturo Hernandez, author of *Peace in the Streets: Breaking the Cycle of Gang Violence* (2006), claims that 60 percent of all gangs do not allow female members, although some of these may allow females to hang out and party with them (Hernandez 2012). Females usually enjoy higher levels of respect from male gang members than girls in auxiliary gangs. This higher status is a result of their coed status, a status that is achieved through merit. Females in coed gangs are given an opportunity to prove themselves on a regular basis because they are entrusted with critical gang matters such as hiding and selling drugs and access to weapons and money. Female gang members may be the primary persons responsible for bringing drugs into correctional facilities for gang members (Eghigian and Kirby 2006). Incarcerated coed female gang members generally enjoy a top position in the prison hierarchy because they have a male gang to back them up on the streets (e.g., if a woman gives a coed gang member a hard time in prison, she can have the woman's loved ones threatened or hurt). Hernandez (2012) points out, however, that the majority of the estimated 14,000 girls in correctional placement are gang members. Thus, all of these girls would be on the top of the food chain and they cannot all be leaders. There are instances when female coeds of a gang bond so closely that they may decide to either form an auxiliary to the gang or form their own independent gang.

Independent Female Gangs

There are very few female gangs that are completely independent of any male gang. Hernandez (2012) claims that only 2 percent of all gangs are female only. Historically, these gangs have been short-lived. More recently, however, there appears to be a growing number of independent girl gangs. Campbell (1984) interviewed females from independent girl gangs and Taylor (1993) described a number of independent girl gangs in Detroit. Females who form independent gangs do so for the same reasons as males: They seek a way out of ghetto life, respect, and association with "like-minded" people who share the same values and norms as they possess. As previously mentioned, female independent street gangs are uncommon. Eghigian and Kirby (2006) caution us that some females appear to be gang members but in reality they are wannabes. They describe "party crews"—females who socialize and party together—as an example of a wannabe female gang. Party crews are not loyal to any gang but like going to whichever gang is throwing the best party or whomever they are most attracted to at any give moment. The problem occurs when party crews attend a party thrown by a gang with an auxiliary as the auxiliary gang members will want to fight the party crew for infringing on their turf. The party crews will then have to fight. The fact that party crew females know they may upset other women at a party but attend it anyway demonstrates that they do have some gangsta attitude in them.

One of the most unique independent female gangs, or any gang for that matter, is **Dykes Taking Over (DTO)**. DTO is an African-American lesbian gang formed in Philadelphia as a result of homosexual students being bullied in school (Johnson 2008). That homosexuality is a missing element in nearly all street gangs makes the existence of DTO all the more fascinating. We hear of the problem of bullying, especially in schools, often in the media and public discourse. And while bullying, in some shape or form, has existed throughout history, there exists a concerted effort to try and curtail such activities in school. Generally, we hear about education methods as a means to end bullying. That is, we need to educate children and adults about the harmful effects of bullying and find ways to identify the perpetrators and the victims of bullying. DTO did not want to wait for others to come up with a solution to the bullying of gays in Philadelphia schools. Instead, they took action. DTO members were being bullied by straight students, and in retaliation, they used sexual harassment and intimidation to attack back (Johnson 2008).

It might be tempting to look at DTO as an activist group for the Lesbian Gay Bisexual Queer and Transgendered (LGBQT) community, but in actuality they possess most of the other criteria for a street gang. DTO was not fighting for the rights of all LGBQT persons; instead they were fighting to defend themselves and their space in school; sort of like defending a turf. That marginalized lesbians formed a group, or a gang, as a result of their feeling alienated is typical of most gang members, especially those from lower SES backgrounds. Fighting back verbally and physically is another characteristic that DTO shares with street gangs. Being ostracized by the community (e.g., the school district) is another feature the two share.

Class and Race

Gang members, male and female alike, generally come from lower socioeconomic social classes. Harper and Robinson (1999) found that 96 percent of girl gang families were receiving unemployment or welfare benefits, 56 percent were receiving food stamps, 7 percent received reduced cost or free lunch at school, and 48 percent were from single-parent families. As described in Chapter 3, economics plays an important role in an individual's decision to join a gang. When young people become disheartened by their bleak financial futures, the gang often appears to be an appealing alternative to struggling in conventional society. Minority members are disproportionately found in the lower economic strata, which accounts for their higher participation rates in gang activity. Residing in high-crime urban areas increases the opportunities for youths to join.

In his research on female gangs, Grossi (2011) found a number of all-girl gangs made up of 14- to 16-year-old whites with one of the most visible, **Bitches with Attitude (BWA)**. BWA consists of young girls from middle-class homes, many of whom work after school, and in all reality, are just part-time, or quasi-gangbangers who still live at home with their parents or guardians. BWA is most visible at school functions, on Facebook, MySpace, and YouTube. A Google search reveals a certain amount of activity from BWA, but it is doubtful it qualifies as a "real" gang.

Since a great number of gangs develop spontaneously, it is easy to conclude that many girl gangs developed as a result of girls who grew up together in the same neighborhood or housing project. Chesney-Lind and Shelden (2004, 73) reviewed the research study conducted by Laidler and Hunt (1997), who "found that most of the girl gang members either grew up in the same housing project or knew a relative associated with their group." People who grow up in poverty have two choices: They can work hard, earn an education, and hope to find a good job; or they can adopt the role of victim and respond in nonproductive ways (i.e., do nothing/collect unemployment and/or welfare, or turn to a criminal lifestyle that may or may not include gangs). Thus, poverty often leads directly, as well as indirectly, to gang participation.

Campbell (1984) linked the effects of poverty to the formation of the girl gangs that she studied in New York City. These girls were worried about their dismal conventional futures and believed that joining a gang offered them an alternative that would provide economic success. These girls wanted economic success and freedom from a life destined for unfulfillment. Campbell (1984) concluded that such expectations were unrealistic and points out that the girls want better welfare and health benefits, and more jobs, but they don't want a revolution.

> Girl members as women want to be American, to be free, to be beautiful, to be loved. These girls subscribe to the new woman's dream, the new agenda: No more suffering or poverty. No more lonely, forced "independence," living alone on welfare in a shabby apartment. First, a good husband; strong but not violent, faithful but manly. Second, well-dressed children. Third, a beautiful suburban apartment. Later for the revolution. (Campbell 1984, 267)

Thus, according to Campbell, American gangs do not represent a revolutionary force in society that seeks political and economic change; they are reflections of America's materialism. Gang members seek material success, not a political overthrow of the government. Girl gang members also seek financial success. Unfortunately, they view the gang as the best route to this desired goal. This speaks volumes about the current economic-political state of affairs in American society.

Race is another critical variable in gang participation. As reported by the OJJDP (2001), the 1998 National Youth Gang Survey revealed that Hispanics were the predominant racial/ethnic group among all gang members nationwide. Forty-six percent of all gang members were Hispanic, 34 percent were African American, 12 percent were Caucasian, 6 percent were Asian, and 2 percent were some other category (e.g., Native American). The vast majority of female gangs are also either Hispanic or black. The primary reason cited by researchers for why minority females are more likely to join a gang than white girls is racism. "Kitchen's study in Fort Wayne, Indiana, revealed some strong feelings about race and racism. Her respondents had some very strong feelings about the society they lived in; expressing the belief that racism was fundamental. . . . Kitchen's study demonstrates the dual problems faced by African American women: racism and sexism. The world they inhabit does not afford many legitimate opportunities to succeed. It is a world filled with poverty on the one hand and the ready availability of drugs on the other hand" (Chesney-Lind and Shelden 2004, 71).

As discussed earlier in this chapter, Quicker's study (1983) of girl gangs was exclusively of Hispanics. He found that poverty, sexism, and racism were all common reasons that led girls to join a gang. The barrio represented a safe haven from the outside world, which the girls perceived as out to get them. A study of gang members in San Francisco found that nearly 80 percent of girl gang members were Latina (Lauderback, Hansen, and Waldorf 1992). Miller (2001, 93) studied gangs in Columbus and St. Louis and found that both class and race were important factors in gang participation. In St. Louis, with its high rate of poverty, 89 percent of the girl gang members were African American; the rest were other minorities. In Columbus, a city with a lower poverty level, 25 percent of the girl gang members were white. Joe and Chesney-Lind (1995) found that girl gang members in Hawaii were minority members, the majority of them being either Filipino or Samoan.

CRIMINAL ACTIVITIES

Like their male counterparts, female gang members spend a great deal of their time just hanging out. Nonetheless, girls who join gangs are delinquents by implication, and they are often criminal in behavior as well. Bjerregard and Smith (1993) reported that female gang members had a higher rate of delinquent offenses than did nongang females. Regoli and Hewitt (2003, 318–319) agreed, adding

> Gang girls are much more likely to be involved in delinquency, especially serious delinquency, than are nongang females. In general, gang girls commit fewer violent crimes than gang boys and are inclined to commit property crime and status offenses. And like males who join gangs, girls' involvement in crime increases with gang membership and tends to decline after leaving the gang. . . . Gang girls are much less likely to be victims of violence than are gang boys, although much more likely than nongang females.

The lower rates of violent victimization among female gang members are attributed to a number of factors beginning with the realization that males are reluctant to include females in violent clashes with rivals. Furthermore, the peripheral or auxiliary status of most female gang members reduces their chances of being targets of violence by rival gang members. Auxiliary female members will also be protected by male gang members against predatory males in the neighborhood (Regoli and Hewitt 2003).

As an example of female gang members being more likely to be involved in crime than non-gang girls, we can look at Rochester, New York. As reported by Moore and Hagedorn (2001), in Rochester, 66 percent of female gang members reported involvement in at least one serious delinquent act, compared with just 7 percent of nongang females. In the same study, it was also revealed that 82 percent of male gang members had committed at least one serious offense compared with 11 percent of nongang males. Growing evidence indicates that some female gang members are as violent as male gang members. For example, Fagan (1996) found that gang girls in Chicago, Los Angeles, and San Diego were heavily involved in serious violent offenses. In general, however, female gang members commit fewer violent crimes than male gang members, but girls are three times more likely than boys to be involved in property offenses and larceny (*Female Gangs* 2003). In short, female gang members may be involved with all the same types of criminal activities as males.

Crime

It was well established in Chapter 1 that very few girls, compared to boys, are arrested for juvenile crimes. Logic would also dictate that far fewer female gang members, compared to males, are arrested for criminal activities. As Hernandez (2012) states, "Female gang members commit fewer crimes and violence: Their incarcerations tend to be for drug use, larceny, petty theft, status offenses or domestic issues (e.g., fights with parents and runaway)." Information about girl gangs and their criminal activities generally comes from three major sources: law enforcement agency reports, surveys of at-risk youths, and field studies. Law enforcement reports are limited to actual arrest statistics available on female gang members. This information does reveal that female gang members in jails or prisons usually make up only approximately 5–10 percent of the total inmate population (*Female Gangs* 2003). (Contrast this to the dramatically increasing number of male gangsters found in jails and prisons.) Police reliance on arrest statistics is one of the leading contributors to the perceived underreporting of female gang membership, however. In many cases, female gangsters' involvement in crime is understated so as not to reflect the presence of female gangs. Some agencies "as a matter of policy" do not report female gang crimes as gang-related crimes. Furthermore, jurisdictions often differ in the labeling of offenses as "gang related" (Moore and Hagedorn 2001, 4).

Surveys of at-risk youths provide a much different perspective on female gang participation in criminal acts. The questionnaires ask youths about their involvement in a gang and whether, and how often, they have committed certain criminal offenses. But these surveys are anonymous, therefore making them difficult to verify. The statistics generated from these types of surveys generally indicate a higher rate of crime than do police agency reports.

Field studies provide the most in-depth analysis of gang life. "Many of these studies, however, do not raise the issue of criminality, and most are confined to one time and one place, making it difficult to generalize from findings" (Moore and Hagedorn 2001, 4). Additionally, the limited research on female gangs makes it difficult to come up with any reliable generalizations. It should be noted, however, that getting to interview female gangs is more difficult (for a variety of reasons, including lack of entry to the gang, the small number of female gangs, and the dominant nature of male gangs). All texts written on gangs rely heavily on field studies conducted by other researchers; this book is no different—although it does contain original research on gangs from a city generally neglected by field researchers.

Female gangsters may commit a variety of different offenses, ranging in severity from the mild (status offenses such as running away from home and truancy), the moderate (property offenses), to the extreme (assault, kidnapping, and murder). Although the amount and degree of criminal acts committed by female gang members vary from one gang to the next (some may not commit any crimes), the violence is disproportionate to that of nongang females. Furthermore, female gang members are more likely to engage in violent behaviors and be victims of violent crimes than nongang girls (Deschenes and Esbensen 2001).

Eghigian and Kirby (2006) found that girl gang members as young as 11 and 12 are skipping school, drinking, experimenting with drugs, and committing low-level crimes and engaging in sexual activity. By age 13 or 14, female gangsters are quite active in property crime, such as larceny/theft, motor theft and burglary, as well as weapons offenses and violent assault. Ages 15 through 18 represent the hard-core years of criminal activity for female gang members. Committing murder peaks at age 18. From the age of 19 and over, the female is likely to be pregnant or is a mother. She will need to take care of her baby. And as mentioned previously, this is the best way for a female to leave the gang. On the other hand, if she stays in the gang she will need to make money. For single-mother gang members, there are limited options in making money and most of them are illegal, including selling drugs, go in to prostituting, or committing other crimes such as burglary and robbery.

Among the specific crimes committed by girl gangs are theft, robbery, and acts of physical violence (fights, stabbings, assaults, mob action, drive-by shootings, and murder). These activities serve to generate money for the gang and to protect its turf. They are also perceived as methods of obtaining respect and initiating new members. In Miller's study (2001) of girl gangs in St. Louis and Columbus, he found that "when comparing male and female gang members, there were no significant differences in their levels of crime: girls were about as likely as boys to steal things, joyride in stolen cars, damage or destroy things, intimidate or threaten people, attack with the intent to seriously hurt them (62 percent of males and 55 percent of females participated in this offense), and sell drugs" (Chesney-Lind and Shelden 2004, 74). Sikes (2001) found that female gang members do not seek out violence; rather, it is an activity that is taken for granted and has become commonplace. Valdez's research puts into question Sikes's conclusion that females do not seek out violence. Valdez (2009b) found that 94 percent of female gang members under study admitted they had engaged in a physical fight; 68 percent said they got into fights in the neighborhood against rivals; and 84 percent admitted to getting into fights within the household. Sixty-four percent had also been in a fight in school (Valdez 2009b). In more than half (51%) of the fights, drugs and alcohol were involved. Twenty-three percent of the neighborhood fights involved the use of weapons. And, in 39 percent of the neighborhood fights the police responded. Fourteen percent of the school fights involving a female gang member involved a weapon. Like male gang members, female gang members report that they too get into fights because of jealousy. Female gang members may also get jealous over their boyfriend's ex-girlfriend(s) and start fights. Female gangsters may start fights if they feel like they are being disrespected. Arguments that form from disrespect are more likely to occur in public places, in front of an audience. Females like to fight in front of people, like males, to prove how tough they are and to show that they demand respect. When alcohol is involved, the chances of fights occurring increases (Valdez 2009b).

Sikes found that Los Angeles' female gang members equate money with power. Equating money with power follows Campbell's conclusion that gangs embrace capitalism, that they have internalized American culture. Unfortunately, they seek the desired goal of economic success by illegitimate means. Female gang members justify this behavior in a number of ways. (*Note*: These techniques will be discussed later in this chapter.)

There are times when male gang members use female gang members to "set up" rival gangs. In her research on female gangs in Los Angeles, San Antonio, and Milwaukee, Gini Sikes

(2001) was told repeatedly how the girls would seduce rival gang members in secluded areas so that the males could jump them and either beat or murder them. Female gang members might be required to have sex with rival gang members in order to gain information. Rival gang members usually realize that they are being set up because they do the same thing.

Female gang members are capable of committing murder, but their homicide rate is much lower compared with males. Less than 1 percent of the 1,072 gang-related homicides documented in Curry's study (1998) were committed by females. Research conducted by Loper and Cornell (1995) led to the revelation that "girls' homicides are more likely to grow out of an interpersonal dispute with the victim (79%), while homicides committed by boys are more likely to be crime related (57%); that is, occurring during the commission of another crime, such as robbery" (Chesney-Lind and Shelden 2004, 68). All evidence clearly indicates that female gang members do not commit a great number of homicides (Hagedorn 2009).

Kitchen (1995) found that gang girls do not want to participate in the conventional job market that most likely would relegate them to lower-paying, menial jobs. Instead, they see dollar signs flashing before their eyes when they consider selling drugs like crack on the street. He pointed out that females who sell drugs must be particularly aggressive and violent. The very nature of the underground drug market necessitates the willingness to fight, even with deadly force. Female gangs that sell drugs have to be tough enough to fight against males in order to protect their market. Laidler and Hunt (1997) suggested that female gang members must be tough because they are challenging the traditional gender roles, where even on the streets, toughness is measured by patriarchal norms. Many of the female gang members in Hawaii studied by Joe and Chesney-Lind (1995) had extensive arrest records, with about 25 percent having 10 or more arrests. "Their offenses were mostly property offenses, but many (about one-third of the girls) had been arrested for violent offenses. Not surprisingly, girls were about equally likely to have committed status offenses as any other type of offense" (Chesney-Lind and Shelden 2004, 77).

In research conducted by Miller and Decker, 85 percent of the girls reported having hit someone with the idea of hurting them. In a study conducted by Finn-Aage Esbensen and his colleagues, 39 percent of gang girls revealed that they attacked someone with a weapon; 78 percent had been involved in gang fights; 65 percent had carried weapons; and 21 percent said that they had shot someone (Regoli and Hewitt 2003, 319). Gearty and Hutchinson (2001) conducted field research on the Bloodettes, a female auxiliary to the Bloods in New York. They found the Bloodettes to be "as criminally cunning and ruthless as the Bloods." The Bloodettes were used by the Bloods as a source of income for the gang. The girls would dupe nongang citizens by obtaining credit cards and/or credit card information in order to conduct such crimes as credit card fraud and identity theft schemes. The Bloodettes are also accused of a number of violent offenses, including the 2000 pipe beating of a woman in the Bronx. Leon Bing, author of *Do or Die*, a book written about the rival Los Angeles gangs, the Bloods and the Crips, conducted research on female gang members in Los Angeles. Some of his research was made available in his *Rolling Stone* article "Homegirls" (2001). In this article, Bing recounts his interview with Claudia, a former Crip member who retired after being blinded in a shotgun attack. Claudia was living with her mother and two children—Nelson, 13, and Kaleesha, 10—who were already getting in trouble at school for fighting and hanging out with known gang members. Bing described how, in the hard-core gang areas of Los Angeles, Watts, Compton, Inglewood, and Baldwin Hills ("the jungle"), school girls with gang affiliation spell out their allegiance to a Blood or Crip set in fancy block lettering on their denim notebooks. These girls were ready to fight any other girl who professed loyalty to a rival set, and this was just the beginning of the violent and criminal activities that Los Angeles gang girls engage in. Female gang members carry weapons for the males and might drive a car for a drive-by shooting. There are some females quite skilled in fighting whom gangsters refer to as "gangsta-lettes" or "riders"—an expression of respect used to describe females with fierce fighting skills (Bing 2001a). In general, male gang members look at their female counterparts as trophies, conveniences, or troublemakers. Bing recalls one of the longest-standing (and lethal) internecine battles between two Crip sets that was started on a schoolyard when a girl, Kaleesha, broke up with one boy to go out with a kid from another neighborhood. "They're living in an environment where they know things are certain way, and they do what they have to do to survive. Things happen to them in their environment: There are one or two shootings in South Central every day, and they're trying to deal with pregnancies and raising their kids and just trying to survive as females" (Bing 2001b, 80). In this environment, Kaleesha became another victim of gang-related homicides in Watts, as she was shot and killed while sitting on the front porch of her mother's house (Bing 2001b).

Bing conducted interviews with a number of female gang members, and it is clear that they were actively involved in violent criminal offenses. They robbed and beat people up. And when one of their members is killed, they seek out their own revenge instead of having their homeboys take care of it. They participated in drive-by shootings and face-to-face murders. In these neighborhoods of Los Angeles, despair is commonplace. The lack of high-paying, low-skill jobs limits the opportunities of gang members, who are generally poorly educated. This is especially true for inner-city minority females. One interviewee stated:

> I'm a black female gangbanger. No education, no trade, no experience with anything except gangbanging. I can't tell you how to work no computer. I can't make up no payroll. I can tell you how to load a gun and shoot it, how to sag yo' pants and tie yo' blue rag. I thought about getting a GED, but in the situation I am—single, young, black and the mother of two kids—I don't have time to go back to school. I got some welfare, and I'm tryin' to find work. (Bing 2001b, 85)

This quote reflects a general feeling shared by many females in the inner city. Economic hopelessness leads many people to the underground market, where street-smarts are the valued job attributes. Among the most financially attractive underground economic opportunities believed to lead to riches is drug-trafficking.

Drugs

Many female gangs are involved with drugs for both recreational purposes and profit via drug-trafficking. Drug violations are among the most common offenses committed by female gang members along with violent offenses. Females may sell drugs to raise enough money so that they can "party," or they may sell drugs for profit. "Most female dealers are working for someone else, although there are a few powerful female career dealers" (Moore and Hagedorn 2001, 5). A study conducted by Moore and Mata in the 1980s found that nearly 20 percent of all Mexican-American female gang members dealt heroin at some point during their time with the gang. Within any gang, the younger members are generally the ones sent out to sell drugs for the higher-ranking gang leaders. Some male gangs have girls sell drugs for them as well. Many female gang members begin to sell drugs when their husbands (or boyfriends) go to prison because they need the money to support themselves and their families.

Moore (1991) described in detail the common occurrence of drug use in the families of the gang members she interviewed. Heroin was always the drug of choice for these cholo gang members, even during the crack cocaine "epidemic" of the late 1980s. Moore referred to this phenomenon as the **tecato lifestyle**. (A **tecato** is a term for heroin addict.) Moore stated that very few of the women in the earlier cliques (1950s and 1960s) used heroin; in fact, most of the gang members did not use heroin until they joined the gang. Mere membership in the gang meant that the label *tecato* would be placed on all gang members whether they used heroin or not. Moore found that female gang members who used heroin were likely to have come from a family where heroin was used in the house. In contrast, Lauderback and associates (1992) found that drug use among girl gang members in San Francisco was nearly as common as among male members, with marijuana being the most popular among the females.

A study of African-American and Latina female gang members in Milwaukee during the 1990s found that approximately 50 percent of the female gangsters dealt drugs, especially cocaine (Moore and Hagedorn 2001). There was a significant difference between these two racial groups, as 72 percent of the Latina females sold drugs compared to just 31 percent of black female gang members. As a rule, males were found to be more heavily involved in the sale of drugs than females. In 1993, Taylor conducted an extensive study of female drug offenders, focusing on Detroit's corporate gangs—gangs designed for profit (Moore and Hagedorn 2001). He concluded that female gangbangers became involved with the drug trade in the early 1990s and predicted that the role of females in drug-trafficking would increase as a result of decreased economic opportunities. Miller (2001) found that girls sold drugs in both St. Louis and Columbus, although to a higher degree in St. Louis. The girls reported that "most of the proceeds of drug selling were used to 'party.' " Also, the drug selling was sporadic rather than a daily event. Kitchen (1995) found that female gang members sold crack cocaine because it was such a profitable business enterprise. Selling crack cocaine is not only lucrative, it is dangerous. The girls that sell rock must be willing to act aggressively and violently to protect their stash and money, let alone their very lives. In their study of San Francisco gangs, Lauderback and associates (1992) found that the girls had an easier time selling drugs than their male counterparts because they generally did not wear their gang colors and were therefore less likely to be harassed by the police. Crack cocaine sales were handled differently. "Most of their crack sales are conducted in rock houses. These houses are usually a neighbor's residence that is rented in exchange for drugs" (Chesney-Lind and Shelden 2004, 77).

Female gangsters generally face the world with a sense of hopelessness. They do not want to be poor and suffer through a life of misery. Lacking the necessary education and job skills needed to advance in the current socioeconomic system, these girls have learned to justify their violent and criminal behaviors through such techniques as neutralization and an overall lack of a guilty conscience. Sykes and Matza's analysis of neutralization was discussed in Chapter 3, but we will now briefly discuss neutralization techniques among female gangsters.

Denial of responsibility is a common neutralization technique used by gang members and nongang members alike. It is the most common response heard from the guilty—"I didn't do it!" Female gang members will often deny their involvement in criminal activities. *Denial of injury* is a common defense for property crime and vandalism. Gang members believe that "marking" their territory is an acceptable form of behavior—it meets the standards of their norms. *Denial of a victim* is common among females who get into fights with other girls over boys. Fighting a rival is deemed appropriate behavior, especially if one can claim that she was the original victim. *Condemnation of the condemners* is similar to the tactic of the best defense being a good offense. Rather than take the defensive approach of proving one's innocence, some gang members attempt to turn the tables on their accusers by claiming they were beaten by the police or that the police planted drugs on them. Female gang members can accuse male police officers of inappropriate sexual contact. *Appeal to higher loyalties* is an essential technique of neutralization for female gang members. The higher loyalty can be to both the gang and the family that she has created with a male gang member. The mother status is highly respected by gang members.

As with many criminals, female gang members may not feel the need for any neutralization technique because they lack a guilty conscience. As we have seen, female gang members are capable of committing a wide range of criminal offenses, and they may not feel any guilt about them. For female gang members, this lack of conscience developed within the gang subcultural context. If someone honestly doesn't believe that she is guilty of committing a crime or violating a societal norm, she will not feel remorse for such behavior. Furthermore, some theories (see Chapter 3) suggest criminals are born as "bad seeds" and therefore are incapable, or unwilling, to feel remorse for criminal activities.

Violating the laws of society may lead to incarceration. Believe it or not, incarceration may be the best thing to happen to a gang girl. She is less likely to die in prison than she is on the streets. In addition, female prisons are not as dominated by gangs as male prisons are. Once a female gang member is incarcerated, she is generally forgotten by the rest of her gang as they move on with business as usual. While in prison, the female gang member speaks of leaving the gang forever, although departure seldom occurs. When a female gang member is released from prison, she generally returns to the old neighborhood and resumes friendships with old acquaintances that draw her back into the gang lifestyle. Frustrated by the lack of legitimate job opportunities for ex-inmate female gang members, the lure of the gang becomes even stronger.

RELATIONSHIPS WITH MALES AND SCHOOL

The relationship that female gang members have with their male counterparts varies a great deal from gang to gang. As for their school experiences, nearly all girl gang members had experienced a number of problems while they attended school.

Relationships with Males

As we have said, females and males appear to join gangs for similar reasons: respect, a sense of belonging, family, identity, protection, economic success, and for thrills and excitement. There are, however, several differences between male and female gang members. First, females tend to drop out of the gang at an earlier age than males, mostly because of pregnancy. "Females leave gangs at the end of their teens, as opposed to less than 25 percent of men in male gangs. The reasons why females left varied: most of them said they grew out of gangs; others said that their parents left the neighborhood, ending their membership. Two-thirds of the women became teen mothers and more than 90 percent were mothers before their mid-twenties" (Tonry and Moore 1998, 388). It is not surprising that girls in gangs get pregnant at an early age, as females who are involved in a gang tend to become involved in sexual activity at a much earlier age than girls not in a gang. This is attributed to the fact that gang involvement is a risky behavior and girls attracted to gang life are attracted to other risky behaviors such as having sex earlier and more frequently than nongang girls. Compared to national rates, females in gangs have a higher number of sexual partners and births than nongang females (Valdez 2009a). Once in a gang, females also tend to change their perception of self. They do not view themselves as candidates for a traditional, stable marriage; as a good partner for a conventional husband; finishing school; let alone going to college, or going to church and being thought of as a "good" woman (Giordano 1978). Then again, this introduces the concept of the self-fulfilling prophecy, as the females who join a gang generally do so because they view the gang as a refuge from their home lives which was far from the idealized middle-class family life that most people are taught to strive and attain (Nurge 2003).

Another difference between female and male gang members is the fact that generally women are less violent than men. Males often use guns; women are more likely to engage in fist fights and use knives. And although males and females are equally affected by the economic shift (and the loss of high-paying factory jobs), women were affected far more severely by cuts in welfare than were men. "In 1990, welfare reforms were introduced that reduced or eliminated welfare payments. Because female gang members often face significant barriers to legitimate employment, it is unclear what they will do to replace welfare support" (Moore and Hagedorn 2001, 3). It appears that many female gangsters have decided to sell drugs and engage in more violent criminal activities as their response to welfare reform.

As mentioned several times earlier in this chapter, historically, female gangs have been auxiliary to males. The very term *auxiliary* implies a secondary role and is defined in terms of "providing help" and "functioning in a subsidiary capacity." Furthermore, when considering the fact that most males report that they prefer their girlfriends not to be in a gang, it is easy to understand why, for the most part, female gang members are not well respected by males. For example, Fishman (1995) described how the Vice Kings reported that their primary relationship with the Vice Queens was sexual. The Queens were expected to have sex with the Kings. The girls interviewed by Laidler and Hunt (1997) reported that their boyfriends were "possessive, controlling, and often violent." All of the male gang members that Totten (2001, 163) interviewed admitted that they committed some form of abuse against their girlfriends, with many admitting that they used sexual force. The "sexing in" initiation practice highlights the subordinate role that women play to men in the gang world.

Thus, just as is sometimes found in the general society, female gang members find themselves victims of sexism. Males do not deny their sexist position and often report that they consider female gang members as "possessions" (Moore and Hagedorn 2001). Sometimes, females are treated as sex objects within the gang. Traditionally, gangs have used their female counterparts: "Girls were useful to them because the police were less suspicious of them. Girls could stand on street corners and serve as decoys while boys committed robberies. Girls could hold weapons or drugs in their clothes, knowing the police would be less likely to frisk them. Gang members often treated girls like guns or knives, passed along from member to member" (Goldentyer 1994, 52). In some cases, females themselves affirm their secondary status to male gangs when they take feminized versions of their names. However, as noted earlier, there are currently more female gangs existing independently of male gangs and that are autonomous, as well as being allied with a male gang. Moore's study (1991) of Mexican-American gangs in Los Angeles found that two-thirds of women, both older and younger, denied being treated like a possession. However, "more of the men—especially the younger men—agreed that the boys treated the girls like possessions (41 percent of the older men and 56 percent of the younger men, reflecting the increase). Among those who denied such sexism, the keynote was that the gang was like a family" (Moore 1991, 53). In a study of Mexican-American gangs in San Antonio, Egley, Maxson, Miller, and Klein (2006) found that male gang members often looked at female gangsters as "possession" and inferior, and as a result, they treated the girls as sex objects. However, two-thirds of the female gang members denied they were treated like possessions. These females said that they were respected because so few girls and women were allowed into the gang in the first place. What seems to be the case is males exaggerate about the control they have over female gang members. Nonetheless, there are many cases of sexual exploitation by males over the females (Egley et al. 2006).

Many females, especially minority women, claim that they are not respected in the legitimate job market and believe that, despite the sexism found within the gang world, they have a better chance of survival in the underground market. "Sexism was a topic that Kitchen explored with her respondents. Women (especially African-American women) do not appear to get much respect within the legitimate business world, but in the informal economy of drug dealing, they command respect as long as they are tough and do not sell themselves" (Chesney-Lind and Shelden 2004, 86). Girls who sell themselves for drugs or money are not respected. The girls are aware of this double standard and told Kitchen that it is easier for a male to get respect because all he has to do is beat someone up, commit a crime, or have sex with lots of women. Female gang members will not be respected if they have a lot of sex (Kitchen 1995). "These types of roles tend to suggest a no-win situation for gang girls. As Sex Objects they are cheap women rejected by other girls, parents, social workers, and ironically often by the boys themselves. As Tomboys, they are resented by boys and ridiculed by family and friends who wait patiently for them to grow out of it (Campbell 1987).

Sex comes into play in other ways as well. Gang members may rape the girlfriends of rival gang members as a form of intimidation or retaliation. Equally disturbing, if a female gang member breaks up with her boyfriend, the male may instruct members of his crew to sexually violate her. Thus, rape is a big part of a female gang member's life. She may have been raped by her male gang counterparts as part of her initiation, she may be set up as a decoy by trading her body for information from rivals, she may be raped by rival gang members, and she may become victimized by her own boyfriend and gang affiliation. Many studies of female gangs reveal that girls admit to being raped by gang members, family members, or boyfriends. Female gang members will not report these heinous crimes to authorities because they know that they risk death (Sikes 2001). Often, female gang members who are victims of rape do not even receive sympathy from the rest of the girls in the gang. They blame the victim and believe that she should have defended herself better. Female gang members particularly loathe women who "cry rape" (those not really raped but falsely accuse someone of rape) (Sikes 2001).

Like most males, gang members want to have sex with females and they want it often. As a result, male gang members often report seeing their female counterparts as distractions. If they are trying to hook up with the girls, their minds are not paying attention to business and survival. The males also acknowledge that females can break the bonds between male members. Male gang members believe that females are demanding of their time and attention, which further takes away time from the group. Gangs generally discourage a deep interest in a specific female for all these reasons. Males are supposed to be interested in hooking up with females, but they are never to get too invested in one specific woman. When a girl joins a gang she is viewed as a gang member, but when she develops into a young woman she is no longer viewed as "one of the boys" and this is when "problems" arise (Hagedorn 2007).

There are still other issues related to sex for the female gang member. For instance, they assume that their boyfriends will cheat on them. The girls place all the responsibility for these types of occurrences on the other girls rather than on their boyfriends. The 1993 film *Mi Vida Loca*, a story about two young Mexican-American female gang members from Echo Park, Los Angeles, named Sad Girl and Mousie, describes the drama between two friends when one (Sad Girl) gets pregnant by the other girl's boyfriend, Ernesto (See "Connecting Street Gangs and Popular Culture" Box 7.2). The two blame each other instead of Ernesto and become enemies. Mousie considers killing Sad Girl but in the end they bond over mutual socioeconomic realities, including the fact that Ernesto also got Mousie pregnant and now they are both single mothers. The gang girls interviewed by Sikes (2001) stated that they believed that it was up to them to keep their boyfriends happy. They believed that if they flaunted themselves in front of guys, guys would respond. And if that guy already had a girlfriend, she would have to fight to keep him. This low expectation of men was obviously learned—most likely in the home and especially in single-parent households. And although the threat of HIV/AIDS has been around for decades now, gang girls run a relatively high risk of acquiring this disease (along with other sexually transmitted diseases), considering the likelihood of rape, promiscuity, and drug and alcohol use. The risk is high primarily because the males engaging in sexual behavior with gang women generally do not use contraceptives.

Moore (1991) also described how girls who are raped by male gang members are in a bad position because if they complain to the police they are labeled a "rat" or "snitch" and also their own homegirls will not support them against the accused rapist. So seemingly, the males have all the power in the gang. But once again, just as often occurs in general society, the female is capable of manipulating males to behave in the manner they wish. Intergang dating is a leading cause of fights among the gangs that Moore studied. This common occurrence led to many wars between rival gangs. Female gang members can also be successful in convincing males not to fight rival gang members. However, while in the gang, both males and females prefer dating gang members rather than nongang members ("squares" or conventional people). Those lucky few who get out of a gang generally prefer to date nongang members, but people who are not too "square." They prefer those labeled "hip-square" (street-smart, but not gangbanging).

In Gini Sikes' study of the Lennox-13 El Salvadorian female gang in Los Angeles, she found that the relationship between boys and girls varied over time. "The level of girls' involvement in the Lennox cliques went in cycles over the years. At times the boys' gangs welcomed girls, at other times they pushed them aside, denigrating them as whores, bitches, snitches, and spies. Girls frequently found themselves in a catch-22: male leaders would order the prettiest to infiltrate an enemy party to set up or lure a rival—at high risk to herself—only to resent her and all females for making men vulnerable" (Sikes 2001, 244). The male gang members also had an interesting viewpoint toward lesbians:

> Many male gang members welcomed lesbians in their ranks with an acceptance that extended beyond anything I'd witnessed in mainstream society. Though at first this surprised me, in time it made sense. Both boys and girls in gangs prize aggressive masculinity above nearly any other trait. Extremely butch homosexual women win respect precisely because they appear almost indistinguishable from men, favoring the same clothes, right down to their boxer shorts. They stay active far later in life than straight women because usually they do not have kids. (Sikes 2001, 248)

Since masculine attributes are the most highly valued in the gang, terms like *bitch*, *girl*, or *faggot* are considered the worst insults that one can sling at a man (Sikes 2001).

Thus, the feminine role in gangs is complicated. "Although some feminine girls secure a role beyond that of seductive informer or spy—I have encountered petite, frail girls who could reduce many men to a pulp, their seemingly innocent faces an effective surprise weapon— inevitably their biology holds them back. Sooner or later, most become pregnant and in Latino gangs a woman on the street who has children at home is an object of scorn" (Sikes 2001, 248). Ultimately, girls, like boys, seek respect, and they fight hard to keep it. Fighting is something that the Lennox-13 gang is good at; after all, "their native country's civil war prepared them well for the streets of LA" (Sikes 2001, 250).

Relationships with the Schools

It is common for gang members to have had problems with schoolwork. They are classic underachievers and generally lack the stable family environment that would support academic pursuits. Youngsters who enter school unprepared (lacking basic skills) risk falling behind at an early age and being placed in "special" classes—and consequently, they run the risk of negative labeling. Students who do not have family members, primarily parents, to help them with their daily homework fall even further behind. Eventually, the child becomes frustrated and loses interest in schoolwork. If the child is from a gang neighborhood, the disinterest in academic knowledge is often replaced by a thirst for a street education. In short, problems with school are a high risk factor for turning to gangs. Furthermore, as researchers like Joan Moore have indicated, many individuals join a gang because the gang has a presence in the school. Thus, the school itself is a risk factor for turning to gangs.

Minority children often believe that they are victimized in school because of their race or ethnicity. Some of the gang members in Moore's study revealed how they discovered their "Mexican-ness" while in school: White kids generally brought sandwiches with them to school for lunch; Mexicans brought tacos. And as Mexican-Americans, these kids struggled with their English skills, which also hurt them in their pursuit of academic knowledge. Moore cautioned, however, against reading too much into the school experience as a factor for ethnic minorities turning to gangs. "It is easy to make too much of such identity confusion. It was undoubtedly shared by other youngsters in the barrios: these gang members were by no means unusually Mexican for their times" (Moore 1991, 85).

Felix Padilla also examined the role of the school environment as a factor for youths joining gangs. Many of the "Diamonds" reported to him that they were routinely negatively labeled by teachers, especially in elementary school. In essence, the early seed of future ganghood was planted for these youths in elementary school. Padilla (1992, 69) blamed the teachers and staff for the negative feelings experienced by the Diamonds in school, stating that they "refused to understand and respect their cultural and socioeconomic class background." Padilla also pointed out the influence of the self-fulfilling prophecy. These youths were told repeatedly by their teachers that they were no good. Over time, these youngsters began to internalize these negative labels and also started to act like deviants (by getting into fights, not doing their homework, etc.); thus, they turned out to be deviants.

Negative feelings toward school experiences are generally a more important contributing cause of joining a gang for males than for females. Girls have an easier time in school, for they are less likely to receive the negative labels of "deviant" and "troublemaker" than are boys. Even so, many minority females become equally disenchanted by the whole school experience. "Many have noted that school is often deemed irrelevant to the lives of gang members and presents a motivation to drop out and become part of a gang" (Chesney-Lind and Shelden 2004, 94). Davis (1999, 257) reported that gang girls considered school as "a road that leads to nowhere." Harris (1997) found that none of the chola gang girls in her study graduated from high school. In his study of the Vice Queens in Chicago, Fishman (1995) reported that most of the gang members attended school only occasionally, eventually just dropping out. Kitchen (1995) found that even though 70 percent of the gang members he interviewed had graduated from high school, most of them felt unprepared to compete in conventional society. They felt that the teachers did not care about them and that, in general, school was a waste of time.

Considering that most gang members are likely to drop out of school by the 10th grade, one has to wonder if teachers' predictions of such behavior by certain children are not warranted. After all, risk factors are easy to identify as early as elementary school. The key, then, is to find some way to keep these youths interested in school. Interest in school begins with individual motivation and responsibility, followed by a supportive family, qualified teachers, and proper funding of all schools.

GANG FAMILIES

Ideally, a family is a social institution that provides a nurturing and safe, loving environment in which children are raised. Unfortunately, this is not always the case. Many children are brought into the world by people who are unwilling or unprepared to raise them properly. Currently, the family social structure appears to be in peril. At the very least, it is changing dramatically, and some of these changes have led to negative consequences. For example, broken homes and single-parent families are a leading contributor to the increased numbers of gang members (although, certainly there is not a cause-and-effect relationship). Some point to the existence of female gangs as further evidence of the decline of the family. "Young women's involvement in gangs is disquieting precisely because females in gangs are perceived to be outside the traditional arena of family control. More specifically, female gang participation generates alarm because it signifies, yet again, fears about the decline of the 'traditional family' " (Hunt et al. 2004, 49). If the family cannot fulfill its traditional role as an ideal socializing and control agent, and females, along with males, feel the need to join a gang to gain a substitute family, then the family as an institution is indeed in turmoil.

The Dysfunctional Home Family

Hunt and associates (2004) believe that "normal" girls do not become involved in gangs and that therefore the reasons certain young females join a gang must lie within deeply troubled families. "Accordingly, the female gang member is viewed within the larger framework of family disintegration and violence. From this viewpoint, aggression and violence in the family are regarded, by definition, as dysfunctional and deviant forms of family disintegration. Consequently, young gang women adopt a lifestyle of violence only as a result of an early and damaging experience, and in compensation for such an experience" (Hunt et al. 2004, 50). The gang, then, provides for the troubled girl a substitute family that is more nurturing than the one in which she was raised.

As a general rule, females who turn to gangs have either been victimized at home or witnessed victimization and abusive relationships at home. These girls may have experienced verbal, sexual, and/or physical abuse. "Females most at risk for gang involvement come from homes in crisis" (Chesney-Lind and Shelden 2004, 90). The majority of the girls interviewed by Totten (2001) indicated that they saw their mothers being abused by both their biological fathers and by "social father-figures" (stepfathers, boyfriends). One common form of abuse suffered by girls who turn to gangs is incest. Moore (1991) found that 29 percent of the female gang members she interviewed reported that some member of the family had raped them. She speculated that more gang girls had actually been victims of rape than reported it. Moore (1991, 96) described how incest is fairly common in traditional Mexican families because of their patriarchal design.

> Fathers of incest victims were more likely to beat their wives, and they were more likely to be strict with and depreciatory of their daughters. Incest victims were also more likely to see their fathers as alcoholics, but they were not significantly more likely to feel that their fathers were trying to set themselves up unequivocally as heads of the household or to control their mothers' visitors—other indicators of patriarchy. In most cases the assailant was the father, but uncles, brothers, and grandfathers were among the culprits. And the

experiences occurred at all ages, ranging from 5 to 17, with a median age of about 11½. In about 40 percent of the cases, only one approach was made, but the remainder reported repeated sexual encounters.

Alcohol and heroin abuse were additional problems found in the homes of the gang members interviewed by Moore. These and other drugs are commonly abused in the families of girl gang members.

Research conducted by Joe and Chesney-Lind (1995) found that the majority of both girls and boys lived with both parents, but most of them (55% of the boys and 62% of the girls) reported being physically abused. A significant difference was that 62 percent of the girls indicated that they had been sexually abused or sexually assaulted (Chesney-Lind and Shelden 2004, 92). Flowers (1995, 181) stated, "Girls join gangs for all the things their families haven't given them: devotion, support, acceptance and love." The gang becomes a refuge for young women who have been victimized at home. These abused girls run away from home and join a gang in order to obtain protection from abusive families. He further explained that joining a gang can be an assertion of independence not only from family, but also from cultural and class constraints. The gang may provide them with a sense of meaning and identity, a place that they can call "home." In summary, the females most likely to join a gang are those who witness physical violence between adults in the family, were abused by a family member, lived in a house with alcohol and drug abuse, whose family had multiple problems (violence, criminality, a family member in jail), and had a family member already in the gang (Miller 2001).

It should be mentioned that some gang members retain a relatively solid relationship with their family members. The families disapprove of their activity but nonetheless still accept them as family members. Geoffrey Hunt and associates (2004, 67) offer this conclusion about the relationship between gang females and their families:

> In our analysis we have tried to illuminate the relationship and meaning of family among homegirls. In doing so, we have tried to dispel popular conceptions about the disintegration of contemporary inner-city families of color, and about the pushing of young minority youths onto the streets. Family relationships, particularly homegirls' ties to mothers, sisters, grandmothers, and other extended kin, are based on reciprocal and mutual forms of emotional and practical support. Not surprisingly, we have found . . . that although homegirls make a heavy investment of time in gang friendships, related activities, and loyalty to the gang, almost all of the women named family members as the most important people or role models in their lives.

Hunt and associates found that many of the other women (outside of the gang) homegirls admired were from their immediate or extended families. Then again, in many instances, homegirls' blood sisters, female cousins, and aunts are part of a gang. Familial and gang loyalties combined are bonds that are difficult to overcome. And in some cases, the homegirls managed to find a way to keep their blood and gang ties strong while raising the next generation in less than ideal social environments. This conclusion raises an interesting question: Is the gang a "legitimate" form of family? As more and more gang women have children and raise them in a gang environment, the gang may in fact take on the role of an extended family, which is quite common in many cultures according to the concept of "it takes a village to raise a child." What if a village consists entirely of gangbangers?

Pregnancy and Starting One's Own Family

Nearly all female gang members eventually get pregnant, something that is, of course, similar to the majority of women in the general population. These children are almost always fathered by male gang members, who typically do not take responsibility for them. The struggle and burden of raising gang children is generally left to the mother. Sometimes she can depend on her extended family. "The Latino cultural emphasis on extended family may play an important role in the support system for these gang members as they negotiate womanhood in a patriarchal environment at home and on the street. Scholars have shown that African American families develop strong real and fictive kinship networks for both emotional and practical support" (Hunt et al. 2004, 52). The gang becomes an extended kinship system that can assist in the raising of the next generation.

There are some advantages to pregnancy. The female may now gain a new status and sense of purpose. "A large part of her identity is provided by the baby under her care and guidance, and for many street-oriented girls there is no quicker way to grow up. Becoming a mother can be a strong play for authority, maturity, and respect, but it is also a shortsighted and naïve gamble because the girl often fails to realize that her life will be suddenly burdened and her choices significantly limited" (Anderson 1999, 148). The gang girl who is now a mother must try to break the cycle of ganghood, or her child will face the same negative environment growing up that she did.

When the gang woman has her baby, she realizes that the father is not likely to stick around. Generally, she would prefer to have a family man in her life who would help raise the child. "Aware of many abandoned young mothers, many a girl fervently hopes that her man is the one who will be different. In addition, her peer group supports her pursuit of the dream, implicitly upholding her belief in the young man's good faith. When a girl does become engaged to be married, there is much excitement, with relatives and friends oohing and ahhing over their prospective life. But seldom does this happen, because for the immediate future, the boy is generally not interested in 'playing house,' as his peers derisively refer to domestic life" (Anderson 1999, 152). The boy does not want to be labeled a "square." His male counterparts try to convince him that he was tricked into getting married because his girlfriend got pregnant on purpose. "Up to the point of pregnancy, given the norms of his peer groups, the young man could simply be said to be messing around. Pregnancy suddenly introduces an element of reality into the relationship. Life-altering events have occurred, and the situation is usually perceived as serious" (Anderson 1999, 156).

Even when the father sticks around and starts a family, it is common for him to rejoin gang activities whenever he gets bored hanging around the house. Lauderback et al. (1992) found in their study of girl gang members that the gang fathers almost never got involved in the lives of the children. Obviously, gangbanging activity is not conducive to a fully functioning family. The father/husband maintains his relationship with the gang for many reasons. His loyalty is often stronger to the gang than to his wife and child and the gang may not allow him to leave. "Hanging out with the gang led to problems for the family, because the gang remained of central importance to the man, even more than the marriage. Also, when there were problems in the marriage, the gang became a convenient escape" (Chesney-Lind and Shelden 2004, 92). It has become increasingly common for women to maintain their allegiance to the gang as well. But when both the mother and father are actively gangbanging, the family and marriage are in big trouble. In short, gang marriages do not last.

Summary

Women have been involved in criminal activity for nearly as long as men, only never to the same extent. This is also true with gangs, as there have been documented cases of female gang members fighting alongside of males for as long as there have been male gangs. The total number of female gang members, however, pales in comparison to that of males. There is conflicting research as to exactly how many female gangs exist in total, but there seems to be a general consensus that approximately 10 percent of all gang members are females. Most female gang members either belong to an auxiliary gang or are coed. There are very few independent female gangs but their numbers are slowing increasing. Female gang members are very capable of committing violent criminal acts but not in the same proportion as male gang members.

Female gang members join gangs for the same reasons as males, the primary ones being to seek refuge, economic success, a substitute family, and respect. Initiation into a gang is a key element in the distinction between male and female recruits as it is common for girls to be "sexed" into a gang. The sexed-in ritual is demeaning enough for girls but it also sets the tone for them being viewed as sex objects and less than full equals. That so many female gang members come from abusive homes in the first place adds to this cruel twist of irony. Girl gang members join the gang at an earlier age than boys but are also more likely to leave the gang earlier than their male counterparts. Like male gang members, female gang members have a difficult time in school and drop out at an early age. Lacking the basic high school education more or less places their futures in socioeconomic peril.

Over the years, research on female gangs has been increasing, but much more is needed in order to gain a greater understanding of this social phenomenon. The single fact that so many female gang members come from abusive and sexually exploitive environments is a strong reason for considering female gang membership a serious social problem. Most female gang members have children, and since the fathers generally refuse to take on family responsibility, the fiscal burden is often shifted onto society in the form of welfare programs. As gang children age, they inevitably become active in gangbanging themselves. Thus, another generation of gang members is guaranteed and their numbers will continue to increase.

8

Criminal Activities of Street Gangs

American street gang members spend the greater part of their time engaged in "normal" activities, such as sleeping, eating, and hanging out. In this regard, gang members are not so different from most people. They play ball, go to movies and ballgames, hang out with their friends, play video games, date, become parents, and so on. If their behavior was restricted to these activities, society would not have to worry about street gangs. However, as we all know, gang members do participate in criminal activities and these are the actions that concern society in general, gang victims, and especially law enforcement officers. The amount of time gang members spend on committing criminal acts is not important. What is important is the fact that gang members *are* involved in a large number of serious delinquent and criminal acts. Gang members are responsible for greater levels of crime and violence than nongang members, and gang-related delinquency is far more violent than nongang-related delinquency.

The type of criminal activities committed by gang members varies from gang to gang; some are involved in a "buffet-style" pattern of offenses, and others are engaged in acts of violence or the sale and distribution of drugs. Generally, gangs are involved in four major categories of **criminal activities**: violent offenses; property crimes; the use, sale, distribution, and trafficking of drugs; and nontraditional (for street gangs) and white-collar crime. Often, all of these criminal activities are intertwined. Violence and drug-trafficking go hand in hand with contemporary street gangs, and in the past, violence and drug use, including alcohol, were synonymous with gangs. In fact, drinking is most likely the second-most popular activity among all gang members (hanging out would be number one) (Fagan 2004). Even the pursuit of "legitimate" activities such as partying may entail criminal action. After all, *partying* implies using recreational drugs, which are illegal, and drinking alcohol (which includes many underaged persons). Drugs and alcohol cost money, and since most gang members do not have high-paying legitimate jobs, they will have to commit some type of crime to raise the money necessary to party. Robberies are a common way to cover the costs. Some gang members sell drugs so that they have enough money to party. Other gangs, of course, are responsible for a great deal of drug sales that, in essence, allow other people with the means to party.

CRIME AND PUNISHMENT

Historically, gangs have formed to ensure the basic survival of their members and to protect their neighborhoods from outsiders who intended to cause harm to local residents. Gangs have also always been known for their criminal activities and their high degree of violent behavior. Much has changed over the course of the past two centuries as street gangs are less concerned about an ideal of protecting their neighborhood from outside threats than they are about protecting their drug marketplaces. The profitability involved in the sale of drugs has led to increased levels of violence and overall criminal activity. **Crime** can be defined as any deviant behavior, or omission (failure to act when called upon to do so either by law or by law enforcement representatives), that violates a law of the land. Crime contains two aspects: an *act* (or, again, the failure to act when the law requires it) and *criminal intent* (in legal terminology, *mens rea*, or "guilty mind"). Intent varies by degree, ranging from willful conduct at one extreme to negligence (meaning that the criminal act was not deliberate) at the other. Prosecutors consider the degree of intent in determining whether, for example, to charge someone with first-degree murder, second-degree murder, negligent manslaughter, or justifiable homicide (e.g., self-defense). As Table 8.1 indicates, there is a great deal of violent and property crime committed in the United States. Murder, forcible rape, robbery, and aggravated assaults are categorized as examples of violent crime, and burglary, larceny-theft, and motor vehicle theft are examples of property crime. There is a violent crime committed every 23.9 seconds and a property crime committed every 3.4 seconds in the United States (U.S. Department of Justice 2010). It's a little frightening to think of the number of violent and property crimes that were committed while you were in class today, isn't it? And street gangs are involved in far more criminal activities than violent and property crimes. They are also heavily involved in the use, sale, distribution, and trafficking of drugs, and they are involved in nontraditional gang crimes and organized crime.

The statistics shown in Table 8.1 come from Uniform Crime Report (UCR) data provided by the U.S. Department of Justice. The department notes that the statistics are the result of total crimes committed in 2009 and that crime is not fixed to time intervals.

TABLE 8.1 Frequency of Select Violent and Property Crimes Committed in the United States (in 2009)	
Type of Crime	**Frequency**
Violent crime	
Murder	One every 34.5 minutes
Forcible rape	One every 6.0 minutes
Robbery	One every 1.3 minutes
Aggravated assault	One every 39.1 seconds
Property crime	
Burglary	One every 14.3 seconds
Larceny-theft	One every 5.0 seconds
Motor vehicle theft	One every 39.7 seconds

Source: U.S. Department of Justice (2010)

Tita and Ridgeway (2007) point out that although street gangs typically form in areas that have higher crime rates than other areas in the first place, once they do form, they generate even higher levels of crime. As discussed in Chapter 1, the Office of Juvenile Justice and Delinquency Prevention (OJJDP) reported 731,000 total gang members in 2009 (Egley and Howell, 2011b), and the FBI reported that there were over 1.1 million total gang members in 2011 (FBI 2011a). Regardless of the citation we trust the most, and the FBI's figures seem more accurate, there are a lot of street gangsters. Street gangs, by implication, commit (mostly) street crimes, and they commit a great deal of them. Just how much crime street gangs are responsible for varies from jurisdiction to jurisdiction. The FBI (2011a) reports in its 2011 National Gang Threat Assessments that criminal street gangs are responsible for an average of 48 percent of violent crime in most jurisdictions and up to 90 percent in several others (e.g., in Arizona, California, Colorado, Illinois, Massachusetts, Oklahoma, and Texas). The FBI (2009c) also reports that street gangs commit as much as 80 percent of the overall crime in many communities, with the typical crimes committed being alien smuggling, armed robbery, assault, auto theft, drug-trafficking, extortion, fraud, home invasions, identity theft, murder, and weapons trafficking.

With all of this crime occurring, what is the United States doing about it? We will pay closer attention to intervention, suppression, and treatment efforts in Chapter 9, but now we can provide a quick answer: arrests and incarceration. A lot of Americans are committing crime. In fact, there were 92 million Americans with a criminal record in 2011, and the vast majority of them are not gang members (*The Post-Standard* 2011). To be fair, most Americans are committing petty crime and are not incarcerated. However, no other country in the world has a higher incarceration rate than the United States. According to the Pew Center on the States (2009), at the beginning of 2009, there were 2.3 million incarcerated American adults. To put this figure in perspective, consider that the far more populous nation of China ranked second, with 1.5 million citizens behind bars, and Russia was a distant third with 890,000 inmates (Pew Center on the States 2009). In addition, if we add the number of people on probation or parole in the United States, there are more than 7.3 million Americans in the corrections system. This figure equates to 1 in every 31 U.S. adults. In 1985, the rate was 1 in 77 adults (Delaney 2012). The United States has 5 percent of the world's population, and yet it houses nearly 25 percent of the world's reported prisoners (Webb 2009). The United States currently incarcerates 756 inmates per 100,000 residents, a rate nearly five times the average worldwide of 158 for every 100,000 (Webb 2009).

The United States is certainly fond of putting people behind bars. But it is more than our get-tough-on-criminals mentality that accounts for our alarming incarceration rate, as a large number of these inmates are nonviolent drug offenders. According to the data provided by the Congress's Joint Economic Committee, drug offenders constitute nearly 33 percent of the prison population. An estimated 60 percent of incarcerated drug offenders are nonviolent (passive users or minor dealers) (Webb 2009). Furthermore, more than one in eight prisoners in the United States have serious mental illness (Foster, Orr, and Laing 2009). Imprisoning violent offenders, especially gang members, with passive recreational drug users is a highly questionable social policy. Regarding correctional facilities, one can ask the obvious question, "What is being corrected? Correctional facilities are troublesome enough for correctional officers because of the estimated 231,000 total gang members incarcerated; why subject nonviolent offenders to such an element?" Many consumer groups question why taxpayer dollars are used to house nonviolent offenders. It is questionable too, as to how effective the correctional system really is; after all, 44 percent of released prisoners are rearrested within one year of release (*The Post-Standard* 2011). Our concern here is not about the social policy of incarceration in the United States. Rather, we are interested in the criminal activities of street gang members that will inevitably lead to their incarceration, or death.

In the remainder of this chapter we will examine, by category, a number of crimes that are committed by street gangs. We begin our discussion with a look at violence.

VIOLENT CRIMES

Violent crimes include homicide, robbery, assault, forcible rape, extortion, and witness intimidation. When it comes to gang life, all of these examples of violent crime are applicable and can come about in the form of violence among members of the same gang and toward rival gangs, toward law enforcement personnel, and toward innocent citizens. Most gang violence is directed toward rival gang members. However, the criminal violent acts of robbery, extortion, and witness intimidation are almost always directed toward nongang members. This introduces an interesting point; whereas gang-against-gang violence is mutually understood and expected by all participants, gang-versus-nongang assaults include a reluctant participant. According to the FBI (2011a), the three leading causes of gang violence are control over drug distribution and disputes over drug territory; conflict with gang migration into rival territory; and the release of incarcerated gang members back into the community.

Violence

The very essence of street gangs implies violent behavior. The Violence Protection Alliance defines **violence** as "the intentional use of physical force or power, threatened or actual, against oneself, another person, or against a group or community, that either results in or has a high likelihood of resulting in injury, death, psychological harm, maldevelopment, or deprivation" (World Health Organization 2012b). Violence is self-directed when the perpetrator and the victim are the same individual and is subdivided into "self-abuse" and suicide. *Interpersonal violence* refers to violence between individuals and can include family and intimate partner violence and community violence. *Collective violence* refers to violence committed by larger groups or multiple individuals and can be subdivided into social, political, and economic violence (WHO, 2012b). The last two types of violence are most applicable to the study of street gangs.

Recreational drug use is often categorized as victimless crime; that is to say, when adult participants freely engage in drug use they are not harming anyone except possibly themselves. When street gangs are involved in the sale, distribution, and trafficking of drugs, there are occasions wherein victimization occurs. Generally, such violence occurs via intergang confrontations. The violence that occurs is the result of trying to gain something (money via drug sales) rather than initiate harm. This type of violence is known as *instrumental violence*. In contrast, *expressive violence* occurs when bodily harm is intended, such as gang fights over turf or revenge attacks. The only goal in these types of scenarios is to cause harm.

Violence in a gang begins with the initiation process in which new recruits are given the opportunity to prove themselves worthy of the group. Taking a beating in the name of the gang reflects the recruit's loyalty to the group. It also exhibits the recruit's strength and willingness to accept pain for the greater good of the gang. The gang initiation is a type of expressive violence. As Dorais and Corriveau (2009, 25) state, "By inflicting physical suffering, the right of initiation confirms the recruit's manliness to the whole group. More crucially, the pain endured serves as proof of loyalty and complicity." With expressive violence there is no material gain; the point is simply to be violent (Tobin 2009). Gang members engage in violence with rival gang members, nongang members, law enforcement officers, and often among themselves. Gangs use violence to protect turf and to acquire turf. And when the turf represents a profitable marketplace (i.e., for selling drugs), the level of violence involved often escalates to murder. The use of violence by youth street gangs to protect their turf is not unique; the use of violence for this purpose by non–street gang, adult criminal organizations (e.g., the Mafia) is well established, and many youth street gangs are dominated by adult members. As Howell and Decker (1999a, 4) explained, "The relationship between drugs and violence is widely accepted in adult criminal organizations such as drug cartels and prison gangs; in some instances, however, it is difficult to distinguish these adult criminal organizations from youth gangs." The very concept of a youth street gang seems to be disappearing, as most gang members are now in for life, and it is common for gangs to have active members well into their adult lives. Additionally, as described earlier in this chapter, since the advent of crack cocaine, a number of drug gangs have come into existence. A drug gang is as much a criminal organization as the American or Russian Mafia.

Some researchers have concluded that the introduction of crack cocaine to the streets has led to increased levels of violence (Taylor 1989). Fagan (1996) found that the level of violence increased with the sale of crack for a number of reasons: "Violence associated with crack co-caine was linked to organizational competition for market share and profits; protection of drug-trafficking territory; regulation of employees in the new selling organization; the urge among habitual users for money to buy crack; its liquid value among the poor; and, for a small group, its psychoactive effects" (Howell and Decker 1999a, 4). Goldstein (1985) detailed three possible relationships between drugs, drug-trafficking, and violent crime:

1. The "pharmacological" effects of the drug on the user can induce violent behavior.
2. The high cost of drug use often impels users to commit "economic compulsive" violent crime to support continued drug use (e.g., robbery for the purpose of securing money to buy drugs).
3. "Systematic" violence is a common feature of the drug-distribution system, including protection or expansion of the drug distribution market share, retaliation against market participants who violate the rules that govern transactions, or maintenance of the drug-trafficking organizations. (Howell and Decker 1999a, 5)

More recent data have shown that Goldstein was correct that gangs would establish systematic drug distribution networks. (*Note*: Evidence of street gangs operating in violent manners has been presented throughout this book and especially in Chapters 2 and 6.) It should be noted, however, that there is little or no evidence to support the claim that drug use, aside from alcohol and PCP, leads to violence. The opposite would be expected for marijuana users. But the *NDIC National Street Gang Survey Report—1998* revealed that many law enforcement agencies say that drugs contribute to gang violence. The Phoenix Police Department, for one, reported that most of the violent crimes involving gangs are the result of their drug-trafficking. The Akron, Ohio, police department stated that gangs are heavily tied to the drug trade in their city and that this involvement has led directly to an increase in violence and gang-related shootings (NAGIA 2002). Because of the high cost of illegal recreational drugs, it is clear that the economically poor will often engage in petty crimes to raise enough money to purchase the desired drugs. If most recreational drugs were legalized, street crime and violence would be dramatically reduced.

The violence associated with drug-trafficking is primarily directed at law enforcement officers but is not limited to the police. Border patrol agents on both the Mexican and American sides risk attack by individuals with ties to Mexican drug cartels. There are reports that drug cartels have offered rewards up to $10,000 for the home addresses of border patrol agents and have also offered bounties on the lives of agents on duty. The U.S. Drug Enforcement Agency estimates that Mexican-based gangs and their connections (usually from Colombia) are responsible for the estimated 770 tons of cocaine, 5.5 to 6.5 tons of heroin, and 7,700 tons of marijuana that enter the United States annually. Once the drugs enter the country, a wide variety of people, including street gangs, become responsible for their distribution. We will take a closer look at gangs and drug use, sale, distribution, and trafficking later in this chapter.

Gangs are also involved with a great deal of violence unrelated to drugs. They are the cause of much violence in America's schools and streets. It has been established that most gangs develop naturally or spontaneously from friendship groups formed in schools or local neighborhoods. School officials often miss or ignore (gang denial) the early warning signs that gangs are developing in their schools. They may view certain delinquent behaviors committed by students as simply a part of "growing up"; since most students will not become involved in gangs, there is some validity to this idea. At other times, school officials mistakenly label juvenile delinquents as "wannabes" (Trump 1996). As a result, nongang students usually notice the presence of gangs before school officials do. "Once a gang problem has developed, it is usually too late to simply put a stop to it. In many cases, by the time officials begin to recognize the existence of a gang problem within their school and attempt to respond to it, the gangs have already established a foothold of power. Students know long before school officials whether there is a gang presence within their school" (Thompkins 2004, 196). When school officials acknowledge the existence of a gang in their school, they typically create an "us-versus-them" relationship, "which paradoxically, leads to many gangs' gaining a level of credibility and increased power. As real and suspected gang members are singled out and punished for what is determined to be gang behavior, students may come to fear the gangs even more. Moreover, the 'us versus them' relationship has the potential to draw some students to the gangs precisely because they want to be recognized as outsiders, as someone who breaks the rules and challenges authority" (Thompkins 2004, 196). As the gang gains in strength in the school, the environment becomes increasingly violent because the gang is driven by a desire for power and respect. Innocent students become the unwilling victims of the gangs and marginalized students are drawn to the aura of the gang. There have always been bullies in schools; gang members have become the new ones.

> As gangs begin to appear on school campuses, they become the bullies, and the level of fear and violence escalates. Gang members commit both individual and group acts of violence, and students know, or at least they believe, that if they retaliate against an act of aggression committed by one gang member, they will have to deal with the entire gang. This can lead to students' suffering increased levels of fear and stress, which not only disrupt their learning process but can also lead to the formation of new gangs. Previously unaffiliated students have been known to come together or "clique up" and form their own gang for protection against other gangs. (Thompkins 2004, 197)

Once rival gangs develop within a school, the level of violence escalates even further. Rival gangs fight for space and respect, and students who are in school to learn face even bigger challenges in their desire to earn a quality education.

Gangs are also responsible for a great deal of violence on the streets, especially in certain urban neighborhoods. Innocent citizens in these neighborhoods are always at risk of being victimized by gangs. Young males who remain neutral to gangs, for example, may find themselves victims because of misidentification. The greatest risk of violence, however, is to gang members. Just by identifying themselves as gang members makes them a target. Being in a gang increases the probability that one will either be victimized by violence or commit violence to another. As described in Chapter 4, some gang members simply love the idea of violence. They get a rush from inflicting pain on others. Those who were victimized by violence in the home find gang activity a catharsis, a release of pent-up frustration. Many members feed off this adrenaline rush. In short, many gang members are attracted to gang life because of the violence. Studies have consistently shown that, overall, violence is more common among gang adolescents than nongang adolescents. Although nongang members are less likely to be involved in violence, many such people enjoy playing video games that depict gang violence. See "Connecting Street Gangs and Popular Culture" Box 8.1 for a closer look at gangs in video games.

Box 8.1   *Connecting Street Gangs and Popular Culture*

Street Gangs in Video Games

Playing video games is among the favorite recreational activities of many youths and young adults, especially males (research indicates that approximately 60% of gamers are male). although some people of all ages enjoy gaming. If people find enjoyment in any activity, including playing video games, and they are not harming others, why should we care? Perhaps parents might want to guard against their children playing violent video games, as there is a debate about the influence of video violence on the effects of the player's behavior in the real world. For example, does playing violent video games de-sanitize gamers to real-life violence? Does it contribute to violent acts by players? Or, are violent people attracted to violent video games? The answers to such questions are beyond the scope of this discussion. We do hear of stories where individuals watch violent video games and commit acts of violence, but these stories are rare. One such example, however, involves Anders Behring Breivik, the Norwegian who slaughtered dozens of people in Norway before he was shot by police. Breivik told authorities that he sharpened his aim by playing the video game "Call of Duty: Modern Warfare" for hours on end. He also told an Oslo court that he took steroids to build his physical strength and meditated to "de-emotionalize" himself before the bombing and shooting rampage that left 77 people dead (*The Post-Standard* 2012b). His lack of remorse and matter-of-fact description of weapons and tactics—he even considered using a flame thrower—were deeply disturbing to the families of the victims. In *Call of Duty*, players compete to complete military strategies. Players can manipulate air strikes, use attack helicopters, and achieve consecutive killstreaks. In essence, players earn points by how may kills they make. Breivik's "skills" were developed playing *Call of Duty*, but was playing a video game the cause of his rampage? Or did he have other issues beyond gaming? What about the role of meditation; did that contribute to his ability to kill innocent people?

There are many violent video games that feature street gangs. Among them are *The Warriors* (2007) and *The Warriors: Street Brawl* (2009), both based on the 1979 film *The Warriors*. The plot centers on the Warriors, an interracial (black and white) street gang from Coney Island, Brooklyn, who send representatives to an all-gangs summit called by Cyrus, the leader of the Gramercy Riffs gang, the most powerful gang in New York City. Cyrus has requested that all gangs send nine unarmed representatives to Van Cortlandt Park in the Bronx to discuss a city-wide truce and unification among all street gangs so that that they can rule the city. Most of the gangs are in favor of this idea, but Luther, leader of the Rogues, shoots Cyrus and frames Cleon, the leader of the Warriors. Cleon is jumped and his fate is unknown. With all the gangs and the police after them, the Warriors attempt the difficult challenge of returning home. At times they get split up. One Warrior is killed by a police officer who throws him in front of a moving train during an arrest attempt. Gang members call in to a radio DJ who gives play-by-play updates on the Warriors' progress. The video game, *The Warriors*, released in 2005 for PlayStation 2 and Xbox and in 2007 for PlayStation Portable, is a game based on the film that takes place in a 1970s New York City and expands to the five city boroughs. The game is about survival and relies heavily on violent brawls. The gamer participates in many gang-related activities, including spray painting turf and disrespecting rivals.

In the film, the Warriors come across a female gang called "The Lizzies." The Lizzies are tough and claim a turf known as Union. The Lizzies are waiting at Union Station when the Warriors get off the train and befriend and seduce the gang. The Lizzies bring them back to their hangout to party. Before long, however, they pull guns and start shooting the trio of Warriors. The Lizzies, with new video characters, are among the gangs to make an appearance on the follow-up *Warriors* game called *The Warriors: Street Brawl*. This game was released on the Mac OS X, Microsoft Windows, and Xbox Live Arcade in 2009. It has six playable characters and comes with 12 achievements worth a total of 200 gamerscore. Gamers participate in gang-related behaviors in 3D. They can punch, kick, or use weapons (e.g., knives, wrenches, pipes, and bats). The punching is realistic and so too are the many impact sounds (from punching and weapons). Perhaps reflecting the male predominance in gaming, the Lizzies in the video game are dressed provocatively, wearing skirts, halter tops, and strapless shirts. In the film the Lizzies were dressed more realistically in jeans and shirts that did not flatter the body; they are gang members after all, not models. Nonetheless, gamers find *Street Brawl* fun and exciting.

Another popular video game featuring street gangs is *Saints Row 3*, an action-adventure–based game that was released in 2011 for Microsoft Windows, PlayStation 3, and Xbox 360. In this game, the player controls the leader of the Third Street Saints, a gang that operates in the fictional city of Steelport. The Saints are at war with three other gangs, the Morningstar, Deckers, and Luchadores. Successful completion of missions earns the player in-game money, weapons, cars, and gang respect. Players can earn enough points to set off a gigantic bomb to demolish one of the enemy skyscrapers in the city. There are consequences to blowing up the skyscrapers, so players have to weigh decisions carefully. Ultimately, the game involves players killing and maiming others.

One of the most popular video games of the violence genre is the *Grand Theft Auto* collection. One of the most popular versions is *Grand Theft Auto: San Andreas* (2004). This action-adventure video game, developed by Rockstar North, is the third 3D game in the *Grand Theft* franchise. Originally released for PlayStation 2, the game can now be played on Xbox and Microsoft Windows (PC). The gameplay consists primarily of a third-person shooter and a driving game. The player's character is capable of walking, running, sprinting, swimming, climbing, jumping, and using weapons and various hand-to-hand combat moves. The game is set in the fictional state of San Andreas, which contains three metropolitan cities: Los Santos (based on Los Angeles), San Fierro (based on San Francisco), and Las Venturas (based on Las Vegas). All of these sub-areas take on many of the same characteristics of their late 1992 corresponding cities. The game play and ambiance of the game borrow heavily from the "gangsta rap" scene of Los Angeles in the same time period. Everything from clothing to music is reminiscent of the area and era. The action in *San Andreas* centers on a group of young gang members, with the primary gang the Grove Street Family. The lead character is Carl "CJ" Johnson, who returns home to Los Santos from Liberty City after learning of his mother's murder. During the course of playing the game, CJ learns of the plot behind his mother's murder. CJ also has a younger sister, Kendl, who is also a member of the Grove gang. She is a peripheral gang member, not hardcore. Still she dresses in the gang color (green) and associates with the other gang members. Like most female gang members, Kendl is dating a member of Grove Street. Other real-life gang experiences include battles with rivals whenever a player ventures into enemy territory, attempts to claim turf to generate more money, and marks turf.

For gamers, playing video games provides hours of entertainment. Playing gang-related games provides the player with a rush. Clearly, the rush of playing a gangbanger pales in comparison to being a gangbanger who actually performs acts of violence and commits crimes. Playing video games is generally a substitute for real-life gang activity. In a few cases, it may inspire young gamers to try out the real thing. But, most gamers know the difference between reality and playing a game.

When gang members confront rivals, violence is nearly inevitable, but there are many reasons for gang violence: invasion of turf, dating rivalries, chance meetings between rival gangs in neutral locations (e.g., a shopping mall), sporting events, and personal issues in which the gang is brought in as reinforcement to back up an individual gang member. The level of violence varies from one gang clique to another and by situation. For traditional gangs, violence is a sign of masculinity or machismo. Getting into a fight is a coming-of-age rite for young boys, especially among the lower socioeconomic classes. Generally speaking, there are six types of gang violence: violence between members of the same gang (beginning with the initiation process and including violent violation ceremonies for those who disobey gang rules); violence in conjunction with fights against rival gangs; violence against conventional folks within the gang neighborhood; violence directed toward conventional folks outside of the gang neighborhood; violence in the form of attacks on property (e.g., vandalism and graffiti) in one's own neighborhood; and violence against property outside of one's own neighborhood.

A particularly disturbing story of street gang violence involving an attack on a gang recruit and an attack on a nongang resident in their own community occurred in the Bronx, New York, in December 2010. Police arrested eight members (one other was at large after the initial arrests) of the **Latin King Goonies** for torturing gays in their Bronx neighborhood. The gang members ranged in ages from 16 to 23 (*USA Today* 2010). According to police reports, the Goonies heard that a 17-year-old recruit was gay and had sex with a 30-year-old man from the neighborhood. The recruit was stripped, beaten, and sodomized with a plunger handle until he confessed to having sex with the 30-year-old man who lived a couple of blocks away. The gang found a second teen they suspected was gay and tortured him too, police said. Finally, they located the 30-year-old man, invited him to a house party, and when he arrived, they burned, beat, and tortured him for hours. The attack included sodomizing him with a miniature baseball bat. The gang members were charged with robbery, assault, sexual abuse, and unlawful imprisonment as a hate crime (*USA Today* 2010). Certainly, such violent brutality underscores the lack of respect many gang members have toward others. Another example of a gang attack on residents of the same community involves a case in San Bernardino, California. In 2011, a teenage street gang member, acting on his own, opened fire on a family as they gathered outside their family home. An hour earlier, a man at the house stopped the same gangbanger from beating a woman on a sidewalk a few doors away. Feeling disrespected, the gangbanger went home, got a gun, and returned to open fire on the innocent community members. The gang member was arrested for homicide and an additional seven counts of attempted murder (Willon 2011).

The influence of incarcerated gang members after they have been released into the community and are back in street gangs is a subject area that has drawn increased attention and concern for the past decade or so. Nearly 700,000 prison inmates arrive in communities throughout the United States each year (Sabol, Minton, and Harrison 2007). There are approximately 2.3 million people incarcerated in the United States, and nearly a quarter million, or roughly 10 percent of them are identified gang members. Thus, one could conclude that nearly 70,000 gang members return to their communities from lockup every year. What will these ex-con gang members bring to the community? New job skills and a willingness to lead a conventional life? Values that one might hope they learned at a "correctional" facility? In the vast majority of the cases, these gangbangers will go right back to gang life, more hardened than they were before incarceration. In some gangs these ex-cons will be revered as Original Gangsters (OGs) with their reputations firmly in hand. Other gangs may be threatened by these OGs and see them as a threat. In other cases, especially with Surenos and Norte gangs, gangsters may have taken orders from these OGs while these OGs were still in prison. As for the communities themselves, the return of all these bitter and violent gang members is not good news. The news is bad because the recidivism rate in the United States is approximately 67.5 percent (Bureau of Justice Statistics 2012). *Recidivism* refers to a relapse into a previous condition or mode of behavior. In other words, the released inmate reverts to his/her criminal ways after release from incarceration. To be sent back to prison means that the released inmate was convicted of a crime. Chances are, such a person committed numerous crimes before being caught. Thus, approximately two-thirds of all released inmates committed enough crime to be arrested, convicted, and sent back to prison. In a study conducted by Olson and Dooley (2006), nearly one-quarter of the adult inmates released from Illinois prisons during 2000 were identified as gang members and 75 percent of them had a new arrest within two years of their release. Gang members are rearrested more quickly following release from prison, and are more likely to be arrested for violent and drug offenses (than are nongang members). In their study, Olson and Dooley (2006) found that 55 percent of the gang members released from prison in 2000 were readmitted to Illinois prisons within two years. There is a vicious trend of young people committing acts of violence, getting sent to prison, then being released back to the streets just as violent, or more so as is generally the case, as before, and then committing more acts of violence. And, so the cycle of violence continues.

Gang violence is a real presence in many U.S. communities. "As gangs and the gang subculture spread across the country, the gang-related violence that was previously limited to urban areas now reaches into suburban and rural communities. The National Institute of Justice estimates that the financial costs of violent crime to American society are well over $400 billion a year. Adding pain and suffering, as well as the reduced quality of life, the total climbs to $450 billion each year—roughly $1,800 for each man, woman, and child in the country. The figures do not include the cost of running the criminal justice system or private actions taken to cut crime—such as hiring guards or buying security systems" (NAGIA 2002, 4–5). Street gangs and their violence thus represent a high cost to American society, both in terms of money and in quality of life.

Homicide

Homicide is the killing of one human being by another, but not all homicides are criminal. There are two forms of homicide: noncriminal and criminal. Noncriminal homicide includes excusable and justifiable homicide. Excusable homicides are accidents or misfortunes where neither negligence nor unlawful intent is involved (e.g., hunting accidents). Justifiable homicides are killings that result from necessity or lawful duty to protect oneself or others (e.g., a police officer who kills a suspect within the line-of-duty guidelines, and self-defense cases, such as when an intruder enters someone's home and attacks the occupant). Most relevant to the study of street gangs are criminal homicides—causing the death of another person without legal justification or excuse. Criminal homicides include murder and manslaughter. Gang members are often involved in both *premeditated murder*, also known as first-degree murder ("murder 1" in police jargon), in which the killing is planned ahead of time; and *felony murder*, which refers to killings that occur during the commission of a felony such as rape or robbery. As the category of felony murder implies, often a number of other crimes are committed during the commission of a homicide.

The impact of street gangs on a community is often measured in terms of the number of gang-related criminal homicides. Such was the case in the discussion of specific street gangs in chapters 2 and 6. In Chapter 6, for example, the number of homicides committed by street gangs in Syracuse, Rochester, and Buffalo was used to illustrate the seriousness of gang activities in those jurisdictions. Often the term *gang-related homicide* is used by jurisdictions when either the perpetrator or the victim of a homicide is a gang member. Using the term *gang related* not only helps to classify certain homicides as gang related or not gang related, it is also used to highlight a gang problem in the community.

It is very difficult to determine, for a number of reasons, the total number of gang homicides. First, many gang homicides go unreported. Second, some police agencies choose not to respond to surveys on gang homicide. Third, some agencies report a gang homicide only if it is committed in relation to a gang function (e.g., a street battle or drugs). Fourth, some agencies choose not to identify certain crimes as gang related—for a variety a reasons, including gang denial (OJJDP 2000, 26). What is certain is that most gang-related homicides occur in cities with populations greater than 50,000 and their adjacent suburban counties (Egley, Howell, and Major 2006). According to Egley and Ritz (2006), more than half of the 2004 reported homicides in Los Angeles and Chicago were gang related. Law enforcement in the remaining 171 cities that responded to the "2006 National Youth Gang Survey" reported that street gangs were responsible for approximately 25 percent of the homicides in their respective communities. Egley and Howell (2011b) report that in cities greater than 100,000 persons, the percentage of gang-related homicides has increased throughout the first decade of the 2000s: 7 percent increase in 2005 from 2004 and an 11 percent increase in 2008 from 2005. Thus, it can be expected that the percentage of gang-related homicides in larger cities is higher than 50 percent. This would certainly be the case in such cities as Syracuse, Rochester, and Buffalo, let alone in Los Angeles and Chicago.

Year after year, the number of gang-related homicides increases. Hispanics and blacks are most likely to be the perpetrators and/or victims of gang-related homicides. In 2004, former California State Senator Tom Hayden (2004) reported that more than 25,000 young people, nearly all of them African American or Hispanic, were slain in street violence during the previous two decades. Gang researchers, law enforcement agencies, and gang members themselves indicate that the primary reason for the continued growth in the number of gang-related homicides is the increased availability and firepower of weapons and gang members' willingness to use firearms as a way to handle problems. The mere presence of firearms increases the likelihood of murder. Routine use of firearms among gang members began in the 1980s (Miller 1992). Each new generation of street gangs ups the ante in their willingness to use firearms to settle beefs and control drug markets.

Gang members have numerous ways to acquire guns, both legally (at a variety of gun shops and online) and illegally (they may steal guns from homes or other places) or through any number of street methods. High-powered weapons have dramatically changed the lethality of violence and have become the primary method of settling disputes and challenges to respect and honor (Klein 1995). The use of guns has become so intertwined as a subcultural norm that gang members now assume rivals are packing and therefore feel it necessary to pack a gun as well. Thus, it is fairly common that in any given gang, all will be heavily armed wherever they are, in private or in public. The possession of a gun gives the holder a feeling of power and invincibility—until he runs into someone else who is also "carrying" and who makes the drop on him first. "Skewed conceptions of power and masculinity have developed in these contexts, fueling a violent response to disputes" (Fagan 2004, 237). Recent studies have shown that firearms are prevalent in nearly all youth gangs today, and gang members of any age are capable of blasting away an enemy for something as simple as perceived disrespect. Using data collected from interviews in 1995 with arrested juveniles in the Drug Use Forecasting study, Decker and colleagues (1997) found that gang members are much more likely than nongang juveniles to carry guns most or all of the time (31% versus 20%). In addition, percentages of arrestees who reported using a gun to commit a crime were higher among adolescents who sold drugs (42%) or belonged to a gang (50%) than among other juveniles (33%) (Howell and Decker 1999a, 6).

Youth gang homicides are characterized by periodic spurts and declines but have been increasing overall nationwide. Evidence indicates that this trend will continue, especially in certain cities (Maxson 1998). The spurts are usually explained by disputes between warring gangs (Block and Block 1993), for gang homicides do not occur throughout a city but are usually confined to specific neighborhoods. Gang battles that lead to homicide generally take place within small, fairly intimate local neighborhoods (Reiner 1992). Most victims of gang homicides are gang members (as opposed to innocent civilians). In fact, some marvel at how accurate gang hits are. Gang members show no remorse and often stand over their victim. If they have the chance, they will take their victim's flag and maybe rob him of any drugs and money.

A number of characteristics distinguish gang homicides from nongang homicides. Decker and Curry (2003, 76) provide these distinctions:

1. Gang violence is more likely than other crimes of violence to involve firearms, particularly handguns.
2. The victims of gang homicides resemble their killers; that is, the victims of gang homicide are more likely to be in the same race, age, sex, and neighborhood where they live as the people who kill them.

Decker and Curry (2003) also indicate that most gang homicides are not tied to drug-trafficking, but are instead motivated by revenge or battles over turf. Klein and Maxson (1989) focused on additional characteristics of gang homicides as distinct from nongang homicides:

1. Gang homicide is more likely to occur on the streets (as opposed to most other homicides, which occur inside people's homes).
2. Gang homicide is more likely to involve a gun and less likely to be committed in conjunction with a robbery.
3. Gang-related homicides involve more participants than nongang ones.
4. Gang-related homicides have a much higher rate of youth suspects than nongang homicides.

Gang homicides are also more likely to involve minority males and the use of automobiles and to take place in public places. Gang-related homicide perpetrators and victims are much younger than those in nongang-related homicides (Decker and Curry 2002).

A specific category of gang homicide, or attempted homicide, the **drive-by shooting**, involves the use of automobiles. Variations of **drive-bys** can be traced back to the 1920s, the era of Al Capone and other gangsters. These incidents were sporadic, however, and never caught on among all criminals in the decades that followed. Klein (1971) stated that early drive-bys were called *japing*, after the hit-and-run tactics of Japanese soldiers in World War II. (*Japing* is considered a racist term today and would not be used by academic researchers. Bill Parcells, former head coach of the Dallas Cowboys, got into trouble when he used the term *Jap plays* in a 2004 press conference to describe the "sneaky" plays he uses in football games.) Miller (1966) referred to mobile attacks as "forays." The victim of a drive-by shooting may be walking the streets, riding in another automobile or bus, or at home (Howell 2004b, 210). Most drive-by shootings involve assailants shooting at intended victims from a moving car. However, gang members may also use a different variation of the drive-by. In these cases, the gang will drive to a specific location, find the target, jump out of the car and chase the victim down, shoot the victim, and then escape in a fleeing automobile. Beyond the obvious act of killing an enemy, the drive-by shooting serves as a very powerful act of intimidation to promote fear.

By the 1980s, drive-by shootings had become fairly common in most major urban cities, especially in Los Angeles. As a former resident of Los Angeles who often drove the highways during this era, I can personally attest to the conscious awareness most motorists had with regard to motorists who might represent a risk of committing a drive-by. That my work often brought me to such areas as South Central and East Los Angeles only heightened my awareness. But, such is life in the big city. Most residents deal with urban crime and a few die because of it. Drive-by shootings have replaced the idea of a fair fight. The "old-school" gangs always maintained a "fair-fight" mentality; that is, they fought with fists and knives and stopped fighting when a victor was clearly established. Furthermore, they fought face-to-face; anything else would be considered an act of cowardice. They would never utilize a "drive-by shooting" because it violated gang norms that dictated the "honorable" fair fight. The introduction of *mobile gangs* violated this concept. Contemporary gangs do not follow the fair-fight concept—they have a win-at-any-cost mentality—a primitive way of thinking that often has deadly consequences and demonstrates a blatant disregard for human life. Often, when drive-bys are conducted, innocent bystanders—nongang youth, children, and older people—are victimized. Without fair warning, these people have no chance of defending themselves. Contemporary gangs view drive-by shootings as a means toward an end. The shootings serve many purposes:

1. They provide individual members an opportunity to prove themselves.
2. They may be used as part of an initiation rite for a new member.
3. They are a means of resolving arguments.
4. They can be viewed as preemptive attacks to intimidate rival gangs to not try the same thing.
5. They are used to eliminate competition in illegal businesses.
6. They are used to settle turf fights.
7. They are used as a means of retaliation against rivals for a previous attack.
8. The "shooting fish in a barrel" mentality provides gang members with an adrenaline rush and provides them with the "courage" to strike against rivals.
9. Drive-bys are, in a sense, safer for gang members because they go into a rival turf and surprise attack targets.

This is not meant to be an exhaustive list, but it does demonstrate that today's gangs view the drive-by shooting as a reasonable way of dealing with rivals. The fact that innocent citizens may be harmed or killed is of little concern. Although drive-bys have certain advantages, there is a corresponding downside: counterstrikes by rivals and the possibility of police involvement because of the amount of attention drive-by shootings create.

Economics is correlated with gang homicides. In a study of the staggering number of homicides in Los Angeles, researchers found that employment and per capita income were more closely associated with the city's gang homicide rate than any other variable—including demographic factors (e.g., race), level of education, or the proportion of single-parent family households. Age is also an important factor in homicides, as the highest gang homicide rates were recorded in communities where the population under 20 years of age was a sizable 40 percent. The lowest murder rates are found in communities where a quarter or less of the population fell below the age of 20.

According to the National Alliance of Gang Investigators Associations, there is an additional cost of up to $2 million per homicide when four suspects are arrested, a figure determined by adding up trial costs, crime scene investigation, medical treatment, autopsy, and incarceration costs if the four suspects are convicted and serve 20 years. These costs are a burden on taxpayers and, more importantly, derived from an activity that detracts from the overall quality of American life.

Robbery

Robbery is the unlawful taking or attempted taking of property that belongs to another by use of force or threat of force. A robbery is a serious crime and a crime of violence because it puts the victim's life in jeopardy. Most robberies occur on the streets as opposed to inside the home. Siegel (1995, 317) created a typology of robberies:

1. Robbery of persons who, as part of their employment, are in charge of money or goods. For gang members, convenience stores and banks represent easy targets for quick cash.
2. Robbery in an open area. These robberies include street offenses, muggings, purse snatchings, and other attacks. In urban areas, this type of robbery constitutes about 60 percent of reported totals. Street robbery is most commonly known as muggings.
3. Robbery on private premises. This type of robbery involves robbing people after breaking into their homes. The FBI reports that this type of robbery accounts for about 10 percent of all offenses.
4. Robbery after preliminary association of short duration. This type of robbery comes in the aftermath of chance meeting—in a bar, at a party, or after a sexual encounter.
5. Robbery after previous association of some duration between the victim and offender.

The gangs most likely to commit a "robbery on a private premise" are Asian gangs (see Chapter 6). These crimes are described as "home invasions." The most common type of robbery committed by gang members is known as a "jacking" or mugging. **Jackings** are street robberies against innocent individuals (Sanders 1994). Jackings are generally not planned, but rather are crimes of opportunity. Even so, gang members put themselves in places where such opportunities present themselves. For example, gang members will loiter near ATMs in order to rob people who have just taken cash out of the machine or near bars where they can take advantage of drunken patrons. Convenience store robberies have continued to rise ever since these stores came into existence. The phrase "stop and rob" has become synonymous with convenience stores because of their high incidence of robberies. Gang members are highly visible and draw the attention of store clerks. "Since they are often seen taking goods from stores, they are challenged by the clerk or store owner. When this occurs, they threaten the clerk and transform a petty theft misdemeanor into a felony crime" (Sanders 1994, 115). As someone who once, long ago, worked as a cashier at Los Angeles convenience stores (c-stores or "stop and robs" as we called them even then) during the graveyard shift, I realized that the graveyard reference has more than one meaning! During my years in management at Los Angeles c-stores, I learned of many horror stories about cashiers who were brutally victimized by robbers, gang members and nongang members alike. There are few jobs scarier than being a convenience store cashier late at night in certain neighborhoods. Cashiers can't run, they can't hide, and they don't carry weapons (generally speaking).

Research on street gangs and robberies is limited. What we do know is that street gangs have committed a small percentage of the overall total number of robberies in the United States. According to the statistics compiled by the OJJDP (2000), gang members are responsible for "most or all" robberies in just 3 percent of jurisdictions, 30 percent of the jurisdictions reported that gangs are responsible for "some" of the robberies, 49 percent reported a "few" robberies, and 19 percent reported that gangs are responsible for "none" of the robberies in their jurisdictions. The following represents a mere sampling of the robberies committed by gang members. Authorities in Denver, however, attribute a recent increase of bank robberies to street gangs. As of May 31, 2011, Denver had experienced a 25 percent increase in bank robberies, and this increase was attributed to more violent, takeover-style robberies at the hands of local street gangs, FBI spokesperson Dave Joly explained (Burnett 2011). Authorities in Merced County, California, solved a drive-by shooting while investigating gangbangers who were involved in a strong-arm robbery. Four gangbangers driving in a car noticed three teenaged boys standing and talking at a bus stop in El Nido on March 5, 2010. They flashed gang signs, turned the car around, got out of the car, and asked the boys what gang they "claim" or "bang." The boys said they did not belong to a gang and that they did not want any trouble. That's when the gangbangers beat up one of the boys and stole the others' cell phones. As it turned out these gangbangers, who were later apprehended by Merced County Sheriff's Deputy Tom Mackenzie, were also involved in an earlier drive-by. In January 2012, the FBI (2012m) indicted five members of the **Brentwood Locos Salvatruchas** (MS-13 Street Gang) for murder, conspiracy, assault, and armed robbery in connection with their attack on rival gang members at a house party on American Boulevard in Brentwood, Long Island, New York. The rival gang was robbed at gun point at the house party.

Assault and Battery

Assault and battery is another violent offense. Many people believe that the terms *assault* and *battery* refer to a single act, when actually they are two separate crimes. The main distinction between the two offenses is the existence or nonexistence of touch or contact, with contact as an essential element of battery and the absence of contact for assault. Sometimes assault is defined loosely to include battery. Thus, **battery** requires offensive touch, such as slapping, hitting, or punching a victim, while **assault** requires no actual touch but involves either attempted battery or intentionally frightening the victim by word or deed. Generally these offenses are treated as felonies, especially when the perpetrator uses a weapon or if they occur during the commission of a felony (assaulting a victim during a robbery). Assault with the intention to inflict serious bodily harm is referred to as **aggravated assault**. **Simple assault** is applied to acts of violence on the person that inflict less than serious bodily injury without a deadly weapon (e.g., punching someone in the gut over a disagreement).

The OJJDP (2000) compiled data on law enforcement responses to youth gang involvement in criminal activity that reveal gang members are responsible for a great number of assaults. Twelve percent of the respondents reported that gangs are responsible for "most/all" assaults, 43 percent reported that gangs are responsible for "some" of the assaults, 40 percent said "few," and just 6 percent reported that gangs are responsible for "none" of the assaults. Gang members commit a large number of assault and battery violent acts against nongang members, rival gang members, and law enforcement. "Many assaults and fights have involved gang members attacking non-gang members. While most of the cases involve clear instances of gang members initiating the violence, some cases do not involve gang initiation" (Sanders 1994, 116). As a rule, people who are not gang members go to great lengths to avoid contact with gang members. However, there are times when the gang forces itself upon innocent victims and conflict becomes inevitable. Obviously, rival gangs commit assault and battery against one another on a regular basis; it's the nature of their very design. And, as we have already learned, gangs also commit assault and battery against their own members. As is often the case, gang members commit numerous crimes in conjunction with related incidents. In 2009, 19 members of the **Royal Lion Tribe Latin Kings** in Rockville, Maryland, were arrested on federal racketeering charges and were accused of committing robberies, beatings, and murder plots (Glod 2009). The crew tossed molotov cocktails at an occupied house in Rockville, agreed to kill a security guard at a Langley Park apartment complex, and beat another gang member for breaking the gang's rules (a violation ceremony), according to authorities.

Law enforcement personnel are constant targets of street gang assaults and battery. Five Chicago police officers were killed in the line of duty in 2010. In one case, a police officer, in full uniform, was "gathering evidence from a car break-in when someone walked into the garage and shot him and the car's owner in the head, then fired another bullet into their heads as they lay on the ground" (Babwin 2010). In 2009, there were just under 3,300 reports of battery on a police officer, more than twice as many as were reported in 2002 and nearly triple the number reported in 1999 (Babwin 2010).

Rape

Rape has existed throughout human history. In early civilization, rape was a common occurrence; only it was never labeled "rape" because the concept of rape did not exist; it was a matter of men claiming ownership of women by forcibly abducting them and having their way with them. This practice led to males' solidification of power and their historical domination of women (Siegel 1995). Siegel (1995) explains that during the Middle Ages, it was a common practice for ambitious men to abduct and rape wealthy women in an attempt to force them into marriage.

> The practice of "heiress stealing" illustrates how feudal law gave little thought or protection to women and equated them with property. It was only in the late fifteenth century that forcible sex was outlawed and then only if the victim was of the nobility; peasant women and married women were not considered rape victims until well into the fifteenth century. . . . Throughout recorded history, rape has also been associated with warfare. Soldiers of conquering armies have considered sexual possession of their enemies' women one of the spoils of war . . . [this has been true] from the Crusades to the war in Vietnam. (Siegel 1995, 298)

Siegel is correct to say that rape is associated with war, but it did not end with Vietnam, it has continued with every war since he discussed this topic nearly two decades ago. Rape is also associated with intimidation and fear. It is a means of one person dominating another against the other's will. In prison, alpha males demonstrate their power within the system by claiming "lesser" men for their own and raping them to show dominance. In any type of scenario, rape is a heinous, violent crime. And it is worth noting that there are indeed different scenarios of rape as the FBI's UCR distinguishes among three categories of rape: (1) forcible rape, (2) statutory rape, and (3) attempted forcible rape. "Some jurisdictions draw a distinction between forcible rape with the use of a weapon and forcible rape without the use of a weapon. Although the UCR . . . does not make such a distinction, it does, however, record statistics on the use of weapons associated with the crime of rape. Other types of rapes include spousal rape, gang rape, and homosexual rape" (Schmalleger 2004, 54). So, as we can see, rape is not simply rape; there are different categories. However, there is one thing that links all the categories of rape and that is what allows us to define **rape** as the unlawful compelling of a person, or persons, through the use of physical force, or the threat of physical force, or duress to have sexual intercourse. Sociologists consider rape to be a violent, coercive act of aggression against individuals as a means of forcible dominance having little or nothing to do with sexual attraction.

Most victims of rape and sexual assault are women (91%), and nearly 1 in 5 women have been raped in their lifetimes while 1 in 71 men have been raped in their lifetimes (U.S. Department of Justice Office on Violence Against Women 2012). In 80 percent of rape cases, victims knew the perpetrators and more than half (51.1%) of female victims of rape reported being raped by an intimate partner (U.S. Department of Justice Office on Violence Against Women 2012). As described in Chapter 7, female gang members are often victimized by rape. In some cases, it is used as a form of initiation, and in other cases, it is used as a method of punishment. The issue of whether a girl can claim rape if she agrees to a roll-in was one of the issues that came up in the film *Havoc* when the character Emily tried to claim she was raped even though she agreed to roll-in (See "Connecting Street Gangs and Popular Culture" Box 7.1). If she was underage, it is still rape (one has to be of legal age to give consent). In the case of "sexed-in" initiations, the female recruit will likely have some knowledge of the identity of males who have sex with her, but not necessarily all of them. In Chapter 7 we also learned that many male gang members treat women as possessions and such a mentality makes it easier for the males to rape females and easily justify their behavior. When rape is committed, a number of other crimes may also occur. For example, in New York City in May 2003, two male gang members who had sex with three 14-year-old girls as part of the girls' initiation into the Crips street gang were eventually arrested for rape and aggravated sexual assault, possessing and creating child pornography, child endangerment, and initiation into a criminal street gang (*New York Post* 2003). Gang members may also rape innocent victims. In especially horrific examples, a large number of gang members attack a female (e.g., a female jogging alone in a park), taunt her, and then take turns raping her. This is known as **gang wilding**.

As described in Chapter 6, MS-13 is often considered the most dangerous street gang of them all. They have a strong presence in Virginia and the Washington, D.C., area. When speaking about gangs in northern Virginia, FBI Special Agent Robert G. Saale states, "MS-13 is the strongest gang, the biggest gang. They are the strongest thing going in terms of organized gangs. MS-13's motto is kill, rape and control" (Wilber 2010). With tactics such as these, it almost sounds as though MS-13 is a war. But MS-13 is not alone when it comes to using rape as a weapon and means to intimidate and demonstrate power. In fact, there are too many examples of gang-related rapes to record here, but a couple examples are warranted. In 2010, three members of an Osceola County (Florida) Crips gang received lengthy prison terms after being convicted of abducting and raping a 19-year-old woman after drugging her drink at a nightclub. The gang members brought her back to a rental home and brutally raped her though she pleaded for them to stop. A Folk gang member who was at the house did not participate but did not intervene. A fourth Crip member who helped to set the young woman up (by bringing her to the club for his follow gangsters to take advantage of her) did not participate in the gang rape because he felt sorry for her but also did not intervene because he knew his homies would jump him if he did (Curtis 2010). Law enforcement officials in Osceola report 20 street gangs with more than 500 total members. In 2009, in Anaheim, California, a gang member broke into a residential home and raped a 9-year-old girl. He then threatened to kill her 15-year-old sister if she said anything (KTLA News 2009).

Extortion

Gangs may be involved in two types of **extortion**. The first involves schoolchildren. Gang members who are still in school may extort lunch money and articles of clothing from other students in school or other youths outside school. Beyond the monetary benefits of extortion, it also serves the valuable function of instilling fear of the gangs (Sanders 1994). A second type of extortion by gangs is extortion against businesses. In this scenario, gang members demand "protection" money from shop owners. If they refuse to pay for the gang's "insurance," the proprietors risk property and personal harm. Generally, the shop owners who end up paying for this protection are in high-crime areas and realize that they will fall victim to someone; therefore, they don't mind paying one gang protection money because that alleviates their fear of attack from other gangs. Asian gangs often commit extortion crimes against members of their own community. Extortion, like the other examples of crimes we have discussed, is often linked with other crimes.

As an extreme example of the complexities of street gang extortion, we look at Los Angeles where the Department of Justice's Drug Enforcement Agency deployed 800 law enforcement officers on February 1, 2011, to arrest 87 targeted members and associates of the **38th Street Gang** who were named in a federal racketeering indictment that alleged a host of violent crimes, large-scale drug-trafficking, extortion of both drug dealers and legitimate businesses, and witness intimidation (United States Drug Enforcement Administration 2011). Among other things, the 38th Street Gang extorted drug dealers and local businesses threatening them with bodily harm and death if they refused to make payments. The 38th Street Gang had to raise money to pay their own "taxes" to the Mexican Mafia, who rules them from inside prison. La Eme gave authorization to the 38th Street Gang to commit certain criminal acts including extortion and murder. The gang targeted vendors at the Alameda Swap Meet to meet these needs. The 38th Street Gang also sold drugs at the Swap Meet. On an occasion, the 38th Street Gang dressed as FBI agents to extort and rob money from rival gangs in South Gate (United States Drug Enforcement Administration 2011). To run this operation, the 38th Street Gang was heavily armed; 80 firearms were seized during the raid.

Witness Intimidation

Gangs thrive on creating an environment of fear and intimidation. It has been well documented by this point that gangs are very violent and willing to murder their enemies. Apprehending gang members who commit crimes presents a challenge to law enforcement officials. Criminal prosecutors often have trouble convicting gang members because of witness intimidation. **Witness intimidation** involves a process wherein witnesses to a court proceeding are threatened in order to pressure or extort them not to testify. Witness intimidation has long been recognized as a problem for law enforcement officials. "President Clinton announced during his weekly radio broadcast on January 11, 1997, 'One of the most difficult problems facing law enforcement is the power of gang members to thwart the criminal justice system by threatening and intimidating the witnesses against them' " (NAGIA 2002, 5). Gang members did not create witness intimidation; it is a problem that has confronted law officials throughout the era of civil law. In a Justice Department survey on gang and drug-related witness intimidation, "192 prosecutors found that intimidation of victims and witnesses was a major problem for 51 percent of prosecutors in large jurisdictions (counties with populations greater than 250,000) and 43 percent of prosecutors in small jurisdictions. An additional 30 percent of prosecutors in large jurisdictions and 25 percent in small jurisdictions considered intimidation a moderately serious problem. Several prosecutors estimated that witness intimidation occurs in up to 75 to 100 percent of the violent crimes committed in some gang-dominated neighborhoods" (NAGIA 2002, 5).

It is actually quite difficult to ascertain the true extent of witness intimidation, as citizens who are threatened may be reluctant to tell the police. This is especially true for witnesses who live in the same neighborhood of those doing the threatening. Some witnesses may not be directly intimidated but fear reprisals if they don't cast a favorable vote. Despite any potential compromise on accurate data collection, a number of small-scale studies and surveys of police and prosecutors suggest that witness intimidation is pervasive and increasing. A study of witnesses appearing in criminal courts in Bronx County, New York, revealed that 36 percent of witnesses had been directly threatened; among those who had not been threatened directly, 57 percent feared reprisals (Center for Problem-Oriented Policing 2012). According to the Center for Problem-Oriented Policing (2012), prosecutors estimate that witness intimidation plays a role in 75 to 100% of violent crime committed in gang-dominated neighborhoods. Understandably, many people fear jury duty when it involves a violent, gang-related crime in gang communities. The role of witness intimidation is less severe in violent crime cases found in communities not dominated by gangs and drugs.

Witness intimidation occurs at many levels. A juror who is glared at by a gang member during a court proceeding may feel threatened or fear for the lives of loved ones. Outside the courtroom, fellow gang members of the accused may intimidate family members of jurors. In many cases, the gangs follow through on their threats. An example is the case of Trevis Ragsdale, a Blood member from Brooklyn who was sentenced to 25 years to life for killing a witness less than 48 hours before the victim was to testify against the half-brother of a reputed gang leader. Ragsdale received orders from a local Bloods leader to kill witness Bobby Gibson (*The Post-Standard* 2004f). Offenders attempt to intimidate victims and witnesses for a variety of reasons. "Gang members may use intimidation to subdue challenges to their authority or to reclaim lost gang status. Gang members and other offenders use intimidation to avoid detection by police and to avoid conviction once they are arrested" (Center for Problem-Oriented Policing 2012). Furthermore, the penalties for witness intimidation are less severe than the other violent crime charges the offender may be facing. One final factor is connected to the increased sophistication of DNA and other forensic testing in that deterring witness cooperation may be one of the only ways left available to weaken the prosecution's case (Center for Problem-Oriented Policing 2012).

Being a witness requires telling authority figures information about an event that is unbeknownst to them, and yet important. For example, when police officers discover a dead body, they look for clues and witnesses to the crime. When the police find someone who may have witnessed the act, they need the witness's cooperation and testimony. Thus, in some ways, and depending on how you look at it, being a witness is like being a snitch. And in some circles, being a snitch is not honorable. To learn about snitching, see "Connecting Street Gangs and Popular Culture" Box 8.2.

Box 8.2   *Connecting Street Gangs and Popular Culture*

Stop Snitchin: A Video Warning to Gang Crime Witnesses

While growing up, many of us wondered how our mothers seemed to know everything we did. Mom would say, "I have eyes in the back of my head." When you're young, and never get away with anything, you begin to wonder if it's true. Such a scenario was played out in an episode ("The Telling") of ABC's *The Middle*, a television show about a middle-class Kansas (located in "the middle" of the country) family. The family is gathered at the dinner table discussing the day's events when Frankie, the mother, cleverly informs her eldest son, Axl, that she is aware of his latest juvenile delinquent behavior. He tries  to explain himself but realizes his efforts are futile. Exasperated, he asks, "How did you find out about this anyway?" Frankie replies, "Moms know everything." Frankie then turns her attention to her daughter Sue and lets her know she has been busted for something she did (took her mom's earrings without permission) but tried to hide. Sue also questions her mom's knowledge and Mike, the father, interrupts by saying, "When are you going to realize, your mom has eyes in the back of her head?" At nighttime, Mike finds out that his wife gets all of her information from their youngest son, Brick. Upset by this, Mike asks, "Brick is a snitch?" To which Frankie replies, "I prefer the term whistle-blower." Justifying her use of Brick as a snitch against the other two kids, Frankie explains to her husband, "They are young and crafty and there are more of them. We need every advantage possible."

Street gang members are young, crafty, and large in numbers, and law enforcement certainly needs every advantage they can muster in their attempt to curtail gang activity. Understandably, gang members, like all criminals, do not like snitches. In fact, most people, even law-abiding citizens, do not like snitches. Mike, from *The Middle*, was not at all pleased to learn that his youngest son was a snitch. Mike informs Brick that it's wrong to snitch and tells him, "don't tell me anything" (as a snitch). Law enforcement relies on witnesses, informants, and snitches. Informants and witnesses to crimes are respected but snitches not so much. As civilians we may wonder whether friends can be trusted if they are willing to snitch on us.

After all, how can you trust someone who gives away secrets or confidential information? We expect our friends and loved ones to keep our secrets. But what if one of your friends or family members commits a crime, a serious crime, would you snitch? When kids snitch they are tattling; when a friend does so, he/she has violated a trust. What about witnesses to a crime, should they tell the police what they saw? If you, or a loved one, were a victim of crime, would you want a witness to step forward?

Witnesses to crimes are often critical for prosecutors seeking convictions. Generally, law-abiding citizens want to cooperate with law enforcement; however, as described in the text, serious crimes, especially gang-related crimes, present potentially dangerous situations for witnesses. Consider these three real-life scenarios. In Boston, a witness to a shooting by a member of a street gang found copies of his grand-jury testimony taped to all the doors in the housing project where he lived (Butterfield 2005). In Baltimore, Rickey Prince, a 17-year-old who witnessed a gang murder and agreed to testify against the killer was shot in the back of the head a few days after a prosecutor read Prince's name aloud in a packed courtroom (Butterfield 2005). In West Palm Beach, Florida, a witness who planned to testify against Futo Charles was gunned down in a parking lot. Charles is the leader of one of South Florida's most violent gangs, **Top 6**, a 400-member gang linked to 14 homicides and more than 150 shootings (*The Citizen* 2011b). In Baltimore and Boston, CDs and DVDs titled *Stop Snitching* have been made, identifying the names of some people whom street gangs suspect of being witnesses against them and warning people who cooperate with the police that they will be killed. The Baltimore video appears to show three dead bodies on its back cover above the words *snitch prevention* (Butterfield 2005).

The Baltimore video received a great deal of publicity in the world of popular culture and mainstream news because it featured NBA star Carmelo Anthony. The video shows alleged drug dealers talking about what happens to people who cooperate with the police and Anthony is standing next to one of them. In one segment, Anthony stands on a street, wearing a red shirt and baseball hat and laughing while another man talks about life on the street, snitches, and the NBA. Anthony does not respond to any of the comments. In fact, it was later learned that Anthony, a native of Baltimore, had no idea that he was being included in an anti-snitching video and that his image was edited to make him look like he took part in it. His agent, Calvin Andrews, explained that Anthony was just hanging out with some guys that he probably knew growing up (Denver ABC News 2004). Law enforcement ruled that Anthony had no criminal involvement in the video. Nonetheless, community activists in Baltimore's inner city say Anthony's appearance in the DVD, even if unintentional, could make their jobs harder because of his fame and street credibility (Denver ABC News 2004). The slogan "stop snitching" has been around since at least 1999, when it was popularized by Boston rapper Tangg da Juice (Kahn 2007). Baltimore rapper, Rodney Thomas, a.k.a. Skinny Suge, took the *stop snitching* message and made an underground DVD titled *Stop F*cking Snitching*, which began circulating in Baltimore in November 2004 (Kahn 2007). The video is now known as *Stop Snitchin*. It would have remained underground if not for Anthony's appearance in it.

What concerns law enforcement, and most conventional folks is the existence of a culture that accepts the notion that snitches, or witnesses to crimes, should be killed. Furthermore, that people are willing to film themselves promoting "death to snitches" says a lot about contemporary culture. The video is now a part of popular culture and freely available on YouTube.

PROPERTY CRIMES

Many of us worry, or take certain precautions, about being a victim of violent crime. Understandably so, when you consider what constitutes a violent crime; we don't want to be murdered, raped, beaten, robbed, or extorted. In reality, however, we are much more likely to be a victim of property offenses than of street crime offenses. Property crime occurs when something of value is taken from its owner by a perpetrator(s). Among the categories of property offenses are burglary, larceny-theft, motor vehicle theft, and vandalism.

Burglary

Burglary accounted for nearly one out of four (23.6%) property crimes committed in the United States in 2009. **Burglary** is defined as the unlawful entry of a structure to commit a felony or theft (FBI 2009f). To classify an offense as a burglary, the use of force to gain entry need not have occurred. The UCR Program has three subdivisions for burglary: forcible entry, unlawful entry where no force is used, and attempted forcible entry. The category of "attempted forcible entry" makes it clear that a person need not be successful in his/her attempt to burglarize a structure. A structure can include an apartment, barn, house, trailer, or houseboat when used as a permanent dwelling, office, railroad car (but not automobile), stable, and vessel (i.e., ship) (FBI 2009f). In 2009, there were nearly 2.2 million burglaries. Because the potential threat to home occupants (even if they were not home at the time of the initial break-in) is so high, most jurisdictions punish burglary as a felony. It is also common for states to enact laws creating different degrees of burglary. For example, nighttime forced entry into a home is more heavily punished than a daytime entry into a nonresidential structure by an unarmed offender (Siegel 1995). Of all burglaries, 61 percent involved forcible entry, 32.6 percent were unlawful entries (without force), and 6.5 percent were forcible entry attempts. Nearly three out of four (72.6%) burglaries are of residential properties (FBI 2009f).

Gang members are well equipped to commit this particular crime. Breaking into and entering someone's home, especially while he/she is home, takes a certain amount of courage. The risks are high and the payoffs are sometimes low. On the other hand, the payoff can be very beneficial from the financial standpoint of the burglar. According to the OJJDP (2000), gang members are responsible for 13 percent of burglaries in "most/all" jurisdictions, 45 percent in "some," 36 percent in a "few," and just 6 percent in "none" of the jurisdictions. Interestingly, rural jurisdictions reported the highest percentage of gang members who committed most/all of the burglaries (21% compared to 11% in large cities). Street gangs may commit burglaries for a number of reasons, but two in particular stand out—as an initiation for a new recruit and as a means of financing gangs. In Tampa Bay, a 14-year-old member of a Blood gang recruited other teens to join the gang. The recruits were told they could choose between a "beat-in" and committing a crime. One boy chose to commit a crime, burglarizing a vacant home on Treehaven Drive in Spring Hill. He caused about $1,000 worth of damage by painting the world "BLOOD" on the carpet. He and the recruiter were both arrested for burglary. The recruiter was also charged with soliciting street gang members. It is a third-degree felony in Florida to "intentionally cause, encourage, solicit, or recruit another person to join a criminal street gang that requires as a condition of membership . . . the commission of any crime" (Marrero 2010). In Santa Fe, New Mexico, the recession and street gangs are being blamed for the rise in the city's residential burglary rate (Auslander 2009). The residential burglary rate in the second quarter of 2009 jumped 105 percent compared to the second quarter of 2008, according to statistics provided by the Santa Fe police department (Auslander 2009).

Larceny-Theft

With an estimated number of larceny-thefts nearing 6.2 million in 2010, larceny-theft accounted for an estimated 68.1 percent of property crimes nationwide (FBI 2010g). The FBI's UCR Program defines larceny-theft as the unlawful taking, carrying, leading, or riding away of property from the possession or constructive possession of another (FBI 2010g). Examples are thefts of bicycles, motor vehicle parts and accessories, shoplifting, pocket-picking, or the stealing of any property or article that is not taken by force and violence or by fraud. Attempted larcenies are considered larcenies. Crimes that are not included as larcenies include embezzlement, confidence games, forgery, and check fraud (FBI 2010g). The average value of property taken during larceny-thefts was $998 in 2010. Applying this average value to the estimated number of larceny-thefts reveals that the total loss to victims nationally was over $6.1 billion. Petty larceny involves small dollar amounts, usually leading to a misdemeanor sentencing; grand larceny involves merchandise of higher dollar value and is considered a felony punishable by prison. According to the OJJDP (2000), gang members are responsible for a great deal of larceny-theft offenses. The percentage of gang members to nongang members (in the "most/all" category) arrested for larceny-theft (17%) is second only to drug sale offenses (27%). Survey respondents in suburban counties reported the highest levels of gang involvement in motor vehicle theft, larceny-theft, and drug sales.

Motor Vehicle Theft

Motor vehicle theft is a common type of larceny offense. However, because of its frequency and seriousness, it is treated as a separate category in the UCRs. The UCR Program defines **motor vehicle theft** as "the theft or attempted theft of a motor vehicle" (FBI 2010h). A motor vehicle is a self-propelled vehicle that runs on land surfaces and not rails. Examples of motor vehicles include sport utility vehicles, automobiles, trucks, buses, motorcycles, motor scooters, all-terrain vehicles, and snowmobiles. "Motor vehicle theft does not include farm equipment, bulldozers, airplanes, construction equipment, or water craft such as motorboats, sailboats, houseboats, or jet skis" (FBI 2010h). Auto theft is attractive to a number of people. Gang members may steal a car to use it in a crime, to sell it on the black market or for parts at chop shops, for their own personal transportation (e.g., to take their girlfriends out on a date or a road trip), or for the simple thrill of stealing a car. **Carjacking** is a type of auto theft that involves the armed robber approaching a car and forcing the owner to give up the keys. In many cases, car owners make the mistake of reacting too slowly and end up dead.

There are numerous examples across the nation of street gangs involved in motor vehicle theft rings. For example, in Lehigh Valley, Pennsylvania, several members of the **Handsome Boys (HB)** were charged with operating an auto theft ring in April 2012. The gang members, who are mostly teenagers in/from Allen High School, started their scheme in the fall of 2011 and stole 16 mid-1990s Hondas (Gamiz 2012). The popularity of older Hondas makes the stolen parts market very lucrative, and the HB gang was trying to take advantage of this. In addition to motor vehicle theft, the boys were charged with other crimes, including receiving stolen property and unauthorized use of an automobile. Street gangs are involved in auto theft in Miami Gardens. In an attempt to combat motor vehicle theft, the Miami Gardens Police Department's Auto Theft Unit promotes using anti-theft deterrents such as ignition kill switches, collars or steering wheel lock bars and V.I.N. etching. "Lo Jack" is especially recommended as the Miami Gardens Police Department has 14 police cars equipped with Lo Jack units to assist in locating stolen vehicles (Miami Gardens Police Department 2008).

Vandalism

The term *vandalism* can be traced back to the Vandals, a Germanic people associated with senseless destruction as a result of their sack of Rome under King Genseric in 455 C.E. **Vandalism** involves the willful or malicious destruction, damaging, or defacing of public or private property. Recklessly damaging property is called **criminal damage**. As defined by Arizona state law (A.R.S. 13-1602A&B), *criminal damage* may be defined as a misdemeanor or a felony, depending on the amount of damage. Defacing property, which includes the scratching or painting of property (including buildings, furniture, vehicles, cemeteries, signs, and freeway overpasses), is also considered criminal damage. One of the more common forms of vandalism involves the use of graffiti by gang members. In the state of California, vandalism up to $400 may result in up to less than one year in county jail and a fine of no more than $5,000 as it is considered a misdemeanor offense. If the amount of damage exceeds $400, the consequences may include time in prison or county jail for no more than one year and a fine of $10,000, as it is considered a felony offense (Penal Code 594 PC). Simply using a magic marker and writing your initials on a public window, such as a coffee shop, is a misdemeanor offense, even though nail polish remover will easily erase marker and paint impressions. Other examples of vandalism include salting lawns, cutting trees without permission, egg throwing, placing glue into locks, "keying" an automobile, clogging a sink and leaving the water running, and painting graffiti.

Graffiti represents an attack on property and on society as a whole. Graffiti, one of the worst eyesores in a community, is despised by law-abiding citizens. A great deal of graffiti is gang related. Graffiti in the community is often the first sign that gangs are taking over a neighborhood. For gangs (and those who can read the language, including law enforcement, gang researchers, and street-smart residents), graffiti is like a newspaper, containing messages about turf boundaries and advertising gang exploits. The costs of graffiti are immense. Schools, businesses, local governments, and property owners spend millions of dollars each year to clean graffiti, repair buildings, or replace vandalized equipment. Local governments pass the costs on to taxpayers, and businesses pass the costs of vandalism on to customers through higher prices. According to GraffitiHurts.com (2012), the annual clean-up costs of graffiti vandalism in the United States average taxpayers about $1–3 per person per year. Caltrans and Metro in Los Angeles County estimated that the cost of graffiti removal was about $28 million in 2006. According to the Metropolitan Transportation Authority, graffiti costs New York City residents $50 million a year (Carter 1999). Graffiti announces gangsters' power in a neighborhood, but it is also a major form of disrespect directed toward the local residents. Graffiti lowers property values, heightens fear among residents, and diminishes a community's quality of life. Many cities, such as Stockton, California, have established "Graffiti Hotlines" so that residents can report the location of graffiti. Stockton, a city with just under 300,000 residents, spent $900,000 in graffiti removal in 2006, putting this city firmly in the $3.00 per person category (City of Stockton 2012).

Not all graffiti criminals are members of street gangs. The most common nongang members to utilize graffiti are **taggers**. A tagger does not (necessarily) belong to a gang; instead, he/she enjoys defacing the property of others by "tagging" his/her "name" (an alias is common) on numerous forms of property. Tagger crews also exist. They typically lack the relatively formal organization of gangs, but some carry weapons for protection against rival tagger crews. Regardless of who creates it, graffiti is a scourge against civil society. In an attempt to curtain the blight of gang graffiti, a number of jurisdictions have created vandal-resistant murals. In Los Angeles, for example, the Caltrans' Mural Replica Project is responsible for putting up a number of 14- by 16-foot, vandal-resistant plastic-and-vinyl murals along busy highways (e.g., the 101 Freeway at North Main Street in Los Angeles).

Realizing that there are delinquents who find it appealing to paint walls, some organizations and private business people have established areas where it is okay to paint their property. One of the most popular places is the 5Pointz Institute of Higher Burnin', otherwise known as the 5Points Aerosol Art Center and outdoor art exhibit space considered to be the world's premiere "graffiti mecca." Located in an area in Long Island City, by the 7 Train, graffiti artists are allowed to paint colorful pieces on the walls of the 200,000 square foot factory building. The warehouse itself houses numerous studios for artists, and as a result, using the building for painting graffiti seems like a natural solution. After all, if people are going to deface other people's property, it is best that they have the okay of the owner(s).

DRUGS: USE, SALE, DISTRIBUTION, AND TRAFFICKING

In a study by McCorkle and Miethe (1998, 2002) it was suggested that it is a myth that street gangs have taken over the drug market. Things have certainly changed since then. According to the FBI (2009c), gang members are the primary retail-level distributors of most illicit drugs. Street gangs are also increasingly distributing wholesale-level quantities of marijuana and cocaine in most urban and suburban communities. Law enforcement views drug-related activity among street gangs as the strongest factor influencing local gang violence (Howell 2012). The reported increased levels of gang violence in a significant portion of locales across the United States in 2006 (e.g., 55% in aggravate assaults; 45% reported increase in robbery; 39% increase in larceny-theft; 37% increase in burglary; and 30% increase in auto theft) compared to the previous year is attributed to the increase in gang participation of drug sales, distribution, and trafficking (Egley and O'Donnell 2006).

The 2005 "National Gang Threat Assessment" reported that street gangs are also increasingly associating themselves with organized crime groups, such as Mexican drug organizations and Asian and Russian organized crime. "Imprisoning gang members is thought to do little to curb their activities, and the return of previously imprisoned gang members to communities is believed to intensify criminal activity, drug trafficking, and violence in those communities" (*Encyclopedia.com* 2009). Mexican drug cartels have increased their level of violence to expand their drug distribution and trafficking operations. They have assassinated politicians, journalists, and law enforcement officers. In May 2012, the Zetas drug cartel killed 49 people and left their decapitated and mutilated bodies on a highway connecting the northern Mexican metropolis of Monterrey to the U.S. border. The Zetas cut off the heads, hands, and feet of the victims to make identification difficult (Ramirez 2012). The dead were tattooed with Santa Muerte, a sacred figure adored by criminals and drug traffickers in Mexico. The tattoos generally depict the saint as a skeletal figure clad in a long robe and carrying one or more objects, usually a scythe and a globe (*Notitas de Noticias* 2012). The dead were members of a rival cartel (Sinaloa) who are waging an increasingly bloody war to control smuggling routes, the local drug market, and extortion rackets, including shakedowns of migrants seeking to reach the United States (Ramirez 2012). The Sinaloa cartel had massacred a group of Zetas previously in an apparent bid to take over the territory that had been dominated by the Zetas for a long time. Like any gang war, only much more extreme than U.S. street gang wars, the Mexican cartels massacre one another back and forth. In 2011, officials found 193 bodies in mass graves believed to have been migrants killed by Zetas drug cartel (Ramirez 2012). And these cartels are examples of the groups American street gangs are working with to bring drugs into the United States. One could argue that a simple solution to all this would be to legalize recreational drugs in the United States and all this violence, death, destruction, and financial costs would disappear. Current American drug policies, however, do not work with that idea in mind and so we have street gang involvement with drugs.

Drug Use

Street gang members spend a great deal of time hanging out "partying," and as previously described, *partying* implies drinking and taking recreational drugs (or stolen prescription drugs). Alcohol, marijuana, heroin, PCP, and amphetamines are among the more popular drugs used by gang members. Gang members **use drugs** for a variety of reasons. Drugs such as marijuana and crack cocaine are welcome party favors for gang members who are hanging out. They serve as a social "lubricant" during times of collective relaxation (Vigil 1988a). "Research conducted in the 1980s and 1990s has documented extensive youth and adult gang member involvement in drug use and generally higher levels of use compared with nongang members" (Howell and Decker 1999b, 2). Drugs may also be consumed for ritualistic reasons (e.g., "toasting" a fallen comrade or smoking pot at 4:20 PM). Drugs are also used in conjunction with acts of aggression. Vigil found that Chicano gang members often prepared for imminent fights with other gangs by drinking and smoking PCP-laced cigarettes. The drug PCP makes the user feel invincible and the adrenalin rush that the user experiences makes him/her a much better fighter. (Think of Rodney King withstanding the repeated blows of the Los Angeles Police Department—he was so high on PCP the baton blows could not hurt him or bring him down, causing the officers to use excessive force.) Hispanic gang members in Los Angeles smoke marijuana joints laced with PCP, commonly referred to as "dusters." It is interesting to note that the gang members studied by Vigil were able to use PCP with alcohol for both relaxation when hanging out and as a way to amp up for battle. "Evidently, gang members had substantial knowledge about the effects of alcohol (and its reactivity to PCP), and they had developed processes to adjust their reactions to the mood and behaviors they wanted" (Fagan 2004, 238). Of course, marijuana smokers do the same thing. They can smoke weed to get high or to "veg-out," a fact research on the effects of marijuana often fails to address. Alcohol users can also control the effects of the drugs. Sometimes the alcohol user drinks to get high; other times, to unwind or relax.

It is important to note that in some gangs drug use is forbidden. Spergel (1995) described how gang members who used heroin were forced out of gangs because they could not be relied on in fights with other gangs. Research conducted by Chin (1990) revealed that New York City Chinese gangs disallowed the use of drugs and alcohol, especially when they could interfere with conducting gang business. Gang leaders do not want their drug sellers high when they sell because they might mess up business.

Drug Sales

The **sale of drugs** has been a source of income for gangs for a long time, and many indications point to a large number of gangs resorting to the selling of drugs for profit in order to operate the gang. "Selling small amounts of drugs, especially marijuana . . . has been a common feature of gang life for decades. But the cocaine and crack crises of the 1980s created opportunities for gang and nongang youth alike to participate in drug selling and increase their incomes" (Fagan 2004, 239). Decker (2004) had suggested that most research shows that gang members sell drugs as individuals and that the gang exerts little instrumental control over the patterns of sales and the profits made by their members. This would not be true today, as street gangs have become increasingly organized in their drug sale operations. The fact that so many gangs are brought down by RICO violations (see discussions in Chapters 2 and 6) which involved establishing an organizational component that includes a hierarchy where orders come from the top and are carried through by those on the bottom would show that gangs do exert control over patterns of sales and profits.

As FBI evidence reveals, street gangs are taking over the retail drug sales market. There are two primary interconnected reasons why street gangs are involved with drug sales. First, selling drugs is a way of making money. As we discussed in Chapter 4, socioeconomic factors play an important role in gang formation. The historical gang that consisted of youths who felt they were protecting turf while having some kicks and thrills was merely a rite of passage until adulthood when they would find jobs to make a living. During much of the 1900s until the late 1970s and early 1980s, young adult gangbangers, like nongang persons, could find relatively high-paying factory jobs. The shifting labor market changed all that. The decline of American industry was a stimulus for increased gang membership. The second reason that gangs are involved in drug sales is the amount of money that can be made selling drugs. When people have desires for good and services that are either illegal or not readily available, inevitably a black market will be created to meet these needs. This simple fact helps to explain a lot of criminal activity beginning with the formation of the Russian Mafia and the establishment of an illegal drug market. The Russian Mafia was formed to meet the needs of the Russian people. Evidence of the Russian Mafia dates to at least the eighteenth century. Nicholas II, Russia's last czar, could not control the Mafia, neither could Joseph Stalin, who led the Soviet Union until 1953 with an iron fist. In fact the Mafia actually flourished during Stalin's reign (Delaney 2004b). The U.S. government keeps the use of recreational drugs illegal, thus guaranteeing a black market. The U.S. government has failed as miserably as Stalin in its attempt to control the drug market. Consequently, street gangs and other liked-minded criminals flourish, violence increases, and the incarceration rate supercedes any sort of acceptable standard for a civilized society. As drug retailers, street gangs may have achieved a formation that is similar to a mafia, that is, they have found a way to organize a complex market at all levels: sales, distribution and trafficking, and a means of protecting the marketplace (through violence).

One might wonder just how much money gang members make selling drugs. The answer varies dramatically from gang to gang and by individual pusher. It was determined during the RICO trial of Syracuse's Boot Camp gang leader Karo Brown that each gang member made between $400 and $2,000 a week selling crack cocaine. An average of 15 gang members were dealing drugs at once. Thus, the gang's annual profit was between $312,000 and $1.6 million (O'Brien 2004c). Bear in mind, Boot Camp was just one of many gangs selling drugs and making that kind of money, in Syracuse, for that matter. Imagine how much money can be made selling drugs in larger U.S. markets.

Drug Distribution and Trafficking

The definition of **drug distribution** is subject to local jurisdiction parameters but generally refers to the purchase and sale, or distribution, of a quantity of drugs that can be divided into smaller quantities (to be sold on the street). The definition of **drug-trafficking** may also vary from one jurisdiction to another but generally involves the transport of drugs from one jurisdiction to another and usually involves large quantities or involves an established pattern of drug sales. It is not surprising that street gangs have become actively involved in drug-trafficking; after all, drug-trafficking is the number-one criminal enterprise in the world (followed by weapons trafficking and art theft) according to Interpol (*Parade Magazine* 2003a). As far as gang members are concerned, the sale and distribution of drugs is like any other business enterprise. One of the earliest and most comprehensive pictures of a street gang involved in drug-trafficking was provided by Felix Padilla in *The Gang as an American Enterprise* (1992). In this book, Padilla described the entire evolution of the fictitiously named Diamonds. The Diamonds, a Puerto Rican gang, started off as a musical group that performed in local Chicago nightclubs. In 1971, one of the members was mistaken for a gang member and killed by gunshot fired by a rival gang. The incident sparked the reorganization of the group into a violent criminal youth gang. For six years, the Diamonds were on a course of vengeance and retaliation, often provoking fights with other gangs. Throughout the early years, the Diamonds' involvement with drugs was strictly recreational. By the late 1970s, however, the gang decided that it could make money by selling drugs. The Diamonds set up numerous **puntos** (a number of street-corner marketplaces; translated, *punto* means "points") and took control of their neighborhood by running off the previously established drug dealers. They created a hierarchical structure with the distributors at the top; the thieves were at the low end of the hierarchy. Above the thieves were the runners and then the street dealers, who reported directly to the distributors. As in any business enterprise, members of the Diamonds hoped to climb the ranks, as each level represented more income and respect. As Padilla clearly illustrated, the Diamonds had become a criminal enterprise with a highly entrepreneurial spirit.

An increasing number of gangs are engaged in drug distribution and trafficking. Our discussion of MS-13 and M-18 in Chapter 6 provided a glimpse of their extensive network, one that includes drug distribution and drug-trafficking. Drug distribution and trafficking is not restricted to nation or transnational gangs however, as Syracuse's Boot Camp provides us with a model of how a local street gang near a border can develop a drug network. If you recall, Boot Camp was the first Syracuse street gang to be indicted with RICO violations. It was gang leader Karo Brown's intent to make money, a lot of money. He wanted to be a millionaire, and he thought he could do it by selling drugs and protecting his market through intimidation, violent assaults, and homicide. Located in the center of the state of New York, Syracuse is a city where drugs are usually imported, not exported. Brown knew that he would have to secure extremely large quantities of drugs from a supplier at the very top of the drug distribution hierarchy if Boot Camp was to make the level of profits he envisioned. He could not afford to pay wholesale price (buying from dealers in larger cities like New York, Boston, or Philadelphia as most drug dealers in Syracuse do) if he wanted to make money as a retailer and wholesaler himself. Brown and his gang tried to negotiate with biker gangs in Canada near Buffalo, but the Buffalo gangs were too big and powerful and pushed Boot Camp away from their turf. Next, Boot Camp went north of Syracuse on Interstate 81 to the Akwesasne Mohawk Reservation. Akwesasne is the Mohawk name for the reservation; most people outside of the reservation call it the St. Regis Mohawk Reservation. The reservation is adjacent to the Akwesasne reserve in Ontario and Quebec in Canada and the U.S. (New York) villages of Hogansburg and St. Regis. The Mohawks consider the entire community as one reservation. There is a dispute among the Mohawks from the old culture and traditional chiefs and the new culture and the elected chiefs. The elected chiefs voted in favor of gambling, going against the traditional chiefs' wishes. Today, the reservation is home to the Akwesasne Mohawk Casino and the Mohawk Bingo Palace. As a sovereign nation, U.S. law enforcement officials do not have jurisdiction on the reserve. There are a number of Mohawks who have decided to make money based on the reservation's strategic location between two countries, where one, Canada, is home to suppliers of large quantities of drugs and the other, the United States, has a large appetite for drugs. Members of Boot Camp worked in concert with Mohawks to traffic drugs from Canada into the reservation which the gang took to Syracuse. Before long, Boot Camp's operation was so large, they exported drugs to larger cities like Philadelphia, Boston, and New York and ran a very profitable street business in Syracuse. Street gangs are not the only criminal element working deals with members of the Mohawk tribe, as the reservation has become a center for smuggling many items, including liquor, cigarettes, and drugs. The smuggling of cigarettes goes both directions (the United States and Canada). When Canada raised its cigarette taxes over a decade ago, drug runners began smuggling cigarettes made in an underground factory on the northern New York side of Akwesasne. The number of cigarette seizures in Canada increased ten-fold between 2001 and 2006 (Gifford 2007).

As acknowledged by the FBI (2009c), street gangs, such as Syracuse's Boot Camp gang, work with Outlaw Motorcycle Gangs (OMGs) along the U.S.-Canada border. They work together with

Canada-based gangs and criminal organizations to facilitate various criminal activities, including drug smuggling into the United States. We have previously discussed the role of OMGs in drug-trafficking (see Chapter 1), all along the northern border from the West Coast to the East Coast. OMGs operate in small towns and large cities. They also operate along Canadian reserves and American Indian reservations. No other criminal organization than the Hells Angels so dominates the drug trade along the American–Canadian border. As described in Chapter 1, law enforcement officials on both sides of the border have attempted for decades to bring OMGs under control. Hells Angels, in particular, have been targets of international law enforcement agencies since the late 1970s. Hells Angels are responsible for importing drugs from Canada into the United States through border cities like Niagara Falls.

Street gangs use drug-trafficking as a means of generating money. According to the 2005 National Gang Threat Assessment, 31.5 percent of all law enforcement respondents to the survey indicated that gangs in their communities were *highly* involved in selling drugs; this was especially true in the distribution of marijuana (64.8%), followed by crack cocaine (47.3%), methamphetamine (39.1%), powdered cocaine (38.2%), heroin (27%), and MDMA (the chemical abbreviation for 3,4-methylenedioxymethamphetamine, more commonly known as ecstasy) (23.7%) (*Encyclopedia.com* 2009; National Institute on Drug Abuse 2010). The FBI (2011a) reports that gang involvement and control of the retail drug trade poses a serious threat to public safety and stability in most major cities and in many mid-cities because drug distribution and trafficking activities are routinely associated with lethal violence. Violent disputes over control of drug territory and enforcement of drug debts frequently occur among gangs in both urban and suburban areas, as street gangs expand their control of drug distribution in many jurisdictions. Furthermore, law enforcement reporting indicates that gang-related drug distribution and trafficking has resulted in an increase in kidnappings, assaults, robberies, and homicides along the U.S. Southwest border region (FBI 2011a). As a last statistic designed to leave an impression, in 2010, 69 percent of U.S. law enforcement agencies reported gang involvement in drug distribution (FBI 2011a).

Many prison gangs work with major Mexican drug-trafficking organizations (MDTO), such as Arellano Felix, Beltran Leyva, Fuentes, Gulf Cartel, Los Zetas, Sinaloa, La Familia, and Michoacana, to traffic drugs. Among the U.S. prison gangs to work with MDTOs are La Eme, the Texas Syndicate, and Barrio Azteca. The U.S. prison gangs work in conjunction with street gangs such as the Latin Kings, MS-13, Surenos, and Nortenos to serve as go-betweens with the MDTOs. Street gang members, who are legal U.S. citizens, are used to cross the border, both to get the drugs from the Mexican cartels and then to return to the States with the drugs for sale. The prison gangs ensure cooperation between the two entities and receive a cut of the profits.

This brief coverage of drug use, sale, distribution, and trafficking of illicit drugs by street gangs clearly indicates that street gangs are taking over the black market in many communities. The U.S. government's War on Drugs has failed. It is time for a new policy.

NONTRADITIONAL AND WHITE-COLLAR CRIME

The final category of crime committed by street gangs is an umbrella grouping that includes crimes not traditionally associated with street gangs, such as alien smuggling, human trafficking, and prostitution, along with crimes typically associated with organized crime syndicates and white-collar criminals (e.g., counterfeiting, identity theft, and mortgage fraud).

Gang involvement in alien smuggling, human trafficking, and prostitution is increasing primarily because of their high profitability and lower risks of detection and punishment than that of drug and weapons trafficking. In 2011, federal, state, and local law enforcement officials in at least 35 states and U.S. territories reported that gangs in their jurisdictions are involved in alien smuggling, human trafficking, or prostitution (FBI 2011a).

Alien Smuggling

Street gangs are involved in **alien smuggling** because it is a source of revenue that can be quite lucrative and it is less risky than the illicit drug trade. In some cases, gang members are the ones being smuggled into the United States following their deportation. In other instances, gang members are facilitating the movement of migrants across the border (primarily the U.S.-Mexico border, but also the Canadian border). Alien smuggling has been growing at an alarming rate in the Southwest, according to Janice L. Kephart, Director of National Security Policy. In a report to the House Committee on Homeland Security, Kephart (2010) points out that "Operation Gatekeeper" successfully pushed much of the illegal border crossings to Arizona. Hidden camera footage in Arizona has revealed that hundreds of aliens cross the border into Arizona on a daily basis. (*Note*: Videos are available on YouTube.) You might wonder how this happens. There are simple, and yet alarming, answers to this query. In Yuma, located in far western Arizona, there have been thousands of illegal aliens entering the United States since at the least the early 2000s and they did so unabated because there wasn't a fence to stop them. Agents were regularly assaulted with rocks and weapons and were outnumbered 50 to 1 (Kephart 2010). In 2005, more than 2,700 load trucks full of aliens and drugs illegally breached that sector. Smugglers were leading the masses through the desert, leaving the sick and wounded to die. By 2010, the U.S. Border Patrol claimed that Yuma was under control due to the introduction of a seven-mile long "floating fence." A lack of proper fencing and low personnel numbers are two reasons for the influx of aliens into the United States via the desert Southwest. Corruption is another reason. "In a troubling admission to Congress, a high-ranking official from the Department of Homeland Security (DHS) has revealed that the agency charged with protecting the nation's borders is plagued with internal corruption that could put the U.S. at risk" (Judicial Watch 2012). In the last eight years (2004–2012), 138 agents from the Customs and Border Protection agency have been charged with corruption and more than 2,000 have been charged in other criminal cases (Judicial Watch 2012).

According to the FBI (2011a), there is increased coordination between Mexican drug cartels and U.S. street gangs in the establishment of alien smuggling networks that operate along the Southwest border. The Mexican drug cartels charge $1,200 to $2,500 per illegal alien for entry into the United States. The fee is considerably higher for aliens smuggled from countries other than Mexico (FBI 2011a). It is easy to see how criminals earn billions of dollars each year by smuggling aliens through Mexico into the United States. Many of these aliens are indebted to the cartels and become gang members to pay off their debt. Street gangs often work with the cartels to make sure that both entities profit. The FBI (2011a) reports that the Barrio Azteca, Mexican Mafia, MS-13, 18th Street Gang, and Somali gangs are all involved in alien smuggling. In 2009, members of the Drew Street clique of the Avenues (Sureno) street gang were arrested for running a drug and alien smuggling ring that brought more than 200 illegal aliens per year into the United States from Mexico. The aliens were concealed in hidden compartments of vehicles and then hid in a storehouse in Los Angeles (FBI 2011a).

Human Trafficking

Human trafficking involves the illegal trade of human beings. According to the U.S. Department of State (2008), in order for a situation to be **human trafficking**, it must have at least one of the elements within each of the three criteria areas of process, means/ways, and goal. *Process* elements include recruitment, transportation, transferring, harboring, or receiving; *Means/ways* include threat, coercion, abduction, fraud, deceit, deception, or abuse of power; and *Goal* refers to prostitution, pornography, violence/sexual exploitation, forced labor, involuntary servitude, debt bondage (with unfair wages), or slavery/similar practices. If one condition is met from each category, the result is human trafficking. For adults, victim consent is irrelevant if one of the "means" elements is employed. For children consent is irrelevant with or without the "means" category. The FBI (2011a) reports that 18,000 to 20,000 individuals are trafficked into the United States each year and that 12.3 million individuals worldwide are victims of forced labor, bonded labor, and prostitution. The word *victim* is appropriate, as women being sold on the streets in America are often victims rather than criminals (Kristof, 2012b). Some pimps are known to brand their women and girls. As Kristof (2012b) explains, some pimps brand their names on the prostitutes' necks or backs. In one case, a girl was tattooed with her pimp's name on her pubic area, along with a dollar sign—to make it clear that she was his property. The United Nations (2008) reports that 161 countries are affected by human trafficking by being a source, transit, or destination and that people are reported to be trafficked from 127 countries to be exploited in 137 countries, affecting every continent and every type of economy. The majority of the trafficking victims are between 18 and 24 years of age. In addition, an estimated 1.2 million children are trafficked each year. Recognizing the growing number of humans trafficked in the United States, there are 45 states with anti-trafficking criminal statutes and 48 states with anti-labor trafficking criminal statutes (Polaris Project 2012). Also, in the first five months of 2012, states passed more than 40 laws relating to human trafficking (Polaris Project 2012). That the estimated global annual profit made from the exploitation of all trafficked forced labor exceeds $31.6 billion (U.S. dollars) explains why criminals, including street gangs, participate in human trafficking (United Nations 2008).

The new mantra of large street gangs, especially transnational gangs, is to make money by any means necessary. Human trafficking is one of those means. Street gangs may be involved in human trafficking rings that extend beyond the U.S. border or they may be engaged in more localized versions of human exploitation. As an example of the former, the FBI (2011a) reports that the Bloods, MS-13, Surenos, and Somali gangs are involved in human trafficking. In New England, some gangs are combining human trafficking with drug-trafficking operations, where females are used to courier drugs and participate in prostitution. In November 2010, federal law enforcement officials indicted 29 members of a Somali gang in Minneapolis for operating an interstate sex trafficking ring that sold and transported underage African-American and Somalian females from Minneapolis, Minnesota, to Columbus, Ohio, and Nashville, Tennessee, for prostitution (FBI 2011a). As an example of localized human trafficking, a teenager from Santa Ana, California, who lied to her boyfriend about being pregnant hatched an elaborate scheme to kidnap her roommate's two-week-old baby. The girl allegedly asked gang members to steal the child. She then planned to ride with the gangsters to her boyfriend's home where she would pass the baby off as her own (*Daily Mail* 2011).

Prostitution

Prostitution refers to the commission by a person of any natural or unnatural sexual act, deviate sexual intercourse, or sexual contact for monetary consideration or other thing of value (U.S. Legal 2012). Prostitution is categorized as a "victimless crime" in some criminal categorical schemes. It is considered a victimless crime, however, only when all the direct participants are willing and consenting adults. If a minor is involved or if any of the parties involved are not willing participants, it is not a victimless crime. Even when all parties are consenting adults, participants can be victimized. For example, one of the persons involved can be physically harmed or a sexually transmitted disease could be transmitted from one person to another. In some cases, perhaps a majority of them, the prostitutes are not willing participants; instead, they have been coerced into performing sexual acts by unscrupulous others. Human trafficking in adults and children for purposes of prostitution occurs all around the world, including the United States.

Prostitution is another criminal activity that generates profits for street gangs. Gang members may serve as pimps, lure or force at-risk young females (especially runaways) into prostitution, and control them through violence and psychological abuse. According to the FBI (2011a), Asian gangs, Bloods, Crips, Gangster Disciples, MS-13, Surenos, Vice Lords, and members of OMGs are involved in prostitution operations. In San Diego, prostitution is reportedly the second-largest source of income for street gangs, especially black gangs who pimp young girls (FBI 2011a). In 2012, eight members of the notorious Rolling 60s Crip gang of Los Angeles were indicted on charges of running an underage sex ring. The Rolling 60s served as pimps, and their prostitutes were recruited by young female associates who recruited high school girls from Inland Empire schools. One of the go-betweens (described as the "lead prostitute"), Kimberly Alberti lured underage girls by promising them a glamorous life of a working girl wherein they would attain all sorts of material awards and cash. Instead, the girls were beaten, raped, and locked up along with being forced to have sex with clients (Kim 2012).

White-Collar Crime

White-collar crime was coined by sociologist Edwin Sutherland in his 1939 presidential address to the American Sociological Association. *White-collar crime* has since become recognized throughout the world but its meaning has been modified since Sutherland's (1983[1949]) initial definition of "crime committed by a person of respectable and high status in the course of his occupation" (7). The term *white-collar crime* beckons to an era when professional officer workers wore white shirts with ties; the term is also used to contrast certain crimes from street crime (by implication, committed by "blue"-collar, nonprofessional, workers). *White-collar crime* still refers to certain business-related crimes (e.g., tax evasion, counterfeiting, identity theft, mortgage fraud, embezzlement, and money laundering) although it is now recognized that many nonprofessionals commit such crimes. White-collar crimes are difficult to prosecute because the perpetrators use sophisticated means to conceal their activities through a series of complex transactions. White-collar crimes are nonviolent crimes usually committed in commercial situations for financial gain.

That white-collar crime provides situations for financial gain and leads us to our connection with street gangs. The evolving criminal schemes, which include mortgage fraud, counterfeiting, bank and credit card fraud, and identity theft, are attractive because they are less risky than traditional gang-related crimes. In essence, gangs are "killing" people financially instead of physically, when they commit white-collar crime. Financial crime has increased significantly in the past few years because of technological advances. Gangs such as the Bloods, Crips, Gangster Disciples, Vice Lords, Latin Kings, Mexican Mafia, Surenos, Nortenos, La Nuestra Familia, Texas Syndicate, Aryan Brotherhood, various OMGs, Asian gangs, and a number of local gangs are undertaking white-collar crime by recruiting members who possess the necessary high-tech skill sets. The level of sophistication demonstrated by some gangs reveals that they might be better equipped to run commercial operations than some professionals (Booton 2011). Street gangs engage in counterfeiting, for example, because of its low risks and high financial rewards. This does not mean that law enforcement is powerless against street gang white-collar crime activity. In July 2010, a Florencia 13 gang member was arrested in Los Angeles for operating a lab from his home that manufactured pirated video games, and, in April 2010, a member of the East Coast Crips was arrested in Los Angeles for the sale of counterfeit goods and drug-trafficking at a clothing store he co-owned (police confiscated 824 counterfeit items from the store) (FBI 2011a). According to the FBI (2011a), street gangs launder profits from criminal activities such as drug-trafficking and prostitution through front companies such as music businesses, beauty shops, auto repair shops, law firms, and medical offices. Members of the Black Guerilla Family in Maryland used prepaid debit cards as virtual currency inside Maryland prisons to purchase drugs and further gang interests. In April 2009, members of the Bloods in San Diego were charged with racketeering and mortgage fraud.

One problem most law-abiding citizens do not have involves having so much cash they do not know what to do with it. Illegal enterprises, such as drug-trafficking, generate huge sums of money for transnational gangs and drug cartels. Eventually, these criminals must find a way to channel their money into legal business, because depositing large sums of cash into banks, especially American banks, raises many questions (e.g., "How did you acquire all this cash?") and subjects the depositor to questioning from law enforcement officials. The Mexican drug cartel Los Zetas provides us with one example of money laundering conducted by gangs. Miguel Angel Trevino Morales, the second in command and lead enforcer of the Mexican Zetas drug-trafficking organization, along with his younger brother Jose Trevino Morales, established a prominent horse breeding operation, Tremor Enterprises (with ranches throughout the southwest United States), that allowed them to launder millions of dollars in drug money, according to current and former federal law enforcement officials (Thompson 2012). Miguel Morales, who is known for dismembering his victims while they are still alive, and who is a man on the run (from the law), teamed with his brother Jose, who has legal residency in the United States and possesses a keen eye for a good horse, managed to combine a passion for horses with their need to launder money. "As much as Tremor was a money-laundering operation, the Morales brothers' quarter horse venture allowed them to mix business with pleasure. Horses have long been considered a status symbol in Latin America and drug traffickers have been among the region's most avid collectors" (Thompson 2012). The Morales brothers also have several ranches and racetracks in Mexico and Guatemala which further allows for money laundering. The Morales brothers were successfully laundering as much as $1 million a month into buying quarter horses in the United States, according to authorities. A Justice Department affidavit reveals that law enforcement authorities first became suspicious of Tremor Enterprises when the Zetas paid more than $1 million in a single day for two broodmares (Rubenfeld 2012). The affidavit also indicates that the Justice Department raised eyebrows when four Tremor horses were fielded in the same prestigious race at Los Alamitos Race Course, near Los Angeles. Tremor horses started winning at the All American Futurity, considered the Kentucky Derby of quarter horses, and in one September 2010 race, a Tremor horse won a million-dollar prize with a long-shot colt named Mr. Piloto. Leading the revelry at the track was Mr. Piloto's owner, Jose Trevino Morales. Attempting to launder millions of dollars earned through drug-trafficking into horse racing had actually earned the Zetas millions of dollars. One might think that this is an example of a time when crime *does* pay. However, a federal grand jury in Texas voted to return an indictment against 14 defendants in connection with a conspiracy to launder Los Zetas drug money, by buying, training, breeding, and racing American quarter horses in the United States. Both of the Morales brothers were included, along with another brother Oscar Omar Trevino Morales (Rubenfeld 2012).

As this review of crime, in all its variations, indicates, the days of street gang activity being limited to street crime are over. Gangs are involved in any sort of activity that makes money. Perhaps the one common thread is the willingness of street gangs to commit extreme acts of violence, including homicide, to protect any, and all, of its money-making ventures.

Summary

Although street gang members spend most of their time engaged in regular activities such as sleeping, eating, dating, and playing video games, they also commit a great deal of crime. In this chapter we distinguished street gang criminal activities into four categories: violent offenses; property crimes; the use, sale, distribution, and trafficking of drugs; and white-collar crime and other nontraditional (for street gangs) crime. Often, all of these criminal activities, and especially drugs, violence, and homicide, are intertwined. According to data provided by the FBI in its 2011 "National Gang Threat Assessements," criminal street gangs are responsible for an average of 48 percent of violent crime in most jurisdictions and up to 90 percent in several others. In some communities, street gangs may commit up to 80 percent of the overall crime.

Violent crimes include homicide, robbery, assault, forcible rape, extortion, and witness intimidation. The larger the gang, the greater the likelihood it is involved in all of these activities. The leading causes of gang violence are control over drug distribution and disputes over drug territory; conflict with gang migration into rival territory; and the release of incarcerated gang members back into the community. Property crime occurs when something of value is taken from its owner by a perpetrator(s). Among the categories of property offenses are burglary, larceny-theft, motor vehicle theft, and vandalism. Street gangs are involved in all types of property crime, but they are not responsible for nearly as much proportionately as they are with violent crimes. Street gang members are involved in the use, sale, distribution, and trafficking of illicit drugs. According to the FBI, gang members are the primary retail-level distributors of most illicit drugs. Street gangs are also increasingly distributing wholesale-level quantities of marijuana and cocaine in most urban and suburban communities. A number of street gangs, especially nation and transnational gangs, are working with Mexican drug cartels and outlaw motorcycle gangs to traffic drugs into the United States from border nations. Perhaps nothing illustrates the scope of street gang criminal activity involvement more than the realization that street gangs are involved in many types of crime that past gangs would never had considered, including alien smuggling, human trafficking, and prostitution; along with crimes typically associated with organized crime syndicates and white-collar criminals (e.g., money laundering, counterfeiting, identity theft, and mortgage fraud).

9

Street Gang Intervention: Prevention, Suppression, and Treatment

This chapter discusses various intervention techniques designed to fight the strength and increasing numbers of street gangs in society. It is important to remember that there are numerous reasons why individuals decide to join a gang, and therefore a variety of efforts to combat gangs must also be utilized. The techniques implemented by various policy makers are determined by their ultimate goals. Prevention efforts are those methods designed to stop youths from joining a gang in the first place. Suppression efforts are attempts by law enforcement and judicial bodies to curtail and punish existing gang members. Treatment programs are designed to help rehabilitate gang members so that they can become positive members of society.

The OJJDP (2009) recommends in its "Comprehensive Gang Model" that the first step any community must take before creating intervention programs is to analyze its gang problem. For example, do youths need anger management courses, tutors for youths struggling in school, job placement referrals, or does the community need additional patrols and resources where gang activity takes place in order to suppress such activities? After assessment, the community needs to make a plan and specify specific goals. It is critical that any intervention program implemented be evaluated in order to determine its effectiveness.

Our review of gang intervention programs begins with prevention strategies, which are designed to prevent youths from joining a gang.

PREVENTION STRATEGIES

The discussion in Chapter 1 highlights the importance of recognizing the role of juvenile delinquency on street gangs, in part, because delinquency generally precedes gang membership. As the OJJDP (2011b) indicates, most gang members join between the ages of 12 and 15, and these youths are not, typically, those who have been squeaky clean, well-integrated members of society. Although individuals join street gangs for many different reasons, prevention strategies should be directed toward those most at risk of joining. *At risk* refers to pregang youths who have shown some interest in gangs, by either fantasizing or experimenting by wearing gang attire and talking the talk of gang members. Since most gang members come from lower socioeconomic status backgrounds and share certain attributes (see Chapter 4), these at-risk youths should be targeted with prevention strategies. Furthermore, because most gang members come from certain backgrounds, the OJJDP recommends that specific neighborhoods and schools should be targeted for prevention strategies (Esbensen 2000). Intervening prevention programs, then, are designed to reduce the criminal activities of gangs by coaxing the next generation of youths away from joining gangs.

The goal of prevention strategies is to identify the warning signs that indicate a youth has shown an interest in joining a gang and to combat the many socioeconomic factors that lead to the view that the gang is the most suitable option for socioeconomic success. In essence, **prevention strategies** are the various techniques used to steer youths away from the temptations of "turning" to gangs and keep them on the straight path toward "conventional" lifestyles. As Travis Hirschi articulated, youths need to form a social bond to family, community, and society. Providing troubled youths with viable long-term goals is an important ingredient in forming a successful bond with society.

Prevention strategies, in general, fall into two categories: community programs and national programs. The role of families, schools, and local business within a community is also important. Discussion begins with a brief review of the history of community prevention strategies along with a number of examples of community programs.

Community Prevention Programs

The origin of gangs is in local communities—communities that, for the most part, have failed to provide youths with hope for a positive future. The community, then, becomes the cornerstone for the existence of gangs and is the focal point of attempts to prevent youths from their initial involvement with a gang. As described throughout this book, factors such as poverty, unemployment, and the absence of meaningful jobs contribute to the presence of urban street gangs. Although it is clear that gangs may form in any social environment (e.g., the suburbs, rural areas, prisons, and Native-American reservations), for the most part, gangs reside in urban areas characterized by social disorganization and economic marginalization. They tend to reside in housing projects and barrios. The largest number of gang members can be found in the largest cities starting with Los Angeles, Chicago, and New York City. Many youths are born into social environments filled with violence and hopelessness. "Further, large numbers of America's youth, especially in public housing and inner city areas, are slipping into a quagmire from which return is extremely difficult" (Pope and Lovell 2004, 355). In short, a number of inner-city youths are at risk simply because they were born into certain neighborhoods.

The history of gang intervention programs can be traced back to Chicago and the creation of the **Chicago Area Project (CAP)** in 1934 by University of Chicago sociologist Clifford Shaw. Shaw believed that every neighborhood could reduce juvenile delinquency by improving community life (CAP 2012a). Shaw had endorsed the "social disorganization" approach that was popular with the Chicago School explanation of gang formation (see Chapter 3 for a review of this theoretical perspective). From this perspective, the disorganization found in many of Chicago's communities was explained in terms of the rapidly changing environment. The core poverty areas were plagued by a number of social problems, including poor schools and a lack of social services. The original mission of CAP has not changed since Shaw's inception of the program. CAP works with the notion that community problems such as delinquency, gang violence, substance abuse, and unemployment can best be solved locally. As a result, CAP is not a single organization but rather a network of more than 40 grassroots organizations and special projects aimed at promoting positive youth development and preventing juvenile delinquency through community-building (CAP 2012a). Each affiliate agency is independent and provides its own service toward CAP's goal of reducing juvenile delinquency and social disorganization. Among the programs offered by CAP (2012b) are career development, community initiatives, consumer skills, after-school programs that stress reading and other educational skills, self-sufficiency skills training, student internship, anti-violence, and youth leadership skills.

CAP was formed to involve local community groups and organizations in a combined effort to help prevent delinquency and street gangs. CAP also invented the idea of "detached workers" (agency representatives detached from their offices and assigned to communities) and the community gang worker role (Howell 2004a). It was in the 1940s that CAP introduced its detached-worker program, which focused on either at-risk youths (secondary prevention) or, in some instances, current gang members (tertiary intervention). Hundreds of community committees were formed, resulting in numerous local programs that sponsored such activities as recreation, mediation services, advocacy assistance with probation and parole, and school reforms. The CAP program was massive—it extended throughout the city of Chicago, making evaluation difficult. Howell (2004a) suggests that the only effective way of measuring the success of such a huge "community" program would be by comparison to another city.

The success of CAP's detached-worker component led to many other community-based programs. In New York City in the late 1940s, for example, community organizations designed to prevent youths from joining gangs relied almost exclusively on detached workers and led to eventual formation of the **New York City Youth Board** (1960). Even though the effectiveness of this program was never evaluated, it served as the forerunner of such later detached-worker programs as the Mid-City Project in Boston.

The **Mid-City Project** was a community-wide project that consisted of three major program components: community organization, family service, and gang work. Established in the Roxbury section of Boston in 1954, the Mid-City Project staff worked with 400 members of 21 street corner gangs, providing intensive services to seven gangs. Miller's (1962) rigorous evaluation of the Mid-City Project concluded that the project was ineffective.

Although the benefit of a community-involved intervention program as an effective means of combating gangs seemed obvious, the detached-worker programs appeared to be ineffective across the nation. In Los Angeles, a detached-worker program begun in 1961 with the emergence of African-American gangs in South Central was designed in such a way that workers were to employ "group guidance" as a means of intervention. Staff members of the **Group Guidance Program** (of the Los Angeles Probation Department) created such activities as tutoring, individual counseling, and advocacy with community agencies and organizations as means of providing guidance to a nongang way of thinking about and dealing with adverse conditions. Klein (1995) found, however, that the number of official arrests actually increased during the period that the Guidance Program operated. In the 1960s, he had conducted the Ladino Hills Project, a carefully designed implementation and evaluation of the detached-worker program. Klein found that the detached workers created an unintended outcome: increased gang cohesiveness, which resulted in increased gang crime. "Klein's research focused on detached workers targeting gang members (tertiary prevention), but the overall effectiveness of the CAP model remains in question. . . . To date . . . the evaluations of this strategy have not reported a reduction in gangs or gang activity" (Esbensen 2000, 7). An evaluation of Boston's Mid-City Project had similarly documented that the program failed to reduce delinquency and gang activity.

In the late 1960s, **The House of Umoja** community-based gang program was started in Philadelphia and modeled after CAP. The Umoja Project consists of residential and nonresidential (outreach) programs for gang members and other delinquency youths in hopes of providing them with a sanctuary from street life. The targeted youths for this program were those who came from broken homes (non-intact families) and/or those with emotional problems and other debilitating issues (House of Umoja 2006). The program was often able to negotiate gang summits and truces that were instrumental in reducing the gang homicides in the city during the late 1970s. The truces were generally short-lived. In 2006, the House of Umoja introduced a faith-based program: Peace in the Hood.

The overall effectiveness of the detached-worker approach to community intervention is mixed at best, and unsuccessful in most cases. Because the reasons that gang members join a gang are complicated, such relatively simple approaches to gang intervention as detached-worker strategies and other community-based programs have a hard time succeeding because they merely address the symptoms of the problem and do not properly address the complex issues of why juveniles join gangs. Detached-worker programs, then, should include other forms of intervention as well, such as job skills training, emotional counseling, mentoring programs, recreation centers for youths, drug and alcohol rehabilitation facilities, family counseling, and legal services.

Beginning in the 1970s, **crisis intervention** was a service commonly provided by detached workers. For example, in 1974, the Philadelphia Crisis Intervention Network (CIN) was formed. During the 1960s and 1970s, Philadelphia was a city transforming from mostly white to a city with a rapidly increasing black population. Tensions between racial groups often erupted into violence. Many of the newly arriving blacks were poor and included a number of future gang members. Violence was especially common in the southwest side of Philly during this era. The CIN program was designed to reduce tensions between whites and blacks and to curb the growing gang problem. The CIN program assigned gang workers to work specific geographic areas, but not specific gangs. They patrolled gang hot spots and attempted to defuse potentially violent situations. CIN officials have declared the program a success in reducing gang violence, and its success led to the development of other Philadelphia programs including the Philadelphia Anti-Drug Anti-Violence Network (Heavens 2012). A variation of Philadelphia's CIN program, named the **Community Youth Gang Services (CYGS)** program, was used in Los Angeles. Like CIN, the CYGS used such suppression tactics as dispatching patrol teams in specially marked cars, social intervention, group programming and outings for gang members, and truce meetings (Klein 1995). During the 1990s, emergency room intervention and victim programs were established in many high-crime communities. Emergency room intervention programs for injured victims may help curtail the cycle of gang violence. Other intervention programs have involved providing counseling for victims of drive-by shootings to reduce the traumatic effects of victimization and to discourage retaliation (Groves, Zuckerman, Marans, and Cohen 1993; Hutson, Anglin, Kyriacou, Hart, and Spears 1995; Hutson, Anglin, Pratts 1994).

In most major urban cities, there exists a proliferation of programs designed to prevent delinquency and gangs. In Richmond, Virginia, there exists the Richmond **Gang Reduction Intervention Program (GRIP)**. GRIP, originally funded by the OJJDP, is a collaborative effort among Richmond, federal, state, and local partners focusing on targeted neighborhoods designed to prevent delinquency and street gangs. Programs are designed to address the full range of personal, family, and community factors that contribute to delinquency and gangs. GRIP believes that people have the capacity to make better choices if they have better choices available to them (Cuccinelli 2012a). The GRIP includes over 40 programs on the strategic areas of primary prevention (targets the entire population in high-crime, high-risk communities); secondary prevention (targets at-risk youths, ages 7–14); intervention (targets active gang members and their associates, ages 10–24); reentry (targets multiple offenders about to reenter the local community); and suppression (targets gang leaders) (Cuccinelli 2012b).

As demonstrated in Chapter 6, Syracuse has its share of gang problems. In an effort to combat delinquency and street gangs in this city, a number of community groups and organizations have formed alliances. In the 1990s, the Crisis Response Team was formed under the defunct **Syracuse Partnership to Reduce Gun Violence** (founded by Julius Edwards). The Partnership, now defunct, was the center of a controversy when three staff members were arrested on Racketeer Influenced and Corrupt Organizations (RICO) violations because of their past association with the notorious Boot Camp street gang. The committee that hired these three men (Antonio Owens, Ridwan Othman, and Cheiron Thomas) included representatives of the Syracuse Police Department and the Onondaga County district attorney's office. Owens was hired as a peer counselor at an alternative high school for students with behavioral problems and Othman and Thomas as recreation aides at an evening program run by the Boys & Girls Club at Danforth School and the former St. Anthony's School (O'Brien and Sieh 2003b). Thus, the actual employer of the three men was the Partnership and not local schools. As it turns out, the police were already investigating the three former Boot Camp members but failed to inform the Partnership. Edwards acknowledged that the three men were former members of Boot Camp, but denied knowing they were involved in a major drug enterprise (O'Brien and Sieh 2003b). The Partnership had initially planned on not hiring anyone with a criminal record. However, as community members of the Partnership pointed out, the only way an outreach program would have any success with troubled youths would be by using counselors who had been in trouble and had turned their lives around. Former gang members have street credibility and the respect of at-risk youths, which are critical assets for counselors who hope to reach these youths. Therefore, banning former gang members (as some Syracuse citizens had demanded) is not advisable. The most successful counselors are those who have experienced firsthand the troubles these youths face. An extensive background check should be conducted, however, to ensure that they are no longer actively involved in gang or criminal activities (including outstanding warrants). In 2009, the Syracuse Police Department announced the formation of The Trauma Response Team, an initiative designed to help families and others affected by street violence (Sieh 2009). The team includes members of the clergy and Mothers Against Gun Violence. Syracuse also has the **Violence Intervention Program (VIP)**, a community-based intervention strategy to reduce youth, street, and gang violence. Like CAP, the program has member affiliates that operate independently from one another but each bearing its strengths toward the common VIP mission of improving the quality of life of individuals between the ages of 7 and 30 who are at risk of becoming and/or perpetrators of gang-related violence by empowering clients to make productive choices, effectively address life challenges, reduce the number of victims of violence, and decrease the number of juvenile perpetrators (Syracuse Urban Youth Development Coalition 2009).

In Los Angeles, one of most well-known gang intervention programs is **Homeboy Industries**, which has the catchy motto "Nothing stops a bullet like a job." Homeboy started as a jobs program offering alternatives to gang violence in one of the toughest neighborhoods in Los Angeles by assisting "at-risk, recently released, and formerly gang-involved youth to become contributing members of their communities through a variety of services in response to their multiple needs" (Homeboy Industries 2010). Free programs include counseling (with case managers closely monitoring individual progress and ensuring that participants receive the services they need); education (e.g., helping clients with literacy issues and preparation for the G.E.D. exam); legal services (a full-time lawyer on site provides workshops, one-on-one guidance, and so on); solar panel installation training and certification (a growing field that will provide job opportunities); mental health counseling; provision of job training and job placement skills (e.g., how to interview for a job, fill out resumes and job applications); tattoo removal (Homeboy provides over 4,000 treatments of visible gang tattoo removal a year); and substance abuse and addiction assistance (Twelve Steps meetings).

In Santa Cruz, California, there is the California Coalition of **Barrios Unidos**, a community-based peace movement in the violent streets of urban California. Incorporated in 1993, Barrios Unidos has as a mission to prevent and curtail violence against youths within Santa Cruz by providing them with life-enhancing alternatives (Santa Cruz Barrios Unidos 2012a). Barrios Unidos promotes five strategies to achieve its goal: leadership and human capital development (provides culturally based education, skills development, and service opportunities within the community); community economic development (promotes self-sufficiency through community-based land development, education, job preparedness, skills building, and family micro-business); civic participation and community mobilization (assures access to community resources and requires multi-sector involvement and collaboration); cultural arts and recreational activities (assures common space for the arts, music, dance, literature, etc.); and coalition building (as the name of the program implies, assures a united community among all the barrio/affiliate organizations). One of the more unique programs the Barrios Unidos participates in is the annual (in September) "Warriors Circle" retreat in the mountains of Aptos, California. The event draws boys and young men from around California to spend a weekend in the wilderness connecting with indigenous traditions that teach respect to nature and one another instead of the violence approach so common in gang-infested neighborhoods (Santa Cruz Barrios Unidos 2012b).

Any American city with a gang problem has created some variation of a gang prevention program, and it would be impossible to cover them all here. Among the others reviewed are **Elements** (created in Hanover, North Carolina), a 12-month program designed to prevent children from joining gangs by working with the notion that gangs serve as a coping mechanism for those interested or involved in them; **Aggression Replacement Training (ART)**, a program established in Brooklyn designed to teach at-risk youths anger control and common morality; and **Ceasefire** (Chicago), a public education program that sends the message that gun violence, or any violence, is unacceptable (Howell 2010a; Hughes, Devan Griner, Guarino, Drabik-Medeiros, and Williams 2012).

One of the few community-based prevention programs to provide a comprehensive evaluative data is the **Montreal Preventative Treatment Program** (also known as the Montreal Longitudinal Study and the Montreal Prevention Experiment). Although the focus of this book is American street gangs, Montreal, like any big North American city, has its share of gang problems and the reasons why youths join gangs are similar to those found in American communities. The Montreal Preventative Treatment Program is "a multi-component program designed to prevent antisocial behavior of boys who display early, problem behavior" (National Dropout Prevention Center/Network 2012). The program is designed to intervene the negative behavior of boys aged 7–9 who show potential for delinquent, criminal, or gang behavior. At-risk youths are determined on the basis of many risk factors, including antisocial/delinquent beliefs, early and persistent noncompliant behavior, early onset of aggression/violence, hyperactivity, low intelligence quotient, mental health problems, poor refusal skills, and victimization (e.g., child maltreatment and exposure to violence). Families that might produce at-risk youths are also targeted. Family risk factors include abusive parents, antisocial parents, broken home/change in caretaker, family violence, parent proviolent attitudes, parental use of physical punishment/harsh and/or erratic discipline practices, poor parental supervision, and unhappy parents. School risk factors include bullying, frequent school transitions, identified as learning disabled, low academic aspirations, low school attachment/bonding/motivation/commitment to school, old for grade/repeated grade, and poor student–teacher relations (Montreal Preventive Treatment Program 2012). The Preventive Treatment Program combines parent training with individual social skills training.

Parents receive an average of 17 sessions that focus on monitoring their children's behavior, giving positive reinforcement for prosocial behavior, using punishment effectively, and managing family crisis. The boys receive 19 sessions aimed at improving prosocial skills and self-control. Evaluation of the program is conducted when the boys turn age 12. Among the conclusions were the following: Treated boys were less likely to have engaged in offenses such as trespassing, petty theft, including bicycle theft; treated boys were less likely to get into fights than nontreated boys; 29 percent of treated boys were rated as "well-adjusted" in school, compared to 19 percent of the untreated boys; 22 percent of the treated boys, compared to 44 percent of the untreated boys, displayed less serious difficulties in school; and 23 percent of the treated boys, compared to 43 percent of the untreated boys, were held back in school or placed in special education. By age 15, those boys receiving the prevention treatment were less likely than untreated boys to report gang involvement, having been drunk or taken drugs in the past 12 months, and having friends arrested by the police (Montreal Preventive Treatment Program 2012). The data would seem to support the effectiveness of the Montreal program (Public Health Agency of Canada 2012).

Community prevention programs seem to work best when there is a cooperative effort between multiple key parties, especially families, schools, and local businesses. Realizing this, the OJJDP officially promotes the Spergel Comprehensive Gang Model as a means of responding to the threat of gangs. This model consists of five strategies:

1. Mobilizing community leaders and residents to plan, strengthen, or create new opportunities or linkages to existing organizations for gang-involved or at-risk youths
2. Using outreach workers to engage gang-involved youth
3. Providing or facilitating access to academic, economic, and social opportunities
4. Conducting gang suppression activities and holding gang-involved youths accountable
5. Facilitating organizational change and development to help community agencies better address gang problems through a team "problem-solving" approach that is consistent with the philosophy of community-oriented policing (Burch and Kane 1999; Howell 2000).

As this model indicates, community prevention interventions strategies should include such social institutions as the family, schools, and local businesses (as well as the police and suppression intervention efforts to be discussed later in this chapter).

It Takes an Entire Community: Families, Schools, Law Enforcement, and Local Business

The role and influence of the family in gang life has been discussed throughout this book. Clearly, all individuals are ultimately responsible for their own behaviors, but in many cases the options available are so limited that joining a gang seems like the best option. But before society can be blamed for "disappointing" the individual, the family must be held responsible for failing to keep a youth out of a gang. The first line of defense in gang prevention, then, is the family. Many community organizations such as preschool/Head Start programs and parent training/support programs have been designed to assist parents with at-risk youths. Most troubled youths have problems at school and most gang members are high school dropouts, and so families with school-age children can find assistance from programs that generally come under the collective umbrella of **compensatory education**. Compensatory education programs are U.S.-government-funded programs designed to help preschool children from lower socio-economic classes. Perhaps the best known such program is **Head Start**. The Head Start program is designed to promote "school readiness by enhancing the social and cognitive development of children through the provision of educational, health, nutritional, social and other services to enrolled children and families" (U.S. Department of Health and Human Services 2008).

Although Head Start is federally funded, and partially funded at that, each community runs its own office. Among the many consequences of this are the inconsistency in the effectiveness of the program, the evaluation of the program, and the supplies and services available at each office. As a result, there are mixed reviews about the overall effectiveness of Head Start. There are reports that children score higher on IQ and achievement tests, are less likely to be placed in special education classes or to fail a grade, have higher self-images, and get more encouragement from their parents to get a good education than similar children who have not gone through the program (Farley 1998). However, results from a 2010 study were less than encouraging: "The study demonstrated that children's attendance in Head Start had no demonstrable impact on their academic, socio-emotional, or health status at the end of first grade" (Whitehurst 2010). The Head Start Program is budgeted at $7.235 billion annually for programs serving approximately 1 million children (Whitehurst 2010). As previously mentioned, however, all programs are not funded equally; the Head Start program in Auburn (Cayuga County), New York, is looking for ideas on how to raise local funding to match federal grants. And it is this reality that enlightens us to the funding problem; the local programs cannot survive on federal money alone. "Leadership Cayuga" finds it challenging to sustain fundraising efforts (Long 2012). They look to local businesses for help, in many cases simple help like allowing a small cardboard box for donations, or asking local businesses to advertise fundraising events. Many local businesses donate money to the program. When programs like Head Start in Auburn have to search for nickels and dimes, it might be hard to make the positive impact on children that one would hope.

The school environment is like a "make or break" opportunity for gang prevention. If a student has a positive experience in school, he/she is less likely to join a gang. Conversely, a student who lacks a connection with his/her school is a high-risk candidate for delinquency and street gangs. School-based intervention is a very important factor in the war against gangs. The days of student-related problems being confined to the occasional playground fight or someone playing hooky are long gone. "Today, we are seeing the problems of crime, violence, gangs, guns and drugs spilling over from the streets into our schools. These criminal activities are not exclusive to the inner city schools. They are occurring in rural and suburban areas as well" (Illinois State Police 2002). The schools, especially public ones, can spearhead efforts to prevent youngsters from turning to gangs. Among the school-based intervention programs that are available are social skills training programs, law-related education, classroom management programs that focus on ways of strengthening the bond between teachers and students, alternative schools, cooperative learning programs, and antidrug education programs. The need for schools and families to work together to intervene between youths and gangs is fundamental. The very success of any school program is contingent on reinforcement from the family. But if it is the family that is the cause of the youth's delinquency, effective social programs may identify and correct this problem. Program advocates (teachers and other professionals) in school-based programs can work with youths and family members to improve communication and educate them in an attempt to deter youths from gangs and other deviant pursuits.

By middle school, many at-risk youths have been clearly identified by school teachers and administrators. Many educational problems become quite evident by middle school as well. Some children inevitably begin to struggle with classwork. They may have trouble understanding the material (as a result of a non- or misdiagnosed learning disability), lack family support in reviewing the school material at home, or have ineffective teachers or teaching methods. Many of these students are held back because of their poor academic grades, which lowers their self-esteem.

Of course, the much more harmful option (than failing a student) is passing a student who has not met the course requirements—this is known as "social promotion." Social promotion serves no redeeming purpose in education. Youths who struggle at the lower level will most assuredly struggle and fail at a higher level because they are not prepared to handle the progressively more difficult course material. If they are passed along then, too, the problem will only continue. As a result, the socially promoted child will suffer an even greater blow to self esteem and self-image. The disgruntled student will seek solace outside the school. For some, the gang becomes a welcoming social group, as gang members warmly accept another convert. It is also not acceptable for administrators, in hopes of keeping academically marginal students in school, to resort to policies that force teachers to dumb down the curriculum just because a few students cannot handle the material. By doing so, they are cheating the rest of the students out of their right to a quality education. It is up to school officials to find a course curriculum that is right for students who do poorly in school, for whatever reason (e.g., vocational training, skills improvement programs). Once youths become school dropouts, their chances of finding a quality job disappear, further dooming them to lives that potentially involve deviance, criminality, and gang membership.

Many schools, and especially public ones, provide violence, drug, and other social problem prevention programs. Among the most effective and recognized gang and violence prevention programs is **Gang Resistance Education And Training (GREAT)**. GREAT was first introduced by the Phoenix Police Department in 1991, and it was modeled after the **Drug Abuse Resistance Education (DARE)** program. DARE was founded in 1983, and its primary mission is to provide youths with the necessary skills to avoid drugs and violence. While the topic of gangs may be addressed in the curriculum, it is not a stated specific goal in its mission. GREAT is built around school-based, law enforcement officer–instructed classroom curricula. "The program is intended as an immunization against delinquency, youth violence, and gang membership for children in the years immediately before the prime ages for introduction into gangs and delinquent behavior" (GREAT 2012a). The program has developed partnerships with nationally recognized organizations, such as the Boys & Girls Clubs of America, along with local parents, schools, law enforcement, and local businesses. GREAT attempts to provide life skills to students that help them choose courses of action other than delinquency or violence. The program's goal is to provide educators with effective gang prevention strategies that will help them create school environments which are safe havens of learning, achieving, and teaching necessary skills to youths. The GREAT program consists of four components: 13 sessions for middle-school curriculum, an elementary school curriculum, a summer program, and families training. Each component has outlined lessons to fit the target group's needs and skills while satisfying age-appropriate goals. Perhaps the most important component is the middle-school curriculum, as it is the only mandatory program for schools where GREAT is implemented. The curriculum is designed to teach youths the skills they need to act properly and create an environment that facilitates teaching, a positive school environment, and cooperation. The 13 sessions each last about 30–45 minutes. The middle-school program's goal is "to prevent youth crime, violence, and gang involvement while developing a positive relationship among law enforcement, families, among our young people to create safer communities" (GREAT 2012b). After students complete the program, they are acknowledged in a graduation ceremony.

How effective is GREAT? Program evaluation results published by Esbensen and associates (2011) indicate that five out of nine variables studied showed significant differences. Students in the program displayed more positive attitude toward the police, less positive attitudes toward gangs, more frequent use of refusal skills, greater resistance to peer pressure, and lower rates of gang membership. That the program has helped to change the attitudes of so many students makes it a success. Critics counter, however, the program has not equated to gang reduction in the community. Nonetheless, the GREAT program has been adopted in all 50 states and several countries.

Another school-based prevention program of note is Chicago's **Broader Urban Involvement and Leadership Development (BUILD).** Established in 1969, BUILD combines several popular gang prevention strategies in an attempt to curtail gang violence in some of the city's most depressed and crime-ridden communities (OJJDP 2012a). BUILD was established on the principle that youths join gangs because they lack other, more constructive alternatives and outlets. Open to males and females of any race between the ages of 10 and 17, BUILD is an academic skills enhancement program that provides after-school recreation and teaches community awareness and gang prevention. The target population ranges from less serious to serious offenders, truants and dropouts, and at-risk youths. The prevention component of BUILD consists of a gang prevention curriculum and an after-school program. Students selected for this program attend 12 sessions of instruction over a 12-week period and are taught about gang violence, substance abuse, gang recruitment strategies, and consequences of gang membership. The after-school program provides recreational activities, job skills training workshops, educational assistance programs, and social activities. Rigorous evaluation of this program has shown it to have great promise in keeping targeted youths out of gangs. For example, in the 1990s, the Center for Latino Research at DePaul University conducted an 18-month evaluation and found that the program's objectives were accomplished and in many instances exceeded expectations. The researchers gave credit to the efforts of the BUILD staff (OJJDP 2012a). In 1999, a team of researchers from Loyola University found that BUILD youths had significantly lower recidivism rates than their counterparts from a control group. According to the study's results, only 33 percent of BUILD youths recidivated within one year, compared to 57 percent of non-BUILD students (OJJDP 2012a).

In response to the increasing incidence of gang violence in Illinois schools, the Illinois State Police have developed a school-based gang prevention program called **Violence Education & Gang Awareness (VEGA).** "VEGA was designed to meet the needs of all communities regardless of the level of school violence and gang involvement. VEGA's goals are to stress the importance of resolving conflicts without the use of violence, and to provide young people with a better understanding of the consequences they face when joining gangs and participating in acts of violence" (Illinois State Police 2002). The program is taught to fifth- and sixth graders and is meant to complement any existing gang prevention program taught in individual school districts. The program curriculum consists of police officers teaching five lessons over five consecutive weeks, emphasizing cooperative learning strategies. The lessons deal in a straightforward manner with the tough situations youths are experiencing. The five VEGA lessons are the following:

1. Gangs Are a Matter of Choice—This lesson helps to teach children the basic facts about gangs and the destructive consequences of gang membership.
2. Violence and Its Victims—This lesson helps students discover what causes conflict and why violence is not a constructive solution. This lesson emphasizes that gang life is not glamorous.
3. The Circle of Violence—The third VEGA lesson continues to investigate the sources of violence and conflict by discussing how different ideas and feelings cause people to disagree. This lesson emphasizes how violence not only fails to solve conflicts with others, it actually escalates the problem.
4. Peacemakers, Not Peacebreakers—This lesson focuses on problem-solving skills and prosocial skills which can help people evaluate the risks involved in a situation. Students are taught how to apply these skills in order to resolve conflicts.

5. Thinking Ahead—A Look at Tomorrow—The fifth VEGA lesson helps students to understand and be empathetic to the effect people have on one another. Children learn to take the perspective of others (Illinois State Police 2002).

In Hinsdale, Illinois, the police target sixth-grade students after they take the DARE curriculum. It offers prevention strategies to deal with students at risk of gang involvement and violence (Hinsdale Police Department 2012). The Hinsdale police teach youths a modified version of the original VEGA principles: (1) All students are capable of understanding, learning, and performing leadership tasks; (2) the most effective student groups are those which include diverse background; (3) students need to learn to recognize and value their dependence upon each other; (4) working in a group requires certain social skills which can be taught and learned; (5) when students learn to resolve their problems, without violence, and without teacher intervention, they become more autonomous and self-sufficient (Hinsdale Police Department 2012). The police invite parents and community members to become actively involved in the VEGA program. Students and attendees are asked to share their ideas on how to combat gangs, and these ideas are then discussed in an open environment.

There are numerous other school-related gang prevention programs, for example, the Los Angeles Police Department (LAPD) developed the **Jeopardy** program for boys and girls aged 8 through 17 and their parents. Jeopardy combines the influence of the community, neighborhood schools, and the police department to effect positive, lifelong attitudinal changes in youths to have a positive impact on the community. The **Soledad Enrichment Action (SEA)** program in California provides gang and violence prevention strategies to high-risk youths and their families through education services, mental health therapy, drug and alcohol counseling, field trips, and after-school tutoring including arts and crafts activities. The SEA program was founded in 1972 by mothers from East Los Angeles whose sons had been killed by gang violence (Soledad Enrichment Action 2012). The primary goals of SEA are to reduce school dropout rates and increase high school graduation rates among high-risk youths who have either been expelled from or have dropped out of their home school and likely to test significantly below their peers academically. The SEA, in many cases, is a last chance for troubled youths to turn their lives around before becoming indoctrinated in gang life. One final program that combines the efforts of multiple entities to be discussed is **Schools and Families Educating Children (SAFE Children)**. SAFE is a community and school-based program that targets children aged 5–6, who are making the transition into elementary school and live in inner-city high-risk neighborhoods (Promising Practices Network 2012). The program seeks to help children attain a successful first year of school and assist families manage educational and child development. The program is delivered over a period of 20 weeks and includes sessions with just the children, just the families, and both the children and families (Promising Practices Network 2012). Children are also tutored in the hope that they will become successful students both in the short term and in the long run.

While most of the programs discussed here involved some combination of families, schools, and law enforcement, there are many instances where the funding and success of these programs are dependent, or partially dependent, on local business. Time and space limitations make it impossible to provide any sort of comprehensive review of the programs that involve local businesses. Furthermore, the length of time a business is involved with a violence and gang prevention program is subject to change, making it difficult to cite, or track, specific examples. Some local programs disappear quickly as well, making it increasingly difficult to acknowledge local businesses in a timely manner. Suffice it to say, there are numerous local businesses that "give back" to the community in nearly all cities across the United States. Some businesses donate time (e.g., through job-training programs they provide), goods and services (e.g., computers and computer training), and money to help support violence and gang prevention for altruistic purposes, that is, they enjoy giving back to the community because it's the "right thing" to do. Other businesses realize that by helping to keep youths out of gangs, they are keeping their neighborhoods safer and that is just good business sense. Helping to fund violence and gang prevention programs, then, indirectly helps business.

Community involvement with gang prevention programs takes on a number of interesting partnerships. One of the most interesting combinations of community gang prevention would have to be Snoop Dogg's involvement with youth football. See "Connecting Street Gangs and Popular Culture" Box 9.1 for a closer look.

Box 9.1 *Connecting Street Gangs and Popular Culture*

The Price Is Right for Snoop Dogg and His Snoop Youth Football League

One of the most famous gang members in the United States is a rap star named Calvin Cordozar Broadus Jr. better known as Snoop Dogg (formerly known as Snoop Doggy Dogg). Calvin received his Snoop Dogg nickname from his parents who thought he looked like the *Peanuts* character, Snoopy. Calvin was born on October 20, 1971, at the Los Altos Hospital in Long Beach, California. At an early age he sang in the Golgotha Trinity Baptist Church on East 14th Street in Long Beach. He attended Long Beach Polytechnic High School when he became a member of the notorious East Side Rollin' 20 Crips gang in the Eastside of Long Beach. As discussed in Chapter 6, Snoop claims to have given up his days of *crippin*, but he still pays homage to his homies in his song lyrics. Shortly after graduating from high school, Snoop was convicted for cocaine possession and served six months at the Wayside County jail. He was in and out of jail for much of the first three years following his high school days. His arrest on charges of being a murder accomplice certainly strengthened his early myth and helped his debut album *Doggystyle* (1993) become the first rap debut album to enter the charts at number one (Erlewine 2012). The accomplice to murder charge was filed because Snoop was the driver during a drive-by shooting of Philip Woldermarian. Snoop claimed that his bodyguard shot Woldermarian in self-defense because Woldermarian was stalking him. Snoop turned himself in to the police following the MTV Music Awards ceremony in September 1993 (Erlewine 2012). Snoop will be arrested and convicted numerous times throughout his life for a variety of offenses including drugs and weapons charges (Forsyth 2012). As of this writing, the most recent was in January 2012, when he was arrested after border control agents found a small amount of marijuana on his tour bus. Snoop was stopped at the same Sierra Blanca, Texas, checkpoint as country singer Willie Nelson when he was arrested for marijuana possession in 2010. Interestingly, Snoop Dogg and Willie Nelson collaborated on the song and music video "My Medicine," a thinly veiled homage to marijuana. Both artists have made their appreciation and participation in smoking pot part of their public personas (Forsyth 2012).

It is the pleasant public persona of Snoop Dogg that makes him such a cult figure in the world of popular culture. His impact on the world of music, especially with the gangsta and hip-hop genre, makes Snoop nearly omnipresent. He seems to be a fixture on television and in films. In 1998, he had a cameo appearance in the film *Half Baked* as the "Scavenger Smoker." In 2001, he lent his voice to the animated show *King of the Hill*, in which he played a white pimp named Alabaster Jones. (Interestingly, Snoop told *Rolling Stone* magazine that he was a professional pimp from 2003 to 2004, but quit so that he could spend more time with his family.) Snoop played a lead character in the movie *The Wash* with Dr. Dre. He portrayed a drug dealer in a wheelchair in the film *Training Day*, which features Denzel Washington. He has appeared on a variety of cable shows; an MTV sketch comedy show; a cameo in the television movie *It's a Very Muppet Christmas Movie* (2002); played himself on two episodes of the ABC soap opera *One Life to Live* (with a new opening theme he recorded for those two episodes); an episode of *I Get That a Lot*; participated in Comedy Central's Roast of Donald Trump in March 2011; and, on January 2, 2012, Snoop appeared on *The Price Is Right*.

Although I have met Snoop and watched him in nearly all the appearances described above (plus the many not specifically mentioned), it seemed particularly odd, for me, to see him on *The Price Is Right*. I had heard the promo for his appearance and knew I had to watch the show. Would he be in the audience? Would we hear, "Snoop Dogg, come on down! You're the next contestant on the *Price Is Right!*" He was not among the audience members to be, or not to be, called down to play a pricing game. Instead, he was there to raise money for his charity, "Snoop Youth Football League." Snoop joined as co-host with Drew Carey and helped contestants make decisions while they played pricing games. CBS matched the earnings of all the winners to give to Snoop for his charity. Snoop raised $72,585 for his football league. Apparently, it was a big thrill for him to be on the show as he watched it as a child; and now, he was able to help his own son and his peers (*Huffington Post* 2012b).

The **Snoop Youth Football League (SYFL)** is a non-profit, community-based prevention program established by Snoop Dogg to provide an opportunity for inner-city children to participate in youth sports. The SYFL serves children between the ages of 7 and 14, teaching them the values of teamwork, good sportsmanship, discipline, and self-respect, while also stressing the importance of academics (Black Celebrity Giving 2011). There are a number of different levels of the football league to accommodate the different ages of the participants: Jr. Midgets; Pee Wees; Jr. Pee Wees, Sr. Pee Wees; Sr. Clinic, Junior Clinic; Futures; and Flag (Sportability 2011). The SYFL started in Los Angeles but is now active in Chicago; not coincidentally, the two cities with the largest population of gang members. Snoop started the SYFL because of his own son's interest in playing football when he was eight years old. Snoop explains that he was just like any other father on the sidelines watching his son play football and when he saw things he did not like he would ask the coach about it. The coach made him an assistant. The following year Snoop became the head coach of his son's team. And from there, he decided to start his own league (Black Celebrity Kids 2010). In a 2010 interview, Snoop said that his football league is "dedicated to the inner city, to save lives, to help kids, and just give back in general. And we've been running for 6 years now, we have over 3,500 kids in our leagues. We have our first batch of kids in college this year, and we have 4 kids who are at Division I schools playing college football" (Black Celebrity Kids 2010). Clearly, Snoop is proud of his league, and for good reason.

The Chicago SYFL really helps to reveal its design as a community-based prevention program that incorporates families, school/education, and local business, as it has added financial literacy to its scholastic program. Chicago SYFL partners with the Federal Reserve Bank of Chicago to help empower youths in underserved communities through financial literacy. Through a series of programs the Chicago SYFL student athletes are taught the basics of money, including saving and investing in fun and exciting ways (Black Celebrity Giving 2011). The program, not surprisingly, also incorporates various elements of hip-hop and the entertainment business to help deliver the message of financial empowerment to youths. The youths do, of course, play football. As with any football league, a number of values including teamwork, hard work, loyalty, strength (both mental and physical), respect for authority, and communal bonding are emphasized. As Snoop sums it up, "sports and education, they're better than violence and gangs" (Holiday 2011).

It is worth noting that Snoop still embraces smoking marijuana. So much so, that following an August 2012 trip to Jamaica, Snoop converted to Rastafarianism, a religion that professes the benefits of smoking pot. Snoop also announced that he wanted to be known as Snoop Lion. In the Rasta religion, calling someone a dog is an insult and calling oneself a dog is an indication of a lack of self-knowledge (Burke 2012). Unlike dogs, lions hold a place of pride in Rasta theology, as the lion is symbol of Solomon's Tribe of Judah. Perhaps the most famous Rastafarian, Bob Marley, expresses this belief most clearly (in the popular culture realm) when he sang the "lion of Zion" (Burke 2012).

National/Broad-Based Prevention Strategies

More and more, community and school-based intervention strategies have turned to the federal government for assistance, especially when local programs involve drug prevention and education. Drug treatment programs are almost entirely dependent upon federal financial assistance. The poor families from which at-risk youths primarily come are generally incapable of providing adequate health and mental health coverage for their children, and local social services are generally ill-prepared to take on such a financial responsibility. Gang members are also often victims of, or witnesses to, domestic violence and abuse. Local communities often rely on the federal government for assistance in providing shelters and counseling. For any community, providing jobs is the most important task, but finding jobs for underskilled, at-risk, and former gang members is extremely difficult. Many reformers have called for an increase in the minimum wage to make lower-paying jobs more attractive. In general, there needs to be a federal job creation program designed to keep people employed and, thus, positive contributors to society. The federal government also needs to be involved because many gangs have ties outside of the immediate community and some have a national allegiance (e.g., Crips and Bloods), which implies that multiple police agencies need to be involved when dealing with local gangs.

An example of a national program designed to address the issue of family violence as a contributor to gang involvement is the National Center for Neighborhood Enterprise and its development of **Violence-Free Zones**. Conceptually similar to "drug-free school zones" (which involve increased penalties for drug violations within a certain distance from a school), Violence-Free Zones represent grassroots community intervention for youth and gang-related violence through federal assistance. The Violence-Free Zone model is based on the premise that the breakdown of the family structure is a key risk factor for gang involvement and a major contributor to destructive behavior (National Gang Center 2012). (*Note*: This model is based on the House of Umoja program.) The breakdown of the traditional family is especially important with this model because it echoes the commonly held foundation in the study of street gangs that most members come from fatherless families in which mothers struggle to meet the economic and individual needs of their children. The children, especially males, are not receiving the necessary guidance they need to avoid violence and gangs. The Violence-Free program provides mentors to fill this void. Job training and work opportunities are also provided. The Violence-Free program identifies a number of risk factors at different levels: individual (e.g., drug dealing, fewer social ties, general involvement in delinquency, high alcohol/drug use, illegal gun ownership/carrying, physical violence/aggression, and violent victimization); family (broken home/changes in caretaker, poor parent–children relations, or lack of communication); school (poor attitude/performance, academic failure); community (availability of firearms, community disorganization, economic deprivation/poverty, exposure to violence and racial prejudice, feeling unsafe, and high-crime neighborhood); peer (association with antisocial/delinquent peers, association with gang peers/relatives, gang membership). Youths who have successfully gone through the program often assist other youths in other communities to expand Violence-Free Zones.

The gang world is increasingly becoming a drug world, as we have seen. Historically, gang members have used drugs recreationally, but, as illustrated in Chapter 8, gangs have become increasingly involved in drug-trafficking and distribution. Many federal programs have attempted to prevent youths from taking drugs, one of them being **Operation Weed and Seed**. "Operation Weed and Seed has involved a multidimensional strategy with a primary emphasis on addressing the problems of gangs, drugs, violence, crime and community recovery from drug problems and violent gang activity. The thrust of the overall strategy was based upon an awareness that in various communities a coordinated comprehensive approach was needed" (Pope and Lovell 2004, 356). This program integrates governmental and private organizations' efforts to reduce criminal activity by having law enforcement weed out criminals who participate in violent crime, gang activity, drug use, and drug-trafficking and by stimulating community recovery by "seeding" a variety of human services to the area, restoring it through social and economic revitalization (U.S. Department of Justice 2009). As explained by Pope and Lovell (2004, 356–357), the Weed and Seed program includes four strategies:

1. Suppression—enforcement, adjudication, prosecution, and supervision of those who account for a disproportionate percentage of criminal activity
2. Community-oriented policing—providing a "bridge" between law enforcement activities and neighborhood reclamation and revitalization activities
3. Prevention, intervention, and treatment—focusing on youth services, school programs, community and social programs, and support groups
4. Neighborhood reclamation and revitalization—focusing on economic development activities designed to assist legitimate community institutions

Operation Weed and Seed provides the resources for local communities in designated areas to help eliminate gang activity and reduce the number of at-risk youths who turn to gangs. In Salisbury, Maryland, the Weed and Seed program has been in existence since 2005; in addition to law enforcement efforts, the program has established a number of safe havens for youths and young adults. Officials in Salisbury report that significant strides in neighborhood restoration have been made as a result of the Weed and Seed program. In Cedar Rapids, Iowa, officials report that arrests made in the Wellington neighborhood decreased by 20 percent during the four-year period after the Weed and Seed was implemented versus pre-Weed and Seed (Central Cedar Rapids Weed and Seed 2012).

One of the most well-known national gang prevention programs is the **Boys and Girls Clubs of America (BGCA)**. The BGCA is a national organization of local chapters which provides after-school programs for youths. The roots of the BGCA can be traced back to 1860 in Hartford, Connecticut, where three women believed that boys who were roaming the streets should have a positive alternative (Philanthropedia 2012). And so a cause centered on character development was born. In 1906, representatives from 53 independent boys' clubs met in Boston to form a national organization, the Federated Boys' Clubs of America. In 1990, the organization was modified to its current name. There are well over 4,000 autonomous local clubs in existence today, serving more than 4 million boys and girls. Clubs can be found in all 50 states, Puerto Rico, the Virgin Islands, and U.S. military bases. The organization maintains a commitment to its core beliefs of character development and keeping kids of the streets safe in a community facility under adult supervision. Clubs provided a wide variety of activities, including sports, recreation, arts and science education, and opportunities to learn life skills that will help form a solid foundation for youths as they become adults. BGCA helps to connect youths with a strong positive network of adults and has been praised for its broad reach in programs offered. The club works cooperatively with other existing programs. For example, it was an ideal partner to Weed and Seed efforts.

The BGCA aggressively attempts to reach with its programs at-risk youths as well as those currently involved in gangs. It performs a needs assessment on all referrals (youths who were referred to BGCA by school officials, parents, police, probation officers, and others) to determine what program is best suited for specific youths. For example, the **Gang Prevention through Targeted Outreach** program is directed toward youths who are at risk of becoming involved with gangs. The program provides structured recreational, educational, and life-skills activities geared toward enhancing the communication skills, problem-solving techniques, and decision-making abilities of at-risk youths, seeking to alter their attitudes and perceptions while at the same time improving their conflict-resolution skills (Esbensen 2000, 8).

An overriding mission of Boys and Girls Clubs is to serve youths from disadvantaged backgrounds. It attempts to build the self-esteem of youths, while instilling honest values and a desire to pursue productive futures. Essentially, the BGCA is designed to prevent youths from joining a gang by providing alternatives to gang life, especially through education and employment. The BGCA also provides life-skills development and works to establish truces among rival gangs and to reduce the incidence of gang violence. The BGCA has been very successful in providing young people jobs as outreach workers in a variety of programs. Evaluation of the BGCA has led to positive conclusions.

The final national violence and gang prevention we will look at is the McGruff House. The **McGruff House** is sponsored by the National Crime Prevention Council to provide a temporary safe haven for children who find themselves in emergency of frightening situations, such as being bullied, followed, or hurt while walking in a neighborhood (Hinsdale Police Department 2012). A McGruff House provides a sense of security and a source of emergency aid for those who need it. It is not an escort service or a guarantee of safety but rather a place for appropriate and necessary short-term help by an adult for a child. People can apply to host a McGruff House through local officials after completing an application and passing a background check. The homeowner is then given a McGruff House sign to place in the window. This signals to children in the community that your home is a safe place to go if they are in need of adult assistance.

SUPPRESSION STRATEGIES

The dramatic increase in the shear numbers of gangs and gang-related crimes has led to numerous suppression strategies in the war against gangs. Many prevention intervention programs have failed in their attempt to curb gang violence, and many of the programs that do work take an extended period of time to be effective; or, the funding gets cut and the program disappears. As stated in a *USA Today* 2007 article, "Anti-gang legislation and police crackdowns are failing so badly that they are strengthening the criminal organizations and making U.S. cities more dangerous." This conclusion was reached following the publication of *Gang Wars: The Failure of Enforcement Tactics and the Need for Effective Public Safety Strategies* wherein the authors (Judith Green and Kevin Pranis) indicate, what we have already learned, that gang members who are incarcerated maintain and strengthen gang alliance while in prison and then return to the streets more hardened than when they went in. Meanwhile, many innocent (along with not-so-innocent) citizens continue to fall victim to gang violence. Alarmed community members and concerned politicians who want "something to be done about gangs" cling to the hope and belief that the best intervention strategy is some form of suppression. The idea that something must be done is reflected by the popularity of law enforcement TV shows, movies, and video games. (See "Connecting Street Gangs and Popular Culture" Box 9.2.). *Suppression* refers to efforts to put to an end to something, like taking a cough suppressant to end a cough. With regard to street gangs, then, **suppression strategies** are any attempts by law enforcement and the full force of law to forcibly end, dissolve, or prohibit the criminal activities of street gangs. Suppression strategies generally come in two forms: law enforcement responses and judicial/legislative responses. We begin our discussion with law enforcement as they represent the first line of defense in gang *suppression* (the family was the first line of defense in gang *prevention*).

Box 9.2   Connecting Street Gangs and Popular Culture

Perception and Law Enforcement Suppression Efforts

There exists a general perception that law enforcement's role in society is to "serve and protect." There is, however, a difference in perception as to whom the police are serving and protecting. Some argue that law enforcement serves and protects the interest of the social elites often at the expense of regular folks. Others suggest that law enforcement protects the everyday citizen from criminals. Depending on what side of the law one resides has a great deal to do with how law enforcement officials are perceived. Race also plays a role. As Weitzer and Tuch (2004) explain, "Blacks and whites often perceive American social institutions in starkly different terms, and views of criminal justice are no exception . . . Blacks are more likely than whites to express dissatisfaction with various aspects of policing" (305). What accounts for such a disparity in perception of policing? Weitzer and Tuch (2004) propose the *group-position* theoretical model, a variation of conflict theory, as a possible explanation. The group-position model suggests that people from within one group (e.g., a racial category of people) show favoritism toward their own members and disdain, or distrust, toward members of another group because they are fighting for scarce resources (e.g., material rewards, power, and status). This theory seems feasible as it is applicable to not only law enforcement, but street gangs, sports teams, individuals competing for the affections of another, and so on. As for law enforcement, "Whites tend to hold a favorable opinion of the police, favor aggressive law enforcement, and are skeptical of criticisms of the police . . . Many whites view blacks as inclined to criminal or violent behavior" (Weitzer and Tuch 2004, 306). Blacks and Hispanics, on the other hand, tend to view the police as a visible sign of the power group's domination. Certainly, one's experiences with law enforcement also help to shape his/her perception. That is, people who have been treated fairly and respectfully by law enforcement tend to look at them more favorably. Wentz and Schlimgen (2012) argue that the contact (including response time) between the police and other citizens in their neighborhood is a critical variable in how law enforcement is perceived. The manner in which law enforcement is portrayed in the media also helps to shape one's perception of their performance. When law enforcement fails to capture a criminal in a timely manner, or not at all, people look at them with less respect. In brief, law enforcement is looked upon favorably and unfavorably, and as competent and incompetent. It should come as no surprise then that within popular culture, especially television, film, and video games, law enforcement is also shown in favorable, unfavorable, competent, and incompetent manners.

That popular culture attempts to reach the greatest number of people possible underscores why law enforcement is shown in radically different ways. In some instances, such as the popular TV show *COPS*, the viewing audience rides along with police as a film crew records police officers as they perform their duties. This documentary/reality show first aired in 1989 is still broadcasting new episodes. The audience perception may or may not be swayed by the interactions between the cops and perpetrators, but the show is designed to show that police officers are human and sometimes make mistakes and sometimes perform heroic deeds as they interact with the public. On occasion, *COPS* episodes involve street gangs, but generally, the aired content is fairly mild. The show *Southland* is set up like *COPS*, that is, as a documentary/reality show, but it is staged (*Southland* 2012). The South Los Angeles backdrop, filmed on the real streets of Los Angeles, gives the show a sense of reality. Because *Southland* is staged, however, we learn more about the private lives (both positive and negative) of police officers and how that influences their daily interactions with, and perceptions of, citizens. With South Los Angeles as the setting, street gangs often play a prominent role. In the *Southland* episode "Risk," the street gang lifestyle is in full display, from the importance of marking turf with graffiti, intergang rivalries, and the violence they cause within the community. In this same episode, a patrol car is hit in a gang drive-by and then hit by another passenger vehicle. A pregnant detective is attacked and stabbed by a perpetrator. Such is the real life of police officers in gangland. Speaking of gangland, there is a documentary television series that airs on The History Channel (and is syndicated on the Spike channel) called *Gangland*. *Gangland*, which premiered on November 1, 2007, explores the history of some of America's most violent and notorious gangs. The theme song is performed by Buckshot of the Boot Camp Clik, a rap group that inspired the naming of the Syracuse gang, Boot Camp (see Chapter 6). The interactions between law enforcement and gangs displayed in this show are gritty and very real.

Although law enforcement may be shown in a mostly positive light in shows such as *COPS*, *Southland*, and *Gangland* (not to mention dozens of other shows about cops on TV during the past few decades including *Hill Street Blues*, *NYPD Blue*, *NYC 22*, *Rookie Blue*, *Law and Order*, *Hawaii Five-O*, and *The Wire*), it is also shown in very unflattering manners. *RENO 911*, for example, is a spoof of *COPS*, and involves a film crew following Reno, Nevada, police officers as they perform their daily duties. The law enforcement officers come across as buffoons and it's a wonder there is any law and order whatsoever in Reno. Law enforcement officers are often shown as incompetent in many films as well. The *Naked Gun* movies, while generally funny, makes one wonder once again, how is law and order possible? In other films, such as *Die Hard* and *Lethal Weapon*, the police are shown in a mostly positive manner, but even in these movies, many officers are negatively portrayed. There are millions of fans of law enforcement officers being shown as tough guys where they are admired, by some, even when they break the law and act like vigilantes. Clint Eastwood as "Dirty Harry" comes to mind. Law enforcement is shown both negatively and positively in the more than 60 video games that exist utilizing the police and their suppression efforts.

Undoubtedly, while you were reading this, you thought of many other shows and movies that include law enforcement. Dozens of other examples came to my mind as well. In fact, an entire book could be written on the topic of law enforcement portrayal in the media. However, this glimpse of law enforcement and how they are perceived by members of society reflects the complicated role of policing in America. As they are portrayed in the media, law enforcement officers sometimes put their lives on the line to protect people, they provide initial response to a distress call, they fight crime, including street gangs, but they are humans who are capable of failing and potentially corruptible. How each individual looks at law enforcement depends upon his/her perception of the police and perception is shaped by many social factors, including popular culture.

Law Enforcement Suppression

As the first line of defense against street crime in general, and street gangs in particular, it is the function of law enforcement to use bodily force when necessary. The continued growth and increasingly violent nature of street gangs is often met with an equally violent show of force by law enforcement, especially by specific gang task force units. How the police are perceived by citizens varies "based on global attitudes toward crime and social justice, past experiences with governmental agencies, and social status" (Gaines and Kappeler 2011, 12). Research indicates that people who do not have contact with the police, presumably because they are law-abiding, have more favorable views of the police than citizens who do have contact with them (Gaines and Kappeler 2011). Law enforcement suppression efforts are rather involved and start with the allocation of personnel (to deal with a particular set of problems in the community), receiving and managing calls for service or the identification of problem while on patrol, deploying personnel to a call, methods of patrol (e.g., foot, horse, bicycle, aircraft, watercraft, cruiser, and one-person or two-person patrols), deciding whether or not force is necessary and what type of force (e.g., use of a taser, nightstick, or firearm), investigating a call or crime, deciding when to use discretion in making an arrest, booking and fingerprinting, incarceration, and turning the case over to prosecutors.

Law enforcement officers on patrol are always on the lookout for criminal activities; it's a part of their normal routine. Officers work within certain parameters, including beat boundaries. When not called for service, officers are expected to patrol their areas. When patrols involve street gangs, law enforcement suppression efforts generally take two forms: *proactive strategies* and *reactive strategies* (Sanders 1994). **Proactive strategies** is a crime suppression method that relies on officers' initiative to confront gang members in both friendly and unfriendly manners. While the unfriendly approach involves the apprehension of gang members, the friendly manner assists the intelligence gathering aspect of proactive strategies. Investigators attempt to document gang members, make contacts with them, learn their names, identify gang tattoos and graffiti, and cultivate informants. Gathering this information allows the police an opportunity to prevent illegal gang activities and to catch those involved in such activities (Sanders 1994). Documenting tattoos is often fruitful as individuals have self-identified themselves as belonging to a gang. Law enforcement officers flip through snapshots of tattooed gang members looking for clues. Los Angeles County Sheriff's homicide investigator Kevin Lloyd found a photo that caught his eye. It seems that in some instances, gang members make it too easy for the police. Case in point, Lloyd looked at an inked Pico Rivera gangster named Anthony Garcia who had been picked up and released on a minor offense. Garcia had immortalized his killing of a rival at a liquor store in an elaborate tattoo of the crime scene on his chest. Each detail was there in ink: the Christmas lights that lined the roof of the liquor store, the direction his body fell, the bowed street lamp across the way, and the street sign—all under the chilling banner of RIVERA KILLS. The 2008 discovery by Investigator Lloyd closed a case he had been working on for four years. Garcia was convicted of first-degree murder in April 2011 (Faturechi 2011). This should serve as a warning to all undected or would-be criminals, including gang members; don't get tattoos that are distinctive in any way, as it may lead to your identification, arrest, prosecution, and incarceration. Increasingly, a number of gangs are forgoing visible tattoos.

A typical fact-gathering strategy employed by police is to go to a place where several gang members are known to hang out, search them for weapons and/or drugs, and if illegal weapons or drugs are found, make an arrest. If no arrests can be made, the police attempt to gather information about the gang and its activities through interrogation. The gathered information is entered into a computer program, such as COMPSTAT. **COMPSTAT** was first developed by the New York City Police Department in 1994 and is an acronym for "computer statistics" or "comparative statistics" (Gaines and Kappeler 2011). Many larger law enforcement agencies, and especially those with a street gang problem, have adopted COMPSTAT as it is seen as a strategic management tool. "It gives decision-makers immediate access to information relevant to problems and tactical decision they are facing" (Gaines and Kappeler 2011, 162–163). COMPSTAT has six core elements: mission clarification (allows for the establishment of specific goals and smooth communication of these goals from commanders to officers); internal accountability (operational commanders can be held accountable for the actions of their officers); geographic organization of operational command (assigned patrols to specific geographic areas can be held accountable); organizational flexibility (commanders can move patrols based on arising problems); data-drive analysis (allows for assessments and evaluation of commanders, officers, and assignments); and innovative problem-solving tactics (allows for flexibility) (Gaines and Kappeler 2011).

Flexibility is especially important when law enforcement officials conclude that conventional policing techniques are ineffective in achieving lasting change in gang, or high-crime, neighborhoods. Traditional methods, such as periodic shows of force, like sting operations and raids that temporarily remove gang members from the streets address only the symptoms, but the problem remains. Consider this analogy: Young children often chase sea gulls on the beach; the sea gulls fly away, but return as soon as the children move on to something else. Increasingly, there are those wondering whether military tactics, such as **counterinsurgency methods**, should be employed. The idea of using counterinsurgency tactics has come in vogue, with the increasing number of military personnel who have served in the Gulf Wars returning home and getting into law enforcement. As Lt. Col. Timothy Alben, a division commander with the Massachusetts State Police states, "You're not going to arrest your way out of this problem. The problem of gangs is something you have to make the community itself responsible for, and that goes back to the mission of Special Forces, whether in Iraq or Afghanistan" (Goode 2012). Such an approach is being implemented in Springfield, Massachusetts, where two state troopers returned to their jobs after deployment with a Green Beret unit in Iraq after they noticed troubling parallels between enemy insurgents in Avgani, Iraq, and Brightwood, Massachusetts, a neighborhood besieged by street gangs. In Brightwood, the officers noticed gang members and drug dealers cruising the streets on motor scooters carrying SKS semiautomatic rifles in broad daylight. Gunfire erupts almost daily. At the core of the counterinsurgency approach is a community meeting, held on a weekly basis, wherein residents, community leaders, landlords, representatives of city agencies and non-profit organizations, local politicians, and law enforcement officers strategize on ways to curtail gang insurgency within the community.

Reactive strategies involve the everyday interaction between the police and gang members who are actively committing a crime. The efficient flow of information from a caller reporting a crime to a police dispatcher to a police officer is critical in the reactive fight against gang crime. At other times, the police come across crimes in progress and pursue the perpetrators on foot or via a chase (by car, horse, boat, bicycle, or aircraft). Unfortunately, as foot soldiers in the battle against gang crime, the police are blamed for social injustices that they did not create and held accountable for labeling citizens as criminals. Social critics view the police as oppressors who protect the privileged at the expense of the poor, disadvantaged, and politically disenfranchised. The police view themselves as practical crime fighters caught in a web of political intrigue (Sanders 1994, 178). As important as proactive policing is, the fact remains that most police work is reactive. "Overall, most of the work the police do is reactive in that their options are limited unless the gangs act criminally" (Sanders 1994, 179). The reactive strategies are the ones that interest the media and the public's curiosity, whereas information gathering isn't likely to excite people. As Webb and Katz (2003, 27) explained:

> Whereas the intelligence function and the sharing of information gives value to gang unit activities and legitimizes the existence of the unit from the perspective of many departmental stakeholders, it is suppression/enforcement that legitimizes the unit in the eyes of the public and the media, and gives them confidence that the unit is actively engaging in enforcement efforts directed at gangs and gang crime.

There are a variety of law enforcement suppression techniques, but one of the most common ones is the neighborhood "sweep." A **sweep** involves a large number of officers who enter (sweep) a specified area (generally a specific neighborhood, house, or building), arresting and detaining known or suspected gang members. Successful sweeps are hyped by the media, which, in turn, makes a large number of citizens and politicians feel better about themselves. A sweep is evidence that something is being done about the gang problem. Another suppression tactic involves "hot-spot targeting" of known gang members and their hideouts. **Hot-spot targeting** involves police targeting a specific gang for intensive or saturated surveillance and harassment in an effort to apply pressure and send a message of deterrence (Regoli and Hewitt 2003). Typically, police patrol certain known gang areas (e.g., minority public housing districts with high crime rates, parks, specific parking lots) where gang members are likely to be hanging out (Webb and Katz 2003). Simply patrolling an area allows the police an opportunity to gather information, intervene in visible criminal activity, and make their presence known to the gangs. Police can also crack down on youth gangs and other violence by setting up **roadblocks (or checkpoints)** and questioning people who act in a suspicious way. Syracuse police have utilized this tactic through the **Gang and Violent Crime Task Force**, which has marked and unmarked cars policing high-crime areas of the city.

In addition to sweeps, hot-spot targeting and saturation patrols, and roadblocks and checkpoints, there are a number of other law enforcement suppression tactics. Among these tactics are the following:

- Zero tolerance—police do not give out any warnings and arrests are made for even minor offenses that would otherwise be ignored (Howell 2000).
- Caravanning—cruising neighborhoods in a caravan of patrol cars (Howell 2000).
- Security guards or dogs—any kind of visible security presence (Bruce 2008).
- Directed patrols—like hot-spot targeting, patrols are sent to specific areas that are known for criminal activities, especially at certain times of the day (e.g., convenience store robberies peak between 9 PM and 11 PM, so patrols look especially close at c-stores during these hours) (Bruce 2008).
- Profile interview patrols—controversial at times, but police utilize this tactic regularly. Anyone who matches the description of the offender will be questioned.
- Phantom car/Scarecrow car—police park unused cars at a high-crime location, hoping to fool offenders into believing an officer is present (Bruce 2008).
- Closures—used fairly regularly, police use legal authority to close businesses, streets, and public areas affected by a crime series (Bruce 2008).
- Killing markets—police identify outlets for stolen goods and then close them or otherwise render them unsuitable (Bruce 2008).
- Visible cameras—cameras not only help apprehend offenders, they can help prevent them if placed in a visible area.
- Warning signs—visible warning signs like "Neighborhood Watch Program in Force" (Bruce 2008).
- Alarms
- General community and media information—warning the public of potential problems (Bruce 2008).

In the battle against street gangs, the most intense law enforcement suppression technique is the anti-gang unit. **Gang units** utilize the "hit them as hard as we can" approach in their battle against street gangs. Police raid teams in gang suppression units are analogous to an enthusiastic football team hitting the field fired up for "battle." Although the criteria can change from jurisdiction to jurisdiction, there are generally four characteristics that make for a good gang task force officer: self-motivation (officers who do not require a great deal of oversight from commanders); prior experience; ability to speak a foreign language (Spanish is especially important, but because of the diversity of street gangs, any language spoken by gangs in a particular area); ethnic diversity (ideally, the task force reflects the targeted community) (Katz and Webb 2006). After being chosen for the task force, officers go through training, both physical and educational (e.g., to learn the profiles of gang members and how to fill out forms specific for their multiagency reporting). The shifts may vary from one agency to another, but it is fairly common for a gang task unit to work from 2 PM to 12 PM, with the possibility of working overtime, working four days and having three days off (Watkins and Ashby 2007). This shift allows the officers to meet with members from different agencies, such as the District Attorney, homicide detectives, patrol officers, and witnesses. Much of their shift time is spent gathering information. When confrontation between gangs occurs, task force officers meet violence with violence.

Among the more notable gang suppression units was the LAPD's **Community Resources Against Street Hoodlums (CRASH)** unit. First created in 1975 as the Total Resource Against Street Hoodlums (TRASH) anti-gang unit, the first in Los Angeles, the name was changed (because the TRASH acronym didn't sit well with political folks); the unit was renamed CRASH. CRASH was created in response to the growing street gang problem in Los Angeles. As described by former LAPD Chief of Police Daryl Gates (1978–1992), CRASH consisted of a number of elite anti-gang units within the LAPD that were set up to suppress the increasing rate of gang violence and crime. CRASH officers were required to get to know gang members, their names, their friends, where they hung out, and the types of criminal activities that gang members participated in. Former CRASH officer Sergeant Brian Liddy described how the primary mission of the CRASH unit was to gather intelligence on criminal street gangs that operated within their geographic division, monitor their activities, and take action when needed. (PBS—*Frontline* 2001). Liddy emphasized that the CRASH unit was a suppression unit and they were assigned with preventing gang members from committing drive-by shootings, robberies, extortion, and spray painting buildings (PBS—*Frontline* 2001). As elite police officers, CRASH members were willing to work extra hard and were not afraid to mix it up with gang members and certainly were not intimidated by gangsters. A phrase commonly used by CRASH officers sums up their attitude: "intimidate those who intimidate."

The various CRASH units were assigned to monitor specific gangs throughout Los Angeles and to gather as much information as possible (e.g., asking gang members who they were currently feuding with, who was committing drive-bys on them, whether the Mexican Mafia was still "taxing" them) and ultimately suppressing their criminal activities. CRASH units would drive by a neighborhood to see who was spray painting apartments and other buildings. As discussed in Chapter 6, gang graffiti is not just "art-work" left behind by criminals; it tells a story about what has happened, or what will happen between rival gangs. It also serves as a marker of claimed territory. When a gang attempts to expand its territory, it will begin by spray painting graffiti on rival turf. The police officers in CRASH would, in effect, be tipped off about impending gang activity simply by being able to properly interpret gang graffiti. Information gathering is a critical aspect of any suppression unit. However, relying on gang members for information presents some problems (they are criminals after all). Because gang members are not always the most trustworthy people, the police have to be careful not to act upon false information, or a false tip. Gang members also sometimes use their relationship with suppression units to serve their own needs by passing along information designed to harm their rivals.

Overall, the LAPD's CRASH units were very successful, citywide, in reducing gang-related crime. They were known on the streets as a quasi-gang that used the same brutal and sometimes illegal tactics as gangs. CRASH units relied heavily on sweeps as their primary tactic, and in 1988, LAPD Chief Gates initiated a CRASH operation known as **Operation Hammer** in South Central Los Angeles. The CRASH unit would arrest as many as 1,000 suspected gang members on any given weekend for a wide variety of offenses, including already existing warrants, traffic citations, and curfew violations. Those arrested were taken to a mobile booking operation often at the Memorial Coliseum (Howell 2000). Most of those arrested were later released without charges, but there were 60 felony arrests (which led to just 32 felony charges). In addition to the arrests, a great deal of information was added to the CRASH unit's data banks. Although the target area, South Central Los Angeles, is predominantly African American, there were accusations that Operation Hammer was a racist suppression effort because 93 percent of those arrested were black. The LAPD, predictably, stood by its belief that gang suppression units were necessary for citizen safety. Then-County Supervisor Kenneth Hahn believed that the gang problem was so serious that the National Guard should be sent into Los Angeles's gang neighborhoods to fight a "war" against gangs.

Accusations of corruption accompanied complaints of racism on the part of the LAPD and especially its CRASH units. The NAACP claimed that hundreds of complaints were filed against LAPD and CRASH. Among the accusations are the following: Police left gang suspects stranded on enemy turf and officers wrote over Crip graffiti with Blood graffiti and vice versa (Davis 1992). But the demise of the CRASH suppression unit finally occurred due to allegations of corruption in the Rampart District. The Rampart District has a notorious reputation in Los Angeles as one of the most violent areas anywhere in the country. In 1990, there were around 150 murders in the division; by 1997, the count was down to about 33 (PBS—*Frontline* 2001). The LAPD claimed the reason for the great reduction in violent crime in that district was due to CRASH. According to the former president of the Los Angeles Police Commission, Gerald Chaleff, the Rampart district has always done things "the Rampart Way" (PBS—*Frontline* 2001). The Rampart unit was in a building away from the main station, without supervision, because of space problems. These officers, sergeants and senior police alike, were used to doing whatever they wanted to. They got away with "questionable" behavior because of the population that they served—many people in that community were recent immigrants from Central and South America and more or less expected the police to be corrupt because that's the way it was in their home countries. Among the behaviors that were a part of the "Rampart Way" of doing things was their secret club and system of reward and recognition. They would give out plaques to officers who shot gang members, and they had their own tattoos and patches that they wore on their jackets. The tattoos and patches displayed a cowboy hat on a skull with aces and eights, which stood for the "dead man's" hand that Wild Bill Hickock had when he was shot playing poker. The plaques also had shell casings engraved on them for the number of times the officer had hit the person he was shooting at. A special, distinctive plaques was awarded for a fatal shooting. Members of the Rampart CRASH unit were known to use "drop guns"—guns recovered previously on the street, but never reported—as "planted" evidence against perpetrators they thought had guns but, as it turned out, did not. They did the same thing with drugs. Thus, if a CRASH officer wanted a gang member to go to prison but could not catch him in the act of committing gang crime, he would plant guns or narcotics on the member. It was also common to pay off informants with confiscated drugs that were never turned in to booking.

Ultimately, the worst scandal in LAPD history would ravage the Rampart unit and lead to its—and the rest of CRASH's—end. Former officer Rafael Perez of the Rampart Division admitted in court in 2000, as part of his plea bargain for drug charges in 1999, that he shot and framed an innocent man. Perez was caught while attempting to steal narcotics from an evidence storage facility and implicated other Rampart Division officers in a variety of abuses. The Rampart scandal led to the investigation of 70 current and former officers and the overturning of some 40 convictions. It is estimated that as many as 99 people may have been wrongly convicted based on false testimony by officers (Feldman 2000). In an attempt to institute changes, and facing political backlash from a number of organizations, LAPD Chief Bernard C. Parks disbanded all CRASH units effective March 12, 2000 (*LAPD Newsletter* 2000). As a result of the disbanding of CRASH, the computer database with files on more than 112,000 purported Los Angeles County gang members (62,000 of whom were identified by CRASH units) was compromised (O'Connor 2000). Many citizens of Los Angeles expressed a concern that without the CRASH units gang activity would escalate once again in the "City of Angels." However, it was clear that a city like Los Angeles, the street gang capital, could not go without a suppression unit, and indeed the CRASH units were replaced by Special Enforcement Units to fight gang activity in Los Angeles.

As acknowledged in the discussion on CRASH, gang units depend on intelligence information. "Both police officials and researchers have identified intelligence gathering and the development and maintenance of gang tracking systems and databases as one of the most important functions carried out by specialized gang units" (Webb and Katz 2003, 26). However, it should also be noted that "although nearly every gang unit engages in some form of intelligence gathering, the importance of this function to the gang unit and to its respective department varies from one department to the next" (Webb and Katz 2003, 26). The intelligence function of the gang unit merely allows it the opportunity to perform its primary function—suppression and enforcement. Making arrests and confiscating illegal contraband is the best way for a gang unit to quantify and justify its existence (to politicians and taxpayers). The various law enforcement agencies all have their own criteria for determining who gets added to a gang database and/or tracking system. The Los Angeles Sheriff's Department instructs its officers to enter a name in the gang database only if the suspect meets at least two of the following gang criteria (O'Connor 2000, A23):

- Professes to be a gang member
- Is deemed a gang member by a reliable source, such as a trusted informant, teacher, or parent
- Is called a gang member by an untested informant with corroboration
- Has gang graffiti on his personal property or clothing
- Is observed, by an officer, using gang hand signs
- Hangs around with gang members
- Is arrested with gang members
- Identifies his gang affiliation when brought to county jail—something authorities say suspects do to avoid being jailed with enemy gang members

The Los Angeles Sheriff's Department attempts to be very careful about whose name is added to a gang list but insists that gang databases are a critical tool in the fight against gang activity. This cautious approach reflects those of other police agencies that seek to avoid violating privacy rights. In Tulsa, Okalahoma, a city with a rising gang problem, officials designate people as possible gang members based on a range of factors (e.g., criminal records, tattoos, brands on skin that claim an allegiance to a specific gang, frequent associations with known gang members). Tulsa's database (2004) includes about 3,300 residents. To avoid privacy concerns, Tulsa's database is restricted to suspected and actual gang members. In 2002, Denver officials were forced to drop a broader database after residents accused the department of compiling "spy files" against innocent people (Johnson 2004). The Denver database included names and information on people who were involved in such legal activities as lawful protests or demonstrations.

Every large city in the United States has a gang suppression unit. In 1991, in Baltimore, the police department created a Violent Crime Task Force now called the **Violent Crimes Division**. The division has several units: the Handgun Recovery Squad, the Operations Unit, the Shooting Squad, the Cold-Case Squad (which works closely with the Shooting Squad), and the Youth Violence Strike Force (which now oversees the Intelligence Unit) (OJJDP 2012b). The gang suppression units are deployed to specific, targeted areas. The Youth Violence Strike Force works closely with the FBI, Bureau of Alcohol, Tobacco, Firearms and Explosives (ATF), U.S. Attorney, school police, and the State Department of Juvenile Justice. The Task Force also works closely with parole officers, probation officers, and judges, holding "Gang Call-In" meetings with youths who are on parole and probation (OJJDP 2012b). In St. Louis, Missouri, law enforcement officials have developed the Consent to Search and Seize protocols in conjunction with its **Firearm Suppression Program**. Once the unit receives information on a gang member, two officers visit the residence of the alleged member, speak with an adult resident, and request permission to search the home for illegal weapons. Residents are told that they will not be charged with the illegal possession of a firearm if they sign the Consent to Search and Seize form (Howell 2000; OJJDP 2012c). In Orange County, California, the **Tri-Agency Resource Gang Enforcement Team (TARGET)** operates to decrease gang crime in the area by incorporating a three-prong approach: (1) selective incarceration of the most violent and repeat gang offenders in the most violent gangs; (2) enforcement of probation controls with younger, less violent gang offenders; and (3) arrests of gang leaders in "hot spots" of gang activity (Howell 2010b, 57). TARGET uses a multijurisdictional model that integrates law enforcement with probation and prosecution efforts (OJJDP 2012b). Riverside, California, utilizes the **Riverside County Gang Task Force** to keep its neighborhoods free of violent crime and gang activity. The Task Force works collaboratively with peace officers, probation officers, parole agents, federal agents, and prosecutors whose common objective is to provide targeted intelligence gathering, enforcement, investigation, and vigorous prosecution of gang members who engage in criminal acts (Riverside County Gang Task Force 2012). In Boston, **Operation Ceasefire** was designed to combat street gangs. First implemented in May 1996 as a coordinated, citywide strategy aimed at deterring juvenile and gang firearm violence, this unit works in collaboration with the Attorney for the Commonwealth of Massachusetts and representatives from federal, state, and local law enforcement; parole and probation officers; the mayor's office; city agencies, clergy; and several universities (OJJDP 2012d). The effectiveness of Operation Ceasefire is currently being evaluated by a research team from Harvard University's Kennedy School of Government. Two previous evaluations showed a marked drop in homicides by persons aged 24 and under and a 70 percent reduction in gun assaults for people of all ages (OJJDP 2012d). In January 2003, in response to a rapidly increasing level of gang violence within the city of Syracuse, New York, members of the Syracuse Police Department met with the U.S. Attorney's Office in an effort to explore options within the federal legal system to combat street gang violence. As a result of that meeting, the **Gang and Violent Crime Task Force** was created. The Task Force works cooperatively with the ATF, Drug Enforcement Agency, the Onondaga County Sheriff's Department, and the New York State Police (Syracuse Police Department 2012). As we learned in Chapter 6, the Task Force has worked cooperatively with all these agencies to arrest and convict numerous street gangs under RICO Act.

The earlier described sample gang task forces represent the trend in gang suppression efforts and work cooperatively with other agencies in an effort to curtail, arrest, and prosecute gang members. Nearly all cities with a gang problem have such a specialized unit.

Community Policing

Another element in law enforcement suppression of street gangs is community policing. **Community policing** represents a shift in thinking of law enforcement as sole watchmen over neighborhoods by giving local community members an active role as overseers. "Community policing is people-based as opposed to being bureaucratic or militaristic. It is about improving people's quality of life" (Kappeler and Gaines 2011, 165). Community policing empowers residents of a community by making them active participants in protecting their neighborhoods. Community policing is rooted in two schools of thought: (1) problem-oriented policing and (2) community-oriented policing (Gaines and Kappeler 2011). As first articulated by Goldstein (1979), traditionally, police have spent most of their time responding to problem calls rather than addressing the root causes of the problems. In other words, the police are primarily addressing the symptoms rather than addressing the problems (problem-solving). Community-oriented policing addresses the fears that citizens have about being victimized from crime. Thus, many citizens spend more time fearing the consequences of crime than they do with actually addressing crime. Community policing brings these two aspects together as citizens confront their fears by addressing the root sources of crime.

Citizens in certain communities are fearful of crime because it is such a reality in their lives. The days of foot patrols are long gone, and yet, it is foot patrols that seem to ease the minds of many folks who live in high-crime areas. The hope of community policing is to instill fear in criminals because of citizen patrols that work in cooperation with law enforcement. Foot patrols are supplemented with bicycle patrols in some communities and boat patrols in others. Ideally, community policing involves police officers becoming more involved in communities that are at a high risk for gang activity. However, because of direct input from citizens in patrolled areas, the police will, ideally, prioritize problems based on citizen input. Unfortunately, one of the biggest problems associated with community policing is poor communication. In most cases, it seems that the communication between the two interested parties—community members and law enforcement—is lacking and uncooperative in application. In their evaluation of community-policing programs, Webb and Katz (2003, 36) found that "the lack of communication between citizens and the gang unit was particularly problematic when the gang unit attempted to carry out enforcement-oriented operations. In particular, we found that enforcement operations that are carried out without any citizen input or awareness, and often without input from other units in the agency, can create serious police–community relations problems." For example, a gang suppression unit in Las Vegas carried out a sweep without informing local community-policing leaders or the Las Vegas district commander of that neighborhood (Webb and Katz 2003). The infamous case of George Zimmerman shooting and killing an unarmed Trayvon Martin, however, provides us with an example of poor communication that leads many police agencies to question the validity of community policing of citizens redundancy. Zimmerman, a community watch coordinator for a gated community in Florida, was to work with the Sanford police department. He called in a "suspicious person" report and the police told Zimmerman not to approach the person in question but to remain in his car. Instead, Zimmerman did approach Martin and shot and killed him. The circumstances of the killing were still being debated at the time of this writing, but Zimmerman claimed he acted in self-defense while lawyers for the family of Trayvon Martin argued that it was murder. Community watchpersons are generally advised not to carry guns, but in Florida, gun laws are quite different than in most states (e.g., Florida has a "Stand Your Ground" law that allows people who reasonably fear for their life to defend themselves through use of deadly force; in most states, such laws are restricted to within-your-home parameters). As Police Chief Bill Lee acknowledged, Zimmerman was not acting outside of the legal boundaries of Florida statute by carrying a weapon when the incident occurred. Nonetheless, if Zimmerman had remained inside his car, Martin would still be alive.

In order for community policing to be effective, patrol officers need to meet the citizens involved with community watch. It is also important to have the same beat officers work the neighborhood watch area so that both parties can learn to understand the needs of the other. In many cases, however there remains a measure of mistrust on the part of both parties with the other. Some citizens groups feel their needs are not being addressed and this leads to resentment. Some police officers have had the misfortune to work with "gone-whole" watch members (like Zimmerman) who act like cowboys in the Wild West. Katz and Webb (2006) studied community policing and found officers in many communities that were against community policing.

There are many examples of community-policing programs. Among the more popular are foot patrols. Historically, foot patrols are the oldest form of police patrol work, but by the late 1990s foot patrols comprised just 6 percent of the total policing activities of police departments (Public Safety Strategies Group 2007). The benefits of foot patrols include community goodwill and improved relationships with local police. On the other hand, many officers are unhappy with the concept of foot patrols, they argue, among other things that they are too expensive and antiquated. Foot patrols are indeed expensive and require government funding separate from the current operating budgets of law enforcement agencies that use them. Two of the earliest cities to implement a foot patrol system were Newark, New Jersey, and Flint, Michigan. The "Safe and Clean Neighborhoods Program" began in New Jersey in 1973 and specifically mandated the use of foot patrol in an effort to enhance community safety. Evaluation of the foot patrol in Newark showed that using foot patrols in combination with other strategies increased the perception of safety. Based on crime statistics, however, there was no significant, measurable decrease in criminal activity over the study period (Public Safety Strategies Group 2007).

The Flint (Michigan) Police Department created the **Flint Neighborhood Foot Patrol Program** in 1979 as part of a greater initiative to integrate citizens into the policing of their neighborhood. Before 1979, all of the Flint police patrols were motorized. The program introduced 22 foot patrol officers assigned to 14 experimental areas, which included about 20 percent of the city's population. Among other things, the program hoped to decrease the actual or perceived amount of criminal activity, increase citizen involvement in crime prevention, decrease the depersonalization of interactions between officers and residents, develop citizen volunteer action, and increase protection for women, children, and the aged (Public Safety Strategies Group 2007; Trojanowicz, Morash, and Schram 2001). It is worth noting that Flint, Michigan, is consistently ranked among the most dangerous cities in the United States (fifth in 2010). Research conducted in the mid-2000s revealed that the foot program reduced the crime rate by about 9 percent; decreased the calls for service by 42 percent, and dramatically changed the perceptions of citizens about the police for the better (Public Safety Strategies Group 2007). The program ran out of money and was in jeopardy of being eliminated until the C.S. Mott Foundation provided the city of Flint with a $1.5 million grant to reinstitute the program (Richards 2010). In addition to the foot patrols, Flint will reopen police mini-stations and establish quarterly reduction targets (Richards 2010). The program is now known as the **Community Oriented Policing Services (COPS)**. Foot patrols are popping up all over the United States, as well internationally, including such places as Washington, D.C.; Los Angeles; Suffolk County, New York; Rochester, New York; Madison, Wisconsin; Minneapolis, Minnesota; and San Francisco.

COPS operates as part of a larger conglomerate under the jurisdiction of U.S. Department of Justice and awards grants to cities that apply for funds. In 2009, for example, four law enforcement agencies in Texas received "Recover Act" grants. The department had over 7,200 applications, requesting $8.3 billion in grants for the $1.1 billion available, and just 1.046 of the 4,600 agencies that applied for grants received them (Chron.com 2009). In Dallas, COPS helped to establish five gang-related programs as part of a community-policing program. Three main suppression strategies were employed by Dallas gang units: saturation patrols/high-visibility patrols in target areas, aggressive curfew enforcement, and aggressive enforcement of truancy laws and regulations. Gang unit officers teamed with community-policing officers to carry out these strategies. Community evaluators examined weekly and monthly police reports (e.g., documented overtime-funded activities) to make sure that the police were in compliance with community expectations (Howell 2000).

The state of Illinois, through the Youth Services Department, has set up the **Gang Crime Prevention Center (GCPC)**, which is dedicated to involving all citizens in the fight against street gangs and the conditions that contribute to their formation and growth. The GCPC utilizes community resources, law enforcement resources, and other means to eliminate and control gangs throughout the state. Among the many programs established by the Youth Services Department is the Cook County Sheriff's **Police and Children Together (PACT) Camp**. The PACT program was created to address the lack of positive role models and recreational activities for vulnerable youth, which sometimes results in youth involvement with delinquent friends, drugs, or violence. The camps are designed to put youth and law enforcement personnel together in a cooperative setting that will ultimately strengthen bonds between youth and police and at the same time provide recreational activities that are fun, healthy, and "community positive." Each PACT Camp must have the following (Cook County Sheriff's Department 2012a):

1. At least one police-related activity
2. Police officers serving as officer counselors and facilitating transportation for the campers
3. At least one community-service project
4. At least one team-building activity that involves police officers on the team (not as activity leaders)
5. Structured, daily physical activities that youths can do at home (probably exercises)
6. A graduation ceremony at the conclusion
7. The presence of the chief for at least a portion of the camp

The PACT Camp is an annual event and the Youth Services Department hopes to create spin-off programs. In addition to the camps, PACT is designed to strengthen the presence of the local police department in the community and, when needed, to provide a needed bridge between families and services (Cook County Sheriff's Department 2012a). To reach this goal, the Cook County's Community Relations goal is to assure that the Sheriff's Department is user-friendly for the citizens of the county. Community Relations representatives regularly attend neighborhood and community watch meetings, update residents on area activity, and often provide safety tips and other useful information. Members of the unit are permanently assigned to Proviso East and Shepard high schools as school resource officers (Cook County Sheriff's Office 2012b).

Perhaps the best-known community-policing organization is the **Guardian Angels**. Their trademark, red berets, make them easily identifiable by law-abiding citizens and criminals alike. The Guardian Angels was founded by Curtis Sliwa in 1979. At that time, Sliwa was a McDonald's night manager in a crime-ridden area of the Bronx. Fed up with the crime in his neighborhood, Sliwa formed a voluntary, weapon-free patrol of 13 members, who patrolled subways and city streets in an effort to rid the community of criminals. Once criticized as vigilantes, the Guardian Angels are now an acclaimed example of a successful community-policing group. The Guardian Angels do not merely protect the innocent from criminals—they attempt to teach citizens how to protect themselves and encourage citizens to take responsibility for their neighborhoods (GuardianAngels.org 2004). The Angels have grown from their initial foot patrols to the launching of CyberAngels (1998), an Internet-based cyber safety program (GuardianAngels.org 2004). Today, the Angels have undertaken many school-based initiatives in an effort to empower people to help themselves. As of 2012, the Guardian Angels has more than 130 chapters in 17 countries. They provide safety patrols, as volunteers, on the streets, subways, and other public areas from dusk until dawn, without weapons (GuardianAngels.org 2012).

Community-policing programs appear to have some success in dealing with youth gangs and gang-related problems. If nothing else, they make local citizens feel safer and perception often plays a role in community–police relations. It is unfortunate that citizens have to rely on their police departments receiving grants in order to provide street patrols and other services. If more groups like the Guardian Angels were to emerge in communities, perhaps the crime rate would decrease.

Judicial and Legislative Suppression Efforts

Keeping youths out of gangs begins with individual choice—deciding whether to join a gang or not. The parents and/or legal guardians are the primary agents of socialization that is designed to keep kids out of gangs and/or committing other acts of delinquency. Schools implement many programs that are also designed to keep students out of gangs. Despite all of these efforts at gang prevention, however, youths still turn to gangs. Inevitably, they come in contact with the police and their gang suppression activities. Assisting the police in their "war" against gangs are the courts and legislative bodies. It is the responsibility of the court to prosecute criminals and send them to detention centers or prison. The legislative body attempts to write laws that further assist the police and their efforts at suppression.

JUDICIAL SUPPRESSION EFFORTS **Judicial efforts** include such strategies as the following:

- Injunctions—the banning of gang members from certain areas or congregating in public
- Curfews—attempts to keep youths off the streets late at night and therefore away from gang and criminal activities
- Truancy laws—efforts to keep youths in school
- Banning certain attire—articles of clothing typically associated with gangs. This is often very controversial because one of the most common items banned is the six-pointed star worn by some gangs (e.g., the Gangster Disciples) but also by Jewish people
- Banning gang colors—especially do-rags that indicate gang allegiance
- Housing—housing authorities are authorized by HUD (Department of Housing and Urban Development) to evict gang members caught possessing or using guns (National Drug Strategy Networks 1996)
- Prosecution—punishing gang members by sending them to detention centers, jail, or prison
- Nuisance abatement laws—efforts to reduce gang or juvenile activities that cause harm to members of the community (e.g., banning the drinking of alcohol on sidewalks and in parks, noise limitations on stereos—especially car stereos)
- Loitering restrictions—efforts to stop gang members from hanging out together in public places even if they are not presently committing criminal acts

Injunctions against gangs are one of the favorite judicial suppression efforts. They make use of loitering restrictions by banning gangsters from hanging out with each other in public places. Although there is no official agency responsible for tracking the use of injunctions against street gangs, according to Maxson, Hennigan, and Sloan (2003), "the first reported use of a civil injunction for gang abatement was in Santa Ana, California, in 1980, although site abatements for other disorder problems like drugs or pornography were not uncommon. The Santa Ana city attorney obtained an injunction prohibiting youths from gathering and partying at a known gang hangout." From that point on, injunctions have been used routinely in a number of jurisdictions in southern California. For the most part, these injunctions escaped public attention or interest, but periodically debates over the legality of specific injunctions become sensationalized in the media by political activists and attention-seekers. For example, in 1987 a widely publicized injunction was issued against the Playboy Gangster Crips. The American Civil Liberties Union (ACLU) lodged a court complaint against the legality of this injunction. "The challenge was partly successful in that an attorney was appointed to represent the gang and only illegal behaviors were included in the injunction in December 1987" (Maxson et al. 2003, 249). The ACLU would continue to play "watchdog" over future injunctions, especially after receiving numerous complaints from citizens concerned about the basic civil right to congregate, peacefully, in public. Most citizens support injunctions because they are generally successful in curtailing gang activities in targeted areas.

In order to continue using injunctions, district attorney's offices are careful with their wording. In 1992, the Burbank City Attorney's Office obtained an injunction against 34 members of the **Barrio Elmwood Rifa** gang. This was the first injunction to constrain gang members from associating with one another. It prohibited them from standing, sitting, walking, driving, gathering, or appearing anywhere in public view of each other (Castorena 1998). Prohibiting gang members from public association has remained a staple of court-ordered injunctions. For example, in 1992, Chicago officials adopted the **Gang Congregation Ordinance**, which was essentially an **antiloitering law** targeting street gangs. The ordinance dictates that police officers who observe a person they believe to be a criminal street gang member loitering in any public place with one or more other suspected gang members are to disperse and remove from the area such suspects who are standing around "with no apparent purpose." Any person who does not comply with this order is in violation of the ordinance. In 1993, a Jesus Morales and other individuals charged with violating the Chicago ordinance petitioned Cook County Circuit Court to dismiss the charges, claiming that the ordinance was unconstitutional and violated their rights under the First, Fourth, and Fourteenth Amendments to the Constitution. The court agreed and allowed a motion for dismissal of the charges. The city appealed all the way to the U.S. Supreme Court (losing each step of the way), which found that the ordinance was unconstitutional. The Supreme Court, in a 6–3 decision, ruled that the city's 1992 antiloitering ordinance, which resulted in 45,000 arrests in the three years it was enforced, violated the rights of the defendants because it failed to give citizens adequate notice of what was forbidden (Carelli 1999). In other words, this antiloitering statute was unconstitutional because it was overly broad and vague; it did not even offer a definition of a gang.

Meanwhile, in southern California, at least 30 gang injunctions were issued from 1993 to 2000. In 1993, the Los Angeles County district attorney was granted an injunction banning the **Blythe Street Gang** from congregating in public areas. This Hispanic gang, with more than 500 members, had terrorized a formerly quiet San Fernando Valley neighborhood and turned it into an occupied zone. In 1997, the California Supreme Court ruled that this court injunction was an acceptable gang suppression tactic (Howell 2000). In July 1997, a court-ordered injunction was issued against the notorious Los Angeles **18th Street Gang**. Judge Alan G. Buckner approved the injunction in an unprecedented move in Los Angeles's long and frustrating war on gangs (Rosenzweig and Gold 1997). The injunction specifically targeted 18 members of one set of the 18th Street Gang, barring 3 or more of the 18 from associating in public view at any time and including prohibitions related to graffiti, blocking sidewalks and harassing residents, and acting as lookouts to warn against the approach of police. A month later, a new injunction with the same provisions was directed against all the sets of this gang found in the Pico-Union areas west of downtown (near the Los Angeles Convention Center), comprising more than 300 members (Krikorian and Connell 1997). But despite these injunctions, the gang continues to exist and flourish. In an attempt to dismantle the 18th Street Gang, in 2004 the Los Angeles city attorney's office won a permanent injunction against it that bars members from recruiting young people. The injunction covers gang members around Wilshire Boulevard in the mid-city area. Also in 2004, Los Angeles city attorney Rocky Delgadillo successfully received court approval for an injunction against the **Rolling 60s** gang in South Los Angeles to prevent members from driving together into a rival gang's territory (Garrison 2004). (It is interesting to note that city officials in Los Angeles no longer use "South Central Los Angeles" to refer to that specific area of the city, because of the term's historically negative connotation. This crime-ridden area of the city is now called South Los Angeles, but city officials are naïve, at best, if they think renaming an area of a city will change its character. After all, "a rose by any other name, is still a rose." Los Angeles officials need to spend more time and effort improving the socioeconomic conditions of South Central Los Angeles than on convincing residents that the area now called South Los Angeles has a better image.)

The use of injunctions remains controversial. In southern California, law enforcement agencies have been fairly successful in implementing injunctions against gangs; however, in other areas of the country (e.g., Chicago), injunctions have been shot down as unconstitutional. Unlike the broad Chicago ordinance that was struck down by the U.S. Supreme Court, the injunctions in Los Angeles name specific gang members and accuse them of being involved in criminal activity. Furthermore, the Los Angeles injunctions apply only to the gang's neighborhood, not an unrestricted geographical area. Citizens in embattled communities that are confronted by the lawlessness of street gangs remain the strongest proponents of injunctions, as they see and feel the benefits immediately. Furthermore, law enforcement agencies that have used injunctions typically view them as successful. Unfortunately, injunctions are often little more than quick fixes to a complicated problem that cannot be solved by simply banning the association of gang members. On the other hand, many communities need a quick fix to the gang problem in their neighborhoods.

On February 2, 2011, Carmen A. Trutanich, City Attorney for the City of Los Angeles, petitioned the Superior Court of the State of California (for Los Angeles County) an amended judgment granting permanent injunction (abate a public nuisance) against the **Grape Street Crips** (City Attorney of Los Angeles 2011). The injunction was designed to keep the gang members out of the "Central City Recovery Zone" (CCRZ) (commonly known as "Skid Row") and was very specific in defining the parameters of the CCRZ boundary. The specific nature of Los Angeles's court injunctions is why they generally hold up in court. In November 2011, the first two gang members were charged with violating the injunction. The injunction was the latest step in the city's crackdown on crime on skid row. As part of his problem to clean up the CCRZ, Mayor Antonio Villaraigosa and then Police Chief William J. Bratton deployed 50 additional officers to the area as part of "Safer City Initiative" (Blankstein 2011).

In August 2011, Suffolk County (New York) officials petitioned for an injunction to keep two Bloods street gangs, the **Wyandanch Bloods** and the **Braveheart Bloods**, from gathering with other known gang members within a two-square-mile "safety zone" (Stelloh 2011). Modeling their injunction after the successful injunctions in southern California, the Suffolk County injunction named 37 individuals. By identifying specific individuals, it was believed that the injunction would be safe from appeal by any civil rights groups. The details were so precise that the injunction included a photo, identified specific tattoos, and provided aliases for each of the 37 gang members (Order to Show Cause, Index No.: 2011). Suffolk County executive Steve Levy commented, "We're not talking about seeking an injunction against an individual who happens to be walking down the street randomly or might be wearing a certain color. This is specifically targeted toward 37 individuals who have already been convicted of some major crimes and are self-confessed members of the [Wyandanch] Bloods or the Braveheart Bloods" (Stelloh 2011).

The New York Civil Liberties Union (NYCLU) was opposed to the injunction from its inception. As an expert in the field of gang studies, I was asked by the New York Civil Liberties (NYCLU) Clinic for input on the proposed injunction, so I have been following this case with heightened interest. As summarized by Corey Stoughton, Senior Staff Attorney & Litigation Coordinator for the NYCLU, through a combination of advocacy and fortuitous political change the August application for injunction was intervened in September. The judge set a schedule to dismiss the injunction based on constitutional grounds. In the meantime, there was an election in November 2011, and a new County Executive (D-Steve Bellone) was elected. The NYCLU worked diligently to get Bellone to recognize that the injunction was unconstitutional and bad crime policy, and he agreed. The county then voluntarily withdrew the application, and the judge dismissed the case with prejudice in February. Since the injunction was never issued, no Blood gang members were arrested (because of the proposed injunction). Suffolk County officials are now attempting to form a variation of community policing in an effort to ensure better relations with community members and more community involvement.

Juvenile curfew ordinances are another important tactic in judicial gang suppression efforts. As of July 2009, at least 500 cities had curfews on teenage youths, including 78 of the 92 cities with a population greater than 180,000 (Favro 2009). In most cities, curfews prohibit children under 18 from being on the streets between 11 PM and 5 AM during the week and after midnight on weekends. Approximately 100 cities have daytime curfews to keep children off the streets during school hours (Favro 2009). Curfews are popular because they represent an inexpensive judicial gang and delinquency intervention option. The first youth curfew was adopted by Omaha, Nebraska, in 1880. In 1884, President Benjamin Harrison described curfews as "the most important municipal regulation for the protection of children in American homes from the vices of the street" (Favro 2009). Many jurisdictions report a reduction in crime after instituting a curfew. The Dallas police reported a drop in juvenile victimization (17.7%) and juvenile arrests (14.6%) from the year prior to the curfew during the hours of curfew enforcement. Statistics from the Phoenix police showed that 21 percent of all curfew violators were gang members and that there was a 10 percent drop in juvenile arrests for violent crimes after implementing an aggressive curfew program (Fritsch, Caeti, and Taylor 2003). Three years after San Antonio, Texas, enacted a curfew, the victimization of youth dropped 84 percent. Detroit, Cincinnati, New Orleans, and other cities report comparable results (Favro 2009). Just as there are legal concerns about the constitutionality of injunctions, there are those who wonder whether curfew ordinances infringe on the rights of individuals. A federal appeals court ruled in 1999 that teenagers do not have an unrestricted right to roam the streets late at night and that youth curfews are constitutional. However, the ACLU has launched several challenges to curfews, arguing that they infringe upon the free speech rights of youths. And in some cases they have found favorable rulings. In Rochester, New York, for example, the ACLU was successful in convincing the New York Court of Appeals (in 2009) that the 2007 curfew the city enacted was unconstitutional. The judges cited the infringement of free speech argument presented by the ACLU as one of the prime reasons for overturning the curfew law (NYCLU 2009; Walsh 2010). The judges also cited data that shows 83.6 to 87.8 percent of violent crime committed by youths occurs outside of curfew hours. Upset with the ruling, Rochester mayor Robert Duffy countered that a curfew is a "common-sense" public safety tool.

Truancy, commonly called "skipping school," is defined by all states as unexcused absences from school without the knowledge of a parent or guardian. The concept of skipping school has been romanticized in popular culture by characters such as Tom Sawyer or Ferris Bueller as harmless mischief that youths tend to do. As a result, truancy is often regarded as a minor offense; some call it a **status offense** (relatively minor offenses that may serve as precursors to more serious forms of delinquency). But truancy comes at many costs. For schools, it can cost them government dollars. But the youths themselves are missing out on opportunities to learn in the short term and potential high-paying occupations in the future. Equally important is the realization that if kids are not in school, they are put in a situation where other forms of delinquency, such as drug and alcohol use, become tempting ways to fill the time void. Furthermore, truants, if caught, are subject to fines that can range in cost from $250 to $5,000. There is no national data on truancy, but many cities indicate that truancy is a significant problem. Truancy is often the first indicator that a juvenile is in trouble or on the way to trouble. As obvious as it may seem that truancy leads to delinquency, "the impact of aggressive truancy enforcement on crime rates remains essentially unevaluated" (Fritsch et al. 2003, 271).

Many school districts throughout the country believe that establishing a dress code policy is a good way of providing a positive learning environment. This idea is based on the assumption that most gangs are identified by **specific colors and styles of clothing**. Iowa law (279.58) gives the board of directors of a school district the right to adopt a dress code policy that prohibits students from wearing gang-related or other specific apparel deemed inappropriate. Nevada law 392.4635 allows the board of trustees of each school district the right to forbid "(a) a pupil from wearing any clothing or carrying any symbol on school property that denotes membership in or an affiliation with a criminal gang; and (b) any activity that encourages participation in a criminal gang or facilitates illegal acts of a criminal gang." School officials have the right to suspend or expel any student found in violation of this policy. California law (35183) declares that California children have the right to an effective public school education free from the threat of violence; "gang-related apparel" is deemed hazardous to the health and safety of the school environment. Section 7 of this law encourages school districts to establish a school dress uniform as a means of establishing a "coming together feeling" among members of the student body. In addition to banning certain attire, many have empowered school districts with the authority to combat gangs in a variety of other ways. Utah law 53A-11-902 establishes conduct and discipline policies and procedures. Section 7 of this law establishes "specific provisions for preventing and responding to gang-related activities in the school, on school grounds, on school vehicles, or in connection with school-related activities or events." Washington law (148-120-100) prohibits gang activity on school grounds. Claiming membership in, association with, affiliation with, or participation in a gang or gang-related activities at school or during school-related functions is not allowed in any way.

Nuisance abatement laws address the problem of gangbangers congregating on premises where they are unwelcomed, such as schools and other public places. In 1999, Dade County (Miami), Florida, enacted Ord. No. 99-43, Nuisance Abatement. Section 2-98.4 declares that "any places or premises which are used as the site of the unlawful sale or delivery of controlled substances, prostitution, youth and street gang activity, gambling, illegal sale or consumption of alcoholic beverages, or lewd or lascivious behavior may be a public nuisance that adversely affects the public health, safety, morals, and welfare." Also in 1999, the city of Miami enacted its own public nuisance code legislation (Ord. No. 11797). Section 46-1 set the parameters as "any building, place or premises located in the city which has been used on three or more occasions, documented by substantiated incidences, as the site of the unlawful sale or delivery of controlled substances" or any other criminal act (as defined by Florida law) "within a six-month period from the date of the first substantiated incident, at the same location, is declared an unlawful public nuisance." In 1999, Houston, Texas, passed nuisance abatement legislation (Ord. No. 99-1201) in an attempt to increase the quality of life of its residents as well as to fight criminal activity by both gang members and nongang members. Reno, Nevada (Chapter 8.22, Sec. 8.22.020), has passed nuisance abatement ordinances as a means of keeping its community, including property, buildings, and premises within its limits, safe and as aesthetically pleasing as possible by forbidding a number of criminal activities, especially the use of graffiti by gang members.

Prosecution is a critical element in gang suppression efforts. The prosecutor is supposed to act in the best interests of the state (or the people). As the first line of defense against crime, law enforcement officers arrest people whom they suspect of criminal activity. After an arrest is made, there is little else (beyond offering testimony at trial) that the officer can do to assure that suspects are prosecuted and incarcerated for their crimes. It is the prosecutor's job to present enough evidence to find the accused guilty of a crime. The prosecutor, then, is the second line of defense in the suppression of street gang criminal activity. There are times when prosecutors may feel the evidence presented to them (by the police) is not substantial enough to go to court to seek a conviction. Strength of evidence is just one variable in a prosecutor's decision to proceed with a court case, however. Other factors may include special circumstances (e.g., a motorist who plows his car into a group of people because he suffered a heart attack while driving the car), the severity of the offense (the more serious offenses are the most likely to lead to prosecution), and public sentiment.

An interesting example of how public sentiment may sway a prosecutor's decision to go to court involves an incident that took place in Los Angeles. Graffiti scars the city of Los Angeles, and its residents have no tolerance for taggers and certainly do not view graffiti as some sort of "urban art" (in contrast, New York City commissions graffiti "artists" to paint murals). In 1995, William Masters confronted two taggers and asked them to stop defacing the property (support columns under a freeway) they were spray painting. The taggers refused, confronted Masters, and Masters took out a gun and fired at both of them. Masters freely confessed to killing one man and injuring the other. On the surface, this is an "airtight" case for any prosecutor to win. However, the Los Angeles public treated Masters like a hero, and radio call-in shows were dominated by citizens praising Masters for taking a "bite out of crime"—albeit, vigilante-style. (New York City once had its own public-favorite vigilante in Bernhard Goetz, the "Subway Shooter.") Masters went so far as to brag, "Where are you going to find 12 citizens to convict me?" (Estrich 1995, 11A). Not in Los Angeles. The district attorney's office announced that Masters would not be prosecuted, realizing that public sentiment was clearly on Masters' side.

There are still other conditions under which prosecutors may choose not to prosecute a particular case: when the victim expresses a desire not to prosecute the offender; the judicial costs are too high to justify prosecution; when prosecution results in undue harm to an offender (e.g., an elderly disabled person); when the accused assists prosecutors in other cases; and when amends can be made in ways other than incarceration (e.g., paying restitution) (LaFave and Israel 1992). It is worth noting the political role of prosecutors; they are, after all, elected persons. Consequently, they are swayed by public sentiment, the private interests of donators, and the whims of politicians. Thus, the prosecutor may not always be working in the best interest of the people (the state), and it is also possible for a prosecutor to carry out a personal vendetta against individuals. On the other hand, prosecutors have the discretion to give deserving individuals second chances, and they have the freedom to look into the individual circumstances that led up to the criminal act.

In Los Angeles, a special prosecutorial gang suppression program, **Hardcore Gang Investigations Unit** (formerly known as **Operation Hardcore**) exists to improve the prosecution of gang cases. Formed in 1979, the unit targets habitual gang offenders countywide and prosecutes them in either juvenile or criminal court (OJJDP 2012e). The unit is self-contained with the Los Angeles District Attorney's Office and offers gang cases high-priority prosecutorial handling in terms of the caliber of attorneys assigned to the cases (OJJDP 2012e). Operation Hardcore is an example of vertical prosecution (working through all the levels of the prosecutorial process), utilizes an effective witness protection program, issues special warrants, and provides increased training for prosecutors involved in gang cases (Parker, Negola, Rudy, Asencio, and Asencio 2008). Evaluation of the unit finds that defendants prosecuted by Operation Hardcore were prosecuted at a significantly higher rate than two comparison groups, 95 percent versus 78 percent and 71 percent (OJJDP 2012e). The witness protection aspect of the Hardcore Gang Investigations Unit is especially important with gang cases due to the regular acts of witness intimidation commonly associated with gang prosecution cases (see Chapter 8 for a discussion on gang witness intimidation). The presentation of the case, by prosecutors in court, is a critical element in gaining a conviction and in gang cases, "civilian witness may shut down completely" (Wolf 2009, 60). Jarrett Wolf, president of his own law firm and former Assistant State Attorney and DEA Agent in Miami (2009) explains that witnesses in a gang case generally fall into one of three categories:

1. Members of the victim's gang who usually prefer retaliation over prosecution
2. Members of the defendant's gang who will not testify against their fellow gang member, and
3. Members of the community who live in fear of the gangs and refuse to get involved

Wolf adds that each of these types of witnesses must be handled differently and resourcefully. Specially designed prosecutorial anti-gang units, such as the Hardcore Gang Investigations Unit, are among the best trained.

The court is the legal foundation of the criminal justice system. The court is presumed to consist of an independent judge free from bias who runs trials based on preexisting legal norms and rules that do not change on a case-by-case basis, due process, and (generally) a jury of peers. The court is the setting of legal procedures where objectivity is supposed to reign. Ideally, if the police make a clean and accurate arrest of a suspect, the prosecutor does a good job in presenting the case, and the judge oversees the proceedings objectively; the perpetrator, if guilty, will be given a sentence of some sort, and if innocent, will be freed. The courts are in a strong position to assist suppression efforts against gangs. They provide the injunctions and establish the curfews that police officers need to fight the war on the streets. The judge, like the prosecutor, attained his/her position, as a rule, through an election. Consequently, this position is very political and a judge's personal bias, subjectivity, and political ambition may interfere with the objectivity of the judicial proceedings.

It is important to remember that many gang members are still youths. Consequently, many of them are tried in juvenile court or family court. The legal basis for juvenile court can be traced back to the concept of *parens patriae* (a Latin phrase that literally means "the parent of the country" and refers to the belief that the state has both the right and duty to direct and protect those of its citizens who need help, especially the young and mentally challenged). The basic idea is that young people are too immature to understand the meaning of their behaviors. In other words, they cannot, or should not, be held accountable for certain actions. Many people who work with gangs state that gang members are very aware of what they are doing, even in the early teen years. Juvenile status has been a loophole that has allowed a great number of juvenile gang members to get away with less severe punishments for crimes. There is a movement among many legislatures to modify these legal restrictions.

LEGISLATIVE SUPPRESSION EFFORTS It is the role of the police to enforce current laws. In other words, they must "play the hand that they were dealt." Arresting people for committing crimes against various laws is their greatest contribution to suppression efforts. Even prosecutors and judges with personal ambition for higher office must still work within the letter of the law. Thus, all three elements responsible for suppressing gang activity are dependent on legislators and the laws that they create in the fight against crime. Legislative bodies respond to demands from law enforcement and the general public, who elected them and who are the people that legislators represent in performing their jobs.

In regard to gang suppression, legislative bodies have worked diligently to create laws that are constitutional, enforceable, and yet do not interfere with individual civil rights guaranteed by the U.S. Constitution. Along with the creation of new laws, legislators may modify existing ones. Often the bills they introduce are not passed. For example, in 2001, legislation addressing the issue of adding "thrill" killings and gang-initiation slayings to the list of crimes eligible for the death penalty under New York's capital-punishment law was introduced in the New York State Senate. Thrill killing was described in Bill S.5409, Section 6, paragraph xiv, as "the defendant committed the *killing for the pleasure of it*." According to State Senator Michael F. Nozzolio (2004), the measure was not voted on during the 2001–2002 legislative session and has not been reintroduced since. In fact, New York State's highest court ruled the death penalty itself as unconstitutional on June 24, 2004, as a result of the *People v. Stephen Lavalle* case (Death Penalty Information Center 2012). An example of legislation modified for gang-related purposes is the "aiding and abetting" laws. Some jurisdictions may charge gang leaders involved in criminal enterprises, such as selling drugs, with aiding and abetting even if they are not actually caught selling drugs. In addition, gang members who ride along with others who commit a crime may be found guilty of aiding and abetting even if they never left the car to participate in the criminal act (Howell 2000).

A number of laws that target gang-related activities have been passed by legislative bodies. A few examples are provided here. In an effort to curtail gang graffiti in New York State, legislators passed **New York 125.60**. This law forbids any person from putting graffiti (defined as "the etching, painting, covering, drawing upon or otherwise placing of a mark upon public or private property with intent to damage such property") of any type on any building without the express permission of the owner or operator of said property. **New York 145.65** makes the possession of graffiti tools a class B misdemeanor. Graffiti tools are described as "any tool, instrument, article, substance, solution or other compound designed or commonly used to etch, paint, cover, draw upon or otherwise mark upon a piece of property for which that person has no permission or authority." In an effort to address gang assault, New York State passed **New York S 120.06** (gang assault in the second degree) and **New York S 120.07** (gang assault in the first degree). "A person is guilty of gang assault in the second degree when, with intent to cause physical injury to another person and when aided by two or more other persons actually present, he causes serious physical injury to such person or to a third person (New York S 120.06)." "A person is guilty of gang assault in the first degree when, with intent to cause serious physical injury to another person and when aided by two or more persons actually present, he causes serious physical injury to such person or to a third person" (New York S 120.07).

In the state of California, legislators passed **California 13825.2**, which established the California Gang, Crime, and Violence Prevention Partnership Program, a program administered by the Department of Justice for the purposes of reducing gang, criminal activity, and youth violence in communities with a high incidence of gang violence. **California 14000** established the Community Law Enforcement and Recovery (CLEAR) Demonstration Project, a multiagency gang intervention program under the joint jurisdiction of the Los Angeles County Sheriff's Department, the Los Angeles County District Attorney's office, the Los Angeles County Probation Department, and the LAPD. Among the primary roles of the district attorney under CLEAR is the preparation and prosecution of civil injunctions against gang activities occurring within targeted areas. Law enforcement and probation officials are to share information with each other as well as the District Attorney's office. **California 14005** authorized an independent evaluation of CLEAR.

The District of Columbia passed legislation establishing a juvenile curfew. The Council of the District of Columbia (known as the Council) has determined that persons under the age of 17 years are particularly susceptible, due to their lack of maturity and experience, to participating in unlawful and gang-related activities and to becoming victims of older perpetrators of crime. To protect minors from each other and other persons, legislators enacted **District of Columbia 2-1541**, a curfew for those under the age of 17. The Council also passed legislation, making it unlawful for a person to congregate in groups of two or more persons in public space on public property within the perimeter of a drug-free zone (**District of Columbia 48-1004**).

In an effort to fight gang intimidation, the state of Florida passed the Street Terrorism Enforcement and Prevention (STEP) Act of 1990 (**Florida 874**). In brief, the state legislature established that every person has a legal right to be free from, and protected from, fear, intimidation, and physical harm caused by the activities of criminal street gangs and their members (**Florida 874.02**). Any person found to be victimized by gang intimidation has the right to pursue a civil case against the gang (**Florida 874.06**). Florida legislators consider gangs to be terrorist groups that represent a "clear and present danger" to citizens. It is the intent of the legislature, through the Street Terrorism act, to eradicate the terror created by criminal street gangs and their members by providing enhanced penalties and eliminating the patterns, profits, instrumentation, and property facilitating criminal street gang activity, including criminal street gang recruitment. The state of Illinois, in an attempt to protect witnesses to gang-related crimes from intimidation and retaliation, established the Gang Crime Witness Protection Fund (**725 ILCS 172/5-20**).

In addition to the creation of new laws, a few of which have just been described, legislators may also reconsider appropriate penalties to be attached to a violation. This reconsideration results in stricter penalties and punishments against street gangs. For example, in May 2012, the state of Illinois passed the "Emanuel Anti-Gang" law that makes it easier to prosecute people who organize illegal activities but use others to commit the actual crime. In essence, the bill creates a state version of the federal racketeering statutes (Groeninger 2012). Senator Tony Munoz, D-Chicago, sponsor of the bill, said that the new law will provide an additional way for law enforcement to go after gang kingpins who orchestrate gang activity but have others, usually youths as young as 10 years old, sell the drugs (Groeninger 2012).

The Emanuel Anti-Gang law is described as a state version of federal racketeering statutes, but it is the federal RICO Act that has been used most efficiently throughout the United States. RICO Act leads the way in legislative efforts to combat gangs. As demonstrated throughout the text (especially Chapters 2, 6, and 8), RICO Act has been used as a gang suppression tool against numerous street gangs; six alone in Syracuse during 2004–2012. Prosecutors learned years ago that old legislation was not enough to handle the growing gang problem. Designed to confront organization crime, RICO Act has been made applicable to street gangs due to legislative and prosecutorial efforts. As an example of how this works, Syracuse law enforcement officials used RICO legislation in their battle against the Boot Camp gang. A great deal of the recent youth gang violence that has plagued Syracuse is the result of Boot Camp's drug enterprise. Homicide, gun dealing, violence, and drug-trafficking were trademark criminal acts committed by Boot Camp. Prosecutors reasoned that bringing these thugs up on RICO charges would eventually lead to the strictest and harshest penalties allowed by law. Under RICO Act, a person can be found guilty of any charge that anyone in the group is accused of, regardless of whether these individuals were directly involved in the criminal acts or not. In the Syracuse case, three former Boot Camp members were arrested on RICO violations, which introduced the concept that even *former* gang members could be arrested under the RICO Act. The Syracuse Partnership to Reduce Juvenile Gun Violence and the newly formed Families Against Injustice argued that it is not constitutional to include former gang members in RICO dragnets. Defense attorneys for the Boot Camp gang members took another tack—they did not deny the criminal activities of their defendants but argued that Boot Camp was nothing more than a group of guys who committed crimes independently. Defense attorneys also stated that Boot Camp members only hung out together to protect themselves from rival gangs. Boot Camp defendants admitted to committing a number of crimes, including murder, during the 2004 RICO hearings, but insisted that they did not report to anyone (e.g., alleged gang leader Karo Brown). The importance of this is that in any RICO case against gang members, prosecutors must prove that the gang worked in unison as a criminal enterprise. As stated earlier (in Chapter 6), Karo Brown was ultimately found guilty of violating the RICO Act. The federal jury believed that Brown did run the violent street gang Boot Camp as a criminal business.

In addition to RICO Act, gang suppression efforts have been assisted by other legislation, including the **STEP** acts, based on the RICO model, and the **safe school zone** laws. STEP (California 186.20) was created by the California legislature to protect citizens from fear, intimidation, and physical harm caused by the activities of violent groups and individuals. In the statute, the Legislature states that "the State of California is in a state of crisis which has been caused by violent street gangs whose members threaten, terrorize, and commit a multitude of crimes against peaceful citizens of their neighborhoods" (California 186.20 1988). Some states have enacted safe school zone laws that increase the penalties for certain weapons violations that occur within 1,000 feet of a school, public housing property, or a public park. It should be noted that the Supreme Court deemed unconstitutional a federal safe school zone law that prohibits the mere possession of a gun within 1,000 feet of a school.

Local governments and jurisdictions have adapted existing laws and created new ones to combat the growing presence of gangs. When laws are created, civilians are expected to abide by them, police officers are expected to enforce them, prosecutors are supposed to present a case for conviction, and the courts are to serve as objective viewers of the whole process. The fact that some laws fail to produce the intended results and other laws are not looked upon favorably by a segment of the population is another problem altogether.

GANG TREATMENT PROGRAMS

Although gang prevention programs have likely contributed to keeping many youths out of street gangs, the number of total gang members continues to grow. And while suppression efforts have been successful in locking up large numbers of gang members, the threat of incarceration is not enough to deter youths from joining gangs as the number of gangsters continues to rise. As a result, gangs exist throughout America. A number of agencies take a different approach to gang intervention—they attempt to *treat* the problem of gangbanging behavior. These professionals hope to rehabilitate gang members so that they can reenter conventional society. Gang treatment advocates look for alternatives to secure detention and secure confinement of juvenile offenders in the hope that they can still be rescued from a life of gangism; they apply specific methods of treatment to rehabilitate gang members and create programs for gang members in prison and ex-convicts who need to find a way to conform to conventional society. Gang treatment programs represent the last chance of intervention strategies to get individuals out of gangs and back in society as productive citizens.

Alternatives to Secure Detention and Secure Confinement

Court officials must take into account the interests of public safety with the needs of the individual facing incarceration. Offenders who commit serious and/or violent crimes are more likely to face incarceration than nonviolent, less serious violators. With regard to gang members, juveniles are the most viable candidates for alternatives to secure detention (jails) and secure confinement.

There are many examples of alternatives to secure detention beginning with **outright release**. There are scant published studies on the effectiveness of outright release of offenders. Generally speaking, when courts adhere to the strict guidelines for deciding who to release outright, there is no increase in the number of rearrests prior to final case disposition (Austin, Johnson, and Weitzer 2005; Kilm and Block 1982). In some cases, an offender may be released upon making restitution or performing community service. In cases where the offenses committed involve property damage, property loss, or personal injuries to victims, restitution may be deemed appropriate. **Restitution** programs have been designed to help offenders pay for the damage they caused. One option involves working at specific job sites chosen by the court for which the offender does not receive a salary; instead, the money is taken by the court for payment to the victim. Delinquent youths, especially gang members, commonly deface property, especially with graffiti; they make good candidates for restitution. **Community service** programs are a good option for release too, as they are less expensive to operate than restitution programs and involve far less paperwork for administrators.

Supervised release applies when the offender is deemed too risky for outright release, because he/she is either unlikely to appear for adjudication or likely to commit new offenses (Austin et al. 2005). **Supervised release** still implies a certain level of trust however; otherwise the offender would have been sentenced to detention. Supervised release comes in many forms, including home detention, probation, and electronic monitoring. **Home detention** requires offenders to remain at home during specified time periods: (1) at all times, (2) at all times except when in school or working, (3) at night (curfews). Additionally supervisory conditions may also apply (e.g., drug testing). Descriptive evaluative studies on home detention programs report high levels of success (Austin et al. 2005). **Probation** represents another type of supervised release designed to keep offenders out of lockup. Probation can be both informal (when compliance is voluntary) and formal (mandatory compliance in lieu of formal adjudication). There are a wide variety of probation programs and specifics that vary case by case, state to state, and by jurisdiction. Probation involves the offender checking in with a probation officer at a specified time and place. In some cases, accounting for one's actions may be more severe and include **electronic monitoring**. Offenders under house confinement generally are fitted with electronic monitoring devices, usually an ankle or wrist attachment. Electronic monitoring was designed to reduce the costs of supervision, reduce institutional populations, allow the offender to remain in school or at work while under supervision, and enhance the potential for rehabilitation by keeping offenders at home and in close contact with family members. A study of youth detained at home in Lake County, Indiana, conducted by Roy and Brown (1995) reveals that those assigned to electronic monitoring had a higher program completion rate (90% versus 75%) and a lower recidivism rate (17% versus 26%) than youths who were not monitored electronically (Austin et al. 2005). Supervised release is an excellent diversionary tool for deserving offenders because it allows them an opportunity to remain in the community. If their behavior is positive, and they meet all the requirements of probation, they are free at the end of a designated period of time without having served jail time.

Although many intensive supervision programs (ISP) function primarily as alternatives to confinement, they are also an option to secure detention. As the name implies, **intensive supervision** allows the offender to avoid incarceration but only with strict and regular supervision. One example is the San Francisco **Detention Diversion Advocacy Program (DDAP)**, an ISP that combines rehabilitative treatments with the specific needs of the offender. Started in 1993, this pre-adjudication program targets the highest risk youth in the juvenile justice system and offers them intensive case management and a comprehensive range of community services. DDAP concentrates its services on chronic repeat offenders who present the greatest challenges to the juvenile justice system. "DDAP is presently the only alternative to detention program recognized by the United States Department of Justice as a best practice model in the juvenile justice field" (Center on Juvenile and Criminal Justice 2012). DDAP (2012) concentrates its efforts on chronic offenders because it recognizes that 70 percent of first-time offenders never offend again. Referrals for DDAP come from defense attorneys, courts, parents, or community-based service providers.

Once accepted into the custody of DDAP, the youth is assigned a case manager to carry out a designated case plan. Evaluation of DDAP is very promising. According to a University of Nevada Las Vegas study, DDAP participants were 25 percent less likely to recidivate when compared to detained youths, and in 2007, DDAP served 149 youths with an 85 percent success rate (DDAP 2012). Among the reasons cited for the success of DDAP are the small caseloads of caseworkers, the caseworkers' freedom from bureaucratic restriction of the juvenile justice system, the similar backgrounds of DDAP caseworkers and clients, and an emphasis on rehabilitative services coupled with specific goals to track clients' progress (Austin et al. 2005; Shelden 1999).

Day and evening reporting centers represent another alternative to secure detention. The centers are nonresidential programs that require offenders to report daily activities to case managers. They are different from ISPs because they provide services such as drug treatment, job training referrals, life-skills services, and counseling (Austin et al. 2005). According to Austin and associates (2005), there is little research on the effectiveness of reporting centers. **Skills training programs** are another example of a nonresidential alternative to secure detention. One example is the **Fresh Start** program that serves youth and communities in Baltimore and Washington, D.C. Fresh Start is a 40-week job skills training program that serves out-of-school youths, aged 16–19, most of whom are referred by the Maryland Department of Juvenile Services. The program provides on-job training in the use of tools, carpentry, and boat repair along with academic skills training in reading, writing, math, history, and science (Fresh Start 2012). Fresh Start tracks the progress of its students for three years following their program induction. In Baltimore, graduates from 1997 to 2000 had a rearrest rate of 19 percent and a reincarceration rate of just 7 percent, well below the rearrest rate of 75 percent that other Maryland Department of Juvenile Justice programs reported (Austin et al. 2005). One last alternative to secure detention to be discussed is the residential programs. **Residential programs** are for youths awaiting adjudication and include home programs, detention homes, and programs for runaways that serve as alternatives to secure detention.

Alternatives to secure confinement include ISP and diversion. The ISP alternative was described in the previous discussion of alternatives to secure detention. The difference here involves the reality that offenders are facing incarceration in a secure confinement facility. One example of a successful ISP is the **Tarrant County Advocate Program (TCAP)**, a home-based program that utilizes paid, trained adults (advocates) who live in the same communities as the youths to develop relationships with the department's most at-risk youths and families. Advocates work intensively with assigned youths and their families to assist in the resolution of practical, material, and interpersonal needs. Advocates spend between 7.5 and 30 hours per week in contact with youths and families (Tarrant County Advocate Program 2004). During 2002, TCAP served 527 youths and their families, with 385 families completing project services. Of those, 96 percent were successfully maintained in the community, or were diverted from out-of-home placement or secure confinement (TCAP 2004). TCAP is just one program under the Youth Advocates Program (YAP). YAP provides community-based alternatives to the placement of juvenile offenders for Juvenile Probation Departments. YAP operates in Texas, Florida, South Carolina, New York, New Jersey, Ohio, Pennsylvania, Arizona, Louisiana, and the District of Columbia (Youth Advocate Programs 2012). Eligible youths are those deemed by the courts to be in need of residential care. In addition to assigning eligible youths to TCAP, other YAP alternatives include local Young Men's Christian Associations or Young Women's Christian Associations, scouting, church groups, or other community activities. Unskilled and poorly educated offenders, who represent the "typical" juvenile offender, may also be assigned to the **Supported Work Program**, a subsidized employment service offered in many communities under YAP. While participating in the program, the youth is assigned an advocate who monitors the site for the duration of the youth's employment and is available to provide "coaching" to help resolve problems with the youth on the site, should there be a need (YAP 2012).

A number of professionals are in a position to divert youths away from formal court action, including police officers and court personnel. Police officers and court personnel "give a break" to many juvenile delinquents, who eventually grow out of their delinquent ways and become productive members of society. Their discretion, although flawed at times, can help "save" the lives of juveniles who were simply enjoying adolescent fun that, technically, violated the law. **Diversion**, then, takes place when law enforcement and court personnel exercise their discretion to keep an individual from entering the judicial system. Diversion is one of the most important and commonly used alternatives to court processing, detention, and confinement. There are two types of diversion—conditional and unconditional. As implied, a conditional diversion sentence involves the individual meeting certain requirements in order to stay out of the system. Conditions could include attending drug and alcohol lectures, individual or group therapy, or simply staying out of trouble or risk being incarcerated. Unconditional diversion is also straightforward, as the individual is kept out of jail without having to meet any further requirements.

The **Sacramento Diversion Project**, created in 1970, provides us with an early example of how diversionary processing works. The program was designed to help keep runaways and troubled youths out of jail. These juveniles attend a meeting where police and social workers attempt to convince the youths to call their parents (or guardians) so that they could avoid formal detention. Follow-up counseling sessions were established between professionals and the family on a volunteer basis. Two years later, additional minor offenses were covered by the diversion program. Many youths were successfully diverted ("treated") away from criminal proceedings, and the success of the Sacramento Diversion Project led many other communities to duplicate this alternative to court processing. In addition to helping keep an individual out of the system, alternatives to secure detention and confinement help reduce the overcrowding of juveniles in most detention and confinement facilities. Crowding can create dangerous situations for facility management and is detrimental to the rehabilitation and treatment of youth who are confined. Secondly, it is argued that alternatives to secure detention and confinement is needed because the effectiveness of detention and confinement is unproven (Austin et al. 2005).

A more severe diversionary tactic is to assign juvenile offenders to specialized "**boot camps.**" This alternative to court processing is modeled after military boot camps where young men are put through rigorous training activities. The modified version of juvenile boot camps includes rigorous physical exercise, but with a more important, ultimate goal of building youths' self-esteem and confidence through hard work. The rehabilitative aspect of the boot camps attempts to reduce future criminal activity by changing the offender's attitudes and behavior (Trojanowicz et al. 2001). Juvenile boot camps are utilized by youths who would otherwise be confined in a facility. Youths selected for boot camps are more hardcore than those who might receive probation and yet are viewed as "treatable," but only under more extreme forms of diversion. Advocates of boot camps argue that the incarceration period is shorter than regular incarceration and therefore saves taxpayer money. Additionally, it is believed that many of these youths may disassociate themselves from the gang after successfully completing the program. Opponents argue that military-style training, in which officers yell and scream at youths, is hardly an effective diversionary treatment.

Juvenile boot camps were also inspired by Colorado's **Outward Bound** or **Wilderness Training** program. Outward Bound programs engage youths in rigorous physical work in forestry camps. Interestingly, the forestry camps for juvenile offenders were developed in the 1930s in the Los Angeles County Forestry Department. The juvenile offenders helped clear brush, learned about conservation, worked on road construction, did farm work, and so on. Wilderness Programs attempt to help build the self-esteem of troubled youths by involving them in such physical activities as rock climbing, rappelling, canoeing, backpacking, hiking, and cave exploring. The effectiveness of wilderness programs remains unclear, with some more successful than others (Trojanowicz et al. 2001).

Methods of Treatment

Gang members in treatment programs often have already been incarcerated. In the hope of keeping them out of trouble after release, many are placed on **parole**. Parole is a type of "aftercare" and is similar to probation, except for the fact that parolees have been incarcerated. When comparing these different populations, it is not surprising that the treatment success rate of parolees is much lower than those of probationers (Trojanowicz et al. 2001). Parole is granted when some governing body (e.g., a prison review board) determines that the violator has met community and rehabilitative objectives. The treatment aspect is handled by trained officers (who, unfortunately, are greatly overworked). Parole and probation officers have three functions to perform (Trojanowicz et al. 2001):

1. They must maintain surveillance of the offender. Continuous association reminds the offender of his/her community obligations and of the threat of incarceration.
2. They must make the offender aware of the community services available to assist him/her in his/her rehabilitation.
3. They must counsel the offender and family and make them understand the conditions that led to criminal problems in the first place so as to eliminate the underlying causes of delinquency.

Parole and probation officers generally carry heavy caseloads, and as a result, the treatment aspect of parole and probation takes on a secondary role to the surveillance demands. To counter this, a number of specific treatment programs and therapies have been designed to help keep offenders out of gang specifically and out of trouble in general.

There are numerous types of treatment programs available to parolees and those on probation. One such treatment approach involves **transactional analysis**, which can be used both individually and in groups. This approach is primarily concerned with evaluating and interpreting interpersonal relationships and the dynamic transactions between the gang member (client) and the environment. The therapist examines clients' demeanor, gestures, vocabulary, and voice to gain insights into why they behave the way they do. This treatment appears to be fun because it involves playing games, by which the therapist learns a great deal about the client. Ultimately, the treatment attempts to teach clients redundancy how to act appropriately in a group setting.

Cognitive therapies involve confronting and challenging the offenders' irrational thoughts and behavioral patterns. It is a problem-focused approach to helping people identify and change dysfunctional beliefs, thoughts, and patterns of behaviors that contribute to their problems (OJJDP 2012f). The offender is taught to take control and responsibility for his/her own actions as well as emotions. The therapist attempts to demonstrate to the gang member how his/her behavior is overly emotional and not rational—from a societal standpoint. In order to correct the irrational behavior of gang members (or other offenders), therapists employ cognitive skills development exercises. Particular emphasis is placed on developing decision-making skills, moral education, and replacing aggressive behavior. For example, if a young person has a hard time completing a math problem and thinks to himself, "I'm stupid, I am not a good student," he is taught to think, "this problem is difficult, I will ask for help." Just as negative thoughts are replaced through therapy, so too are negative behaviors. The new, preferred behavior is rewarded and the offender comes to view new behaviors as cognitively better. Studies have shown that cognitive therapies are associated with significant and clinically meaningful changes (OJJDP 2012f).

Vocational training is an atypical treatment approach, in that it does not address the interpersonal dynamics of human behavior or spend a large time on diagnosis. Vocational training provides the client with vocational counseling in order to increase the client's knowledge of career choices and how to address job specifications and qualification requirements (Trojanowicz et al. 2001). Vocational training is a diversionary treatment method as it keeps offenders busy with jobs and career aspirations after successful training, in which they are taught job and computer skills. Job placement is a key to the success of vocational training as an effective diversion method.

Behavior therapy, better known as **behavior modification**, is based on principles of learning theory as well as of experimental psychology (Trojanowicz et al. 2001). This form of therapy attempts to modify the undesired behaviors of juvenile offenders through a series of therapeutic sessions. Behavior modification therapists believe that just about any behavior can be modified, especially if the client is striving to change. The client goes through a series of "baby steps" toward the desired goal. Punishments and rewards are used as reinforcers. Positive behavior is rewarded; negative behavior is punished using a point system. The punishments for gang members need to be far more severe, because they are more adapted to violence than most nongang members. In general, behavior modification programs are most effective for those who want to change their behavior (e.g., someone who is afraid of heights and wants to overcome the fear) and less so for those who are forced into therapy (as are most gang members). Additionally, behavior modification treatments have positive results while the client is in the program, but the modified behavior usually reverts once the client is out of the program.

There a number of community-based treatment and therapy programs available to offenders, for example, **multisystemic therapy (MST)**, which has been introduced to dozens of communities in the United States and Canada. MST is an intensive family- and community-based treatment program that focuses on the entire world of chronic and violent juvenile offenders; that is, their homes and families, schools and teachers, neighborhoods and friends (MST Services 2010a). MST is designed for the toughest offenders, both male and female, between the ages of 12 and 17 who have long arrest histories. The prime directive of MST is to keep adolescents who have exhibited serious clinical problems (e.g., drug abuse, violence, severe and emotional disturbance) at home, in school, and out of trouble. MST has been evaluated for three decades and has consistently demonstrated very positive results. The results show that long-term rearrest rates reduced by 25–70 percent; out-of-home placements reduced by 47–64 percent; families functioned much better; substance use decreased; and mental health problems for serious juvenile offenders decreased (MST Services 2010b). A 14-year follow-up study by the Missouri Delinquency Project reveals that youths who received MST had up to 54 percent fewer rearrests; up to 57 percent fewer days of incarceration; up to 68 percent fewer drug-related arrests; and up to 43 percent fewer days on adult probation (MST Services 2010b).

Community residential centers are an alternative treatment option, generally reserved for nonviolent offenders. Community residential centers include group homes and treatment foster care (TFC). One example of a group home, **VisionQuest**, founded in 1973, combines a wilderness challenge program followed by five months in a residential home. Both males and females, aged 11–18, are potentially eligible for the VisionQuest program. The wilderness challenge provides an alternative to incarceration for serious juvenile offenders. The wilderness program provides youths with a consistent educational program that extends throughout the program. Program youths spend 12 to 15 months in various challenging outdoor impact programs. There are three specific phases of the program: (1) three months in an orientation wilderness camp, (2) five months in an adventure program, and (3) five months in a community residential program (OJJDP 2012g). In phase 1, youths live outdoors in tepees, with a tepee family of 6 to 10 youths and a counselor. Juveniles receive orientation into the program and undergo educational, psychological, and behavioral evaluations. They also go through an intensive physical conditioning program in addition to their regular schoolwork. In the second phase, the participants go on outdoor adventures, like wagon trains, where youths help to care for animals, set up nightly camps, and still complete their academic studies. In the last phase, youths enter the residential program where they live in group homes. The third phase is designed to reacquaint and prepare youths to live back home with their families and be a positive part of the community (OJJDP 2012g). An evaluation of VisionQuest reveals that while it is an expensive treatment program, it produces positive results. Youths who went through the VisionQuest program were substantially less likely to be rearrested in the first year after release than those who did not go through the program (55 percent compared with 71 percent). TFC programs, however, are more effective as an intervention agency. **Treatment foster care** is a distinct, powerful, and unique model of care that provides children with a combination of the best aspects of traditional foster care and residential treatment centers (Foster Family-Based Treatment Association 2004). Youths are referred to TFC programs to address their serious levels of emotional, behavioral, and medical problems.

Prison Treatment Programs

The great influx of gangs in confinement has led detention centers and correctional facilities officials to create programs that attempt to break the individual's alliance to the gang. This is a necessary undertaking, as most incarcerated gang members will eventually be released back into the community.

Jails (also known as detention centers) confine people during the adjudication process (i.e., arraignment, criminal court, grand jury, hearings, trial, and sentencing). Jails contain individuals who have not yet been sentenced (called detainees) and the short-term incarcerated. The sociodynamics of jails vary according to their geographic location; inmates housed in rural jails are often familiar with other inmates, while those incarcerated in large city jails have less chance of being housed with someone they know. Treatment programs in jails present many serious challenges most of them tied directly to the small amount of time available, both in terms of scheduling treatment and in terms of the duration of jail incarceration (Center for Substance Abuse Treatment 2005). Time constraints are a significant factor in the evaluation of the effectiveness of a program, as there is a direct correlation between the length of time in treatment and a positive outcome. Staffing and other financial constraints may limit the treatment offered to detainees. Many times, detainees may have to choose between a treatment and an educational program. Among the types of treatment offered at jails are substance cravings, urges and relapse prevention; self-help programs; basic cognitive skills; strengths building (improve on positive skills already possessed by the individual); communication skills; anger management; domestic violence; problem-solving; and social skills training.

Correctional facilities afford far greater time and opportunity for the implantation of treatment programs. Among the types of treatment offered at correctional facilities are drug treatment; counseling, including group, cognitive-behavioral groups, specialty, family, individual, and self-help; educational and vocational training; and therapeutic techniques, including role playing, video feedback, and blended approaches (Center for Substance Abuse Treatment 2005). In some jurisdictions, drug treatment programs are offered as an alternative to prison. For example, the **Drug Treatment Alternative to Prison (DTAP)** program was developed by the Kings County

District Attorney's Office in Brooklyn, New York, and is the first prosecution-led residential drug treatment diversion program in the country (Office of Justice Programs 2012). The program's objective is to reduce recidivism and drug use by diverting nonviolent felony drug offenders to community-based residential treatment facilities. The program targets felons with previous felony convictions who are prison-bound. DTAP uses a deferred-sentencing model wherein defendants accepted into the program plead guilty to a felony but the prison sentence is deferred while participants enter intensive residential drug treatment, followed by optional aftercare services (Office of Justice Programs 2012). The DTAP participants can expect to stay in the program for 15 to 24 months. Evaluation of the program shows positive results. Those who complete DTAP have significantly lower rearrest rates during the three-year follow-up of the program, compared to program failures and nonparticipants (23% of those who complete the program have been rearrested compared to 47% of nonparticipants and 52% of the failures) (Office of Justice Programs 2012).

Correctional facilities are inundated with gang members, some of whom are willing to participate in treatment, some who are not, and some who cause trouble for nongang inmates seeking treatment. At many prisons, gang members are separated from the nongang inmate population, with treatment programs specifically designed to help each category of the population. Gary Mohr, the director of the **Ohio Department of Rehabilitation and Correction**, unveiled a plan in March 2012 that reorganized state prisons into a tiered system based on levels of control. Disruptive, violent inmates would be separated from the rest of the prison population making other inmates safer and allowing officials to concentrate on rehabilitating inmates in the general population and reintegration groups (Toledo Blade.com 2012). Under the reforms, inmates who complete the rehabilitation program will gain privileges and move up to less-controlled settings, while those who get into trouble lose privileges and move to more secure environments. Inmates at reintegration facilities will get job training, with a goal of having jobs waiting for them when they are released. The tiered system is designed to encourage inmates to see the benefits of rehabilitation. Mohr acknowledged that the Ohio prison system may seem politically liberal, but he countered that he is not a liberal; instead, it was his four decades in the business that has led him to conclude that the best way to cut crime, reduce recidivism, and save money is to give inmates hope and tools to build a better life (Toledo Blade.com 2012). It sounds like a reasonable approach. If it works in Ohio, perhaps other states will examine their system.

Many people find, or claim to find, religion while in prison. Religious advocates have seized the opportunity to provide religion to inmates as a type of treatment program. There are numerous examples of religious treatments in prison; one is the **California Youth Outreach (CYO)**. CYO first attempts to prevent youths from joining a gang by providing a number of outreach programs. CYO's mission statement best sums up its ambition by stating that it is "dedicated to reaching out to all gang impacted youth, families and their communities by means of education services, intervention programs and resource opportunities that support a positive and healthy lifestyle" (California Youth Outreach 2010). CYO first started as Breakout Prison Outreach (CYO 2012). CYO originally provided direct services in the California State Prisons and the California Youth Authorities through live-in adult and youth homes in the city of San Jose, California. CYO attempts to intervene prior to the youth's decision to join the gang, while he/she is in the gang, and when he/she tries to leave the gang.

Among the more interesting prison treatment programs is the gang-busting program at the **Connecticut Garner Correctional Institution**. The facility incarcerates both pretrial and sentenced offenders. "Through proven programmatic innovation and intervention, the Garner Correctional Institution provides positive alternatives for inmates to assist in their successful reintegration into the community as productive members of society" (Department of Correction

2011). Since its inception in 1992, the Garner Correctional Institution has modified its treatment programs to meet contemporary needs. Among the programs offered at the Connecticut program are those that target gangs. The gang-busting program attempts to build trust, and even friendships, among gangsters who might otherwise stab each other. Prison officials put rival gang members together in a prison gym and have them engage in activities where each other's safety is in the hands of a rival. One exercise involves a gang member dangling from a rope wrapped around his waist and looped over a metal rafter. Whether he falls to the hardwood floor below or is lowered slowly and safely depends on the rival gang member who is holding the rope. Prison officials hope that through these activities rival gang members will develop a trust in each other that will last outside prison. The Garner program treats gang affiliation as an addiction and uses a 12-step process, implemented over five months, designed to sever gang ties among inmates forever. Inmates who fail to participate in the program or refuse to renounce their gang ties after the program are separated from the rest of the prison population (*The Post-Standard* 1997a). Individualized treatment plans are also implemented based on the mental health needs of offenders, both during pretrial and their being sentenced to Garner. The Garner program is designed to return as many of these offenders as possible back into the community as productive members of society (Department of Correction 2011).

Jim Brown, former NFL great and Hall of Fame running back for the famed Cleveland Browns, has had his share of run-ins with the law. Retiring after nine short years, Brown left Cleveland for Hollywood to make movies and further increase his fame, but he never forgot about the people who were less fortunate. Jim Brown formed the **Black Economic Union** to help finance new black businesses (O'Keeffe 2011), and he is the founder and president of the **Amer-I-can** program (founded in 1988), which helps inmates, ex-convicts, gang members, and troubled youths to manage their lives better. Most of the skills taught in the Amer-I-can program are job skills, such as how to dress for a job, face a prospective employer, and communicate effectively. At its beginning, the Amer-I-can program was driven by two basic principles: Everyone must take responsibility for his/her behavior and, most importantly, no one is cursed from birth. Brown has risked his life for the program, acting as mediator for rival gangs in his own home. One night, Brown's chief of staff was shot 11 times by a gang that wanted Brown's program to fail. Brown's program has not failed.

More recently, the Amer-I-Can program is about enabling individuals to meet their academic potential, conform their behavior to acceptable society standards, and improve the quality of their lives by equipping them with critical life management skills to succeed with confidence (Amer-I-Can 2012). The program is especially concerned with improving the self-esteem of the individuals, arguing that poor self-image and self-esteem is the root cause of destructive behaviors. The program itself is designed to assist the development of each trainee's personal life skills in nine critical areas. These life skills are all linked and therefore must all be addressed if an individual is to reach his/her full potential. The nine areas are motivation, conditions, attitudes and habits; goal-setting; problem-solving and decision-making; emotional control; family relationships; financial stability; effective communication; job search and retention; and drug and alcohol abuse treatment (Amer-I-Can 2012). The curriculum is a 15-chapter, 60-hour self-esteem and life management course that incorporates the aforementioned nine skills areas. The program works within the structure of a self-help, peer group relationship, with a trained facilitator to monitor the group's achievements. The class size ranges from 15 to 30 trainees per facilitator.

This concludes our look at treatment intervention programs. As we have learned, some programs are quite effective; conversely, there are, seemingly, many people who will never rehabilitate their lives. And what do we, as a society, do about those folks?

Summary

In this chapter, three categories of gang intervention, prevention, suppression, and treatment, were discussed. The goal of prevention strategies is to identify the warning signs that indicate a youth has shown an interest in joining a gang and to combat the many socioeconomic factors that lead to the view that gang membership is the most viable option for success. In essence, prevention strategies are techniques used to steer youths away from the temptations of turning to gangs, to prevent them from joining a gang. Gang prevention strategies are subdivided into three classification schemes: community prevention programs; prevention involving a combination of families, schools, law enforcement, and local businesses; and national/broad-based prevention strategies. The community prevention programs discussed were Chicago Area Project (CAP); Mid-City Project; the Group Guidance Program, House of Umoja; crisis intervention; Community Youth Gang Services; Gang Reduction Intervention Program (GRIP); Syracuse Partnership to Reduce Guns; Homeboy Industries; Element; and the Montreal Prevention Program. Youths and young adults turn to gangs for many reasons, and most of the reasons are connecting to problems found within the community. As a result, many prevention strategies at the community level attempt to incorporate the "it takes a village" approach by involving families, schools, law enforcement, and local businesses. Many communities seek the help of the federal government in their pursuit to prevent youths from joining street gangs. This leads to national/broad-based prevention strategies. The national prevention strategies discussed in this chapter include Violence-free Zones; Operation Weed and Seed; Boys and Girls Clubs of America; Gang Prevention through Targeted Outreach; and the McGruff House.

Despite the success of many prevention strategies, there are roughly 1 million street gang members (depending on whether one cites the FBI or OJJDP for gang statistics) in the United States, and they commit a great deal of crime. As a result, the public demands to be protected from street gangs and this leads to suppression efforts. Suppression strategies generally come in two forms: law enforcement responses and judicial and legislative responses. Law enforcement suppression efforts include proactive and reactive strategies; counterinsurgency methods; sweeps; hot-spot targeting; roadblocks; community policing; and the creation of gang task force units. Judicial and legislative responses include injunctions; curfews; banning certain attire; and creating laws designed to curtail gang activity.

Once in a gang, a number of agencies work to get gang members out of the gang; this is referred to as gang treatment intervention strategies. The hope of gang treatment programs is to rehabilitate gang members so that they can reenter conventional society. Gang treatment advocates look for alternatives to secure detention and secure confinement of juvenile offenders in the hope that they can still be rescued from a life of gangism; they apply specific methods of treatment to rehabilitate gang members and create programs for gang members in prison and ex-convicts who need to find a way to conform to conventional society. Many gang members will be sent to prison, and most of them will return to their communities. As a result, a number of prison anti-gang treatment programs exist. Gang treatment programs represent the last chance of intervention strategies to get individuals out of the gang and back in society as productive citizens.

A number of intervention strategies and programs have been evaluated to determine whether they are successful. In many cases, they are successful, relatively speaking, that is. The optimist might look at the many successful intervention programs and say, "without these programs, there would be far more gang members in American society." The pessimist might look at the continuously growing number of street gang members found in American communities and conclude, "intervention programs are a failure, just look at all the gang violence, mayhem and crime street gangs commit in our neighborhoods." The realist might conclude that both scenarios are correct. One thing seems certain: If gang intervention remains ineffective, overall, the negative impact of street gangs on American society will continue to increase. And that should concern, if not scare, everyone.

10

What's Trending with Street Gangs

The word *trend* refers to the general direction in which something tends to move; it also refers to a current style or happening, or something that is in vogue. The term *trending* has become very popular in contemporary culture as a verb and refers to a general tendency or inclination. The use of the term *trending* is certainly applicable with regard to street gangs, as a number of trends have revealed themselves throughout the text. For example, it would be accurate to say, "Street gang involvement in the sale, distribution, and trafficking of illicit street drugs is trending upward." In this final chapter, a quick review of the previous nine chapters will be presented; followed by a discussion of a number of specific trends in the gang world; and concluded with a few parting thoughts. The discussion of what's trending with street gangs will help the reader to understand the implications of street gangs for the future.

A REVIEW

The perception that people have of street gangs is generally shaped by their level of contact with them. Most Americans have little or no direct contact with gangs and therefore they tend to view gang members merely as punks and criminals who need to be locked up, and this limited view is often distorted by popular media portrayals of gangbangers. The people whose lives are daily affected by direct contact with gangs come to view America's street gangs as intimidating thugs. Law enforcement officers on the whole view gang members simply as criminals who need to be incarcerated. Gang researchers generally come to the realization that the development and maintenance of gangs in society is very much intertwined with the socioeconomic conditions that lead individuals to turn to gangs in the first place. For most gang members, the gang is a refuge from a world filled with disenchantment and perceived hopelessness. Ideally, after reading the entire text, readers, both those who already knew something about street gangs and those who did not, have a fuller understanding of the relatively complex and extremely violent nature of street gangs. The complexity of street gangs was first revealed in Chapter 1 as we learned that there is no universal definition of what constitutes a gang.

In Chapter 1, the topic of juvenile delinquency was discussed and deemed important because most individuals join a street gang as youths. While it remains true that most gang members join the gang when they are minors, what's trending is the length of time individuals remain in a gang; it is not uncommon for many larger gangs to have gangbangers in their 30s, 40s, or older. Still, most gangbangers were juvenile delinquents first. It is also true that gang leaders still have underaged members participate in many street crimes, especially selling drugs at the retail level. Although the parameters that establish the labeling of particular groups as gangs are generally agreed upon from one law enforcement jurisdiction to another, there is no universally agreed upon definition of a street gang. The definition is important in order to establish civil policy. It is also important in order to provide an accurate statistical account of the number of gangs and gang members. Nonetheless, statistics are available and according to the Office of Juvenile Justice and Delinquency Prevention (OJJDP), there were 28,100 street gangs and 731,000 gang members in 2009. The FBI, however, reports that there were 30,313 street gangs and more than 1.1 million gang members in 2011. In addition to gangs on the street, nearly all correctional facilities are now home to prison gangs, some of which exert so much power that they control the streets from behind bars. There are also a large number of outlaw motorcycle gangs who are linked to street gangs via drug distribution operations.

Chapter 2 provided a rather extensive history of gangs. The existence of gangs, in one form or another, has been documented for over eight centuries. Street gangs, however, have a shorter history, with the first one, the Forty Thieves, originating from New York City's Five Points slums in the mid-1820s. The Forty Thieves, like many of the earliest American street gangs, were of Irish decent. The young Irish-Americans felt it necessary to protect their turf from outsiders who disapproved of their very existence. As the Irish slowly became assimilated into the surrounding culture, other ethnic groups took their place as victims of racial and ethnic prejudice and mistreatment. This pattern continued throughout the twentieth century and still exists today. New York City remained the epicenter of the growing gang epidemic throughout the 1800s. However, by the mid-1800s and late 1800s, street gangs were found in other parts of the Northeast, especially Boston and Philadelphia, and in such Southern cities as New Orleans, Baltimore, and Richmond. By the early 1900s, many larger cities, such as Detroit and Chicago, played witness to street gangs. In the mid-1900s, street gangs began to flourish in Los Angeles and southern California. The formation of the Crips in Los Angeles and their counterparts the Bloods led to the emergence of "nation" gangs who would develop a loose confederation of affiliates throughout the nation by the start of the 2000s. Meanwhile, in Chicago, two other nation gangs were being formed—the People and the Folks. By the start of the twenty-first century, gangs had proliferated in nearly all geographical areas of the United States. Gangs can now be found in all major cities, most smaller cities, the suburbs, and in some rural areas.

From a sociological standpoint, one of the more intriguing questions regarding street gangs is, "Why do gangs exist?"Chapters 3 and 4 attempt to address this rather simple question, but as we discovered, the answers are multifaceted and illustrate, once again, the complex nature of street gangs. Chapter 3 offers a great number of theoretical explanations, including biological and psychological explanations and many of the traditional sociological theories: social disorganization (Chicago School), anomie/strain, subculture/social bond, social learning/differential learning, labeling, and Marxist. Sociological theories are grounded by the belief that gang formation and participation are the result of social factors. Although each of the sociological approaches offers great insights in the study of gang behavior and have been applied to real case scenarios, theoretical approaches alone cannot completely explain why gangs exist. Chapter 4 offers different explanations of why gangs exist and persist in society. Instead of theoretical constructs, the focus of this chapter is on the socioeconomic explanations. Chief among these socioeconomic factors is the shifting labor market that has left unskilled workers without work, which in turn has led to the development of an underclass in many urban inner-city neighborhoods; poverty; the feminization of poverty (an important variable when considering the fact that a great number of gang members come from single-parent families headed by economically poor women); the lack of a male role model; poor levels of educational attainment; and a general sense of frustration and hopelessness that many youths experience with their life circumstances. Job opportunities would address nearly all of these socioeconomic concerns as a good-paying job allows someone a higher standard of living and a sense of pride and self-fulfillment.

Another very important consideration as to why someone joins a gang is the realization that many individuals, youths and adults find the deviant lifestyle preferable to the conventional one. Legitimate society has its "thrill-seekers," people who need to live on the edge in order to feel alive. Well, many gang members have this same attitude; they join a gang simply because they find that the criminal and violent lifestyle is exciting and thrilling. I have asked many gang members, "Why did you join your gang?" And not a single one ever cited a theoretical perspective as the reason (e.g., "I joined the gang because of the labeling theory"). And while many gang members will acknowledge that they joined their gang for a socioeconomic reason(s), many simply respond that it is fun to be in a gang. They experience a rush of excitement and genuinely enjoy the gangbanging lifestyle. Owning a firearm, for example, provides gang members with a sense of power, something that they lack in the capitalistic system. Having power is certainly more fun than being powerless. The adrenaline rush experienced by gang members because of the life they lead would be difficult to duplicate by legitimate means. Thus, the "rush factor" becomes a potentially major contributing explanation of why an individual chooses to join a gang. Removing these individuals from the gang will be a most difficult task, because they are not looking for a job—they are looking for kicks and thrills.

Any comprehensive review of gangs must include a discussion on gang structure and process. Chapter 5 addresses these issues by examining the organizational component of gangs. As Thrasher (1927) explained, many street gangs emerge from childhood playgroups. Peers have the same experiences as one another and tend to take on the characteristics of a group in a given environment. The social environment produces a wide variety of street gangs and as such a corresponding diversity of organizational structures. Some gangs are so highly structured that they resemble the military, whereas others are loosely confederated groups of youths and young adults who view the gang as a temporary aspect of life. At least one pair of researchers believe that gangs are so violent that they could be compared to a violent, murderous Amazonian tribe. The organizational structure of some gangs may resemble the Greek-letter organizations as well. Despite the differences among street gangs, a number of different typologies have been established to categorize street gangs, including age, degree of criminality, degree of attachment to and involvement in the gang, type of activity, and racial and ethnic distinctions. Other discussed processes include the procedures involved in joining a gang, initiations, leadership, belief systems, leaving the gang, and the code of the streets reveal the sociological makeup of gangs. Especially important to gangs is symbolism: the use of graffiti, hand signals, gang colors, and clothing. Graffiti is a primary means of communication among gang members; it also provides law enforcement officials a written account of what is going on in the streets (e.g., what gangs are at war with each other, what gang is attempting to enlarge its territory, and so on).

Chapter 6 began with an examination of the proliferation of street gangs across the United States, some of which have influence in multiple nations. Our look at street gangs began with rural and suburban street gangs. We generally think of street gangs as limited to urban areas of big cities, but this not reality as an increasing number of rural and suburban law enforcement agencies are reporting problems with gangs. Next, we discussed the impact of urban local street gangs with a focus on gangs in Syracuse, Rochester, and Buffalo, three cities in New York State. Large gangs that are found throughout most of the United States are referred to as nation gangs and include two Los Angeles-based nation gangs, the Crips and Bloods, and two Chicago-based nation gangs, the People and Folks. The Bloods and People have a loose confederation and so do the Crips and Folks. *The People* and *Folks* are actually umbrella terms used to describe an alliance between many individual gangs. The People, for example, have Latin Kings and Vice Lords under their nation flag and the Folks have the Black Gangster Disciples, Latin Disciples, and Simon City Royals under their flag. Nations gangs are the ones we usually hear about in the news as they represent the bulk of all street gangs. We learned about two transnational gangs, the 18th Street Gang, also known as M-18, and Mara Salvatrucha, a.k.a. MS-13. Chapter 6 also included a discussion of historical and contemporary Asian-American gangs.

Female gang members were the topic of Chapter 7. Females have always also been involved in crime, just not to the extent of males. Since the time of the New York City Irish gangs of the mid-1800s, females have fought alongside their male gangster counterparts. There is conflicting data on just how many female gang members exist in the United States, but generally 10 percent is used as a benchmark figure. Most female gang members either belong to an auxiliary gang or a coed gang. There are very few independent female gangs, but their numbers are slowing increasing. Female gang members are very capable of committing violent criminal acts; but, they do not do so in the same proportion as male gang members. Other topics covered in this chapter include reasons why females join gangs, recruitment, initiation, affiliation to male gangs, criminal activities, relationships with males and schools, pregnancy, and family relationships. It appears that females, for the most part, join a gang for the same reasons as their male counterparts, although a distinguishing feature is the fact that a great number of female gang members were victimized, or witness victimization, in the home. They turn to a gang looking for a family substitute.

The primary reason the general public is concerned about street gangs is because of their criminal activities. In Chapter 8, we distinguished four categories of street gang criminal activities: violent offenses; property crimes; the use, sale, distribution, and trafficking of drugs; and white-collar crimes and other nontraditional (for street gangs) crimes. Often, all of these criminal activities, and especially drugs, violence, and homicide are intertwined. There is a great deal of crime committed in the United States, and street gangs are responsible for an increasingly amount of it. Street gangs are especially responsible for a large number of violent crimes. According to data provided by the FBI in its 2011 "National Gang Threat Assessments," criminal street gangs are responsible for an average of 48 percent of violent crime in most jurisdictions and up to 90 percent in several others. In some communities, street gangs may commit up to 80 percent of the overall crime. Another big concern for law enforcement agencies is the increasingly dominant role street gangs are playing with the use, sale, distribution, and trafficking of illicit drugs. Gangs are engaged in an ever-expanding spectrum of crimes, having branched out to committing such crimes as alien smuggling, human trafficking, and prostitution, along with, crimes typically associated with organized crime syndicates and white-collar criminals (e.g., counterfeiting, identity theft, and mortgage fraud). Gang members participate in criminal activities for many reasons, but like most criminals, their crimes center on economic considerations. However, it is important to point out that gangs also commit crime for the rush experienced in gangbanging, some gang members engage in violent and nonviolent crime because they find it exciting.

In Chapter 9, three categories of gang intervention—prevention, suppression, and treatment—were discussed. The goal of prevention intervention programs is to divert youth away from gang life before they ever join. In many jurisdictions, at-risk youths are identified and indoctrinated into anti-gang programs. Prevention strategies were subdivided into three classification schemes: community prevention programs; prevention involving a combination of families, schools, law enforcement, and local businesses; and national/broad-based prevention strategies. A number of specific programs were discussed, including many that are quite successful in preventing youth from joining gangs. Despite the relative success of prevention programs, there are roughly 1 million street gang members (depending on whether one cites the FBI or OJJDP gang statistics) in the United States and they commit a great deal of crime. Because of this, the public demands that something be done about gangs. Thus, the introduction of suppression efforts. Suppression strategies generally come in two forms: law enforcement responses and judicial and legislative responses. Once someone is in a gang, there are efforts to intervene through a variety of treatment strategies. Treatment programs have also been established to help break gang members' ties with the gang so that they can become productive members of society. Gang treatment programs represent the last chance of intervention strategies to get individuals out of the gang and back in society as productive citizens.

TRENDS

The quick recap of the previous nine chapters provides us with a glimpse at a number of trends with street gangs. In the discussion that follows, we will look at some of the gang-related trends that have revealed themselves so far and conclude with other examples of what's trending in the world of street gangs.

First, a Juvenile Delinquent, and Then . . .

To be fair, most juvenile delinquents do not become gang members. However, juvenile delinquency nearly always precedes membership in a gang. This has been a trend throughout most of the history of street gangs; it continues today and will continue into the future. Youths who are frustrated for any number and variety of socioeconomic reasons who become delinquents are candidates for gang membership. The bravado of youth combined with the search for kicks and thrills creates a persona of invincibility. When like-minded youths form deviant cohort groups, especially in certain neighborhoods, we have the ingredients for a street gang. Add dashes of weaponry, violent-intent, and a disregard for life (one's own and others'), we have the stew that is a contemporary street gang. Existing gangs look to youth much like cigarette companies do, that is, they need new participants to replace those who have died off (literally and figuratively speaking). Like any group or organization, newer members start at the bottom of the hierarchy (unless they have special skills) and have to prove themselves to established associates. Gang leaders often have the youngest members perform the grunt work, such as, serving as lookouts while the gang performs some sort of crime, committing petty crimes, or selling drugs at the retail level. Underage gang members are great for such tasks because they not only can prove themselves to older gang members but receive juvenile status in the court system. Having youth perform many tasks has traditionally kept the gang leaders free of arrest, as they merely gave out the orders, but did not commit the crimes. The increasing usage of the Racketeer Influenced and Corrupt Organizations (RICO) Act by law enforcement agencies against street gangs reveals a very important trend that allows the judicial system to arrest gang leaders if they can establish a direct, organizational link. RICO has been used against street gangs for over a decade now because of the growing presence of street gangs nearly everywhere in the United States. The number of total gangs and gang members is certainly trending upward. Furthermore, because of the growing number of street gang members, people who eventually get arrested and incarcerated, the number of prison gangs has also trended upward. The growing presence of gang members in prison will only cause greater problems for those who work in corrections.

Street Gangs as Fixtures of History

One of the clearest trends involving street gangs is their historical fixture status in societies across the globe. If we use the concept of a "gang" more loosely than we presently interpret its meaning, gangs have been around for over 800 years, dating back to the *thugz* in India (A.D. 1200). In American history, the first street gangs were of Irish decent. Among the more primary reasons why the Irish formed street gangs was their status as second-class citizens. The Irish immigrants could not speak English, were poorly educated, lacked the necessary job skills to succeed in the New World, and were victims of prejudice and discrimination. Once the Irish became assimilated to the American culture their status improved, their involvement with street gangs trended downward, and they were replaced by the next ethnic peoples to be discriminated against. And so the trend has continued: one ethnic/racial category of people after another, coming to the United States and having a hard time adjusting. Their youth act out, and in some cases become delinquents and gang members. This pattern is likely to continue. What really distinguishes the contemporary era to past eras, however, is the magnitude of gang proliferation across the United States, as well as other nations. In the United States, there are gangs in every major city, many smaller cities, suburbs, and some rural areas; they are trending throughout the nation and internationally. The scope and seriousness of the gang problem in Canada is a matter of debate. In brief, many of the socioeconomic conditions that lead individuals to join a gang in the United States are the same in Canada. "Each country's gangs emerge from social, cultural, political, and economic conditions. In this respect, Canada's gang problem appears similar to the U.S. gang situation except on an infinitely smaller scale" (Howell 2012, 190). The Canadian population is roughly 11 percent of the U.S. population, so we would expect lower total crimes committed by Canadian gang members. If Canadian gangs follow the trend established by American gangsters, we can expect more incidents like the gang shooting in a Toronto mall on June 2, 2012. Toronto police reported that the violent shooting at the Toronto Eaton Centre involved one gang member who brazenly murdered a rival gang member who was at the Food Court (CTVNews 2012). Ahmed Hassan was killed and seven other people were injured. The shooter initially escaped but was later apprehended. Gangs have been documented in Europe for centuries, but they were not institutionalized fixtures like contemporary gangs. The presence of modern-day gangs in Europe, however, is more prevalent and led to the establishment of Eurogang Programme in 1997 (Howell 2012). "Just as is the case in the United States, street gangs and troublesome youth groups in Europe vary considerably with respect to key features—including demographic characteristics, background, social, and economic elements—as well as structural components, particularly the degree of organization" (Howell 2012, 192). Like Canada, street gangs in Europe are not as predominant as in the United States. However, there are signs that indicate gangs trending upward in Europe. While acknowledging that street gangs are still most closely associated with American cities, Hagedorn (2009) indicates that gangs are entrenched worldwide and that they play a significant role in a wide range of activities, from drug dealing to extortion to religious and political violence.

Filling the Socioeconomic Void

Graduate from college and the door to economic security awaits, or so millions of graduates each year hope. If many college graduates are having a hard time finding a career, or a high-paying job at the least, and they are, imagine how difficult it is to find a job if you are a high school dropout. Being a high school dropout is just one social variable that contributes to delinquency and gangism. As demonstrated in Chapter 4, there are many socioeconomic conditions that contribute to the trending of gang members from mostly lower socioeconomic status (SES) neighborhoods. The American economic system is designed to allow a few to flourish, the majority to get by, and guarantees a lower socioeconomic class. The gang is perceived by some as the only hope of fulfilling an economic void. In some neighborhoods the people with the cash, big shinny car, and flashy jewelry are the gang members. For disenchanted youth, the gang looks like an ATM. With this in mind, it is easy to comprehend why there will always be street gangs in American society. (That is, unless the economic-political system changes.) Hagedorn (2009) describes the trending of gangs around the world as a consequence of the ravages of the socioeconomic phenomenon of globalization. The author of *A World of Gangs*, Hagedorn (2009) suggests that for the more than 1 billion people in the world who now live in urban slums, gangs are ubiquitous features of daily life. Worldwide, then, individuals are increasingly turning to gang life as a way of filling the socioeconomic void. A very important contributing social element to gang participation is the opportunity a gang provides the individual for thrills and excitement. Nearly all of us enjoy some level of excitement, but some people enjoy the thrill of living on the edge so intensely that they join a gang just to feel alive. Most people enjoy an adrenaline rush from time to time; crave adrenaline a little too much and you find yourself participating in dangerous situations. Because there appears to be an abundance of adrenaline junkies who perceive gang life as fun, exciting, and an acceptable way of life, we can expect street gangs to continue to exist in the future to help fuel this addiction.

Street Gangs: Made in America, But Available as an Export

It's nothing to be proud of, but American society has certainly produced some of the most violent gangs in the world. And much to the chagrin of foreign governments, the United States is exporting franchises of American street gangs internationally. Gangs are being made in towns as small as a couple of thousand people and as large as New York City. In rural areas and smaller cities, many of the street gangs are local products that developed spontaneously from playgroups. In cities like Syracuse, Rochester, and Buffalo, and across the country gangs are becoming increasingly violent and committing a wider array of crimes. Some gangs, such as the Crips, Bloods, People, and Folks are so large they extend across the United States and have attained "nation" status. In addition to the trend of an ever-increasing number of gangs in American society is the trending phenomenon of transnational gangs. Transnational gangs are those that exist in multiple nations. While there are a number of gangs, like the Crips and Bloods, with sets in different countries, right now there are two trending international gangs: the 18th Street Gang, a.k.a. M-18 and Mara Salvatrucha, a.k.a. MS-13. Transnational gangs present the most problems for law enforcement agencies because their influence extends beyond U.S. jurisdiction to many Central American nations. MS-13 and M-18, considered the most dangerous gangs in Central America, are increasingly involved in international crimes that either originate or end in the United States.

Third Generation Gangs

The establishment of transnational gangs leads to the trending concept of "third generation gangs." **Third generation gangs (TGG)**, such as MS-13 and M-18, are gangs that conduct business internationally, especially throughout the Americas. The TGG designation extends beyond geographical parameters; it represents an evolutionary view of street gangs. With the TGG concept in mind, first generation gangs are the traditional or historical American street gangs that were primarily concerned with protecting a specific home neighborhood, or turf, from outside threats. First generation gangs are characterized by lower SES persons who were trying to protect the few assets they possessed—local streets, parks, and schools. Second generation gangs are those who attempt to establish a market place to make money selling drugs. Local gangs, such as those described in Chapter 6, qualify as second generation gangs because they are more interested in protecting drug-selling turfs that make money than they are concerned with protecting their neighborhood streets. Second generation gangs, however, are mostly nation gangs, such as the Crips and Bloods, who have established sets or cliques throughout the nation in attempt to expand power and create as many marketplaces as possible. The small, but growing numbers of third generation gangs are internationalized and seek money-making opportunities both domestically and internationally. One cannot help but notice that the establishment of second and third generation gangs is representative of capitalist ideology—reduce labor costs, expand geographic markets, and maximize profits regardless of the consequences. It often seems that corporate capitalists run such operations unabated, even when many of their tactics are illegal, immoral, and unethical. Gang members also engage in illegal, immoral, and unethical tactics to extend their capitalistic marketplaces, but they are more readily challenged by the vigor of law enforcement.

Gangs and Their Buffet-Style Involvement in Criminal Activity

American street gangs have always participated in criminal behavior, but what's really trending with street gangs is the increased level of violence; their expanding role in the sale, distribution, and trafficking of drugs; and the wide variety of crimes contemporary gangs are participating in compared to the past. As described earlier in this chapter (as well as Chapter 8), American street gangs are responsible for an average of 48 percent of violent crime in most jurisdictions and up to 90 percent in several others. If this trend continues, we can expect the number of gang-related shootings and murders to climb higher than ever before. The increase in gang violence is directly connected to control over drug markets. Proportionately, street gangs commit a smaller percentage of property-related crimes than the general public. Considering the fact that street gangs make more money committing other types of crime, it is doubtful that we will witness a substantial increase in the percentage of property crimes they commit. Street gangs are taking over a sizeable chunk of the illicit drug market. They have taken over drug markets in many neighborhoods across the country. In some instances gangs that are otherwise bitter enemies might work together to secure economic profits. In Rockaway Peninsula, a Queens neighborhood, individual members of a Bloods gang from a different New York City borough worked with Crips sets (the **Hassock Boys**; the **Gang of Apes**, or **GOA**; **Wildmeda**; and **Get It in Bricks**, or **GIB**) in an effort to take over control of a drug marketplace dominated by local Bloods, according to Kevin Ryan, a spokesman for the Queens district attorney's office (*The Citizen* 2010). After years of blood battles that left numerous gang members dead, law enforcement arrested nearly 100 gang members in April, 2010 on a variety of murder, weapons, shootings, and narcotics trafficking charges. The interesting point of this story is the glimpse it provides of the emerging trend in the gang world that money makes for better alliances than nation affiliation. One does not have to think too long to imagine what street gangs are willing to do to nongang members who try to sell drugs on their turf; after all, they are willing to betray their "brothers" from another set and murder their rivals. This helps to explain why, according to the Justice Department's National Gang Intelligence Center (NGIC), gangs have become the "primary retail-level distributors of most illicit drugs" (Johnson, K. 2009). A rising number of street gangs, especially MS-13 and the 18th Street Gang, are now working with foreign drug-trafficking organizations. Drug-trafficking has become so profitable and violent that today's transnational gangs and their interactions with others are reminiscent of scenes depicted in the 1983 film *Scarface* (see "Connecting Street Gangs and Popular Culture" Box 10.1). The criminal activities of transnational gangs are trending beyond drugs as they are working with Mexican cartels (among others) on alien smuggling, human trafficking, and prostitution. In addition to committing all these crimes, street gangs are becoming increasingly involved in a number of white-collar crimes, such as counterfeiting, identity theft, and mortgage fraud. In sum, gangs have always been associated with violence and crime, but their buffet-style involvement in criminal activity is trending upward.

Box 10.1   *Connecting Street Gangs and Popular Culture*

Drug Trafficking: *Scarface*-Style

In 1983, the film *Scarface*, directed by Brian De Palma and written by Oliver Stone was released to mixed reviews. This contemporary remake of the original 1932 film of the same name tells the fictional story of Tony Montana, a Cuban refugee who arrives in the United States as a result of the Mariel Boatlift and rises to power as a Miami drug lord. The Mariel Boatlift officially began on April 15, 1980 and ended on October 31, 1980, with the arrival of over 125,000 Cubans to Southern Florida from the Port of Mariel, Cuba. These Cubans were exiled by Fidel Castro because they did not support communism on the island nation. In essence Castro was ridding his country of "undesirables," and these undesirables included nearly 25,000 criminals who were released from Cuban jails. U.S. officials tried to downplay the number of criminals involved in the Mariel Boatlift, claiming that the number of criminals were around 2,746 (Global Security 2011). Among these criminals (in the film) were Tony Montana (Al Pacino) and his close friend Manny Ribera (Steven Bauer). When these Cuban exiles arrived in Miami, they went through an immigration process that involved some people, including Montana and Ribera, being interviewed by the Immigration and Naturalization Service (INS). The INS agents ask him about his tattoo, a pitchfork over a heart, on his hand. The INS knows that Montana's tattoo symbolizes that he is an assassin. Montana, however, claims to be a "political refugee." Because President Jimmy Carter promised citizenship to the Cuban refugees (a political move meant to stick it to Castro), Montana, Ribera, and all the other criminals, along with the law-abiding Cubans were admitted into the country. For a time, they are housed in "Freedomtown," a makeshift temporary quarters for the Cubans that was located underneath a connection of I-95 highway overpass in Miami.

Like so many other immigrants to arrive in the United States, these Cubans lack the necessary job skills to excel in the legitimate socioeconomic world. Montana has ambitions. He wants to be rich and powerful; he does not want to struggle, economically speaking. As a criminal in Cuba, Montana has a few connections in the underworld that reside in Miami. Montana is asked to perform "a hit" (kill someone) on a guy in Freedomtown who once tortured Cubans for the communists. In return, Montana and his friends will receive green cards and jobs more quickly. Montana agrees and kills his target. Waiting for their big break—a chance to work for a wealthy drug trafficker named Frank Lopez (Robert Loggia)—Tony tells Manny, "We should be picking up gold from the streets." Such is Montana's goal, he wants riches beyond reason. The only way to accomplish this, with his job-skills limitations, is through illegal means (e.g., drug-trafficking). Their first job entails Tony and his crew making a buy (purchasing cocaine) from some dangerous Columbians. At this time, Columbian drug lords enjoyed a reputation as the most brutal of all the crime syndicates. (MS-13 or the Mexican drug cartels have that distinction today.) The Columbians are trying to set Tony up and keep the coke and money, but Tony and his crew are ready for the challenge. Tony's friend Angel is killed during a violent exchange of bullets. Montana's crew prevails, killing all the Columbians and retrieving both the cash and cocaine. He brings them both to Frank, who is so impressed by Montana that he takes him under his wing. Lopez warns Montana with two drug-trafficking lessons: (1) "Don't underestimate the other guy's greed," and (2) "Don't get high on your own supply." Tony will eventually violate both of these lessons.

As the film progresses, Montana is in Bolivia, representing Lopez. He brokers a deal with a Bolivian drug lord named Alejandro Sosa (Paul Shennar). But Tony commits to purchase far more cocaine that Lopez feels he can sell on the streets. Lopez is not pleased and worries how he will come up with the initial $5 million. Tony counters that he can make a few deals on the streets, raise the seed money, and then points out how the deal will earn Lopez $75 million. Lopez is not as ambitious as Montana and he is worried that the other Miami drug lords will feel that he is taking over their turfs. Montana, on the other hand, is very ambitions. He wants to set up a distribution ring that extends to New York, Chicago, and Los Angeles. Lopez becomes even more upset with Tony when he realizes that Tony is trying to steal his girlfriend, Elvira (Michelle Pfeiffer). As a result, Lopez orders a hit on Montana, but Tony survives. Montana confronts Lopez and his law enforcement buddy Mel Bernstein (Harris Yulin). Lopez admits his guilt and Tony has Manny kill him. As he turns his sight on Mel, Tony says, "Every dog has his day." Tony then kills Mel. He takes over Frank's entire drug operation and his girlfriend. As the film progresses, Montana becomes a drug kingpin, marries Elvira, and opens up a beauty parlor for his sister Gina. He is making so much cash that he cannot legitimately account for it all. He has to pay his banker a fee (10%) just to keep his money in the bank. Tony states that the reason drugs are kept illegal is the banks (via transfer fees) and corrupt government officials can generate free and untraceable money. When people have as much cash as Montana, but cannot document it through legitimate sources, they draw the attention of the feds. Tony is eventually charged with money laundering and tax evasion. (*Note*: This is a similar scenario to the money laundering scheme of Los Zetas described in the discussion on money laundering in Chapter 8.) His lawyer works out a deal wherein Tony will pay a huge fine and serve 1–3 years in jail. But Montana says he will never go back to jail. Tony's drug partner in Bolivia, Sosa, uses his connections in government to keep him out of jail (reinforcing Tony's belief that drugs are kept illegal so that certain government officials can benefit from the exchange of money between them and international drug dealers). But Montana must accompany Sosa's henchman, Alberto (Mark Margolis) to New York City to assassinate a Bolivian journalist intent on exposing Sosa. Montana agrees to the deal. In New York, Alberto places a bomb in the journalist's car, but when Tony sees that the journalist's entire family is in the car he calls off the hit and shoots and kills Alberto who insisted that the hit go through as planned. Sosa is very upset when he learns about what happened. Tony returns to Miami and looks for Manny, but he cannot find him. Tony is told that both Manny and his sister Gina have been missing for days. Tony does not know that Manny and Gina have been secretly dating. Tony had warned his best friend to stay away from his sister. Tony's mother informs him that she followed Gina to a mansion in Coconut Grove. Tony goes to mansion, knocks on the door and is shocked to find that Manny lives there. When he sees Gina standing behind Manny at an upstairs balcony wearing just a sexy negligee. Tony becomes enraged. He turns back to Manny, gives him the stink eye, and shoots his best friend at point-blank range. Gina is horrified and runs down the stairs and tells her brother that she and Manny had married the day before, and they were going to surprise him with the news. Gina is distraught. Tony's body guards take Gina out of the house, and they all head back to Tony's mansion.

As the film reaches its violent climax Tony's world is completely falling apart. His wife has left him, his best friend is dead, his beloved sister hates him, and his enemies are about to descend upon him. Montana has long been getting very high on his own supply. His mind is not nearly as sharp as it once was. Sosa has sent an army of hit men to Miami to bring Tony down. As his guards are picked off one at a time, Sosa's men work their way inside Tony's mansion. Montana is armed with an M16 equipped with an under-barrel M203 grenade launcher and extended magazines. Just prior to his opening fire on dozens of Sosa's men, Montana yells out one of the most famous and popular lines in film history—"Say hello, to my little friend!" Tony kills many of Sosa's men, but he is shot from behind. Tony's corpse falls from atop the staircase into a fountain in the foyer with a statue in it that reads, "The World is Yours." What once led to Montana's partial ownership of the world, drug-trafficking, now led him to his early demise and the countless losses of lives to those who had the misfortune of coming in contact with him.

When this version of *Scarface* was first released, it did well at the box office (over $135 million when adjusted for inflation in 2010 dollars), but its popularity continues today as it has become a cult phenomenon. In some instances people have been known to do cocaine while watching the film trying to match the characters' cocaine consumption line for line; something that is very difficult to accomplish toward the end of the film as Montana has mounds of coke in front of him and cuts lines with his hand instead of a razor blade because there is so much cocaine. The music in *Scarface*, often haunting, also helps to establish an undeniably eerie and violent mood. *Scarface* garnered mixed reviews from film critics; some were very displeased with the level of violence. Others found it realistic and acceptable. The level of violence and vulgarity in the film, uncommon for that era, earned it an "X" rating—the kiss of death for a legitimate film trying to reach a mainstream audience. Director Brian De Palma gathered a panel of experts, including real narcotics officers who testified that the film depicted an accurate portrayal of a real-life drug-trafficking world. The film was released on December 9, 1983, in 997 theaters with an unapproved "R" rating. Over the years, a number of critics have changed their once negative view of *Scarface* and now view it more positively. The American Film Institute ranks *Scarface* as the #10 gangster film of all time (American Film Institute 2008).

The fictional account of Tony Montana as a drug lord shocked conventional people and was deemed unrealistic when it was first released. Most citizens had no idea that drug cartels such as this existed and were responsible for trafficking recreational drugs into the United States. While *Scarface* portrayed drug-trafficking of the 1980s realistically—with drug cartels dominating the flow of drugs into the United States through extremely violent means—it would be less accurate today as nation and especially transnational gangs, working with drug cartels control the flow of drugs into this country. Just as depicted in *Scarface*, however, drug traffickers use a great deal of violence in order to assure that the cash keeps rolling in. Today, transnational gangs work with drug lords from Central and South America to assure mass distribution on American streets. Transnational gang members are willing to risk a violent death trafficking in drugs because there is so much money to be made. In that regard, the level of violence shown in *Scarface* is fairly common in the international world of drug-trafficking.

Trying to Make It Illegal to Be a Gang Member

In an attempt to counteract the social institution status of street gangs, a number of intervention programs have been enacted. Intervention comes in the form of prevention (programs designed to stop youths from joining a gang); suppression (attempts to curtail the criminal activities of existing gangs); and treatment (programs designed to help individuals leave a gang). While it is true that the number of gangs and gang members are trending upwards, so are the attempts to intervene. Without intervention programs, the total number of gang members would be much higher. Unfortunately, a number of programs face short life spans because of the lack of funding. Politicians, city leaders, and taxpayers alike have to balance their own budget constraints when considering the value of intervention programs. Considering the costs (both social and financial), gangs already cost society, can we afford not to support intervention programs? Students and nonstudents alike have asked me numerous times, "Why don't they just make it illegal to be a gang member?" a type of ultimate prevention strategy. Trying to make it illegal to be a gang member presents all sorts of potential legal issues, especially the rights of citizens to peacefully assemble in public. Legislative efforts to curtail gang activity fall within the suppression category of intervention. Over the years, a number of anti-gang laws have been introduced, are pending, or have been passed that virtually make it illegal to be a gang member. In 1999, Omaha, Nebraska legislators passed Ordinance No. 34926 as part of its Municipal Code. Sec.18-81 (Declaration of nuisance; notice to abate) states that "any private place or premises within the city which is used as the site of a juvenile gathering is hereby declared to be a public nuisance. No person shall maintain any such nuisance." The police are given authority to abate the nuisance. In Arizona (Arizona 13-2308), assisting in a criminal syndicate is a class 4 felony. If the criminal syndicate is a street gang, such offenses may become class 3 or 2 felonies. California law (186.22) states that "any person who actively participates in any criminal street gang with knowledge that its members engage in or have engaged in a pattern of criminal gang activity, and who willfully promotes, furthers, or assists in any felonious criminal conduct by members of that gang, shall be punished by imprisonment in a county jail for a period not to exceed one year, or by imprisonment in the state prison for 16 months, or two or three years." Georgia law (16-15-4) makes it illegal for any person employed by or associated with a criminal street gang to conduct or participate in a pattern of criminal gang activity. It is also illegal to encourage, solicit, or coerce another person to participate in a criminal street gang. Iowa legislation (723A.2) states that any person who commits a criminal act for the benefit of a criminal street gang is guilty of a class D felony. Louisiana (15:1403), Minnesota (609.229), and Missouri (578.423) state laws make it illegal for any person to participate in a pattern of criminal gang activity. In 2007, then California Governor Arnold Schwarzenegger signed five bills aimed at stemming the tide of killings, including the creation of a state office of gang and youth violence policy to oversee the efforts; a bill that allows judges to order parents of gang members to attend anti-violence classes; and, a bill designed to improve the protection of witnesses of gang killings (McGreevy 2007). Colorado has passed a number of laws to curtail gang activity including laws allowing cities and counties to pass curfew ordinances; laws prohibiting gang recruitment activities; laws prohibiting loitering, graffiti, and other types of criminal mischief; and criminal laws prohibiting gang-related activity (applicable to juveniles and adults) (Bussey 2012). In North Carolina, thanks to the "North Carolina Street Gang Suppression Act" (2008-214, s. 3.), it is illegal to be in a gang. Specifically, the 2008 law makes it unlawful for any person employed by or associated with a criminal street gang to do either of the following: (1) to conduct or participate in a pattern of criminal street gang activity and (2) to acquire or maintain any interest in or control of any real or personal property through a pattern of criminal street gang activity. Law enforcement officials claim that the law gives them more authority to tackle gang problems, but at least one prosecutor believes the law is too complex and legislators have not done enough to prevent teens from joining gangs in the first place (American Police Beat 2010). In an attempt to curtail the growing presence and power of transnational gangs and their negative effect on society, El Salvador passed the "Law Prohibiting Maras, Gangs, Groups, Associations and Organization of a Criminal Nature" in 2010. Among other things, the law carries tougher prison sentences for belonging to a gang; prohibits the existence of gangs; declares gang-related activity of any kind as illegal; and grants the attorney general and applicable judges the power to freeze bank accounts, properties, and assets of gang members (Voices from El Salvador 2010).

Hit 'em Where It Hurts . . . Their Wallets

As described in the previous section, judicial officials in El Salvador have the legal right to freeze bank accounts, properties, and assets of gang members. The law does not apply to minors, who are covered by the Law of the Protection of Childhood and Adolescence (LEPINA), but it is applicable to current inmates already in jail serving prison sentences (Voices from El Salvador 2010). Legislative and judicial efforts "to hit 'em where it hurts" are applicable in the United States as well. In fact, the trend may have started in California. In Los Angeles, a superior court judge ruled that city officials can seek to recover $5 million from a street gang that has long held a monopoly on the downtown heroin trade (*The Post-Standard* 2009b). It was the first such judgment since a 2007 state law (SB 271 [Cedillo]; 2007 STAT. Ch. 34) was passed allowing county and city prosecutors to go after a gang's ill-gotten assets. Under Chapter 34, any district attorney or prosecuting city attorney can sue for damages on behalf of a community injured by a gang-created nuisance when an injunction has been issued (Lee, P. 2012). The law was further amended in 2008 enabling prosecutors to go after gang leaders' personal assets, regardless of whether they were tied to illegal activity (*The Post-Standard* 2009b). With an estimated 250,000 members in over 5,000 gangs in California alone, the law was deemed necessary. Chapter 34 amends section 186.22a of the Penal Code by expanding the group of individuals to pursue an action for damages due to gang-related activities (Lee, P. 2012). Judgments must name gang members who will be held liable for the damages. In the Los Angeles case, penalties collected would be set into a fund to be distributed to the downtown community affected by the damages caused by the gang's operations. City Attorney Rocky Delgadillo said, "This is a whole new front that we're waging against these gang members" (*The Post-Standard* 2009, B-5). Suing gang members for their ill-gotten money is trending, and it may represent a great tactic in combating street gangs. After all, individuals join a gang to make money, if they cannot make money from the gang the incentive is lessened, at least theoretically. Suing gang members for their money is merely theoretical for people like Lawrence Rosenthal, a former federal prosecutor who worked on anti-gang efforts in Chicago, who are skeptical whether a jurisdiction would actually be successful in attaining financial compensation from street gangs even if they were ordered to do so (*The Post-Standard* 2009).

Web Banging: Gangs and the Internet

Social media is certainly trending in contemporary society and gang members are utilizing the Internet just like everyone else. In Chapter 4, "Connecting Street Gangs and Popular Culture" Box 4.2 described how street gangs keep connected via the Internet. It would be pointless to retell that same story here, but it is a trend that is worthy of being acknowledged nonetheless. Sending emails and placing posts online allows law enforcement an opportunity to access gang communications. However, many gangs have learned the same lesson as revolutionists in the Middle East, using Twitter and sending text messages allows for rapid movement, regrouping, and reorganizing large numbers of people. Many gang members use prepaid cell phones to conduct their illegal activities and to avoid being tracked by law enforcement. For more than a decade now, street gangs have established their own websites and have links to "sound-off" pages, "RIP" sections dedicated to fallen members, making threats, photos and bios of gang members, and graffiti and audio messages and music. The Internet is being increasingly used for criminal activities and has proven to be a tool for drug-trafficking. To underscore the trending aspect of street gangs and the Internet, there is now a term for gang activities on the Internet—*Web banging* (Queally 2011). **Web banging** refers to all the activities conducted by gang members online including those just described and access to younger recruits. Using the Internet for recruiting is the new concern for law enforcement as youngsters do not need to have physical contact with gang members; they have virtual contact. In the recent past, the Internet was used to post audio messages and music, now gang members are inviting thousands of people to parties and posting home movies on Facebook and YouTube. According to Anthony Cox, **Violence Interdiction/Intelligence Prosecution Eradication Recidivism (V.I.P.E.R.) Unit** detective (Essex County, New Jersey), these gatherings sometimes turn into recruitment sessions and when the youths see themselves in a gang movie, it makes quite an impression (Queally 2011). V.I.P.E.R. is a New Jersey anti-gang unit that was created in 2008 when the Gang Intelligence Unit was merged with the Narcotics Task Force (Essex County Prosecutor's Office 2012). Web banging is certainly trending, and it is likely to have an even greater impact on gang recruitment in the years to come.

Gangs Infiltrating Law Enforcement and Corrections

As we know, police officers and corrections officers are only human, and like many other citizens, some of them are corruptible. Among other things, police officers and correctional officers are subject to bribes. Why would they take a bribe? For the same reason any number of people might take a bribe, that is, most of the rank and file officers do not earn high salaries. For some, it is a little too tempting to pass up a chance to make some extra cash, even in the form of a bribe. For example, in January 2012 a Los Angeles County Sheriff's deputy, Henry Marin, was indicted for smuggling drugs into a courthouse jail by concealing them in a burrito (Faturechi and Leonard 2012). Inside the bean-and-cheese burrito was heroin. In May, the deputy pleaded no contest (Corrections One 2012). The full scope of smuggling drugs into jails and prisons is difficult to quantify, but the FBI recognizes this as a serious problem. It is disturbing enough to realize that some law enforcement and correctional officers became corrupt and assist criminals, but when we learn that gang members and outlaw motorcycle gangs (OMGs) are infiltrating law enforcement and corrections agencies, we realize that the problem is even bigger. The FBI (2011a) has been aware of gang members infiltrating the ranks of law enforcement and corrections for years. Infiltration into law enforcement and correctional agencies creates serious security threats, as gang members have access to police reports, sensitive information on investigations, access to the names of protected witnesses to gang-related crimes, and so on. The gang members who have infiltrated these agencies have also acquired knowledge and training in police tactics and weapons. Corrupt law enforcement officers and correctional staff have assisted gang members in committing crimes and have impeded investigations in various jurisdictions across the nation. The trending aspect of gang infiltration into law enforcement and corrections is demonstrated with the following:

- The NGIC reports that gang members in at least 57 jurisdictions, including California, Florida, Tennessee, and Virginia, have applied for or gained employment within judicial, police, or correctional agencies (FBI 2011a).
- A Crip gang member applied for a law enforcement position in Oklahoma (FBI 2011a).
- OMGs engage in routine and systematic exploitation and infiltration of law enforcement and government infrastructures to protect and perpetrate their illegal activities. OMGs regularly request information of intelligence value from government and/or law enforcement employees (FBI 2011a).
- The NGIC reports that gang members have compromised or corrupted judicial, law enforcement, or correctional staff in 72 jurisdictions within the past three years (FBI 2011a).
- In November 2010, a parole worker in New York was suspended for relaying confidential information to a Bloods gang member in Albany; in July 2010, a Riverside County, California detention center sheriff deputy was convicted of assisting her incarcerated La Eme boyfriend with murdering two witnesses in her boyfriend's case; and, in April 2010, a former Berwyn, Illinois police officer pleaded guilty to charges of conspiracy to commit racketeering and to obstruct justice for his part in assisting an OMG member in targeting and burglarizing rival businesses (FBI 2011a).
- In 2010, a local gangbanger who'd nearly completed all of his preemployment exams for a police academy in southwest Florida was identified by a local street cop who recognized the candidate's gang tattoo (Grossi 2011).

Gang infiltration into law enforcement and corrections is very problematic. Of (at least) equal concern is trending of gang members in the military. As we shall soon learn, this trend is very well-documented.

Gangs Infiltrating the Military

According to the FBI, members of nearly every major street gang, as well as some prison gangs and OMGs, have been identified on both domestic and international military installations. Military deployments have resulted in gang members among service members and/or dependents on or near overseas bases. In addition, military transfers have resulted in gang members, both service members and their dependents/relatives, moving to new areas and establishing a gang presence (FBI 2009c). Once deployed, or transferred, military-affiliated gang members expand their culture and operations to new regions nationwide and worldwide, undermining security and law enforcement efforts to combat crime (FBI 2011a). Gang members in the military help to fuel the growth of third generation gangs discussed earlier in this chapter. The idea of gang members with military-style training is especially disconcerting for law enforcement officials on the American streets because of their distinctive weapons and combat training skills and their ability to transfer these skills to fellow gang members (FBI 2011a). One of earliest glimpses of a gang member with military experience causing havoc on domestic streets occurred in Ceres, California in 2005 when Andres Raya, a 19-year-old Marine on liberty (a type of military leave) shot two police officers, killing one of them, using a technique he learned in the Marines called "slicing the pie." This approach involves the shooter rapid firing to clear a path while advancing on his target. Using a semiautomatic rifle, Raya drew officers into an ambush outside a liquor store in Ceres (CNN 2005). Police officers were finally able to return fire and kill Raya. Upon investigation, it was discovered that Raya was a current member of the Nortenos Gang (Roberts 2005). He was on leave and had already served a tour in Iraq. The Raya incident provides us with an example of how a gang member can learn a new skill set in the military and apply it to his gang life back home. One merely has to recall the discussion of the origin of MS-13 (see Chapter 6) and their current status as one of, if not *the*, most dangerous street gangs in the world to understand the concern over American street gang members with combat experience. In brief, the original members of MS-13 in the United States were young people with military training and combat experience in the El Salvador civil war. The NGIC indicates that law enforcement officials in at least 100 jurisdictions have come in contact with, detained, or arrested an active duty or former military gang member within the past three years (FBI 2011a). Although gang members have been identified in every branch of the U.S. military, the largest proportion of these gang members are affiliated with the U.S. Army, Army Reserves, and National Guard branches (FBI 2011a). Look closely at news footage of the current wars and you are likely to find gang graffiti in the background. In the 2011 National Gang Threat Assessments, there is a photo of a U.S. military vehicle in Iraq with "Support your local Hells Angels" graffiti on it and another photo of a soldier in a combat zone throwing gang signs.

The phenomenon of gang members in the military has been trending for quite a while now, and the warning signs were visible but mostly ignored. In the early 2000s, the FBI and the U.S. Army Criminal Investigations Department (CID) identified nearly 40 gang members affiliated with the Folk Nation (primarily Gangster Disciples [GD]) stationed at Fort Bliss Army Base in Texas; another 40 gang members at Fort Hood Army Base in Texas; and nearly 130 gang and extremist group members at Fort Lewis Army Installation in Washington (National Gang Intelligence Center 2007). Military-affiliated gang members are responsible for a disproportionate amount of crime and misconduct committed on military bases. The Southern Poverty Law Center (SPLC) reports that gang members in the military are just the latest example of the trend of a "few bad men" to serve in the armed forces. The SPLC provides a timeline of extremism and the military in its 2006 Intelligence Report (Holthouse 2006). This timeline chronicles a number of high-ranking military people with ties to anti-Semitic groups in the 1950s (i.e., the 1953 formation of the American Nazi Party by retired U.S. Naval Commander George Lincoln Rockwell); the infiltration of KKK members in the military during the 1970s and continuing for decades; the formation of the White Patriot Party, a paramilitary Klan offshoot set up in 1980 with members trained in guerilla warfare and weapons stolen from the military provided by active military personnel; the training and weapons provision to a number of white hate groups by military personnel throughout the 1990s; and now, the influx of primarily nonwhite gang members into the military (Holthouse 2006).

A warning sign that should have received far greater attention was the death of U.S. Army Sergeant Juwan Johnson. In 2005, while stationed at Kaiserslautern Army Base in Germany, Johnson decided to join the Gangster Disciples (GD). On July 3, Johnson went to park not far from his base to be initiated. He was jumped by up to 10 GD soldiers. Sgt. Johnson lost consciousness during the "jump in" and was carried back to his bed by his new gang brothers. However, Johnson never woke up and died later that night from his injuries (Stars and Stripes 2009). In 2008, Rico Rodrigus Williams, a former Air Force senior airman, was charged in a federal indictment with one count of second-degree murder and three counts of tampering with a witness in the beating death of Johnson. Williams unleashed the first punch and the rest of the gang members joined in during the six-minute beating (Stars and Stripes 2009). Johnson's death should have served as a major wake–up call to top military and political figures that gang infiltration is a very serious trending issue. Perhaps the reality of fighting multiple wars provided a challenge too daunting to military higher-ups to address the issue of gang members in the military. If this is true, then we are in even bigger trouble than already thought. The United States seems to always be engaged in war—something that once went against American socio-political ideology—so we cannot wait for the end of war to address the growing problem of gang members in the military. Furthermore, because of America's constant participation in war, the opportunities for gang members to join the armed forces, become trained in the latest military tactics, have access to superior weaponry, and then return to the streets to wreak havoc will only continue to increase. Again, the signs are there: Marines in gang attire on Parris Island; paratroopers flashing gang hand signals at a nightclub near Ft. Bragg; and, infantrymen showing off gang tattoos at Ft. Hood (Klatell 2011). The FBI is certainly paying attention. In the 2011 National Gang Threat Assessments reports, the FBI (2011a) provides a table with headings of "Gang Name," "Type" (Street, Prison, or OMG), and "Military Branch." The table provides an alphabetical list of gangs beginning with the 18th Street Gang and the Aryan Brotherhood through the Wah Ching Gang and Warlocks, 52 gangs in total. With all this information, one would hope something would be done to curtail the upward trend of gang members serving in the military.

Gangs Are Trending Everywhere

At this point, having read the entire text, it would seem to be an understatement to say that gangs are trending everywhere. Gangs can be found in rural, suburban, and urban areas, on Native-American reservations, and in prisons. In Chapter 5, a description of the similarities and differences between street gangs and the military was provided. We discovered that these two social institutions share many of the same characteristics, such as distinctive clothing, use of symbols and acronyms, rituals and ceremonies of status, reasons for joining, initiations, and a hierarchal structure. With our discussion of gang infiltration into the military, we can see a partial fusing of the two social institutions. In this chapter, gang infiltration into law enforcement and corrections was also briefly described. The fact is gang members are infiltrating all of America's social institutions. They can be found in a variety of workplace environments working an angle that leads to the profitability of the gang. The trend of gang members participating in white-collar crime implies that a number of gang members are working in the professions. Gang members have long been engaged in politics. Their influence was first noted in New York City in the era of Tammany Hall, whose corrupt political officials hired gang members to intimidate would-be voters. In contemporary America, it would be difficult for gangs to have this same influence; however, if gang members were to register to vote and voted as a block, they could have a significant influence on local-level politics. Gangs—the Conservative Vice Lords, for example—have always been involved in local politics and some attempt to elect their own candidates. In New York City, the Almighty Latin King Nation is involved in voter registration, distributes campaign fliers for favorite candidates, and has been accused of intimidating voters into favoring its chosen candidates (NAGIA 2002). The corruption inherent in politics makes this social institution an attractive environment for business-savvy gang leaders, who could easily take advantage of money-laundering opportunities through monetary contributions to candidates.

PARTING THOUGHTS

Street gangs are a permanent fixture in American society. They have existed for nearly 200 years. When gangs first formed in the United States the gang members felt like they were adhering to a type of "call to duty" to protect their neighborhood and families from outside threats. Although often violent and murderous, the activities of these first generation-style street gangs were generally confined to specific local geographic locations. They engaged in what would now be described as expected or traditional criminal activities. These first generation-style gang members were usually youths frustrated with the socioeconomic hand dealt to them. Most would leave the gang in early adulthood, pursue a conventional job, and raise a family—hopefully under better socioeconomic conditions than their parents. The advent of nation gangs led to the creation of the second generation-styled gangs. Less concerned about local geographic areas under the idealized view that such turfs needed to be protected from outsiders (a defensive strategy), nation gangs went on the offensive (taking over other people's turf). Second generation gangs are characterized by making money, regardless of the costs to themselves, rival gangs, and innocent people. Third generation gangs have expanded their influence beyond the United States and like second generation gangs make most of their money selling drugs. Americans have a huge appetite for drugs and yet the government has criminalized many of the drugs people crave. The government legalizes some of the most deadly drugs known to humankind (i.e., nicotine and alcohol) and yet still refuses to legalize recreational drugs (i.e., marijuana and cocaine). History has repeatedly shown that when people want goods or services not allowed or provided by the government, a black market will emerge to fill this void. Second and third generation gangs have increasingly taken over the illicit drug market and are heavily involved in the sale, distribution, and trafficking of recreational drugs. In order to protect their economic empires, street gangs engage in violent and murderous battles with one another leaving a wake of terrorized citizens wherever they roam.

It has often been proposed by a wide variety of folks from all walks of life that if recreational drugs (e.g., marijuana and cocaine) were legalized, the number of drug-selling gangs would diminish, the level of violence in many jurisdictions would decrease significantly, and a source of taxable income for governments at all levels (local, state, and federal) would be provided. In other words, crime would go down, citizens would feel safer, and the government would generate revenue. Nation gangs and transnational gangs are fueled by a seemingly endless supply of cash provided via drug sales. Gangs exist in many areas simply because of illegality of recreational drugs. A great example of this is found in Anchorage, Alaska. It would be easy to think of Alaska as gang-free, but street gangs have existed in the state's largest city of Anchorage since the mid-1970s. And there is one simple reason they exist: money. Ever since the oil boom of the 1970s people from all over the world have moved to Alaska to make money, and there is great deal of free time and disposable income among many of these workers. Like people everywhere, the folks with disposable income in Alaska want to party and partying means doing illicit drugs. The *Gangland* (2009b) episode "Ice Cold Killers" documents the history of gangs in Anchorage. Alaska has more guns per capita than any other U.S. state. There are gun shops and homes filled with guns, and they make for perfect targets for gang members looking to increase their arsenals of weapons. Anchorage is dominated by Crips, mostly from Los Angeles. A Crips member who was interviewed for the documentary said, "Crips don't die, they multiply." And over the years, they certainly multiplied in Anchorage. The *Gangland* episode described in great deal how the 1977 oil boom created workers with disposable income and how the gangs migrated to Alaska because they were shocked to learn how easy it was to make more cash than imaginable. Many families from lower SES neighborhoods moved to Alaska in the 1980s to escape the devastation of the "crack epidemic" on their neighborhoods, viewing Anchorage as a safe haven. The youth of these migrating families brought with them the gang culture and soon Crip graffiti sprung up all around Anchorage. Incidents of street and school violence increased, but the local officials referred to these youths as wannabes. The Crip members were insulted by this and stepped up their level of violence and brazen attempt to control drug sales throughout the Anchorage region. The **Hamo Tribe**, a Samoan Crip gang dominated during the 1990s, caused violent chaos on the streets until the FBI's Safe Street Unit (which equates to more detectives and more prosecutors) was set up in 1995. By 1998, the Hamo Tribe members were put behind bars. Following the 9/11 attacks, the Safe Street Unit was deployed back to the Lower 48. This turned out to be a big mistake as the number of Crips migrating to Alaska increased dramatically in the early 2000s. In 2006, the Safe Streets Unit was revitalized. Because these gangs are more loosely organized than Crips found outside Alaska, the FBI had a harder time using RICO racketeering violations. Instead, the feds used gun crime laws to put gang members away; federal gun offenses dramatically increase the sentences of violators. The Crips are still the largest gang presence in Anchorage although there are some Bloods and small gangs as well. A female Crip was interviewed by the *Gangland* crew and she was quoted saying, "money makes people funny"—a reference to the willingness of gang members to kill each other because the amount of money being made on the streets of Anchorage is so huge. The drugs being sold in Anchorage by street gangs are primarily marijuana and cocaine. If these two drugs were legal, the gangs would have never gone to Anchorage.

As each year goes by, there appears to be greater acceptance of the idea of legalizing, or at the very least, decriminalizing certain recreational drugs. In many states, people can purchase marijuana legally if they can provide medical evidence that the drug is being used for medical purposes. The state of New York once had the harshest drug laws (known as the Rockefeller laws) in the country. But the laws are lessening in New York. In June, 2012, New York Governor Andrew Cuomo proposed lowering the penalty for public possession of a small amount of marijuana, reducing it from a misdemeanor to a violation with a fine up to $100. The Democrat governor has the support of New York City prosecutors, Republican New York City Mayor Michael Bloomberg, and an endorsement from Police Commissioner Raymond Kelly (Weaver 2012). Although this law, if passed, would not suffice to reduce marijuana gang-related crime in New York State (marijuana would have to be legalized for that to happen), it does represent a change in ideology in a state once very intolerant toward recreational drug users.

In April 2012, President Obama attended a Latin American regional summit in Cartagena, Columbia to discuss trade and business opportunities, but other leaders upstaged him by pushing to legalize marijuana and other illicit drugs in an attempt to stem the rampant trafficking. Latin American leaders point out that it is Americans' desire for recreational drugs that causes drug-trafficking–related problems in their nations. Latin leaders want Obama to legalize recreational drugs in the United States in an attempt to stem the rampant trafficking in their nations. The Latin perspective is steadfast that the "American demand for illegal drugs has caused fierce bloodshed, plus political and economic turmoil, across much of the region" (Parsons and Bennett 2012). Obama opposes decriminalization and supports the hard-line approach where law enforcement goes after the narcotic traffickers in an attempt to arrest and incarcerate them and also goes after the coca growers to destroy the coca bushes. Just as the American war on drugs failed miserably in the United States, so has this policy failed wretchedly in Latin American nations. "The crackdown on criminal cartels in Mexico, for example, launched when President Felipe Calderon took office in 2006, has resulted in more than 40,000 deaths and had little impact on drug trafficking along the border with the United States, some say" (Epatko 2012). Other Latin American countries are concerned about what happens in Mexico and its relationship with the United States because Mexico-based drug cartels are moving south into Central America. As previously described, transnational gangs based in the United States are working with these Mexico-based cartels. The drug issue came up on Saturday, April 14, during the 2012 summit. Obama was hesitant to make any move toward decriminalizing drugs in the United States because of fears of a political backlash. Legalizing recreational drugs would support the idea of "hitting 'em where it hurts" approach; that is, if the drugs that gangs are selling were legal, it would take all the drug money out of the gangs' pockets. (Interestingly, in the film *Scarface*, Tony, Manny, and Elvira watch a news report on TV and a commentator suggested that drugs should be legalized as an effort to curtail gang violence.) Many Americans oppose the idea of legalizing recreational drugs. Opponents worry that if recreational drugs were legalized problems might get worse. One thing is for sure, American street gang involvement in drug-trafficking is at an all-time high right now. Current policy has failed.

Joining a gang has always been tied to socioeconomic realities. Many youth, especially those from lower SES backgrounds grow up perceiving the local gang as economically successful, especially compared to most of the other folks in their neighborhoods. When youth see gang members with cash, cars, jewelry, and all the material comfort commodities, it is easy to see why some might view a gang favorably. Taking drug money out of the pockets of street gangs would reduce their power and lower their economic status. This would have a negative impact on recruitment. But much more has to be accomplished. Youth need to feel as though the conventional life will provide opportunities to become successful. They need quality education in safe schools. They need to be taught job and social skills. They need to be taught academic subjects that will allow them to attend college where their life chances will improve all the more. They need job opportunities. If all this sounds like something conventional youth and young adults like college students crave, that's the point. When at-risk youth have hope and start thinking like conventional folks and not as thugs, they are less likely to join a gang. Hope helps to establish the critical bonds that individuals need to feel a part of society and therefore have a vested interest in its maintenance and smooth operation. A number of people, including those who work with gang intervention programs, social workers, educators, everyday citizens and politicians, want to help change the culture of gangism—a culture that embraces a thug mentality. Senator Eric Adams, D-Brooklyn, believes that young people should take pride in their image reasoning that having pride is counter to the thug mentality. One of the things that really bothers Adams is the saggy pants delinquent youths wear. Under his sponsorship, messages intended principally for young black men went up on several billboards in Brooklyn that read: "We are better than this! Stop the Sag!" In between the two sentences is a photo of two young blacks with pants sagging so low you can see most of their underwear. The billboards also have the Senator's photo on them with a message at the bottom reading: "Raise Your Pants, Raise Your Image!" Adams argues that raised trousers mean raised respect (*The Post-Standard* 4/4/10). Another helpful way to change the culture of acceptance of thugism involves community members, along with social policy makers, taking a stand against gang members through a variety of means including anti-gang videos. The State of Virginia, for example, is utilizing a video titled "The Wrong Family" in its attempt to fulfill Governor McDonnell's cry to make Virginia a Gang-Free Zone. See "Connecting Street Gangs and Popular Culture" Box 10.2 for a discussion on Virginia's anti-gang video "The Wrong Family."

Box 10.2   *Connecting Street Gangs and Popular Culture*

"The Wrong Family": An Educational Anti-Gang Video

While serving as the Virginia Attorney General (2006–2009), Robert (Bob) McDonnell proposed the idea that Virginia should be a gang-free state. Despite the naiveté of the idea of ridding the state of all gangs, it is a worthy dream. Among the many obstacles in succeeding with his gang-free utopian state is the public apathy and a lack of knowledge of the dangers gangs present. Clearly, the people who live in and near gang areas understand the horrors gangs represent, but law enforcement felt that the general public lacked enough knowledge about gangs. It was reasoned that once the public was educated on the extent of gang criminal activity, Virginia citizens would stand united with law enforcement in their effort to rid the state of gang members. In 2007, in response to suggestions of local law enforcement who noted the need to raise awareness about gangs, the Attorney General's Office began production of an anti-gang video made up of interviews and footage shot entirely in Virginia. The video was titled: "The Wrong Family: Virginia Fights Back Against Gangs" and was created with federal grant funds and funds seized by the Office of the Attorney General from criminals around the Commonwealth (Commonwealth of Virginia Office of Attorney General 2011). The aim of the video is to serve as a prevention intervention strategy to keep kids from joining gangs, educate parents about the warning signs of gang activity and their criminal activities, and to educate law enforcement on the ways to monitor and recognize gang involvement.

The video is a 25-minute documentary and is not the gang version of the famous prison documentary *Scared Straight*, but rather, a "straight talk" teaching tool for law enforcement and anti-gang community organizations to preach gang education and prevention among at-risk youth in the commonwealth (Nolan 2008). The video features parents whose children have been affected by gang involvement, and law enforcement officers who confront gang activity in the urban and rural regions of the state of Virginia. It includes footage of the emergency room of VCU Medical Center, where doctors with blood literally on their hands try to stitch together lives ripped apart by gang-related violence (Nolan 2008). A gang member named Paradise C states in the video, "Love your kids. It's not hard. It's a simple concept"—a warning from a gang member who knows. A warning that should be heeded by parents everywhere, not just in Virginia. A paralyzed former gangbanger named Christopher Robinson describes how he was looking for a family, a place where he could fit it. He turned to a gang for his substitute family. Robinson states, "It wasn't a family for me at all. We as a community have got to save our kids. We can't let them choose the wrong family" (Nolan 2008). The video's title is connected to this last quote, as the "wrong family" is the gang family. The warning is directed at parents to be good role models, to be there for their children, because if they are not, their children may turn to the wrong family—a gang. And for Robinson, the gang was the wrong family. Robinson belonged to Richmond gang and he was shot in gang fight. His legs were paralyzed by a bullet. He recalls on the video overhearing the doctor say that he might not survive. Robinson did survive, but he lost the use of legs because of a gang fire-fight. Robinson describes how he would give anything to go back in time and not join the gang, the wrong family (Fiske 2008).

"Basically, we sell drugs and shoot people," says another young man named Tong G on "The Wrong Family" video (Fiske 2008). Tony G has been a member of a Crips gang since he was 14 years old. The video describes how gangs are appealing to youth because they have money and because gangs promise to provide recruits a sense of family, a message that is appealing because most gang members come from single-parent families (Fiske 2008). Law enforcement officers also describe the need for after-school care and activities such as night basketball leagues to keep youths too busy to join a gang. The video was not released on the Internet, but it is available to local police departments and commonwealth attorneys, who can make it available for groups who want to watch it (Fiske 2008). As the video gained popularity, it received two awards (in 2009): "The Bronze Telly Award for Social Issues" and the "Communicator Award of Distinction for Social Issues" (Commonwealth of Virginia Office of Attorney General 2011). In 2009, the video was translated in Spanish and some scenes were reshot with bilingual participants speaking Spanish. In addition, to complement "The Wrong Family" video, the Office of Attorney General developed an additional anti-gang video specifically targeting youth: "The Big Lie, Unmasking the Truth Behind Gangs." The Big Lie is a documentary exposing the lies gangs tell recruits in an attempt to lure them in. The documentary also illustrates healthy lifestyle choices kids can make to avoid gangs (Commonwealth of Virginia Office of Attorney General 2011).

The video, which is designed as a type of "tough love" approach to parents, is just one aspect of McDonnell's attempt to rid Virginia of gangs. The then-attorney general also recognizes the need for community programs to keep youths busy and off the streets. Riding the success of this office's two successful anti-gang videos, McDonnell ran for Governor of Virginia. During his 2009 campaign, McDonnell proclaimed that "combating criminal street gangs will be one of my top public safety priorities" (McDonnell 2009). Among his ideas was expanding the "drug-free school zones" to "gang-free zones" and then expand those zones to include the entire state (Gorman 2011). Drug-free and gang-free zones provide enhanced penalties for gang-related crime occurring within them. McDonnell also proposed appointing a State Anti-Gang Coordinator, expanding the successful GRIP program (Gang Reduction Intervention Program), expanding prevention programs, and increasing penalties for gang recruitment. McDonnell was successful in his bid for Virginia's governor's office and took office in January 2010. Shortly after, he backed a House bill that called for expanding the anti-gang zones.

McDonnell is to be commended on his ambition to rid his state of gangs, even if this is a futile effort. He realizes, however, that to combat gangs it takes more than suppression efforts, it takes prevention and intervention programs, and it takes attempts at reaching regular citizens through popular culture means (the use of videos). Seemingly, every nongang member in the United States supports his attempts in ridding the state of street gangs. If it works in Virginia, the concept of anti-gang zones could be expanded nationwide.

It is very important that intervention programs continue. While prevention programs cannot keep everyone out of gangs, they are making a difference. Suppression efforts are necessary to protect citizens from gang crime, but suppression alone will not stop gang activity. Treatment programs have been successful in helping some individuals leave gangs. All of the intervention strategies require funding. Intervention programs more or less pay for themselves because they offset the damages that would have been caused by the gang members had they not been successfully intervened. Intervention programs also depend on well-meaning individuals who truly possess a desire to make American society a better one in which to live. School intervention programs are of particular importance. Many students today live in constant fear of violence, and this violence is no longer limited to the bully in the school. There are still individual bullies, but at many schools the bullies are gangs. The constant threat of gang violence has led to the development and implementation of safe-school plans. Many schools have banned the wearing of alleged gang-related colors on school campuses. Unfortunately, it is difficult to ascertain whether such policies have any appreciable effect on the levels of school violence.

Summary

As this chapter itself served as a summary, of sorts, of the entire text, a brief synopsis is offered here. It would be nice to conclude on an upbeat note. But any astute reader of this text, let alone experts in the field of street gangs, should be able to ascertain that the gang problem is trending upward. There are more gangs and gang members than ever before. They are more violent than ever before, and they are increasingly taking over the illicit drug trade.

The increased level of violence committed by street gangs is directly correlated to their increased control of drug markets. And as long as recreational drugs are illegal and the public demand for drugs remains high, street gangs will continue to profit from drug-trafficking. It will take drastic changes in the economy, government policy, and cultural norms and values to turn the tide of increased gang activity.

REFERENCES

Abbott, Greg. 2012. "Gangs and the Internet." Available: http://staffweb.esc12.net/~mbooth/resources_general/Internet_Cyberbullying_bullying/Mohler_Handout%20Gangs%20and%20the%20internet%20Sept%2008.pdf.

Adams, E., and Richard T. Serpe. 2000. "Social Integration, Fear of Crime, and Life Satisfaction." *Sociological Perspectives*, 43(4):605–29.

Albanese, Jay. 2002. *Criminal Justice*, 2nd ed. Boston, MA: Allyn & Bacon.

Aleman, Marcos. 2012. "El Salvador Mara Salvatrucha, Mara 18 Gangs Reach Truce." *Huffington Post*, March 23. Available: http://www.huffingtonpost.com/2012/03/24/el-salvador-mara-salvatrucha-mara-18-truce_n_1376955.html.

Ambert, Anne-Marie. 2001. *The Effects of Children on Parents*, 2nd ed. New York: Haworth.

Amer-I-Can. 2012. "The Amer-I-Can Program: Homepage." Available: http://www.amer-i-can.org/index.html.

American Educator. 2011 (Winter 2011–2012). "The Rise of Poverty." Vol. 35, No. 4:2.

American Film Institute. 2008. "Top 10 Gangster." Available: http://www.afi.com/10top10/category.aspx?cat=8.

American Police Beat. 2010. "New Law Takes Aim at Gang Membership." Available: http://www.apbweb.com/featured-articles/1052-new-law-takes-aim-at-gang-membership.html.

Anderson, David C. 1995. *Crime and the Politics of Hysteria: How the Willie Horton Story Changed American Justice*. New York: Times Books.

Anderson, Elijah. 1999. *Code of the Street: Decency, Violence, and the Moral Life of the Inner City*. New York: W. W. Norton.

Anderson, Mark, and Mark Jenkins. 2001. *Dance of Days*. New York: Soft Skull Press.

Anstey, Michael L., Stephen M. Rogers, Swidbert R. Ott, Malcolm Burrows, and S. J. Simpson. 2009. "Serotonin Mediates Behavioral Gregarization Underlying Swarm Formation in Desert Locusts." *Science*, 323(5914):627–30.

Anti-Defamation League. 2005. "The Five Percenter." Available: http://www.adl.org/hate_symbols/Five_Percenters.asp.

———. 2008. "Colorado Racist Prison Gang Leader Sentenced to 112 Years." Available: http://www.adl.org/learn/extremism_in_the_news/White_Supremacy/211+Crew+Danny+Shea+7-08.htm?LEARN_Cat=Extremism&LEARN_SubCat=Extremism_in_the_News.

Archer, John. 1991. "The Influence of Testosterone on Human Aggression." *British Journal of Psychology*, 82(1):1–28.

Archer, Lianne, and Andrew M. Grascia. 2006. "Girls, Gangs and Crime: Profile of the Young Female Offender." *Journal of Gang Research*, 13(2):37–49.

Asbury, Herbert. 2002. "The Gangs of New York," in *Gangs*. Ed. Sean Donohue. New York: Thunder's Mouth Press. (Originally published in 1927 by Knopf.): pp. 55–86.

Associated Press. 1998. "Injunction Targets Hollywood Gang." Available: http://www.streetgangs.com/topics/1998/041498.html.

Auslander, Jason. 2009. "City Burglaries Jump Amid Recession, Gangs." *The New Mexican*, July 26. Available: http://www.santafenewmexican.com/Local%20News/City-burglaries-jump-amid-recession—gangs.

Austin, James, Kelly Dedel Johnson, and Ronald Weitzer. 2005 (September). "Alternatives to the Secure Detention and Confinement of Juvenile Offenders." *OJJDP*. Washington, DC: U.S. Department of Justice.

Babwin, Don. 2010. "Chicago Police See Spike in Cop Killings, Assaults." *Associated Press*, December 4. Available: http://www.streetgangs.com/news/120410_chicago_cop_killings.

Baker, Geoffrey. 2011. "Preachers, Gangsters, Pranksters: MC Solaar and Hip-Hop as Over and Covert Revolt." *The Journal of Popular Culture*, 44(2):233–55.

Baker, Robert A. 2010. "Syracuse Toddler's Death Blamed on Gang Revenge." Available: http://www.syracuse.com/news/index.ssf/2010/12/toddlers_death_blamed_on_gang.html.

Bandura, Albert, and Richard Walters. 1963. *Social Learning and Personality Development*. New York: Holt, Rinehart and Winston.

Barger, Ralph "Sonny." 2001. *Hell's Angels*. New York: Perennial.

Bartollas, Clemens, and Stuart J. Miller. 2001. *Juvenile Justice in America*, 3rd ed. Upper Saddle River, NJ: Prentice Hall.

Basu, Dipa. 1998. "What Is Real About 'Keeping it Real?'" *Postcolonial Studies*, 1(3):371–87.

Becker, Howard. 1963. *Outsiders: Studies in the Sociology of Deviance*. New York: Free Press.

Belknap, Joanne. 2001. *The Invisible Woman: Gender, Crime and Justice*, 2nd ed. Belmont, CA: Wadsworth.

Bennett, Shea. 2012. "Twitter on Track for 500 Million Users by March, 250 Million Active Users by End of 2012." Available:http://www.mediabistro.com/alltwitter/twitter-active-total-users_b17655.

Berry, Bonnie. 1998. "Criminal Criminologist Newsletter." Available: http://www.sun.soci.niu.edu.

Best, Joel, and David F. Luckenbill. 1994. *Organizing Deviance*, 2nd ed. Englewood Cliffs, NJ: Prentice Hall.

Bing, Leon. 2001a. "Do or Die," in *Gangs*. Ed. Sean Donohue. New York: Thunder's Mouth Press.

———. 2001b. "Homegirls." *Rolling Stone*, April 12:76–86.

Black Celebrity Giving. 2011. "Snoop Youth Football League Partners with Federal Reserve Bank of Chicago to Make Money Smart Kids!" July 27. Available: http://www.blackcelebritygiving.com/2011/07/snoop-youth-football-league-partners-with-federal-reserve-bank-of-chicago-to-make-money-smart-kids/.

Black Celebrity Kids. 2010. "Snoop's Youth Football League: Helping to Keep Kids off the Streets." July 27. Available: http://www.blackcelebkids.com/2010/07/snoops-youth-football-league-helping-to-keep-kids-of-the-streets/.

Black Guerilla Family. 2003. "Activity of the Black Guerilla Family." Available: http://www.knowgangs.com/gang_resources/black_guerilla_family/bgf_001.htm.

Black Panther Organization. 2012. "There Is No New Black Panther Party: An Open Letter from the Dr. Huey P. Newton Foundation." Available: http://www.blackpanther.org/newsalert.htm.

Black Panther Party. 1999. "The FBI's War on the Black Panther Party's Southern California Chapter." Available: http://www.itsabouttimebbp.com/Chapter_History/FBI_War_LA_Chapter.html.

Black Perspective and Introspection. 2005. "Repping Your Gang Affiliation in Hip Hop." Available: http://blackintrospection.blogspot.com/2005/01/repping-your-gang-affiliation-in-hip.html.

Blankstein, Andrew. 2011. "2 Charge with Violating Skid Row Injunction." *Los Angeles Times*, November 18. Available: http://articles.latimes.com/print/2011/nov/18/local/la-me-downtown-drugs-20111118.

Bilchik, Shay. 1998. "Youth Gangs: An Overview." *Journal Justice Bulletin: Office of Juvenile Justice and Delinquency Prevention*. Washington, DC: U.S. Department of Justice.

Billings Gazette. 1995. "Nuke Photos of Students Off Limits," January 21:1A.

Bjerregard, B., and C. Smith. 1993. "Gender Differences in Gang Participation, Delinquency and Substance Abuse." *Journal of Quantitative Criminology*, 4:329–55.

Block, Carolyn R., and Richard Block. 1993. "Street Gang Crime in Chicago." Washington, DC: National Institute of Justice, U.S. Department of Justice. Research in Brief.

Blumenthal, Ralph. 1990. "The City's Rough Past: Frighteningly Familiar." *The New York Times*, August 26. Available: http://www.nytimes.com/1990/08/26/weekinreview/the-region-the-city-s-rough-past-frighteningly-familar.html?pagewanted=3&src=pm.

Booth, Martin. 1999. *The Dragon Syndicates: The Global Phenomenon of the Triads*. New York: Oxford.

Booton, Jennifer. 2011. "From the Streets to Cyberspace: U.S. Gangs Turn to White-Collar Crime." *Fox Business*, October 28. Available: http://www.foxbusiness.com/technology/2011/10/28/from-streets-to-cyberspace-us-gangs-turn-to-white-collar-crime/.

Borges, Jorge Luis. 2002. "Monk Eastman, Purveyor of Iniquities," in *Gangs*. Ed. Sean Donohue. New York: Thunder's Mouth Press.

Bracken, Michael B., and Stanislav K. Kasl. 1975. "First and Repeat Abortions: A Study of Decision-Making and Delay." *Journal of Biosocial Science*, 7:374–491.

Brignall, Robert. 2009. "Feds, State Help Detroit Police Fight Violent Gangs." *Detroit Crime Examiner*, September 11. Available: http://www.examiner.com/crime-in-detroit/feds-state-help-detroit-police-fight-violent-gangs.

Brooks, David. 2012. "Confronting the Killer Within Us." Syndicated column as it appeared in the *Post-Standard*, March 21:A-12.

Bruce, Christopher W. 2008. "Police Strategies and Tactics: What Every Analyst Should Know." *International Association of Crime Analysts*, July 31. Available: http://www.iaca.net/Resources/Articles/PoliceStrategiesTactics.pdf.

Buffalo News. 1999. "Gang Members Indicted in Drug and Murder Case," March 5:B4.

Burch, J., and C. Kane. 1999. *Implementing the OJJDP Comprehensive Gang Model*. Fact Sheet. Washington, DC: U.S. Department of Justice, Office of Justice Programs, Office of Juvenile Justice and Delinquency Prevention.

Bureau of Alcohol, Tobacco, Firearms and Explosives (ATF). 2009. "New York Field Division." Available: http://www.atf.gov/field/newyork/.

Bureau of Justice Statistics. 2012. "Recidivism: Summary Findings." Available: http://bjs.ojp.usdoj.gov/index.cfm?ty=tp&tid=17.

Bureau of Labor Statistics. 2012. "Manufacturing: NAICS 31-33." Available: http://www.bls.gov/iag/tgs/iag31-33.htm#workforce.

Burke, Daniel. 2012. "How a Dogg Became a Lion." *Daily Breeze*, August 4:A13.

Burnett, Sara. 2011. "Gangs Linked to Heists as Metro-Denver Bank Robberies Rise 25%." *Denver Post*, May 31. Available: http://www.denverpost.com/news/ci_18172487.

Bussey, Timothy R. 2012. "Gang-Related Crimes/Affiliation." The Law Office of Timothy R. Bussey. Available: http://www.coloradospringsjuvenileattorneys.com/gang-related-crimes.html.

Butterfield, Fox. 2005. "Boston Street Gangs Master Intimidation." January 16, as it appeared in *The Seattle Times*. Available: http://seattletimes.nwsource.com/html/nationworld/2002152199_gangs16.html.

Bynum, Timothy S., and Sean P. Varano. 2003. "The Anti-Gang Initiative in Detroit," in *Policing Gangs and Youth Violence*. Ed. Scott H. Decker. Belmont, CA: Wadsworth.

California Youth Outreach. 2010. "Our Mission Statement." Available: http://www.cyoutreach.org/01/index.html.

_____. 2012. "Bible Resources." Available: http://www.cathedral-offaith.org/min_community.html.

Callanan, Valerie J. 2012. "Media Consumption, Perceptions of Crime Risk and Fear of Crime: Examining Race/Ethnic Differences." *Sociological Perspectives*, 55(1):93–115.

Campbell, Anne. 1984. *The Girls in the Gang*. New York: Basic Blackwell.

_____. 1987. "Self Definition by Rejection: The Case of Girl Gangs," in *Female Gangs in America*. Ed. Meda Chesney-Lind and John M. Hagedorn. Chicago, IL: Lake View Press.

Campo-Flores, Arian. 2003. "Gangland's New Face: The South Sees a Surge in Violence by Latino Groups." *Newsweek*, December 8.

Carelli, Richard. 1999. "Chicago Anti-Loitering Law Against Gangs Struck Down." *Buffalo News*, June 10:A1.

Carlson, Peter. 2003. "Tupac's Mother Quite Radical Herself." *The Post-Standard*, October 20:D4.

Carter, Chelsea J. 1999. "One Time Miscreants Turn Talents Elsewhere by Making Legitimate Art Out of American Graffiti." *Buffalo News*, January 10:A13.

_____. 2004. "Why Did the 91-Year-Old Man Rob Banks?" *The Post-Standard*, March 28:A13.

Cartwright, Duncan. 2002. *Psychoanalysis, Violence, and Rage-Type Murder*. New York: Brunnel-Routledge.

Case, Dick. 2003. "New Yorkers Need Guts to Clean Albany Slate." *The Post-Standard*, October 11:B1.

Castorena, Deanne. 1998. *The History of the Gang Injunction in California*. Los Angeles, CA: Los Angeles Police Department Hardcore Gang Division.

CBS News. 2009. "Tookie Williams Is Executed." February 11. Available: http://www.cbsnews.com/2100-201_162-1121576.html.

Center for Problem-Oriented Policing. 2012. "Witness Intimidation." Available: http://www.popcenter.org/problems/witness_intimidation/.

Center for Substance Abuse Treatment. 2005. *Treatment Improvement Protocol (TIP), Series, No 44.* Rockville, MD: Substance Abuse and Mental Health Services Administration. Available: http://www.ncbi.nlm.nih.gov/books/NBK64145/.

Center on Juvenile and Criminal Justice. 2012. "Homepage: About Us." Available: http://www.cjcj.org/about_us.

Centers for Disease Control and Prevention. 2009. "Press Release." November 12. Available: www.cdc.gov/media/press-rel/2009/r091112.htm.

———. 2010. "Alcohol Use." Available: http://www.cdc.gov/healthyyouth/alcoholdrug/index.htm.

———. 2011a. "Youth Violence National and State Statistics at a Glance." Available: http://www.cdc.gov/ViolencePrevention/youthviolence/stats_at-a_glance/index.html.

———. 2011b. "Youth Violence: National Statistics." Available: http://www.cdc.gov/ViolencePrevention/youthviolence/stats_at-a_glance/hr_trends.html.

———. 2011c. "Youth Violence: National Statistics." Available: http://www.cdc.gov/ViolencePrevention/youthviolence/stats_at-a_glance/hr_male.html.

Central Cedar Rapids Weed and Seed. 2012. "Latest Weed and Seed Information." Available: http://www.crweedandseed.com/.

Century, Douglas. 2004. "Big Trouble in Little China." *Blender*, April: 82–88.

Chamberlain, Ted. 2003. " 'Gangs of New York': Fact vs. Fiction." *National Geographic News*. Available: http://news.nationalgeographic.com/news/pf/26219736.html.

Chambliss, William. 1964. "A Sociological Analysis of the Law of Vagrancy." *Social Problems*, 12:67–77.

———. 1993. "State Organized Crime," in *Making Law: The State, the Law and Structural Contradictions*. Ed. William J. Chambliss and Majorie Zatz. Bloomington, IN: Indiana University Press.

———. 1998. *On the Take*, 2nd ed. Bloomington, IN: Indiana University Press.

Chambliss, William, and Robert Seidman. 1971. *Law, Order, and Power*. Reading, MA: Addison-Wesley.

Champion, Dean John. 2004. *The Juvenile Justice System*, 4th ed. Upper Saddle River, NJ: Prentice Hall.

Cheektowaga Times. 2003. "Police Are Alerted to Gang's Agenda," December 18:1. Available: http://www.cheektowatimes.com/News/2003/1218/Front_Page/004.html.

Chesney-Lind, Meda. 1997. *The Female Offender: Girls, Women, and Crime*. Thousand Oaks, CA: Sage.

Chesney-Lind, Meda, and Randall G. Shelden. 2004. *Girls, Delinquency and Juvenile Justice*, 3rd ed. Belmont, CA: Wadsworth.

Chesterton, Gilbert K. 1994. *Orthodoxy*. Published by Project Guttenberg and available: http://www.gutenberg.org/cache/epub/130/pg130.html.

Chicago Area Project. 2012a. "About Chicago Area Project." Available: http://www.chicagoareaproject.org/about-us.

———. 2012b. "Programs." Available: http://www.chicagoareaproject.org/programs.

Chin, K. 1986. *Chinese Triad Societies, Tongs, Organized Crime, and Street Gangs in Asia and the United States*. Ann Arbor, MI: University Microfilms International.

Chin, Ko-Lin. 1990. *Chinese Subculture and Criminality: Non-traditional Crime Groups in America*. Westport, CT: Greenwood.

———. 1996. *Chinatown Gangs: Extortion, Enterprise, and Ethnicity*. New York: Oxford.

Chron.com. 2009. "Texas on the Potomac: Washington News with a Texas Accent." Available: http://blog.chron.com/txpotomac/2009/07/galveston-gets-stimulus-police-grants-houston-left-out/.

City Attorney of Los Angeles. 2011. "Case No. BC435316: Amended Judgment Granting Permanent Injunction, Set 1." Filed February 1, in the Superior Court of the State of California for the County of Los Angeles.

City-Data.com. 2012a. "Crime in Buffalo, New York (NY): Murders, Rapes, Robberies, Assaults, Burglaries, Theft, Auto Thefts, Arson, Law Enforcement Employees, Police Officers." Available: http://www.city-data.com/crime/crime-Buffalo-New-York.html.

———. 2012b. "Crime in Rochester, New York (NY): Murders, Rapes, Robberies, Assaults, Burglaries, Theft, Auto Thefts, Arson, Law Enforcement Employees, Police Officers." Available: http://www.city-data.com/crime/crime-Rochester-New-York.html.

CityRating.com. 2012a. "Buffalo Crime Rate Report." Available: http://www.cityrating.com/crime-statistics/new-york/buffalo.html.

———. 2012b. "Rochester Crime Rate Report." Available: http://www.cityrating.com/crime-statistics/new-york/rochester.html.

———. 2012c. "Syracuse Crime Rate Report." Available: http://www.cityrating.com/crime-statistics/new-york/syracuse.html.

City of Rochester. 2009. "News Release: Richard Vega to Retire as City Public Integrity Director." December 4. Available:http://www.cityofrochester.gov/article.aspx?id=8589940745.

City of Rochester Comprehensive Plan. 2002. "Comprehensive Annual Financial Report." Available: http://search.aol.com/aol/search?s_it=topsearchbox.search&v_t=comsearch50ct16&q=City+of+Rochester+Comprehensive+Plan%2C+1999.

City of Stockton. 2012. "Graffiti Removal." Available: http://www.stocktongov.com/government/departments/police/psGraf.html.

City of Syracuse. 2012. "Westside." Available: http://www.syracuse.ny.us/Home_Westside.aspx.

Cloward, Richard. 1959. "Illegitimate Means, Anomie, and Deviant Behavior." *American Sociological Review*, 24:164–76.

Cloward, Richard, and Lloyd Ohlin. 1960. *Delinquency and Opportunity: A Theory of Delinquent Gangs*. New York: Free Press.

CNN. 2005. "Marine on Liberty Dies in Gun Battle with Police." January 12. Available: http://articles.cnn.com/2005-01-11/us/marine.shooting_1_sam-ryno-andres-raya-police-officer?_s=PM:US.

Coakley, Jay. 2001. *Sport in Society*, 7th ed. Boston, MA: McGraw Hill.

Cohen, Albert. 1955. *Delinquent Boys: The Culture of the Gang*. New York: Free Press.

Cohen, Rich. 2002. "Tough Jews," in *Gangs*. Ed. Sean Donohue. New York: Thunder's Mouth Press.

Cohen, Stanley. 1980. *Folk Devils and Moral Panics: The Creation of the Gang*. Glencoe, IL: Free Press.

Coldren, James R., and Daniel F. Higgins. 2003. "Evaluating Nuisance Abatement at Gang and Drug Houses in Chicago," in *Policing Gangs and Youth Violence*. Ed. Scott H. Decker. Belmont, CA: Wadsworth.

Colorado Department of Natural Resources. 2003. "Help Catch a Thief and Preserve the Future of Hunting." Available: http://www.dnr.state.co.us/news/press.

Commonwealth of Virginia Department of State Police. 2008. "Bloods Street Gang Intelligence Report." November. Available: http://info.publicintelligence.net/BloodsStreetGangIntelligenceReport.pdf.

Commonwealth of Virginia Office of Attorney General. 2011. "Gangs in Virginia: Resources and Information for Citizens of the Commonwealth." Available: http://www.ag.virginia.gov/Programs%20and%20Resources/Gangs/GANGS_Wrong_Family.html.

Connors, Dennis. 2012. "Black History Month: Riots Targeting African Americans Among Darkest Days of Civil War." *The Post-Standard*, February 23:A-6.

_____. 2012a. "Community Relations Section." Available: http://www.cookcountysheriff.org/sheriffs_police/ccspd_Patrol_CommunityRelations.html.

Cook County Sheriff's Department. 2012b. "Police and Children Together (PACT) Camp." Available: http://www.cookcountysheriff.org/backup/jail_diversion/youthservices_specialprojects_pact.html.

Cooley, Charles. 1909. *Social Organization*. New York: Scribner.

Corrections One. 2012. "Deputy Pleads No Contest in Burrito Drug Smuggling." May 1. Available: http://www.correctionsone.com/contraband/articles/5483232-Deputy-pleads-no-contest-in-burrito-drug-smuggling/.

Coventry, Andrea. 2007. "FBI's 30th Most Dangerous City: Rochester, New York." Available: http://voices.yahoo.com/fbis-30th-most-dangerous-city-rochester-york-667803.html?cat=17.

Covey, Herbert C., Scott Menard, and Robert J. Franzese. 1992. *Juvenile Gangs*. Springfield, IL: Charles C. Thomas.

Criminal Justice Degrees Schools. 2012. "Gang Criminal Justice Directory." Available: http://www.criminaljusticedegree-schools.com/criminal-justice-resources/gang-directory/.

Crip History. 2003. "Crip History." Available: http://www.36rovals.8m.com/crip.

CTVNews. 2012. "Gang Ties Possible in Eaton Centre Shooting: Police." CTVNews.ca, June 3. Available: http://www.ctv.ca/CTVNews/Canada/20120603/toronto-police-eaton-centre-shooting-investigation-120603/.

Cuccinelli II, Kenneth (Attorney General of Virginia). 2012a. "Gangs: Richmond Gang Reduction and Intervention Program." Available:http://www.oag.state.va.us/Programs%20and%20Resources/GRIP/index.html.

_____. 2012b. "GRIP: Strategies." Available: http://www.oag.state.va.us/Programs%20and%20Resources/GRIP/GRIP_Strategies.html.

Cummings, Melbourne S., and Abhik Roy. 2002. "Manifestations of Afrocentricity in Rap Music." *Howard Journal of Communications*, 13:59–76.

Curran, Daniel, and Claire Renzetti. 1994. *Theories of Crime*. Boston, MA: Allyn & Bacon.

Curry, G. David. 1998. "Female Gang Involvement." *Journal of Research in Crime and Delinquency*, 35(1):100–18.

Curry, G. David, and Scott H. Decker. 2003. *Confronting Gangs: Crime and Community*, 2nd ed. Los Angeles, CA: Roxbury.

Curtis, Henry Pierson. 2010. "Crips Gang Rape: Attack on Young Woman Highlights Osceola County's Gang Problem." *Orlando Sentinel*, May 12. Available: http://articles.orlandosentinel.com/2010-05-12/news/os-gang-rape-kissimmee-20100511_1_crips-gang-gang-problem-street-gangs.

Daily Herald. 2011. "How Many Native American Tribes Are in the U.S.?" June 7. Available: http://www.dailyherald.com/article/20110607/news/706079944/.

Daily Mail. 2011. "Teenager Who Lied to Her Fiancé About Being Pregnant Enlisted Two Gang Members to Steal Her Friend's Baby so She Could Pass It Off as Her Own," December 4. Available: http://www.gossiprocks.com/forum/crime-punishment/167556-girl-enlists-gang-members-steal-baby.html.

Dale, Alzina Stone. 1997/2002. *Mystery Readers Walking Guide: New York*. (Originally published by Passport Books.) Available: http://books.google.com/books?id=BLJtOzQHjggC&pg=PA26&lpg=PA26&dq=%22five+points%22+%22al+capone%22+%22never+left%22&source=web&ots=DlE_68fTze&sig=Edx0CN-Df0QFCCk5Me30xcM0B8w#v=onepage&q=%22five%20points%22%20%22al%20capone%22%20%22never%20left%22&f=false.

Daniels, Douglas Henry. 1997. "Los Angeles Zoot: Race 'Riot,' the Pachuco, and Black Music Culture." *Journal of Negro History*, 82(2, Spring):201–20.

Danitz, Tiffany. 1998. "The Gangs Behind Bars." *Insight on the News*. Available: http://www.findarticles.com.

Dannen, Fredric. 2002. "Bo Ying," in *Gangs*. Ed. Sean Donohue. New York: Thunder's Mouth Press.

Davis, M. 1992. *City of Quartz*. New York: Vintage Books.

Davis, N. 1999. *Youth Crisis*. Westport, CT: Praeger.

Davis, Roger H. 1995. "Cruising for Trouble: Gang-Related Drive-By Shootings." *The FBI Enforcement Bulletin*, 64(1):16–23.

Dawley, David. 1992. *A Nation of Lords: The Autobiography of the Vice Lords*, 2nd ed. Prospect Heights, IL: Waveland.

Death Penalty Information Center. 2012. "New York's Death Penalty Law Declared Unconstitutional DPIC Summary: People v. Stephen LaValle." Available: http://www.deathpenaltyinfo.org/node/1199.

Decker, Scott H. and G. David Curry. 2002. "Gangs," pp. 755–760 in Encyclopedia of Crime and Punishment, Vol. 2. Thousand Oaks, CA: Sage.

Decker, Scott H. 2004. "Legitimating Drug Use," in *Understanding Contemporary Gangs in America*. Ed. Rebecca D. Petersen. Upper Saddle River, NJ: Prentice Hall.

Decker, Scott H., and Barrik van Winkle. 1996. *Life in the Gang: Family, Friends, and Violence*. New York: Cambridge University Press.

Decker, Scott H., and G. David Curry. 2002. "Gangs," pp. 755–60 in *Encyclopedia of Crime and Punishment*, Vol. 2. Thousand Oaks, CA: Sage.

_____. 2003. "Suppression Without Prevention, Prevention Without Suppression," in *Policing Gangs and Youth Violence*. Ed. Scott H. Decker. Belmont, CA: Wadsworth.

Delaney, Tim. 2001. *Community, Sport, and Leisure*. Auburn, NY: Legend Books.

_____. 2004a. *Classical Social Theory: Investigation and Application.* Upper Saddle River, NJ: Prentice Hall.

_____. 2004b. "The Russian Mafia in the United States," in *Social Diseases: Mafia, Terrorism and Totalitarianism.* Ed. Tim Delaney, Valerii Kuvakin, and Tim Madigan. Moscow, Russia: Russian Humanist Society Press.

_____. 2005. *Contemporary Social Theory: Investigation and Application.* Upper Saddle River, NJ: Prentice Hall.

_____. 2006. *Seinology: The Sociology of Seinfeld.* Amherst, NY: Prometheus.

_____. 2012. *Connecting Sociology to Our Lives: An Introduction to Sociology.* Boulder, CO: Paradigm.

Delaney, Tim, and Allene Wilcox. 2002. "Sports and the Role of the Media," in *Values, Society & Evolution.* Ed. Tim Delaney. Auburn, NY: Legend Books.

Delaney, Tim, and Tim Madigan. 2009. *The Sociology of Sports: An Introduction.* Jefferson, NC: McFarland.

Delgadillo, Rocky. 2008. "Going Global to Fight Gangs." *Los Angeles Times,* August 18. Available: http://www.latimes.com/news/opinion/commentary/la-oe-delgadillo18-2008aug18,0,3286181.story.

Denfeld, Rene. 2006. "Inside the EK: Born in Prison, the European Kindred Leaves Its Mark on Both Sides of the Bars." *The Portland Tribune,* November 3. Available: http://www.portlandtribune.com/news/story.php?story_id=116251110953381300.

Denver ABC News. 2004. "Carmelo Anthony Featured in a Drug Video." December 2. Available: http://www.thedenverchannel.com/sports/3967329/detail.html.

Denver Westword News. 2011. "Raped and Extorted by a Prison Gang, Scott Howard was Called a 'Drama Queen' by Corrections Officials." Available: http://www.westword.com/2011-02-03/news/211-crew-rapes-extorts-scott-howard-colorado-prison/.

Department of Correction, State of Connecticut. 2011. "Garner Correctional Institution." Available: http://www.ct.gov/doc/cwp/view.asp?a=1499&q=265410.

Deschenes, Elizabeth Piper, and Finn-Aage Esbensen. 2001. "Violence Among Girls: Does Gang Membership Make a Difference," in *Female Gangs in America.* Ed. Meda Chesney-Lind and John M. Hagedorn. Chicago, IL: Lake View Press.

Detention Diversion Advocacy Center (DDAP). 2012. "Detention Diversion Advocacy Program: Overview." Available: http://www.cjcj.org/detention_diversion_advocacy_program.

Dickens, Charles. 1842. *American Notes for General Circulation.* Echo Library. Available: http://www.amazon.com/American-General-Circulation-Charles-Dickens/dp/1406800570/ref=sr_1_2?s=books&ie=UTF8&qid=1331482556&sr=1-2.

Dishion, Thomas J., Sarah E. Nelson, and Miwa Yasui. 2005. "Predicting Early Adolescent Gang Involvement from Middle School Adaptation." *Journal of Clinical Child and Adolescent Psychology,* 34(1):62–73.

Ditota, Donna. 2012. "Scoop, A Player Transformed: From Dangerous Streets to a Career to Celebrate." *The Post-Standard,* March 1:B1–B2.

Dohrmann, George. 2008a. "How Dreams Die." *Sports Illustrated,* June 30: 54–57, 59–60.

_____. 2008b. "The Hardest Loss." *Sports Illustrated,* June 30: 58–59.

Donahue, Sean. 2001. *Gangs: Stories of Life and Death from the Streets.* New York: Thunder's Mouth Press.

Dorais, Michel, and Patrice Corriveau. 2009. *Gangs and Girls: Understanding Juvenile Prostitution.* Montreal: McGill-Queen's University Press.

Dowdy, Zachary R. 2004. "Patchwork of Gang Violence." *Newsday.com,* October 14. Available: http://www.newsday.com.

Duffy, Lori. 1996a. "Expert Says Gangs Offer Acceptance." *The Post-Standard,* November 7:A16.

_____. 1996b. "Shootings Spark Concerns About Role of Latin Kings." *The Post-Standard,* November 7:A1.

Eghigian, Mars, and Katherine Kirby. 2006. "Girls in the Gangs: On the Rise in America." A report for the Chicago Crime Commission. Available: http://www.aca.org/fileupload/177/prasannak/Eghigian-Kirby-21.pdf.

Egley, Jr., Arlen, and Christina E. O'Donnell. 2006. "OJJDP Fact Sheet: Highlights of the 2006 National Youth Gang Survey." Washington, DC: U.S. Department of Justice. Available: https://www.ncjrs.gov/pdffiles1/ojjdp/fs200805.pdf.

Egley, Jr., Arlen, and Christina E. Ritz. 2006. *Highlights of the 2004 National Youth Gang Survey* (OJJDP Fact Sheet). Washington, DC: U.S. Department of Justice Office of Juvenile and Delinquency Prevention.

Egley, Jr., Arlen, and James C. Howell. 2011a. *Highlights of the 2009 National Youth Gang Survey.* Washington, DC: Office of Juvenile Justice and Delinquency Prevention.

Egley, Jr., Arlen, and James C. Howell. 2011b (June). "OJJDP Fact Sheet: Highlights of the 2009 National Youth Gang Survey." Available: http://www.ncjrs.gov/pdffiles1/ojjdp/233581.pdf.

Egley, Jr., Arlen, Cheryl L. Maxson, Jody Miller, and Malcolm W. Klein. 2006. *The Modern Gang Reader,* 3rd ed. Los Angeles, CA: Roxbury.

Egley, Jr., Arlen, James C. Howell, and A. K. Major. 2006. *National Youth Gang Survey: 1999–2001.* Washington, DC: U.S. Department of Justice, Office of Juvenile Justice and Delinquency Prevention.

Elon University. 2012. "Greek Life: History of Greek Life in the United States." Available: http://www.elon.edu/e-web/students/greek_life/glhistory.xhtml.

Elsner, Alan. 2003. "Gang Violence Rising on Indian Reservation in S.D." *USA Today,* December 23:13A.

Empey, Lamar. 1982. *American Delinquency,* rev. ed. Lexington, MA: D. C. Heath.

Encyclopedia Americana—International Edition. 1998. Danbury, CT: Grolier.

Encyclopedia.com. 2009. "Violence and Gangs." Available: http://www.encyclopedia.com/topic/Violence_and_Gangs.aspx.

English, T. J. 1995. *Born to Kill.* New York: William Morrow and Company.

Epatko, Larisa. 2012. "Legalizing Drugs: Why Some Latin American Leaders Are Ok with It." PBS. April 16. Available: http://www.pbs.org/newshour/rundown/2012/04/legalizing-drugs.html.

Erlewine, Stephen Thomas. 2012. "Snoop Dogg: Biography." *Allmusic.* Available: http://www.allmusic.com/artist/snoop-dogg-mn0000029086.

Ernst, Tom. 2002. "Program Seeks to Deter Growth of Gangs." *Buffalo News,* March 22:B3.

Esbensen, Finn-Aage. 2000 (September). "Preventing Adolescent Gang Involvement." *Juvenile Justice Bulletin*. Washington, DC: Office of Juvenile Justice and Delinquency Prevention (OJJDP).

Esbensen, Finn-Aage, Dana Peterson, Terrance J. Taylor, Adrienne Freng, D. Wayne Osgood, Dena C. Carson, and Kristy Matsuda. 2011. "Evaluation and Evolution of the Gang Resistance Education and Training (G.R.E.A.T.) Program." *Journal of School Violence*, 10:53–70.

Esbensen, Finn-Aage, and D. W. Osgood. 1997. *National Evaluation of G.R.E.A.T.* Washington, DC: U.S. Department of Justice, National Institute of Justice.

Esbensen, Finn-Aage, Elizabeth Piper Deschenes, and L. Thomas Winfree, Jr. 2004. "Differences Between Gang Girls and Gang Boys," in *Understanding Contemporary Gangs in America*. Ed. Rebecca D. Petersen. Upper Saddle River, NJ: Prentice Hall.

Essex County Prosecutor's Office. 2012. "VIPER Gang—Narcotics Task Force." Available: http://www.njecpo.org/narcotics.htm.

Estrich, Susan. 1995. "Public Cheers Killer as Justice Fails." *USA Today*, February 9: 11A.

Ewen, R. B. 1988. *An Introduction to Theories of Personality*. Hillsdale, NJ: Lawrence Erlbaum Associates.

Fagan, Jeffrey. 1996. "Gangs, Drugs, and Neighborhood Change," in *Gangs in America*, 2nd ed. Ed. C. R. Huff. Thousand Oaks, CA: Sage.

———. 2004. "Gangs, Drugs, and Neighborhood Change," in *Understanding Contemporary Gangs in America*. Ed. Rebecca D. Petersen. Upper Saddle River, NJ: Prentice Hall.

Farley, John. 1998. *Sociology*, 4th ed. Upper Saddle River, NJ: Prentice Hall.

Farley, Reynolds, Sheldon Danziger, and Harry J. Holzer. 2000. *Detroit Divided*. New York: Russell Sage Foundation.

Faturechi, Robert. 2011. "Gang Tattoo Leads to a Murder Conviction." *Los Angeles Times*, April 22. Available: http://articles.latimes.com/2011/apr/22/local/la-me-tattoo-20110422.

Faturechi, Robert, and Jack Leonard. 2012. "Heroin in a Burrito Allegedly Smuggled by L.A. County Deputy into Courthouse Jail." *Los Angeles Times*, January 12. Available: http://articles.latimes.com/2012/jan/12/local/la-me-deputy-smuggling-20120112.

Favro, Tony. 2009. "Youth Curfews Popular with American Cities but Effectiveness and Legality Are Question." *City Mayors Society*, 13. Available: http://www.citymayors.com/society/usa-youth-curfews.html.

Federal Bureau of Investigation (FBI). 2001. "Law Enforcement Bulletin." Available: http://www.fbi.gov/stats-services/publications/law-enforcement-bulletin/2001-pdfs/dec01leb.pdf.

———. 2005. "Serial Murder: Multi-Disciplinary Perspectives for Investigators." Available: http://www.fbi.gov/stats-services/publications/serial-murder.

———. 2006. "Crime in the United States, 2004." *Uniform Crime Reports*. Available: http://www2.fbi.gov/ucr/cius_04/offenses_reported/violent_crime/murder.html.

———. 2009a. "Anti-Gang Effort Leads to Hefty Sentences as 10 Members and Associates of the Texas Syndicate Street/Prison Gang Sentenced." Available: http://www.fbi.gov/houston/press-releases/2009/ho092309.htm.

———. 2009b. "Crime in the United States 2009: Burglary." Available: http://www2.fbi.gov/ucr/cius2009/offenses/property_crime/burglary.html.

———. 2009c. "Fourteen Motorcycle Gang Leaders and Members Plead Guilty in Detroit to Violent Crime, Drug and Firearms Charges." Available: http://www.fbi.gov/detroit/press-releases/2009/de073009.htm.

———. 2009d. "National Gang Threat Assessment 2009." Available: http://www.fbi.gov/stats-services/publications/national-gang-threat-assessment-2009-pdf.

———. 2009e. "Sharing Intelligence to Fight Transnational Gangs." August 11. Available: http://www.fbi.gov/news/stories/2009/august/gangs_081109.

———. 2009f. "RICO Indictment Expands Case Against Clique of 18th Street Gang Involved in Murder of 3-Week-Old Child, a Cold Case Murder Committed in 2001, and Other Crimes." June 16. Available: http://www.fbi.gov/losangels/press-releases/2009/la061609.htm.

———. 2010a. "Crime in the United States 2010: Larceny-Theft. Available: http://www.fbi.gov/about-us/cjis/ucr/crime-in-the-u.s/2010/crime-in-the-u.s.-2010/property-crime/larcenytheftmain.

———. 2010b. "Crime in the United States 2010: Motor Vehicle Theft." Available: http://www.fbi.gov/about-us/cjis/ucr/crime-in-the-u.s/2010/crime-in-the-u.s.-2010/property-crime/mvtheftmain.

———. 2010c. "Defendants Receive Lengthy Sentences in Major Drug Trafficking Conspiracy." Available: http://www.fbi.gov/dallas/press-releases/2010/dl012110.htm.

———. 2010d. "Founding Member of White Supremacist Prison Gang European Kindred (EK) Sentenced to 90 Months in Federal Prison Metro Gang Task Force Investigation Results in Two Portland Residents Convicted of Providing a Firearm to a Convicted Felon." Available: http://www.fbi.gov/portland/press-releases/2010/pd020910.htm.

———. 2010e. "Major Gang Takedown: 78 Bloods, Latin Kings Indicted." Available: http://www.fbi.gov/news/stories/2010/may/gangs_051310.

———. 2010f. "Member of the Krazy Locos Criminal Street Gang Sentenced to Life Imprisonment Following Convictions for Two Homicides, Robbery, and Firearms Charges." Available: http://www.fbi.gov/miami/pressreleases/2010/mm102210a.htm.

———. 2010g. "Nearly 100 Alleged Traveling Vice Lords Street Gang Members and Associates Facing State or Federal Narcotics Charges." November 17. Available: http://www.fbi.gov/chicago/press-releases/2010/cg111710a.htm.

———. 2010h. "Twenty-Seven Members of American Outlaw Association Motorcycle Gang Indicted." Available: http://www.fbi.gov/boston/press-releases/2010/bs061510a.htm.

———. 2011a. "2011 National Gang Threat Assessment—Emerging Trends." Available: http://www.fbi.gov/stats-services/publications/2011-national-gang-threat-assessment.

———. 2011b. "BGF Leader Sentenced to over 12 Years in Prison for Participating in a Racketeering Conspiracy." Available:http://www.fbi.gov/baltimore/press-releases/2011/bgf-leader-sentenced-to-over-12-years-inprison-for-participating-in-a-racketeering-conspiracy.

———. 2011c. "Eight Members of Miami Garden Gang Convicted of Narcotics, Firearms, and Identity Theft Charges." Available:http://www.fbi.gov/miami/press-releases/2011/eight-members-of-miami-gardens-gangconvicted-of-narcotics-firearms-and-identity-theft-charges.

_____. 2011d. "Eleven Gang Members and Associates Indicted Federally." November 10. Available: http://www.fbi.gov/saltlakecity/press-releases/2011/elevengang-members-and-associates-indicted-federally.

_____. 2011e. "Federal, State and Local Authorities Arrest 23 Hondo and Uvalde-Based Texas Syndicate Members and Associates." Available: http://www.fbi.gov/sanantonio/press-releases/2011/federal-state-and-local-authorities-arrest-23-hondo-and-uvalde-based-texas-syndicate-members-and-associates.

_____. 2011f. "Forty-One Gang Members and Associates in Five Districts Charged with Crimes Including Racketeering, Murder, Drug Trafficking, and Firearms Trafficking." Available: http://www.fbi.gov/news/pressrel/press-releases/forty-one-gang-members-and-associates-in-five-districtscharged-with-crimes-including-racketeering-murderdrug-trafficking-and-firearms-trafficking.

_____. 2011g. "Leader of the Krazy Locos Criminal Street Gang and Five Gang Associates Sentenced on Charges Related to Two Homicides, Robbery, Narcotics, Firearms, and Obstruction of Justice." Available: http://www.fbi.gov/miami/press-releases/2011/leader-of-the-krazylocos-criminal-street-gang-and-five-gang-associatessentenced-on-harges-related-to-two-omicides-robbery-narcotics-firearms-and-obstruction-of-justice.

_____. 2011h. "Member of Aryan Brotherhood Sentenced to 450 Months in Prison in Connection with Hate Crime Involving Church Arson and Attempted Murder of Disabled African-American in Texas." Available: http://www.fbi.gov/elpaso/press-releases/2011/member-of-aryan-brotherhood-sentenced-to-450-months-in-prison-in-connection-with-hate-crime-involving-church-arson-and-attempted-murder-of-disabled-african-american-in-texas.

_____. 2011i. "Member of United Aryan Brotherhood Pleads Guilty to Hate-Motivated Assault of Jewish Inmate in Texas." Available:http://www.fbi.gov/dallas/press-releases/2011/member-of-united-aryan-brotherhood-pleads-guilty-to-hate-motivated-assault-of-jewish-inmate-in-texas.

_____. 2011j. "Trinitarios Gang Leader Sentenced to 90 Months in Federal Prison." Available: http://www.fbi.gov/boston/press-releases/2011/trinitarios-gang-leader-sentenced-to-90-months-in-federal-prison.

_____. 2011k. "U.S. Attorney for the Southern District of New York Charges 20 Members and Associates of Newburgh-Based Bloods Gang with Racketeering, Murder, Assault, Robbery, and Narcotics Trafficking." Available: http://www.fbi.gov/newyork/press-releases/2011/u.s.-attorney-for-the-southern-district-of-new-york-charges-20-members-and-associates-of-newburgh-based-bloods-gang-with-racketeering-murder-assault-robbery-and-narcotics-trafficking.

_____. 2011l. "Vice Lord Gang Members and Associates Indicted on Drug and Firearms Charges." September 19. Available: http://www.fbi.gov/memphis/press-releases/2011/vice-lord-gang-members-and-associates-indicted-on-drug-and-firearms-charges.

_____. 2012a. "Asian Criminal Enterprises." Available: http://www.fbi.gov/about-us/investigate/organizedcrime/asian.

_____. 2012b. "Crime in the United States: Expanded Homicide Data." Available: http://www.fbi.gov/about-us/cjis/ucr/crime-in-the-u.s/2010/crime-inthe-u.s.-2010/offenses-known-to-law-enforcement/expanded/expandhomicidemain.

_____. 2012c. "Five Members of the MS-13 Street Gang Indicted for Murder, Conspiracy, Assault, and Armed Robbery." January 23. Available: http://www.fbi.gov/newyork/press-releases/2012/five-members-of-the-ms-13-street-gang-indicted-for-murder-conspiracy-assaultand-armed-robbery.

_____. 2012d. "Indictment Returned Charging Three Additional Men in Major Street Gang RICO Conspiracy." April 11. Available:http://www.fbi.gov/indianapolis/press-releases/2012/indictment-returned-charging-three-additional-men-in-major-street-gang-rico-conspiracy.

_____. 2012e. "Latin Kings' Nationwide Leader Augustin Zambrano Sentenced to 60 Years in Prison for RICO Conspiracy and Related Gang Charges." January 11. Available: http://www.fbi.gov/chicago/press-releases/2012/latin-kings-nationwide-leader-augustinzambrano-sentenced-to-60-years-in-prison-for-ricoconspiracy-and-related-gang-crimes.

_____. 2012f. "Leader of Bloods Street Gang Indicted for Racketeering, Including Three Murders and Three Attempted Murders." February 13. Available: http://www.fbi.gov/newyork/press-releases/2012/leader-of-bloodsstreet-gang-indicted-for-racketeering-including-threemurders-and-three-attempted-murders.

_____. 2012g. "Member of the 10th Street Gang Pleads Guilty to Racketeering and Admits Murdering Rival Gang Member." March 26. Available: http://www.fbi.gov/buffalo/press-releases/2012/member-of-10thstreet-gang-pleads-guilty-to-racketeering-and-admitsmurdering-rival-gang-member.

_____. 2012h. "Meth-Dealing Gang Associate Gets 121 Months in Federal Prison." April 25. Available: http://www.fbi.gov/saltlakecity/press-releases/2012/methdealing-gang-associate-gets-121-months-in-federalprison.

_____. 2012i. "Six Charged in Connection with Buffalo Gang Case." March 8. Available: http://www.fbi.gov/buffalo/press-releases/2012/ix-charged-in-connection-with-buffalo-gang-case.

_____. 2012j. "Texas Mexican Mafia Member Sentenced to Federal Prison." Available: http://www.fbi.gov/sanantonio/press-releases/2012/texas-mexican-mafia-member-sentenced-to-federal-prison.

_____. 2012k. "Two Additional Former 10th Street Gang Members Charged with Attempted Murder." March 29. Available: http://www.fbi.gov/buffalo/press-releases/2012/two-additional-former-10th-street-gang-members-charged-with-attempted-murder.

_____. 2012l. "Two Mexican Mafia Members and 117 San Diego County, California Street Gang Members and Associates with Ties to the Mexican Mafia Charged with Racketeering Conspiracy, Drug Trafficking Violations, and Firearms Offenses." Available: http://www.fbi.gov/sandiego/press-releases/2012/two-mexican-mafiamembers-and-117-san-diego-county-californiastreet-gang-members-and-associates-with-ties-tothemexican-mafia-charged-with-racketeering-conspiracydrug-trafficking-violations-and-firearms-offenses.

_____. 2012m. "U.S. Attorney's Office Announces Sentencing, Prosecution of Louisville-Area Cocaine Ring." April 12. Available:http://www.fbi.gov/indianapolis/pressreleases/2012/u.s.-attorneys-office-announces-sentencing-prosecution-of-louisville-area-cocaine-ring.

Feldman, Charles. 2000. "Anti-Gang Units a Casualty of Los Angeles Police Scandal." March 13. Available: http://www.cnn.com.

Feldman, Steven R., Anthony Liguori, Michael Kucenic, Stephen R. Rapp, Alan B. Fleischer, Jr., Wei Lang, and Mandeep Kaur. 2004. "Ultraviolet Exposure Is a Reinforcing Stimulus in Frequent Indoor Tanners." *Journal of the American Academy of Dermatology*, 51(1): 45–51.

Female Gangs. 2003. *Female Gang Member Relationships.* Available: http://www.uic.edu/orgs/kbc/Hagedorn/girlgangs.html.

Filmsite Movie Review. 2012. "West Side Story (1961)." Available: http://www.filmsite.org/wests.html.

Fink, Arthur E. 1938. *Causes of Crime.* New York: A. S. Barnes.

Fiore, Faye. 1997. "Professor Compares a Violent Tribe to Gangs." *Los Angeles Times*, November 30:A1.

Fishman, Laura T. 1995. "Differences Between Gang Girls and Gang Boys," in M. Klein, C. Maxson, and J. Miller, *The Modern Gang Reader.* Los Angeles, CA: Roxbury.

Fiske, Warren. 2008. "Virginia Takes 'Tough Love' Approach with Anti-Gang Video." *The Virginian Pilot*, November 18. Available: http://hamptonroads.com/2008/11/virginia-takes-tough-love-approach-antigang-video.

Fitzgerald, Patrick, and Brian Lambkin. 2008. *Migration in Irish History, 1607–2007.* Basingstoke, England: Palgrave Macmillan

Flanigan, Patrick. 2003a. "Cops Come Down hard on Gang." *Rochester Democrat and Chronicle*, December 22:1A.

_____. 2003b. "Neighborhood Mum on Gang." *Rochester Democrat and Chronicle*, December 23:1A.

Fleisher, Mark S., and Jessie L. Krienert. 2004. "Life-Course Events, Social Networks, and the Emergence of Violence Among Female Gang Members." *Journal of Community Psychology*, 32(5):607–22.

Florida Department of Corrections. 2009. "Gang and Security Threat Group Awareness." Available: http://www.dc.state.fl.us/pub/gangs/index.html

Flowers, R. Barri. 1995. *Female Crime, Criminals and Cellmates: An Exploration of Female Criminality and Delinquency.* Jefferson, NC: McFarland.

Fong, Robert S. 1990. "The Organizational Structure of Prison Gangs: A Texas Case Study." *Federal Probation,* 54(1):36–43.

_____. 1991. "The Detection of Prison Gang Development: An Empirical Assessment." *Federal Probation,* 55(1):66–69.

Fontana, Andrea. 1973. "Labeling Theory Reconsidered," in *Outsiders: Studies in the Sociology of Deviance.* Ed. Howard Becker. New York: Free Press.

Ford, Andrea. 1993. "Man Guilty of Gang Counselor's Murder; Courts: Jose Gilbert Gonzalez, 30, Is Convicted of Killing Ana Lizarraga, a Popular Intervention Worker Who Had Been Involved in the Film 'American Me.'" *The Los Angeles Times*, May 11. Available: http://articles.latimes.com/print/1993-05-11/local/me-33972_1_prison-gang.

Ford, Martin. 2008. "The Gangs of Baltimore," *Humanities* (May/June), 29(3). Available: http://www.neh.gov/news/humanities/2008-05/gangs.html.

Forsyth, Jim. 2012. "Snoop Dogg Arrested on Marijuana Charge." *Reuters*, January 9. Available: http://www.reuters.com/article/2012/01/10/us-snoopdogg-idUSTRE80900220120110.

Foster, Brooke Lea, J. Scott Orr, and Laura Laing. 2009. "The Mentally Ill in Prison." *Parade*, June 28:6.

Foster Family-Based Treatment Association. 2004. "What Is Treatment Foster Care?" Available: http://www.ffta.org/whatis.html.

Fox, James, and Jack Levin. 2002. "Mass Murder," in *Encyclopedia of Crime and Punishment.* Ed. David Levinson. Thousand Oaks, CA: Sage.

Fox59 News. 2010. "Agents Nab 14 Suspected Gang Members in Southern Indiana." August 11. Available: http://www.fox59.com/news/wxin-southern-indiana-gang-arrests-081110,0,4489946.story.

Franco, Celinda. 2008. "CRS Report for Congress: The MS-13 and 18th Street Gangs: Emerging Transnational Gang Threats?" Prepared for Members and Committees of Congress, Order Code RL34233. Available: http://www.fas.org/sgp/crs/row/RL34233.pdf.

Fresh Start. 2012. "Employment Training." Available: http://www.livingclassrooms.org/training/fresh-start.html.

Fried, Albert. 1980. *The Rise and Fall of the Jewish Gangster in America.* New York: Holt, Rinehart and Winston.

Friedman, Thomas L. 2012. "Flash: Average Is Officially Over." Syndicated column as it appeared in *The Post-Standard*, January 27:A-12.

Fritsch, Eric J., Tory J. Caeti, and Robert W. Taylor. 2003. "Gang Suppression Through Saturation Patrol and Aggressive Curfew and Truancy Enforcement," in *Policing Gangs and Youth Violence.* Ed. Scott H. Decker. Belmont, CA: Wadsworth.

Gaines, Larry K., and Victor E. Kappeler. 2011. *Policing in America,* 7th ed. Waltham, MA: Elsevier/Anderson Publishing.

Gamiz, Jr., Manuel. 2012. "Street Gang Members Charged in Lehigh Valley Auto Theft Ring." *The Morning Call*, April 5. Available: http://articles.mcall.com/2012-04-05/news/mc-street-gang-members-charged-in-lehigh-valley-au-20120405_1_auto-theft-ring-motor-vehicle-street-gang.

Gang Resistance Education And Training (G.R.E.A.T.) 2012a. "G.R.E.A.T. Middle School Component." Available: http://www.great-online.org/Components/MiddleSchool.Aspx.

_____. 2012b. "G.R.E.A.T. Website." Available: http://www.great-online.org/

Gangland. 2008a. "The Gotti Boyz of New Orleans." First aired on the History Channel as a documentary on November 2, 2008.

Gangland. 2008b. "Maniacal." First aired on the History Channel as a documentary on March 13.

_____. 2009a. "The Death Hand." First aired on the History Channel as a documentary July 9, 2009.

_____. 2009b. "Circle of Death." First aired on the History Channel as a documentary, July 16, 2009.

_____. 2009c. "Ice Cold Killers." First aired on the History Channel as a documentary May 28, 2009.

Gangs of New York. 2002. Distributor: Miramax.

Garrison, Jessica. 2004. "L.A.'s 18th Street Gang Is Hit with Injunction Forbidding Recruiting." *Los Angeles Times*, July 3:B7.

Gearty, Robert, and Bill Hutchinson. 2001. "Sweeping Up Street Gang Bloods, Bloodettes, Indicted." *Daily News*, 7.

Gerbner, George, and Larry Gross. 1976. "Living with Television: The Violence Profile." *Neiman Reports*, 50(3):10–16.

Gifford, Aaron. 2007. "Authorities See More Crimes by Non-Indians from Syracuse Area." *The Post-Standard*, December 3:A-1, A-4.

Giordano, Peggy. 1978. "Girls, Guys and Gangs: The Changing Social Context of Female Delinquency," pp. 90–99 in *Female Gangs in America: Essays on Girls, Gangs and Gender*. Ed. Meda Chesney-Lind and John M. Hagedorn. Chicago, IL: Lake View Press.

Girardot, Frank. 2009. "Florencia 13 Gang Members Guilty in Federal Conspiracy Case." *San Gabriel Valley*, January 12. Available: http://www.insidesocal.com/sgvcrime/2009/01/florencia-13-gang-members-guil.html.

Glazer, Andrew. 2006. "Authorities Say Gangs Using Internet." *The Washington Post*, July 6. Available: http://www.washingtonpost.com/wp-dyn/content/article/2006/07/06/AR2006070600886.html.

Gleeson, David T. 2001. *The Irish in the South, 1815–1877*. Chapel Hill, NC: University of North Carolina Press.

Global Security. 2011. "Mariel Boatlift." Available: http://www.globalsecurity.org/military/ops/mariel-boatlift.htm.

Glod, Maria. 2009. "19 Alleged Gang Members Charged with Assaults, Murder Plots." *Washington Post*, November 20. Available: http://www.streetgangs.com/news/112009_latinkings.

Godbout, Todd M. 1993. "Employment Change and Sectoral Distribution in 10 Countries, 1970–90." *Monthly Labor Review*, October:3–20.

Goldentyer, Debra. 1994. *Gangs*. Austin, TX: Steck-Vaughn.

Goldman, Leah, and Kevin Lincoln. 2011. "The New Most Dangerous Cities in America." *Business Insider*, September 19. Available: http://www.businessinsider.com/most-dangerous-cities-2011-9.

Goldschein, Eric, and Luke McKenna. 2012. "13 American Gangs That Are Keeping the FBI Up at Night." *Business Insider*, January 15. Available: http://www.businessinsider.com/dangerous-american-gangs-fbi-2011-11?op=1.

Goldstein, Arnold P. 1991. *Delinquent Gangs: A Psychological Perspective*. Champaign, IL: Research Press.

Goldstein, H. 1979. Improving Policing: A Problem-Oriented Approach. *Crime & Delinquency*, 25:236–58.

Goode, Erica. 2012. "With Green Beret Tactics, Combating Gang Warfare." *The New York Times*, April 20. Available: http://www.nytimes.com/2012/05/01/us/springfield-mass-fights-crime-using-green-beret-tactics.html?_r=1&pagewanted=all.

Gorman, Sean. 2011. "Anti-Gang Law Signed in 2010." Available: http://www.politifact.com/virginia/promises/bob-o-meter/promise/1003/seek-law-establishing-gang-free-zones/.

Graber, Doris A. 1980. *Crime News and the Public*. New York: Praeger Publishers.

GraffitiHurts.com. 2012. "Get the Facts: Cost of Graffiti." Available: http://www.graffitihurts.org/getfacts/cost.jsp.

Grann, David. 2004. "The Brand: How the Aryan Brotherhood Became the Most Murderous Prison Gang in America." *The New Yorker*, February 16, 23:157–71.

Grant, Elizabeth. 2002. "Gangsta Rap, the War on Drugs and the Location of African-American Identity in Los Angeles, 1988092." *European Journal of American Culture*, 21(1):4–15.

Green, Judith, and Kevin Pranis. 2007. *Gang Wars: The Failure of Enforcement Tactics and the Need for Effective Public Safety Strategies*. Washington, DC: Justice Policy Institute.

Greenberg, Amy Sophia. 1998. *Cause for Alarm: The Volunteer Fire Department in the Nineteenth-Century City*. Princeton, NJ: Princeton University Press.

Grennan, Sean, Marjie T. Britz, Jeffrey Rush, and Thomas Barker. 2000. *Gangs: An International Approach*. Upper Saddle River, NJ: Prentice Hall.

Groeninger, Alissa. 2012. "Emanuel Anti-Gang Law Passes Illinois Senate." *Chicago Tribune*, May 25. Available: http://articles.chicagotribune.com/2012-05-25/news/chi-emanuel-antigang-law-passes-illinois-senate-20120525_1_gang-leaders-mayor-rahm-emanuel-drug-sales.

Grossi, Dave. 2011. "Street Gang Tactics." *Law Officer Police and Law Enforcement*, May 10. Available: http://www.lawofficer.com/article/training/street-gang-tactics.

Groves, B. M., B. Zuckerman, S. Marans, and D. J. Cohen. 1993. "Silent Victims: Children Who Witness Violence." *Journal of the American Medical Association*, 269:262–64.

GuardianAngels.org. 2004. "Welcome to GuardianAngels.org." Available: http://www.outta-sites.com/clients/guardianangels/webie.

_____. 2012. "Our Safety Patrols." Available: http://www.guardianangels.org/safety.php.

Guilford County OJJDP Comprehensive Gang Assessment. 2010. "Guilford County Gang Assessment: The OJJDP Comprehensive Gang Model, Section: Law Enforcement, Gangs, and Gang-Related Crime." Available: http://www.uncg.edu/csr/files/LawEnforcementGangsandGangRelatedCrime.pdf.

Gurr, T. A. 1989. *Violence in America: Protest and Rebellion*. Newbury Park, CA: Sage.

Gzesh, Susan. 2006. "Central Americans and Asylum Policy in the Reagan Era." *Migration Information Source*. Available: http://www.migrationinformation.org/Feature/print.cfm?ID=384.

Hagedorn, John M. 1988. *People and Folks: Gangs, Crime and the Underclass in a Rustbelt City*. Chicago, IL: Lake View Press.

_____, ed. 2007. *Gangs in the Global City: Alternatives to Traditional Criminology*. Chicago, IL: University of Illinois Press.

_____. 2009. *A World of Gangs: Armed Young Men and Gangsta Culture*. Minneapolis, MN: University of Minnesota Press.

Hamilton-Merritt, Jane. 1993. *Tragic Mountains: The Hmong, the Americans, and the Secret Wars for Laos, 1942–1992*. Bloomington, IN: Indiana University Press.

Hamm, Mark. 1994. *American Skinheads*. Westport, CT: Praeger.

Harper, G., and L. Robinson. 1999. "Pathways to Risk Among Inner-City African American Adolescent Females: The Influence of Gang Membership." *American Journal of Community Psychology*, 27:383–404.

Harris, Julie Aitken, Rushton J. Phillippe, Elizabeth Hampson, and Douglas N. Jackson. 1996. "Salivary Testosterone and Self-Report Aggression and Pro-Social Personality Characteristics in Men and Women." *Aggressive Behavior*, 22:321–31.

Harris, M. G. 1988. *Cholas: Latino Girls and Gangs*. New York: AMS Press.

_____. 1997. "Cholas, Mexican-American Girls, and Gangs," in *Gangs and Gang Behavior*. Ed. G. Larry Mays. Chicago, IL: Nelson-Hall.

Haskins, James. 1974. *Street Gangs: Yesterday and Today*. Wayne, PA: Hastings.

Hay, D., P. Linebaugh, J. Rule, E. P. Thompson, and C. Winslow, eds. 1975. *Albion's Fatal Tree: Crime and Society in Eighteenth-Century England*. New York: Pantheon.

Hayden, Tom. 2004. *Street Wars: Gangs and the Future of Violence.* New York: The New Press.

Healy, Patrick. 2004. "U.S. Indicts 30 in L.I. Gangs Crimes, Including 5 Murders." *The New York Times,* February 5:B8.

Heavens, Alan J. 2012. "Youth Build's Growing Mission." Philly. com, April 6. Available: http://articles.philly.com/2012-04-06/business/31300445_1_youthbuild-usa-dorothy-stoneman-youthbuild-graduates.

Hells Angels. 2012. "Hells Angels Motorcycle Club Homepage: History." Available: http://www.hells-angels.com/?HA=history.

Henderson, Eric, Stephen J. Kunitz, and Jerrold E. Levy. 2004. "The Origins of Navajo Youth Gangs," in *Understanding Contemporary Gangs in America.* Ed. Rebecca D. Petersen. Upper Saddle River, NJ: Prentice Hall.

Henderson, Errol A. 1996. "Black Nationalism and Rap Music." *Journal of Black Studies,* 26(3):308–39.

Heneka, Michael T., Fabian Nadrigny, Tommy Regan, Ana Martinez-Hernandez, Lucia Dumitrescu-Ozimek, Dick Terwel, Daniel Jardanhazi-Kurutz, Jochen Walter, Frank Kirchhoff, Uwe-Karsten Hanisch, and Markus P. Kummer. 2010. "Locus Ceruleus Controls Alzheimer's Disease Pathology by Modulating Microglial Functions Through Norepinephrine." *Proceedings of the National Academy of Sciences of the United States of America,* 107(13):6058–63. Available: http://www.ncbi.nlm.nih.gov/pmc/articles/PMC2851853/.

Herbeck, Dan. 2000. "Fear Strikes Home." *Buffalo News,* July 17:A1.

_____. 2008. "N.Y. Task Force Takes Aim at Latin Kings." *Buffalo News,* September 6. Available: http://www.policeone.com/gangs/articles/1732158-N-Y-task-force-takes-aim-at-Latin-Kings/.

_____. 2012. "Prosecutors File Charges in Roundup of Gang." *Buffalo News,* May 25. Available: http://www.buffalonews.com/city/police-courts/courts/article873320.ece.

Hernandez, Arturo. 2012. "Gang Prevention for Schools and Communities: Statistics." Available: http://www.helpinggangyouth.com/statistics.html.

Hewitt, John, and Randall Stokes. 1975. "Disclaimers." *American Sociological Review,* 40(1):1–11.

Hickey, Eric, ed. 2003. "The Zoot Suit Riots," in *Encyclopedia of Murder & Violent Crime.* Thousand Oaks, CA: Sage.

Hinsdale Police Department. 2012. "Police Department Crime Prevention." Available: http://www.villageofhinsdale.org/pd/crime_prevent.php.

Hirschi, Travis. 1969. *Causes of Delinquency.* Berkeley, CA: University of California Press.

Hirschi, Travis, and Rodney Stark. 1969. "Hellfire and Delinquency." *Social Problems* 17:202–13.

Hmong American Partnership. 2009. "Our History." Available: http://www.hmong.org/history.aspx.

Holiday, Darryl. 2011. "Snoop Dogg's Youth Football League Touches Down Here." *Chicago Sun-Times,* November 2. Available: http://www.suntimes.com/news/metro/6794597-418/snoop-doggs-youth-football-league-touches-down-here.html.

Holthouse, David. 2006. "A Few Bad Men." *Intelligence Report,* published by the Southern Poverty Law Center, Summer, no. 182: 41–50.

_____. 2010a. "Being David Kennedy: The Making of a Gang Boss." *Intelligence Report,* published by The Southern Poverty Law Center, Spring, no. 137: 27–29.

_____. 2010b. "Killer Kindred: An Oregon-Based Racist Prison and Street Gang Has Produced an Incredible Amount of Criminal Violence." *Intelligence Report,* published by The Southern Poverty Law Center, Spring, no. 137: 27–29.

Hom, Taylor. 2012. "Tupac Shakur Hologram that Stunned Coachella Audience May Take Its Act on the Road." *New York Daily News,* April 17. Available: http://www.nydailynews.com/entertainment/music-arts/tupac-shakur-hologram-stunned-coachella-audience-act-road-article-1.1063122.

Homeboy Industries. 2010. "What We Do: Services." Available: http://homeboy-industries.org/index.php/services1/.

House of Umoja. 2006. "The House of UMOJA: Peace in the Hood Program." Available: http://www.houseofumoja.org/peacein-hood.htm.

Howell, James C. 2000. *Youth Gang Programs and Strategies.* Washington, DC: U.S. Department of Justice.

_____. 2004a. "Promising Programs for Youth Gang Violence Prevention and Intervention," in *Understanding Contemporary Gangs in America.* Ed. Rebecca D. Petersen. Upper Saddle River, NJ: Prentice Hall.

_____. 2004b. "Youth Gang Homicides," in *Understanding Contemporary Gangs in America.* Ed. Rebecca D. Petersen. Upper Saddle River, NJ: Prentice Hall.

_____. 2010a (December). "Gang Prevention: An Overview of Research and Programs." *OJJDP Juvenile Justice Bulletin.* Washington, DC: U.S. Department of Justice.

_____. 2010b. "Lessons Learned from Gang Program Evaluations: Prevention, Intervention, Suppression, and Comprehensive Community Approaches," pp. 51–75 in *Youth Gangs and Community Intervention: Research, Practice and Evidence.* Ed. Robert J. Chaskin. New York: Columbia University Press.

_____. 2012. *Gangs in America's Communities.* Thousand Oaks, CA: Sage.

Howell, James C., and Scott H. Decker. 1999a (January). "The Youth Gangs, Drugs, and Violence Connection," in *OJJDP Juvenile Justice Bulletin.* Washington, DC: U.S. Department of Justice.

_____. 1999b (December). "Youth Gang Drug Trafficking," in *OJJDP Juvenile Justice Bulletin.* Washington, DC: U.S. Department of Justice.

Huff, C. R. 1989. "Youth Gangs and Public Policy." *Crime and Delinquency,* 35:524–37.

Huffington Post. 2012a. "NYPD, FBI in Hunt for Devon Rodney, Leader of the Six Tre Outlaw Gangsta Disciples Folk Nation." February 1. Available: http://www.huffingtonpost.com/2012/02/01/nypd-fbi-in-hunt-for-devon-rodney-outlaw-gangsta-disciples-folk-nation_n_1248193.html.

_____. 2012b. "Snoop Dogg on 'The Price is Right': Rapper Co-Hosts, Wins Money." January 2. Available: http://www.huffingtonpost.com/2012/01/02/snoop-dogg-on-the-price-is-right_n_1179797.html.

Hughes, K. Michael, D. O. Devan Griner, Michelle Guarino, Bernie Drabik-Medeiros, and Kristy Williams. 2012. "A Second's Chance: Gang Violence Task Force Prevention Program." *American Surgeon,* 78(1):89–93.

Huizinga, D. 1997. "Gangs and the Volume of Crime." Paper presented at the annual Meeting of the Western Society of Criminology, Honolulu, HI.

Hunt, Geoffrey, Kathleen MacKenzie, and Karen Joe-Laidler. 2004. "I'm Calling My Mom," in *Understanding Contemporary Gangs in America.* Ed. Rebecca D. Petersen. Upper Saddle River, NJ: Prentice Hall.

Huston, Peter. 1995. *Tongs, Gangs, and Triads: Chinese Crime Groups in North America.* Boulder, CO: Paladin.

Hutson, H. R., D. Anglin, and M. J. Pratts. 1994. "Adolescents and Children Injured or Killed in Drive-By Shootings in Los Angeles." *New England Journal of Medicine,* 330(5):324–27.

Hutson, H. R., D. Anglin, N. Kyriacou, J. Hart, and K. Spears. 1995. "The Epidemic of Gang-Related Homicides in Los Angeles County from 1979 Through 1994." *Journal of the American Medical Association,* 274:1031–36.

Illinois State Police. 2002. "Violence Education Gang Awareness." Available: http://www.isp.state.il.us/crime/vega/htm.

Indianapolis Metropolitan Police Department. 2012. "Safe Streets Task Force (Criminal Street Gangs)." Available: http://www.indy.gov/eGov/City/DPS/IMPD/Enforcement/Investigations/Pages/safe-streets.aspx.

Infoplease.com. 2012. "American Indians by the Numbers." Data provided by the U.S. Census Bureau. Available: http://www.infoplease.com/spot/aihmcensus1.html.

Interagency Task Force. 2003. *Girls and Gangs.* Available: http://www.faculty.smsu.edu/m/mku096/nogangs/Girls/girls%20and%20gangs.html.

Jah, Yusuf, and Sister Shah'Keyah, 1995. *Uprising: Crips and Bloods Tell the Story of America's Youth in Crossfire.* New York; Simon and Schuster.

James, Randy. 2009. "The Hell's Angels." *Time,* August 3. Available: http://www.time.com/time/nation/article/0,8599,1914201,00.html.

Jamison, Michael. 2000. "Hell's Angels." *Organized Crime in America.* Belmont, CA: Wadsworth.

Jankowski, Martin Sanchez. 1991. *Islands in the Street: Gangs and American Urban Society.* Berkeley, CA: University of California Press.

Jenkins, Morris. 1995. "Fear of the 'Gangsta': Policy Responses to Gang Activity in the City of Boston." PhD diss., Northeastern University, Department of Law, Policy, and Society.

Jet. 2005. "Stanley 'Tookie' Williams Receives Presidential Award for Good Deeds." September 5. Available: http://findarticles.com/p/articles/mi_m1355/is_10_108/ai_n15655319/.

Joe, K., and Meda Chesney-Lind. 1995. "Just Every Mother's Angel: An Analysis of Gender and Ethnic Variations in Youth Gang Membership." *Gender and Society,* 9:408–31.

Johnson, Bryon. 2012. "Motivating Factors of Gang Affiliation." Unpublished research data results (from 1996–98 research) presented to Tim Delaney by Byron Johnson, April 18.

Johnson, D. R. 1981. *American Law Enforcement: A History.* St. Louis, MO: Forum.

Johnson, Dominique. 2008. "Taking Over the School: Student Gangs as a Strategy for Dealing with Homophobic Bullying in an Urban Public School District." *Journal of Gay & Lesbian Social Services,* 19(3–4):87–104.

Johnson, Kevin. 2004. "Mean Streets Once Again: Gang Activity Surging." *USA Today,* July 21:1A, 2A.

_____. 2009. "FBI: Burgeoning Gangs Behind up to 80% of U.S. Crime." *USA Today,* January 29. Available: http://www.usatoday.com/news/nation/2009-01-29-ms13_N.htm.

Johnson, Marilynn S. 2003. *Street Justice: A History of Police Violence in New York City.* Boston, MA: Beacon.

Johnson, Paula B., and David O. Sears. 1971. "Black Invisibility, the Press, and the Los Angeles Riot." *American Journal of Sociology,* 76(4, January):698–721.

Judicial Watch. 2012. "U.S. CBP Agents Team Up with Mexican Drug Cartels." May 22. Available: http://www.judicialwatch.org/blog/2012/05/u-s-cbp-agents-team-up-with-mexican-drug-cartels/.

Kahn, Jeremy. 2007. "The Story of a Snitch." *The Atlantic,* April. Available: http://www.theatlantic.com/magazine/archive/2007/04/the-story-of-a-snitch/5703/1/.

Kappeler, Victor E. 1989. "St. Louis Police Department," in *The Encyclopedia of Police Science.* Ed. W. G. Bailey. New York: Garland.

Kappeler, Victor E., and Larry K. Gaines. 2011. *Community Policing: A Contemporary Perspective,* 6th ed. Boston, MA: Elsevier/Anderson Publishing.

Katz, Charles, and Stephen M. Schnebly. 2011. "Neighborhood Variation in Gang Member Concentration." *Crime and Delinquency,* 57:377–407.

Katz, Charles, and Vincent J. Webb. 2006. *Policing Gangs in America.* Cambridge, MA: University Press.

Katz, Charles M., Edward R. Maguire, and Dennis Roncek. 2000. "A Macro-Level Analysis of the Creation of Specialized Police Gang Units: An Examination of Rational, Social Threat, and Resource Dependency Perspectives." Unpublished manuscript.

Katz, Jack. 1988. *Seductions of Crime.* New York: Basic.

Kavieff, Paul. 1999. "Detroit's Infamous Purple Gang" (a special to the *Detroit News,* July 16). Available: http://apps.detnews.com/apps/history/index.php?id=183.

_____. 2000. *The Purple Gang.* Fort Lee, NJ: Barricade Books.

Keene, J. 1989. "Asian Organized Crime." *FBI Law Enforcement Bulletin,* 58(10):12–17.

Keiser, R. Lincoln. 1969. *The Vice Lords.* New York: Holt, Rinehart and Winston.

Kelleher, Jennifer Sinco, and John Moreno Gonzales. 2004. "West Coast Gang Built Up and East." *Newsday.com.* Available: http://www.newsday.com/news/local/longisland/ny-liprim.

Keller, Larry. 2010. "From the Ashes." From the Southern Poverty Law Center's *Intelligence Report,* 140 (Winter):12–14.

Kennedy, Kelly. 1998. "Straight Edge: Is it a Gang or a Brotherhood." *Salt Lake City Tribune,* January 31.

Kenney, Dennis J., and James O. Finckenauer. 1995. *Organized Crime in America.* Belmont, CA: Wadsworth.

Kephart, Janice. 2010. "Enhancing DHS' Efforts to Disrupt Alien Smuggling Across Our Border." Testimony provided by Kephart, Director of National Security Policy for the Center for Immigration Studies before the House Committee on Homeland Security. Center for Immigration Studies. Available: http://www.cis.org/node/2109.

Kessler, Robert E., and Andrew Smith. 2004. "Police: Gang Paired in Nassau." Newsday.com, October 13. Available: http://www.newsday.com.

Keyes, Cheryl. 2002. *Rap Music and Street Consciousness.* Urbana, IL: University of Illinois Press.

Kilm, R., and J. Block. 1982. "Response to a Crisis: Reducing the Juvenile Detention Rate in Louisville, Kentucky." *Juvenile and Family Court Journal,* 33(1):37–44.

Kim, Victoria. 2012. "8 Charged in Alleged Underage Sex Ring." *The Los Angeles Times,* August 10:AA1.

Kitchen, D. B. 1995. *Sisters in the Hood*. PhD diss., Western Michigan University.

Kitwana, Bakari. 2002. *The Hip Hop Generation: Young Blacks and the Crisis in African-American Culture*. New York: Basic Books.

Klatell, James M. 2011. "Exclusive: Gangs Spreading in the Military." CBS News. Available: http://www.cbsnews.com/2100-18563_162-31073.html.

Klein, Malcolm. 1971. *Street Gangs and Street Workers*. Englewood Cliffs, NJ: Prentice Hall.

———. 1995. *The American Street Gang*. New York: Oxford University Press.

Klein, Malcolm, and Cheryl L. Maxson. 1989. "Street Gang Violence," in *Violent Crimes, Violent Criminals*. Ed. N. Weiner. Beverly Hills, CA: Sage.

Klein, Malcolm, Cheryl L. Maxson, and L. C. Cunningham. 1991. "'Crack,' Street Gangs, and Violence." *Criminology*, 29(4):623–50.

Klinteberg, Britt. 1989. "Aggressiveness and Hyperactive Behavior as Related to Adrenaline Excretion." *European Journal of Personality*. Available: http://www.search.epnet.com/direct.asp?an=12061706&db=pbh.

Knox, George W. 2000. *An Introduction to Gangs*. Peotone, IL: New Chicago School Press.

———. 2001. "Female Gangs: A Focus on Research." OJJDP Juvenile Justice Bulletin. U.S. Department of Justice: Washington, D.C.

———. 2004. "Gang Threat Analysis: The Black Gangster Disciples." National Gang Crime Research Center. Available: http://www.ngcrc.com/bdprofile.html.

Kodluboy, Donald W. 1996. "Asian Youth Gangs: Basic Issues for Educators." *National Alliance of Gang Investigators Associations*. Available: http://www.nagia.org/asian_youth_gangs1.htm.

Kontos, Louis, and David C. Brotherton, eds. 2008. *Encyclopedia of Gangs*. Westport, CT: Greenwood.

Kotulak, Ronald. 2003. "Poverty, Malnutrition Can Lower a Child's IQ Score," *The Post-Standard* (originally published in the *Chicago Tribune*), December 9:E1.

Kouri, Jim. 2011. "Operation Black Magic Nails 30 Latino Gang Members." *The Examiner*, March 21. Available: http://www.examiner.com/article/operation-black-magic-nails-30-latino-gang-members.

Kratcoski, Peter, and Lucille Dunn Kratcoski. 1996. *Juvenile Delinquency*, 4th ed. Upper Saddle River, NJ: Prentice Hall.

Krikorian, Greg, and Rich Connell. 1997. "Wide Injunction Sought Against 18th Street Gang." *Los Angeles Times*, August 4:A1.

Kristof, Nicholas D. 2012a. "Sioux Reservation: Poverty's Poster Child." Syndicate column as it appeared in *ThePost-Standard*, May 12:A-12.

———. 2012b. "His Name Is Etched on Her." Syndicated column as it appeared in *The Post-Standard*, May 22: A-16.

KTLA News. 2009. "Gang Member Sought in Rape of 9-Year-Old." September 25. Available: http://www.streetgangs.com/news/092509_gangmemberrape.

Kulkus, Emily. 2003. "A Look at Carousel's Curfew, Six Months Later." *The Post-Standard*, December 20:A6.

La Opinion. 1943. "The Battle Between Marines and Pachucos." June 9. Available: http://web.viu.ca/davies/H324War/Zootsit.riots.media.1943.htm.

LaFave, W. R., and J. H. Israel. 1992. *Criminal Procedure*, 2nd ed. St. Paul, MN: West.

Laidler, K. A., and G. Hunt. 1997. "Violence and Social Organization in Female Gangs." *Social Justice*, 24:148–69.

Landre, Rick, Mike Miller, and Dee Porter. 1997. *Gangs: A Handbook for Community Awareness*. New York: Facts On File.

LAPD Newsletter. 2000. "CRASH Units Replaced by New Special Units." April, XLVI(IV):1, 7.

Lardner, James, and Thomas Reppetto. 2000. *NYPD: A City and Its Police*. New York: Henry Holt and Company.

Lauderback, D., J. Hansen, and D. Waldorf. 1992. "'Sisters Are Doin' It for Themselves': A Black Female Gang in San Francisco." *The Gang Journal*, 1:57–72.

Lavigne, Y. 1993. *Good Guy, Bad Guy*. Toronto: Random House.

Lee, Phillip. 2012. "Chapter 34: Hitting Criminal Street Gangs Where It Hurts—Their Wallets." *McGeorge Law Review*, 39:577–636. Available: http://www.mcgeorge.edu/documents/publications/mlr/Vol_39_2/_10_Penal_Master.pdf.

Leibovich, Lori. 2001. "Girl Gangs Are a Growing Problem," pp. 56–69 in *Gangs: Opposing Viewpoints*. Ed. Laura K. Egendorf. San Diego, CA: Greenhaven Press.

Lemann, Nicholas. 1991. "The Other Underclass." *The Atlantic Monthly*. Available: http://www.theatlantic.com/politics/poverty/othurnd.htm.

Lemert, Edwin M. 1951. *Social Pathology*. New York: McGraw Hill.

Levin, Brian. 2005. "Radical Religion in Prison." Available: http://www.splcenter.org/intel/intelreport/article.

Lindberg, Richard. 2003. "Spotlight on Asian Organized Crime." Available: http://www.nasiangangs.htm.

Lombardi, John. 1998. "Scenes from a Bad Movie." *New York*, January 12. Available: http://nymag.com/nymetro/news/people/features/1983/index4.html.

Long, Dorothy. 2012. "Head Start: Auburn Agency Aims to Spread Awareness of Services and Increase Support." *The Post-Standard*, May 10:3 (Neighbors Section).

Lopez, Robert J. 1996. "Actor Named as Alleged Gang Target." *Los Angeles Times*, October 24. Available: http://articles.latimes.com/1996-10-24/local/me-57292_1_prison-gang.

Los Angeles Almanac. 2011. "Los Angeles Zoot Suit Riots." Available: http://www.laalmanac.com/history/hi07t.htm.

Lyman, Michael D., and Gary W. Potter. 2000. *Organized Crime*, 2nd ed. Upper Saddle River, NJ: Prentice Hall.

Mafia Today. 2011. "Mexican Mafia Members Nailed by FBI, Texas Rangers." Available: http://mafiatoday.com/other-mafia0orgs/mexican-mafia-members-nailed-by-fbi-texas-rangers/.

Main, Frank, and Carlos Sadovi. 2002. "Gangs Channel River of Drug Cash from Streets to Shops, Studios—Even Vegas." *Chicago Sun Times*, April 7:6A–9A.

Majithia, Neil. 2012. "Caffeine: Understanding the World's Most Popular Psychoactive Drug." *Journal of Young Investigators*, 23(3):1–5. Available: http://www.jyi.org/features/ft.php?id=1327.

Maps of the World. 2008. "Top Ten Poorest Countries." Available: www.mapsofworld.com/world-top-ten/world-top-ten-poorest-countries-map.html.

Mark, Gregory Yee. 2004. "Oakland Chinatown's First Youth Gang: The Suey Sing Boys," in *Understanding Contemporary Gangs in America*. Ed. Rebecca D. Petersen. Upper Saddle River, NJ: Prentice Hall.

Marrero, Tony. 2010. "Two Spring Hill Teens Face Burglary Charges in Gang Recruiting." *Tampa Bay Times*, December 29. Available: http://www.tampabay.com/news/publicsafety/crime/two-spring-hill-teens-face-burglary-charges-in-gang-recruiting/1142346.

Marshall, George. 1994. *Spirit of '69: A Skinhead Bible*. Scotland: S. T. Publishing.

Martin, Constance. 2000. *Endocrine Physiology*. New York: Oxford University Press.

Martinez, Pila. 1999. "Novel Attempt to Curb Prison Gang Violence." *Christian Science Monitor*, 91(164):2.

Maslow, A. 1951. *Motivation and Personality*. New York: Harper & Row.

Matza, David. 1964. *Delinquency and Drift*. Englewood Cliffs, NJ: Prentice Hall.

Maxson, C. L. 1998. "Gang Homicide," in *Studying and Preventing Homicide*. Ed. D. Smith and M. Zahn. Thousand Oaks, CA: Sage.

Maxson, Cherly L., Karen Hennigan, and David C. Sloan. 2003. "For the Sake of the Neighborhood?" in *Policing Gangs and Youth Violence*. Ed. Scott H. Decker. Belmont, CA: Wadsworth.

Mazon, Mauricio. 1984. *The Zoot-Suit Riots*. Austin, TX: University of Texas Press.

McCorkle, R., and T. Miethe. 1998. "The Political and Organizational Response to Gangs: An Examination of a Moral Panic." *Justice Quarterly*, 15:41–64.

_____. 2002. *Panic: Rhetoric and Reality in the War on Street Gangs*. Upper Saddle River, NJ: Prentice Hall.

McCrary, Gregg O., and Katherine Ramsland. 2003. *The Unknown Darkness: Profiling the Predators Among Us*. New York: William Morrow.

McDevitt, Jack, Anthony A. Braga, Dana Nurge, and Michael Buerger. 2002. "Boston's Youth Violence Prevention Program," in *Policing Gangs and Youth Violence*. Ed. Scott H. Decker. Belmont, CA: Wadsworth.

McDevitt, Jack, Jack Levin, and Susan Bennett. 2002. "Hate Crime Offenders: An Expanded Typology." *Journal of Social Issues*, 58(2):303–18.

McDonnell, Robert. 2009. "Press Release: Make Virginia a Gang-Free Zone." Available: http://www.bobmcdonnell.com/index.php/press_releases/details/mcdonnell_make_virginia_a_gang-free_zone/.

McGarrell, Edmund F., and Steven Chermak. 2003. "Problem Solving to Reduce Gang and Drug-Related Violence in Indianapolis," in *Policing Gangs and Youth Violence*. Ed. Scott H. Decker. Belmont, CA: Wadsworth.

McGoldrick, S. K., and P. Simpson. 2007. "Violence, Police and Riots in New Orleans Political Culture: 1854–1874." *Journal of Historical Sociology*, 20(1–2):72–101.

McGreevy, Patrick. 2007. "Gob. To Sign 5 New Laws to Battle Gangs." *Los Angeles Times*, October 11. Available: http://articles.latimes.com/2007/oct/11/local/me-gangs11.

McPhee, Michele. 2003. "Asian Eagles Ganging Up." *Daily News*, November 24:10.

_____. 2005a. "Eastie Gang Linked to al-Qaeda." *Boston Herald*, January 5. Available: http://news.bostonhearld.com/localRegional/view/bg?articleid=61903&format=text.

_____. 2005b. "U.S. Rep: MS-13 Is a True Terror Threat." *Boston Herald*, January 7. Available: http://news.bostonhearld.com/localRegional/view.bg?articleid=62313.

Melton, Tracy. 2005. *Hanging Henry Gambrill: The Violent Career of Baltimore's Plug Uglies, 1854–1860*. Baltimore, MD: Maryland Historical Society.

Merton, Robert K. 1968. *Social Theory and Social Structure*. Glencoe, IL: Free Press.

Messerschmidt, James. 1997. "From Patriarchy to Gender: Feminist Theory, Criminology, and the Challenge of Diversity," pp. 118–132 in *Female Gangs in America: Essays on Girls, Gangs, and Gender*. Ed. Meda Chesney-Lind and John M. Hagedorn. Chicago, IL: Lake View Press.

Miami-Dade County Police. 2011. "Miami-Dade County Police—Robbery Division." August 12. Available: http://www.miami-dade.gov/mdpd/BureausDivisions/bureau_Robbery.asp.

Miami Gardens Police Department. 2008. "Special Operations." Available: http://www.miamigardenspolice.org/specialoperations.html.

Michel, Lou. 2002. "Homicide Upsurge." *Buffalo News*, January 2:A6.

Mieczkowski, Thomas. 1986. "Geeking Up and Throwing Down: Heroin Street Life in Detroit." *Criminology*, 24:645–66.

Milidor, Christian E. 1996. "Female Gang Members: A Profile of Aggression and Victimization." *Journal of Social Work*, 41(3):251–60.

Militant Islam Monitor. 2005. "Boston Street Gang M-13 Cited as 'True Terror Threat'—Linked to Al Qaeda & Adnan Shukrijumah." January 7. Available:http://www.militantislammonitor.org/article/id/372.

Miller, Jody. 2001. *One of the Guys: Girls, Gangs, and Gender*. New York: Oxford University Press.

Miller, Walter B. 1957. "The Impact of a Community Group Work Program on Delinquent Corner Groups." *Social Science Review*, 41(4):390–406.

_____. 1958. "Lower Class Culture as a Generating Milieu of Gang Delinquency." *Journal of Social Issues*, 14(3):5–19.

_____. 1959. "Preventive Work with Street-Corner Groups: Boston Delinquency Project." *Annals of the American Academy of Political and Social Science*, 322:97–106.

_____. 1962. "The Impact of a 'Total Community' Delinquency Control Project." *Social Problems*, 10:168–91.

_____. 1966. "Violent Crimes in City Gangs." *Annals of the American Academy of Political and Social Science*, 364:96–112.

_____. 1973. "The Molls." *Society*, 11:32–35.

_____. 1992. *Crime by Youth Gangs and Groups in the United States*, 2nd ed. Washington, DC: National Institute of Juvenile Justice and Delinquency Prevention, U.S. Department of Justice.

Miller, Wilbur R. 1977. *Cops and Bobbies: Police Authority in New York and London, 1830–1870*. Chicago, IL: University of Chicago Press.

Mobilia, Jennifer. 2012. "Multiple Arrests in Morning Drug Raid." YNN (Your News Now). January 23. Available: http://buffalo.ynn.com/content/top_stories/571136/multiple-arrests-in-morning-drug-raid/.

Mock, Bretin. 2007. "Sharing the Hate." From the Southern Poverty Law Center's *Intelligence Report*, 125(Spring):15–16.

Montreal Preventive Treatment Program. 2012. "Prevention, ages 7–9." Available: http://www.nationalgangcenter.gov/SPT/Programs/93.

Moore, Jack B. 1993. *Skinheads Shaved for Battle*. Bowling Green, OH: Bowling Green State University Popular Press.

Moore, Joan W. 1991. *Going Down to the Barrio*. Philadelphia, PA: Temple University Press.

———. 1993. "Gangs, Drugs, and Violence," in *Gangs: The Origins and Impact of Contemporary Youth Gangs in the United States*. Ed. Scott Cummings and Daniel J. Monti. Albany, NY: SUNY Press.

Moore, Joan W., and John Hagedorn. 2001 (March). "Female Gangs: A Focus on Research." *OJJDP Juvenile Justice Bulletin*. Available: http:///.ncjrs.org/html/ojjdp/jjbul2001_3_/contents.html

Mordecai, Samuel. 1860. *Virginia, Especially Richmond, in By-Gone Days: With a Glance at the Present: Being Reminiscences and Last Words of an Old Citizen*. Richmond, VA: West and Johnson.

Morgan, Jr., William J. 2009. "The Major Causes of Institutional Violence." *American Jails*, 23(5):62–70.

MST Services. 2010a. "What Is Multisystemic Therapy?" Available: http://mstservices.com/.

———. 2010b. "Proven Results." Available: http://mstservices.com/index.php/proven-results/proven-results.

Mulvaney, Jim. 1993. " 'Skinhead' Founder Renounces His Ties." *Las Vegas Review—Journal*, August 1.

Murray, Maxwell. 1943. "Memo from Maxwell Murray, Major General, U.S. Army Commanding." June 11. Available: http://web.viu.ca/davies/H324War/Zootsit.riots.media.1943.htm.

Myers, David G. 1998. *Psychology*, 5th ed. Holland, MI: Worth.

Nation Master. 2012. "Gun Violence, Homicides, Firearm Homicide Rate per 100,000 by Country." Available: http://www.nationmaster.com/graph/cri_gun_vio_hom_fir_hom_rat_per_100_pop-rate-per-100-000-pop.

National Advisory Committee on Criminal Justice Standards and Goals. 1976. *Organized Crime, Report of the Task Force on Organized Crime*. Washington, DC: Law Enforcement Assistance Administration.

National Alliance of Gang Investigators Associations. 2002. "The National Gang Threat." Available: http://www.nagia.org.

———. 2009. "Quick Guide to Gangs." Available: http://cryptocomb.org/Quickguide%20to%20gangs.pdf.

National Center for Health Statistics. 2009. "Press Release: Increase in Unmarried Childbearing Also Seen in Other Countries." Available: www.cdc.gov/media/pressrel/2009/r090513.htm.

National Criminal Justice Reference Service (NCJRS). 2011. "In the Spotlight: Gangs." Available: http://www.ncjrs.gov/spotlight/gangs/summary.html.

National Dropout Prevention Center/Network. 2012. "Model Program: Preventive Treatment Program." Available: http://www.dropoutprevention.org/modelprograms/show_program.php?pid=62.

National Drug Intelligence Center. 2002 (November). "Drugs and Crime: Gang Profile." Available: http://cryptome.org/gangs/crips.pdf.

National Drug Strategy Network. 1996 (May). "HUD Announces 'One Strike' Rules for Public Housing Tenants." Available: http://www.ndsn.org/may96/onestrik.html.

National Gang Center. 2012. "Violence-Free Zones: Intervention; Ages 15–24." Available: http://www.nationalgangcenter.gov/SPT/Programs/130.

National Institute on Drug Abuse. 2010 (December). "Drug Facts: MDMA (ecstasy)." Available: http://www.drugabuse.gov/publications/drugfacts/mdma-ecstasy.

National Rife Association. 2011. "Firearm Fact Card 2011." Available: http://www.nraila.org/news-issues/fact-sheets/2011/firearm-fact-card-2011.aspx?s=.

National Gang Intelligence Center. 2007. "Gang Related Activity in the US Armed Forces Increasing." January. Available: http://www.militarytimes.com/static/projects/pages/ngic_gangs.pdf.

———. 2009. "National Youth Gang Survey Analysis." Available: http://www.nationalgangcenter.gov/Survey-Analysis/Demographics.

———. 2011a. "2011 National Gang Threat Assessment." Available: http://www.fbi.gov/stats-services/publications/2011-national-gang-threat-assessment/2011%20National%20Gang%20Threat%20Assessment%20%20Emerging%20Trends.pdf.

———. 2011b. "2011 National Gang Threat Assessment—Emerging Trends and the Internet." Available: http://ilookbothways.com/2011/11/07/2011-national-gang-threat-assessment-%E2%80%93-emerging-trends-and-the-internet/.

———. 2011c. "National Youth Gang Survey Analysis: Demographics." Available: http://www.nationalgangcenter.gov/Survey-Analysis/Demographics#anchorregm.

National Poverty Center. 2009. "Poverty in the United States." Available: www.npc.umich.edu/poverty.

1997 National Youth Gang Survey. 1999 (December). U.S. Department of Justice, OJJDP.

Nawojczyk, Steve. 1997. "Street Gang Dynamics." Available: http://www.gangwar.com/dynamics.

New York. 2010. "The New Gangs of New York." October 4:80–81.

New York Post. 2003. "2 Arrested in Gang Sex Rite," May 1:22.

New York Times. 1943. "Not a Race Issue, Mayor Says." June 10. Available: http://web.viu.ca/davies/H324War/Zootsit.riots.media.1943.htm.

———. 2010. "U.S. Service Sector Expanded in September." October 5. Available: www.nytimes.com/2010/10/06/business/economcy/06econ.html?_r=1.

———. 2011. "Soaring Poverty Casts Spotlight on 'Lost Decade.' " September 13. Available: http://www.nytimes.com/2011/09/14/us/14census.html?_r=1&pagewanted=all.

New Zealand Herald. 2011. "Growing Sense of Pride Erodes Mob's Influence." January 7:A6.

Newswire. 2002. "Controversial Detroit Rapper Now Offering Extreme Kidnapping Adventure to Hardcore Thrill Seekers." October 21 (Article A93091592).

Nolan, Jim. 2008. " 'Love Your Kids,' Gang Member Says in Video." *Richmond Times-Dispatch*, November 19. Available: http://www2.godanriver.com/news/2008/nov/19/love_your_kids_gang_member_says_in_video-ar-285566/.

Notitas de Noticias. 2012. "Santa Muerte Cult Members Charged with Murders of Boys, Women." May 18. Available: http://www.hispanicallyspeakingnews.com/notitas-de-noticias/details/santa-muerte-cult-members-charged-with-murders-of-boys-woman/15964/.

Nozzolio, Michael F. 2004. Personal mail correspondence dated January 26, 2004.

Nurge, Dana. 2003. "Liberating Yet Limiting: The Paradox of Female Gang Membership," pp. 161–182 in *Gangs and Society: Alternative Perspectives*. Ed. Louis Kontos, David Brotherton, and Luis Barrios. New York: Columbia University Press.

NYCLU. 2009. "State's Highest Court Rules Rochester Youth Curfew Is Unconstitutional." June 9. Available: http://www.nyclu.org/news/state%E2%80%99s-highest-court-rules-rochester-youth-curfew-unconstitutional.

Nye, F. I. 1958. *Family Relationships and Delinquent Behavior.* New York: Wiley.

NYPD and Department of Correction. 2001. As reported in the *Daily News*, April 8:5.

O'Brien, John. 2003a. "2 Gang Members Enter RICO Pleas." *The Post-Standard*, November 5:B5.

_____. 2003b. "Boot Camp Fugitives Caught in Connecticut." *The Post-Standard*, October 29:A1.

_____. 2003c. "How Boot Camp Ruled a Gang." *The Post-Standard*, September 3:A1.

_____. 2004a. " 'Gang' Was Forbidden Word for Police." *The Post-Standard*, July 20:A1, A8.

_____. 2004b. "I Wanted a Name. I Wanted to Be a Gangster." *The Post-Standard*, July 25:A1, A16.

_____. 2004c. "Evidence Shows Little Boot Camp Opulence." *The Post-Standard*, August 2:A1, A8.

_____. 2011. "City Police Take Down Bricktown Gang." *The Post-Standard*, April 29:A-3.

_____. 2012a. "Feds Charge 11 in Gang Sweep." *The Post-Standard*, May 2:A-1, A-14.

_____. 2012b. "Shutting Down Gang Violence Before It Starts." *The Post-Standard*, September 28:A-9.

O'Brien, John, and Maureen Sieh. 2003a. "Jail Keeps List of Inmates Who Say They're in Gangs." *The Post-Standard*, October 11:A1.

_____. 2003b. "Alleged Gang Members Hired to Work with Kids." *The Post-Standard*, December 7:A1.

O'Brien, Margaret. 1999. "At Least 16,000 Girls in Chicago's Gangs More Violent Than Some Believe, Reports Say." *Chicago Tribune*, September 17:5.

O'Connor, Anne-Marie. 1997. "Tijuana Gunman May Have Mexican American Mafia Tie." *Los Angeles Times*, November 29.

_____. 2000. "Massive Gang Member List Now Clouded by Rampart." *Los Angeles Times*, March 25:A1.

Office of Justice Programs. 2012. "Program Profile: Drug Treatment Alternative to Prison (DTAP)." Crime Solutions. gov. Available:http://www.crimesolutions.gov/ProgramDetails.aspx?ID=89.

Office of Juvenile Justice and Delinquency Prevention (OJJDP). 2000. "1998 National Youth Gang Survey." Washington, DC: U.S. Department of Justice.

_____. 2001. "1999 National Youth Gang Survey." Washington, DC: U.S. Department of Justice.

_____. 2004 (April). "OJJDP Fact Sheet." Washington, DC: U.S. Department of Justice.

_____. 2008 (July). "OJJDP Fact Sheet: Highlights of the 2006 National Youth Gang Survey." Washington, DC: U.S. Department of Justice. Available: https://www.ncjrs.gov/pdffiles1/ojjdp/fs200805.pdf.

_____. 2009 (May). "Comprehensive Gang Model: Planning for Implementation." Washington, DC: U.S. Department of Justice. Available:http://www.nationalgangcenter.org/Content/Documents/Implementation-Manual/Implementation-Manual.pdf.

_____. 2011a. "Comprehensive Anti-Gang Initiative." Available: http://www.ojjdp.gov/programs/antigang/.

_____. 2011b. "Juvenile Arrests." Available: http://www.ojjdp.gov/ojstatbb/crime/qa05101.asp?qaDate=2009.

_____. 2012a. "Baltimore Police Violent Crimes Division and Youth Violence Strike Force—Baltimore, MD," in *Promising Strategies to Reduce Gun Violence*. Washington, DC: U.S. Department of Justice. Available: http://www.ojjdp.gov/pubs/gun_violence/profile18.html.

_____. 2012b. "Broader Urban Involvement and Leadership Development Program (BUILD): Prevention." Washington, DC: U.S. Department of Justice. Available: http://www.ojjdp.gov/mpg/Broader%20Urban%20Involvement%20and%20Leadership%20Development%20Program%20(BUILD)-MPGProgramDetail-662.aspx.

_____. 2012c. "Consent to Search and Seize Firearms—St. Louis, MO," in *Promising Strategies to Reduce Gun Violence*. Washington, DC, U.S. Department of Justice. Available: http://www.ojjdp.gov/pubs/gun_violence/profile15.html.

_____. 2012d. "Operation Ceasefire—Boston, MA," in Promising Strategies to Reduce Gun Violence. Washington, DC: U.S. Department of Justice. Available: http://www.ojjdp.gov/pubs/gun_violence/profile21.html.

_____. 2012e. "Hardcore Gang Investigations Unit—Los Angeles County District Attorney's Office." Washington, DC: U.S. Department of Justice. Available: http://www.ojjdp.gov/mpg/Hardcore%20Gang%20Investigations%20Unit%E2%80%94Los%20Angeles%20County%20District%20Attorney%E2%80%99s%20Office-MPGProgramDetail-596.aspx.

_____. 2012f. "Cognitive Behavioral Treatment." Washington, DC: U.S. Department of Justice. Available: http://www.ojjdp.gov/mpg/progTypesCognitiveInt.aspx.

_____. 2012g. "VisionQuest: Residential Reentry." Washington, DC: U.S. Department of Justice. Available: http://www.ojjdp.gov/mpg/VisionQuest-MPGProgramDetail-77.aspx.

O'Hara, Jim. 2003. "Gang-Related Cases Moving Quickly in Court." *The Post-Standard*, May 19:A1.

O'Keeffe, Michael. 2011. "Jim Brown's Amer-I-Can Makes a Difference." *The Daily News*, November 6. Available: http://articles.nydailynews.com/2011-11-06/news/30364997_1_gang-violence-gang-members-crips.

Oliveiri, Chad. 2004. "The Mess We're in: State of the City." *City*, March 10–16:8.

Olson, David E., and Brendan, Dooley. 2006. "Gang Membership and Community Corrections Populations: Characteristics and Recidivism Rates Relative to Other Offenders," pp. 193–202 in *Studying Youth Gangs*. Ed. J. F. Short and L. A. Hughes. Lanham, MD: AltaMira Press.

O'Neill, Terry. 2002. "Biker Gangs—Stronger Than Ever." *Report* (Alberta), 29(4):18–22.

O'Shaughnessy, Patrice. 2001. "NYPD Beefs Up Units to Fight Growing Menace." *Daily News*, April 8:3, 5.

Padilla, Felix. 1992. *The Gang as an American Enterprise.* New Brunswick, NJ: Rutgers University Press.

Palmer, Craig T., and Christopher F. Tilley. 1995. "Sexual Access to Females as a Motivation for Joining Gangs: An Evolutionary Approach." *Journal of Sex Research*, 32(3):213–217.

Papachristos, A. V., and D. S. Kirk. 2006. "Neighborhood Effects on Street Gang Behavior," pp. 63–84 in *Studying Youth Gangs*. Ed. James F. Short and Lorine A. Hughes. Lanham, MD: Altamira Press.

Papadimitriou, Dimitri. 1998. "Employment Policy, Community Development, and the Underclass." Available: http://www.ideas.repec.org/p/wpa/wuwpma/9802016.html.

Parade Magazine. 2003a. "Gangs Terrorize France," April 28:9.

_____. 2003b. "Thieves' Favorites," August 17:14.

_____. 2009. "Intelligence Report: What's Made in the USA." April 19:10.

Parker, Robert N., Todd Negola, Miranda Rudy, Larry Asencio, and Emily Asencio. 2008. "Treating Gang-Involved Offenders," pp. 171–209 in *Treating the Juvenile Offender.* Ed. Robert D. Hoge, Nancy G. Guerra, and Paul Boxer. New York: Guilford Press.

Parsons, Christi, and Brian Bennett. 2012. "At Latin America Summit, Obama to Face Push for Drug Legalization." *Los Angeles Times,* April 13. Available: http://articles.latimes.com/2012/apr/13/world/la-fg-latin-america-summit-20120414.

PBS—*American Experience.* 2002. "Timeline: Zoot Suit Riots." Available: http://www.pbs.org.

PBS—*Frontline.* 2001. "LAPD Blues: CRASH Culture." Available: http://www.pbs.org/wgbh/pages/frontline/shows/lapd/scandal/crashculture.html.

Pearce, Diana. 1978. "The Feminization of Poverty: Women, Work, and Welfare." *Urban and Social Change Review,* 30(February).

Pearson, G. 1983. *Hooligan: A History of Reportable Fears.* New York: Schocken Books.

Perkins, U. E. 1987. *Explosion of Chicago's Black Street Gangs: 1900 to the Present.* Chicago, IL: Third World Press.

Pew Center on the States. 2009. "One in 100: Behind Bars in America 2008." February 28. Available: www.pewcenteronthestates.org/news_room_detail.aspx?id=35904.

Pew Research Center. 2010. "The New Demography of American Motherhood." Available: http://pewresearch.org/pubs/1586/changing-demographic-characteristics-american-mothers.

Philanthropedia. 2012. "Boys and Girls Clubs of America (BGCA): #2 Expert-Identified At-Risk Youth Nonprofit." Available:http://www.myphilanthropedia.org/blog/2011/09/22/boys-girls-clubs-of-america-bgca-2-expert-identified-at-risk-youth-nonprofit/.

Pitts, Jr., Leonard. 2012. "Let's be Clear; It's About Fear." *Syndicated column as it appeared in The Post-Standard,* March 27:A-8.

Polaris Project. 2012. "Combating Human Trafficking and Modern-Day Slavery: Rated State Laws." Available: http://www.polarisproject.org/what-we-do/policy-advocacy/state-policy/current-laws.

Pope, Carl E., and Rick Lovell. 2004. "Gang Prevention and Intervention Strategies of the Boys and Girls Clubs of America," in *Understanding Contemporary Gangs in America.* Ed. Rebecca D. Petersen. Upper Saddle River, NJ: Prentice Hall.

Port Washington News. 1998. "Port Police Arrest 8 MS-13 Gang Members." March 6.

Portillos, Edwardo Luis. 1997. "Women, Men and Gangs: The Social Construction of Gender in the Barrio," in *Female Gangs in America.* Ed. Meda Chesney-Lind and John M. Hagedorn. Chicago, IL: Lake View Press.

Posner, Gerald L. 1988. *Warlords of Crime: Chinese Societies—The New Mafia.* New York: McGraw-Hill.

Powell, Robert Andrew. 2003. *We Own This Game.* New York: Atlantic Monthly Press.

Promising Practices Network. 2012. "Schools and Families Educating Children (SAFE Children)." Available: http://www.promisingpractices.net/program.asp?programid=244.

Public Health Agency of Canada. 2012. "Preventive Treatment Program." Available: http://cbpp-pcpe.phac-aspc.gc.ca/intervention/243/view-eng.html.

Public Safety Strategies Group. 2007. "Perspectives on Foot Patrols: Lessons Learned from Foot Patrol Programs and an Overview of Foot Patrol in San Francisco." Prepared for the City and County of San Francisco, November 19. Available: http://www.sfcontroller.org/ftp/uploadedfiles/controller/reports/SFPD_Foot_Beat_Report-Final%20_111907.pdf.

Queally, James. 2011. "As N.J. Gangs Adopt Web 2.0 to Talk Shop, Police Keep Tabs." *The Star-Ledger,* October 2. Available: http://www.nj.com/news/index.ssf/2011/10/as_gangs_adopt_web_20_to_talk.html.

Quicker, John. 1983. *Home Girls.* San Diego, CA: International Universities Press.

_____. 1999. "Chicana Girl: A Preliminary Description," pp. 48–56 in *Female Gangs in America: Essays on Girls, Gangs and Gender.* Ed. Meda Chesney-Lind and John M. Hagedorn. Chicago, IL: Lake View Press.

Quinn, Michael. 1996. "Never Shoulda Been Let Out the Penitentiary: Gangsta Rap and the Struggle over Racial Identity." *Cultural Critique,* 34(Autumn):65–89.

Quinney, Richard A. 1970. *The Social Reality of Crime.* Boston, MA: Little, Brown and Company.

_____. 1977. *Class, State, and Crime: On the Theory and Practice of Criminal Justice.* New York: David McKay.

Quinney, Richard A., and J. Wildeman. 1991. *The Problem of Crime: A Peace and Social Justice Perspective,* 3rd ed. Mountain View, CA: Mayfield.

Quinones, Sam. 2010. "Six Florencia 13 Gang Members Sentenced to Life in Prison." *Los Angeles Times,* February 8. Available: http://articles.latimes.com/2010/feb/08/local/la-me-gang8-2010feb08.

Ramirez III, Pedro, and BoNhia Lee. 2006. "Alleged Street Gang Leaders Arrested." *The Post-Standard,* August 23:A-1, A-4.

Ramirez, Porfirio Ibarra. 2012. "Mexican Cartel Kills 49." *The Post-Standard,* May 4:A-9.

Ramos, George. 1997. "3 More Sentenced to Life in Mexican Mafia Case." *Los Angeles Times,* September 4:B3.

Ramsey, Alison L., James O. Rust, and Susan M. Sobel. 2003. "Evaluation of the Gang Resistance and Training (GREAT) Program: A School-Based Prevention Program." *Education,* 124(2):297–309.

Reckless, W. C. 1961. "A New Theory of Delinquency and Crime." *Federal Probation,* 25:42–46.

Regoli, Robert M., and John D. Hewitt. 2003. *Delinquency in Society,* 5th ed. Boston, MA: McGraw-Hill.

Reiner, I. 1992. *Gangs, Crime and Violence in Los Angeles: Findings and Proposals from the District Attorney's Office.* Arlington, VA: National Youth Gang Information Center.

Reiner, Robert. 2007. "Media Made Criminality: The Representation of Crime in the Mass Media," pp. 302–40 in *The Oxford Handbook of Criminology,* 4th ed. Ed. M. Maguire, M. Morgan, and R. Reiner. Oxford, UK: Oxford University Press.

Reiss, Albert. 1951. "Delinquency as the Failure of Personal and Social Controls." *American Sociological Review,* 16:196–207.

Renteria, Nelson. 2012. "El Salvador Heralds 1st Murder-Free Day in Nearly 3 Years." *The Star,* April 15. Available:

http://www.thestar.com/news/world/article/1162146—el-salvador-heralds-1st-murder-free-day-in-nearly-3-years.

Richards, Ann. 2010. "Mott's Legacy in Community Policing Revived with New Grants to City of Flint, MSU." *Charles Stewart Mott Foundation*, March 5. Available: http://www.mott.org/news/news/2010/policing.aspx.

Richardson, Erin, and David Hemenway. 2010. "Homicide, Suicide, and Unintentional Firearm Fatality: Comparing the United States with Other High-Income Countries, 2003." *Journal of Trauma, Injury, Infection and Critical Care*, 70(1):238–43. Available: http://journals.lww.com/jtrauma/Abstract/2011/01000/Homicide,_Suicide,_and_Unintentional_Firearm.35.aspx.

Richardson, John H. 1997. "Secrets of the Kings." *New York*, February 17.

Ried, Robert. 2004. *Central America on a Shoestring*, 5th ed. Melbourne, Australia: Lonely Planet.

Rist, Curtis. 1996. "Don't Be Like Me." *People Weekly*, 46:123. Also available: http://www.people.com/people/archive/article/0,,20142676,00.html.

Rivera, Lirio Gutierrez. 2010. "Discipline and Punish? Youth Gangs' Response to 'Zero-Tolerance' Policies in Honduras." *Bulletin of Latin American Research*, 29(4):492–504.

Rivera, Ray. 2010. "Agents Swarm Newburgh in Raid Against Gangs." *The New York Times*, May 13. Available: http://www.nytimes.com/2010/05/14/nyregion/14newburgh.html.

Riverside County Gang Task Force. 2012. "Mission & Goals." Available: http://www.riversidecountygtf.org/missionGoals.asp.

Robarchek, Clayton, and Carole Robarchek. 1997. *Waorani: The Contents of Violence and War*. New York: Harcourt Brace.

Roberts, Matthew. 2005. "Gang Warfare." *The American Conservative*, 7(9):25–26.

Robinson, Bryan. 2005. "Tookie Williams: Gang Founder Versus Noble-Nominated Peacemaker." *ABC News*, December 8. Available: http://abcnews.go.com/US/LegalCenter/story?id=1377890.

Rodine, Kristin. 2012. "High Court Rules Idaho's Gang-Recruitment Law Is Constitutional, Upholds Caldwell Woman's Conviction." *Idaho Statesman*, January 9. Available: http://www.idahostatesman.com/2012/01/09/1946012/high-court-rules-idahos-gang-recruitment.html.

Rosenzweig, David, and Meta Gold. 1997. "Sweeping Order to Limit Activity of 18th Street Gang." *Los Angeles Times*, July 12:A1.

Roy, S., and M. Brown. 1995. "Juvenile Electronic Monitoring Program in Lake County, Indiana: An Evaluation," in *Intermediate Sanctions: Sentencing in the 1990s*. Ed. J. Smykla and W. Selke. Cincinnati, OH: Anderson Publishing.

Rozanski, Lauren. 2003. An unpublished manuscript of interviews with members of the Mara Salvatrucha Gang.

Rubenfeld, Samuel. 2012. "US Indicts 14 in Drug-Money Laundering Scheme Involving Horses." *Corruption Currents*, June 12. Available: http://blogs.wsj.com/corruption-currents/2012/06/12/us-indicts-14-in-drug-money-laundering-scheme-involving-horses/.

Ryan, Mary P. 1998. *Civic Wars: Democracy and Public Life in the American City During the Nineteenth Century*. Berkeley, CA: University of California Press.

Sabol, William, Todd Minton, and Paige Harrison. 2007. "Prison and Jail Inmates at Midyear 2006." *Bureau of Justice Bulletin*. Washington, DC: U.S. Department of Justice Bureau of Justice Statistics.

Safir, Howard. 2003. *Security: Policing Your Homeland, Your City*. New York: St. Martin's Press.

Sahagun, Louis. 1997. "Tribes Struggle with Violent-Crime Wave." *Los Angeles Times*, November 9:A18.

Sampson, Robert J., and Byron W. Groves. 1989. "Community Structure and Crime: Testing Social Disorganization Theory." *American Journal of Sociology*, 94:774–802.

San Antonio Police Department. 2012 (note, there is no copyright date on this publication, 2012 was used as this was the date the information was retrieved). "Gang Awareness." Available: http://www.sanantonio.gov/sapd/pdf/Awareness.pdf.

Sanders, William B. 1970. *Juvenile Offenders for a Thousand Years*. Chapel Hill, NC: University of North Carolina Press.

_____. 1994. *Gangbangers and Drive-By's: Grounded Culture and Juvenile Gang Violence*. Hawthorne, NY: Aldine DeGryter.

Santa Cruz Barrios Unidos. 2012a. "Homepage: History." Available: http://www.barriosunidos.net/about.html.

_____. 2012b. "Warriors Circle 2011." Available: http://www.barriosunidos.net/.

Sante, Luc 1991. *Low Life: Lures and Snares of Old New York*. New York: Vintage.

Saporito, Bill. 2011. "Where the Jobs Are." *Time*, January 17: 12:14–19.

Savelli, Lou. 2000. "Introduction to East Coast Gangs." *National Alliance of Gang Investigators Associations*. Available: http://www.nagia.org.

Scharf, John Thomas. 1874. *The Chronicles of Baltimore: Being a Complete History of 'Baltimore Town' and Baltimore City from the Earliest Period to the Present Time*. New York: Turnbull.

Schmalleger, Frank. 2004. *Criminology Today*, 3rd ed. Upper Saddle River, NJ: Prentice Hall.

Schmid, Randolph E. 2009. "How Serotonin Turns Solitary Locusts into a Swarm." *The Post-Standard*. February, 9:A-8.

Schneider, Eric C. 1999. *Vampire, Dragons, and Egyptian Kings: Youth Gangs in Postwar New York*. Princeton, NJ: Princeton University Press.

Schneider, Stephen. 2002. "Organized Crime-Global," pp. 1112–18 in *Encyclopedia of Crime and Punishment*. Ed. David Levinson, Vol. 3. Thousand Oaks, CA: Sage.

Schumer, Charles E. 2003. "Press Release." November 26. Available: http://www.senate.gov/~schumer/schumer.

Scott, Marvin B., and Stanford M. Lyman. 1968. "Accounts." *American Sociological Review*, 33(February):46–62.

Seinfeld. 1997. "The Van Buren Boys." First aired date February 6.

Selcraig, Bruce. 1999. "Into the Heart of Darkness." *U.S. News & World Report*, 126(9):18–21.

Severson, Lucky. 2001. "Nobel Peace Nominee." *Religion and Ethics*, February 16. Available: http://www.pbs.org/wnet/religionandethics/week425/cover.html.

Shelden, Randall G., Sharon K. Tracy, and William B. Brown. 2001. *Youth Gangs in American Society*. Belmont, CA: Wadsworth.

Sheldon, William. 1949. *The Varieties of Delinquent Youth*. New York: Harper.

Shepperd, Walt. 2012. "Beyond RICO: The Next Gang Generation." *The Eagle*, May 3. Available: http://www.theeaglecny.com/news/2012/may/03/beyond-rico-next-gang-generation/.

Sherman, Gene. 1943. "Youth Gangs Leading Cause of Delinquencies." *Los Angeles Times*, June 2. Available: http://web.viu.ca/davies/H324War?Zootsuit.riots.1943.htm.

Shibutani, Tamotsu. 1955. "Reference Groups as Perspectives." *American Journal of Sociology*, 6:562–569.

Shippee, Nathan D. 2012. "Victimization, Fear of Crime, and Perceived Risk: Testing a Vulnerability Model of Personal Control." *Sociological Perspectives*, 55(1):117–40.

Shoemaker, Donald. 2000. *Theories of Delinquency*. New York: Oxford University Press.

Short, Jr., James F. 1974. "Collective Behavior, Crime, and Delinquency," in *Handbook of Criminology*. Ed. Daniel Glaser. Chicago, IL: Rand McNally.

Siegel, Larry J. 1995. *Criminology: Theories, Patterns, and Typologies*, 5th ed. Minneapolis/St. Paul, MN: West Publishing.

Siegel, Larry J., Brandon C. Welsh, and Joseph J. Senna. 2003. *Juvenile Delinquency*, 8th ed. Belmont, CA: Wadsworth.

Sieh, Maureen. 2003. "Police, Residents Talk About Gangs." *The Post-Standard*, July, 29:A1.

———. 2009. "Clergy and Community Members Form Team to Respond to Violent Crimes in Syracuse." *The Post-Standard*, April 23. Available: http://blog.syracuse.com/metrovoices/2009/04/syracuse_nytoday_the_syracuse.html.

Sifakis, Carl. 2001. *The Encyclopedia of American Crime*. New York: Facts on File.

Sikes, Gini. 2001. "8 Ball Chicks: A Year in the Violent World of Girl Gangsters," in *Gangs*. Ed. Sean Donahue. New York: Thunder's Mouth Press. (Originally published in 1997 by Anchor Books/Doubleday.)

Simon, David R., and Frank E. Hagan. 1999. *White-Collar Deviance*. Boston, MA: Allyn & Bacon.

Sitkoff, Harvard. 1971. "Racial Militancy and Interracial Violence in the Second World War." *Journal of American History*, 58(3, December):661–81.

Skarbek, David. 2012. "Prison Gangs, Norms, and Organizations." *Journal of Economic Behavior & Organization*, 82(1):702–16.

Smith, Craig. 2005. "France Awakens to Its Own Problems: Second- and Third-Generation Immigrant Underclass Is Increasingly Isolated, Angry." Syndicated column as it appeared in *The Post-Standard*. November 6:A-8.

Smith, Janet, and Ryan Lenz. 2011. "New Soldiers of the Confederacy." From the Southern Poverty Law Center's *Intelligence Report*, 144(Winter):12–14.

Soledad Enrichment Action. 2012. "SEA's History." Available: http://www.seacharter.org/about_us/SEAs_History.html.

Solotaroff, Ivan. 2002. "Gangsta Life, Gangster Death," in *Gangs*. Ed. Sean Donahue. New York: Thunder's Mouth Press.

Southland. 2012. "Risk." Original air date: March 13 on TNT.

Spencer, William. 1987. "Self-Work in Social Interaction: Negotiating Role-Identities." *Social Psychology Quarterly*, 50(2):131–42.

Spergel, Irving. 1995. *The Youth Gang Problem: A Community Approach*. New York: Oxford University Press.

Sportability. 2011. "Snoop Youth Football League." Available: http://www.sportability.com/spx/leagues/client.asp?clientid=333.

Stamford, Bryant. 1987 (December). "The Adrenaline Rush." *The Physician and Sports Medicine*, 15(12):184.

Starbuck, David, James C. Howell, and Donna J. Lindquist. 2001 (December). "Hybrid and Other Modern Gangs" in the *OJDDP Juvenile Justice Bulletin*. Washington, DC: U.S. Department of Justice.

Stars and Stripes. 2009. "Ex-Airman Charge in Beating Death." February 8. Available: http://www.stripes.com/news/ex-airman-charged-in-beating-death-1.87932.

Stelloh, Tim. 2011. "Suffolk Seeks 'Safety Zone' Barring Gang Members." *The New York Times*, August 16. Available: http://www.nytimes.com/2011/08/17/nyregion/suffolk-seeks-to-bar-gang-members-from-safety-zone.html?_r=1.

Stephens, Richard, John Atkins, and Andrew Kingston. 2009. "Swearing as a Response to Pain." *Neuro Report*, 20(12):1056–60.

Stith, John. 2010. "Poverty in US Suburbs Rising, but CNY Steady, Report Says." *The Post-Standard*, January 21:A6.

Straka, Richard. 2003. "The Violence of Hmong Gangs and the Crime of Rape." *FBI Law Enforcement Bulletin*, 72(2):12–16.

Sutherland, Edwin. 1939. *Principles of Criminology*, 3rd ed. Philadelphia, PA: Lippincott.

———. 1947. *Principles of Criminology*, 4th ed. Philadelphia, PA: Lippincott.

———. 1983 [1949]. *White Collar Crime*. New Haven, CT: Yale University Press.

Sutherland, Edwin, and Donald R. Cressey. 1978. *Criminology*, 10th ed. Philadelphia, PA: Lippincott.

Sykes, Gresham, and David Matza. 1957. "Techniques of Neutralization: A Theory of Delinquency." *American Sociological Review*, 22:664–670.

Syracuse Police Department. 2012. "Investigation Bureau: Gang Task Force." Available: http://www.syracusepolice.org/listing.asp?orgId=141&parent=88.

Syracuse Urban Youth Development Coalition. 2009. "Violence Intervention Prevention Program." Available: http://www.suydc.com/Partners/vip.html.

Tannenbaum, Frank. 1938. *Crime and the Community*. Boston, MA: Ginn.

Tarrant County Advocate Program (TCAP). 2004. "Homepage." Available: http://www.tarrantcounty.com/ejuvenile/cwp/view.asp?A=737&Q=427766.

Taylor, Carl S. 1989/1990. *Dangerous Society*. East Lansing, MI: Michigan State University Press.

———. 1990. "Gang Imperialism," in *Gangs in America*. Ed. C. R. Huff. Newbury Park, CA: Sage.

———. 1993. *Girls, Gangs, Women, and Drugs*. East Lansing, MI: Michigan State University Press.

Taylor, Diane. 2001. "Girl-Gang Princess . . . At 18 Months Old." *The Mirror*, 23:15.

Thamel, Pete. 2012. "Waiters: Talented Tough, Turbulent." As it appeared in *The Post-Standard*, March 25:C-10.

The Age. 2003. "Part-Time Work Spawns Rural Underclass," April 25. Available: http://www.theage.com.au/articles/2003/04/25/1050777401309.html">.

The American Heritage Dictionary. 2000. Boston, MA: Houghton Mifflin Company.

The Citizen. 2004. "The Lawless West? Rural Idaho Grapples with Gang Violence," October 29:B6.

———. 2008. "Specially Groomed Eyebrows a Headache," April 30:A2.

———. 2010. "NYPD: Crips Partnered with Bloods in NYC Drug War," April 17:A5.

———. 2011a. "Buffalo Motorcycle Club Targeted in Drug Raids," March 4:A3.

_____. 2011b. "Fla. Gang Leader Gets 65 Years," August 13:A9.

The Crime Encyclopedia. 1998. "The World's Most Notorious Outlaws, Mobsters, and Crooks." Detroit, MI: UXL.

The Daily Mail. 2012. "You've Been Served! Serena Williams Celebrates Olympic Gold by Bringing the Crip Walk to Wimbledon." August 4. Available:http://www.dailymail.co.uk/news/article-2183600/Serena-Williams-crip-walk-Youve-served-Champion-celebrates-Olympic-gold-Wimbledon.html.

The Early Show. 2011. "Gangs and Sports: Protecting Athletes from Growing Violence." Original air date: December 1.

The Economist. 2012. "Central America's Gangs: A Meeting of the Maras." May 12. Available: http://www.economist.com/node/21554521.

The Middle. 2012. "The Telling." ABC television, original air date: May 16, 2011.

The New York Times. 1943. "Not a Race Issue, Mayor Says." June 10. Available: http://web.viu.ca/davies/H324War/Zootsit.riots.media.1943.htm.

_____. 2004. "Oldest Bank Robber Meets a Quiet End." November 23. Available at: http://query.nytimes.com/gst/fullpage.html?res=9906E6D7163EF930A15752C1A9629C8B63.

_____. 2010. "U.S. Service Sector Expanded in September." October 5. Available at: www.nytimes.com/2010/10/06/business/economcy/06econ.html?_r=1.

_____. 2011. "Soaring Poverty Casts Spotlight on 'Lost Decade.'" September 13. Available: http://www.nytimes.com/2011/09/14/us/14census.html?_r=1&pagewanted=all.

The Post-Standard. 1997a. "Program Tries to Sever Gang Ties." March 17:A1.

_____. 1997b. "War and Peace Between the Gangs of Syracuse." December 12:A1, A-8.

_____. 2004a. "Deportations and Arrests Follow Probe of Gang." November 18:A12.

_____. 2004b. "Man Sentenced 25 Years to Life for Killing Witness." September 14:A4.

_____. 2004c. "Hunters' Killings Baffle Authorities, Residents." November 23:A-6.

_____. 2009a. "Gangs Tread More Carefully." December 4:A-15.

_____. 2009b. "Judge: Gang Owes City $5 Million." January 14:B-5 (Originally published in the *Los Angeles Times*).

_____. 2010. "Senator: Pull Up Your Pants." A *New York Times* syndicated article as it appeared in *The Post-Standard*, April 4:A-13.

_____. 2011. "CCA at 30: By the Numbers." December 16:A-10.

_____. 2012a. "Facebook by the Numbers." February, 4:A-1.

_____. 2012b. "Killer Sharpened Aim by Playing Video Game." April 20:A-11.

_____. 2012c. "Bricktown Gang Members Face Prison." July 20:A-9.

_____. 2012d. "Gang Member Sentenced." September 27:A-9.

_____. 2012e. "Man Admits Being in Gang Activities." September 27:A-3.

_____. 2012f. "City Man Admits Role in Street Gang." October 20:A-6.

_____. 2012g. "Serena Will Wait and See About Repeating 'Crip Walk' at U.S. Open." August 15: B-1.

The Southern Poverty Center. 2006 (Spring). "Minuteman Founder Said to Tolerate Neo-Nazis in Campaign." *Intelligence Report*, 121:10–11.

_____. 2009 (Fall). "Nearly 150 Latino Gang Members Indicted for Racist Violence." *Intelligence Report*, 135:3–4.

_____. 2011 (Fall). "10-Year-Old Son of NSM Leader in Held in Father's Slaying." *Intelligence Report*, 143:3–4.

_____. 2012 (Spring). "The Year in Hate & Extremism." *Intelligence Report*, 145:39–42.

Thio, Alex. 2003. *Sociology*. Boston, MA: Allyn & Bacon.

Thomas, Vanessa. 2004. "Meaner Streets." *Buffalo News*, August 22.

Thomas, Vanessa, and T. J. Pignataro. 2003. "Shooting Season." *Buffalo News*, July 25:A1.

Thompkins, Douglas E. 2004. "School Violence," in *Understanding Contemporary Gangs in America*. Ed. Rebecca D. Petersen. Upper Saddle River, NJ: Prentice Hall.

Thompson, Carol Y., Robert L. Young, and Ronald Burns. 2003. "Representing Gangs in the News: Media Construction of Criminal Gangs," in *Readings in Juvenile Delinquency and Juvenile Justice*. Ed. Thomas C. Calhoun and Constance L. Chapple. Upper Saddle River, NJ: Prentice Hall.

_____. 2012. "A Drug Family in the Winner's Circle." *The New York Times*, June 12. Available: http://www.nytimes.com/2012/06/13/us/drug-money-from-mexico-makes-its-way-to-the-racetrack.html?pagewanted=all.

Thompson, Hunter S. 1999. *Hell's Angels, a Strange and Terrible Saga*. New York: Random House.

Thornton, William E., and Lydia Voight. 1992. *Delinquency and Justice*, 3rd ed. New York: McGraw-Hill.

Thrasher, Frederic. 1962/1927. *The Gang*. Chicago, IL: University of Chicago Press.

Tifft, Austin T. 1979. "The Coming Redefinitions of Crime: An Anarchist Perspective." *Social Problems*, 26:392–402.

Tita, George, and Greg Ridgeway. 2007 (May). "The Impact of Gang Formation on Local Patterns of Crime." *Journal of Research in Crime and Delinquency*, 44(2):208–37.

Tobin, Kimberly. 2009. *Gangs: An Individual and Group Perspective*. Upper Saddle River, NJ: Pearson/Prentice Hall.

Toledo Blade.com. 2012. "Prison Reform." March 9. Available: http://www.toledoblade.com/Editorials/2012/03/09/Prison-reform.html.

Tonry, Michael, and Mark H. Moore. 1998. *Youth Violence*. Chicago, IL: University of Chicago Press.

Totten, Mark D. 2001. *Guys, Gangs, & Girlfriend Abuse*. Orchard Park, NY: Broadview.

Towers, Frank. 2004. *The Urban South and the Coming of the Civil War*. Charlottesville, VA: University of Virginia Press.

TRF Policy Map. 2012. "New York City Crime Rate and Statistics." Available: http://www.policymap.com/city-crime-rates/new-york-city-crime-statistics/index.html.

Trojanowicz, Robert C., Merry Morash, and Pamela J. Schram. 2001. *Juvenile Delinquency*, 6th ed. Upper Saddle River, NJ: Prentice Hall.

Trulson, Chad R., James Marquart, and Soraya K. Kawucha. 2006. "Gang Suppression and Institution Control." *Corrections Today*, 68(2):26–30.

Trump, Kenneth S. 1996. "Gangs and School Safety," in *Schools, Violence and Society*. Ed. Allan M. Hoffman. Westport, CT: Praeger.

Turner, Ralph H., and Samuel J. Surace. 1956. "Zoot-Suitors and Mexicans: Symbols in Crowd Behavior." *American Journal of Sociology*, 62(1, July):14–20.

Tyre, Peg. 1997. "New York Turns Up the Heat on Crips, Bloods." *CNN Interactive*, August 27.

_____. 2009. "Coaching Students to Stay in School." *Parade*, June 7:10.

Tyson, Ann Scott. 1997. "Prison Threat: Gangs Grab More Power." *Christian Science Monitor*, 89(160).

United Nations. 2008. "Human Trafficking: The Facts." The Global Initiative to Fight Human Trafficking. Available: http://www.unglobalcompact.org/docs/issues_doc/labour/Forced_labour/HUMAN_TRAFFICKING_-_THE_FACTS_-_final.pdf.

United States Attorney's Office—District of Massachusetts. 2010. "Twelve Alleged Gang Members and Associates in Chelsea Named in Federal and State Charges." Available: http://www.justice.gov/usao/ma/news/2010/January/CrossroadsPR.html.

United States Attorney's Office—Eastern District of Virginia. 2011. "MS-13 Associate Sentenced to 292 Months for Sex Trafficking Teenage Runaway Girls." November 4. Available: http://www.justice.gov/usao/vae/news/2011/11/20111104ormenonr.html.

United States Department of Homeland Security. 2012a. "Drug Enforcement Task Forces." Available: http://www.ice.gov/drug-task-force/.

_____. 2012b. "News Releases: Canadian Police Officer Pleads Guilty to Exporting Drugs From the U.S. Into Canada." Available:http://www.ice.gov/news/releases/1210/121031buffalo.htm.

United States District Court for the Northern District of New York. 2009. "Grand Jury Charges." Indictment against the 100 gang. Available: http://blog.syracuse.com/news/2009/06/2009-06-18-gang-indictment.pdf.

United States Drug Enforcement Administration. 2010. "Evansville, Indiana Drug Trafficking Investigation Leads Results in Twenty-two Charged Federally." Available: http://www.justice.gov/dea/pubs/states/newsrel/2010/chicago020410.html.

_____. 2011. News Release: Los Angeles Roundup Targets 38th Street Gang." February 1. Available: http://www.justice.gov/dea/pubs/states/newsrel/2011/la020111.html.

United States Military. 2012. "The Hip Hop Music History of Boot Camp Clik." Boot Camps. Available: http://www.usmilitarymuscle.com/the-hip-hop-music-history-ofboot-camp-clik.php.

U.S. Bureau of Labor Statistics. 2009. "Employment by Major Industry Sector." Available: www.bls.gov/emp/ep_table_201.htm.

_____. 2012. "Education Pays." Available: http://www.bls.gov/emp/ep_chart_001.htm.

U.S. Census Bureau. 2003. "Poverty: 2002 Highlights." Last revised on September 26, 2003. Available: http://www.census.gov.

_____. 2011. "U.S. Census Bureau Delivers Illinois' 2010 Census Population Totals, Including First Look at Race and Hispanic Origin Data for Legislative Redistricting." Available: http://2010.census.gov/news/releases/operations/cb11-cn31.html.

_____. 2012a. "Boston: Quick Facts from the U.S. Census Bureau." Available: http://quickfacts.census.gov/qfd/states/25/2507000.html.

_____. 2012b. Buffalo: Quick Facts from the U.S. Census Bureau." Available: http://quickfacts.census.gov/qfd/states/36/3611000.html.

_____. 2012c. "Chicago: Quick Facts from the U.S. Census Bureau." Available: http://quickfacts.census.gov/qfd/states/17/1714000.html.

_____. 2012d. "Detroit: Quick Facts from the U.S. Census Bureau." Available: http://quickfacts.census.gov/qfd/states/26/2622000.html.

_____. 2012e. "Guilford County, North Carolina: Quick Facts from the U.S. Census Bureau." Available: http://quickfacts.census.gov/qfd/states/37/37081.html.

_____. 2012f. "Indianapolis (city), Indiana: Quick Facts from the U.S. Census Bureau." Available: http://quickfacts.census.gov/qfd/states/18/1836003.html.

_____. 2012g. "Kansas City, Missouri: Quick Facts from the U.S. Census Bureau." Available: http://quickfacts.census.gov/qfd/states/20/2036000.html.

_____. 2012h. "Los Angeles (city): Quick Facts from the U.S. Census Bureau." Available: http://quickfacts.census.gov/qfd/states/06/0644000.html.

_____. 2012i. "Los Angeles County: Quick Facts from the U.S. Census Bureau." Available: http://quickfacts.census.gov/qfd/states/06/06037.html.

_____. 2012j. "Miami: Quick Facts from the U.S. Census Bureau." Available: http://quickfacts.census.gov/qfd/states/12/12450000.html.

_____. 2012k. "New York (city): Quick Facts from the U.S. Census Bureau." Available: http://quickfacts.census.gov/qfd/states/36/3651000.html.

_____. 2012l. "Rochester: Quick Facts from the U.S. Census Bureau." Available: http://quickfacts.census.gov/qfd/states/36/3663000.html.

_____. 2012m. "Syracuse: Quick Facts from the U.S. Census Bureau." Available: http://quickfacts.census.gov/qfd/states/36/3673000.html.

_____. 2012n. "USA: People Quick Facts from the U.S. Census Bureau." Available: http://quickfacts.census.gov/qfd/states/00000.html.

U.S. Department of Health and Human Services. 2006. "New Surgeon General's Report Focuses on the Effects of Secondhand Smoke." Available: www.hhs.gov/news/press/2006pres/20060627.html.

_____. 2008. "About the Office of Head Start." Available: www.acf.hhs.gov/propgrams/hsh/about/index.html.

_____. 2011. "The HHS Poverty Guidelines for the Remainder of 2010." August. Available: http://aspe.hhs.gov/poverty/10poverty.shtml.

U.S. Department of Justice. 2002. "Drugs and Crime Gang Profile: Crips." November. Available: http://cryptome.org/gangs/crips.pdf.

_____. 2009. "Operation Weed and Seed." Available: http://www.justice.gov/usao/md/Community-Programs/Weed%20and%20Seed/index.html.

_____. 2010. "Crime in the United States: Crime Clock Statistics." Available: http://www2.fbi.gov/ucr/cius2009/about/crime_clock.html.

U.S. Department of Justice Office on Violence Against Women. 2012. "The Facts on the Workplace and Sexual Violence." Available:http://www.workplacesrespond.org/learn/the-facts/the-costs-of-sexual-violence.

U.S. Department of State. 2008. "Human Trafficking Defined." June 4 Trafficking in Persons Report. Available: http://www.state.gov/j/tip/rls/tiprpt/2008/105487.htm.

U.S. Legal. 2012. "Prostitution Law & Legal Definition." US Legal.com. Available: http://definitions.uslegal.com/p/prostitution/.

USA Today. 2007. "Report: Gang Suppression Doesn't Work." July 18. Available: http://www.usatoday.com/news/nation/2007-07-18-gang-report_N.htm.

_____. 2010. "8 Gang Suspects Arraigned in NYC Attack." October 10. Available: http://www.usatoday.com/news/nation/2010-10-09-gang-torture-new-york_N.htm.

Valdez. 2007. *Mexican American Girls and Gang Violence: Beyond Risk*. New York: Palgrave/Macmillan.

_____. 2009a. *Gangs: A Guide to Understanding Street Gangs*. San Clemente, CA: Law/Tech Publishing.

_____. 2009b. "Prison Gangs 101." *Corrections Today*, 71(1):40–43.

Vergano, Dan. 2002. "The 'Gangs' All Here, on a New York Tour." *USA Today*, December 3:8D.

Verhovek, Sam Howe. 1997. "As Texas Executions Mount, They Grow Routine." *New York Times*, May 25:A1 and A6.

Vigil, James D. 1988a. *Barrio Gangs*. Austin, TX: University of Texas Press.

_____. 1988b. "Group Processes and Street Identity: Adolescent Chicano Gang Members." *Ethos* 16:421–445.

_____. 1990. "Cholos and Gangs: Culture Change and Street Youths in Los Angeles," in *Gangs in America*. Ed. C. R. Huff. Newbury Park, CA: Sage.

_____. 1997. "Origins of Mexican American Gangs: Learning from Gangs." *The Mexican American Experience, Eric Digest*. Available: http://www.ed.gov.databases/ERIC_Digests.

Vigil, James D., and J. M. Long. 1990. "Emic and Etic Perspectives on Gang Culture: The Chicano Case," in *Gangs in America*. Ed. C. R. Huff. Newbury Park, CA: Sage.

Voices from El Salvador. 2010. "The New Anti-Gang Law Took Affect This Week." Available: http://voiceselsalvador.wordpress.com/2010/09/23/THE-NEW-ANTI-GANG-LAW-TOOK-AFFECT-THIS-WEEK/.

Vold, G. B. 1958. *Theoretical Criminology*, 2nd ed. New York: Oxford University Press.

Voorhees, Seth. 2011. "Rochester Gathering Tackles Gang Issue." *Your News Now (YNN)*, August 22. Available: http://rochester.ynn.com/content/top_stories/554438/rochester-gathering-tackles-gang-issue/.

Wade, Carole, and Carol Tavris. 2002. "Hormones and Emotions," in *Psychology*, 7th ed. Upper Saddle River, NJ: Prentice Hall.

Walker, Robert. 2012. "18th Street Gang: A Violent Transnational Criminal Street Gang." *Gangs OR Us*. Available: http://www/gangsorus.com/18th_street.hym.

Walker-Barnes, Chanequa J., and Craig A. Mason. 2001. "Perceptions of Risk Factors for Female Gang Involvement Among African American and Hispanic Woman." *Youth and Society*, 32(3):303–336.

Wallace, Charles M. 1938. "The Boys Gangs of Richmond in the Dear Old Days: A Page of the City's Lessor (sic) History Recalled by Charles M. Wallace, an Old Boy," originally appearing in the *Richmond Times-Dispatch*, in Harry Tucker's Column titled, "Main Street." Available: http://www.richmondthenandnow.com/Boy-Gangs-Index.html.

Wallechinsky, David, and Irving Wallace. 2010. "Biography of Gangsters: Arizona Clark Ma Barker." Trivia-Library.com. Available: http://www.trivia-library.com/c/biography-of-gangsters-arizona-clark-ma-barker.htm.

Walsh, Patrice. 2010. "Rochester Curfew Unconstitutional, But—Kids Were Off Streets." 13WHAM.com. Available: http://www.13wham.com/news/local/story/Rochester-Curfew-Unconstitutional-But-Kids-Were/hwUWmVkjaEuzAAXenkB1Ug.cspx.

Warren, Jennifer, and Dan Morian. 2003. "Crips Target of Prison Lockdown." *Los Angeles Times*, July 1:B1.

Washington Regional Threat and Analysis Center. 2008. *Intelligence Bulletin 2008–26: Bloods Gang*. January 31.

Watkins, Derrick, and Richard Ashby. 2007. *Gang Investigation: A Street Cops Guide*. Boston, MA: Jones and Bartlett.

Wayne, Alex. 2012. "Sioux Reservation is Nation's Least-Healthy Place." *The Post-Standard*, April 4: A–11.

Weaver, Teri. 2012. "Cuomo Proposes Changes in Marijuana Laws." *The Post-Standard*, June 5:A-4.

Webb, Jim. 2009. "Why WE Must Fix Our Prisons." *Parade*, March 29, 4–5.

Webb, Vincent J., and Charles M. Katz. 2003. "Policing Gangs in an Era of Community Policing," in *Policing Gangs and Youth Violence*. Ed. Scott H. Decker. Belmont, CA: Wadsworth.

Weibezahl, Sue. 2002. "Gang Violence Task Force Hits the Streets." *The Post-Standard*, June 9:A8.

_____. 2003a. "Auditor: Anti-Drug Tactics Flawed." *The Post-Standard*, December 30:B5.

_____. 2003b. "Police Say It's Working, but Some Residents Are Disagreeing." *The Post-Standard*, May 19:A1.

_____. 2003c. "Street Violence, Killings, Sweep Upstate Big Cities." *The Post-Standard*, August 3:A1.

Weinberg, Daniel H. 2006. "Measuring Poverty in the United States: History and Current Issues." Center for Economic Studies, U.S. Census Bureau. Available: www.ces.census.gov/index.php/cespapers.

Weiser, Benjamin. 2003. "Founder of East Coast Bloods Is Given 50 Years." *New York Times*, April 15:2D.

Weiser, Kathy. 2010. "Old West Legends: Pearl Hart—Lady Bandit of Arizona." Available: http://www.legendsofamerica.com/we-pearlhart.html.

Weisheit, Ralph A., and L. Edward Wells. 2004. "Youth Gangs in Rural America." *NIJJournal*, 5:2–6.

Weisman, Larry. 2002. "Do-Rags Formally Fall Out of Fashion with NFL." *USA Today*, March 29:1C.

Weitzer, Ronald, and Steven A. Tuch. 2004. "Race and Perceptions of Police Misconduct." *Social Problems*, 51(3):305–25.

Welling, Dale A. 1994. "Experts Unite to Combat Street and Prison Gang Activities." *Corrections Today*, 56(5):148–9.

Wentz, Ericka A., and Kristyn A. Schlimgen. 2012. "Citizens' Perception of Police and Police Response to Community Concerns."*Journal of Crime and Justice*, 35(1):114–33.

WHEN-CBS, 2012. "Rewind & Reload: Tournament." Original air date: March 13.

White, Rhindi. 2010. "Detroit Rappers Unite for Rally Against Violence This Weekend." Available: http://www.streetgangs.com/hip-hop/061110_detroit_rappers_unite.

Whitehurst, Grover J. 2010. "Is Head Start Working for American Students?" *Brookings Institution*, January 21. Available: http://www.brookings.edu/up-front/posts/2010/01/21-head-start-whitehurst.

Wilber, Del Quentin. 2010. "MS-13 Gang Out to 'Kill, Rape and Control: FBI Agent." *Washington Post*, January 11. Available: http://voices.washingtonpost.com/crime-scene/gangs/ms-13-gang-out-to-kill-rape-an.html.

Williams, Frank P., and Marilyn D. McShane. 1994. *Criminological Theory*. Englewood Cliffs, NJ: Prentice Hall.

Williams, Schloss P. 1998. "The Serotonin Transporter: A Primary Target for Antidepressant Drugs." *Journal of Psychopharmacol,* 12(2):115–21.

Williams, Stanley Tookie. 1997a. "Tookie's Corner: My Letter to Incarcerated Youth, No.1." Available: http://networkfory outhintransition.org/forum/topics/tookies-corner.

———. 1997b. "Tookie's Corner: The Apology." Available: http://networkforyouthintransition.org/forum/topics/tookies-corner.

———. 2004. *Blue Rage, Black Redemption: A Memoir.* New York: Touchstone.

Williams, Stanly Tookie, and Barbara Cottman Becnel. 2001. *Life in Prison.* San Francisco, CA: Chronicle Books.

Willon, Phil. 2011. "Arrest Made in 3-Year-Old's Slaying." *Los Angeles Times.* September 16:A1.

Wilson, Charles. 2010. "Teen Faces 100 Years in Prison in Indy Shootings." *Associated Press,* July 26. Available: http://www.streetgangs.com/news/072610_indianapolis_shootings.

Wilson, William. 1987. *The Truly Disadvantaged.* Chicago, IL: University of Chicago Press.

———. 1996. *When Work Disappears: The World of the New Urban Poor.* New York: Vintage Books.

Winterdyk, John, and Rick Ruddell. 2010. "Managing Prison Gangs: Results from a Survey of U.S. Prison Systems." *Journal of Criminal Justice,* 38(4):730–6.

Wolf, Daniel R. 1991. *Rebels.* Toronto: University of Toronto Press.

Wolf, Jarrett. 2009. "Presentation of the Case," pp. 60–87 in *Gang Prosecution Manual,* OJJDP. Washington, DC: U.S. Department of Justice.

Women in History. 2012. "Belle Starr." Available: http://www.lkwdpl.org/wihohio/star-bel.htm.

World Bank. 2011. "World Bank Updates Poverty Estimates for the Developing World." Available: http://web.worldbank.org/WBSITE/EXTERNAL/EXTDEC/EXTRESEARCH/0,,contentMDK:21882162~pagePK:64165401~piPK:64165026~theSitePK:469382,00.html.

———. 2012b. "Poverty." Health Topics. Available: http://www.who.int/topics/poverty/en/.

World Health Organization. 2012a. "Definition and Typology of Violence." *Violence Prevention Alliance.* Available: http://www.who.int/violenceprevention/approach/definition/en/index.html.

World Hunger Education Service. 2012. "2012 World Hunger and Poverty Facts and Statistics." Available: http://www.worldhunger.org/articles/Learn/world%20hunger%20facts%202002.htm.

Yablonsky, Lewis. 1959. "The Delinquent Gang as a Near-Group." *Social Problems,* 7:108–117.

———. 1997. *Gangsters: Fifty Years of Madness, Drugs, and Death on the Streets of America.* New York: New York University Press.

Yost, James A. 1981. "Twenty Years of Contact: The Mechanisms of Change in Huao ('Aura') Culture," in *Cultural Transformations and Ethnicity in Modern Ecuador.* Ed. Norman E. Whitten, Jr. Champaign-Urbana, IL: University of Illinois Press.

Your News Now. 2009. "Twelve Indicated for Gang Activity." June 19. Available: http://centralny.ynn.com/content/top_stories/475107/twelve-indicated-for-gang-activity/.

Youth Advocate Programs, Inc. 2012. "Juvenile Justice Alternatives: Program Description." Available: http://www.yapinc.org/index.php?pID=273.

Youth Gangs and Juvenile Violence. 2003. "Indicators of Gang Membership." The Office of the Attorney General, State of Arkansas.

INDEX

Note: Bold locators refer to definition of key terms. Notation "b" and "ex" refers to box and exhibits cited in the text.